CONTENTS

CHAPTER 1 – ALGEBRA
1.1   Types of numbers...5
1.2   Interval notation...10
1.3   Significant figures...13
1.4   Scientific notation...16
1.5   Error analysis..19
1.6   International system of units...................................24
1.7   Currency conversion...28
1.8   Sequences and Series and compound interest.....................31
1.9   Financial applications of sequences and series 44

CHAPTER 2 – STATISTICS
2.1   Introduction to statistics.....................................51
2.2   Frequency diagrams & measures of central tendency.............52
2.3   Measures of dispersion...61

CHAPTER 3 – LOGIC
3.1   Set theory 68
3.2   Logic 79

CHAPTER 4 – PROBABILITY
4.1   Probability..87

CHAPTER 5 – MATHEMATICAL MODELS
5.1   Introduction to functions 99
5.2   Linear functions 108
5.3   Quadratic functions 129
5.4   Exponential functions...160

CHAPTER 6 – TRIGONOMETRY AND GEOMETRY
6.1   Definition of the Trigonometric functions.....................178
6.2   Sine and Cosine Rule..182
6.3   Trigonometric Ratios..187
6.4   3D Geometry...192

CHAPTER 7 – CALCULUS
7.1   Rate of change..200
7.2   Definition of derivative......................................201
7.3   Tangents and normals to functions.............................202
7.4   Stationary points and function analysis.......................210
7.5   Optimization problems...215

CHAPTER 8 – STATISTICS
8.1   Correlation...226
8.2   Chi Squared...233
8.3   Normal distribution...239

ANSWER KEY

CHAPTER 1 – ALGEBRA
1.1 Types of numbers...254
1.2 Interval notation...259
1.3 Significant figures...262
1.4 Scientific notation...264
1.5 Error analysis 266
1.6 International system of units.................................269
1.7 Currency conversion...273
1.8 Sequences and Series and compound interest..............275
1.9 Financial applications of sequences and series 285

CHAPTER 2 – STATISTICS
2.1 Introduction to statistics.....................................289
2.2 Frequency diagrams & measures of central tendency.......290
2.3 Measures of dispersion.......................................299

CHAPTER 3 – LOGIC
3.1 Set theory 303
3.2 Logic 313

CHAPTER 4 – PROBABILITY
4.1 Probability..320

CHAPTER 5 – MATHEMATICAL MODELS
5.1 Introduction to functions 330
5.2 Linear functions 337
5.3 Quadratic functions 352
5.4 Exponential functions...379

CHAPTER 6 – TRIGONOMETRY AND GEOMETRY
6.1 Definition of the Trigonometric functions...................394
6.2 Sine and Cosine Rule...397
6.3 Trigonometric Ratios...402
6.4 3D Geometry..405

CHAPTER 7 – CALCULUS
7.6 Rate of change...410
7.7 Definition of derivative.......................................412
7.8 Tangents and normals to functions..........................417
7.9 Stationary points and function analysis.....................420
7.10 Optimization problems.......................................425

CHAPTER 8 – STATISTICS
8.1 Correlation...428
8.2 Chi Squared...432
8.3 Normal distribution...438

CHAPTER 1 – ALGEBRA

1.1. – TYPES OF NUMBERS

Natural Numbers (N): $N = \{\underset{0}{0}, \underline{1}, \underline{2}, \underline{3}, \underline{4} ...\}$

Integers (Z): $Z = \{..., \underline{-5}, \underline{-4}, \underline{-3}, \underline{-2}, \underline{-1}, 0, \underline{1}, \underline{2}, \underline{3}, \underline{4}, \underline{5} ...\}$

Rational Numbers (Q): $Q = \{\frac{a}{b}, a, b \in Z\}$

Numbers that **can** be written as FRACTION being both the

numerator and the denominator Z INTIGER

Examples: $\frac{1}{1}, \frac{2}{3}, \frac{-7}{3}, \frac{4}{-1}, \frac{5}{10}, 0.5 , \_\_\_\_ ...$

Irrational Numbers (Q'): $Q' \neq \{\frac{a}{b}, a, b \in Z\}$ Numbers that __CAN'T__ be written as

fractions, being both the DENUMER and DENOM NUM Integers.

Examples: $\pi, \sqrt{2}, \_\_ ...$

Real Numbers (R): $R = Q + Q'$ (Rationals and Irrationals)

Represented in a Venn diagram:

NATURAL   WHOLE NUMBER ABOVE 0.
Z INTIGER   WHOLE NUMBER
Q RATIONAL   FRACTIONS
Q' IRRATIONAL   WEIRD FRACTIONS
REAL   ALL

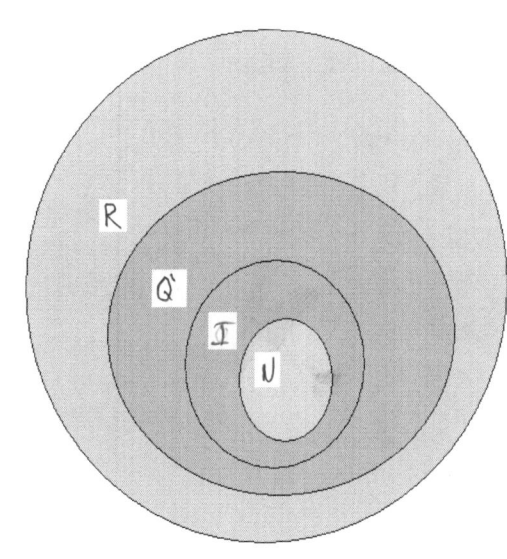

Exercises:

1. Natural numbers are contained in the _INTIGER (Z)_ numbers.

2. Integer numbers are contained in the _RATIONAL (Q)_ numbers

3. Rational numbers are contained in the _IRRATIONAL_ numbers.

4. Irrational numbers are located _____ .

5. Shade the area in which the irrational numbers are located:

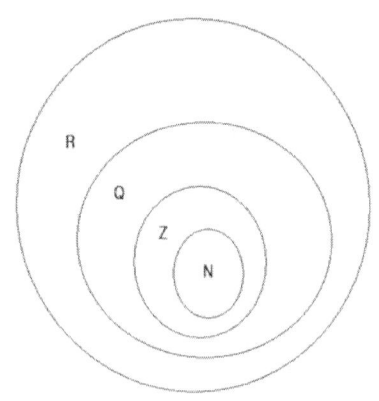

6. True or False:

    a. All Natural numbers are Integers: _____

    b. All Real numbers are Natural: _____

    c. All Rational numbers are Real: _____

    d. All Real numbers are Rational: _____

    e. All Integer numbers are Rational: _____

    f. All Real numbers are Irrational: _____

    g. Some Irrational numbers are Real and some are not: _____

    h. Some Irrational numbers are Integers: _____

    i. Some integers are negative: _____

    j. Some Irrationals are negative: _____

    k. Some Natural numbers are negative: _____

7. Fill the chart with yes or no (follow the example):

Number	Natural	Integer	Rational	Real
-2	no	yes	yes	yes
Π				
$-3.121212....$				
-15.16				
$\sqrt{3}$				
$-2\dfrac{2}{5}$				
$\sqrt[3]{8}$				

8. Fill the numbers column with appropriate numbers and yes or no. Follow the example.

Number	Natural	Integer	Rational	Real
-2	no	yes		
$3/5$		no	yes	yes
2	yes	yes	yes	
π			no	yes
$5/6$		no	yes	yes
			yes	
	no			
		yes	no	

4. Convert the following numbers into the form: $\dfrac{n}{m}$

1. $0.333\ldots =$

2. $1.111\ldots =$

3. $5.3 =$

4. $5.2828\ldots =$

5. $-2.3535\ldots =$

6. $42.67 =$

7. $12.355355\ldots =$

8. $-31.44 =$

9. $0.125125... =$

13. $1.123123... =$

10. $3.22332233... =$

14. $1.22565656... =$

11. $1115.36 =$

15. $1.5696969... =$

12. $122.53 =$

16. $5.540404040... =$

5. Given the following diagram:

Write the following numbers in the appropriate location in the diagram:

a. 2.2
b. -5
c. 3
d. $\dfrac{1}{3}$
e. 5
f. -3.3
g. $1.111...$
h. $\dfrac{1}{\sqrt{3}}$
i. 2π
j. $1+2\pi$
k. $\sqrt{2}+3$
l. $\dfrac{4}{2}$

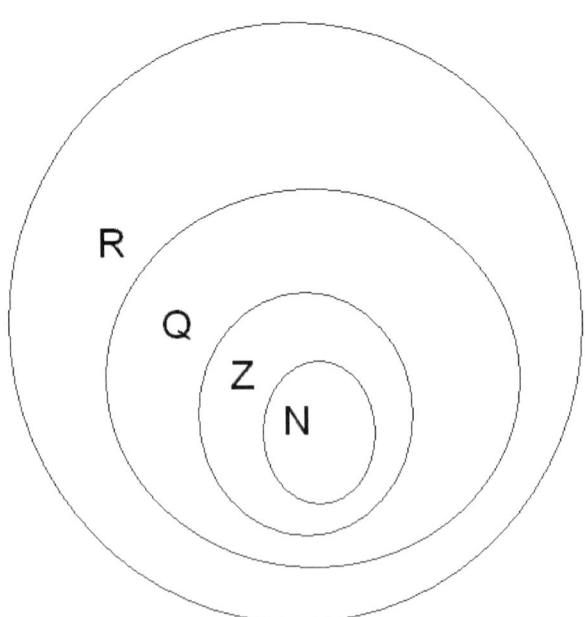

6. Circle the right option. The number –2 is:

   a. Integer and Natural.
   b. Positive
   c. Integer and Rational
   d. Natural and Real
   e. Natural and Rational
   f. None of the above

7. Circle the right option. The number 3.41414141..... is:

   a. Integer and Natural.
   b. Natural
   c. Integer and Real
   d. Rational and Integer
   e. Rational
   f. None of the above

8. Circle the right option. The number 3.41 is:

   a. Integer and Natural.
   b. Integer
   c. Rational and Real
   d. Integer and Real
   e. Rational and negative
   f. None of the above

9. Circle the right option. The number $\sqrt{31}$ is:

   a. Integer and Natural.
   b. Integer
   c. Decimal
   d. Integer and Real
   e. Rational
   f. Irrational

10. Circle the right option. The number 5 is:

   a. Natural.
   b. Integer
   c. Real
   d. Integer and Natural
   e. Rational and Natural
   f. All of the above

1.2. – INTERVAL NOTATION

x ∋ (a, b] or {x| a < x ≤ b} means x is between a and b, not including a and including b.

Exercises:

1. Represent the following Intervals on the real line:

   a. x ∋ (2, 5]

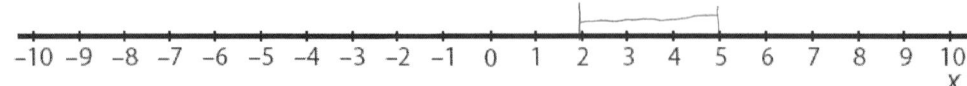

   b. x ∋ (3,6)

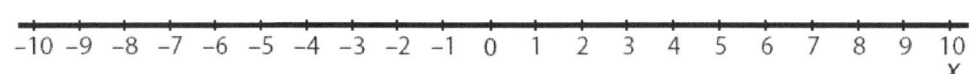

   c. x ∋ [–5,9]

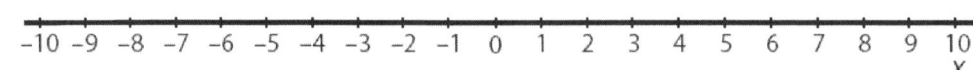

   d. x ∋ [–8,–1)

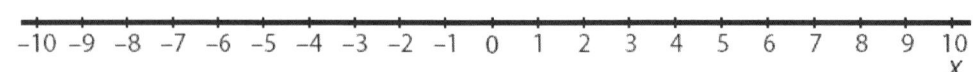

   e. x ∋ [–∞,–1)

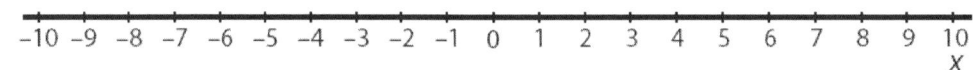

   f. x ∋ [–∞,6]

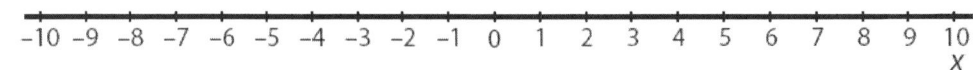

   g. x ∋ (6, ∞]

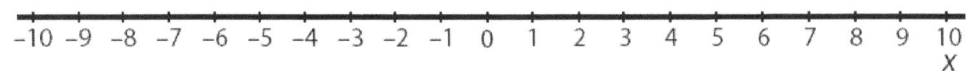

   h. {x| 7 < x < 9}

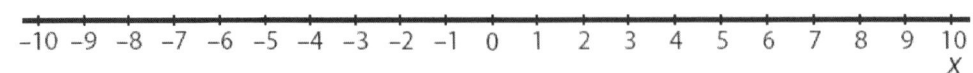

   i. {x| –7 < x < –2}

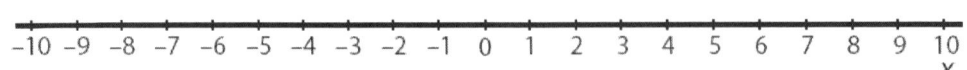

j. $\{x|\ 1 < x < 2\}$

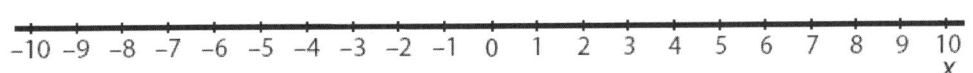

k. $\{x|\ \infty < x < 2\}$

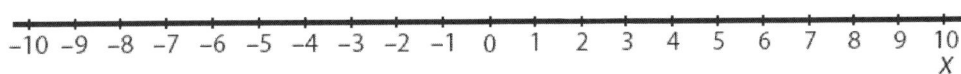

l. $\{x|\ 1 < x < \infty\ \}$

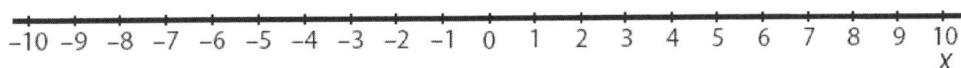

2. Write each one of the Intervals using all types of notations:

a. $x \ni [4, 5]$

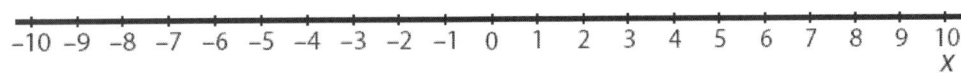

b. $x \ni (-\infty, 5)$

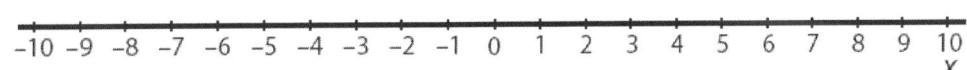

c. $x \ni (4, 5)$

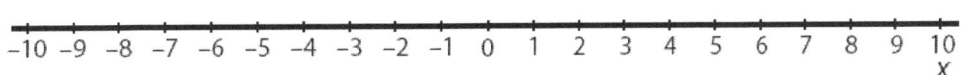

d. $x \ni (3, \infty]$

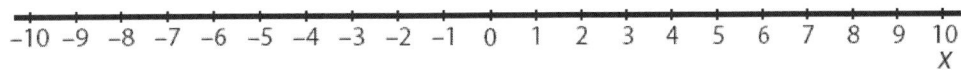

e. $x \ni]-5,9]$

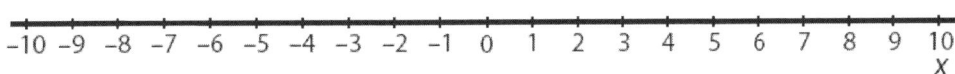

f. $x \ni [-8,-1[$

g. $\{x|\ 7 < x < 9\}$

h. $\{x|\ -7 < x < -2\}$

11

3.

    a. Solve the inequality $3x - 7 \leq 2$

    b. Solve the inequality $-x < -2$.

    c. Represent both solutions on the real line:

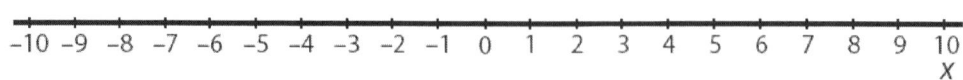

    d. State their intersection: _____.

4.

    a. Solve the inequality $5x - 2 \leq 2$

    b. Solve the inequality $-2x + 1 > -2$.

    c. Represent both solutions on the real line:

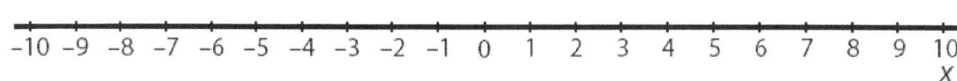

    d. State their intersection: _____.

5.

    a. Solve the inequality $5x - 2 \leq -12$

    b. Solve the inequality $-2x - 3 \leq -2$.

    c. Represent both solutions on the real line:

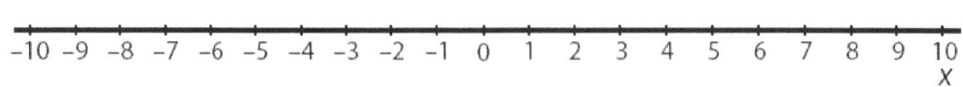

    d. State their intersection: _____

1.3. – SIGNIFICANT FIGURES

Whenever a measurement is performed an error is committed. The error can be caused by insufficient precision of the measuring device used, by the person doing the measurement, etc. Communicating our uncertainty in a measurement is as important as the measurement itself. The following rules help us to communicate our measurements better:

1. Significant figures in a measurement include all of the digits that are known precisely plus one last digit that is estimated.

2. Non-zero digits are always significant: 203.230002

3. All **final zeros** after the decimal point are significant: 2.7450 ; 0.1420

4. Zeros between two other significant digits are always significant: 70.0 ; 1002 ; 9.000

5. Zeros used only for spacing the decimal point are **not** significant: 100 ; 0.000078

6. On adding or subtracting, the answer is rounded to the same number of

    _____ as the measurement with the least

    number of decimal places.

7. On multiplying or dividing two numbers, the answer is rounded off to the

    number of _____ in the least precise term used in the

    calculation

Determine the number of significant digits in each of the following:

1. 273.20 cm _____

2. 4513.01 L_____

3. 2.00011 km _____

4. 0.0001010450 sec _____

5. 4.75 kg _____

6. 1.0 _____

7. 10.0 _____

8. 10 _____

9. 1.0 _____

10. 9.401°C _____

11. 0.2 ml _____

12. 314 kg _____

13. 2000.103 mm _____

14. 704,000 h _____

Answer using proper number of significant figures:

11. 3.414 s + 10.02 s + 58.325 s + 0.00098 s = _____

12. 2.326 h – 0.10408 h = _____

13. 10.19 m x 0.013 m = _____

14. 140.01 cm x 26.042 cm x 0.0159 cm = _____

15. 80.23 m / 2.4 s = _____

16. 4.301 kg / 1.9 cm^3 = _____

17. A Chemical experiment involves the following substances:

    85.238 g of Iron, 32.1 g of Water, 0.0026 g of Oil, 7.13 g of Glass

    a. How many significant digits are there in each measurement?
    b. What is the total mass of substances in this experiment?
    c. How many significant digits are there in the answer to part b?

18. A certain living room was measured to be 12.412m long and 5.212m wide. Determine:

    a. The area of the living room to the correct number of decimal places.

    b. The area of the living room to 3 significant figures.

    c. The area of the living room to 4 significant figures.

    d. The area of the living room to 1 decimal place.

    e. The perimeter of the living room to the correct number of decimal places.

    f. The perimeter of the living room to 3 significant figures.

    g. The perimeter of the living room to 4 significant figures.

    h. The perimeter of the living room to 1 decimal place.

19. You measured 17.40 ml of water in a certain recipient. After a certain experiment 9.0 ml of water was left.

    a. Which measurement is more precise, before or after the experiment? Explain.
    b. How much water was consumed during the experiment?

1.4. – SCIENTIFIC NOTATION

1. How many significant figures does the measurement of 100 mm have? _____ However, what if whoever performed the measurement was accurate to within 1 mm? How can the experimenter report the measurement with the appropriate number of significant figures?

2. Reporting the value as 100.0 suddenly turns the term having one significant digit into a term having _____.

3. The solution to this problem is called "scientific notation". In this case the solution to the problem would be: _____. With this notation, it is clear that three significant digits are intended.

4. Typically a _____ is placed to the left of the decimal, and this number is then multiplied by the appropriate _____. Our experimenter could report the measured quantity as 10.0×10^1 mm, but the first version is more common.

Write the following numbers in scientific notation and indicate the number of significant figures, later write with 3 significant figures:

1. 1026.90 = _____ 3S.F._____

2. 0.03045 = _____ 3S.F._____

3. 12,000 = _____ 3S.F._____

4. 0.00690 = _____ 3S.F._____

Write In scientific notation (use appropriate number of significant figures):

5. 0.11 = _____

6. 0.015 = _____

7. 0.0071 = _____

8. 0.0000001 = _____

9. 1.2 = _____

10. 1.02 = _____

11. 0.3 = _____

12. 0.00004 = _____

13. 0.06023 = _____

14. 0.000345 = _____

15. 0.00155 = _____

16. 0.0000204 = _____

17. 100 = _____

18. 10100 = _____

19. 11.0 = _____

20. 200 = _____

21. 201 = _____

22. 10.00 = _____

23. 101.0 = _____

24. 1.200 = _____

25. 1500 = _____

26. 2000 = _____

27. 51223 = _____

28. 100.80 = _____

29. 209.1 = _____

30. 24.18 = _____

31. 5500 = _____

32. 766600 = _____

33. 54000 = _____

34. 44500 = _____

35. 65000 = _____

36. 0.00545 = _____

37. 0.001545 = _____

38. 0.00020545 = _____

39. 0.050425 = _____

40. 0.0050545 = _____

41. 70000 = _____

Calculate giving your answers in scientific notation with the proper number of significant figures.

42. $(6.6 \cdot 10^{-8}) / (3.30 \cdot 10^{-4}) =$ _____

43. $(1.56 \cdot 10^{-7}) + (2.43 \cdot 10^{-8}) =$ _____

44. $(7.4 \cdot 10^{10}) / (3.7 \cdot 10^{3}) =$ _____

45. $(2.5 \cdot 10^{-8}) \cdot (3.0 \cdot 10^{-7}) =$ _____

46. $(2.67 \cdot 10^{-3}) - (9.5 \cdot 10^{-4}) =$ _____

47. $(2.3 \cdot 10^{-4}) \cdot (2.0 \cdot 10^{-3}) =$ _____

1.5. – ERROR ANALYSIS

1. As was seen earlier, when performing a measurement an error is always committed. The errors are classified in the following way:

2. Absolute error = |_____|

3. Relative error = | |

4. Percentage error = |_____|

5. An error can be negative (True/False).

Exercises

1. 0.33 is used instead of $\dfrac{1}{3}$

     a. Calculate the absolute error committed
     b. Calculate the relative error committed
     c. Calculate the percentage error committed

2. 1.41 is used instead of $\sqrt{2}$

     a. Calculate the absolute error committed
     b. Calculate the relative error committed
     c. Calculate the percentage error committed

3. A bathroom scale measures weights to the nearest 0.5 Kg. If we weigh a box that weights 65 Kg.

      a. Calculate the absolute error committed
      b. Calculate the relative error committed
      c. Calculate the percentage error committed

4. A digital bathroom scale measures weights to the nearest 0.1 Kg. If we weigh a cat that weights 1.9 Kg.

      a. Calculate the absolute error committed
      b. Calculate the relative error committed
      c. Calculate the percentage error committed

5. A certain ruler measures lengths to the nearest millimeter. Find the absolute error, relative error and percentage error committed if we measure lengths of:

     a. 5cm
     b. 1 cm
     c. 0.5 cm
     d. 1 mm
     e. In which case(s) would you say the ruler is not very useful? Explain

6. Given that x = 0.12, y = 0.0316 and z = 808

   a. State the number of significant figures given for each variable: _____

   b. Calculate exactly $\dfrac{z(x^2 + \sqrt{y})}{x - y} =$

   c. Write all the values of x, y and z correct to 1 significant figure.

      x = _____   y = _____   z = _____

   d. Use the values found in c to calculate $\dfrac{z(x^2 + \sqrt{y})}{x - y} =$

   e. Find the absolute, relative and percentage error committed (in part d compared with the exact value calculated in b).

      Absolute error = _____

      Relative error = _____

      Percentage error = _____

   f. Write all the values of x, y and z correct to 2 significant figures.

      x = _____   y = _____   z = _____

   g. Use the values found in e to calculate $\dfrac{z(x^2 + \sqrt{y})}{x - y} =$

   h. Find the absolute, relative and percentage error committed (in part g compared with the exact value calculated in b).

      Absolute error = _____

      Relative error = _____

      Percentage error = _____

7. Given that x = 560°, y = 1.61 and z = 808

   a. State the number of significant figures given for each variable: _____

   b. Calculate exactly $\dfrac{z\sin(x)}{y} =$

   c. Write all the values of x, y and z correct to 1 significant figure.

      x = _____ y = _____ z = _____

   d. Use the values found in c to calculate $\dfrac{z\sin(x)}{y} =$

   e. Find the absolute, relative and percentage error committed (in part d compared with the exact value calculated in b).

      Absolute error = _____

      Relative error = _____

      Percentage error = _____

   f. Write all the values of x, y and z correct to 2 significant figures.

      x = _____ y = _____ z = _____

   g. Use the values found in e to calculate $\dfrac{z\sin(x)}{y} =$

   h. Find the absolute, relative and percentage error committed (in part g compared with the exact value calculated in b).

      Absolute error = _____

      Relative error = _____

      Percentage error = _____

1.6. – INTERNATIONAL SYSTEM OF UNITS

Notation of units units: g – gram, m – metre, s – second

1. Gram is a unit of _____. Other units of _____ are:

2. Metre is a unit of _____. Other units of _____. are:

3. Second is a unit of _____. Other units of _____. are:

4. Celsius is a unit of _____. Other units of _____. are:

5. An area has units of _____

6. A volume has units of _____

7. Velocity has units of _____

8. Kilo = _____ Mili = _____

9. 1 Litre = _____ = _____ = _____

Convert the units in the following exercises, use scientific notation in at least one of each type of exercises:

1. How many metres are 2.5 km? _____

2. How many metres are 0.5 km? _____

3. How many metres are $\frac{1}{3}$ km? _____

4. How many metres are 56 km? _____

5. How many metres are 2500 km? _____

6. How many grams are 1.25 kg? _____

7. How many grams are 0.05 kg? _____

8. How many grams are $\frac{1}{4}$ kg? _____

9. How many grams are 34.5 kg? _____

10. How many grams are 257.31 kg? _____

11. How many km are 26 m? _____

12. How many km are 75 m? _____

13. How many km are 1000 m? _____

14. How many km are $5.2 \bullet 10^7$ m? _____

15. How many km are $5.12 \bullet 10^8$ m? _____

16. How many kg are 5798 g? _____

17. How many kg are 115 g? _____

18. How many kg are 1000 g? _____

19. How many mg are 2.9 kg? _____

20. How many mg are 0.4 g? _____

21. How many mg are 0.55 kg? _____

22. How many mg are 24 g? _____

23. How many mg are 2660 kg? _____

24. How many mg are 2.85 g? _____

25. How many mg are 73 g? _____

26. How many ms are 3.04 s? _____

27. How many ms are 0.5 s? _____

28. How many ms are 1 s? _____

29. How many s are 5 min? _____

30. How many s are 5 hours? _____

31. How many ms are in 2 days? _____

32. How many ms are 2.5 min? _____

33. How many ms are 1.35 min? _____

34. How many ms are $\dfrac{1}{3}$ min? _____

35. How many ms are 56 min? _____

36. How many ml are 3.1 litres? _____

37. How many ml are 0.5 litres? _____

38. How many litres are there in 120 ml? _____

39. How many litres are there in 5420 ml? _____

40. How many litres are there in 17 ml? _____

41. How many litres are there in 12392 ml? _____

42. How many ms are 5.1 s? _____

43. How many ms are 2.2 min? _____

44. How many ml are 13.12 litres? _____

45. How many ml are 10.05 litres? _____

46. 1 m/s = _____ km/s = _____ km/h

47. 1 km/h = _____ km/s = _____ m/s

48. 2 m/s = _____ km/s = _____ km/h

49. 2 km/h = _____ km/s = _____ m/s

50. How many m/s are 50 km/h? _____

51. How many m/s are 0.5 km/h? _____

52. How many m/s are $\frac{5}{2}$ km/h? _____

53. How many m/s are 516 km/h? _____

54. How many km/h are 10 m/s? _____

55. How many km/h are 0.5 m/s? _____

56. How many km/h are $\frac{5}{2}$ m/s? _____

57. How many km/h are 280 m/s? _____

Celsius – Fahrenheit:

$$F = \frac{9}{5}C^{\circ} + 32$$

Convert C° to F

    1. −100° = _____

    2. −50° = _____

    3. 0° = _____

    4. 20° _____

    5. 30° _____

    6. 100° = _____

    7. 200° = _____

    8. 1000° = _____

Convert F to C°

    9. −100F = _____

    10. −50F = _____

    11. 0F = _____

    12. 20F = _____

    13. 30F = _____

    14. 100F = _____

    15. 2000F = _____

1.7. – CURRENCY CONVERSION

1. The Exchange rate from US dollars to Euros is 1 USD = 0.81 EUR

    a. Convert 100 USD to Euros

        81

    b. Convert 255 USD to Euros

        206.55

    c. Convert 67 EUR to USD

        82.72

    d. Convert 332 EUR to USD

        397.53

    e. Diana receives 200 CAD (Canadian dollars) for 150 Euros. Calculate the value of 1 USD in CAD.

        200 : 150

        1.333 : 1

        1.38

    f. Diana receives 1300 MAR (Martian dollars) for 150 Euros. Calculate the value of 1 USD in MAR.

2. Given that 1 USD = 13.2 MXN (Mexican peso). Richard travels to Mexico with 1200 USD. He changes all his money to MXN and later spends 60% of the amount.

    a. How much MXN is he left with at the end of his trip?
    b. Back in the US he changes the MXN he is left with for USD. If the bank charges a commission 3% after the exchange. Calculate how many USD Richard receives.

3. A certain bank presents the following table to clients. The table makes reference to USD:

	Buy	Sell
JPY (Japanese Yenn)	75	85
ARS (Argentina Pesos)	4.4	5.2
COP (Colombian Pesos)	1750	1850

    a. State the amount of JPY obtained for 100 USD.
    b. How many USD will be obtained in case the client switches back to USD? What is the lost in percentage.
    c. A client exchanges 300 ARS to USD and then exchanges the amount obtained to COP. Find the amount of COP obtained.

4. The Exchange rate from US dollars to Euros is 1 USD = 0.73 GBP

    a. Convert 560 GBP to USD.

    b. Jane goes on a trip with 700 USD. She changes the amount to GBP. Later she wins a 100 GBP in a card game and decides to switch back to USD. The bank charges 1% commission on the last operation. Find the amount of GBP Jane will have.

5. The following table presents the exchange rate between EURO and different currencies:

1 EURO	89 JPY (Japanese Yenn)
1 EURO	6 ARS (Argentinean Peso)
1 EURO	2005 COP (Colombian Peso)

    a. State the amount of JPY obtained for 100 EURO.

    b. Find the exchanges rate between ARS and COP.

1.8. – SEQUENCES AND SERIES

Given The following sequences, write the first 3 terms and the term in the 20th position. If possible identify the pattern using text (follow example):

1. $a_n = 3n$ $a_1 = 3$ $a_2 = 6$ $a_3 = 9$ $a_{20} = 60$ Pattern: ___add 3____

2. $a_n = 3n + 1$ $a_1 = \cancel{5}4$ $a_2 = 7$ $a_3 = 10$ $a_{20} = 61$ Pattern: ___ADD3____

3. $a_n = 3n - 5$ $a_1 = -2$ $a_2 = -1$ $a_3 = 4$ $a_{20} = 55$ Pattern: ___ADD 3____

4. $a_n = 2n + 1$ $a_1 =$ $a_2 =$ $a_3 =$ $a_{20} =$ Pattern: _____

5. $a_n = 2n$ $a_1 =$ $a_2 =$ $a_3 =$ $a_{20} =$ Pattern: _____

6. $a_n = 2n - 4$ $a_1 =$ $a_2 =$ $a_3 =$ $a_{20} =$ Pattern: _____

7. $a_n = -4n$ $a_1 =$ $a_2 =$ $a_3 =$ $a_{20} =$ Pattern: _____

8. $a_n = -4n + 10$ $a_1 =$ $a_2 =$ $a_3 =$ $a_{20} =$ Pattern: _____

9. $a_n = -4n - 6$ $a_1 =$ $a_2 =$ $a_3 =$ $a_{20} =$ Pattern: _____

10. $a_n = \dfrac{n}{3}$ $a_1 =$ $a_2 =$ $a_3 =$ $a_{20} =$ Pattern: _____

11. $a_n = \dfrac{n}{2}$ $a_1 =$ $a_2 =$ $a_3 =$ $a_{20} =$ Pattern: _____

12. $a_n = \dfrac{2n}{5} + 1$ $a_1 =$ $a_2 =$ $a_3 =$ $a_{20} =$ Pattern: _____

13. $a_n = \dfrac{-3n}{7} + 5$ $a_1 =$ $a_2 =$ $a_3 =$ $a_{20} =$ Pattern: _____

14. $a_n = \dfrac{n}{9} - 5$ $a_1 =$ $a_2 =$ $a_3 =$ $a_{20} =$ Pattern: _____

15. $a_n = \dfrac{n}{10} - 1$ $a_1 =$ $a_2 =$ $a_3 =$ $a_{20} =$ Pattern: _____

16. $a_n = \dfrac{3n}{4} + 2$ $a_1 =$ $a_2 =$ $a_3 =$ $a_{20} =$ Pattern: _____

17. $a_n = n^2$ $a_1 =$ $a_2 =$ $a_3 =$ $a_{20} =$ Pattern: _____

18. $a_n = n^3$ $a_1 =$ $a_2 =$ $a_3 =$ $a_{20} =$ Pattern: _____

19. $a_n = 2^n$ $a_1 =$ $a_2 =$ $a_3 =$ $a_{20} =$ Pattern: _____

20. $a_n = -2^n$ $a_1 =$ $a_2 =$ $a_3 =$ $a_{20} =$ Pattern: _____

21. $a_n = 2^{-n}$ $a_1 =$ $a_2 =$ $a_3 =$ $a_{20} =$ Pattern: _____

22. $a_n = -2^{-n}$ $a_1=$ $a_2=$ $a_3=$ $a_{20}=$ Pattern: _____

23. $a_n = (-2)^n$ $a_1=$ $a_2=$ $a_3=$ $a_{20}=$ Pattern: _____

24. $a_n = 2^{n-1}$ $a_1=$ $a_2=$ $a_3=$ $a_{20}=$ Pattern: _____

25. $a_n = 2^{n+2}$ $a_1=$ $a_2=$ $a_3=$ $a_{20}=$ Pattern: _____

26. $a_n = 3 \times 2^n$ $a_1=$ $a_2=$ $a_3=$ $a_{20}=$ Pattern: _____

27. $a_n = -5 \times 2^{n-1}$ $a_1=$ $a_2=$ $a_3=$ $a_{20}=$ Pattern: _____

28. $a_n = 5 \times 2^{1-n}$ $a_1=$ $a_2=$ $a_3=$ $a_{20}=$ Pattern: _____

29. $a_n = (-3)^{2-n}$ $a_1=$ $a_2=$ $a_3=$ $a_{20}=$ Pattern: _____

30. $a_n = 2 \times (-3)^n$ $a_1=$ $a_2=$ $a_3=$ $a_{20}=$ Pattern: _____

31. $a_n = 2 \times (-5)^{n-1}$ $a_1=$ $a_2=$ $a_3=$ $a_{20}=$ Pattern: _____

32. $a_n = (-3)^{n+1}$ $a_1=$ $a_2=$ $a_3=$ $a_{20}=$ Pattern: _____

33. $a_n = 1 + 5^{n-2}$ $a_1=$ $a_2=$ $a_3=$ $a_{20}=$ Pattern: _____

34. $a_n = 3 \times 2^n$ $a_1=$ $a_2=$ $a_3=$ $a_{20}=$ Pattern: _____

35. $a_n = -5 \times 2^{n-1}$ $a_1=$ $a_2=$ $a_3=$ $a_{20}=$ Pattern: _____

36. $a_n = 2 \times 3^n$ $a_1=$ $a_2=$ $a_3=$ $a_{20}=$ Pattern: _____

37. $a_n = 5^{n-2} + 3$ $a_1=$ $a_2=$ $a_3=$ $a_{20}=$ Pattern: _____

38. $a_n = (-3)^n$ $a_1=$ $a_2=$ $a_3=$ $a_{20}=$ Pattern: _____

39. $a_n = 2 \times (-3)^n$ $a_1=$ $a_2=$ $a_3=$ $a_{20}=$ Pattern: _____

40. $a_n = 2 \times (-5)^{n-1}$ $a_1=$ $a_2=$ $a_3=$ $a_{20}=$ Pattern: _____

41. $a_n = (-3)^{n+1}$ $a_1= -9$ $a_2= -27$ $a_3= -81$ $a_{20}=$ Pattern: _multiply by 3_ _____

42. $a_n = 1 + 5^{n-2}$ $a_1=$ $a_2=$ $a_3=$ $a_{20}=$ Pattern: _____

43. The sequences in which the pattern is add/subtract a number are called _Arithmetic_

44. The sequences in which the pattern is multiply/divide (pay attention that

     dividing by a is the same as multiplying by _____) a number are called _Geometric_

45. (T/F) Arithmetic and Geometric sequences are most of the sequences that exist.

46. Give an example of a convergent geometric sequence:

47. Give an example of a divergent geometric sequence:

Arithmetic sequence (Pattern – Add a constant):

General term: $a_n = a_1 + (n-1)d$

Sum: $S_n = \dfrac{n}{2}(2a_1 + (n-1)d)$

Geometric Sequence (Pattern – multiply by a constant):

General term: $a_n = a_1 r^{n-1}$

Sum: $S_n = \dfrac{a(r^n - 1)}{r - 1}$

Example

    3, 7, 11, 15…
    Arithmetic sequence.
    Pattern: add 4.
    General term: $a_n = 3 + (n-1)4$
    General term can be written also like this: $a_n = -1 + 4n = 4n - 1$

Given the following sequences:

a. For each one write: arithmetic, geometric convergent, geometric divergent or neither, the <u>next term</u> and their <u>general term</u> (in case they are geometric or arithmetic only).

b. Try to write the general term of the other sequences as well.

48. 1, 2, 3, 4, <u>5</u> …
    +1

50. 1, 3, 5, 7, <u>9</u> …
    +2

49. 1, 2, 4, 8, <u>16</u> …
    × 2

51. 1, 3, 9, 27, <u>71</u> …
    ×3

52. 4, 6, 9, 13, 5, ____ ...

58. 2, 102, 202, 302, ____ ...

53. 4, 1, –2, –5, ____ ...

59. 1, –1, 1, –1, ____

54. 5, 0, –4, –7, ____ ...

60. –2, 2, –2, 2, ____ ...

55. 10, 1000, 100000, ____ ...

61. 3, –6, 12, –24, ____ ...

56. 30, 10, $\frac{10}{3}$, $\frac{10}{9}$, ____ ...

62. –8, 4, –2, 1, ____ ...

57. 2, 10, 50, 250, ____ ...

63. 5, 1, $\frac{1}{5}$, $\frac{1}{25}$, ____ ...

64. $100, 10, 1, \dfrac{1}{10},$ ___..

70. $1, \dfrac{3}{2}, \dfrac{9}{4}, \dfrac{27}{8},$ ___...

65. $\dfrac{3}{4}, \dfrac{3}{8}, \dfrac{3}{16},$ ___...

71. $5, -\dfrac{5}{3}, \dfrac{5}{9}, -\dfrac{5}{27},$ ___...

66. $12, 11, 10, 9,$ ___...

72. $-1, -2, -3,$ ___...

67. $\dfrac{4}{9}, \dfrac{5}{9}, \dfrac{6}{9},$ ___...

73. $-2, 4, -8,$ ___...

68. $9, 8, 6, 5, 3, 2,$ ___...

74. $70, 20, \dfrac{40}{7},$ ___...

69. $5, 9, 13,$ ___...

75. $100, 10, 1,$ ___...

76. $100, -10, 1, \dfrac{-1}{10}, \underline{} \cdots$

77. $3, 24, 192, \underline{} \cdots$

78. $90, 9, \dfrac{9}{10}, \underline{} \cdots$

79. $\dfrac{3}{2}, \dfrac{4}{3}, \dfrac{5}{4}, \underline{} \cdots$

80. $\dfrac{40}{3}, \dfrac{20}{6}, \dfrac{10}{12}, \dfrac{5}{24}, \underline{} \cdots$

81. $\dfrac{2}{3}, -\dfrac{4}{9}, \dfrac{8}{27}, -\dfrac{16}{81}, \underline{} \cdots$

82. $-\dfrac{1}{2}, -\dfrac{1}{4}, -\dfrac{1}{8}, -\dfrac{1}{16}, \underline{} \cdots$

83. $\dfrac{1}{7}, -\dfrac{1}{14}, \dfrac{1}{21}, -\dfrac{1}{28}, \underline{} \cdots$

84. $8, 5, 3, 0, \underline{} \cdots$

85. $3, \dfrac{3}{4}, \dfrac{3}{16}, \underline{} \cdots$

86. $81, -9, 1, -\dfrac{1}{9}, \underline{} \cdots$

87. $2, -10, 50, \underline{} \cdots$

In each one of the following sequences find the term indicated:

88. $1, 4, 7...$ (a_{31})

89. $-8, -5, -2...$ (a_{37})

90. $4, -8, 16...(a_{15})$

91. $32, -8, 2...(a_{11})$

92. $68, -34, 17...(a_9)$

93.   The 4th term of a geometric sequence is 3, the 6th term is $\dfrac{27}{4}$.

      a.   Find the ratio of the sequence.
      b.   Find a_1
      c.   Find a_{12}
      d.   Sum the first 15 terms.

$U_4 = 3$

$U_6 = \dfrac{27}{4}$

94. The 2nd term of a arithmetic sequence is –2, the 6th term is –4.

    a. Find the difference of the sequence.
    b. Find a_1
    c. Find a_{12}
    d. Sum the first 50 terms.

95. The 10th term of a geometric sequence is 5, the 14th term is $\dfrac{80}{81}$

    a. Find the ratio of the sequence.
    b. Find a_1
    c. Find a_7
    d. Sum the first 10 terms.

96. The 7th term of a arithmetic sequence is 120, the 16th term is 201.

     a. Find the difference of the sequence.
     b. Find a_1
     c. Find a_{12}
     d. Sum the first 50 terms.

97. All the terms in a geometric sequence are positive. The first term is 7 and the 3rd term is 28.

     a. Find the common ratio.
     b. Find the sum of the first 14 terms.

98. The fifth term of an arithmetic sequence is –20 and the twelfth term is –44.

  a. Find the common difference.
  b. Find the first term of the sequence.
  c. Calculate the eighty–seventh term.
  d. Calculate the sum of the first 150 terms.

99. Sum the following sequences:

  a. $3 + 6 + 9 + 12 + \ldots + 69 =$

  b. $6 + 14 + 22 + 30 + \ldots + 54 =$

  c. $5 + \dfrac{5}{3} + \dfrac{5}{9} + \ldots =$

d. $1 + 2 + 3 + 4 + \ldots + 158 =$

e. $9 + 18 + 27 + 36 + \ldots + 900 =$

f. $80 + 20 + 5 + \ldots$

100. In a theatre there are 20 seats in the first row, 23 in the 2nd, 26 in the 3rd etc. There are 40 rows in the theatre. Find the total number of seats available.

$U_1 = 20$

$U_2 = 23$ $d = 3$

$U_3 = 26$

$S_{40} = 20 \left(2 \cdot 40 + (39) \cdot 3 \right)$

3140

101. A ball bounces on the floor. It is released from a height of 160 cm. After the 1st bounce it reaches a height of 120 cm and 90 cm after the 2nd. If the patterns continue find:

    a. The height the ball will reach after the 6th bounce.
    b. The total distance the ball passed after a long period o time.

$$U_1 = 120$$
$$U_2 = 90$$
$$U_3$$

102. In a certain forest the current population of rabbits is 200 objects. It is know that the population increases by 20% every year.

    a. Find the population of rabbits after a year.
    b. Find the population of rabbits after 2 years.
    c. What kind of a sequence is it? State the expression for the population after n years.
    d. Find the total number of rabbits after 10 years (assuming none has died).

103. In a research it was observed that the number of defective products produced by a machine per year decreases by 10% every year (due to technological improvements). In a certain year the machine made 300 products.

    a. Find the number of defective products produced a year later.
    b. Find the number of defective products produced 2 years later.
    c. What kind of a sequence is it? State the expression for the number of errors committed after n years.
    d. Find the total number of bad products produced in the first 8 years.

104. In a certain company the pay scale follows a pattern of an arithmetic sequence (every year). This means:

    a. The salary increases by a certain % every year (True/False), explain.

    b. The salary increases by a certain amount every year (True/False), explain

1.9. – FINANCIAL APPLICATIONS OF SEQUENCES AND SERIES

COMPOUND INTEREST

1. 1200$ are put in account that gives 2% per year. Calculate the amount of money in the account after:

   a. 1 year.

   b. 2 years.

2. To increase an amount A by 5% it should be multiplied by _____ .

3. To increase an amount A by 56% it should be multiplied by _____ .

4. To decrease an amount A by 5% it should be multiplied by _____ .

5. To increase an amount A by 15% it should be multiplied by _____ .

6. To decrease an amount A by 12% it should be multiplied by _____ .

7. To increase an amount A by 230% it should be multiplied by _____ .

8. 1000$ are put in account that takes 5% commission per year. Calculate the amount of money in the account after:

   a. 1 year.

   b. 2 years.

9. 2000$ are being put in a deposit that pays 5% (per year).

a. Fill the table:

Number of Years	Interest earned at the end of the year	Amount in deposit ($)
0		2000
1	$\dfrac{5}{100}2000 = 100$	2100
2	$\dfrac{5}{100}2100 = 105$	2205
3	$\dfrac{5}{100}2205 = 110.25$	
4		
5		

b. Observe the numbers in the compound interest column: 2000, 2100, 2205... What kind of a sequence is that? Write its general term.

c. How much money will be in the account after 20 years?

d. Discuss the meaning of writing $a_n = a_1 r^{n-1}$ or writing $a_n = a_0 r^n$. Use the exercise as an example.

10. A loan of 1200$ is made at 12% per year compounded semiannually, over 5 years the debt will grow to:

   a. $\$1200(1 + 0.12)^5$
   b. $\$1200(1 + 0.06)^{10}$
   c. $\$1200(1 + 0.6)^{10}$
   d. $\$1200(1 + 0.06)^5$
   e. $\$1200(1 + 0.12)^{10}$

11. A loan of 23200$ is made at 8% per year compounded quarterly, over 6 years the debt will grow to:

   a. $\$23200(1 + 0.2)^{24}$
   b. $\$23200(1 + 0.08)^6$
   c. $\$23200(1 + 0.02)^{24}$
   d. $\$23200(1 + 0.08)^{24}$
   e. $\$23200(1 + 0.02)^6$

12. A loan of 20$ is made at 12% per year compounded monthly, over 8 years the debt will grow to:

   a. $\$20(1 + 0.12)^{80}$
   b. $\$20(1 + 0.01)^8$
   c. $\$20(1 + 0.012)^{96}$
   d. $\$20(1 + 0.01)^{96}$
   e. $\$20(1 + 0.06)^{12}$

13. A loan of X$ is made at 12% per year compounded every 4 months, over 5 years the debt will grow to:

   a. $\$X(1 + 0.12)^4$
   b. $\$X(1 + 0.3)^5$
   c. $\$X(1 + 0.12)^{15}$
   d. $\$X(1 + 0.03)^{15}$
   e. $\$X(1 + 0.3)^{15}$

14. A loan of X$ is made at i% per year compounded every m months, over n years the debt will grow to:

$$Debt = \_\_(1 + \_)\_$$

15. Calculate the total amount owing after two years on a loan of 1500$ if the interest rate is 11% compounded

     a. Annually

     b. Semiannually

     c. Quarterly

     d. Monthly

16. How much will a client have to repay on a loan of 800$ after 2 years, if the 12% interest is compounded annually.

17. Find the compound interest **earned** by the deposit. Round to the nearest cent. $3000 at 12% compounded semiannually for 10 years

18. How many years will it take to a 100$ to double assuming interest rate is 6%. Compounded semiannually.

19. How many years will it take to a X$ to triple assuming interest rate is 7%. Compounded quarterly

20. Find the interest rate given to a certain person in case he made a deposit of 1000$ and obtained 1200$ after 3 years, compounded monthly.

21. Find the interest rate given to a certain person in case he made a deposit of 2500$ and obtained 3000$ after 10 years, compounded yearly.

ANNUAL DEPRECIATION

1. Depreciation is _____

2. The value of a car is depreciated by 20% every year. Given its initial price is 10000$, find:

   a. Its value after 1 year.
   b. Its value after 2 years.
   c. An expression for its value after n year.

   $10,000 \times 0.80 = 8000 \rightarrow$

   $8000 \times 0.80 = 6400$

   $10,000 \times 0.8^{n}$

3. The value of a flat is depreciated by 12% every year. Given its initial price is 200000$, find:

   a. Its value after 1 year.
   b. Its value after 2 years.
   c. An expression for its value after n year.

4. Given that the price of a product is 200$ when it's bought and 100$ 4 years later, find the percentage in which it's depreciated per year.

5. Given that the price of a product is 1400$ when it's bought and 700$ 10 years later, find the percentage in which it's depreciated per year.

6. The value of a toy is depreciated by 2% every month. Given its current price is 300$, find:

   a. Its value 1 year ago.
   b. Its value 2 years ago.
   c. An expression for its value n years ago.
   d. Its initial price assuming it was bought a year and a half ago.

2.1. – INTRODUCTION TO STATISTICS

In Statistics we try to obtain some conclusions by observing and/or analyzing data.

1. The set of objects that we are trying to study is called _____, the number of elements in the population can be _____ or _____.

2. Usually the _____ is too big and therefore we obtain a _____. This process is called _____.

3. We use the _____ to obtain conclusions about the _____.

Types of DATA

GUALITATIUE → NUMERICAL
QUANTITAPUE → DISCRETE OR CONTINUOD

1. _CATEGORICA_ data.

2. _NUMERICAL_ data that can be divided to _CONTINUO)_ or _DISCRET_ .

3. _N D_ can be counted while _NC_ data can be _MEASURED)_ .

4. Give 3 examples of _____ data:

5. Give 3 examples of _____ _____ data:

6. Give 3 examples of _____ _____ data:

2.2. – FREQUENCY DIAGRAMS & MEASURES OF CENTRAL TENDENCY

1. In a certain math class the following grades were obtained:

68, 79, 75, 89, 54, 81, 88, 62, 67, 75, 64, 85, 97, 77, 79, 90, 75, 89, 76, 68

a. State the number of elements in the set: _____

b. What kind of data is this? _____

c. Fill the table:

Grade	Mid – Grade (Mi)	Frequency (fi)	fi · Mi	Cumulative Frequency (Fi)	Fi (%)
51 – 60					
61 – 70					
71 – 80					
81 – 90					
91 – 100					
Total					

d. Is this the only possible choice for the left column of the table? Why? Discuss the advantages and disadvantages of organizing information in such a way.

e. Design a new table with a different _____

Grade	Mid – Grade (Mi)	Frequency (fi)	fi · Mi	Cumulative Frequency (Fi)	Fi (%)

f. Obtain the mean in both cases:

g. State a formula for the mean:

h. The mean of the <u>population</u> is denoted with the Greek letter mu: _____

   and typically it is _____. The mean of the <u>sample</u> is denoted by

   _____

i. State the mode of the set: _____

j. Find the modal interval in both cases:

k. Find the Median using the original data: _____

l. Find the median using the tables, discuss your answer.

m. In general this method of organizing information is called _____

n. The 1st column is called _____ with upper interval boundary and

   _____ interval boundary.

o. The 2nd column is called _____

p. On the following grid paper sketch the corresponding points.

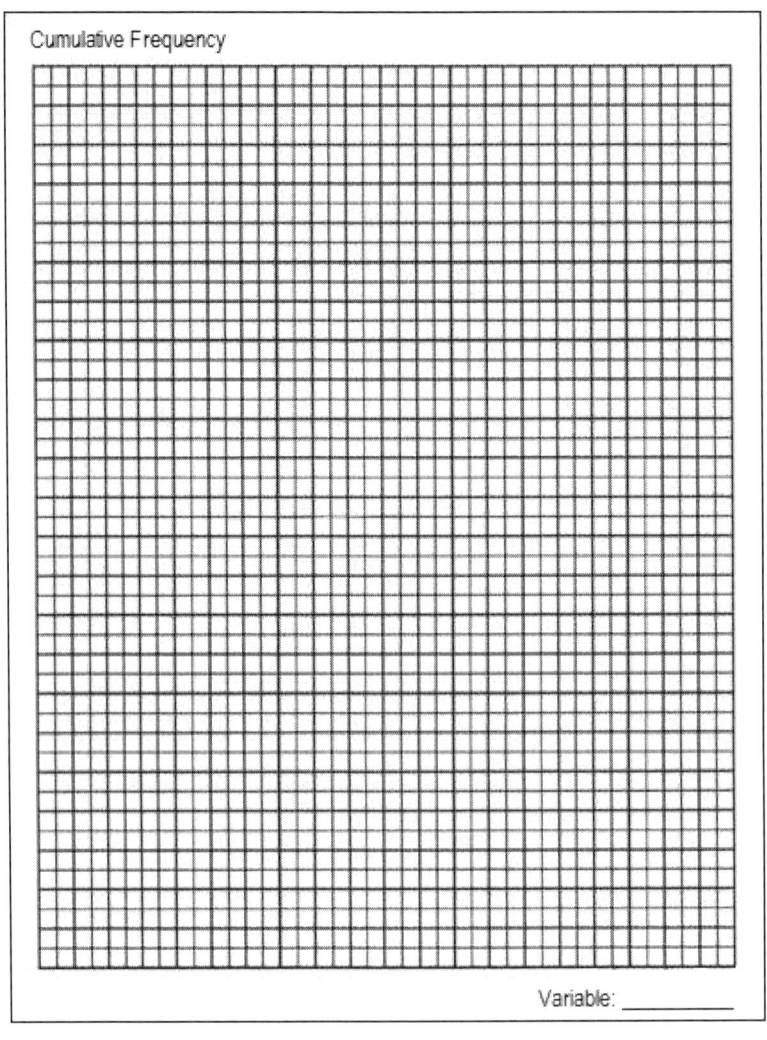

Cumulative Frequency

Variable: _____

q. This graph is called cumulative frequency curve or _____

r. Find the median using the graph: _____

s. Find the first quartile (Q_1) using the graph: Q_1 = _____

t. Find the first quartile (Q_1) using the original data: Q_1 = _____

u. Find the third quartile (Q_3) using the graph: Q_3 = _____

v. Find the first quartile (Q_3) using the original data: Q_3 = _____

w. Find P_{30} using the graph: _____ Find P_{65} using the graph: _____

x. The <u>Inter Quartile Range</u> is in general _____ in this case it is_____

y. Find the answers to all the different parts using your GDC.

2. In a certain class the following heights (in m) of students were collected:

1.77, 1.60, 1.89, 1.54, 1.77, 1.65, 1.86, 1.51, 1.67, 1.94, 1.73, 1.70, 1.66

a. State the number of elements in the set: _____

b. What kind of data is this? _____

c. Fill the table:

Height	Mid – Height (Mi)	Frequency (fi)	fi · Mi	Cumulative Frequency (Fi)	Fi (%)
[1.50 , 1.60)					
[1.60 , 1.70)					
[1.70 , 1.80)					
[1.80 , 1.90)					
[1.90 , 2.00)					
Total					

d. Obtain the mean: _____

e. State the mode of the set: _____

f. Find the modal interval: _____

g. Find the Median using the original data: _____

h. Find the median using the table, discuss your answer.

i. On the following grid paper sketch the corresponding points.

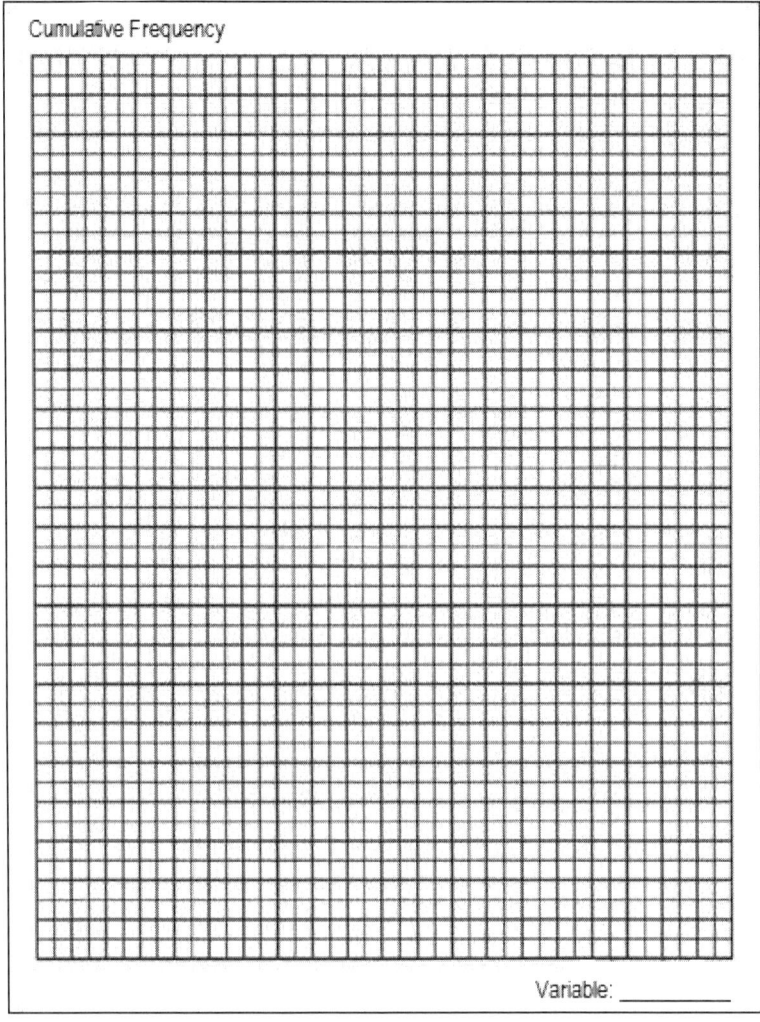

Cumulative Frequency

Variable: _____

j. This graph is called cumulative frequency curve or _____

k. Find the median using the graph: _____

l. Find the first quartile (Q_1) using the graph: Q_1 = _____

m. Find the first quartile (Q_1) using the original data: Q_1 = _____

n. Find the third quartile (Q_3) using the graph: Q_3 = _____

o. Find the first quartile (Q_3) using the original data: Q_3 = _____

p. Find P_{20} using the graph: _____Find P_{80} using the graph: _____

q. The <u>Inter Quartile Range</u> is in general _____ in this case it is_____

r. Find the answers to all the different parts using your GDC.

3. In a certain class students eye color was collected:

Brown, Black, Brown, Blue, Brown, Blue, Green, Brown, Black, Green

    a. State the number of elements in the set: _____

    b. What kind of data is this? _____
    c. Fill the table:

Eye Color	Mid – Color (Mi)	Frequency (fi)	Fi x Mi	Cumulative Frequency (Fi)	Fi (%)
Brown					
Blue					
Green					
Black					
Total					

    d. Obtain the mean: _____

    e. State the mode of the set: _____

    f. Find the modal interval: _____

    g. Find the Median using the original data: _____

    h. Find the median using the table, discuss your answer.

    i. Find the answers to all the different parts using your GDC.

    j. Represent the information in a histogram:

BOX PLOT

1.

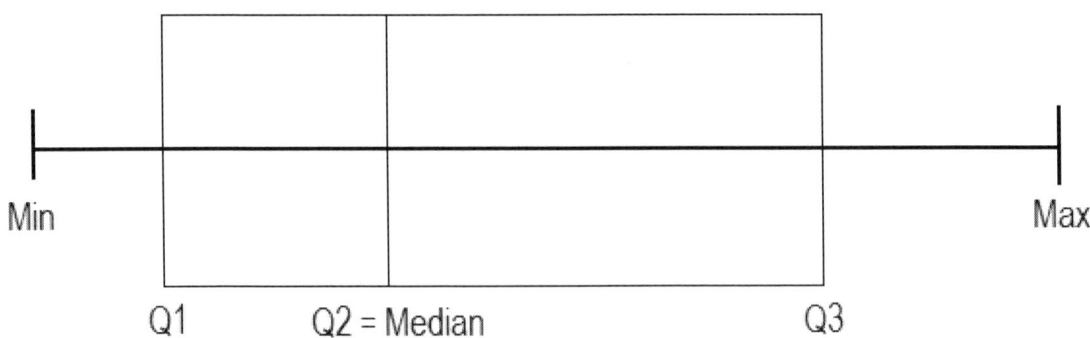

2. The results for 100 m dash competition are displayed in the following diagram:

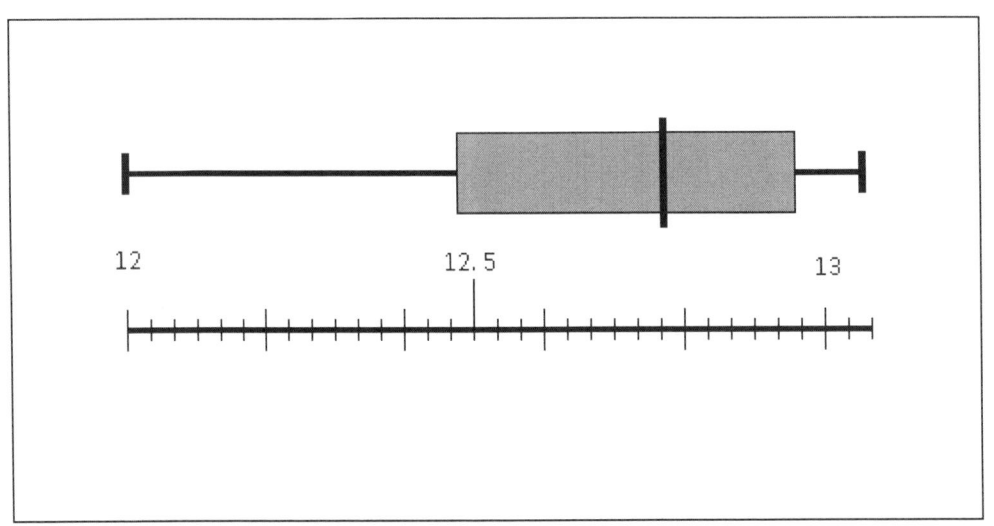

Answer:

a. Min = _____ Max = _____

b. Q_1 = _____ Q_2 = Med = _____ Q_3 = _____

c. Range = _____

d. Inter quartile range = _____

3. Given that in a certain classroom the heights of the students in cm are: 168, 178, 166, 191, 188, 181, 174, 159, 179, 173, 171, 166, 185, 184, 169. Draw a box-and-whisker plot using the graph below.

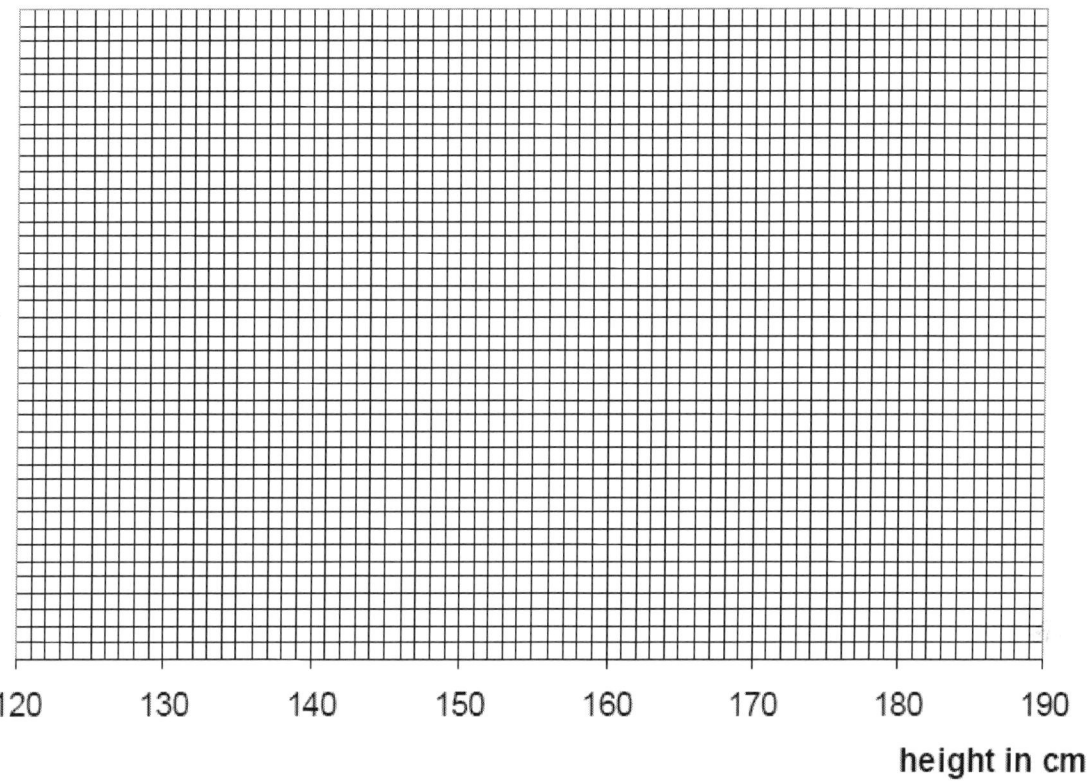

120   130   140   150   160   170   180   190

height in cm

4. In a factory a few machines are being classified according to the number of defective products produced. The following data was collected:

Machine	A	B	C	D	E	F	G	H	I
Number of defective products	0	2	4	1	5	2	1	3	2

a. Mean = _____   Median = _____   Mode = _____

b. Min = _____   Max = _____

c. Q_1 = _____ Q_2 = Med = _____ Q_3 = _____

d. Range = _____   Inter quartile range = _____

STEM AND LEAF DIAGRAMS

1. The following stem and leaf diagram gives the heights of a group of high school students (in cm):

    a. Find the number of students in the classroom _____.

    b. Mean = _____   Median = _____   Mode = _____

    c. Min = _____   Max = _____

    d. Q_1 = _____ Q_2 = Med = _____ Q_3 = _____

    e. Range = _____   Inter quartile range = _____

    f. What percentage of students is less than 165cm tall?

Stem	Leaf
15	7 7 9
16	4 5 6 7 7 8
17	1 3 3 4 8 8
18	2 3 4 8 9 9
19	0 1 3

2. The following stem and leaf diagram gives the grades of a group of high school students in math:

    a. Find the number of students in the classroom _____.

    b. Mean = _____   Median = _____   Mode = _____

    c. Min = _____   Max = _____ h

    d. Q_1 = _____ Q_2 = Med = _____ Q_3 = _____

    e. Range = _____   Inter quartile range = _____

    f. 60 is the passing grade in the class room. How many students failed?

    g. What percentage of students obtained 85 or more?

Stem	Leaf
5	1 3 5 5 8
6	0 1 3 5 6 6 7
7	1 3 4 7 8
8	0 1 1 3 7 8 8
9	2 6 8

2.3. – MEASURES OF DISPERSION

1. In a certain Biology test the following results were obtained: 80, 80, 80, 80,

   a. Obtain the mean: μ = _____

   b. Represent the results using a histogram:

   c. The standard deviation of a set of numbers is defined by:

   $$\sigma = \sqrt{\sum_i f_i(x_i - \mu)^2} = \sqrt{f_1(x_1 - \mu)^2 + f_2(x_2 - \mu)^2 + ...}$$

   In this case $\sigma =$ _____

   d. How spread is this group of grades?

2. In a certain Physics test the following results were obtained: 70, 80, 80, 90

    a. Obtain the mean: μ = _____

    b. Represent the results using a histogram:

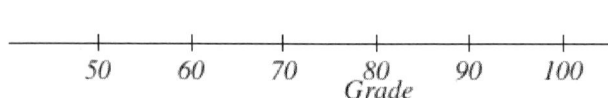

    c. The standard deviation of a set of numbers is defined by:

$$\sigma = \sqrt{\sum_i f_i(x_i - \mu)^2} = \sqrt{f_1(x_1 - \mu)^2 + f_2(x_2 - \mu)^2 + ...}$$

    In this case $\sigma =$ _____

    d. How spread is this group of grades? Is it more spread than the previous one?

3. In a certain math class the following grades were obtained:

68, 79, 75, 89, 54, 81, 88, 62, 67, 75, 64, 85, 97, 77, 79, 90, 75, 89, 76, 68

    a. State the number of elements in the set: _____

    b. What kind of data is this? _____

    c. Fill the table:

Grade	Mid – Grade (Mi)	Frequency (fi)	fi · Mi	$(Mi - \mu)^2$	$fi(Mi - \mu)^2$
51 – 60					
61 – 70					
71 – 80					
81 – 90					
91 – 100					
Total					

    d. Obtain the mean: μ = _____

    e. The numbers in the 6th column give us an idea about the _____

of each _____ to the spread of the data.

    f. The sum of the numbers in the 6th column gives us an idea about the

_____ of the data. In case this number is 0 it means that

_____for example:

    g. Use the table to find the Variance:_____

    h. Use the table to find the Standard Deviation S.D.:_____

    i. Write down the formula for the Variance of a population (σ^2):

    j. Write down the formula for the Standard Deviation of a population (σ):

k. Write down the difference between μ and $\bar{x}$

l. Write down the difference between σ and S_x

m. Find the answers to all the different parts using your GDC.

4. In a certain class the following heights (in m) of students were collected:

   1.77, 1.60, 1.89, 1.54, 1.77, 1.65, 1.86, 1.51, 1.67, 1.94, 1.73, 1.70, 1.66

   a. State the number of elements in the set: _____

   b. What kind of data is this? _____

   c. Fill the table:

Height	Mid – Height (Mi)	Frequency (fi)	Fi · Mi	$(Mi - \mu)^2$	$fi(Mi - \mu)^2$
[1.50 – 1.60)					
[1.60 – 1.70)					
[1.70 – 1.80)					
[1.80 – 1.90)					
[1.90 – 2.00)					
Total					

   d. Obtain the mean: μ = _____

   e. The numbers in the 6th column give us an idea about the _____

      of each _____ to the spread of the data.

   f. The sum of the numbers in the 6th column gives us an idea about the

      _____ of the data. In case this number is 0 it means that

      _____ for example:

   g. Use the table to find the Variance: _____

   h. Use the table to find the Standard Deviation (S.D.): _____

   i. Find the answers to all the different parts using your GDC.

5. The weights in kg of 6 different classes (A, B, C, D, E, F) was collected and represented in the following histograms:

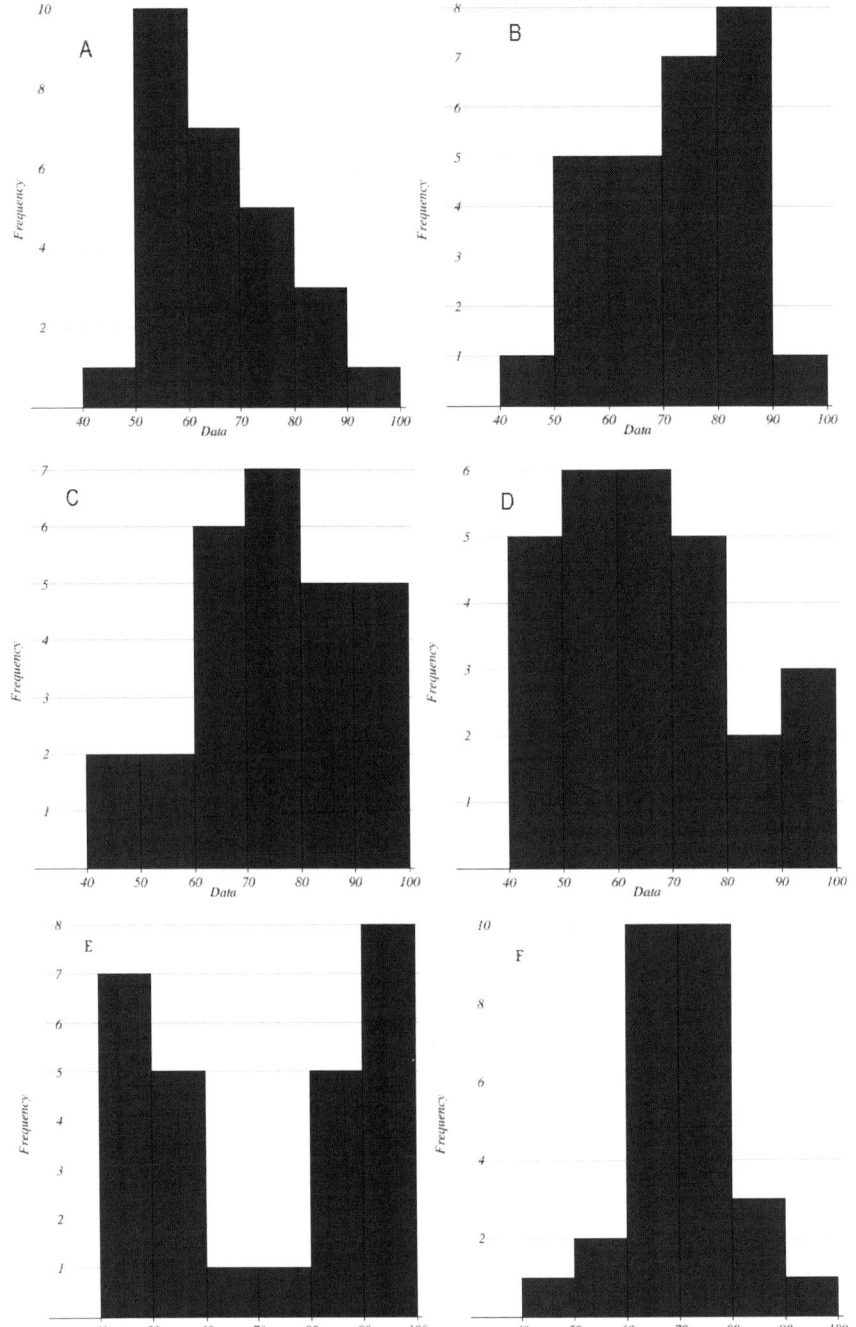

The mean $\bar{x}$ and the S.D. σ are given in the table:

	1	2	3	4	5	6
$\bar{x}$	74.6	65.7	70	72.0	65.7	70.6
σ	14.5	15.6	20.6	12.7	12.1	10.3

a. Find the number of students in the sample: _____

b. Which distribution will the highest SD: _____

c. Which distribution will the lowest SD: _____

d. Match between the histograms and the numerical results. Use the table:

$\bar{x}$ and σ	Class
1	
2	
3	
4	
5	
6	

6. In a certain class students eye color was collected:

Brown, Black, Brown, Blue, Brown, Blue, Green, Brown, Black, Green

a. State the number of elements in the set: _____

b. What kind of data is this? _____

c. Fill the table:

Eye Color	Mid – Color (Mi)	Frequency (fi)	Fi · Mi
Brown			
Blue			
Green			
Black			
Total			

d. What can you say about the measures of spread in this case?

3.1. – SET THEORY

1. A set is _____.

2. Give 3 examples of sets:

3. Consider the set {2, 4, 6, …}

   a. This is the set of _____. The next element is ___

   b. In this set the number of elements is _____It is an _____ set

4. Consider the set {1, 8, 27, …}

   a. This is the set of _____. The next element is ___

   b. In this set the number of elements is _____It is an _____ set

5. Consider the set {Asia, Africa, …}

   a. This is the set of _____. The next element is ___

   b. In this set the number of elements is _____It is an _____ set

6. A **subset** is _____. It is denoted by $A \subseteq B$

7. Given the set L = {A, B, C}

    a. State all the possible subsets of L. include the empty set.

    L1 = _____

    L2 = _____

    L3 = _____

    L4 = _____

    L5 = _____

    L6 = _____

    L7 = _____

    L8 = _____

    b. All the subsets except _____ are called **proper subsets denoted by** $A \subset B$

    c. Explain the difference between a subset and a propersubset.

    d. $A \not\subset B$ means _____

    e. _____ means that A is NOT a subset of B

8. M is the set of perfect square smaller than a 100.

    a. List the elements of M _____

    b. List the subset Q of even numbers in M _____

9. N is the set of prime numbers between 10 and 30.

    a. List the elements of M _____

    b. List the subset Q of even numbers in M _____

10. The **<u>universal set</u>** is particular for _____ and

    contains _____ for the problem. Usually it is

    denoted by the letter _____.

11. The universal set for the students in the classroom is

    U = _____

12. Given the sets U = {John, Raquel, Felix, Shan, Mila, Jessy, Pamela} and the subset of U: B = {Shan, Mila}.

    State the complement of the set B' = _____

13. The **<u>complement of a</u>** set _____

14. The **<u>intersection</u>** of 2 sets is _____. It is denoted by $A \cap B$.

15. The **<u>union</u>** of 2 sets is_____. It is denoted by $A \cup B$

16. For example if S = {1, 2, 3, 4, 5, 6, 7, 8, 9} and M = {2, 6, 10, 12}

    a. $S \cap M =$ _____

    b. $S \cup M =$ _____

17. Given the sets U = {John, Raquel, Felix, Shan, Mila, Jessy, Pamela} and the subset of U: B = {Shan, Mila}.

    a. $U \cap B =$ _____

    b. $U \cup B =$ _____

Venn diagrams

Event	Set Language	Venn diagram	Probability result
Complementary event (A')	Not A		P(A') =
The _____ of A and B (A ∩ B)	Set of elements that belongs to A _____ B		P(A ∪ B) =
The _____ of A and B (A ∪ B)	Set of elements that belongs to A _____ B ____ both		
If (A ∩ B) = ∅ A and B are said to be: _____	The sets A and B are _____		P(A ∪ B) = P(A ∩ B) =

18. Given N, the set of natural numbers, Z the set of integers, Q the set of rationals and R the set of Real numbers.

    a. Write down an element of the set $N \cap Z$: _____

    b. Write down an element of the set $Q \cap Z$: _____

    c. Write down an element of the set $Q \cap Z'$: _____

    d. Write down an element of the set $Q' \cap Z$: _____

    e. Write down an element of the set $R \cap Q$: _____

    f. Write down an element of the set $R \cap Q'$: _____

    g. Write down an element of the set $N \cap N'$: _____

19. Consider the sets: $U = \{x \in N\}$

    $A = \{x \in N \,|\, 11 < x < 21\}$, B={multiples of 4}, and C ={13, 16, 18, 20}

    a. Write all the elements of the set $A \cap B$: _____

    b. Write all the elements of the set $A \cap C$: _____

    c. Write all the elements of the set $B \cap C$: _____

    d. Write all the elements of the set $B \cup C$: _____

    e. Write all the elements of the set $A \cap (B' \cup C)$: _____

    f. Write all the elements of the set $A \cap (B \cup C')$: _____

    g. Write all the elements of the set $A \cap B \cap C')$: _____

    h. True/False: $11 \in A$ True/False: $11 \in A'$

    i. True/False: $13 \in A \cap C$ True/False: $30 \notin B$

    j. True/False: $12 \in A \cap B$ True/False: $30 \notin C$

    k. True/False: $B \subset A$ True/False: $C \subset A$

20. Given the Venn diagram. Shade A∩B

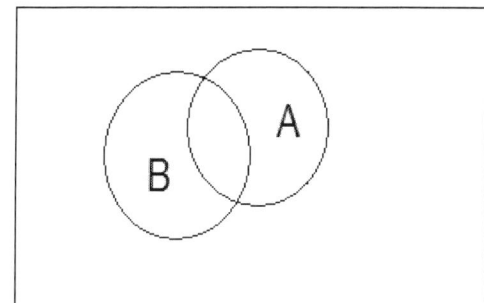

21. Given the Venn diagram. Shade A∩B'

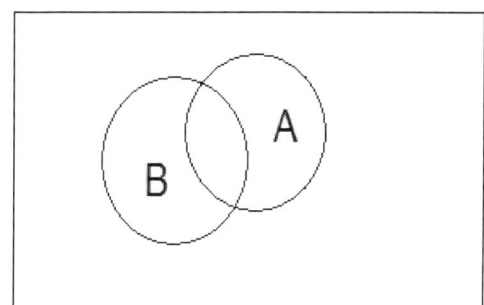

22. Given the Venn diagram. Shade B'

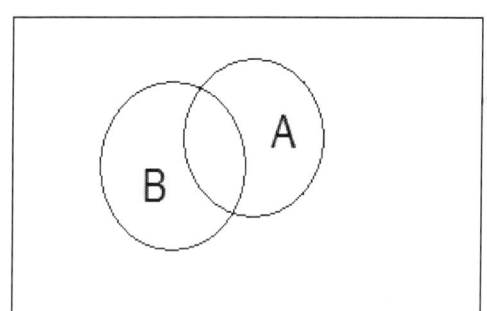

23. Given the Venn diagram. Shade A'∩B'

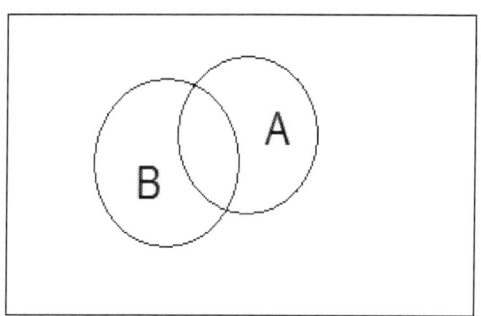

24. Given the Venn diagram. Shade A∪B

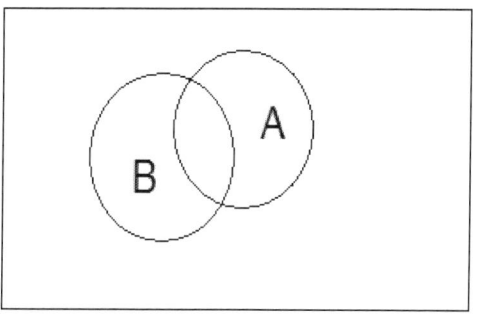

25. Given the Venn diagram. Shade A' ∪ B

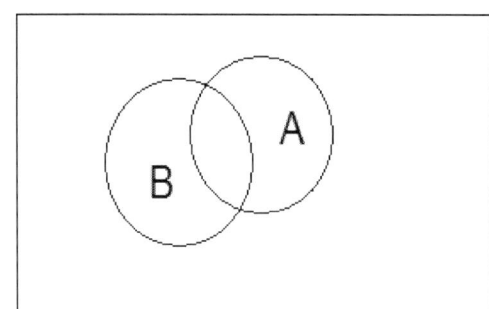

26. Given the Venn diagram. Shade A' ∪ B'

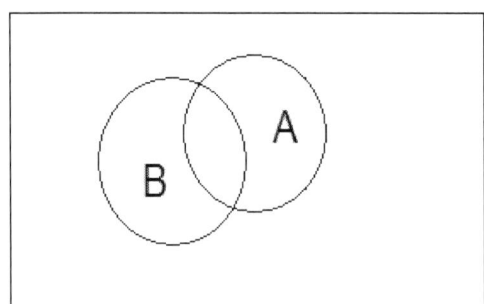

27. Given the Venn diagram. Shade A ∪ B

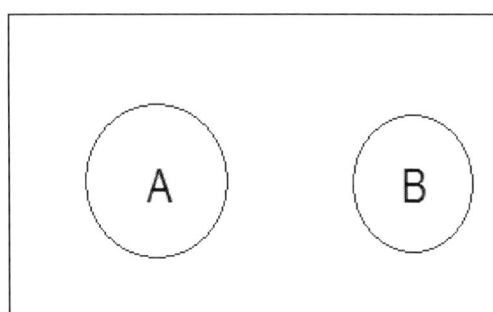

28. Given the Venn diagram. Shade A ∪ B'

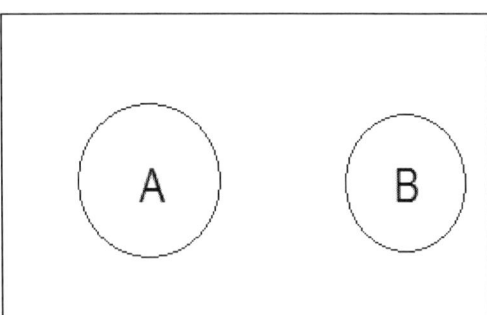

29. Given the Venn diagram. Shade A ∩ B'

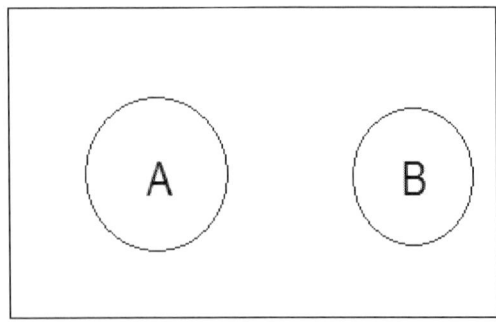

30. Given the Venn diagram. Shade $A \cap B$

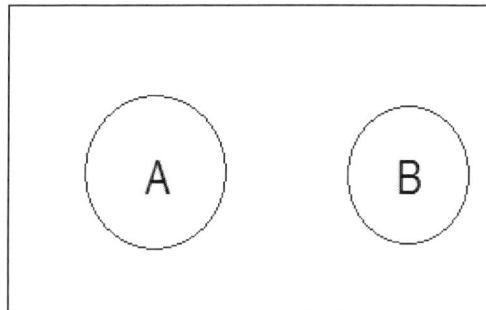

31. Given the Venn diagram. Shade $A \cap B \cap C$

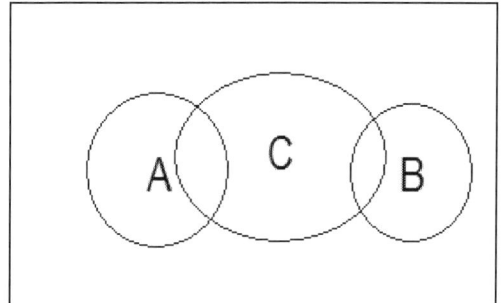

32. Given the Venn diagram. Shade $(A \cup B) \cap C$

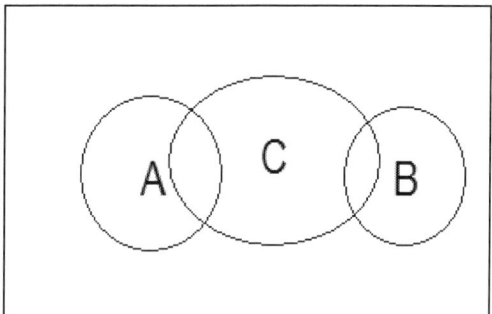

33. Given the Venn diagram. Shade $(A' \cup B) \cap C$

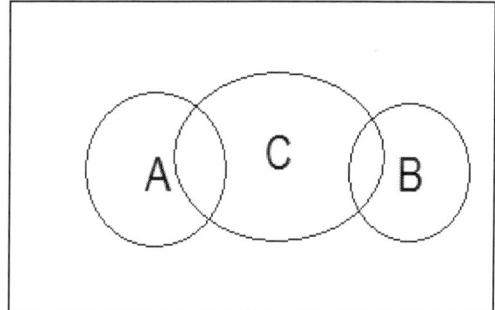

34. Given the Venn diagram. Shade $(A \cup B) \cap C'$

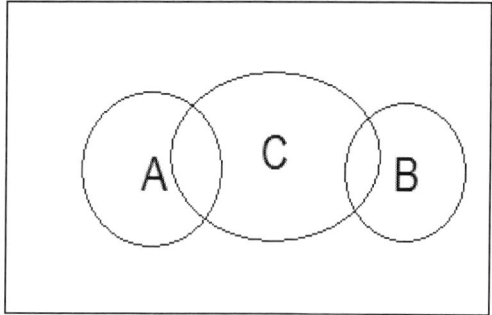

35. Given the Venn diagram. Shade $A \cap B \cap C$

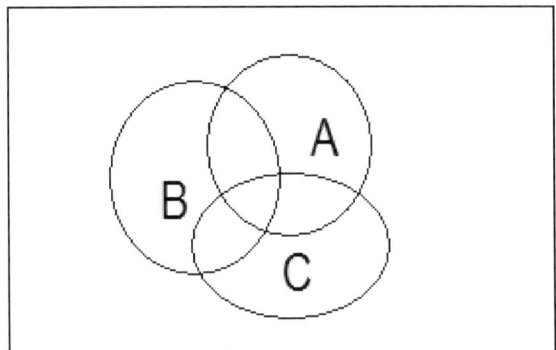

36. Given the Venn diagram. Shade $(A \cap B) \cap C'$

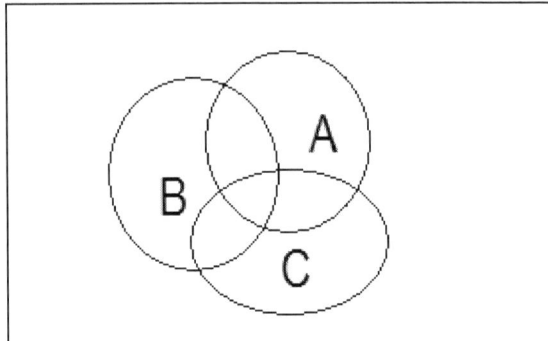

37. Given the Venn diagram. Shade $(A' \cap B) \cap C$

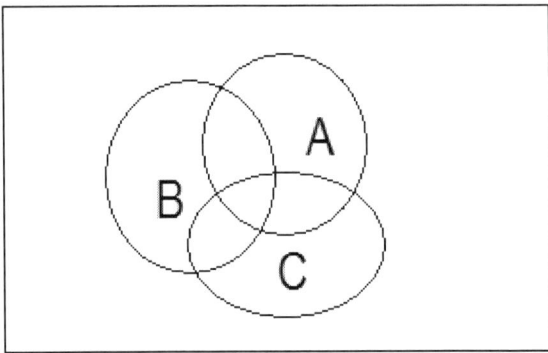

38. Given the Venn diagram. Shade $(A \cap B') \cap C$

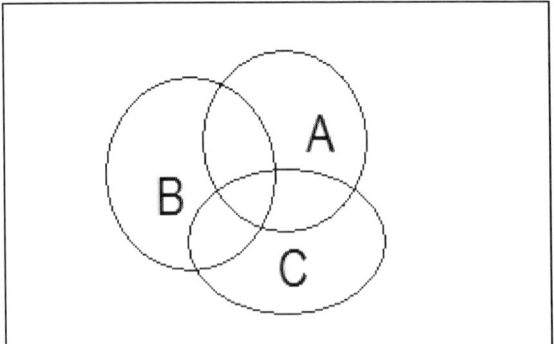

39. 50 drivers were asked about the favourite car colour. 3 choices were given: Red (X), Blue (Y) and White (Z). The results were:

15 liked all three
3 liked red and blue only
9 liked red and white only
7 liked blue and white only
2 liked red only
5 liked white only
1 liked blue only

a. Represent this information in a Venn diagram. Fill the Venn diagram with all the corresponding numbers.
b. Write down the percentage of drivers that did not like any of the 3 colours.

40. Given the sets U = {Real numbers}, A={Negative numbers}, Z={Integers}

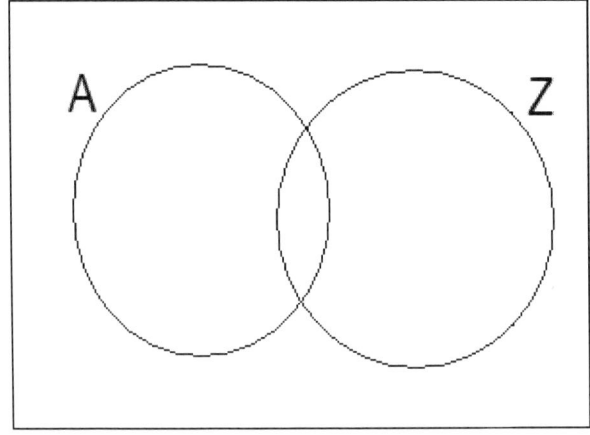

Write the following numbers in the correct region: cos(0), 0.5, $-\pi$, 5^{-2}, -7, 0

41. In a certain hospital in which there are 70 nurses, 20 work in cardiac surgery (C) and 15 others in the intensive care unit (I). 8 nurses work in both units.

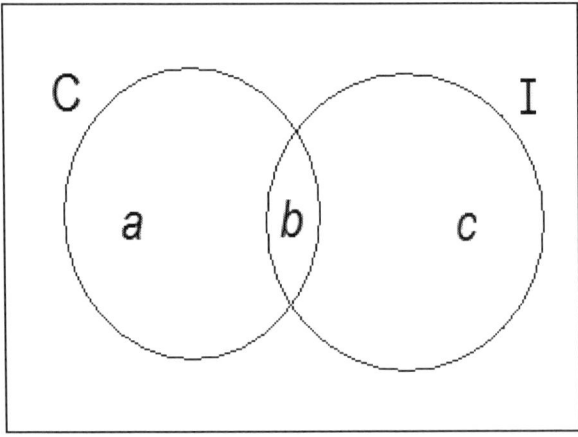

   a.   a = ____   b = ____   c = ____

   b.   Calculate the number of nurses that work outside of the cardiac surgery or intensive care units.

3.2. – LOGIC

1. Logic is a way to describe situations or knowledge in a way that allows drawing new conclusions. It is useful in computer programming, artificial intelligence and better understanding of language.

2. For example:

   a. All swimmers can swim fast
   b. Daniel is a swimmer

   Therefore by using logic, Daniel can _____

3. p: A proposition that is either true or false

   Example: _____

   Example: _____

   Example: _____

   Example that is not a proposition: _____

   Example that is not a proposition: _____

4. $\neg p$ Negation of p

   Example: _____

   Example: _____

   Example: _____

5. Compound statements: A compound statement is:_____

   _____

6. $q \wedge p$ Conjunction: q and p

   Example: _____

   Example: _____

   Example: _____

7. $q \lor p$ Disjunction: q or p

Example: _____

Example: _____

Example: _____

8. $q \veebar p$ Exclusive Disjunction: q or p but not both

Example: _____

Example: _____

Example: _____

9. $p \Rightarrow q$ Implication

Example: _____

Example: _____

Example: _____

10. $p \Leftarrow q$ Converse of an Implication

Example: _____

Example: _____

Example: _____

11. $\neg p \Rightarrow \neg q$ Inverse of an Implication

Example: _____

Example: _____

Example: _____

12. $\neg p \Leftarrow \neg q$ Contrapositive of an Implication

     Example: _____

     Example: _____

     Example: _____

13. $p \Leftrightarrow q$ Equivalence of p and q

     Two statements p, q are equivalent if _____

     If $p \Rightarrow q$ and $p \Leftarrow q$ are both _____ we can say that _____

     Example:

14. Valid arguments: An argument is valid if the conclusion follows the statements, even if the statements are incorrect. For example:

     a. Oranges are white
     b. White fruit are sweet

     Therefore by logic, _____

15. There is a deep analogy between set theory and logic. For example:

     Disjoint: A red chair is never blue, that can be observed in the following sets exercise:

     Sketch the corresponding Venn diagram to the following sets:

     A: Set of red chairs
     B: Set of blue chairs
     C: Set of red chairs with wheels
     D: Set of high chairs

TRUTH TABLES

1. A truth table is a way to show the possibilities of a statement.

2. For example:

    q: Tuesday it will rain
    p: Wednesday it will rain
    r: Thursday it will rain

p	q	$\neg p$	$\neg q$	$q \wedge p$	$q \vee p$	$q \underline{\vee} p$

p	q	r	$\neg r$	$\neg q \wedge r$	$(\neg r \vee p) \wedge q$	$\neg(q \underline{\vee} p)$

3. Tautology: When a statement is always _____ it is considered a tautology.

4. Logical contradiction: When a statement is always _____ it is considered a logical contradiction.

p	$\neg p$	$p \wedge \neg p$	$\neg(p \wedge \neg p)$

5. Implication:

p	q	$q \Rightarrow p$

6. Converse

p	q	$q \Leftarrow p$

7. Given the logic propositions:

   p: Daniel eats ice cream

   q: Daniel plays soccer

   Write in words:

   a. $q \wedge p$ _____

   b. $q \wedge \neg p$ _____

   c. $q \underline{\vee} p$ _____

   d. $q \Rightarrow p$ _____

   e. $q \Rightarrow \neg p$ _____

8. Consider the propositions p and q. Complete the table

p	r	$\neg r$	$p \Rightarrow \neg r$	$\neg p$	$\neg p \Rightarrow r$	$(p \Rightarrow \neg r) \Leftrightarrow (\neg p \Rightarrow r)$
T	T					
T	F					
F	T					
F	F					

9. Consider the propositions p and q. Complete the table

p	r	....	$p \Rightarrow \neg r$
T	T	F	
T	F	F	
F	T	T	
F	F	T	

10. Given the logic propositions:

p: Maria loves to dance.

q: Maria will dance for 2 hours.

r: Maria will go swimming.

Write in symbolic form:

a. Maria does not like to dance   _____

b. If Maria loves to dance then she will dance for 2 hours   _____

c. Maria doesn't love to dance therefore she will not dance for 2 hours _____

d. Maria will dance for 2 hours or she will go swimming   _____

e. Maria will dance for 2 hours or she will go swimming but not both _____

f. Maria will dance for 2 hours and she will go swimming   _____

Write in words:

g. $(q \wedge \neg r) \Rightarrow \neg p$ _____

11. Given the logic propositions:

   p: a number is an integer

   q: a number can be divided by 2

   r: a number is odd

Write in symbolic form:

a. If a number is an integer and it is not odd then it can be divided by 2

b. Write the contrapositive of the previous statement.

c. Write in words:

   $(q \vee r) \Rightarrow p$ _____

   $p \Rightarrow (q \vee r)$ _____

12. complete the table:

p	r	$\neg r$	$\neg r \wedge p$	$\neg p$	$(\neg r \wedge p) \vee (\neg p)$	$(\neg r \wedge p) \vee (\neg p) \Rightarrow r$

4.1. – PROBABILITY

Probability is the science of chance or likelihood of an event happening

If a random experiment is repeated _____ times in such a way that each of the trials is identical and independent, where n(A) is the _____ event A occurred, then:

$$\text{Relative frequency of event A} = P(A) = \frac{n(A)}{N} \quad (N \to \infty)$$

Exercises:

1. In an unbiased coin what is P(head) ? _____

   This probability is called _____.

2. Explain the difference between theoretical probability and "regular" probability.

3. Throw a drawing pin at least 15 times and fill the table:

	Fell pointing upwards	Fell on its side	Total number of throws
Number of events			
Probability			

4. The definition of probability is:

$$P(A) = \frac{Number \underline{\hspace{5cm}}}{Total \underline{\hspace{5cm}}}$$

Properties of probability

1. ___ $\leq P(A) \leq$ ___

2. $P(U) =$ _____

Exercises

1. The events A and B are such $P(A) = 0.2$, $P(B) = 0.4$ and $P(A \cup B) = 0.5$. Find:

    a. $P(A \cap B)$
    b. $P(B')$
    c. Sketch the corresponding Venn diagram.
    d. $P(A' \cap B)$
    e. $P(A' \cap B')$
    f. Are the events A and B Independent? Explain.

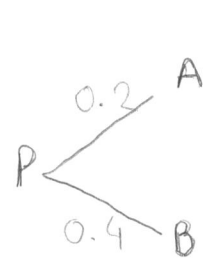

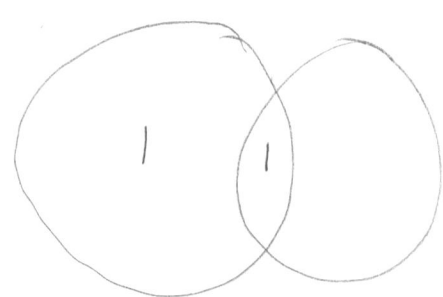

$$P\left(A \cup B\right) = 0.5$$

$$P\left(A \cap B\right) = 0.1$$

2. The events A and B are such $P(A) = 0.15$, $P(B) = 0.3$ and $P(A \cup B) = 0.4$, Find:

   a. $P(A \cap B)$
   b. $P(B')$
   c. Sketch the corresponding Venn diagram.
   d. $P(A' \cap B)$
   e. $P(A' \cap B')$
   f. Are the events A and B Independent? Explain.

3. The events A and B are such $P(A) = 0.3$, $P(B) = 0.6$ and $P(A \cup B) = 0.9$, Find:

   a. $P(A \cap B)$
   b. $P(B')$
   c. Sketch the corresponding Venn diagram.
   d. $P(A' \cap B)$
   e. $P(A' \cap B')$
   f. Are the events A and B Independent? Explain.

4. The events A and B are such $P(A) = 0.2$, $P(B) = 0.9$ and $P(A \cap B) = 0.1$, Find:

    a. $P(A \cup B)$
    b. $P(B')$
    c. Sketch the corresponding Venn diagram.
    d. $P(A' \cap B)$
    e. $P(A' \cap B')$
    f. Are the events A and B Independent? Explain.

5. 20% of certain city census consume alcohol regularly, 40% do sport regularly and 10% do both.

   a. Represent the information in a diagram.
   b. Calculate the probability that someone chosen at random only drinks alcohol regularly.
   c. Calculate the probability that someone chosen at random only drink alcohol regularly or only practices sport regularly (but not both).
   d. Calculate the probability that someone picked at random does not drink alcohol nor practices sport regularly.

6. $P(A) = 0.46$, $P(B) = 0.33$, $P(A \cap B) = 0.15$.

   a. Represent the information in a diagram.
   b. Find the probability that an event is not A nor B.

CONDITIONAL PROBABILITY

Informal definition: **Knowing** that B has happened, what is the probability that A will happen (Written as P(A|B))

Formal definition: The probability of and event A given event B is:

$$P(A|B) = \frac{P(A \cap B)}{P(B)}, \; P(B) \neq 0$$

INDEPENDENT EVENTS

Informal definition: P(B) is not influenced by P(A).

Formal definition : $P(A \cap B) = P(A)P(B)$

Exercises

1. What is the difference between independent events and mutually exclusive events?

2. Give an example of independent events.

3. In a certain town the probability of a rainy day is 0.58 and the probability of strong wind is 0.76. If these are independent events, find the probability of:

    a. A rainy windy day.
    b. A dry windy day.
    c. A dry and not windy day.
    d. 2 consecutive rainy days.
    e. 2 consecutive windy rainy days.

Lattice diagrams

4. Two dice numbered one to six are rolled onto a table.

   a. Sketch a corresponding diagram.
   b. Find the probability that the sum is 7.
   c. Find the probability that the sum is more than 7.
   d. Find the probability that the sum is less than 4.
   e. Find the probability that the sum is even.
   f. Find the probability of obtaining a sum of five given that the sum is seven or less.
   g. Find the probability of obtaining a sum of 4 given that the sum is even.

5. A die and coin are rolled on a table.

   a. Sketch a corresponding diagram.
   b. Find the probability of getting Tail and an even number.
   c. Find the probability of getting Tail and a 4.
   d. Find the probability of obtaining a 5 knowing that a tail was obtained.

TOTAL PROBABILITY

Solved Example

It is known that:

    i.   1% of women aged 40 have breast cancer
    ii.   A mammography test has 80% success rate.
    iii.   A mammography test has 10% false alarm rate

A woman receives a positive mammography test, what is the probability she really has cancer?

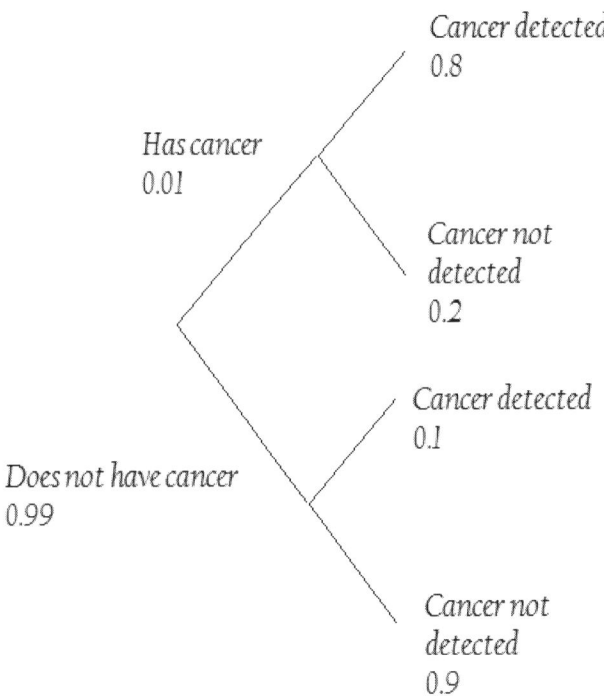

$$P \text{ (True yes} | \text{ (All Yeses)} = \frac{0.01 \cdot 0.8}{0.01 \cdot 0.8 + 0.99 \cdot 0.1} \approx 0.0748$$

The woman has 7.5% probability to have cancer.

TREE DIAGRAMS

6. If the probability of tail is 0.53, find the probability of at least one tail in 2 throws.

7. An urn contains 8 cubes of which 5 are black and the rest are white.

   a. What is the probability to draw a white cube?
   b. Draw a tree diagram in case a 1st cube is drawn, it is **NOT replaced** and then another cube is drawn. Indicate all the probabilities on the tree diagram.
   c. Calculate the probability to draw 2 consecutive black cubes.
   d. Calculate the probability to draw **at least** 1 black cube.
   e. Given that the first cube drawn was white, calculate the probability that the 2nd is black.

8. A bag contains 3 red balls, 4 blue balls and 5 green balls. A ball is chosen at random from the bag and is not replaced. A second ball is chosen. Find the probability of choosing one green ball and one blue ball in any order.

9. Given that events A and B are independent with $P(A \cap B) = 0.4$ and $P(A \cap B')$ = 0. Find $P(A \cup B)$.

10. Given that $P(A) = 0.4$, $P(B) = 0.7$ and $P(A \cup B) = 0.8$. Find:

    a. $P(A \cap B)$
    b. $P(A \mid B)$
    c. Determine if A and B are independent events.

11. Given that $P(A) = 0.4$, $P(B) = 0.6$ and $P(A \cup B) = 0.76$.

    a. Find $P(A \cap B)$
    b. Are events A and B mutually exclusive? Explain.
    c. Are events A and B independent?

12. The events A and B are independent, where A is the event "it will rain today" and B is the event "We will go out for pizza". It is known that

$$P(B) = 0.3, \ P(A \mid B) = 0.6, \ P(A \mid B') = 0.5.$$

a. Complete the following tree diagram.

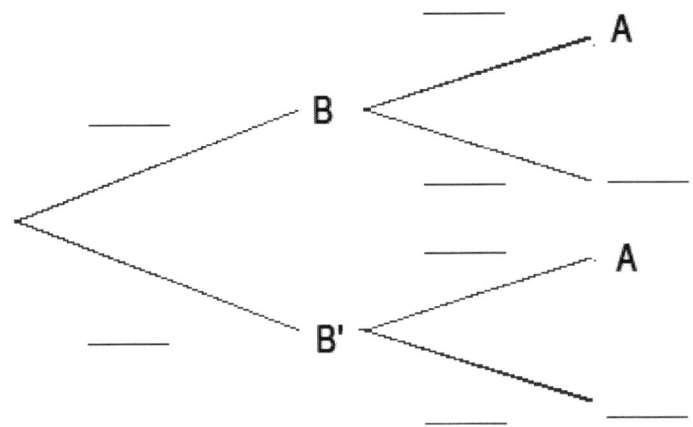

b. Calculate the probability that it rains knowing we went out for pizza.

5.1. – INTRODUCTION TO FUNCTION

1. Write the definition of a function in your own words:

2. Write 2 examples of relations that <u>are</u> functions:

3. Draw a sketch of the functions that describe those relations. Can you write the mathematical expression to describe them?

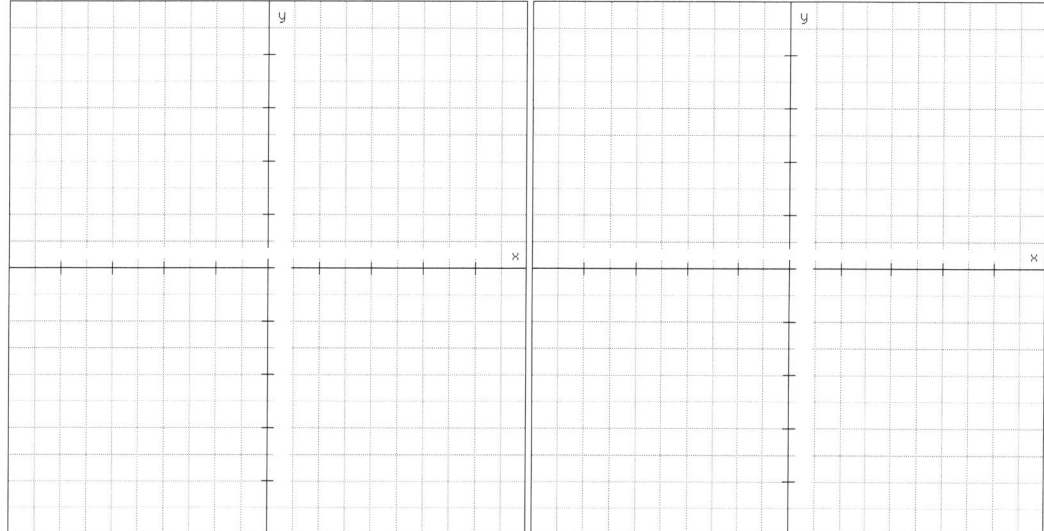

4. Write 2 examples of relations that <u>are not</u> functions:

5. Which one of the following graphs cannot represent function:

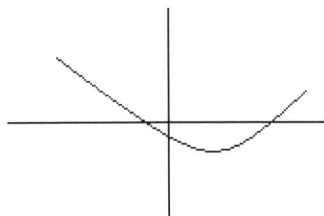
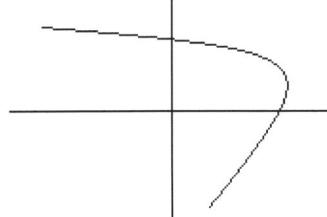

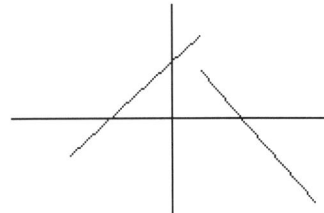
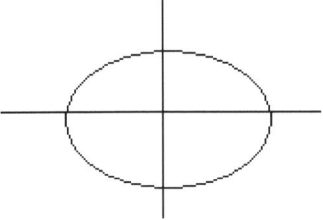

6. Draw an example of a curve that is not a function:

7. Draw an example of a curve that is a function:

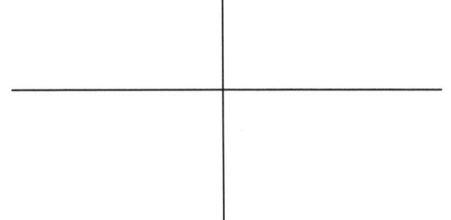

8. The domain of a function is the: _____

9. The Range of a function is the: _____

10. Given the Height – age curve for a human.

a. Sketch an approximate graph:

Height (cm)

|

Age (years)

b. In your sketch Height(0) = _____ , it is the height of _____

c. In your sketch Height(t) = 100cm. Then t is: _____

d. State its domain: _____

e. State its range: _____

11. Out of the following relations circle the ones that are functions:

    a. Person's name → Person's age
    b. City → Number of habitants
    c. City → Names of habitants
    d. Family → Home Address
    e. Satellite's name → Position of satellite
    f. Time → Position of object
    g. One → One
    h. One → Many
    i. Many → One

12. Given the function:

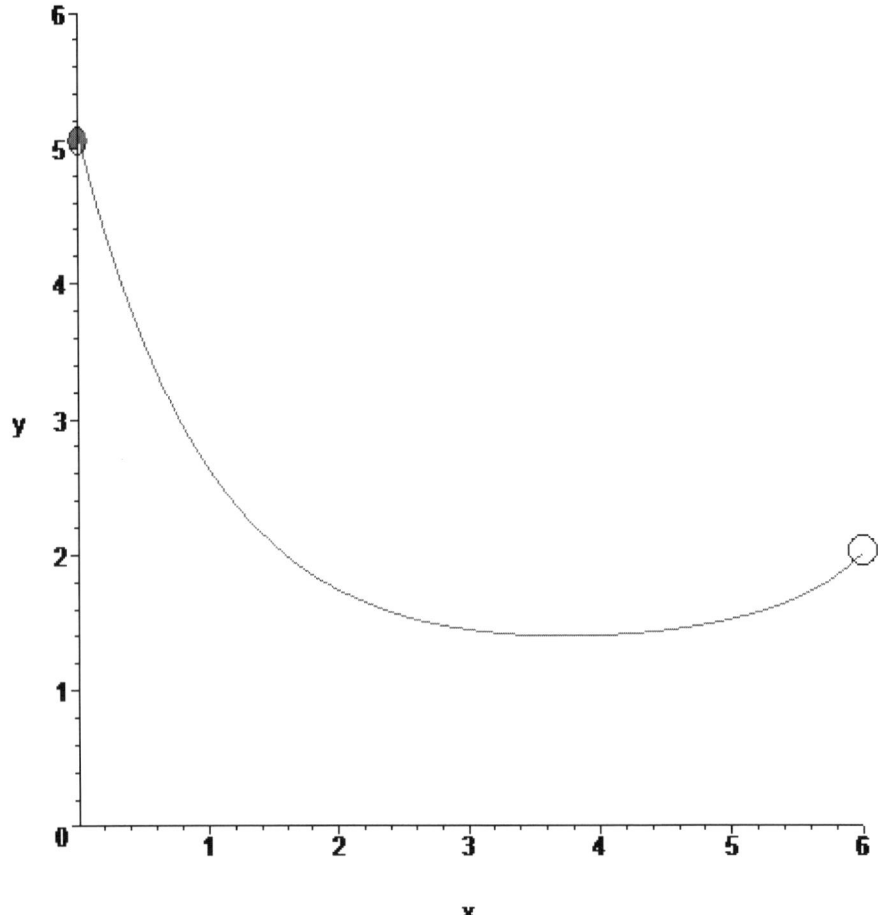

a. f(0) = __5__

b. f(2) = __1.8__ = f(__1.8__)

c. f(7) = _____

d. f(x) = 3, __x = _____

e. f(x) = 2, __x = _____

f. State its domain: _____

g. State its range: _____

h. Is this function one to one? One to many? Explain.

13. Given the function:

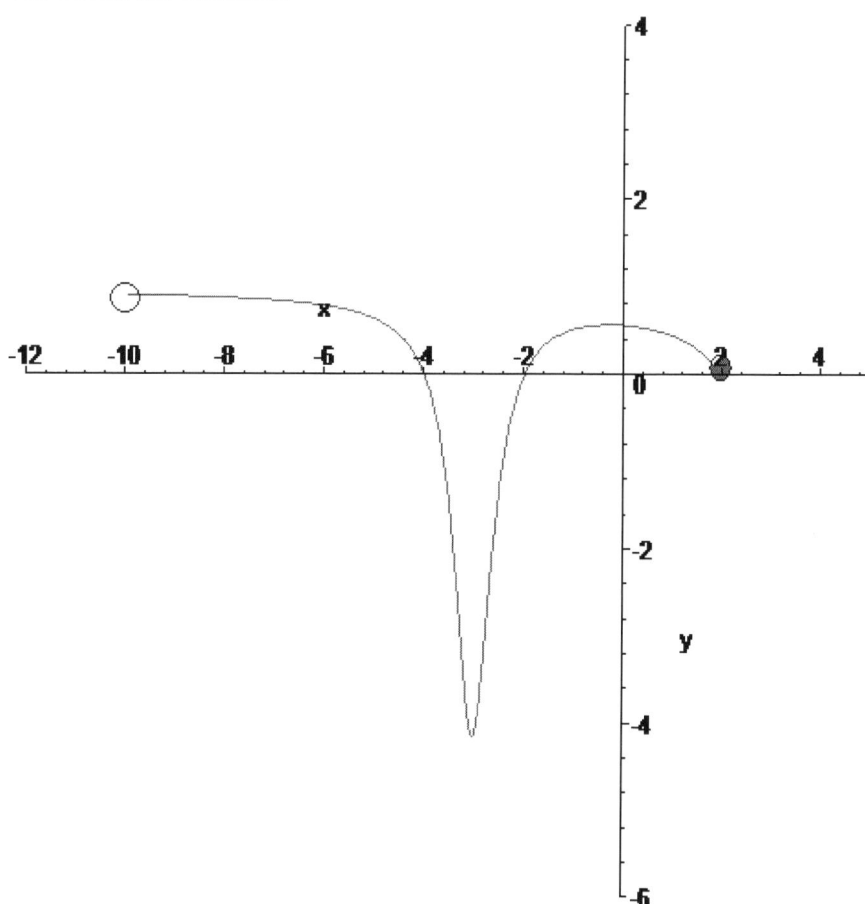

a. f(x) = 0, _____

b. f(0) = _____ =f(__)

c. f(–8) = _____

d. f(–3) = _____

e. f(–4) = _____ =f(__)

f. f(3) = _____

g. State its domain: _____

h. State its range: _____

i. Is this function one to one? One to many? Explain.

14. Given the following function:

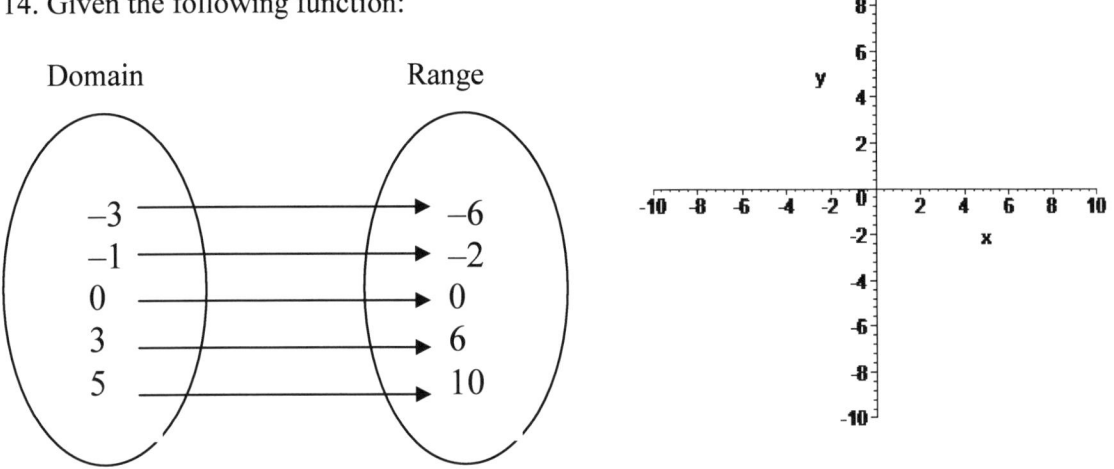

Domain   Range

-3 → -6
-1 → -2
0 → 0
3 → 6
5 → 10

a. What are the allowed values for the independent variable (The domain)?

b. What are the allowed values for the dependent variable (The range)?

c. Sketch the function on the graph.

d. Can you write a mathematical expression to express this function?

15. Given the following function:

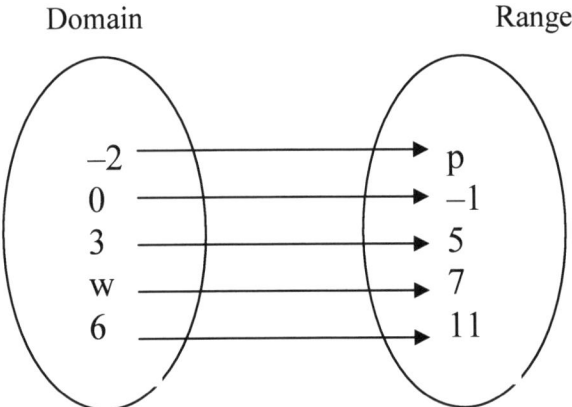

Domain   Range

-2 → p
0 → -1
3 → 5
w → 7
6 → 11

a. Can you write a mathematical expression to express this function?

b. Find p. Find w.

16. Use the graph below to answer the following:

    a. $f(0) =$ ____

    b. $f(7) =$ ____

    c. $f(2) =$ ____

    d. Is $f(-1/2)$ positive or negative?

    e. For what values of x is $f(x) = 0$

    f. Is $f(1) > f(7)$?

    g. For what values of x is $f(x) > 0$?

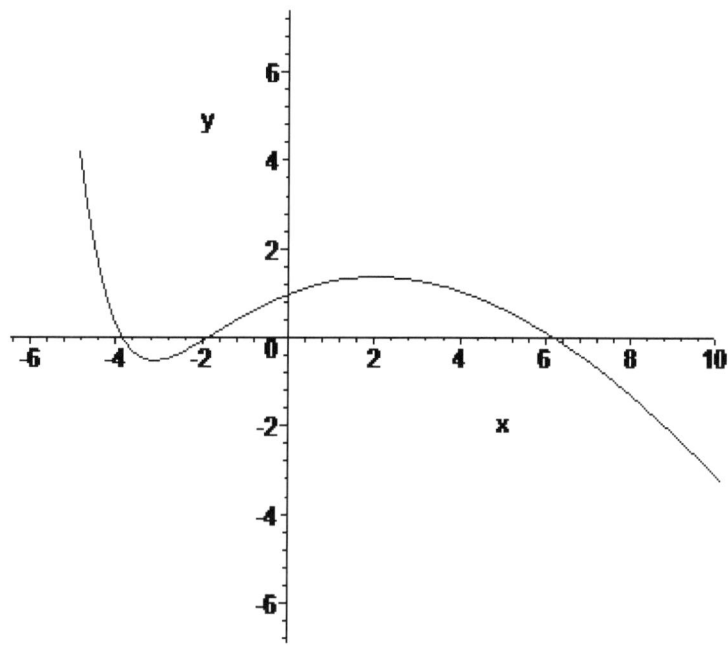

17. Functions can be represented using: _____ or _____.

18. The following graph models the concentration of a drug injected into the blood as a function of the time (in minutes) since the injection. $t = 0$ corresponds to the time of injection.

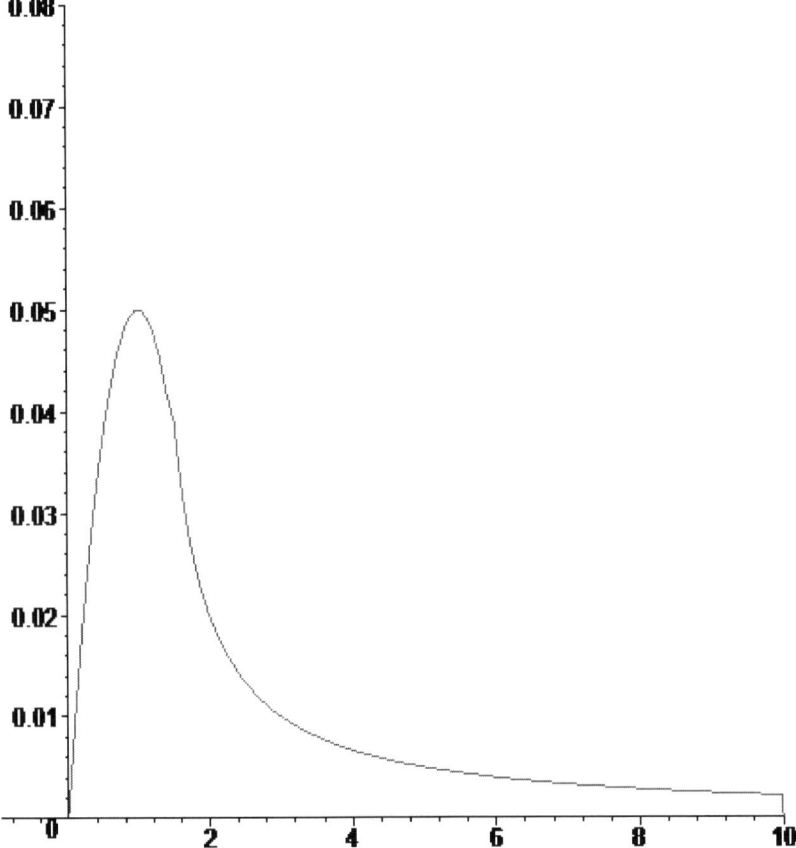

a. What is the concentration of the drug 4 hours after the injection?

b. During what period of time is the concentration increasing?

c. After how long is the concentration maximum?

d. When is the concentration greater than 0.02?

e. State the domain and range of the function.

19. The graph below models the temperature in C° on a particular day as a function of time since midnight.

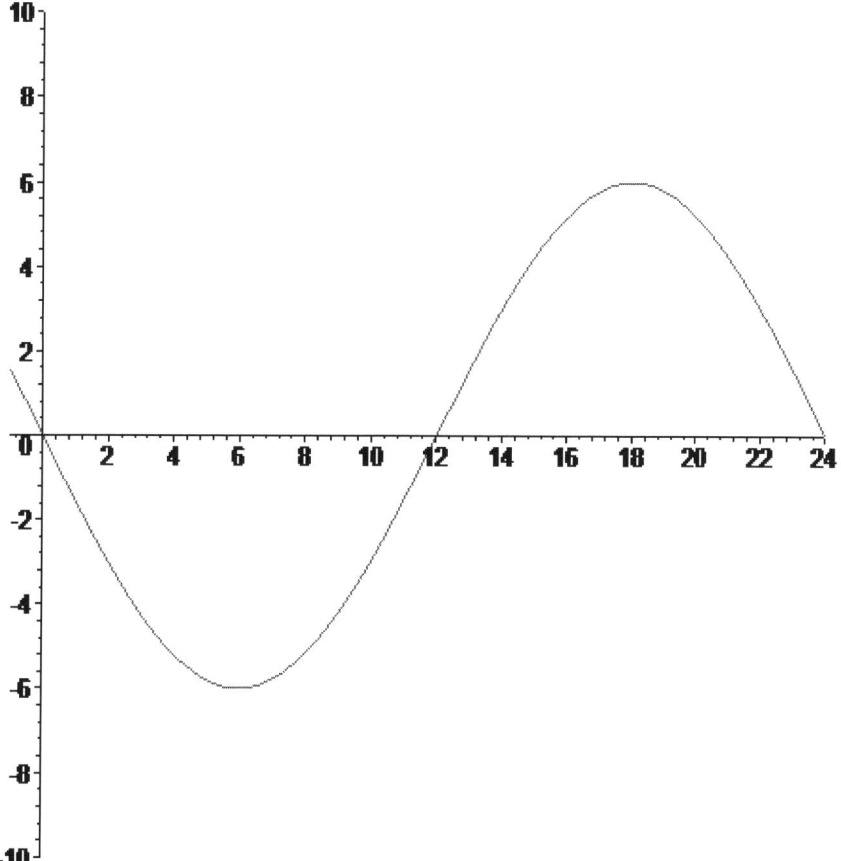

a. What was the temperature at 4:00 a.m.?

b. When was the temperature 4 degrees?

c. When was the temperature below freezing? (less than 0 degrees)

d. When was the temperature increasing?

f. State the domain and range of the function.

5.2. – LINEAR FUNCTIONS

1. Given the function: f(x) = –5

- Complete the following table:

X	–5	–4	–3	–2	–1	0	1	2	3	4	5
f(x)											

- Sketch the points of the chart on a graph (use a ruler).

- State the domain of the function: _____

- State the *y* intercept (sketched on the graph: (____ , ____)

- State the *x* intercept: (____ , ____)

- The function is increasing on the interval: _____

- The function is decreasing on the interval: _____

- Sketch the function of the graph used for the points initially drawn

- State the range of the function: _____

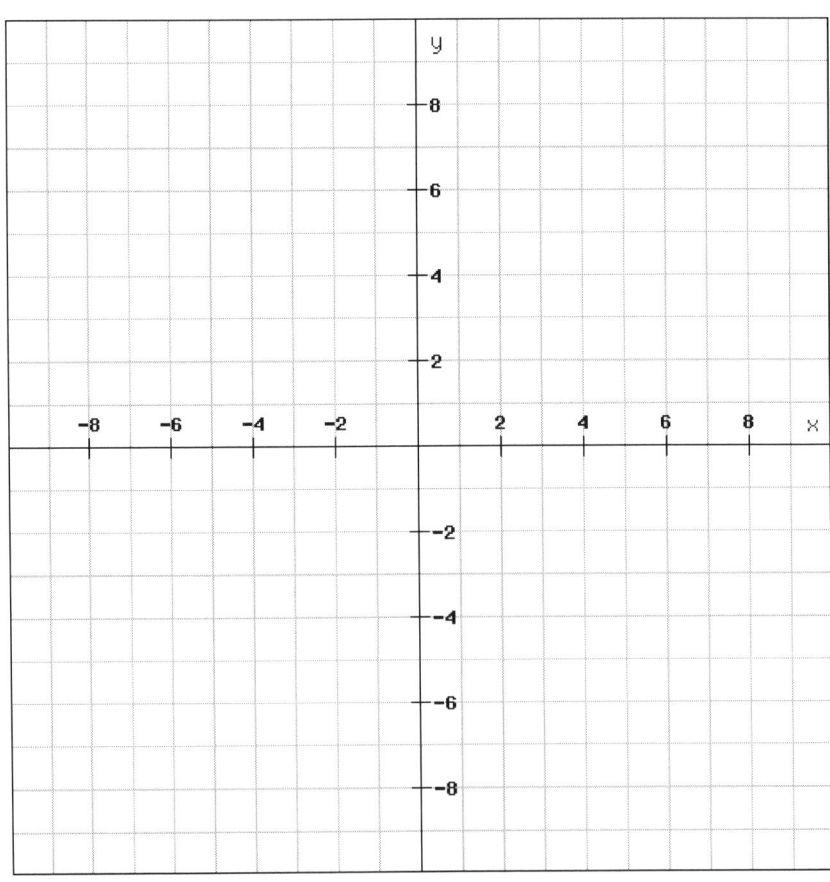

2. Given the function: f(x) = x + 3

- Complete the following table:

x	−5	−4	−3	−2	−1	0	1	2	3	4	5
f(x)											

- Sketch the points of the chart on a graph (use a ruler).

- State the domain of the function: _____

- State the y intercept (sketched on the graph: (____, ____)

- State the x intercept: (____, ____)

- The function is increasing on the interval: _____

- The function is decreasing on the interval: _____

- Sketch the function of the graph used for the points initially drawn

- State the range of the function: _____

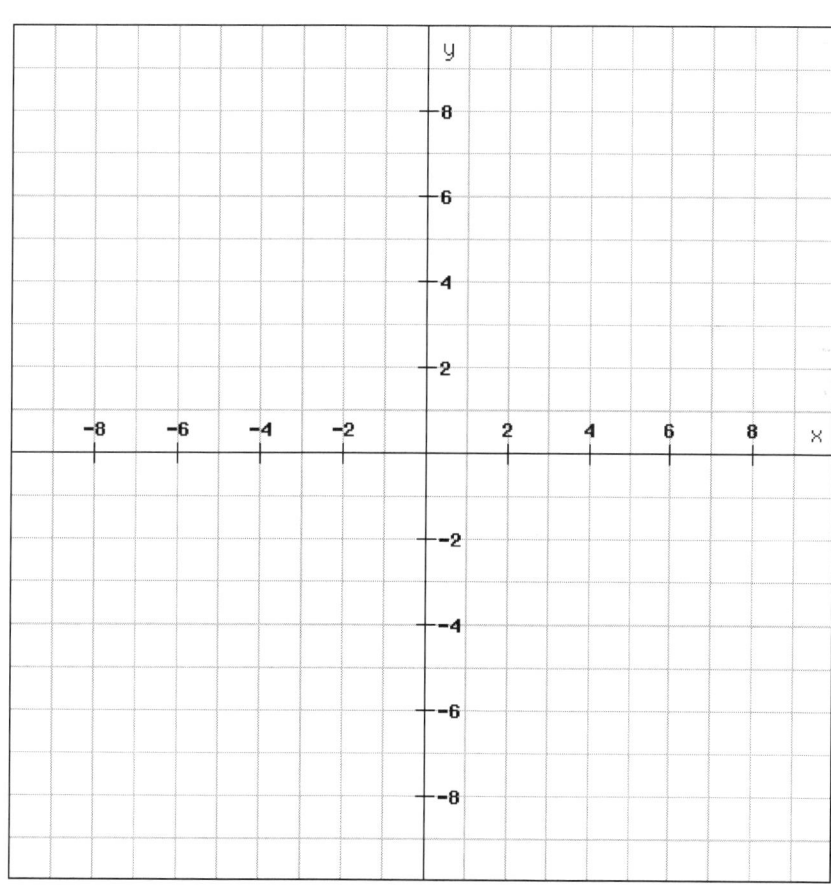

3. Given the function: f(x) = –2x – 5

- Complete the following table:

x	–5	–4	–3	–2	–1	0	1	2	3	4	5
f(x)											

- Sketch the points of the chart on a graph (use a ruler).

- State the domain of the function: _____

- State the y intercept (sketched on the graph: (____, ____)

- State the x intercept: (____, ____)

- The function is increasing on the interval: _____

- The function is decreasing on the interval: _____

- Sketch the function of the graph used for the points initially drawn

- State the range of the function: _____

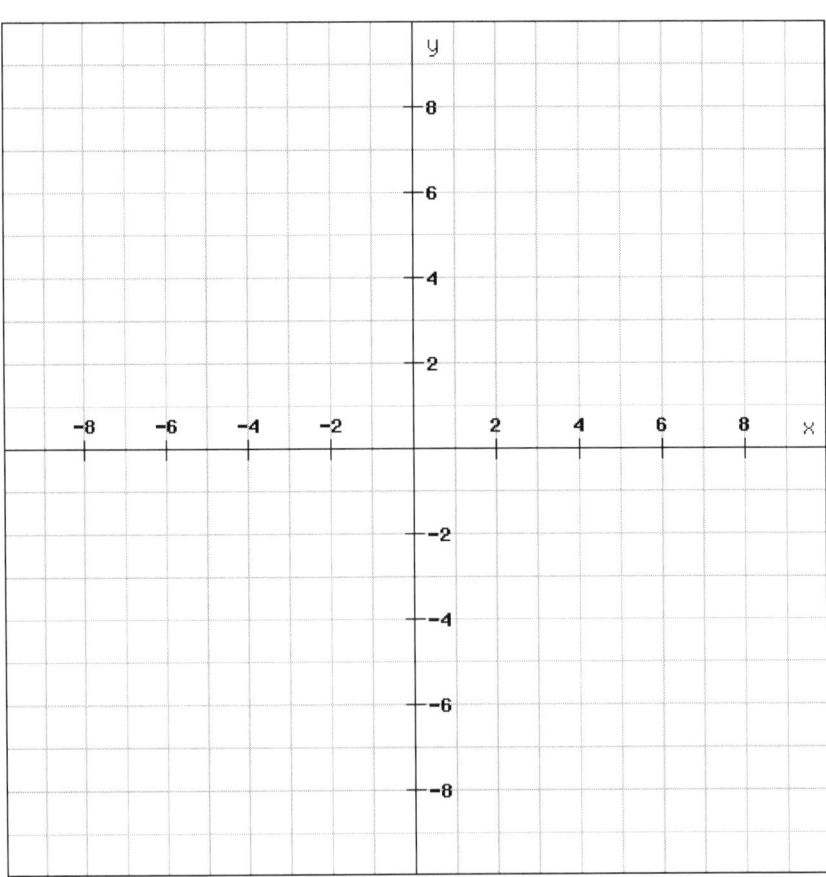

4. Given the function: f(x) = 4x – 3

- Complete the following table:

x	–5	–4	–3	–2	–1	0	1	2	3	4	5
f(x)											

- Sketch the points of the chart on a graph (use a ruler).

- State the domain of the function: _____

- State the y intercept (sketched on the graph: (____ , ____)

- State the x intercept: (____ , ____)

- The function is increasing on the interval: _____

- The function is decreasing on the interval: _____

- Sketch the function of the graph used for the points initially drawn

- State the range of the function: _____

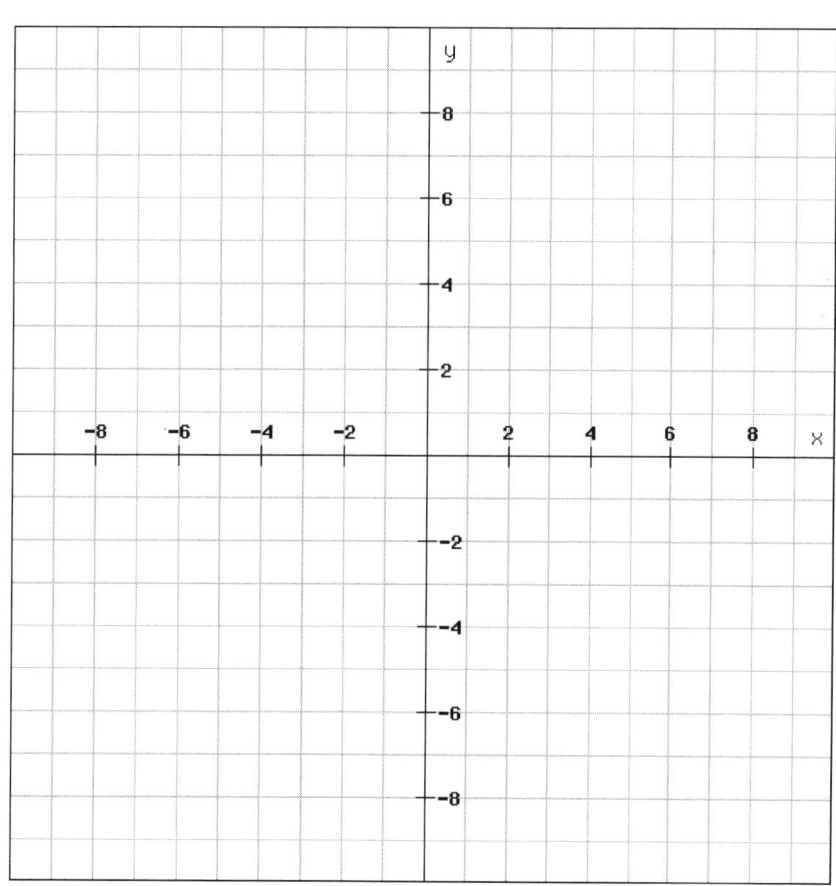

5. Given below are the equations for five different lines. Match the function with its graph.

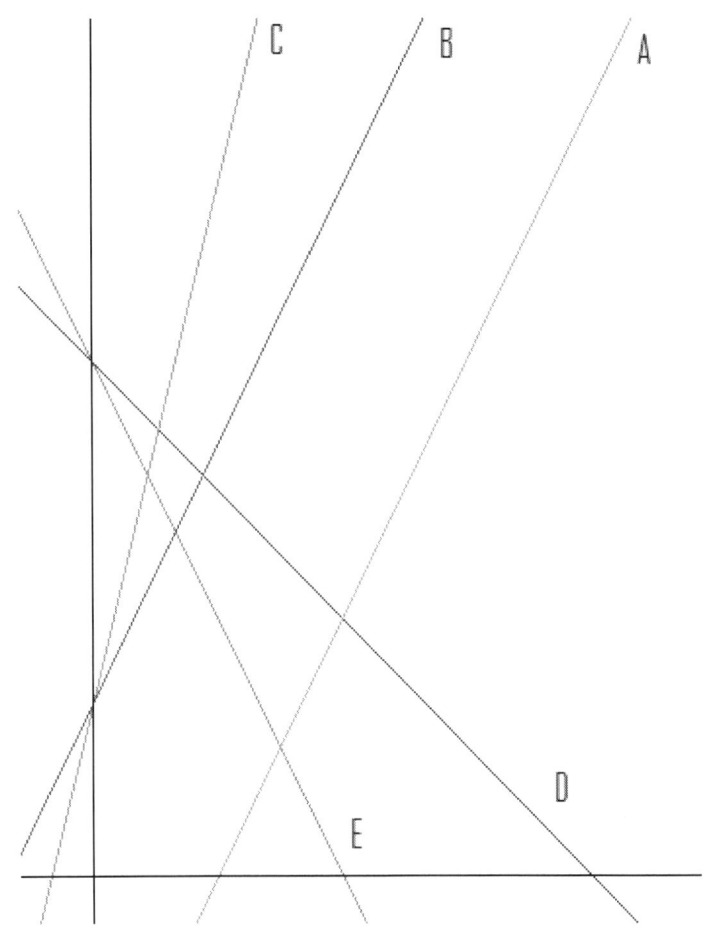

Function	On the graph
f(x) = 20 + 2x	
g(x) = 4x + 20	
s(x) = –30 + 2x	
a(x) = 60 – x	
b(x) = – 2x + 60	

6. The general functions that describes a straight line is _____

7. We know a function is a straight line because _____

8. The y–intercept (also called vertical intercept), tells us where the line crosses the

   _____. The corresponding point is of the form (,   ).

9. The x–intercept (also called horizontal intercept), tells us where the line crosses the

   _____. The corresponding point is of the form (,   ).

10. If m > 0, the line _____ left to right. If _____ the line decreases left to right.

11. In case the line is horizontal m is _____ and the line is of the form _____.

12. The larger the value of m is, the _____ the graph of the line is.

13. Given the graph, write, the slope (m), b and the equation of the line:

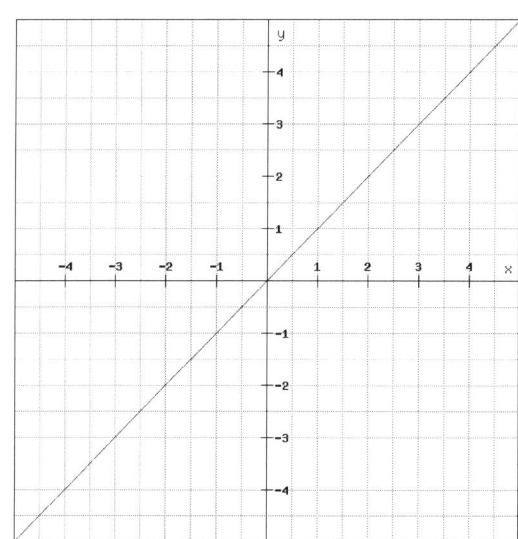

m = _____ b = _____ f(x) = _____

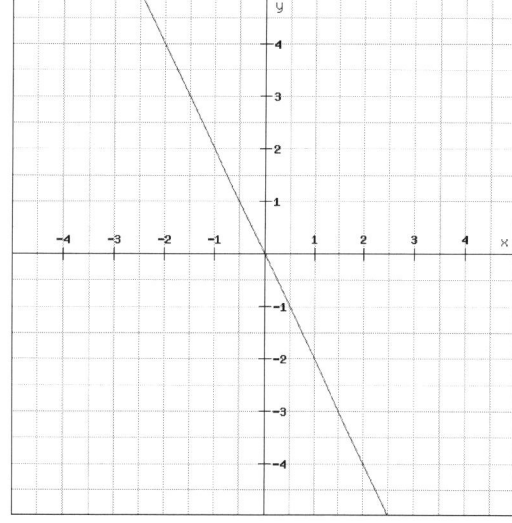

m = _____ b = _____ f(x) = _____

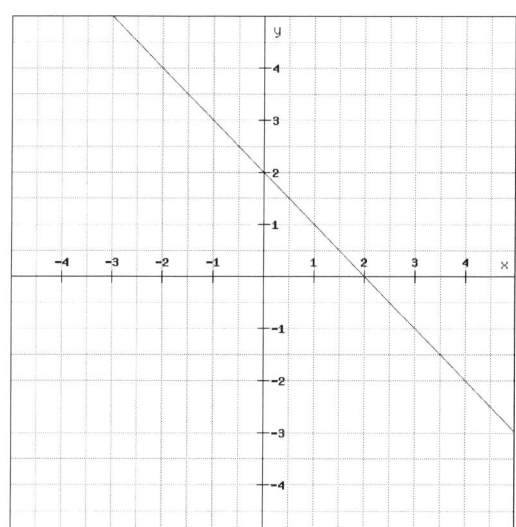

m = _____ b = _____ f(x) = _____

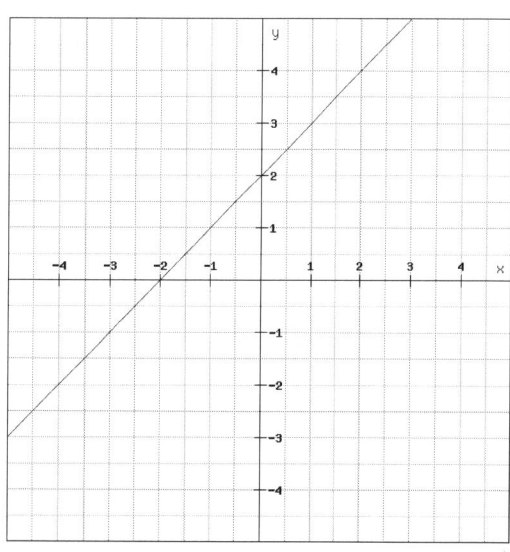

m = _____ b = _____ f(x) = _____

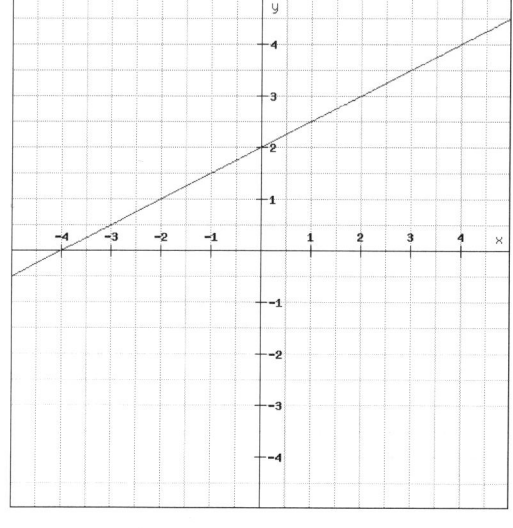

m = _____ b = _____ f(x) = _____

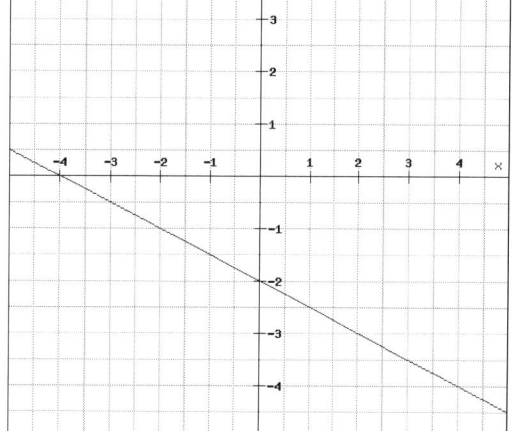

m = _____ b = _____ f(x) = _____

113

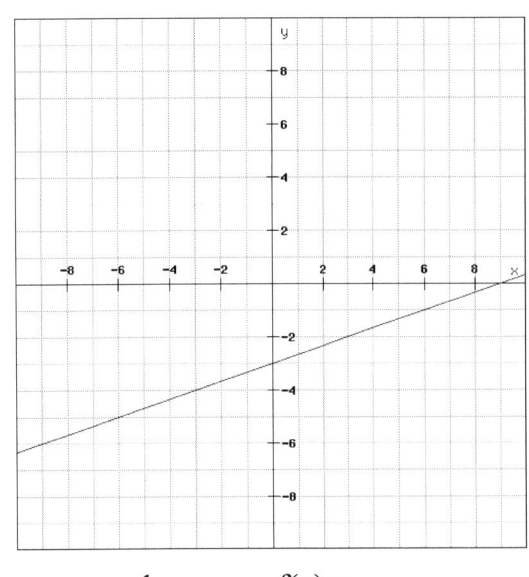

m = _____ b = _____ f(x) = _____

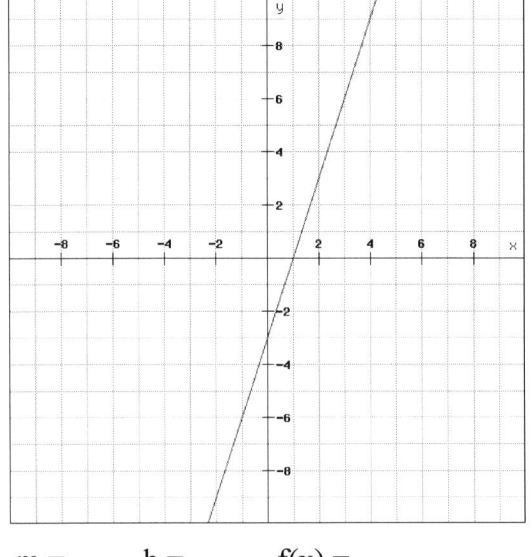

m = _____ b = _____ f(x) = _____

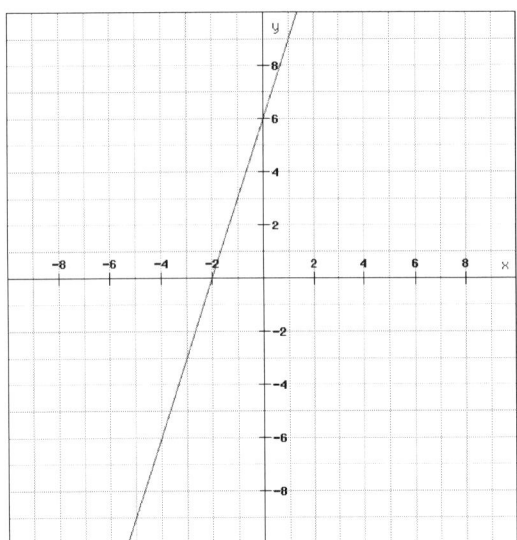

m = _____ b = _____ f(x) = _____

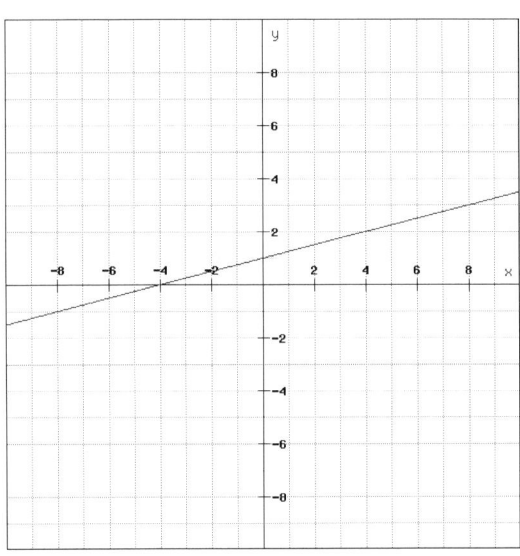

m = _____ b = _____ f(x) = _____

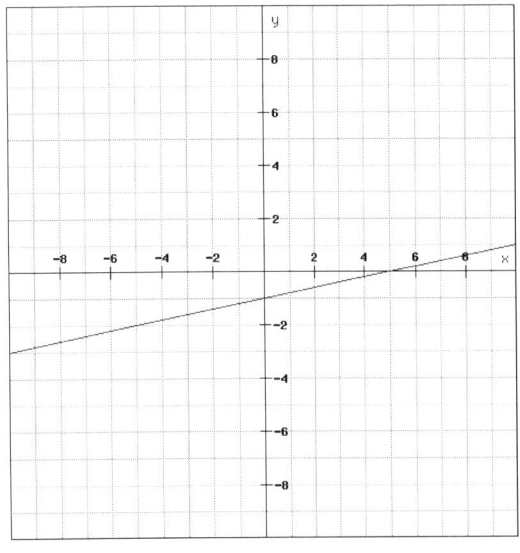

m = _____ b = _____ f(x) = _____

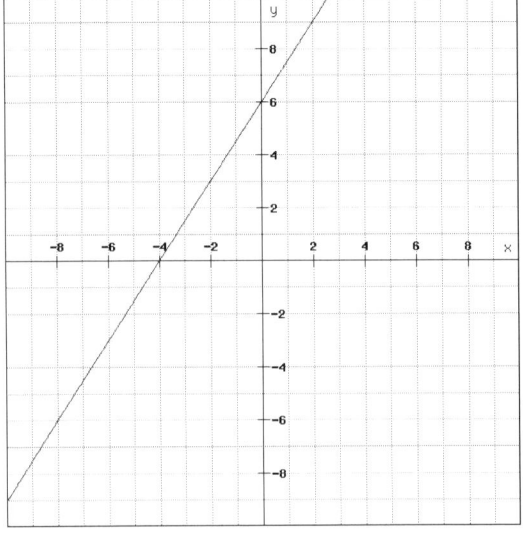

m = _____ b = _____ f(x) = _____

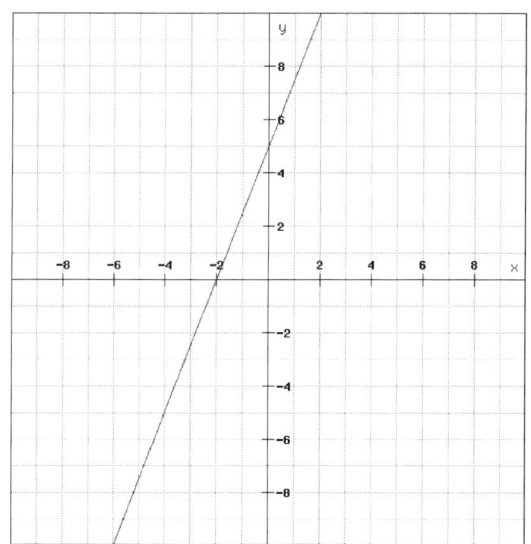

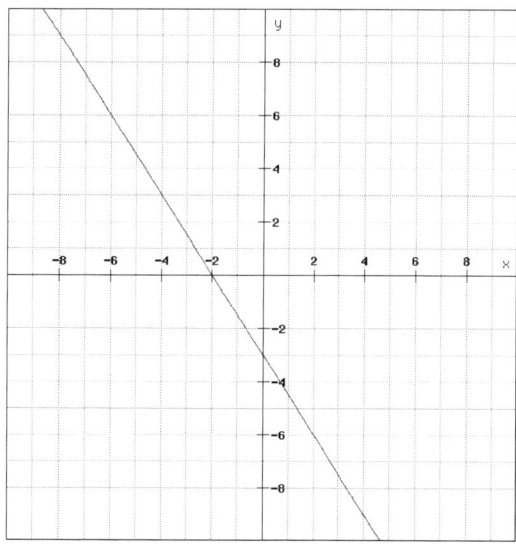

m = _____ b = _____ f(x) = _____

m = _____ b = _____ f(x) = _____

Analyze the following functions:

1. f(x) = 1

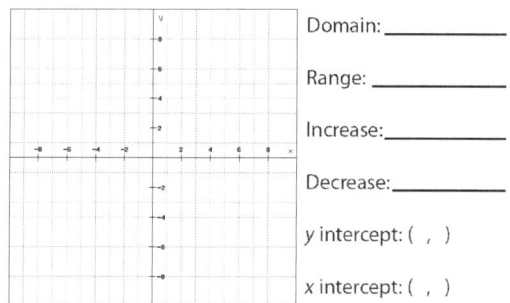

Domain:_____

Range:_____

Increase:_____

Decrease:_____

y intercept: (,)

x intercept: (,)

2. f(x) = 2

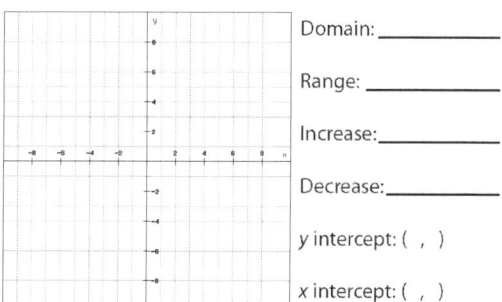

Domain:_____

Range:_____

Increase:_____

Decrease:_____

y intercept: (,)

x intercept: (,)

3. f(x) = −1

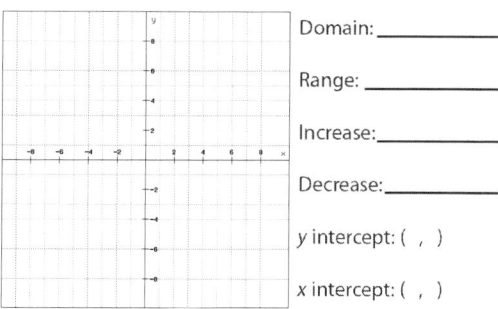

Domain:_____

Range:_____

Increase:_____

Decrease:_____

y intercept: (,)

x intercept: (,)

4. f(x) = 0

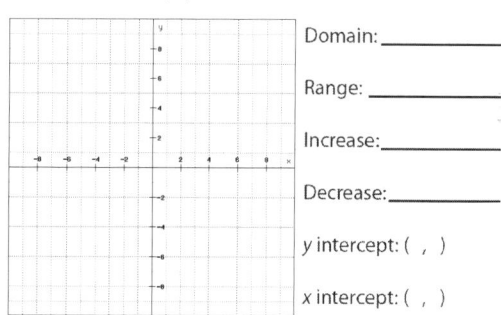

Domain:_____

Range:_____

Increase:_____

Decrease:_____

y intercept: (,)

x intercept: (,)

5. f(x) = x

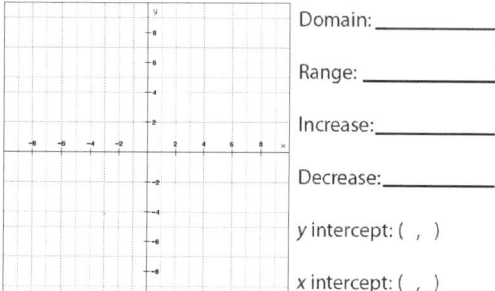

Domain:_____

Range:_____

Increase:_____

Decrease:_____

y intercept: (,)

x intercept: (,)

6. f(x) = x+1

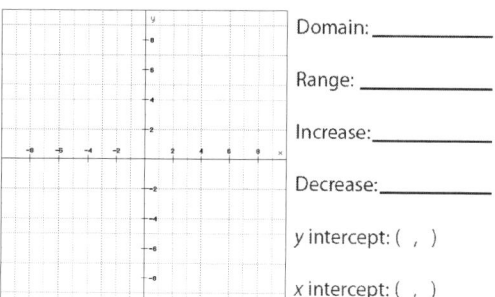

Domain:_____

Range:_____

Increase:_____

Decrease:_____

y intercept: (,)

x intercept: (,)

7. $f(x) = -x$

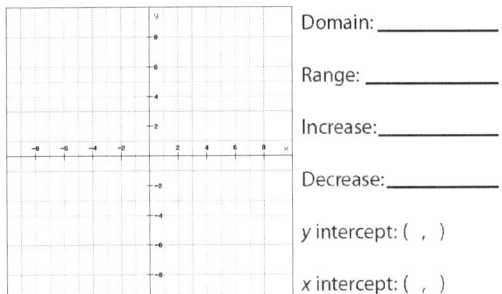

Domain: _____

Range: _____

Increase: _____

Decrease: _____

y intercept: (,)

x intercept: (,)

11. $f(x) = 3 - 2x$

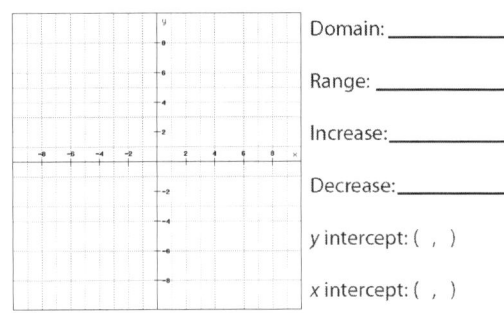

Domain: _____

Range: _____

Increase: _____

Decrease: _____

y intercept: (,)

x intercept: (,)

8. $f(x) = -x - 2$

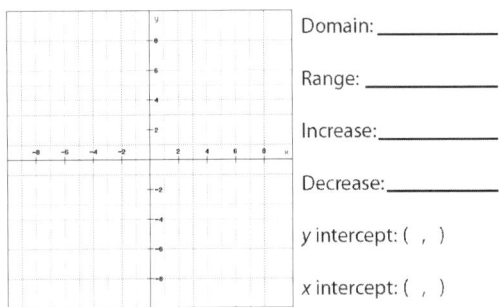

Domain: _____

Range: _____

Increase: _____

Decrease: _____

y intercept: (,)

x intercept: (,)

12. $f(x) = \dfrac{x}{3}$

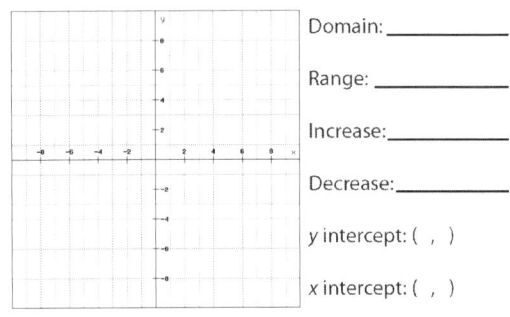

Domain: _____

Range: _____

Increase: _____

Decrease: _____

y intercept: (,)

x intercept: (,)

9. $f(x) = 2x$

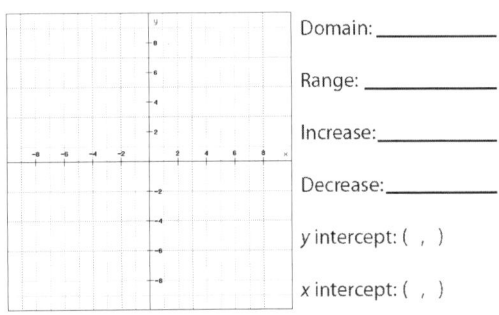

Domain: _____

Range: _____

Increase: _____

Decrease: _____

y intercept: (,)

x intercept: (,)

13. $f(x) = 2x + 1$

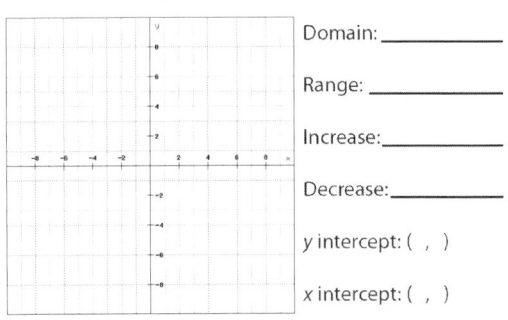

Domain: _____

Range: _____

Increase: _____

Decrease: _____

y intercept: (,)

x intercept: (,)

10. $f(x) = 3x - 5$

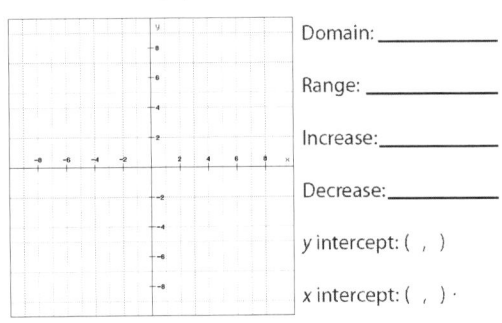

Domain: _____

Range: _____

Increase: _____

Decrease: _____

y intercept: (,)

x intercept: (,) ·

14. $f(x) = 2x - 2$

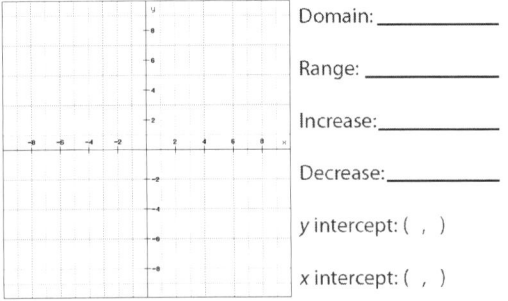

Domain: _____

Range: _____

Increase: _____

Decrease: _____

y intercept: (,)

x intercept: (,)

15. f(x) = 3x+5

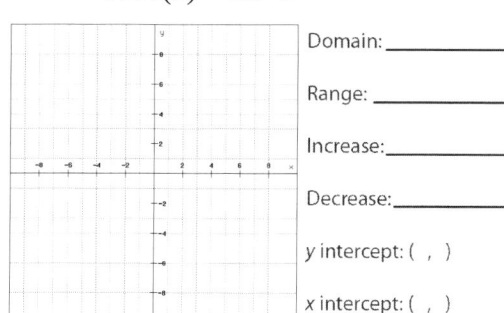

Domain:_____

Range: _____

Increase:_____

Decrease:_____

y intercept: (,)

x intercept: (,)

16. f(x) = $\frac{x}{2}$ − 5

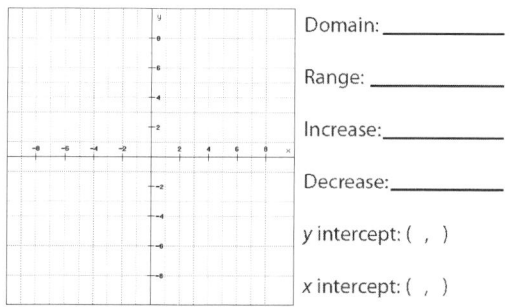

Domain:_____

Range: _____

Increase:_____

Decrease:_____

y intercept: (,)

x intercept: (,)

17. f(x)= $\frac{x}{4}$ + 6

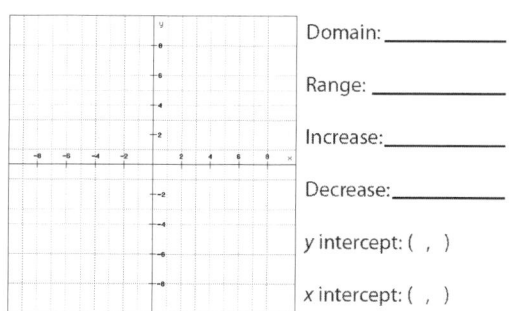

Domain:_____

Range: _____

Increase:_____

Decrease:_____

y intercept: (,)

x intercept: (,)

18. f(x) = $\frac{3}{2}$x − 5

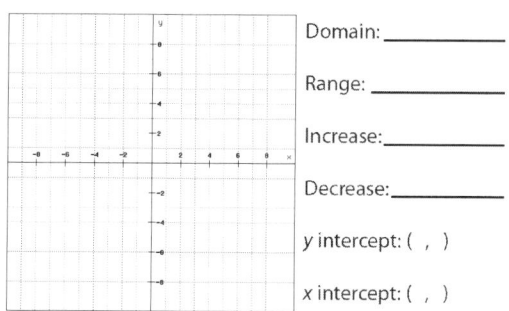

Domain:_____

Range: _____

Increase:_____

Decrease:_____

y intercept: (,)

x intercept: (,)

19. f(x) = $-\frac{3}{2}$x − $\frac{3}{2}$

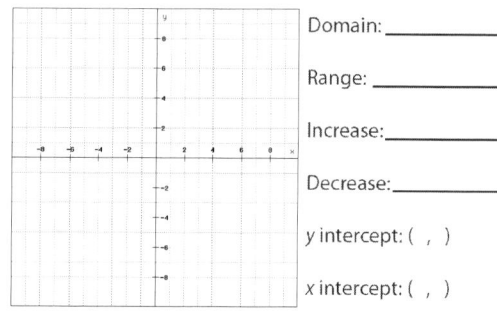

Domain:_____

Range: _____

Increase:_____

Decrease:_____

y intercept: (,)

x intercept: (,)

20. f(x) = $-\frac{1}{2}$x − $\frac{3}{2}$

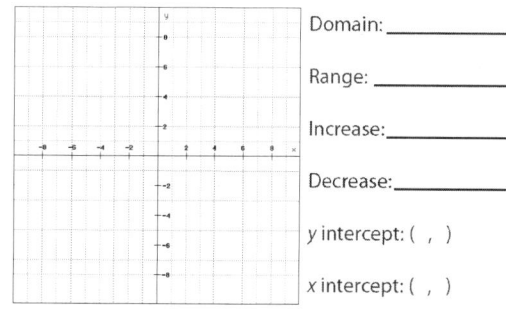

Domain:_____

Range: _____

Increase:_____

Decrease:_____

y intercept: (,)

x intercept: (,)

21. f(x) = $\frac{7}{2}$x − $\frac{1}{4}$

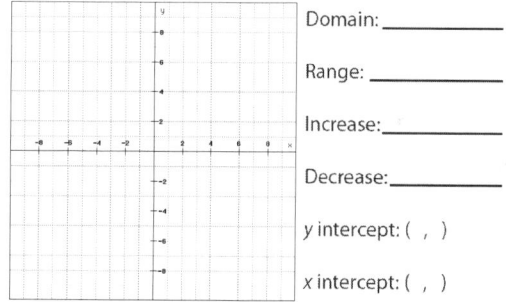

Domain:_____

Range: _____

Increase:_____

Decrease:_____

y intercept: (,)

x intercept: (,)

22. f(x) = $-\frac{9}{5}$x + $\frac{8}{3}$

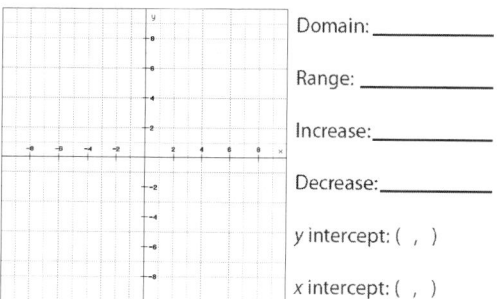

Domain:_____

Range: _____

Increase:_____

Decrease:_____

y intercept: (,)

x intercept: (,)

23. $3x + 2y = 2$

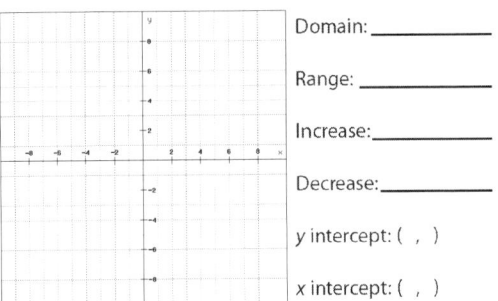

Domain: _____

Range: _____

Increase: _____

Decrease: _____

y intercept: (,)

x intercept: (,)

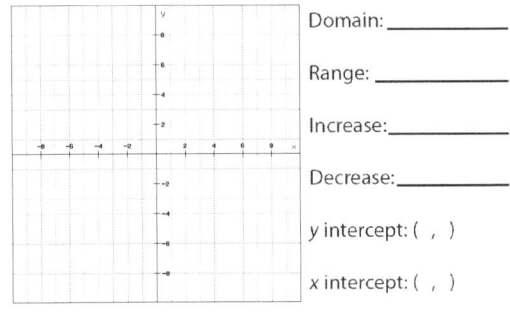

Domain: _____

Range: _____

Increase: _____

Decrease: _____

y intercept: (,)

x intercept: (,)

24. $4x - 2y - 3 = 1$

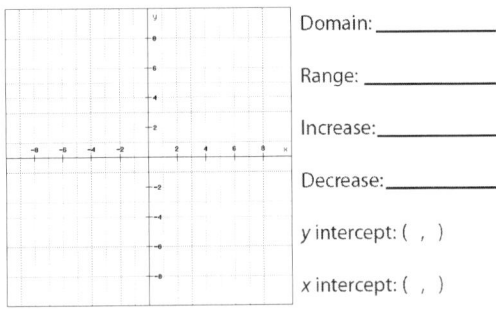

Domain: _____

Range: _____

Increase: _____

Decrease: _____

y intercept: (,)

x intercept: (,)

28. $5y + 5x = 5$

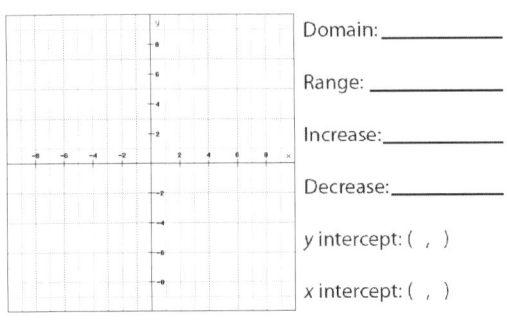

Domain: _____

Range: _____

Increase: _____

Decrease: _____

y intercept: (,)

x intercept: (,)

25. $-2y + 3x = -5$

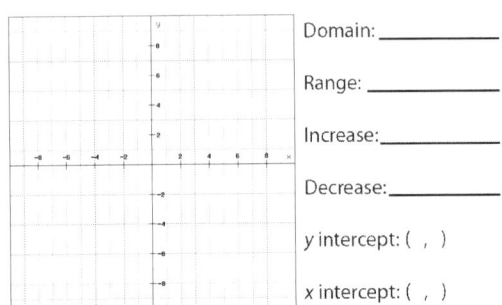

Domain: _____

Range: _____

Increase: _____

Decrease: _____

y intercept: (,)

x intercept: (,)

29. $2x - 2y - 3 = 1$

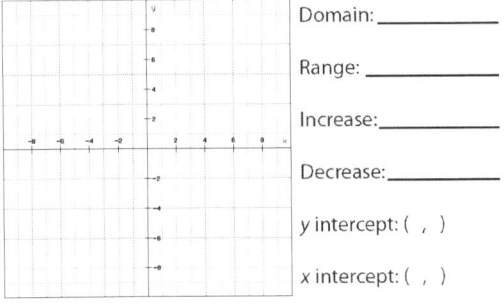

Domain: _____

Range: _____

Increase: _____

Decrease: _____

y intercept: (,)

x intercept: (,)

26. $y - x = 2$

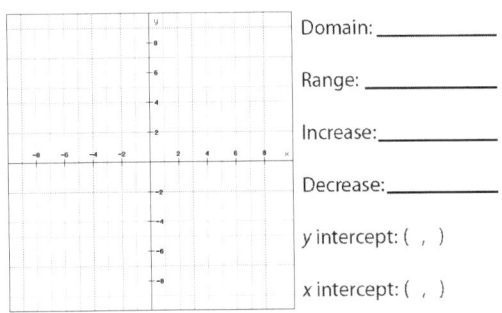

Domain: _____

Range: _____

Increase: _____

Decrease: _____

y intercept: (,)

x intercept: (,)

30. $x - 2y - 150 = 0$

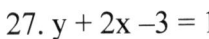

Domain: _____

Range: _____

Increase: _____

Decrease: _____

y intercept: (,)

x intercept: (,)

27. $y + 2x - 3 = 1$

31. Write the equation of the line that has a slope of 2 and passes through the

point (2, 4) in the forms:y = mx + b and ax + by + c = 0, (a, b ∈ Z)

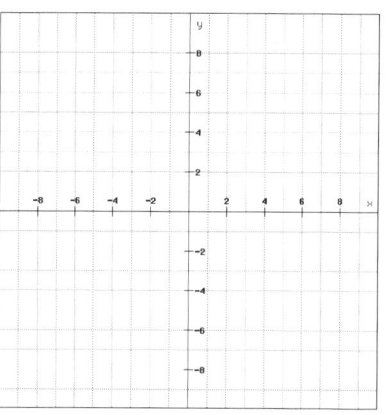

32. Write the equation of the line that has a slope of $-\dfrac{1}{2}$ and passes through the

point (–2, –3) in the forms: y = mx + b and ax + by + c = 0, (a, b ∈ Z)

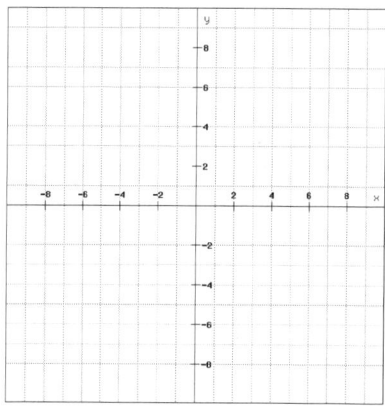

33. Write the equation of the line that has a slope of $-\dfrac{5}{2}$ and passes through the

point (–1, 2) in the forms: y = mx + b and ax + by + c = 0, (a, b ∈ Z)

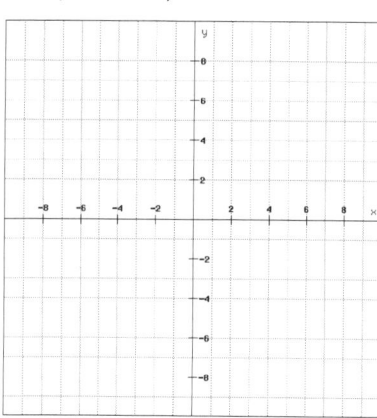

34. Find the equation of the line that passes through the points (1, 1), (2, 4), indicate its y and x intercepts and sketch it. Write its equation in the forms: y = mx + b and ax + by + c = 0, (a, b ∈ Z)

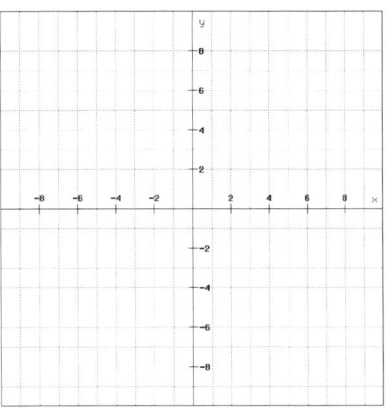

35. Find the equation of the line that passes through the points (–1, –5), (4, 3), indicate its y and x intercepts and sketch it. Write its equation in the forms: y = mx + b and ax + by + c = 0, (a, b ∈ Z)

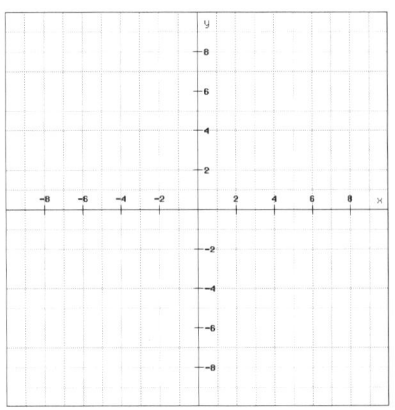

36. Find the equation of the line that passes through the points (–5, 1), (–2, 4), indicate its y and x intercepts, sketch it and write it in both formas y = mx + b and ax + by + c = 0, (a, b ∈ Z)

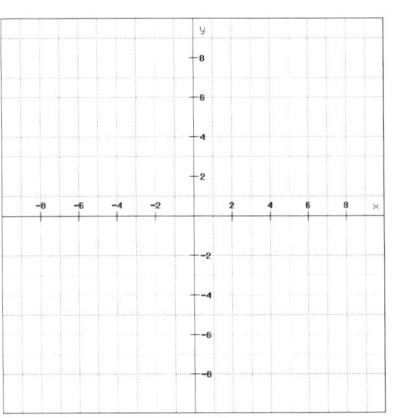

37. Write the equation of the line that is parallel to the line $y = 5x - 2$ and passes through the point $(-2, -1)$. Write its equation in the forms: $y = mx + b$ and $ax + by + c = 0$, $(a, b \in Z)$

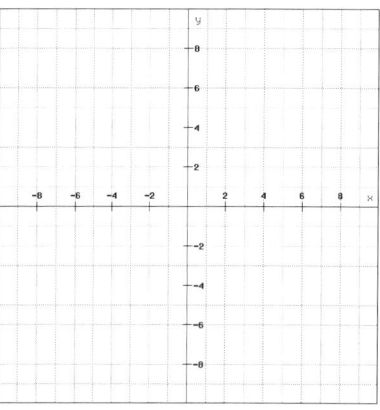

38. Write the equation of the line that is parallel to the line $y = -0.5x - 1$ and passes through the point $(-3, 6)$. Write its equation in the forms: $y = mx + b$ and $ax + by + c = 0$, $(a, b \in Z)$

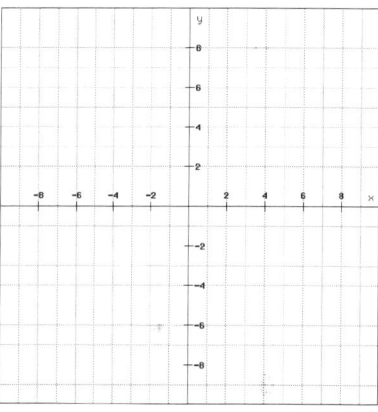

39. Sketch and write the equation of the line with a slope of $-\dfrac{1}{5}$ that passes through the point $(0,2)$.

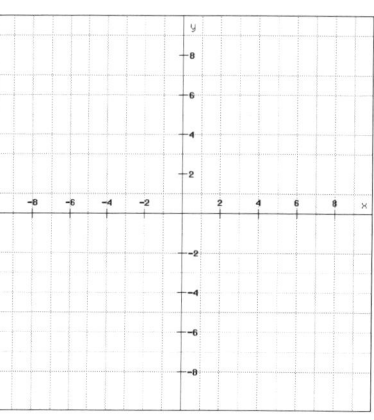

40. Sketch and write the equation of the lines with a slope: 1, 2, –3, –1, $-\dfrac{1}{2}$, $-\dfrac{1}{3}$,

that passes through the point (0,0).

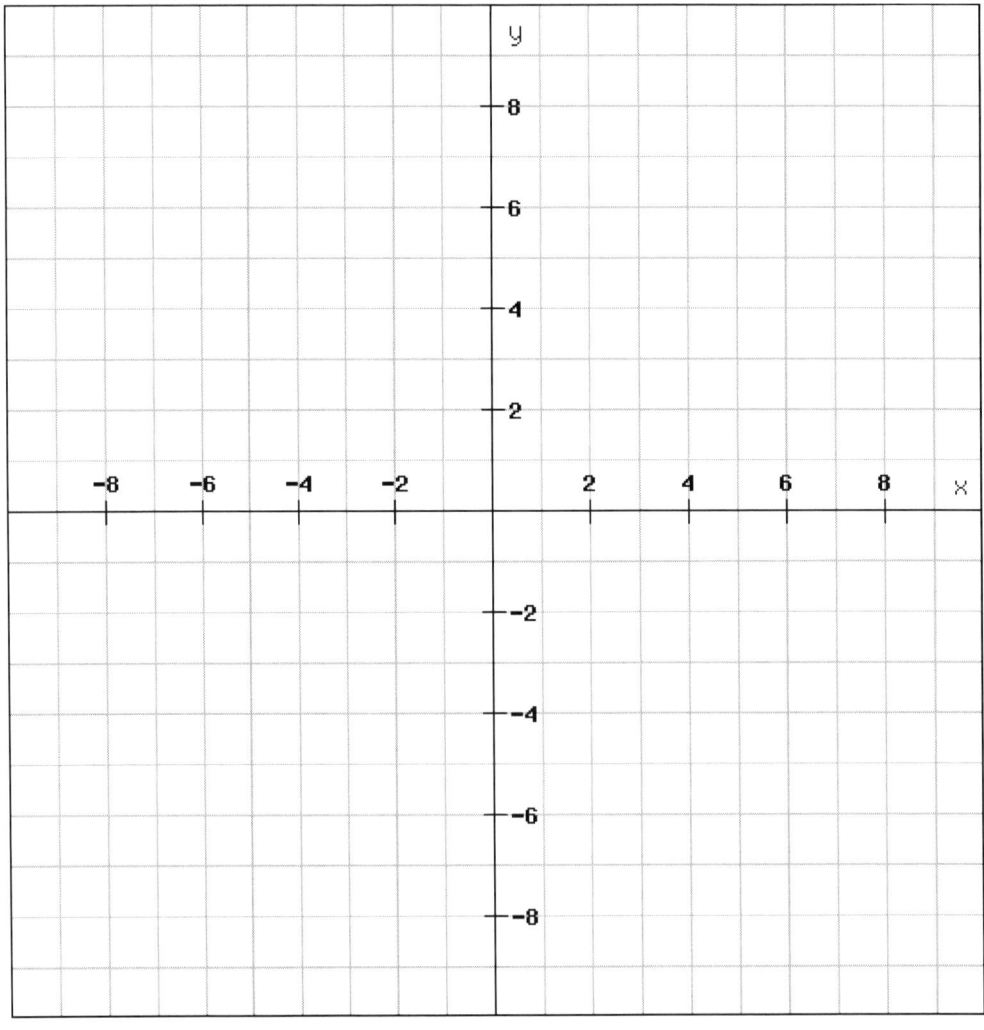

41. Sketch and write the equation of the line with a slope of -3 that passes through the point $(0,-3)$.

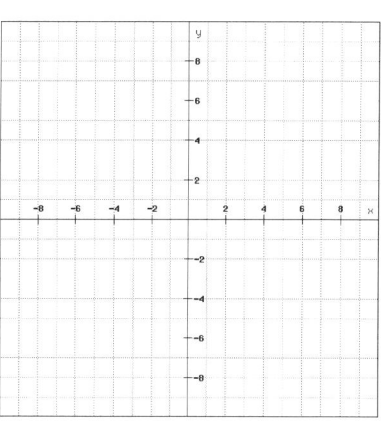

42. Sketch and write the equation of the line with a slope of 2 that passes through the point $(2,0)$

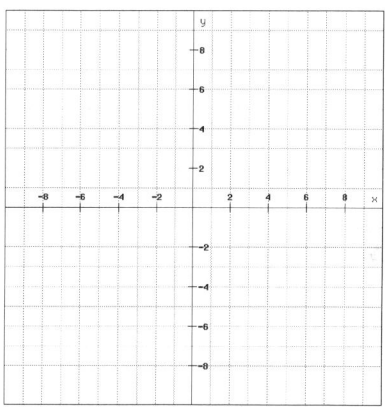

43. Sketch and write the equation of the line with a slope of $-\dfrac{1}{2}$ that passes through the point $(-2,0)$

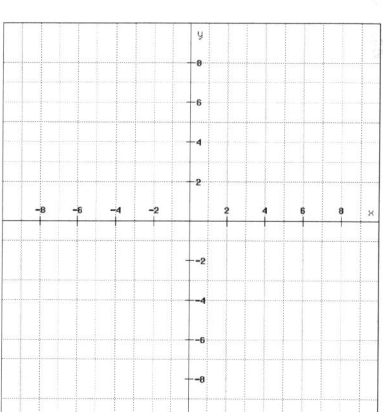

44. Sketch and write the equation of the line with a slope of 2 that passes through the point (–4,2)

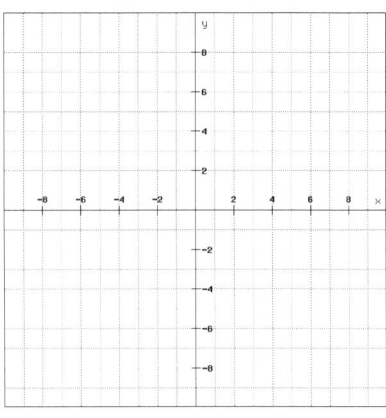

45. Find the intersection between the lines $f(x) = 2x - 3$ and $f(x) = -5x - 2$

46. Find the intersection between the lines $f(x) = -12x - 13$ and $f(x) = 15x + 20$.

DISTANCE AND MIDPOINT BETWEEN 2 POINTS

47. Given the points (1, 2) and (5, 8). Find the distance between them. Find the midpoint. Sketch to illustrate your answer.

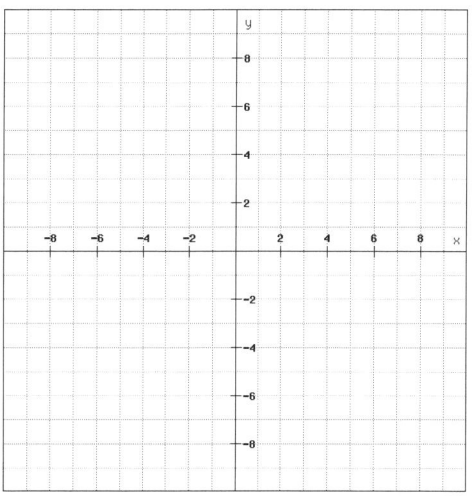

48. Given the points (–3, 2) and (5, –6). Find the distance between them. Find the midpoint. Sketch to illustrate your answer.

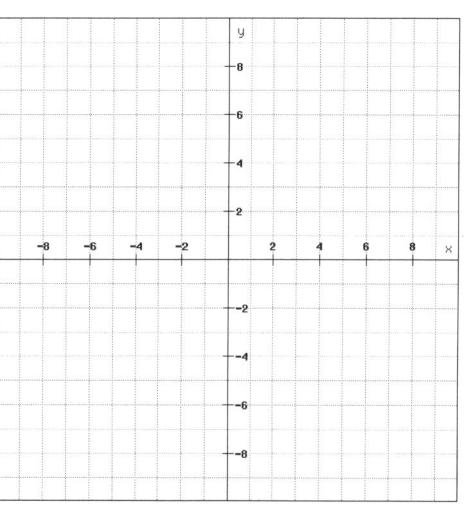

49. Given the points (–1, –6) and (–5, –1). Find the distance between them. Find the midpoint. Sketch to illustrate your answer.

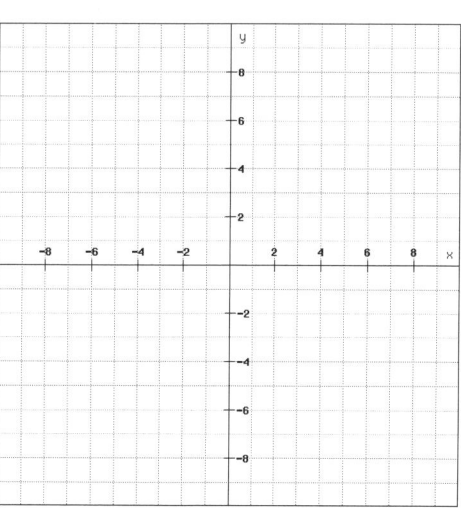

PERPENDICULAR LINES $(m \cdot m\perp = -1)$

50. Find the equation of a line perpendicular to the line $y = 3x - 2$ that passes through the point (3, 12). Sketch to illustrate your answer.

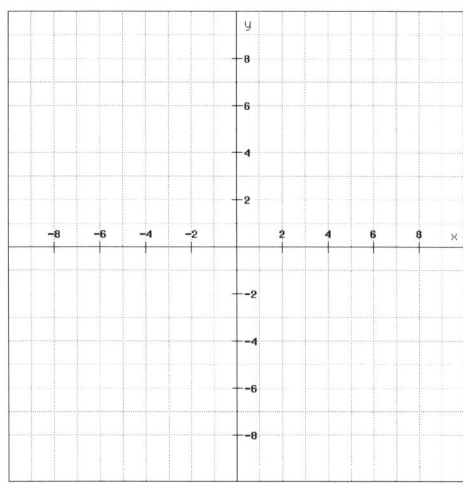

51. Find all the lines perpendicular to the line $y = -3x + 4$. Fin the ones that passes through the point (−3, 1). Sketch to illustrate your answer.

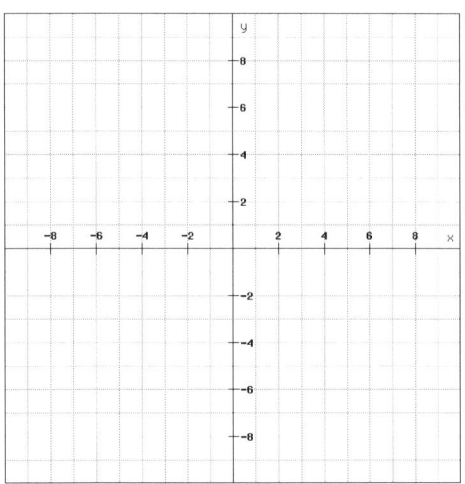

52. Find a line perpendicular to the line $y = -\dfrac{2}{5}x + 1$ that passes through the point (−1, −7). Sketch to illustrate your answer.

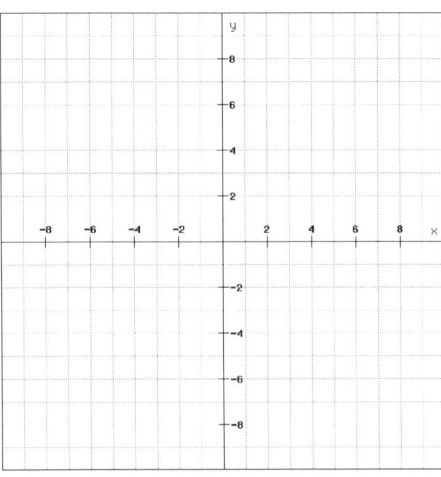

53. Given that the slope of one of the lines is 3 and that the lines are perpendicular, find the **exact** coordinates of the point of intersection of the two lines.

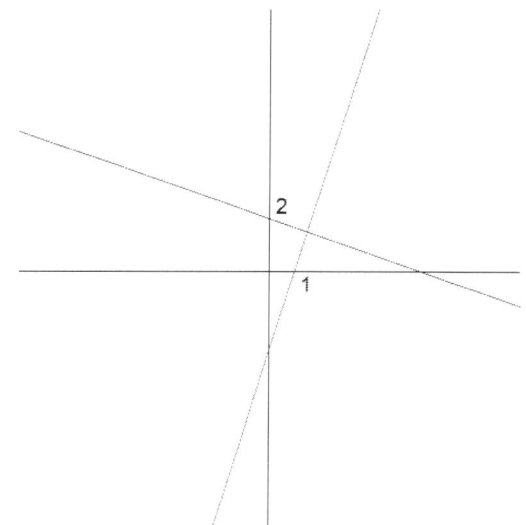

Application

1. The price of a new toy (in US$) is C(t) = 20 – 0.5t, t given in days.

    a. Sketch the corresponding graph.

    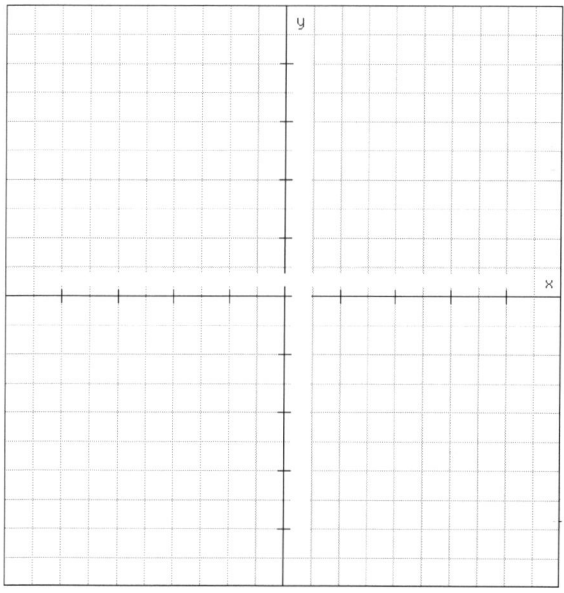

    b. What was the initial price of the toy? _____

    c. Find the price of the toy after 10 days

    d. What is the domain of the function, argument the answer,

    e. What is the range of the function.

    f. What is the meaning of 0.5? Does it have units? What are they?

2. You need to rent a car <u>for one day and</u> to compare the charges of 3 different companies. Company I charges 20$ per day with additional cost of 0.20$ per mile. Company II charges 30$ per day with additional cost of 0.10$ per mile. Company III charges 70$ per day with no additional mileage charge.

    a. Write the cost function for each one of the companies.

    b. Sketch all 3 graphs on the same axes system.

    c. Comment on the circumstances in which renting a car from each one of the companies is best.

5.3. – QUADRATIC FUNCTIONS

1. Given the functions: $f(x) = x^2$, $g(x) = x^2 - 2$. Complete the following table:

x	−5	−4	−3	−2	−1	0	1	2	3	4	5	6
f(x)												
g(x)												

- Sketch the points of the table on a graph (use a ruler).

- State the domain of the function: _____

- State the y intercept (sketched on the graph: (____ , ____)

- State the x intercept(s): (____ , ____), (____ , ____)

- Write in all possible forms:

- Find the max/min point(s): (____ , ____)

- The function is increasing on the interval: _____

- The function is decreasing on the interval: _____

- Sketch the function of the graph used for the points initially drawn

- State the range of the function: _____

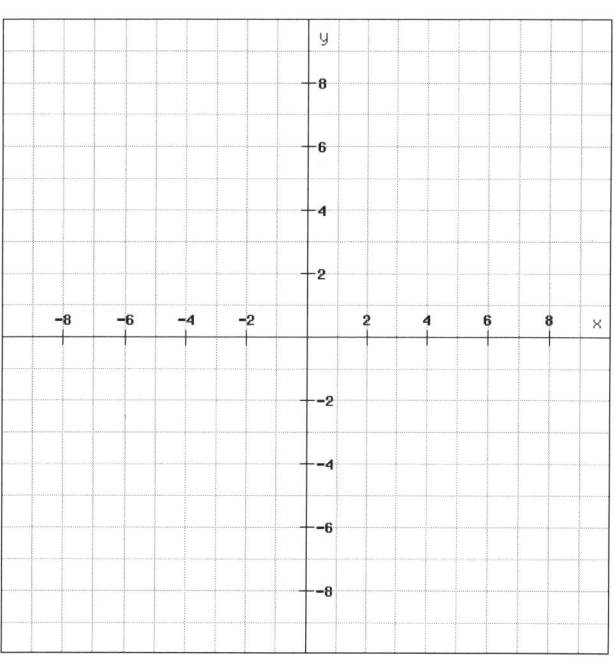

2. Given the functions: $f(x) = (x - 2)^2$, $g(x) = (x + 3)^2 - 2$. Complete the following table:

x	−5	−4	−3	−2	−1	0	1	2	3	4	5	6
f(x)												
g(x)												

- Sketch the points of the table on a graph (use a ruler).

- State the domain of the function: _____

- State the y intercept (sketched on the graph: (____ , ____)

- State the x intercept(s): (____ , ____), (____ , ____)

- Write in all possible forms:

- Find the max/min point(s): (____ , ____)

- The function is increasing on the interval: _____

- The function is decreasing on the interval: _____

- Sketch the function of the graph used for the points initially drawn

- State the range of the function: _____

- State its axes of symmetry: _____

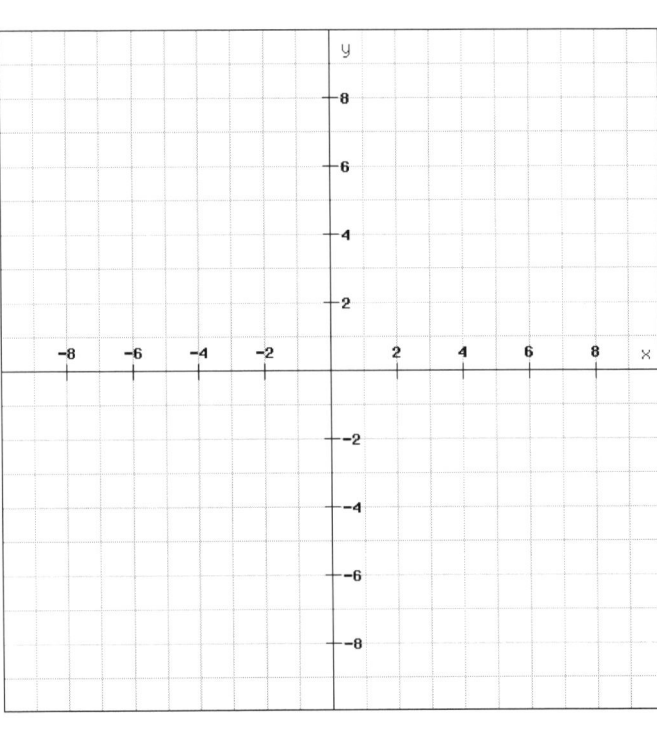

130

3. Given the function: $f(x) = (x + 2)(x - 4)$, $g(x) = 2(x + 2)(x - 4)$ Complete the following table:

x	−5	−4	−3	−2	−1	0	1	2	3	4	5	6
f(x)												
g(x)												

- Sketch the points of the table on a graph (use a ruler).

- State the domain of the function: _____

- State the y intercept (sketched on the graph: (____, ____)

- State the x intercept(s): (____, ____), (____, ____)

- Write in all possible forms:

- Find the max/min point(s): (____, ____)

- The function is increasing on the interval: _____

- The function is decreasing on the interval: _____

- Sketch the function of the graph used for the points initially drawn

- State the range of the function: _____

- State its axes of symmetry: _____

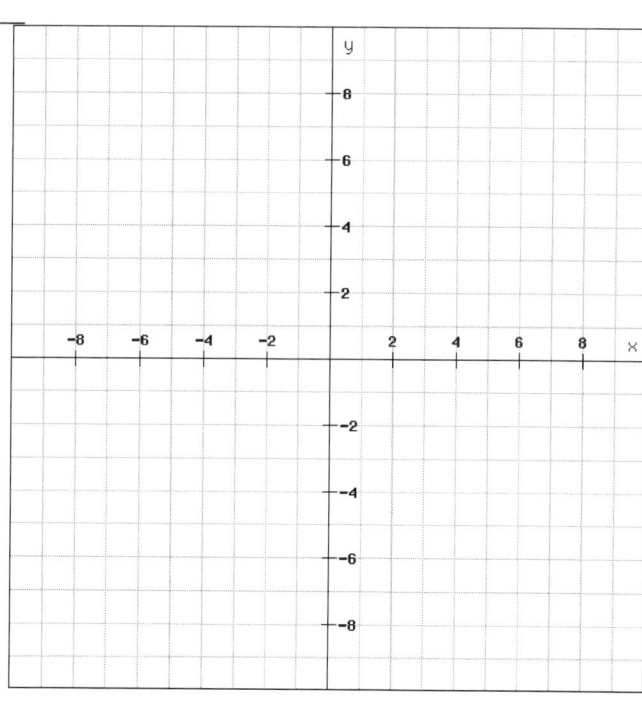

131

In general, a quadratic function f can be written in several different ways:

a. $f(x) = ax^2 + bx + c$ **standard form**, where a, b and c are constants
b. $f(x) = a(x - r)(x - s)$ **factored form**, where a, r and s are constants
c. $f(x) = a(x - h)^2 + k$ **vertex form**, where a, h and k are constants

Example:

Vertex form:	$f(x) = 3(x - 2)^2 - 3$
Partial factored form:	$f(x) = 3(x - 1)(x - 3)$
Standard form:	$f(x) = 3x^2 + 12x + 9$

Complete the sentences:

1. The graph of a quadratic function is called a _____.

2. In factored form, the numbers r and s represent the _____ of f.

3. In vertex form, the point (h, k) is called the _____ of the parabola.
   The axis of symmetry of the parabola is the line _____.

4. The graph of the parabola opens upwards if _____ and
   downwards if _____.

5. In case $f(x) = x^2 + 1$, the function can be written in ____ form(s) only. Why?

6. In case $f(x) = x^2 - 1$, the function can be written in ____ form(s) only. Show
   your answer:

7. A parabola has its vertex at the point (2, 3) and goes through the point (6, 11).
   Find the expression of the function.

8. A parabola has its vertex at the point (− 2, 4) and passes through the point (2, −
   6). Find the expression of the function.

9. Write the analytical expression that corresponds the following functions in all possible forms, assume $a = 1$ or -1 in all cases:

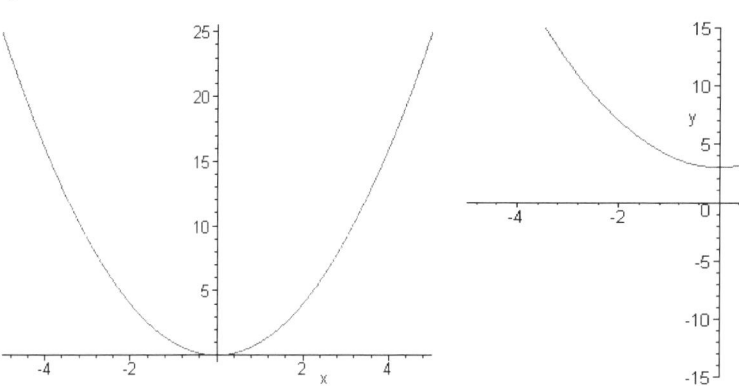

Range: _____ Range: _____

Vertex form: _____ Vertex form: _____

Factorized form:_____ Factorized form:_____

Standard form:_____ Standard form:_____

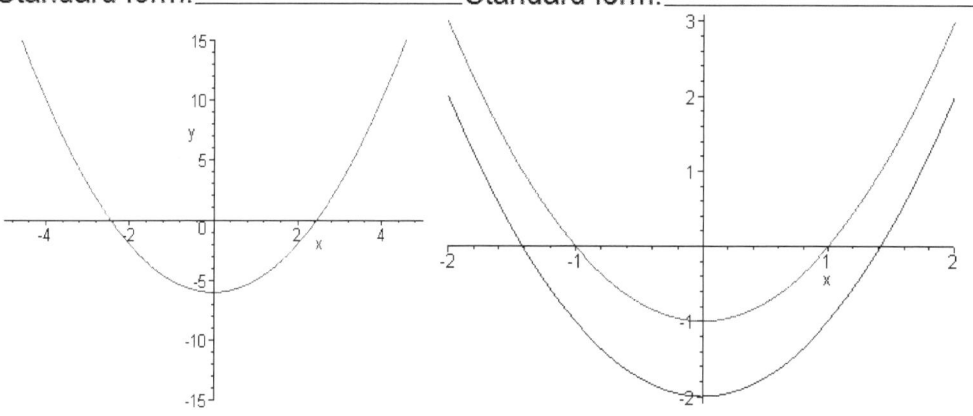

Range: _____ Range: _____

Vertex form: _____ Vertex form: _____

Factorized form:_____ Factorized form:_____

Standard form:_____ Standard form:_____

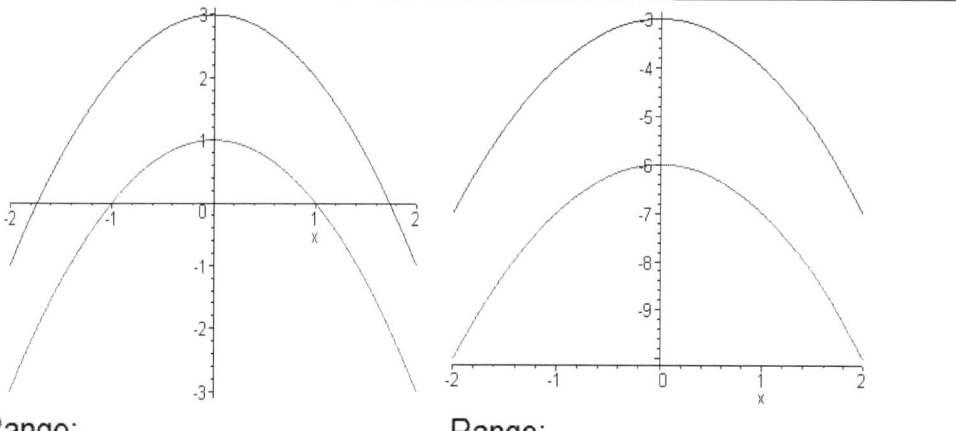

Range: _____ Range: _____

Vertex form: _____ Vertex form: _____

Factorized form:_____ Factorized form:_____

Standard form:_____ Standard form:_____

10. Complete the tables:

Function	On the graph
$f(x) = x^2$	
$f(x) = \dfrac{x^2}{2}$	
$f(x) = \dfrac{x^2}{3}$	
$f(x) = 2x^2$	

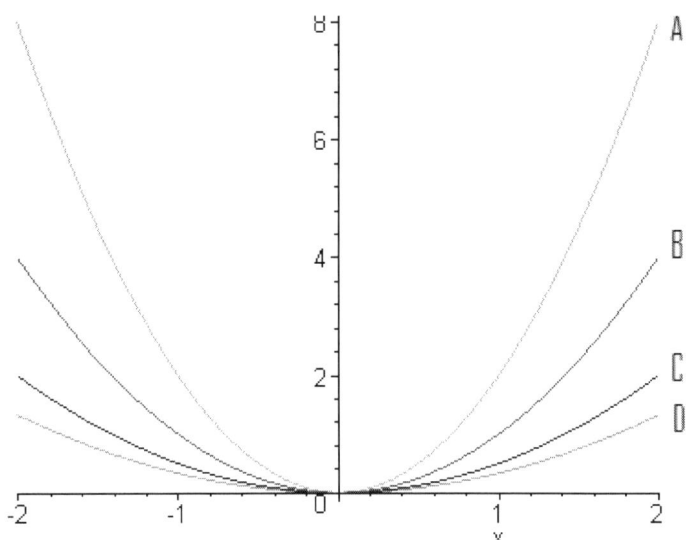

11. Complete the table:

Function	On the graph
$f(x) = x^2 + 2$	
$f(x) = x^2 - 2$	
$f(x) = x^2 - 3$	
$f(x) = 2x^2 + 2$	

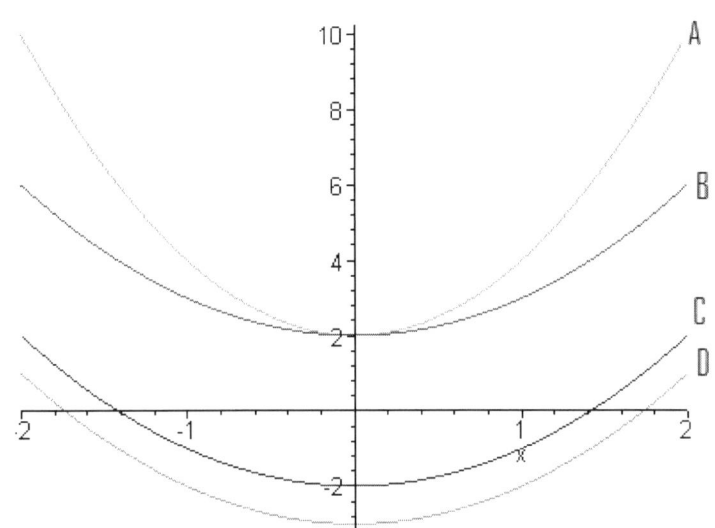

12. Complete the table:

Function	On the graph
$f(x) = -x^2 + 2$	
$f(x) = x^2 - 4$	
$f(x) = -x^2 + 3$	
$f(x) = 2x^2 + 2$	

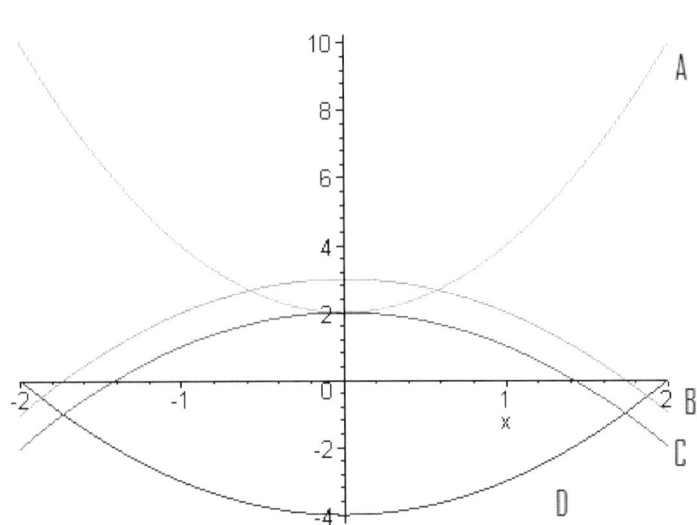

134

13. Write the expression of the function in all possible forms, indicate the range assume $a = 1$ or -1 in all cases. Use GDC to check your answer.

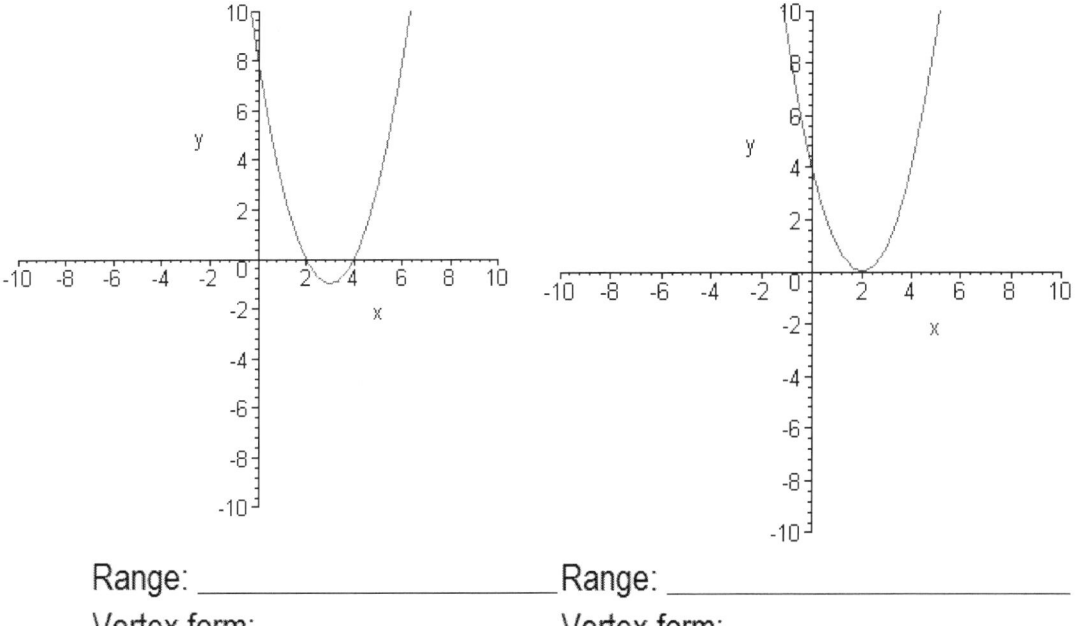

Range: _____ Range: _____

Vertex form: _____ Vertex form: _____

Factorized form:_____ Factorized form:_____

Standard form:_____ Standard form:_____

14. Write the expression of the function in all possible forms, indicate the range assume $a = 1$ or -1 in all cases. Use GDC to check your answer.

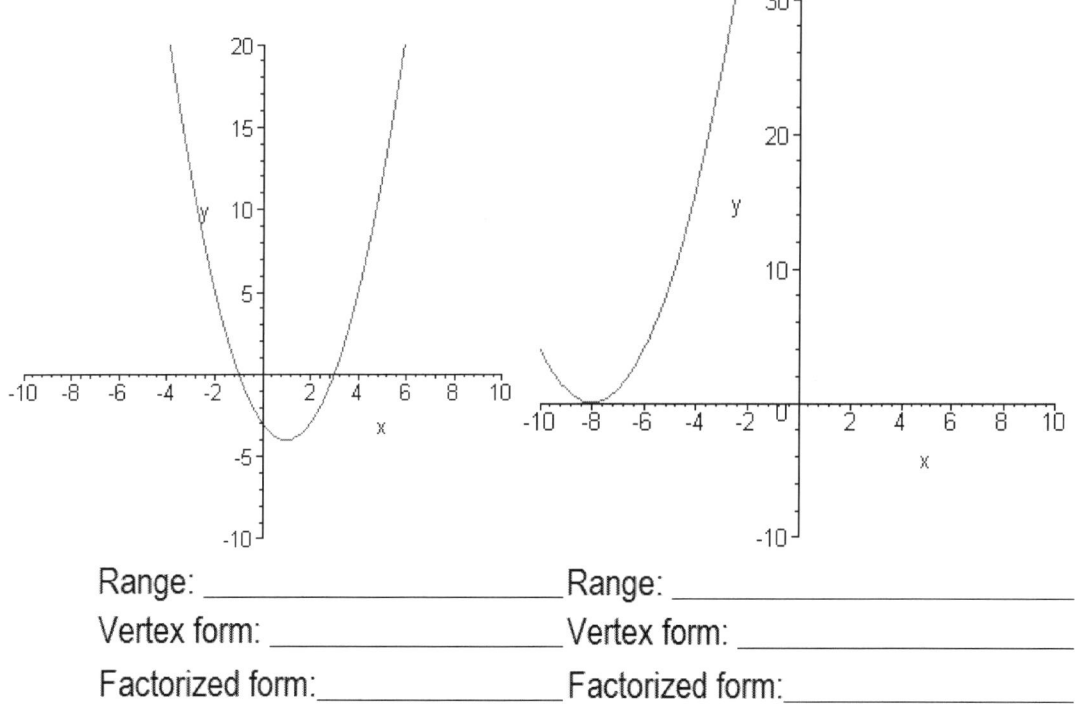

Range: _____ Range: _____

Vertex form: _____ Vertex form: _____

Factorized form:_____ Factorized form:_____

Standard form:_____ Standard form:_____

15. Write the expression of the function in all possible forms, indicate the range assume $a = 1$ or -1 in all cases. Use GDC to check your answer.

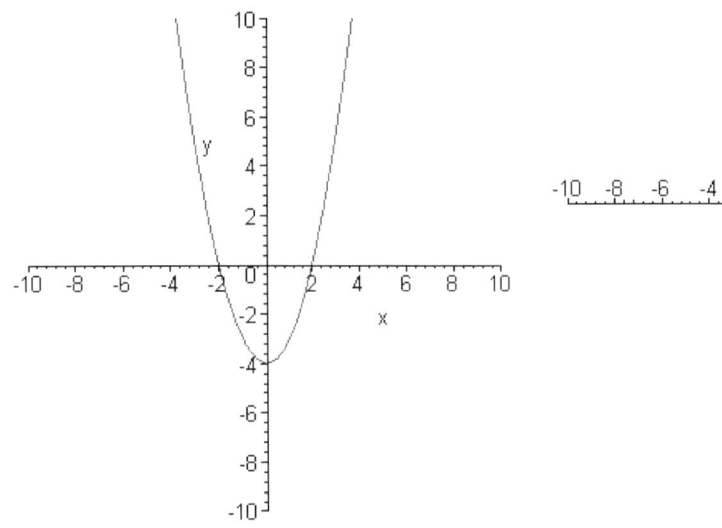 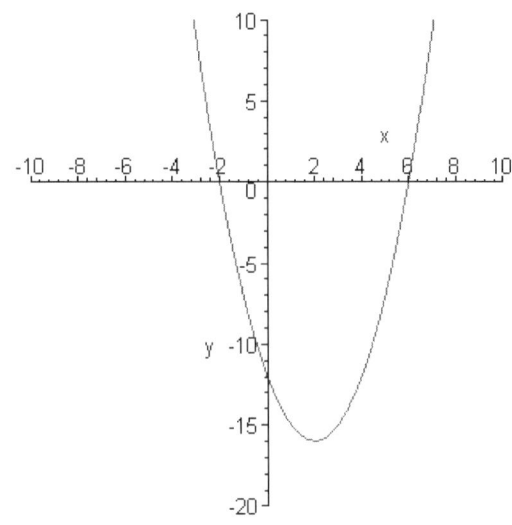

Range: _____ Range: _____

Vertex form: _____ Vertex form: _____

Factorized form:_____ Factorized form:_____

Standard form:_____ Standard form:_____

16. Write the expression of the function in all possible forms, indicate the range assume $a = 1$ or -1 in all cases. Use GDC to check your answer.

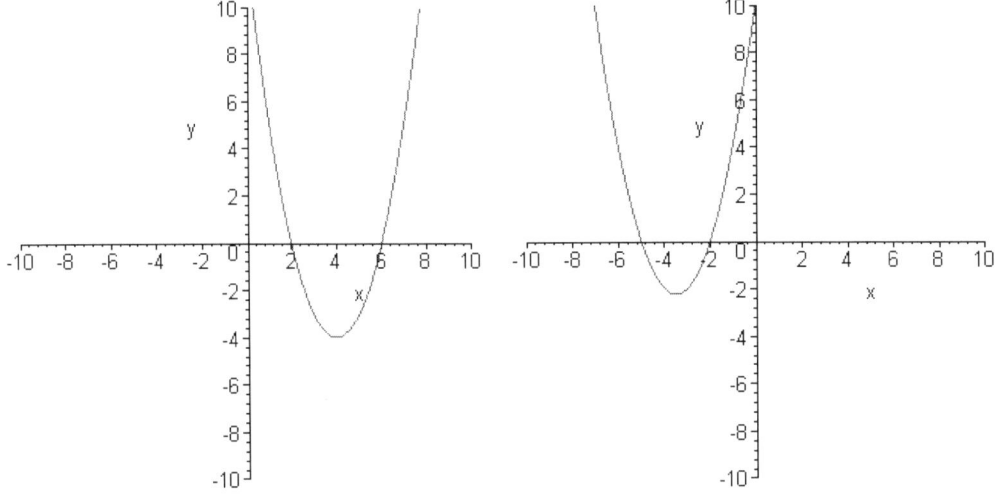

Range: _____ Range: _____

Vertex form: _____ Vertex form: _____

Factorized form:_____ Factorized form:_____

Standard form:_____ Standard form:_____

17. Write the expression of the function in all possible forms, indicate the range assume $a = 1$ or -1 in all cases. Use GDC to check your answer.

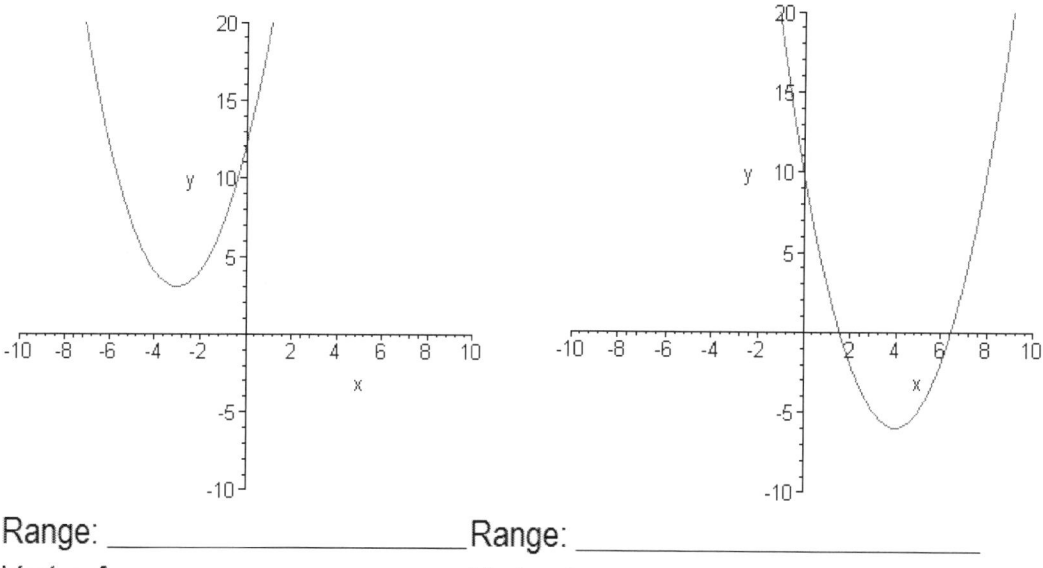

Range: _____   Range: _____
Vertex form: _____   Vertex form: _____
Factorized form: _____   Factorized form: _____
Standard form: _____   Standard form: _____

18. Write the expression of the function in all possible forms, indicate the range assume $a = 1$ or -1 in all cases. Use GDC to check your answer.

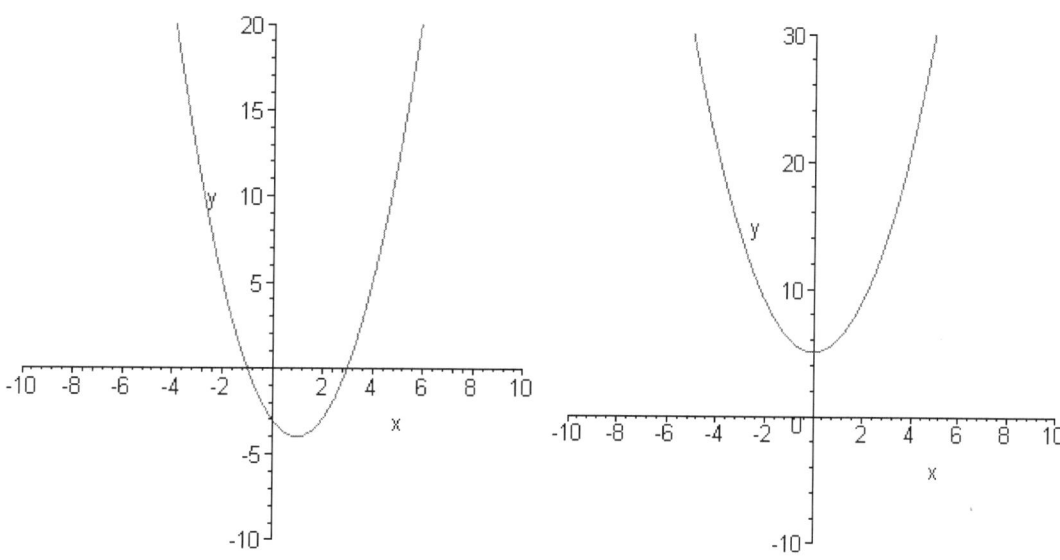

Range: _____   Range: _____
Vertex form: _____   Vertex form: _____
Factorized form: _____   Factorized form: _____
Standard form: _____   Standard form: _____

19. Write the expression of the function in all possible forms, indicate the range assume $a = 1$ or -1 in all cases. Use GDC to check your answer.

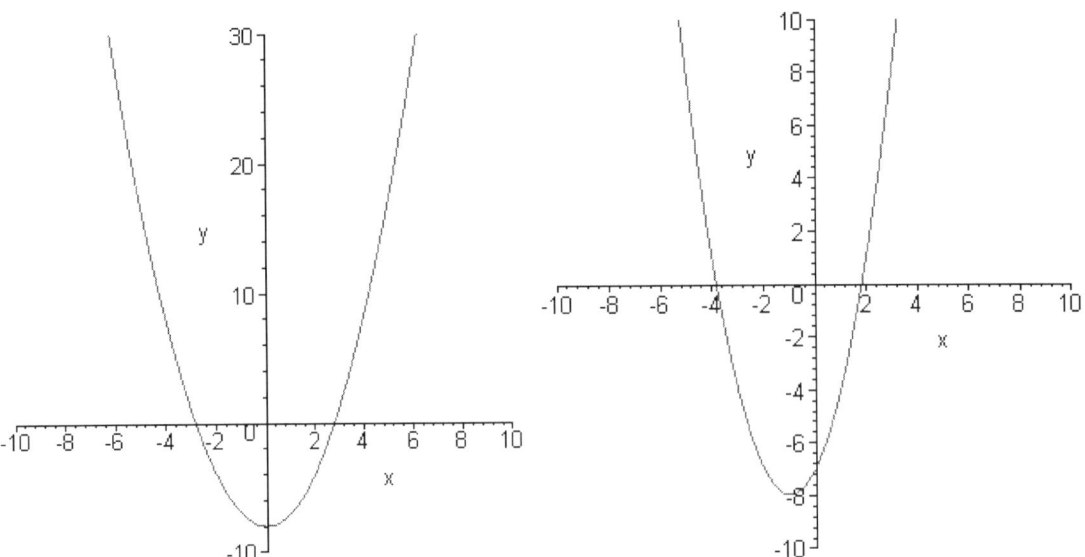

Range: _____ Range: _____
Vertex form: _____ Vertex form: _____
Factorized form:_____ Factorized form:_____
Standard form:_____ Standard form:_____

20. Write the expression of the function in all possible forms, indicate the range assume $a = 1$ or -1 in all cases. Use GDC to check your answer.

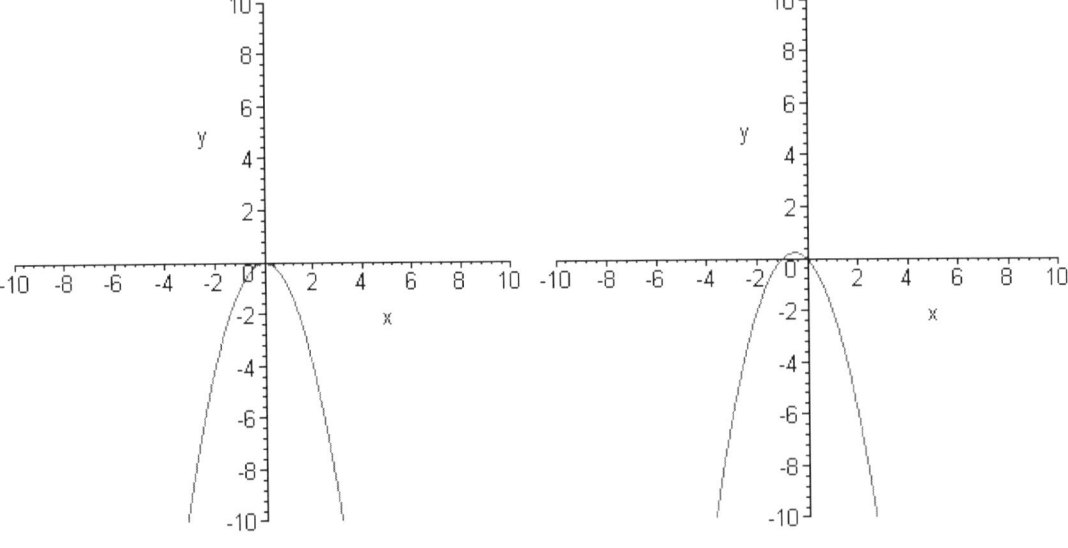

Range: _____ Range: _____
Vertex form: _____ Vertex form: _____
Factorized form:_____ Factorized form:_____
Standard form:_____ Standard form:_____

21. Write the expression of the function in all possible forms, indicate the range assume $a = 1$ or -1 in all cases. Use GDC to check your answer.

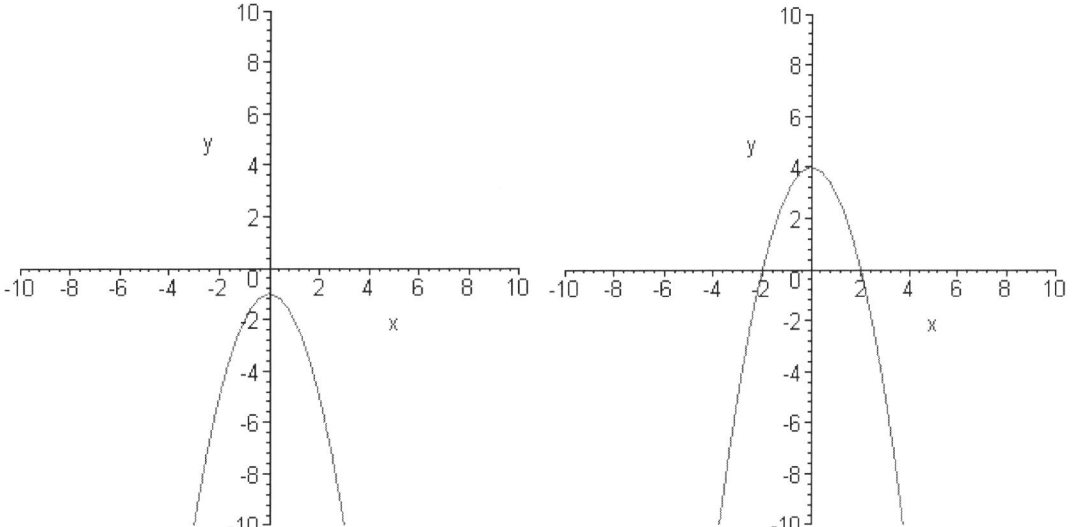

Range: _____   Range: _____

Vertex form: _____   Vertex form: _____

Factorized form:_____   Factorized form:_____

Standard form:_____   Standard form:_____

22. Write the expression of the function in all possible forms, indicate the range assume $a = 1$ or -1 in all cases. Use GDC to check your answer.

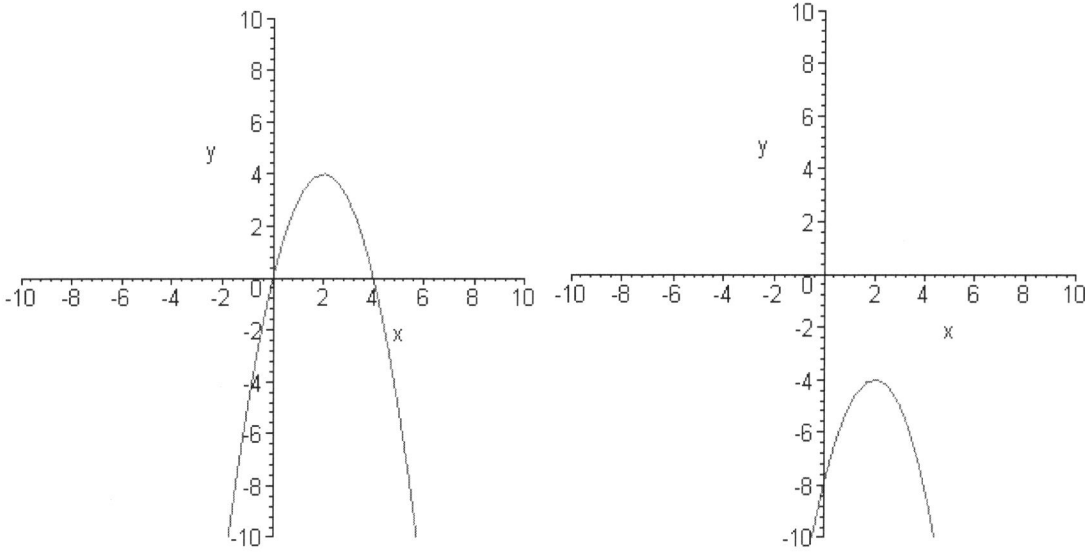

Range: _____   Range: _____

Vertex form: _____   Vertex form: _____

Factorized form:_____   Factorized form:_____

Standard form:_____   Standard form:_____

23. Write the expression of the function in all possible forms, indicate the range assume $a = 1$ or -1 in all cases. Use GDC to check your answer.

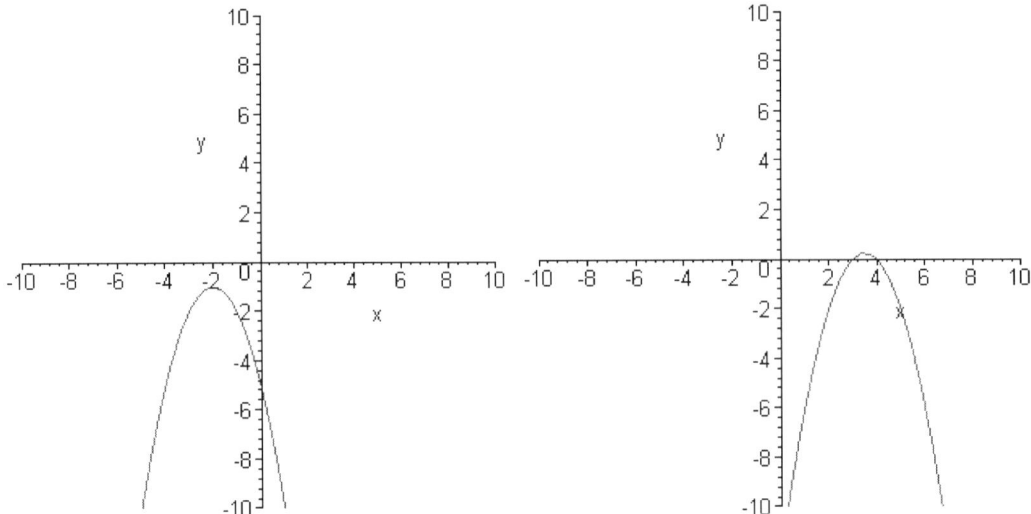

Range: _____ Range: _____

Vertex form: _____ Vertex form: _____

Factorized form:_____ Factorized form:_____

Standard form:_____ Standard form:_____

24. Write the expression of the function in all possible forms, indicate the range assume $a = 1$ or -1 in all cases. Use GDC to check your answer.

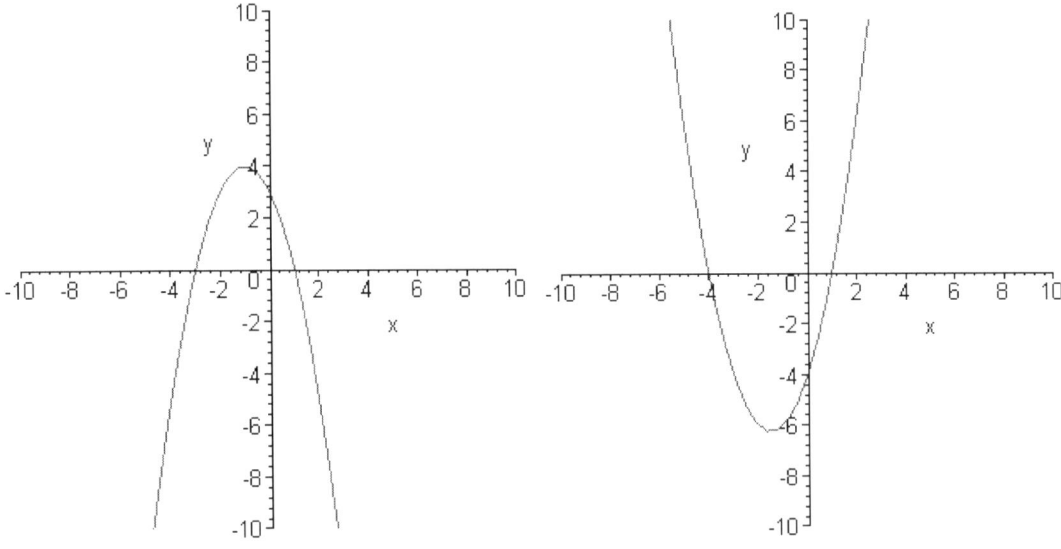

Range: _____ Range: _____

Vertex form: _____ Vertex form: _____

Factorized form:_____ Factorized form:_____

Standard form:_____ Standard form:_____

25. Write the expression of the function in all possible forms, indicate the range assume $a = 1$ or -1 in all cases. Use GDC to check your answer.

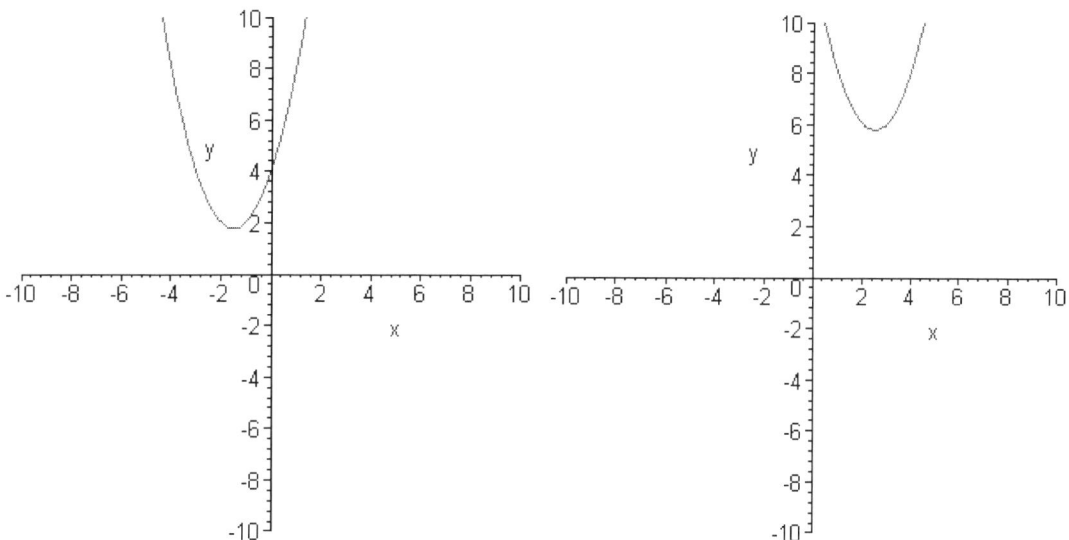

Range: _____   Range: _____
Vertex form: _____   Vertex form: _____
Factorized form:_____   Factorized form:_____
Standard form:_____   Standard form:_____

Analyze the following functions; use GDC to verify your answers.

26. $f(x) = -3$

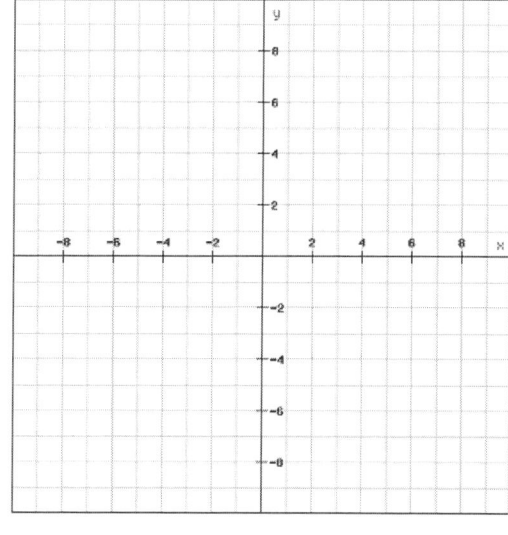

Vertex form: _____

Factorized form:_____

Domain: _____   Range: _____

y intercept:(___, ___)

x intercept(s):(___, ___), (___, ___)

Increases: _____Decreases: _____

27. f(x) = 5x

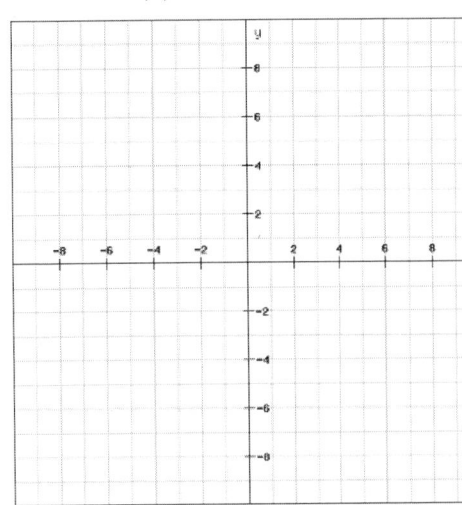

Vertex form: _____

Factorized form:_____

Domain: _____   Range: _____

y intercept:(__, __)   Vertex:(__, __)Max/Min

x intercept(s):(___, ___), (___, ___)

Increases: _____Decreases: _____

28. f(x) = $x^2 + 8x + 19$

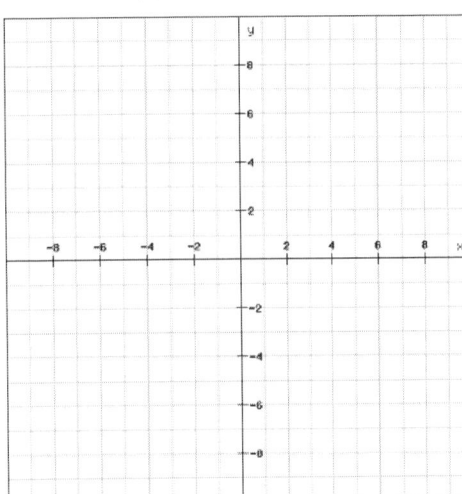

Vertex form: _____

Factorized form:_____

Domain: _____   Range: _____

y intercept:(__, __)   Vertex:(__, __)Max/Min

x intercept(s):(___, ___), (___, ___)

Increases: _____Decreases: _____

29. f(x) = $10x^2 - 8x - 2$

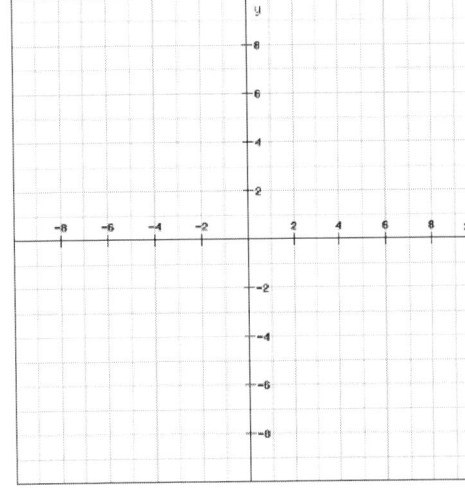

Vertex form: _____

Factorized form:_____

Domain: _____   Range: _____

y intercept:(__, __)   Vertex:(__, __)Max/Min

x intercept(s):(___, ___), (___, ___)

Increases: _____Decreases: _____

30. $f(x) = x^2 + 4x + 1$

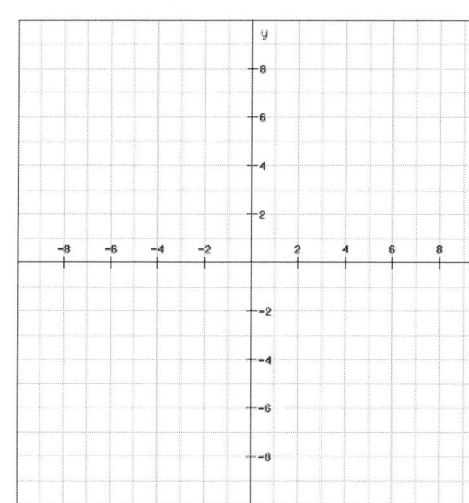

Vertex form: _____

Factorized form: _____

Domain: _____   Range: _____

y intercept:(__, __)   Vertex:(__, __)Max/Min

x intercept(s):(___, ___), (___, ___)

Increases: _____Decreases: _____

31. $f(x) = 4x^2 - 14x + 6$

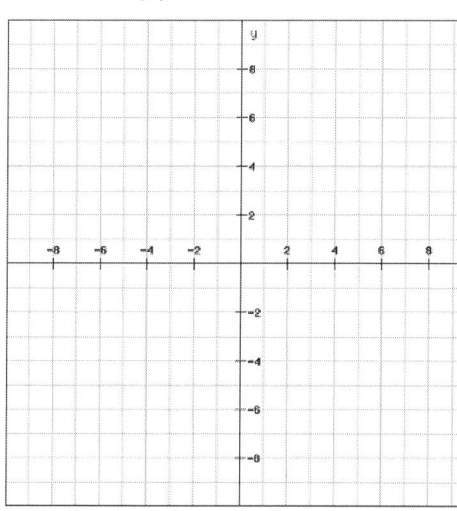

Vertex form: _____

Factorized form: _____

Domain: _____   Range: _____

y intercept:(__, __)   Vertex:(__, __)Max/Min

x intercept(s):(___, ___), (___, ___)

Increases: _____Decreases: _____

32. $f(x) = 2x^2 - 3x - 5$

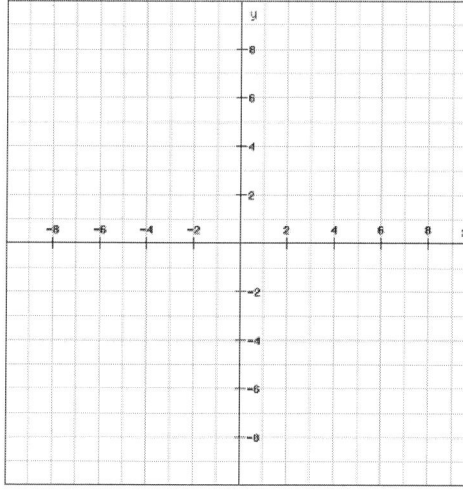

Vertex form: _____

Factorized form: _____

Domain: _____   Range: _____

y intercept:(__, __)   Vertex:(__, __)Max/Min

x intercept(s):(___, ___), (___, ___)

Increases: _____Decreases: _____

33. $f(x) = x^2 + 3x - 10$

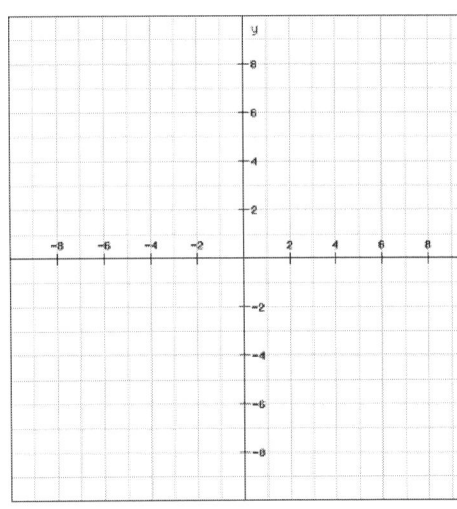

Vertex form: _____

Factorized form:_____

Domain: _____   Range: _____

y intercept:(__, __)   Vertex:(__, __)Max/Min

x intercept(s):(___, ___), (___, ___)

Increases: _____Decreases: _____

34. $f(x) = x^2 + 7x - 1$

Vertex form: _____

Factorized form:_____

Domain: _____   Range: _____

y intercept:(__, __)   Vertex:(__, __)Max/Min

x intercept(s):(___, ___), (___, ___)

Increases: _____Decreases: _____

35. $f(x) = x^2 + 2x + 7$

Vertex form: _____

Factorized form:_____

Domain: _____   Range: _____

y intercept:(__, __)   Vertex:(__, __)Max/Min

x intercept(s):(___, ___), (___, ___)

Increases: _____Decreases: _____

36. f(x) = x² + x −1

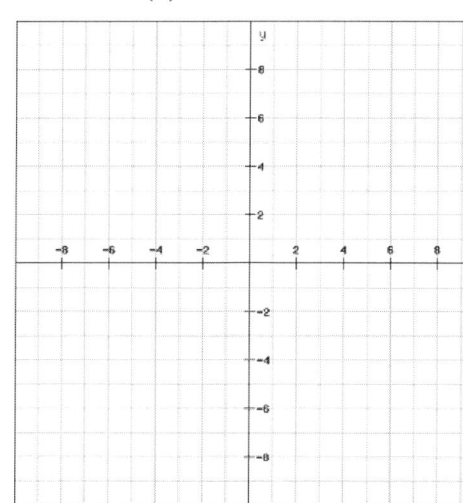

Vertex form: _____

Factorized form:_____

Domain: _____   Range: _____

y intercept:(__, __)   Vertex:(__, __)Max/Min

x intercept(s):(___, ___), (___, ___)

Increases: _____Decreases: _____

37. f(x) = x² + 2x +1

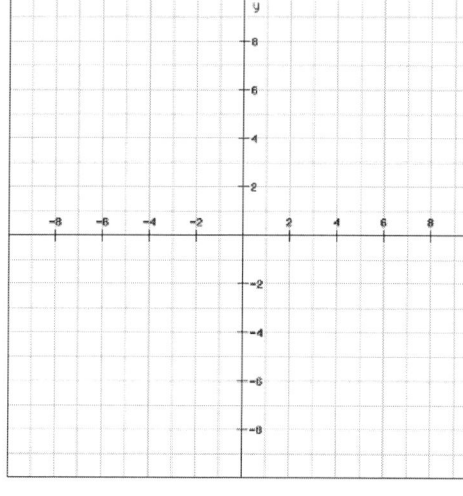

Vertex form: _____

Factorized form:_____

Domain: _____   Range: _____

y intercept:(__, __)   Vertex:(__, __)Max/Min

x intercept(s):(___, ___), (___, ___)

Increases: _____Decreases: _____

38. f(x) = x² + 1

Vertex form: _____

Factorized form:_____

Domain: _____   Range: _____

y intercept:(__, __)   Vertex:(__, __)Max/Min

x intercept(s):(___, ___), (___, ___)

Increases: _____Decreases: _____

39. $f(x) = x^2 - 1$

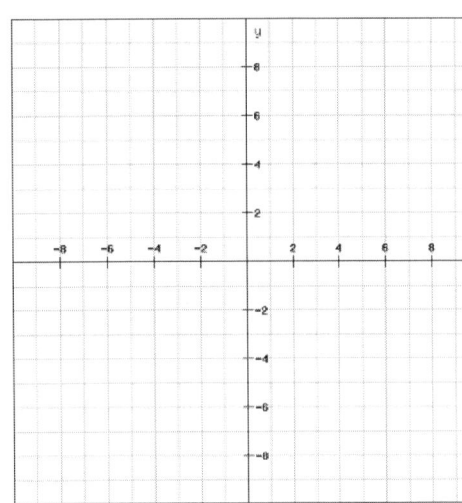

Vertex form: _____

Factorized form: _____

Domain: _____   Range: _____

y intercept:(__, __)   Vertex:(__, __)Max/Min

x intercept(s):(___, ___), (___, ___)

Increases: _____ Decreases: _____

40. $f(x) = x^2 + 3x$

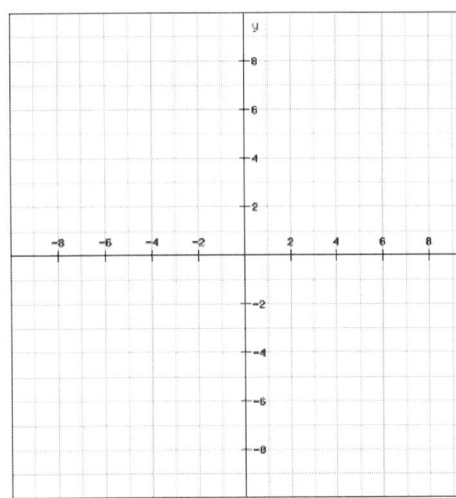

Vertex form: _____

Factorized form: _____

Domain: _____   Range: _____

y intercept:(__, __)   Vertex:(__, __)Max/Min

x intercept(s):(___, ___), (___, ___)

Increases: _____ Decreases: _____

41. $f(x) = x^2 + 5x$

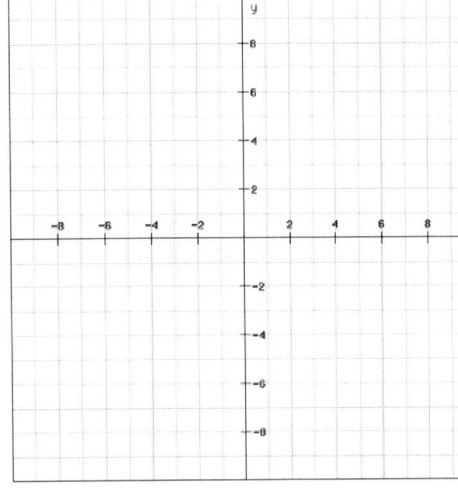

Vertex form: _____

Factorized form: _____

Domain: _____   Range: _____

y intercept:(__, __)   Vertex:(__, __)Max/Min

x intercept(s):(___, ___), (___, ___)

Increases: _____ Decreases: _____

42. $f(x) = x^2 - 3x$

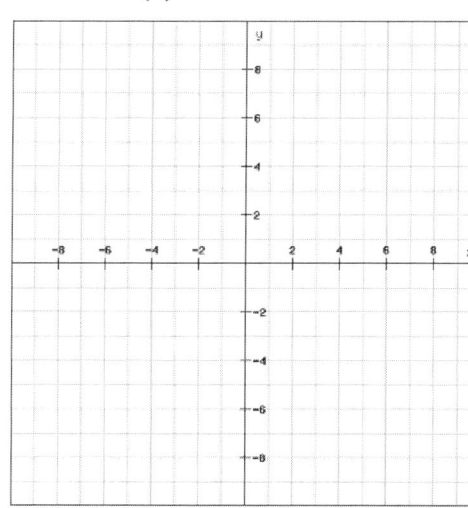

Vertex form: _____

Factorized form: _____

Domain: _____   Range: _____

y intercept:(__, __)   Vertex:(__, __)Max/Min

x intercept(s):(___, ___), (___, ___)

Increases: _____Decreases: _____

43. $f(x) = x^2 - 7x$

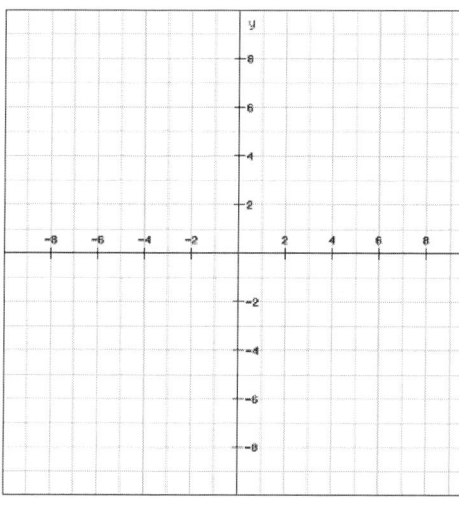

Vertex form: _____

Factorized form: _____

Domain: _____   Range: _____

y intercept:(__, __)   Vertex:(__, __)Max/Min

x intercept(s):(___, ___), (___, ___)

Increases: _____Decreases: _____

44. $f(x) = x^2 + 4x + 6$

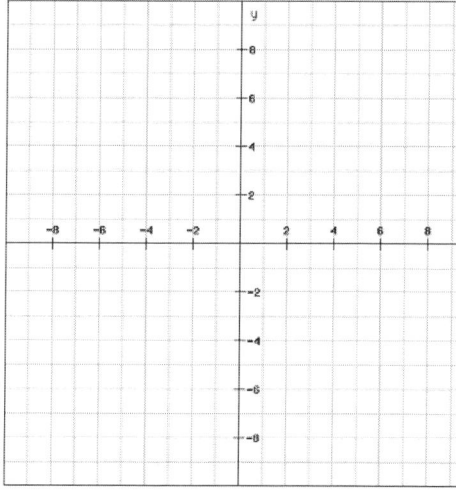

Vertex form: _____

Factorized form: _____

Domain: _____   Range: _____

y intercept:(__, __)   Vertex:(__, __)Max/Min

x intercept(s):(___, ___), (___, ___)

Increases: _____Decreases: _____

45. $f(x) = -2x^2 - 16x - 29$

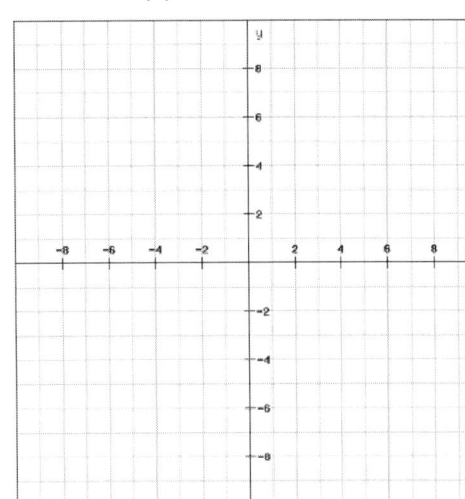

Vertex form: _____

Factorized form:_____

Domain: _____   Range: _____

y intercept:(__, __)   Vertex:(__, __)Max/Min

x intercept(s):(___, ___), (___, ___)

Increases: _____ Decreases: _____

46. $f(x) = x^2 - 6x + 4$

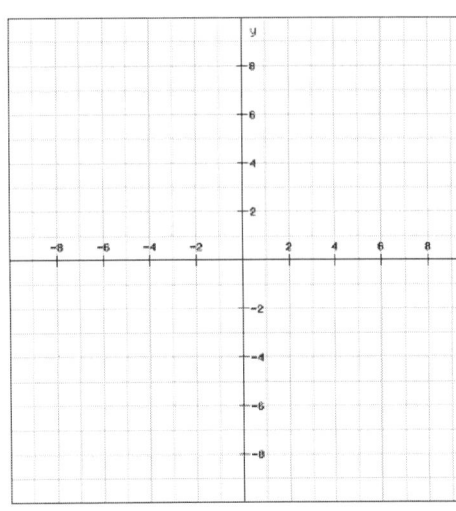

Vertex form: _____

Factorized form:_____

Domain: _____   Range: _____

y intercept:(__, __)   Vertex:(__, __)Max/Min

x intercept(s):(___, ___), (___, ___)

Increases: _____ Decreases: _____

47. $f(x) = x^2 - 7x + 2$

Vertex form: _____

Factorized form:_____

Domain: _____   Range: _____

y intercept:(__, __)   Vertex:(__, __)Max/Min

x intercept(s):(___, ___), (___, ___)

Increases: _____ Decreases: _____

48. $f(x) = x^2 + 3x + 10$

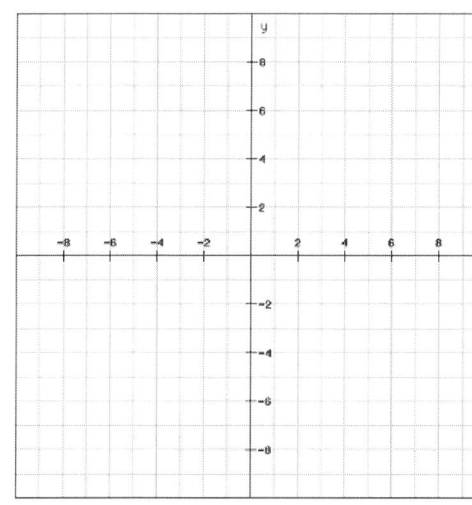

Vertex form: _____

Factorized form:_____

Domain: _____   Range: _____

y intercept:(__, __)   Vertex:(__, __)Max/Min

x intercept(s):(____, ____), (____, ____)

Increases: _____Decreases: _____

49. $f(x) = x^2 + 5$

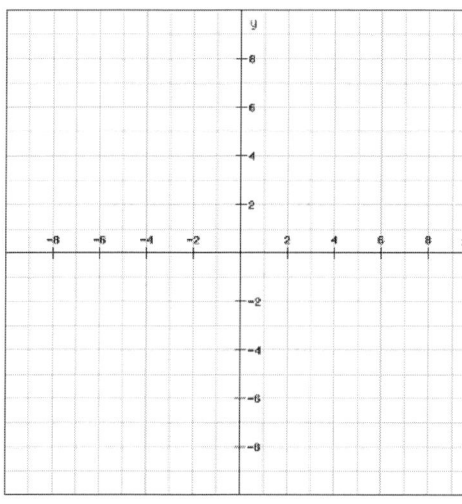

Vertex form: _____

Factorized form:_____

Domain: _____   Range: _____

y intercept:(__, __)   Vertex:(__, __)Max/Min

x intercept(s):(____, ____), (____, ____)

Increases: _____Decreases: _____

50. $f(x) = x^2 - 3$

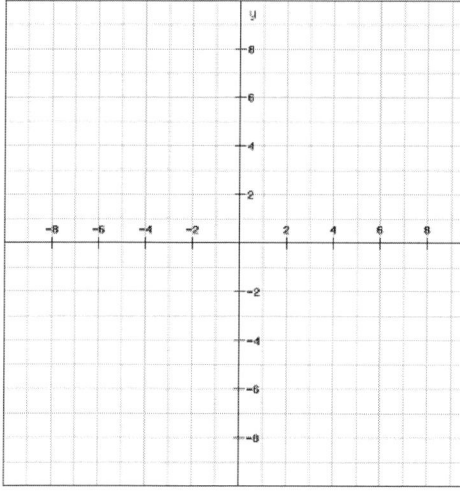

Vertex form: _____

Factorized form:_____

Domain: _____   Range: _____

y intercept:(__, __)   Vertex:(__, __)Max/Min

x intercept(s):(____, ____), (____, ____)

Increases: _____Decreases: _____

51. $f(x) = x^2 - 7x$

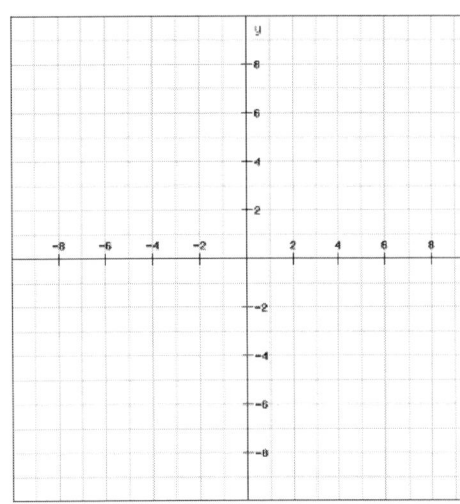

Vertex form: _____

Factorized form:_____

Domain: _____   Range: _____

y intercept:(__, __)   Vertex:(__, __)Max/Min

x intercept(s):(___, ___), (___, ___)

Increases: _____Decreases: _____

52. $f(x) = x^2 + 3x - 5$

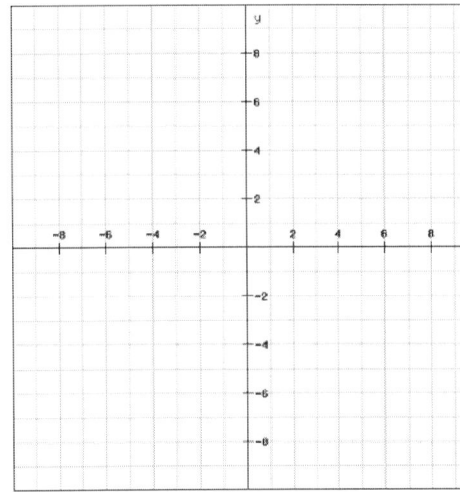

Vertex form: _____

Factorized form:_____

Domain: _____   Range: _____

y intercept:(__, __)   Vertex:(__, __)Max/Min

x intercept(s):(___, ___), (___, ___)

Increases: _____Decreases: _____

53. $f(x) = 5x^2 - 3$

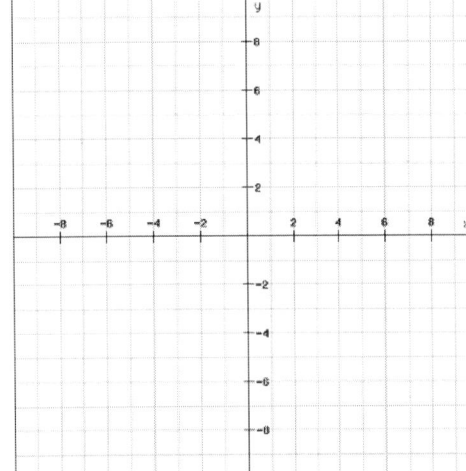

Vertex form: _____

Factorized form:_____

Domain: _____   Range: _____

y intercept:(__, __)   Vertex:(__, __)Max/Min

x intercept(s):(___, ___), (___, ___)

Increases: _____Decreases: _____

54. $f(x) = 5x^2 - 10x$

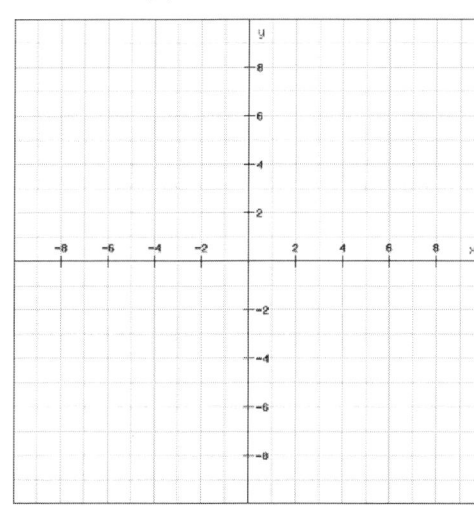

Vertex form: _____

Factorized form:_____

Domain: _____   Range: _____

y intercept:(__, __)   Vertex:(__, __)Max/Min

x intercept(s):(___, ___), (___, ___)

Increases: _____Decreases: _____

55. $f(x) = -5x^2$

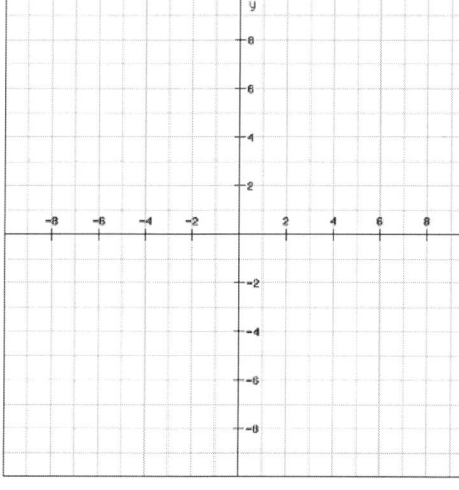

Vertex form: _____

Factorized form:_____

Domain: _____   Range: _____

y intercept:(__, __)   Vertex:(__, __)Max/Min

x intercept(s):(___, ___), (___, ___)

Increases: _____Decreases: _____

56. $f(x) = -x^2 + 6x - 8$

Vertex form: _____

Factorized form:_____

Domain: _____   Range: _____

y intercept:(__, __)   Vertex:(__, __)Max/Min

x intercept(s):(___, ___), (___, ___)

Increases: _____Decreases: _____

57. $f(x) = -x^2 - 6x + 2$

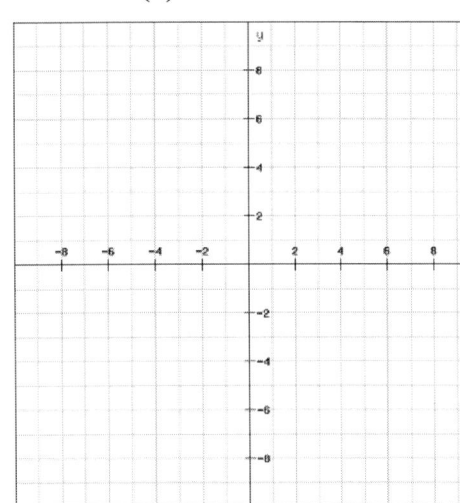

Vertex form: _____

Factorized form: _____

Domain: _____   Range: _____

y intercept:(__, __)   Vertex:(__, __)Max/Min

x intercept(s):(___, ___), (___, ___)

Increases: _____Decreases: _____

58. $f(x) = -x^2 + x - 5$

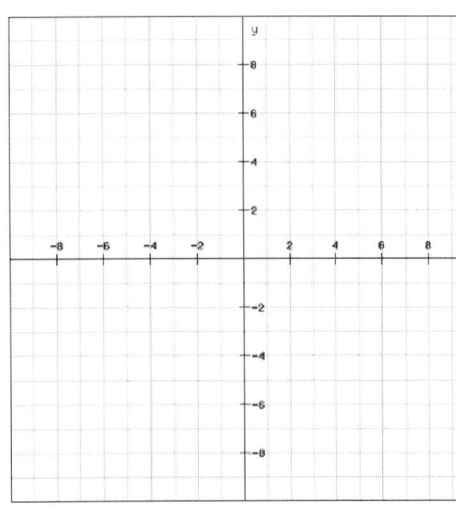

Vertex form: _____

Factorized form: _____

Domain: _____   Range: _____

y intercept:(__, __)   Vertex:(__, __)Max/Min

x intercept(s):(___, ___), (___, ___)

Increases: _____Decreases: _____

59. $f(x) = -x^2 - 4x - 4$

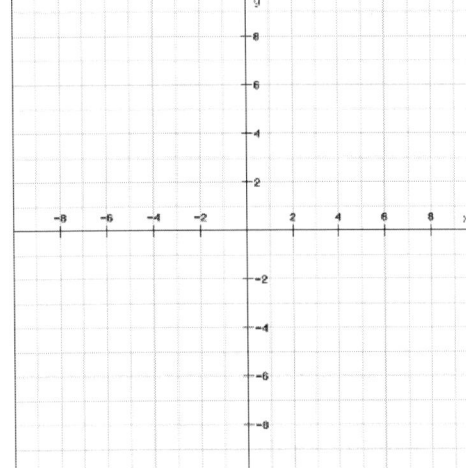

Vertex form: _____

Factorized form: _____

Domain: _____   Range: _____

y intercept:(__, __)   Vertex:(__, __)Max/Min

x intercept(s):(___, ___), (___, ___)

Increases: _____Decreases: _____

60. $f(x) = -x^2 + 3$

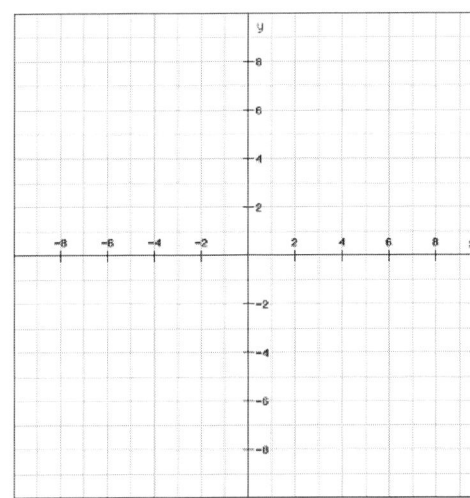

Vertex form: _____

Factorized form:_____

Domain: _____   Range: _____

y intercept:(__, __)   Vertex:(__, __)Max/Min

x intercept(s):(___, ___), (___, ___)

Increases: _____Decreases: _____

61. $f(x) = 3x^2$

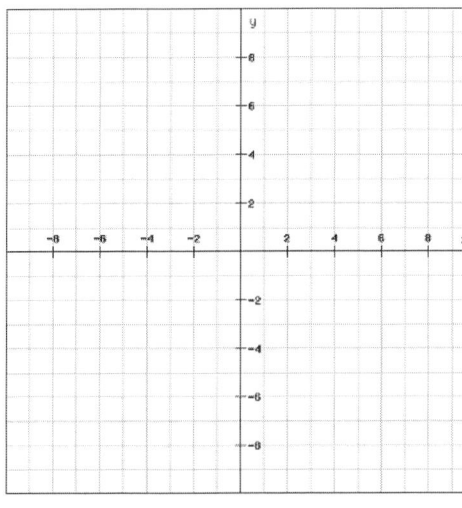

Vertex form: _____

Factorized form:_____

Domain: _____   Range: _____

y intercept:(__, __)   Vertex:(__, __)Max/Min

x intercept(s):(___, ___), (___, ___)

Increases: _____Decreases: _____

62. $f(x) = x^2 + 3x + 4$

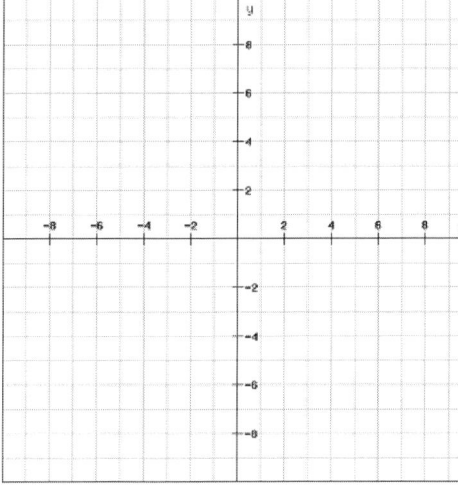

Vertex form: _____

Factorized form:_____

Domain: _____   Range: _____

y intercept:(__, __)   Vertex:(__, __)Max/Min

x intercept(s):(___, ___), (___, ___)

Increases: _____Decreases: _____

63. f(x) = –4x + 3

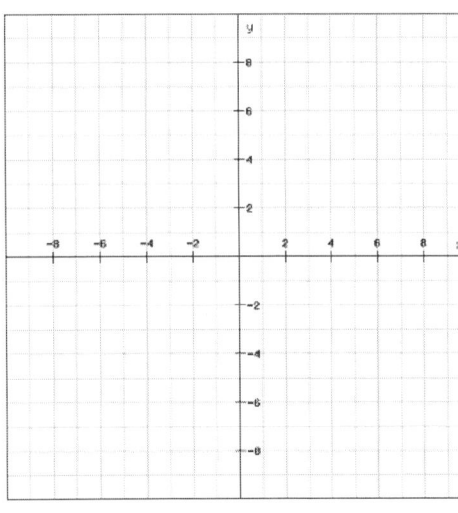

Vertex form: _____

Factorized form:_____

Domain: _____   Range: _____

y intercept:(__, __)   Vertex:(__, __)Max/Min

x intercept(s):(___, ___), (___, ___)

Increases: _____Decreases: _____

64. f(x) = $x^2 - 2$

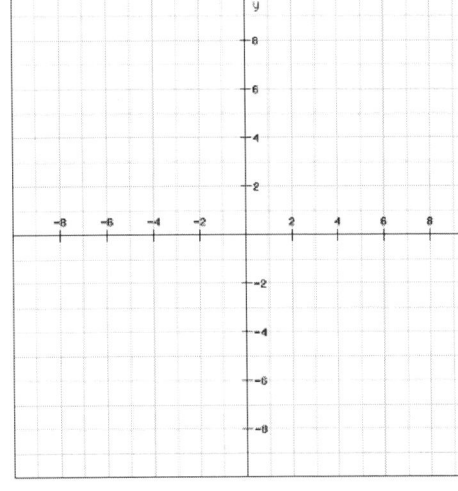

Vertex form: _____

Factorized form:_____

Domain: _____   Range: _____

y intercept:(__, __)   Vertex:(__, __)Max/Min

x intercept(s):(___, ___), (___, ___)

Increases: _____Decreases: _____

65. f(x) = $x^2 - 2x$

Vertex form: _____

Factorized form:_____

Domain: _____   Range: _____

y intercept:(__, __)   Vertex:(__, __)Max/Min

x intercept(s):(___, ___), (___, ___)

Increases: _____Decreases: _____

66. What are the coordinates of the vertex of $y = 7(x + 3)^2 + 4$? (___ , ___). State its axes of symmetry: _____

67. What are the coordinates of the vertex of $y = -2(x - 4)^2 + 2$? (___ , ___). State its axes of symmetry: _____

68. What value of b makes the expression $x^2 + 8x + b$ a perfect square? State its axes of symmetry: _____

69. When a quadratic function can be written as a perfect square on the graph it

means that _____.

70. what are the zeros of the quadratic relation $y = 10x^2 - 20x$. State its axes of symmetry: _____

71. Find the roots (zeros) of the equation $20(6 + 5x)(12 - x) = 0$. State its axes of symmetry: _____

72. The quadratic equation is used to find the _____ of the quadratic function.

n case this equation has no solutions it means the quadratic function is

ompletely _____ or _____ the x axis and the value of $b^2 - 4ac$

_____. In case $b^2 - 4ac$ is _____ the quadratic function will have

_____ and lastly if $b^2 - 4ac$ is _____ the quadratic function

will have _____.

If $b^2 - 4ac$ __ 0 there are _____ Example: _____

If $b^2 - 4ac$ __ 0 there are _____ Example: _____

If $b^2 - 4ac$ __ 0 there are _____ Example: _____

73. Under what conditions will the parabola with equation $y = a(x - h)^2 + k$ have two x–intercepts?

74. How many zeros does the quadratic relation $y = -1.7(x + 13.2)^2 - 3.1$ have?

75. A parabola has its vertex in the third quadrant and opens down. Write a possible function for it.

76. Write the equation, in vertex form, of a parabola that has its vertex in the second quadrant, contains two zeros, and is narrower than $y = x^2$

77. Write the equation, in vertex form, of a parabola that has its vertex in the third quadrant, contains two zeros, and is wider than $y = x^2$

78. Give   the relation $y = -4(x - 2)^2 + 7$, state its axes of symmetry: _____

79. Determine the value of the vertex of the relation $y = -(x - 3)(x + 1)$. Is the vertex a maximum or a minimum? State its axes of symmetry: _____

156

Applications

80. The height of a ball kicked upwards is given by h(t) = 40t − 16t^2 meters, $t \in [0, 2.5]$ where t is measured in seconds.

   a.   Sketch the corresponding function, label the axes.

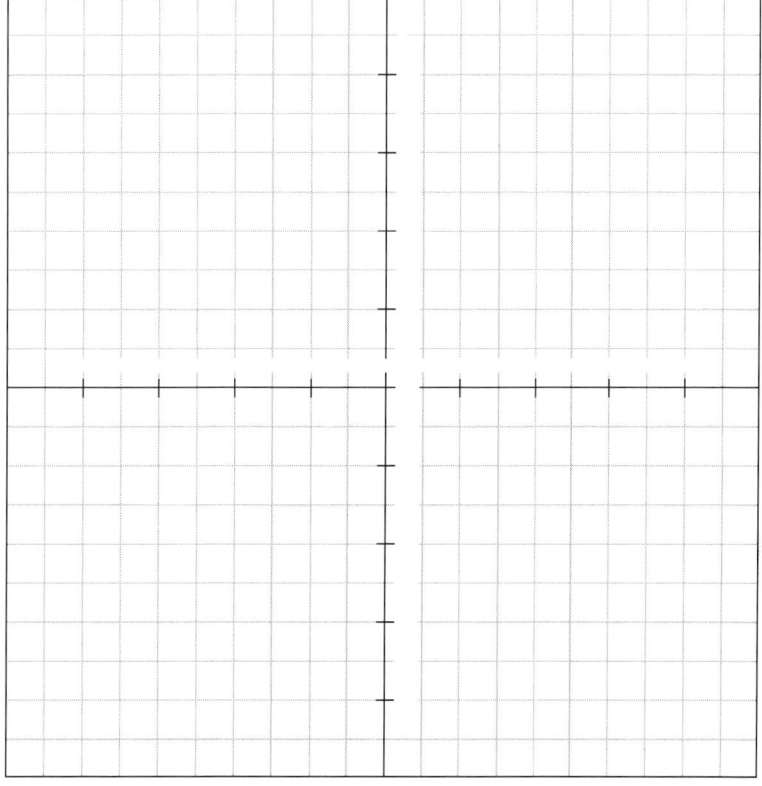

   b

   b.   Calculate h(1) and give a practical interpretation to your answer.

   c.   Calculate the zeros of h(t) and explain the meaning in the context of the problem.

   d.   Solve the equation h(t) = 10 and explain the meaning of the solutions in the context of the problem.

   e.   Obtain the maximum height of the ball and the instant in which it reaches it.

81. The efficiency of an engine as a function of the concentration of a certain chemical component is given by $f(x) = -0.5x^2 + x$, $0 \le x \le 2$.

    f.   Sketch the function in its domain.

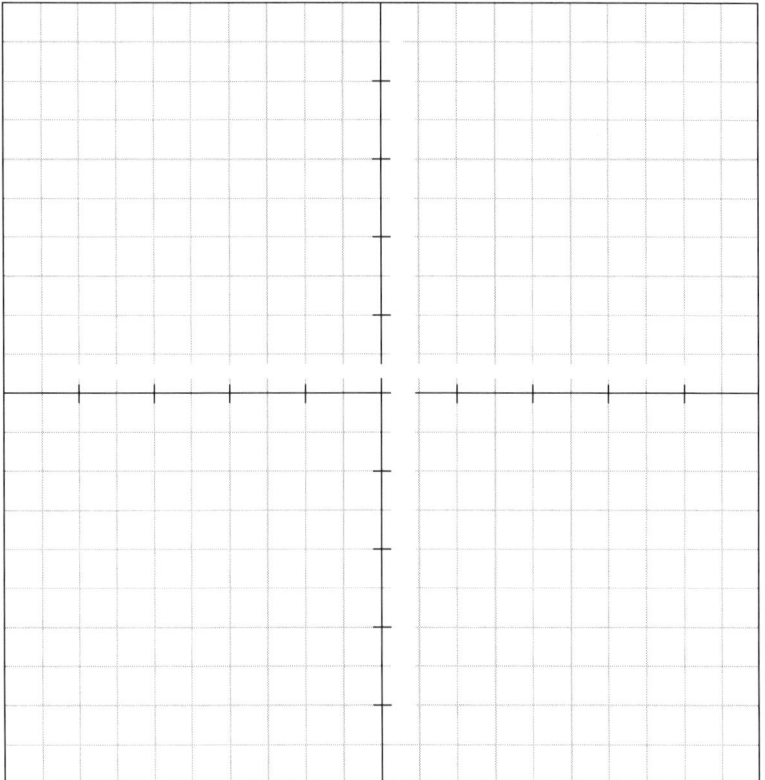

    g.   Find the concentration of the chemical for which the efficiency is maximized. What is the efficiency in this case?

82. A hundred meters of fencing is available to enclose a rectangular field along side of a River, What dimensions will produce the maximum area that can be enclosed?

5.4. – EXPONENTIAL FUNCTIONS

1. Given the functions: $f(x) = 2^x$, $g(x) = 3^x$, Complete the following chart:

x	−5	−4	−3	−2	−1	0	1	2	3	4	5	6
f(x)												
g(x)												

- Sketch the points of the table on a graph.

- State the domain of the function: _____

- State the y intercept (sketched on the graph: (____, ____)

- State the x intercept(s): (____, ____), (____, ____)

- Write the equation of the horizontal asymptote: _____

- Function is increasing on the interval: _____, decreasing on the interval:_____

- Find the max/min point(s): (____, ____)

- State the range of the function: _____

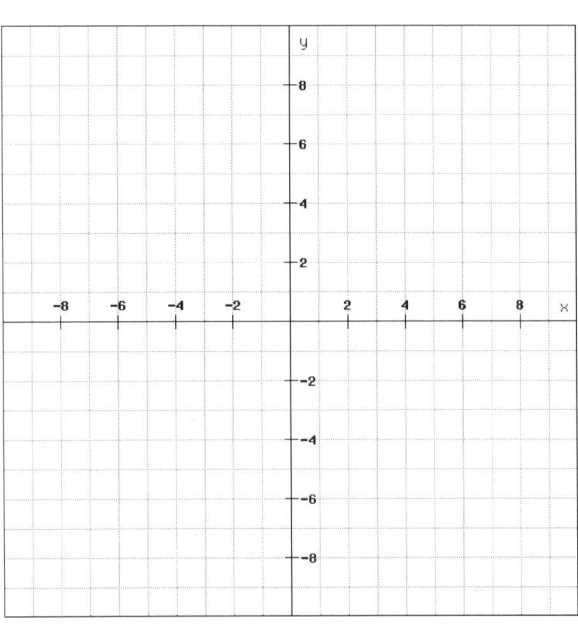

2. Given the functions: $f(x) = 2^{-x}$, $g(x) = 3^{-x}$, Complete the following chart:

x	−5	−4	−3	−2	−1	0	1	2	3	4	5	6
f(x)												
g(x)												

- Sketch the points of the table on a graph.

- State the domain of the function: _____

- State the *y* intercept (sketched on the graph: (____, ____)

- State the *x* intercept(s): (____, ____), (____, ____)

- Write the equation of the horizontal asymptote: _____

- Function is increasing on the interval: _____, decreasing on the interval:_____

- Find the max/min point(s): (____, ____)

- State the range of the function: _____

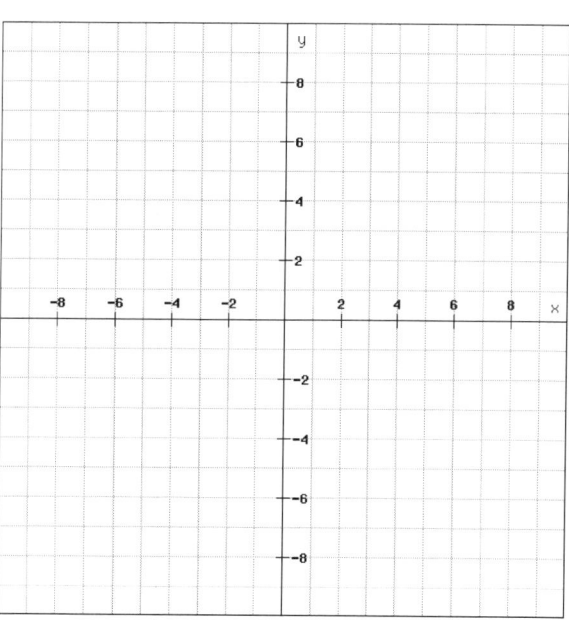

3. Given the functions: $f(x) = -2^x$, $g(x) = -3^x$, Complete the following chart:

x	−5	−4	−3	−2	−1	0	1	2	3	4	5	6
f(x)												
g(x)												

- Sketch the points of the table on a graph.

- State the domain of the function: _____

- State the y intercept (sketched on the graph: (_____, _____)

- State the x intercept(s): (_____, _____), (_____, _____)

- Write the equation of the horizontal asymptote: _____

- Function is increasing on the interval: _____, decreasing on the interval: _____

- Find the max/min point(s): (_____, _____)

- State the range of the function: _____

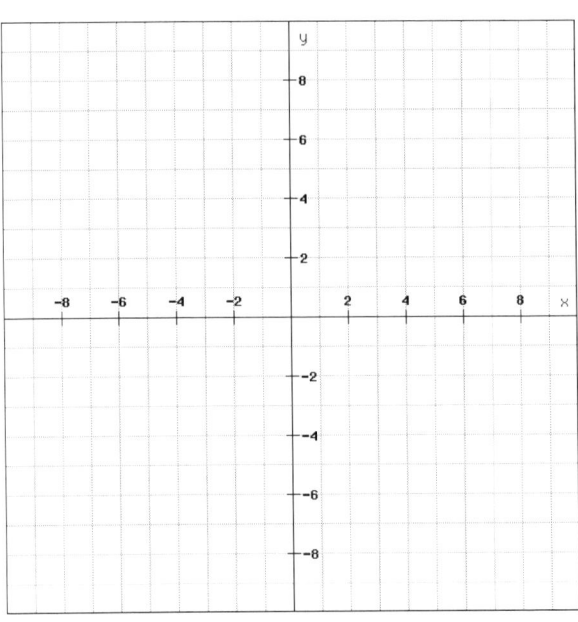

4. Given the functions: $f(x) = -2^{-x}$, $g(x) = -3^{-x}$, Complete the following chart:

x	−5	−4	−3	−2	−1	0	1	2	3	4	5	6
f(x)												
g(x)												

- Sketch the points of the table on a graph.

- State the domain of the function: _____

- State the y intercept (sketched on the graph: (____, ____)

- State the x intercept(s): (____, ____), (____, ____)

- Write the equation of the horizontal asymptote: _____

- Function is increasing on the interval: _____, decreasing on the interval:_____

- Find the max/min point(s): (____, ____)

- State the range of the function: _____

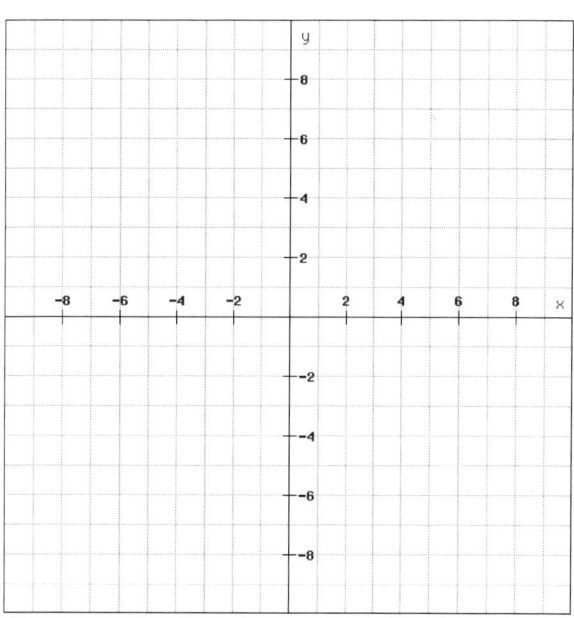

163

5. Given the functions: $f(x) = -5 \times 4^{-2x} + 1$, Complete the following chart:

x	−5	−4	−3	−2	−1	0	1	2	3	4	5	6
f(x)												
g(x)												

- Sketch the points of the table on a graph.

- State the domain of the function: _____

- State the y intercept (sketched on the graph: (____, ____)

- State the x intercept(s): (____, ____), (____, ____)

- Write the equation of the horizontal asymptote: _____

- Function is increasing on the interval: _____, decreasing on the interval:_____

- Find the max/min point(s): (____, ____)

- State the range of the function: _____

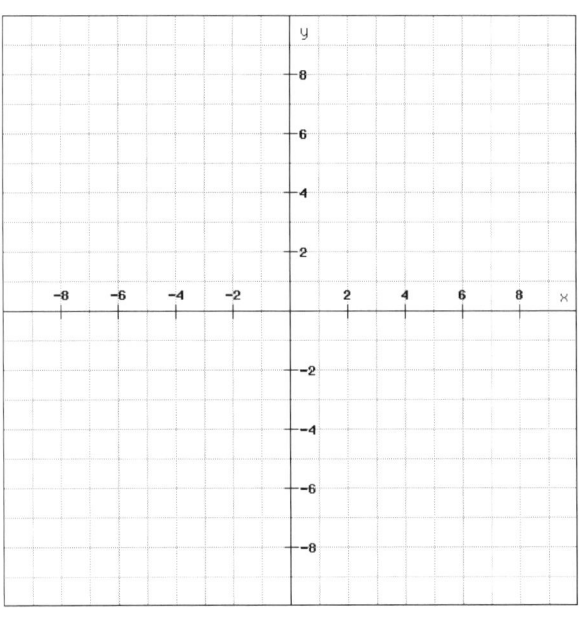

6. Given the graph of the function $f(x) = \left(\dfrac{1}{2}\right)^x = (\underline{})^x = \underline{}$ sketch, on the same set of axes, the graphs of the functions:

$g(x) = \left(\dfrac{1}{2}\right)^{x-2} = (\underline{})^{x-2} = \underline{} = \underline{}$

$d(x) = \left(\dfrac{1}{2}\right)^x - 2 = \underline{}$

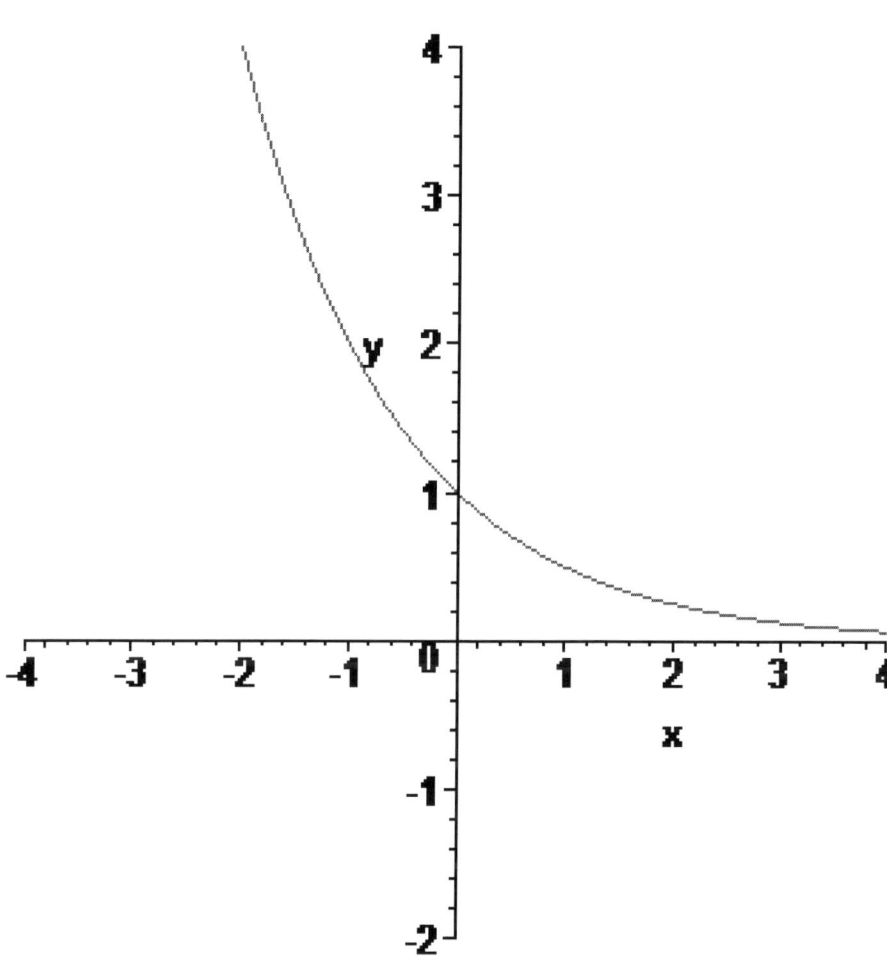

7. Given the graph, complete the table below:

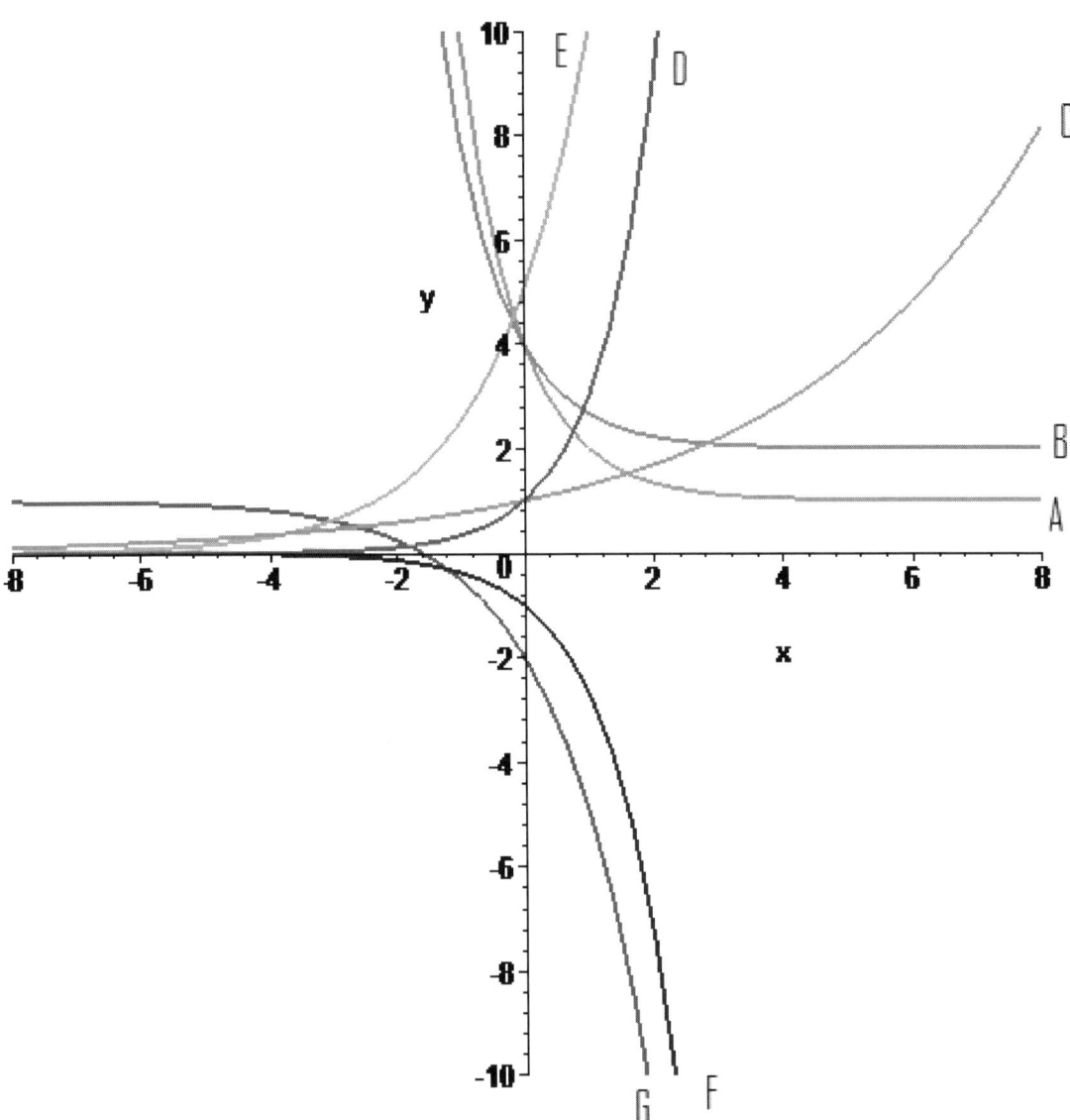

Function	On the graph
$f(x) = 5 \times 2^x$	
$f(x) = 2 + 2 \times 3^{-x}$	
$f(x) = 3 \times 3^{-x} + 1$	
$f(x) = (1.3)^x$	
$f(x) = -e^x$	
$f(x) = 3^x$	
$f(x) = -3 \times 2^x + 1$	

Analyze the functions, using your GDC:

1. $f(x) = 4^x$

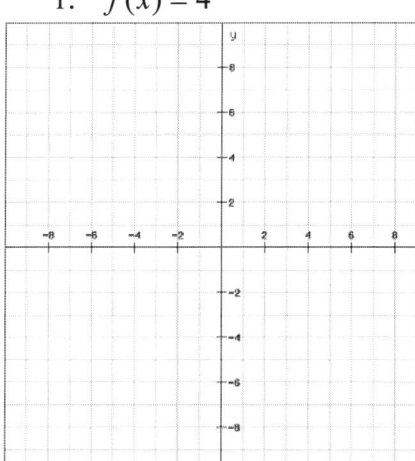

Domain: _____   Range: _____

y intercept:(___, ___)

                   Increases: _____

x intercept:(___, ___)   Decreases: _____

Horizontal asymptote:_____

2. $f(x) = -3^x$

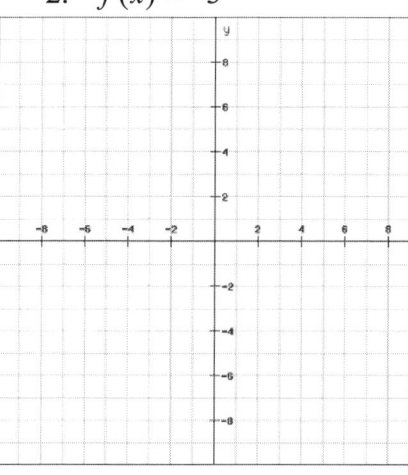

Domain: _____   Range: _____

y intercept:(___, ___)

                   Increases: _____

x intercept:(___, ___)   Decreases: _____

Horizontal asymptote:_____

3. $f(x) = 2^{-x}$

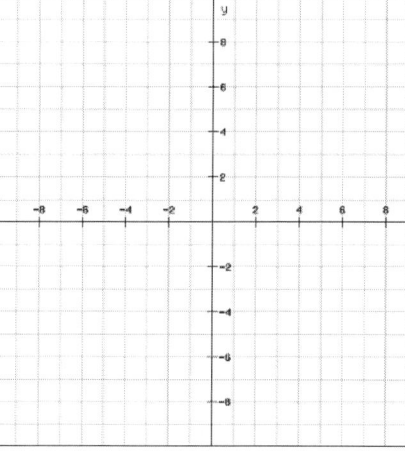

Domain: _____   Range: _____

y intercept:(___, ___)

                   Increases: _____

x intercept:(___, ___)   Decreases: _____

Horizontal asymptote:_____

4. $f(x) = -2^{-x}$

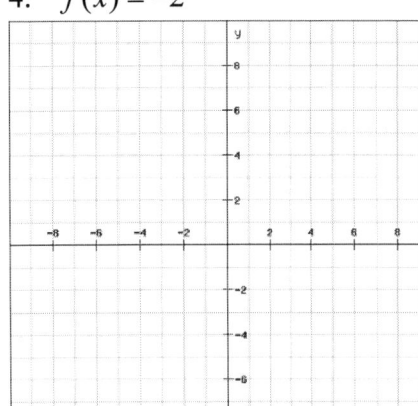

Domain: _____   Range: _____

y intercept:(___, ___)

                               Increases: _____

x intercept:(___, ___)   Decreases: _____

Horizontal asymptote:_____

5. $f(x) = \left(\dfrac{1}{4}\right)^x$

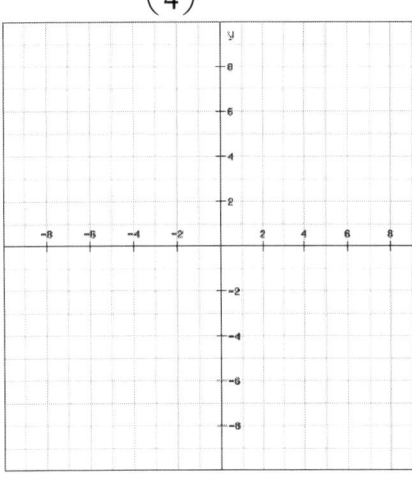

Domain: _____   Range: _____

y intercept:(___, ___)

                               Increases: _____

x intercept:(___, ___)   Decreases: _____

Horizontal asymptote:_____

6. $f(x) = 3\left(\dfrac{2}{7}\right)^x$

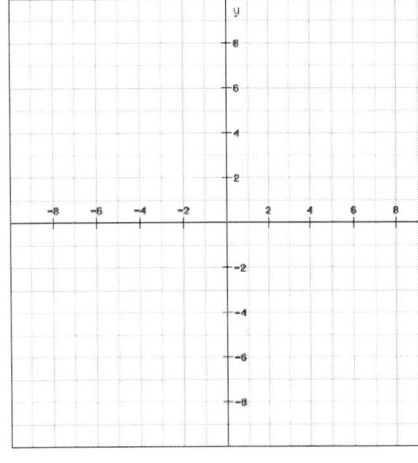

Domain: _____   Range: _____

y intercept:(___, ___)

                               Increases: _____

x intercept:(___, ___)   Decreases: _____

Horizontal asymptote:_____

7. $f(x) = -2^{x+5}$

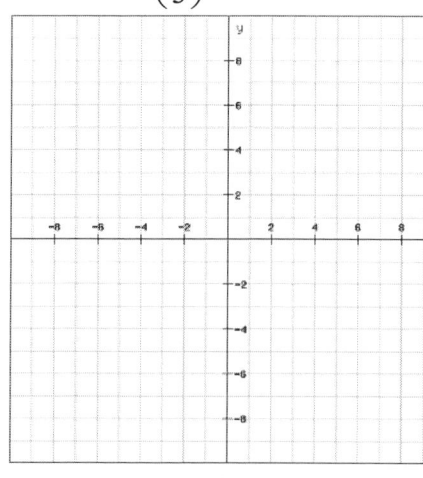

Domain: _____   Range: _____

y intercept:(___, ___)

                            Increases: _____

x intercept:(___, ___)   Decreases: _____

Horizontal asymptote:_____

8. $f(x) = \left(\dfrac{2}{3}\right)^{x}$

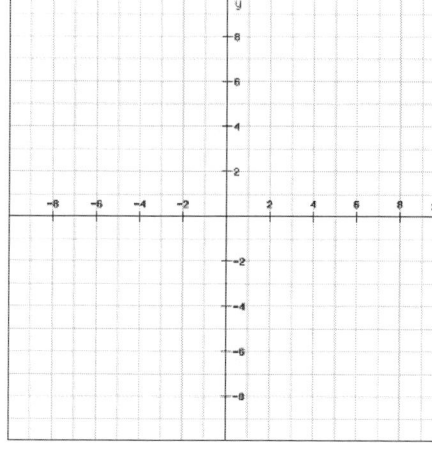

Domain: _____   Range: _____

y intercept:(___, ___)

                            Increases: _____

x intercept:(___, ___)   Decreases: _____

Horizontal asymptote:_____

9. $f(x) = 3 \cdot 7^{x-4}$

Domain: _____   Range: _____

y intercept:(___, ___)

                            Increases: _____

x intercept:(___, ___)   Decreases: _____

Horizontal asymptote:_____

10. $f(x) = -7^{x-2} + 2$

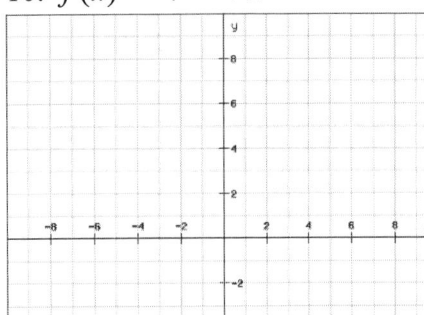

Domain: _____   Range: _____

y intercept:(___, ___)

Increases: _____

x intercept:(___, ___)   Decreases: _____

Horizontal asymptote:_____

11. $f(x) = 2 \cdot 5^{-x-2} - 5$

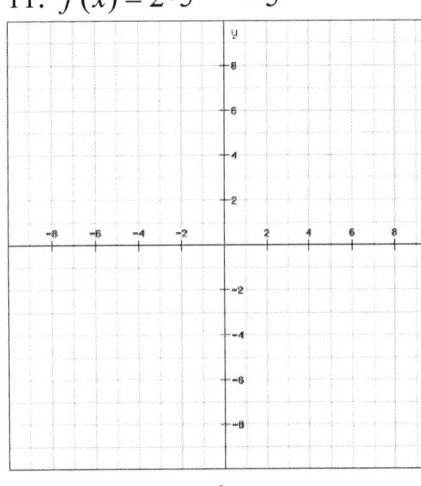

Domain: _____   Range: _____

y intercept:(___, ___)

Increases: _____

x intercept:(___, ___)   Decreases: _____

Horizontal asymptote:_____

12. $f(x) = -3^{-x-3} + 4$

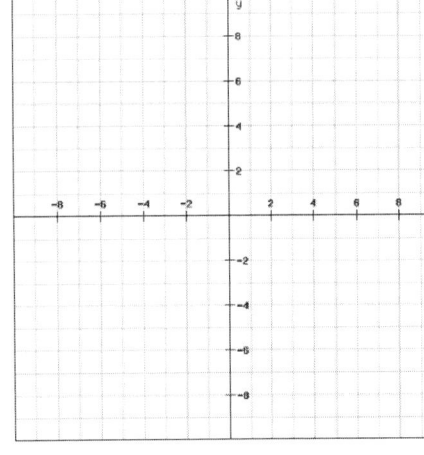

Domain: _____   Range: _____

y intercept:(___, ___)

Increases: _____

x intercept:(___, ___)   Decreases: _____

Horizontal asymptote:_____

13. $f(x) = -e^x$

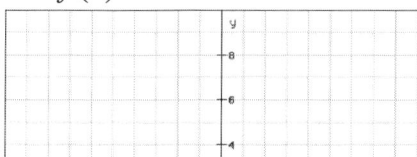

Domain: _____   Range: _____

y intercept:(___, ___)

Increases: _____

x intercept:(___, ___)   Decreases: _____

Horizontal asymptote:_____

14. $f(x) = e^{x+2}$

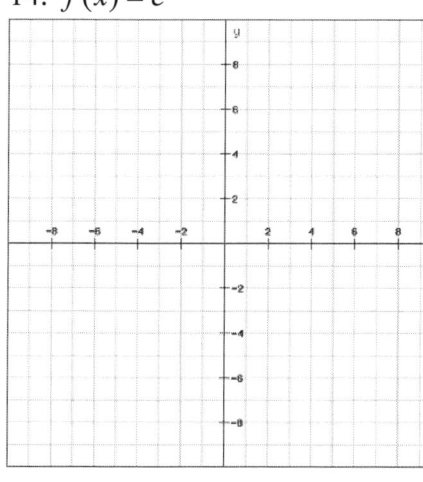

Domain: _____   Range: _____

y intercept:(___, ___)

Increases: _____

x intercept:(___, ___)   Decreases: _____

Horizontal asymptote:_____

15. $f(x) = -e^x + 4$

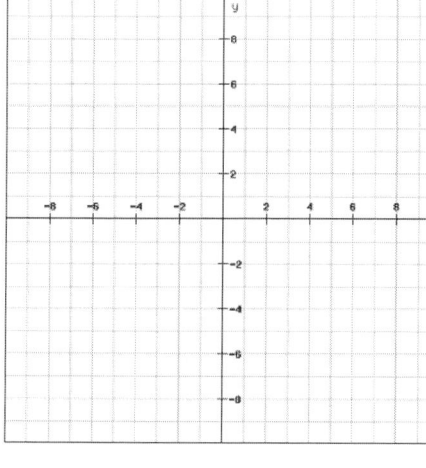

Domain: _____   Range: _____

y intercept:(___, ___)

Increases: _____

x intercept:(___, ___)   Decreases: _____

Horizontal asymptote:_____

16. $f(x) = 0.1e^{x+1} + 2$

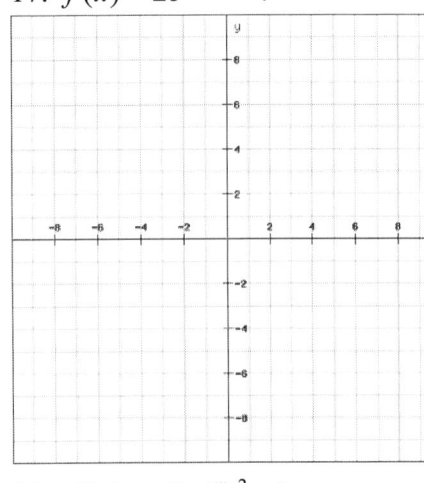

Domain: _____   Range: _____

y intercept:(___, ___)

                                 Increases: _____

x intercept:(___, ___)   Decreases: _____

Horizontal asymptote:_____

17. $f(x) = 2e^{2x+1} - 4$

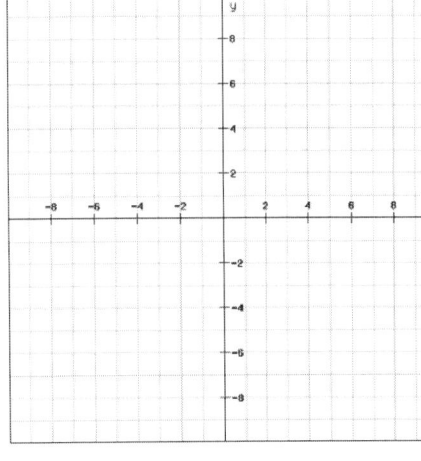

Domain: _____   Range: _____

y intercept:(___, ___)

                                 Increases: _____

x intercept:(___, ___)   Decreases: _____

Horizontal asymptote:_____

18. $f(x) = -2 \cdot 6^{x-2} - 1$

Domain: _____   Range: _____

y intercept:(___, ___)

                                 Increases: _____

x intercept:(___, ___)   Decreases: _____

Horizontal asymptote:_____

19. $f(x) = 2 \cdot 3^{x-2} - 5$

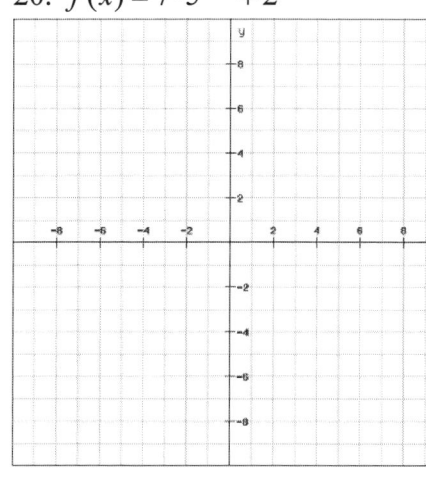

Domain: _____   Range: _____

y intercept:(___, ___)

                                           Increases: _____

x intercept:(___, ___)   Decreases: _____

Horizontal asymptote:_____

20. $f(x) = 7 \cdot 5^{x-2} + 2$

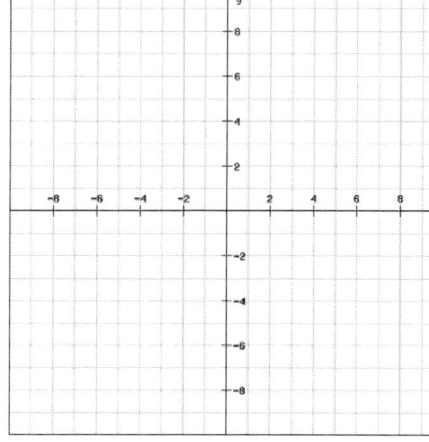

Domain: _____   Range: _____

y intercept:(___, ___)

                                           Increases: _____

x intercept:(___, ___)   Decreases: _____

Horizontal asymptote:_____

21. $f(x) = -2 \cdot 3^{-2x+1} + 4$

Domain: _____   Range: _____

y intercept:(___, ___)

                                           Increases: _____

x intercept:(___, ___)   Decreases: _____

Horizontal asymptote:_____

Applications

1. The number of products sold during the year 2012 in a certain store can be modeled by the following function where t is given in months (t = 1 corresponds the month of January).

$$T(t) = 800 \times (1.02)^{(2.3)t} - 50$$

    a. Find the number of products sold in March.
    b. Sketch the function.
    c. What can be said about the number of products sold?
    d. When will the number of products sold exceed 1000 for the first time?

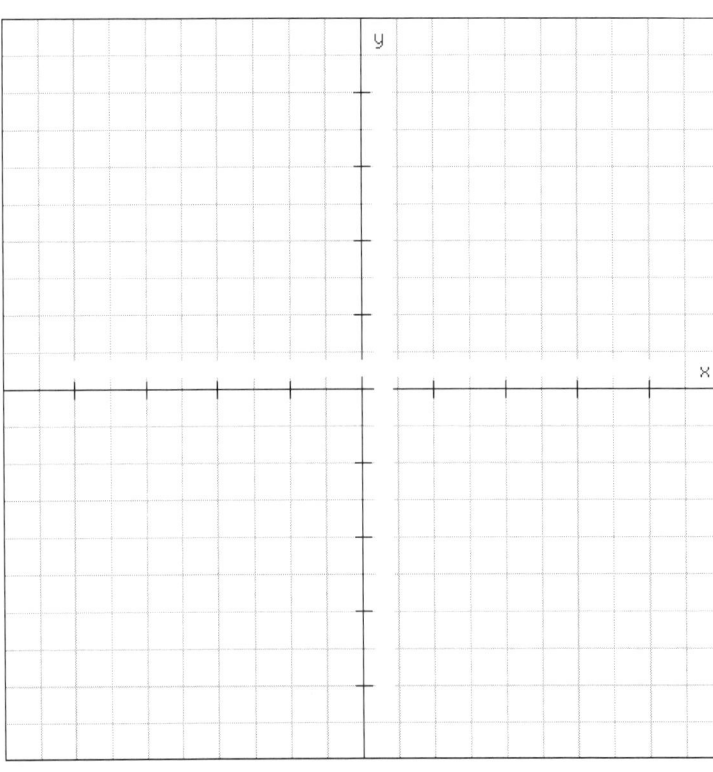

2. The temperature of boiling liquid can be modeled by the following function where t is given in minutes.

$$T(t) = 80 \times \left(\frac{9}{8}\right)^{-2t} + 10$$

    a. Find the initial temperature of the liquid.
    b. Find the temperature of the liquid after 2 minutes.
    c. What will the temperature of the liquid after a long time? Give a practical interpretation to this temperature.
    d. Sketch the function.
    e. How long will it take the temperature of the liquid reach 42°?

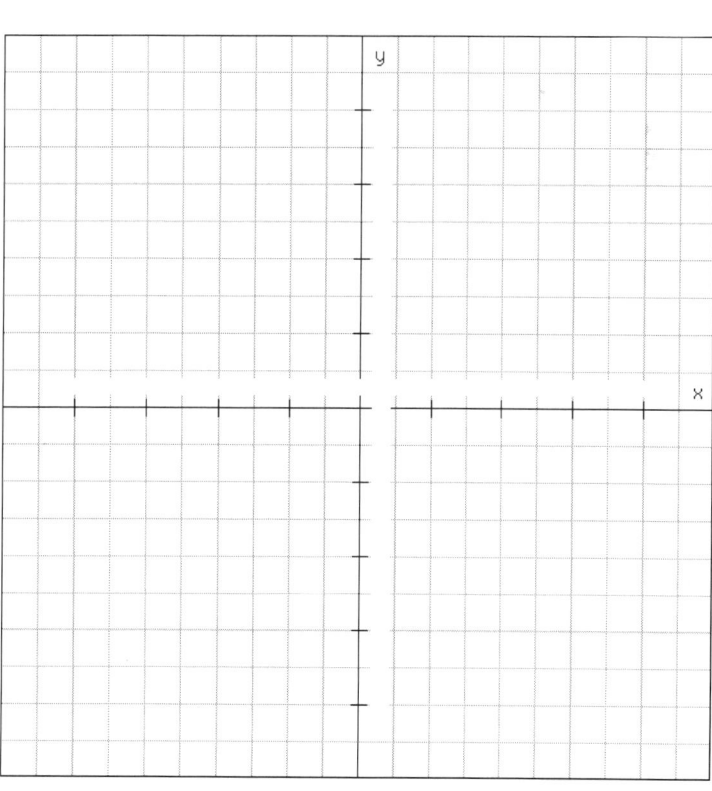

3. The population of a rapidly–growing country starts at 4 million and increases by 10% each year.
    a. Complete the table below:

t(years)	P, population (in millions)	ΔP, increase in population (in millions)
0		
1		
2		
3		
4		

    b. Do you identify a pattern? Can you write a general expression of the population (P) as a function of the time (t)?

    c. Sketch its graph:

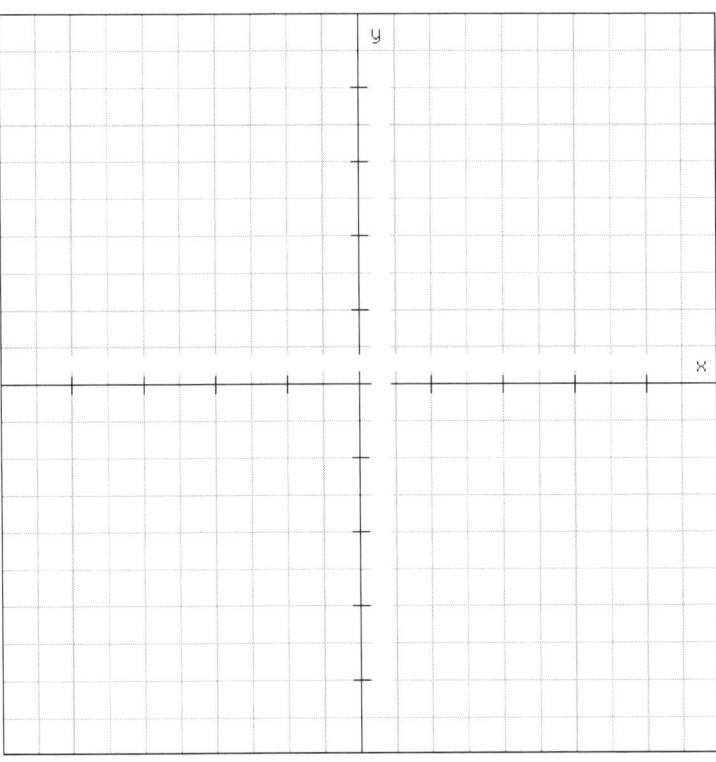

4. A chemical reaction starts with 200 grams of radioactive substance that decays by 20% per year.
   a. First, complete the table below.

t (years)	0	1	2	3	4
Q (grams)					

b. Find the expression of the function A(t), A the amount of substance and t the time in years.

c. Sketch its graph.

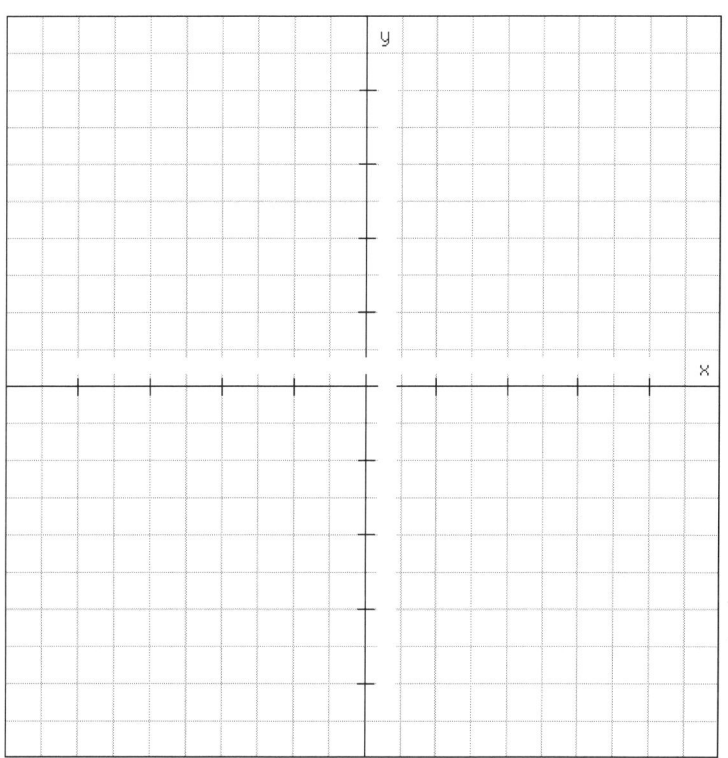

5. Suppose you invest 10000$ in the year 2000 and the investment earns 5.5% annually.

   a. a. Find the expression of the function A(t), A the amount of money and t the time in years.

   b. What will be the investment worth in 2010, 2020, 2030?

6.1. – DEFINITION OF TRIGONOMETRIC FUNCTIONS

Definition: The trigonometric functions are defined using the so called "unit circle" which is simply a circle with radius 1:

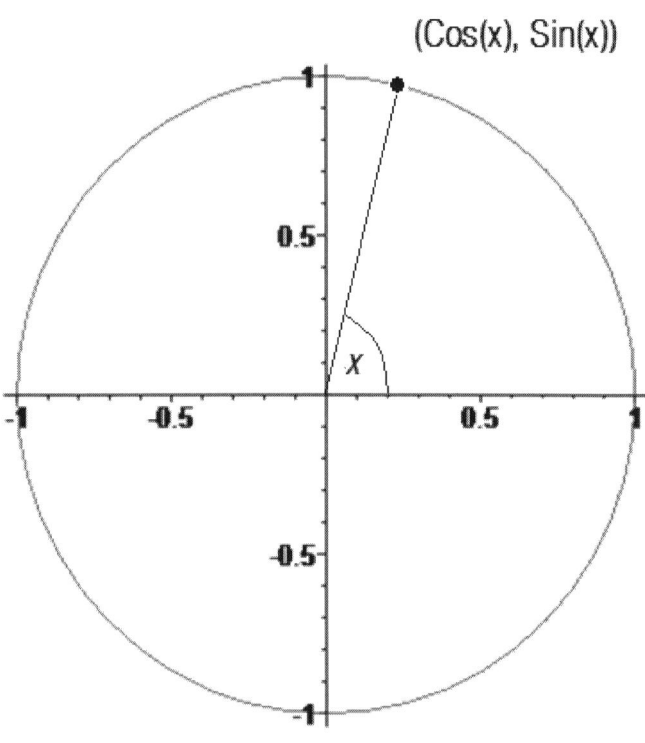

Definition of Sin(x):

1st Quadrant: 3rd Quadrant:

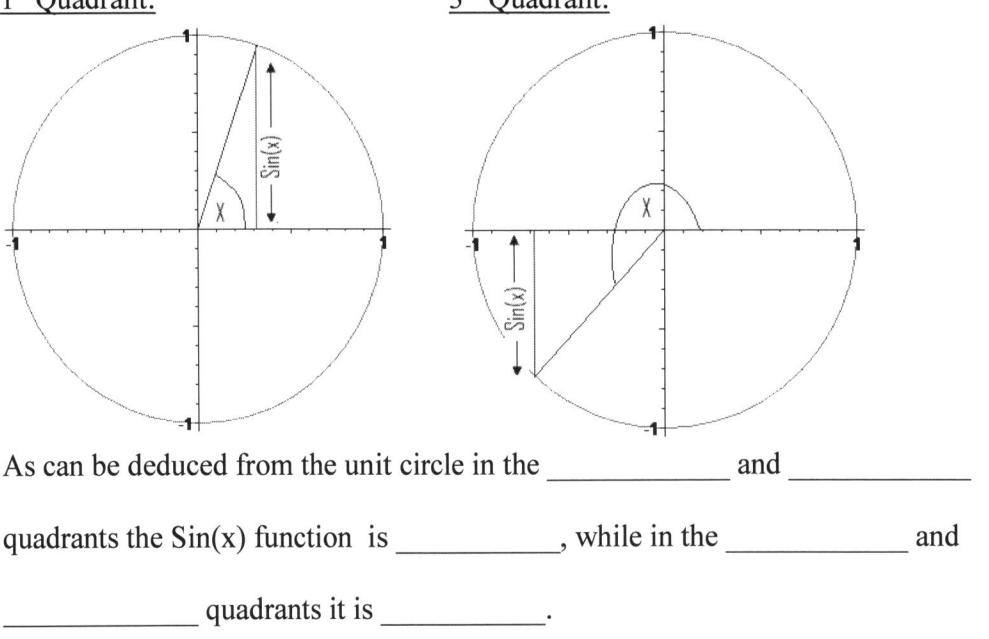

As can be deduced from the unit circle in the _____ and _____

quadrants the Sin(x) function is _____, while in the _____ and

_____ quadrants it is _____.

Definition of Cos(x):

2nd Quadrant: 4th Quadrant:

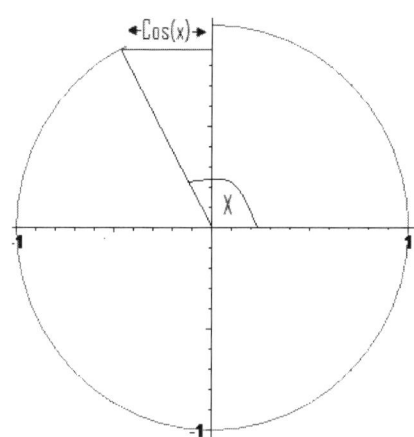

As can be deduced from the unit circle in the _____ and _____

quadrants the Sin(x) function is _____, while in the _____ and

_____ quadrants it is _____.

Exercises:

In each one of the cases sketch the unit circle and the corresponding angle and then find the corresponding value:

1. Sin(0°) =   3. Sin(90°) =

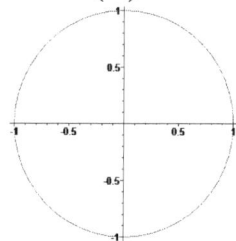   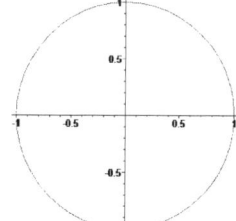

2. Cos(0°) =   4. Cos(225°) =

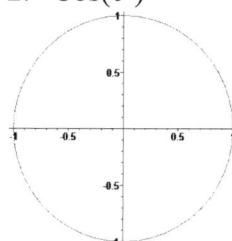   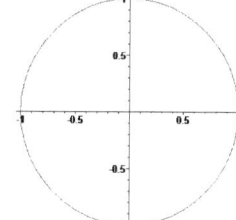

179

5. Sin(225°) =

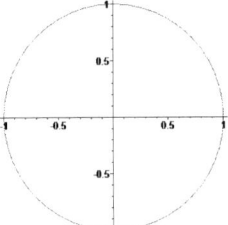

6. Cos(210°) =

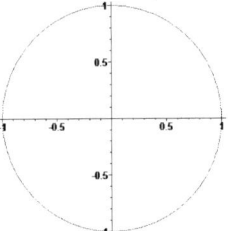

7. Sin(210°) =

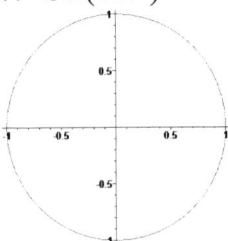

8. Cos(225°) =

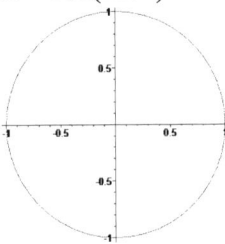

9. Sin(–225°) =

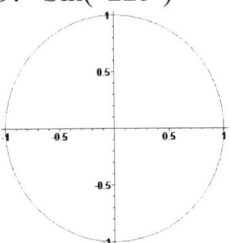

10. Cos(210°) =

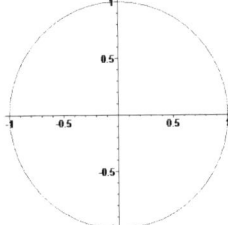

11. Sin(–210°) =

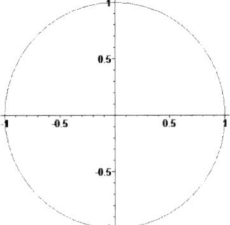

12. Cos(90°) =

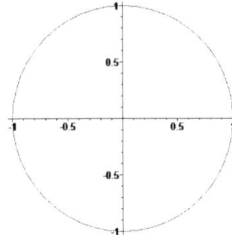

13. Sin(270°) =

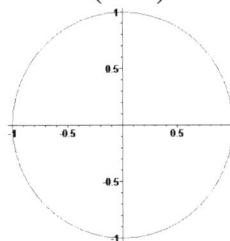

14. Cos(270°) =

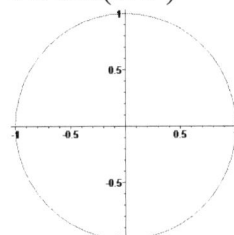

15. Sin(360°) =

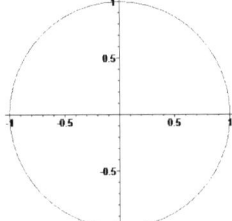

16. Cos(180°) =

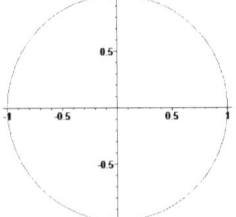

17. Sin(180º) =

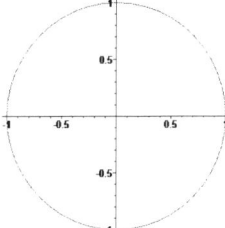

18. Cos(–45º) =

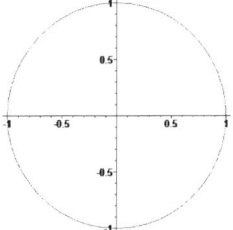

19. Cos(300º) =

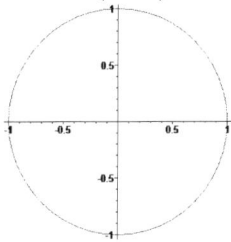

20. Sin(300º) =

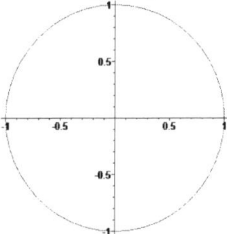

21. Sin(330º) =

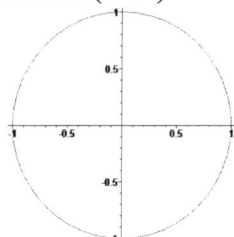

22. Cos(390º) =

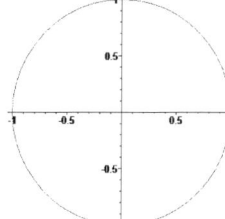

23. Cos(135º) =

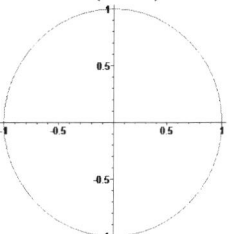

24. Sin(135º) =

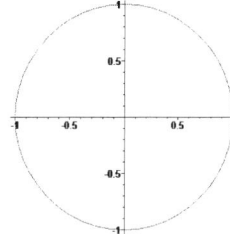

25. Sin(45º) =

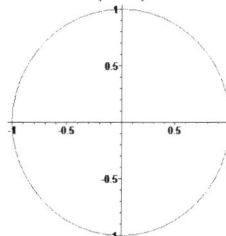

26. Cos(70º) =

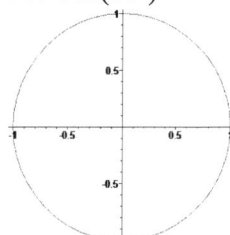

27. Cos(130º) =

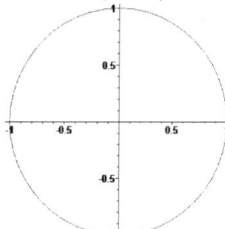

28. Cos(1º) =

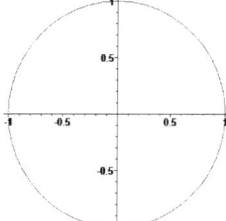

181

6.2. – SINE AND COSINE RULE

<u>The sine rule:</u> For any triangle, given the sides a, b and c and their corresponding opposite angles, A, B and C:

$$\frac{Sin(A)}{a} = \frac{Sin(B)}{b} = \frac{Sin(C)}{c}$$

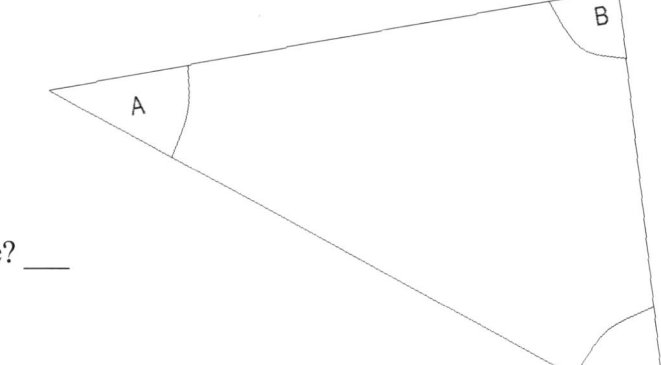

How many equations are written above? ____

    I.   _____

    II.   _____

    III.   _____

<u>The cosine rule:</u> For any triangle, given the sides a, b and c and their corresponding opposite angles, A, B and C:

$$a^2 = b^2 + c^2 - 2bc\cos(A)$$
$$b^2 = a^2 + c^2 - 2ac\cos(B)$$
$$c^2 = \underline{\ } + \underline{\ } - \underline{\quad\quad}$$

Given the following triangle:

    a. Find AD in terms of AC and the angle C.

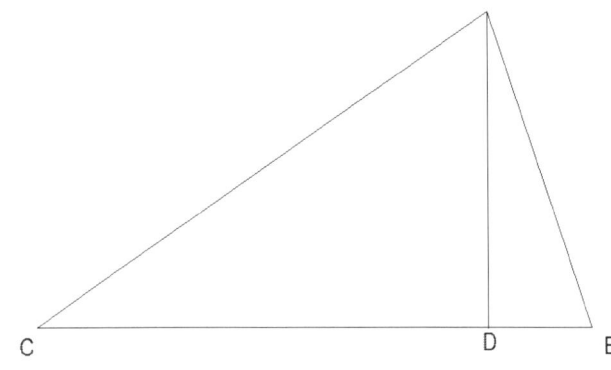

    b. Find the Area of the triangle in terms of AB, BC and the angle C.

    c. Conclusion:

Exercises

1. Sketch a right angled triangle with angles: M, N, G and sides x, y, z. Write the Sine and Cosine rule for this triangle.

2. Find all the missing sides, angles and area of the triangles below. If there is more than one set of solutions, try to find them all.

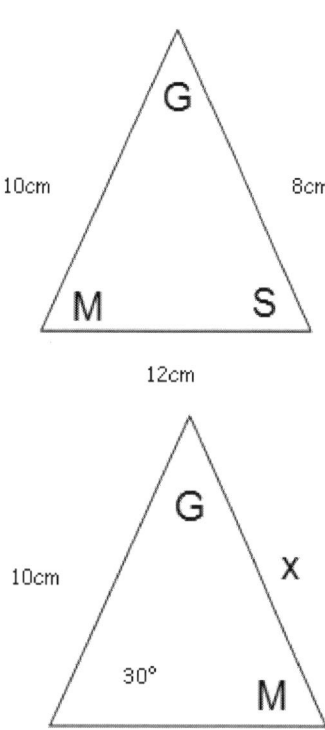

3. Find all the sides, angles and the area of the following triangles:

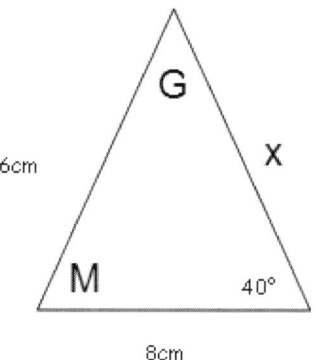

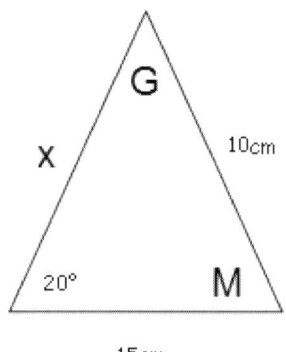

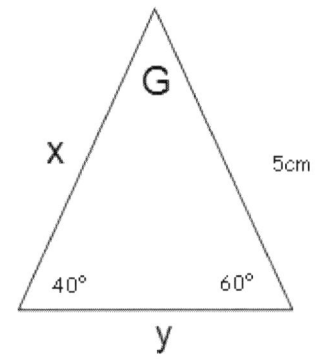

4. Find all the sides, angles and the area of the following triangles:

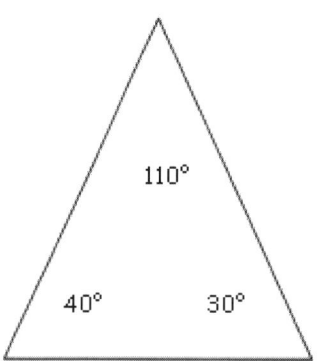

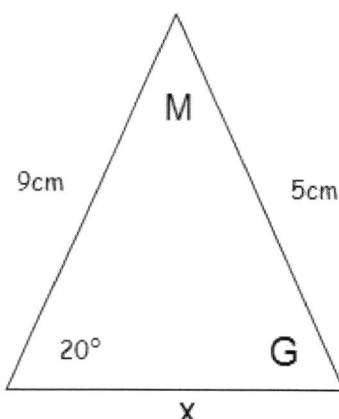

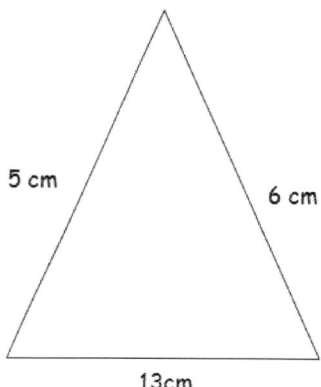

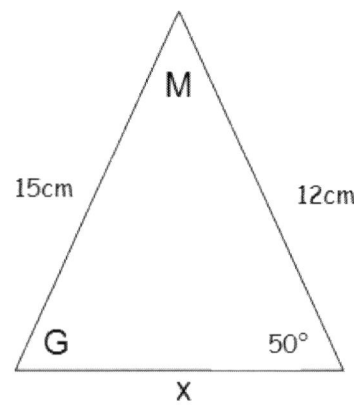

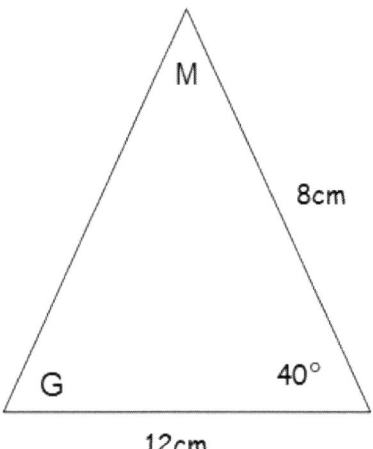

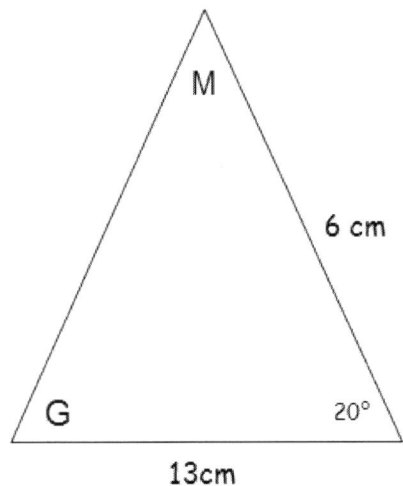

6.3. – TRIGONOMETRIC RATIOS

Following directly from the unit circle are the trigonometric ratios:

$$Sin(x) = \frac{a}{c} = Cos(y)$$

$$Cos(x) = \frac{b}{c} = Sin(y)$$

$$Tan(x) = \frac{a}{b} = \frac{Sin(x)}{Cos(x)}$$

$$Tan(x) = \frac{b}{a} = \frac{Sin(y)}{Cos(y)}$$

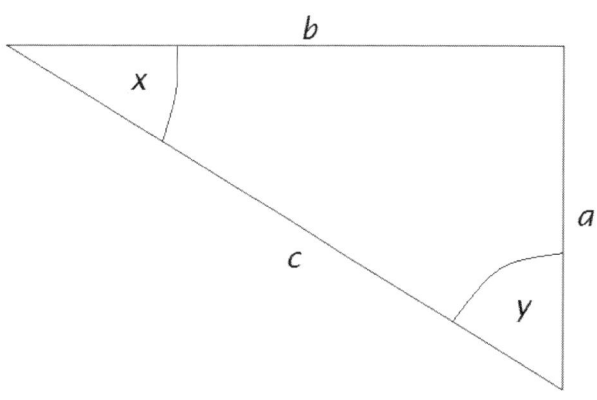

Exercises:

1. Find x and y in the following cases:
   a.

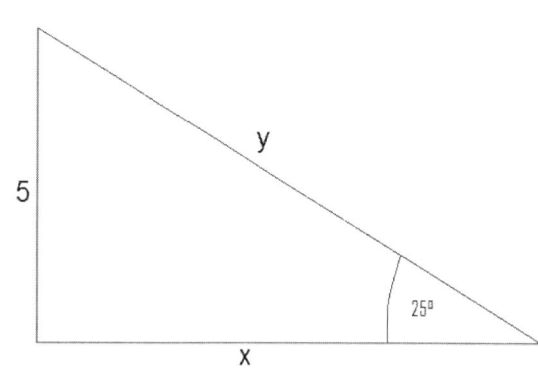

   b.

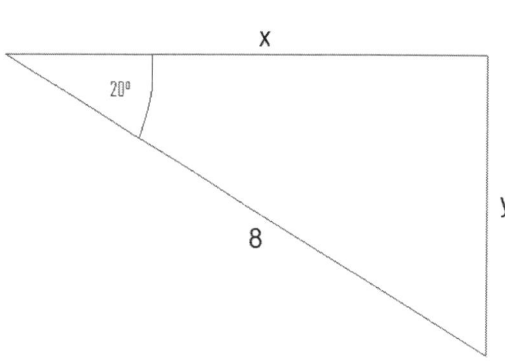

2. The Triangle in the diagram (not to scale) is <u>not</u> right angled, find x and y.

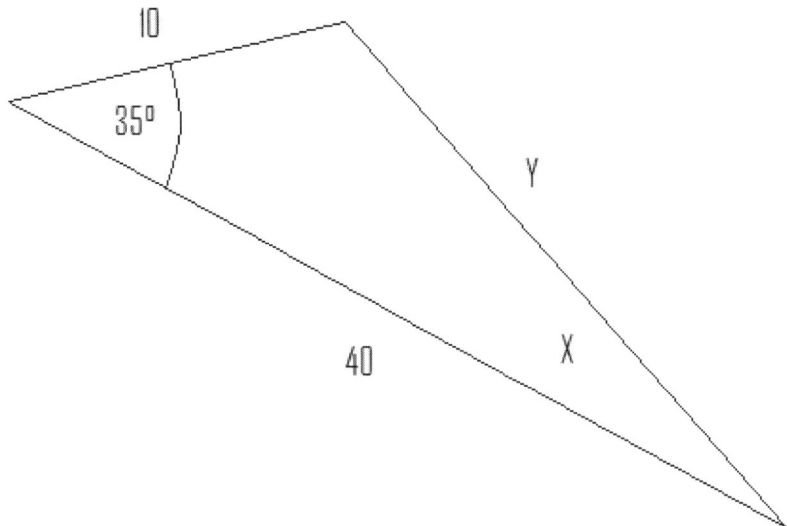

3. The shade formed by building is 100m long. The depression angle of the light as it approaches the ground is 40°.

    a. Sketch a diagram that describes the situation.
    b. Find the height of the building.

4. John who lives next the river wanted to measure its width without crossing the river. He did some measurements and obtained the following data:

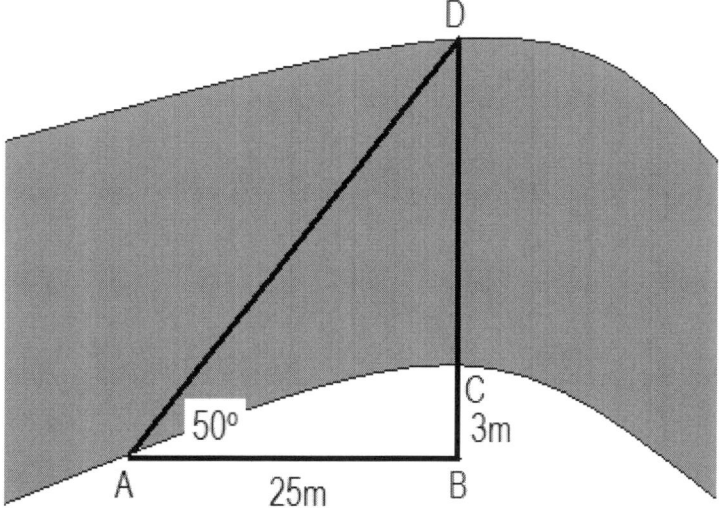

AB = 25m, BC = 3m, B = 90°

Find the width of the river.

5. The height of building is 120m. The depression angle of the light as it approaches the ground is 30°.

   a. Sketch a diagram that describes the situation.
   b. Find the length of the shade on the ground.

6. In its search for food the lion is observing a certain prey located 2 m above the ground. The lion's head forms an angle of 12° with the ground as he looks at his prey.

   a. Sketch a diagram that describes the situation.
   b. Find the distance from the lion's mouth to its prey.

7. Measuring the height and distance of objects:

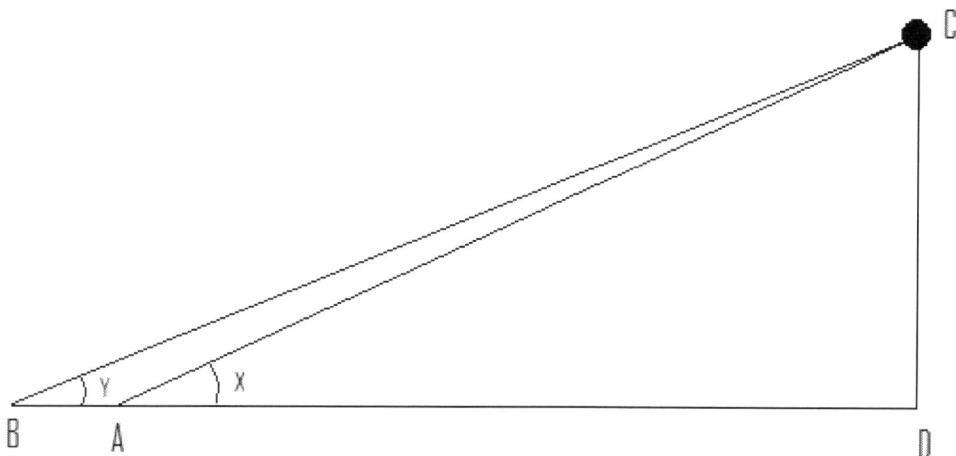

Assuming we start at point A and the object that we want to measure its distance (ground distance AD or Air distance AC) is located at point C. We need to use a device (in real life a **theodolite** is used) the measure the angle x (elevation angle), let's assume that we measured it and got 20°. Later we move a certain distance (backwards or forward) and measure the angle y. Let assume that we moved backwards 4 meters (that is AB = 4m) and the angle y is 18°. Find AD, AC, CD.

6.4. – 3D GEOMETRY

1. Sketch each one of the solids and fill the blanks.

   a. Cuboid   Volume = _____ Surface Area = _____

   b. Right pyramid   Volume = _____ Surface Area = _____

   c. Right prism   Volume = _____ Surface Area = _____

   d. Right cone   Volume = _____ Surface Area = _____

   e. Cylinder   Volume = _____ Surface Area = _____

   f. Sphere   Volume = _____ Surface Area = _____

   g. Hemisphere   Volume = _____ Surface Area = _____

2. In the design process of a certain lamp the following diagram is obtained.

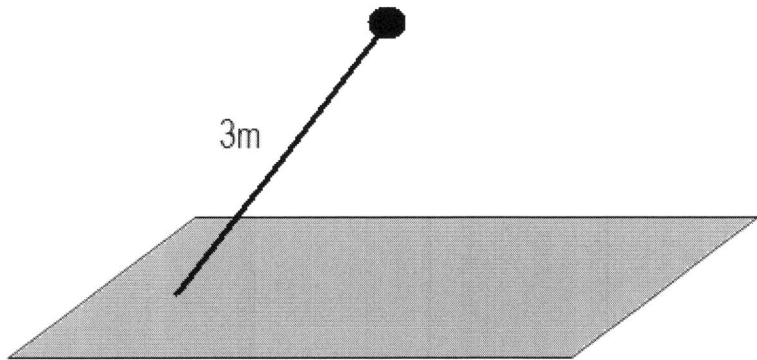

Assuming the sun is directly above the lamp and length of the shadow on the ground is 2.5 meters.

a. Find the angle between the lamp and the ground.
b. Find the height of the lamp above the ground.

3. Given the following diagram (not to scale): ABCD is a rectangle AB = 20 cm, BC = 12 cm, EA = BF = 14 cm. EM = 5 cm.

    a. Find the angle between NB and the base ABCD.
    b. Find the length of the segment MC.
    c. Find the area of MNBC
    d. Find the volume of the cuboid.
    e. Find the surface area of the cuboid.

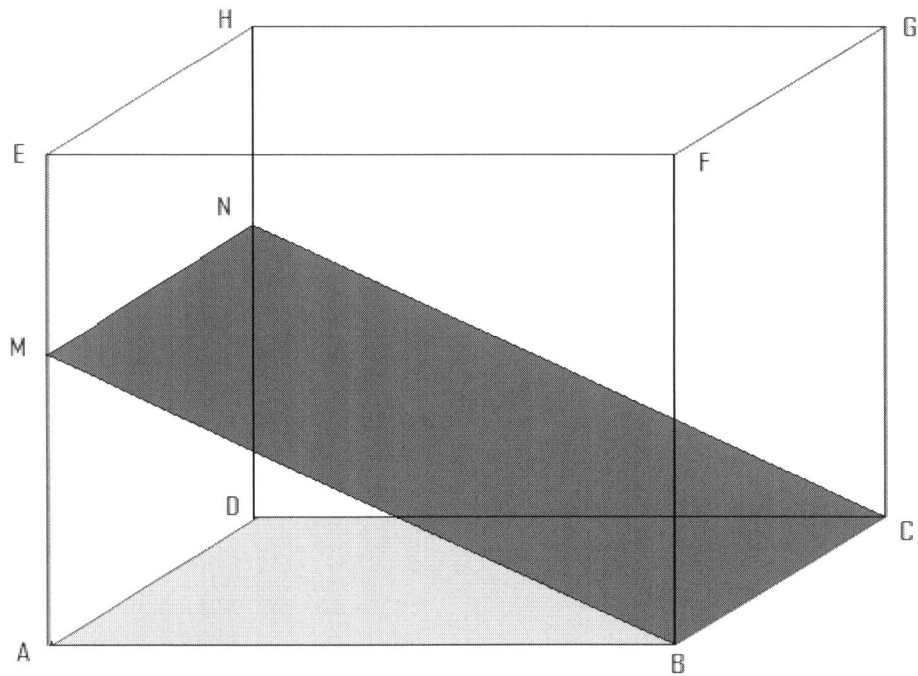

2. Given the following diagram (not to scale): ABCD is a square AB = 10 cm. CG =
   BF = 12 cm. M is the midpoint of DB.

   a. Find the length DB.
   b. Find the angle between DG and the base ABCD.
   c. Find the angle between GM and the base ABCD.
   d. Find the area of BDG.

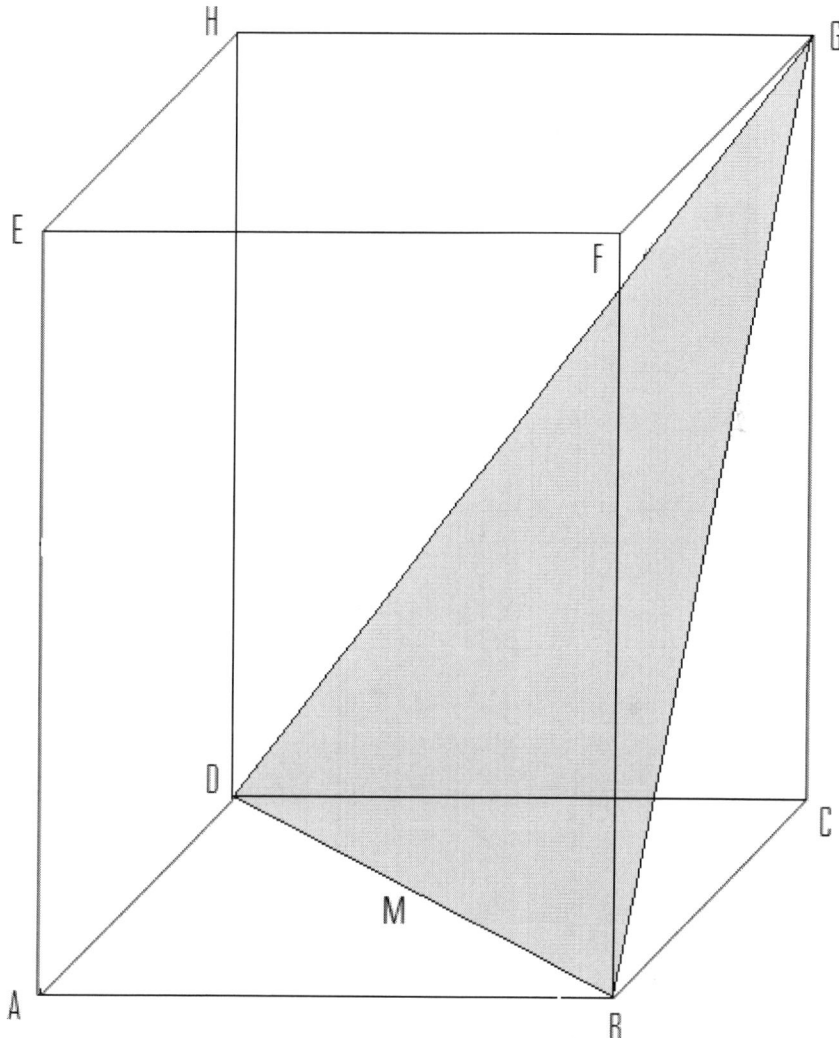

3. In the design process of a modern building a sphere of 5m radius is put on top a cylinder with a radius twice as big. The height of the building is 30m.

    a. Find the volume of the sphere.
    b. Find the height of the cylinder.
    c. Find the volume of the building.
    d. Find the surface area of the building that that is exposed to fresh air.

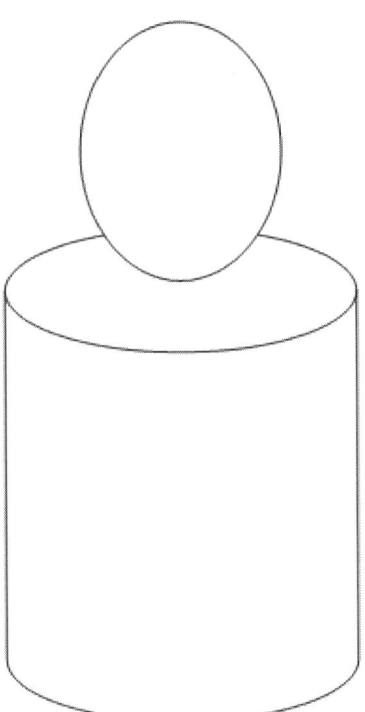

4. Given the following right prism. AB = 12cm, AE = 15cm.

Find:

    a. The length of AD.
    b. The length of ED.
    c. The length of AF.
    d. The angle FAB.
    e. The surface area of the prism.

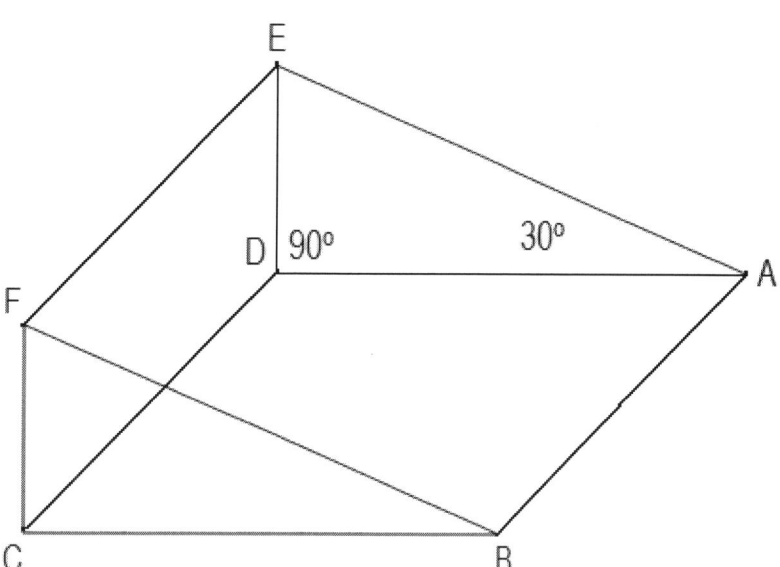

5. An old tower is made of a cone put on top of a cylinder. The radius of both is 5m. The height of the cylinder is 10m. The height of the cone is 60% of the cylinder's height.

   a. Find the height of the tower.
   b. Find the volume of the tower.

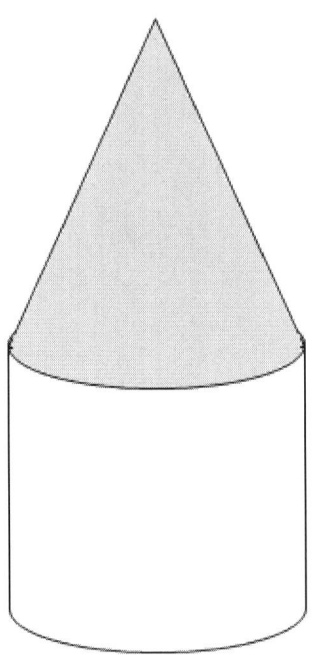

6. Given the following diagram (not to scale): ABCD is a rectangle AB = 9 cm. BC = 7 cm. EF = 10 cm is the height of the right pyramid.

Find:

    a. The length AE.
    b. The length AF.
    c. The angle between AF and the base ABCD.
    d. The length MF.
    e. The angle between MF and the base ABCD.
    f. The area of FBC.
    g. Find the volume of the pyramid.
    h. Find the surface area of the pyramid.

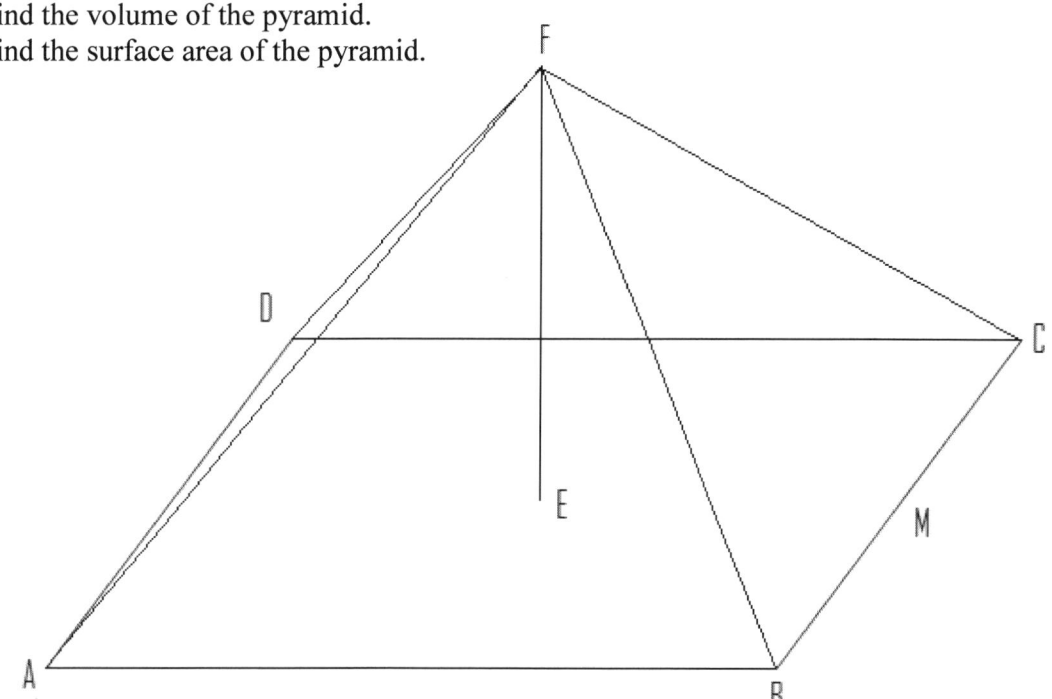

7.1. – RATE OF CHANGE

In the world that surrounds us things change: the temperature, the direction and strength of the wind, the prices of products, the velocity of objects, population size, our height, weight etc.

Example 1: Oil prices, represented as a function of time P(t):

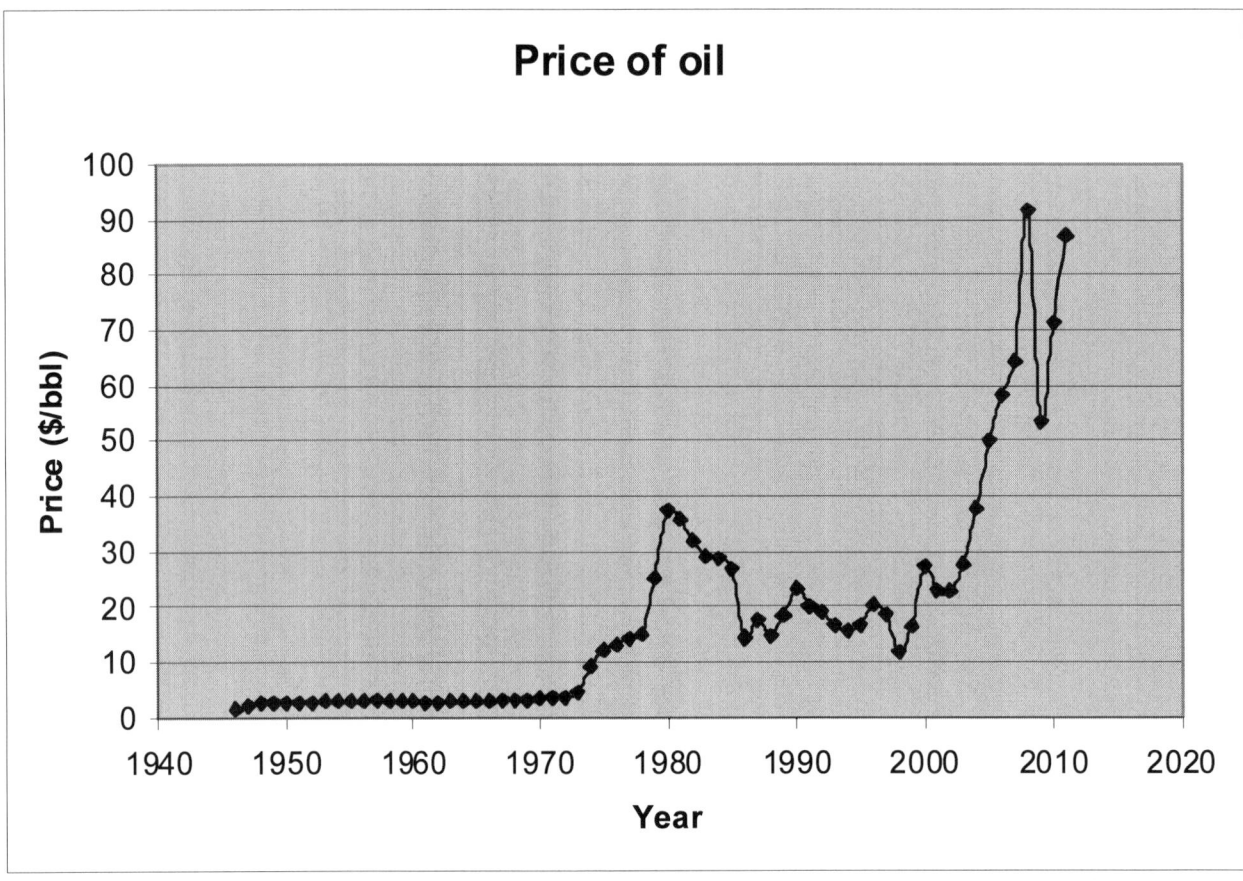

1. As you can see there have been periods of time in history in which the prices have changed slowly, Identify one of them: _____

2. In other periods the prices have been changing very quickly, identify one positive change: _____ and one negative change: _____

3. In this graph what are the <u>units</u> of the <u>change</u> of price: _____

4. Find the <u>average rate of change</u> in oil prices between 1970 and 1985. Is this average similar to the real change in prices? Explain your answer.

5. Find the average rate of change between 1945 and 2005, how can this change be represented graphically?

Example 2: Population of 20 – 29 year olds in southern Europe for example, represented as a function of time P(t):

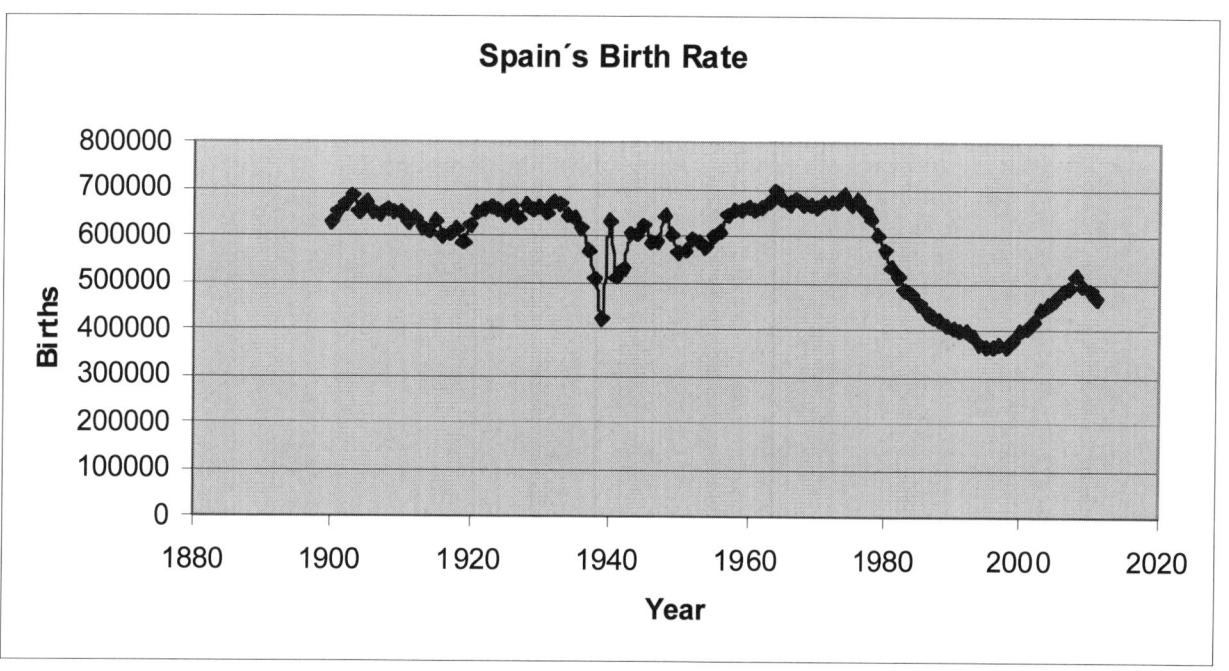

6. During what period of time the fastest change occurs? _____

7. In this graph what are the units of the change of birth:_____

8. Find the average rate of change between 1960 and 2000. Is this average similar to the real change in births? Explain your answer.

9. Find the average rate of change between 2000 and 2010, how can this change be represented graphically?

7.2. – DEFINITION OF DERIVATIVE

Given the function Temp(x) = –x(x – 4) with the points P = (2, 4) and Q = (a, f(a)). Temp is the temperature on the top of a certain mountain, t is given in hours.

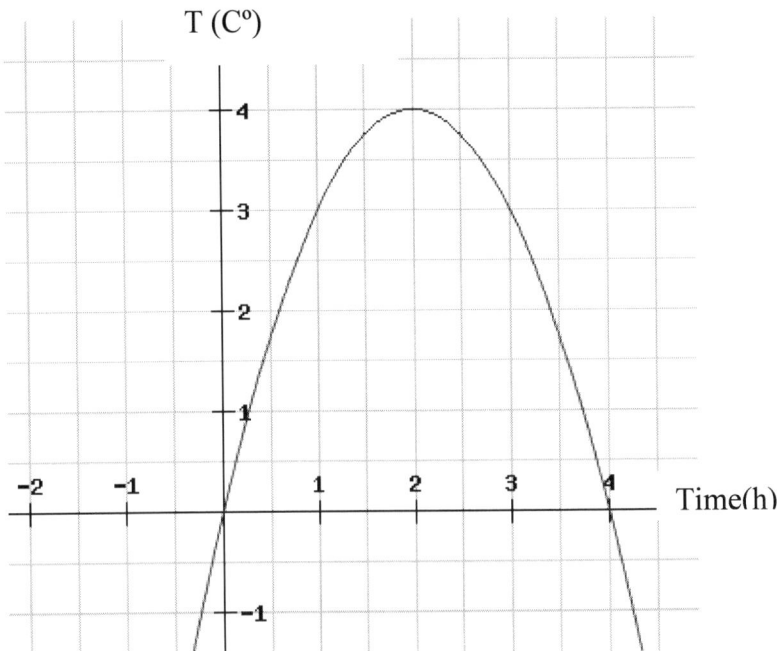

1. Complete the <u>y coordinate</u> of point Q in case a = 3.

2. If a = 2.5 find the slope of the line that connects the points Q and P (and sketch the line).

3. If a = 2.1 find the slope of the line that connects the points Q and P (and sketch the line on the same graph).

4. If a = 2.01 find the slope of the line that connects the points Q and P (and sketch the line on the same graph).

5. If a = 2.001 find the slope of the line that connects the points Q and P (and sketch the line on the same graph).

6. Fill the following table:

a	2.5	2.1	2.01	2.001
Slope of QP				

What is your conclusion?

7. What does the slope **between 2 points** represent? Make reference to temperature and give units.

8. What does the slope of the tangent to the function **at a certain point** represent? Make reference to temperature and give units.

The derivative is the _____

Find the derivative of the following functions

1. $f(x) = 3$ $\dfrac{df}{dx} = f'(x) =$

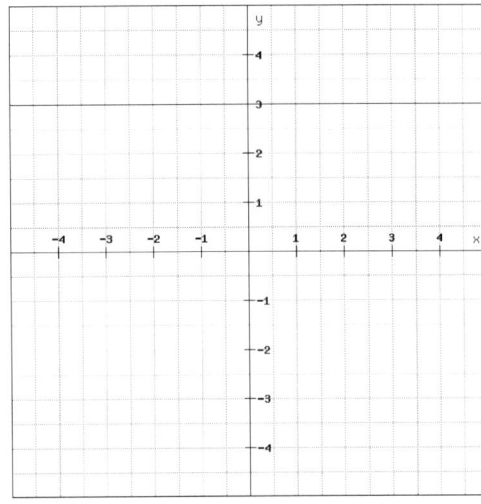

2. $g(x) = 2x - 2$ $\dfrac{dg}{dx} = g'(x) =$

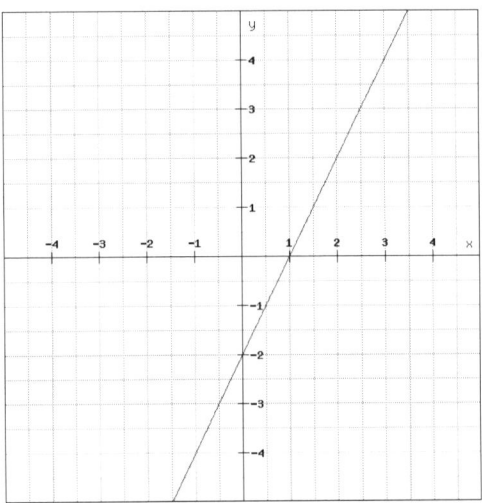

3. $f(x) = -\dfrac{x}{2} + 1$ $\dfrac{df}{dx} = f'(x) =$

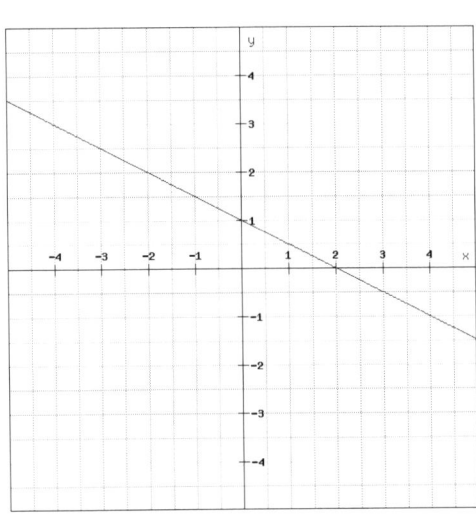

4. $f(x) = -x^2 + 4x$ $\dfrac{df}{dx} = f'(x) =$

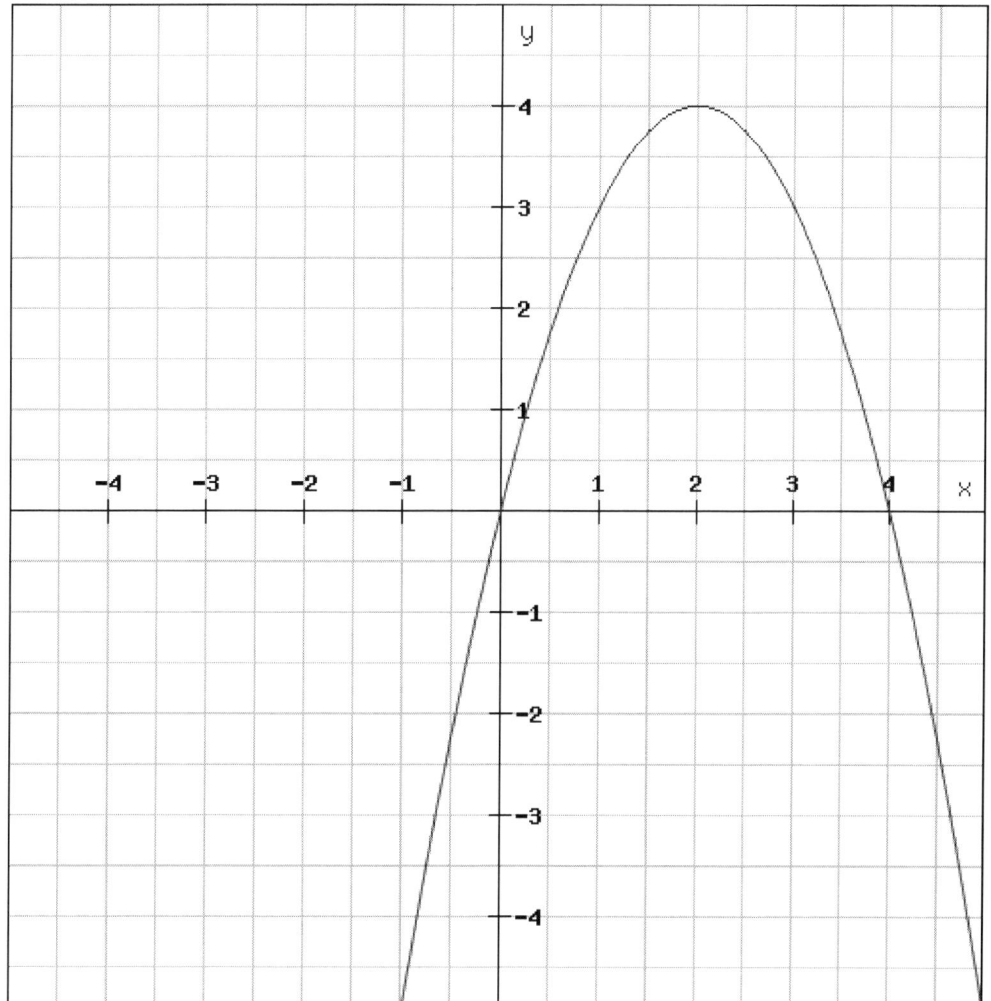

In this case the value of the derivative depends on the _____.

For example:

$$f'(0) = \underline{\quad}$$

$$f'(1) = \underline{\quad}$$

$$f'(2) = \underline{\quad}$$

Sketch the tangent and normal in each one of the cases. State the slope of the normal in each case:

5. Given the function, sketch the tangent in each one of the points:

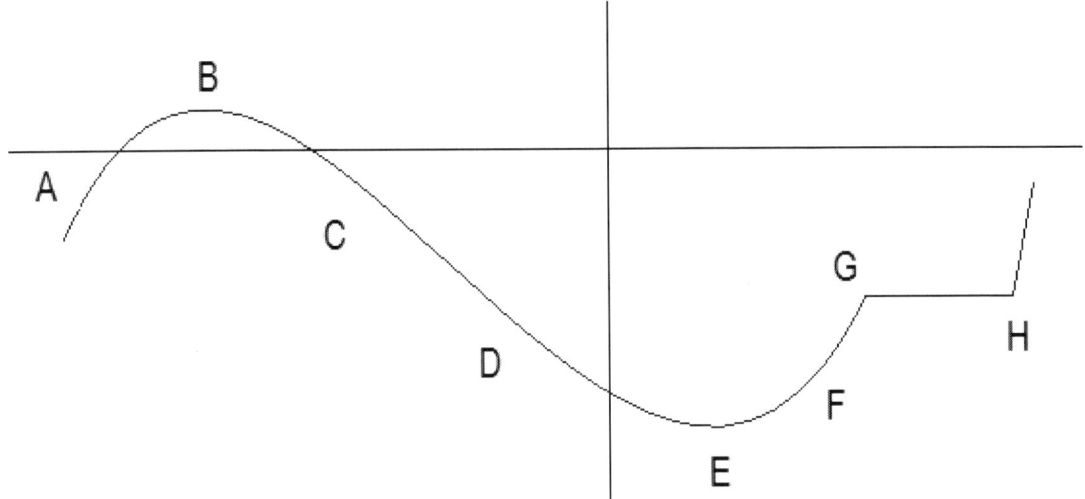

Fill the blanks with the words positive, negative, zero or doesn't exist. The value of the derivative at point

A is _____   B is _____   C is _____   D is _____

E is _____   F is _____   G is _____   H is _____

6. $f(x) = x - 3x^2 + \dfrac{2}{x} + 3$

$\dfrac{df}{dx} = f'(x) = $ ____

$f'(0) = $ ____

$f'(-2) = $ ____

7. $V(r) = 5 - 4r^{-2} - 3r + \dfrac{4}{3r^3}$

$\dfrac{dV}{dr} = V'(r) = $ ____

$V'(-1) = $ ____

$V'(3) = $ ____

8. $S(c) = \dfrac{-2}{c^2} - c^{-3} + 10$

$\dfrac{dS}{dc} = S'(c) = $ ____

$S'(-3) = $ ____

$S'(1) = $ ____

9. $f(x) = 7x^3 - 3 + \dfrac{5}{x^2}$

$f'(x) = $ ____

$f'(2) = $ ____

$f'(-2) = $ ____

Find the derivatives of the following functions

1. $f(x) = -2$

2. $f(x) = x$

3. $f(x) = 5x$

4. $f(x) = 5kx + 1$

5. $f(x) = -2x$

6. $f(x) = -2x - 3$

7. $f(x) = -2x + 3$

8. $f(x) = x^2 + 3x - 10$

9. $f(x) = x^2 + 7x - 1$

10. $f(x) = bx^6 + 2x + 7$

11. $f(x) = x^{22} + x - 1$

12. $f(x) = x^4 + 2x + 1$

13. $f(x) = x^5 + x$

14. $f(x) = x^{22} - \dfrac{1}{x}$

15. $f(x) = x^2 - 2x + \dfrac{1}{x^2}$

16. $f(x) = a\,x^5 - 2x^4 - \dfrac{5}{x^2} + \dfrac{1}{x^3}$

17. $f(x) = 5x^2 - 10x + \dfrac{1}{x^2}$

18. $f(x) = -5x^{20} - \dfrac{1}{x^2} + \dfrac{3}{x^3}$

19. $f(x) = -bx^4 - 4x^2 - 4 + \dfrac{5}{x^2}$

20. $f(x) = -x^{-2} + 3x$

21. $f(x) = 5 - 15x^{-2} - 3x^{-5} + \dfrac{1}{x^5}$

22. $f(x) = \dfrac{5}{2}x^{-3} - b6x + \dfrac{1}{2x^2} + 7$

23. $f(x) = \dfrac{1}{6}x^3 - 3 + \dfrac{3}{x^2} - 5$

24. $f(x) = -12x - 13 + 3bx + 4 + 3x^{-3} + \dfrac{44}{6x^2} - 51$

25. $f(x) = x^2 + 9x - 4 + 3x^2 + \dfrac{2}{7x^{12}} - 12$

26. $f(x) = 8x + 8 + \dfrac{11}{3x^4} + 345$

27. $f(x) = -x^3 + 6x^{22} - 8 - x + \dfrac{8}{3x^7} - 135$

7.3. – TANGENTS AND NORMALS TO FUNCTIONS

1. Given the function $f(x) = 2x^2$.
   Sketch it.

   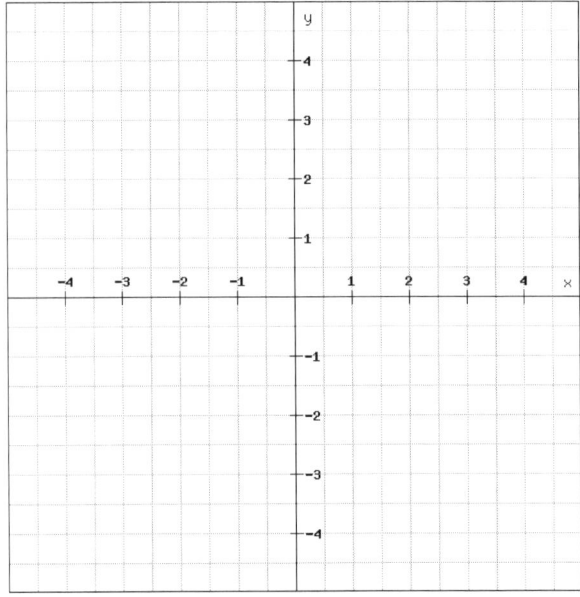

   a. Find its derivative

   b. Find the slope of the tangent to the function at the point with $x = 1$. Show the slope found on the graph.

   c. Find the slope of the tangent to the function at the point with $x = -1$. Show the slope found on the graph.

   d. Find the point in which the slope of the tangent to the function is 3. Show the point and slope on the graph.

   e. Find the point in which the slope of the tangent to the function is –4. Show the point and slope on the graph.

   f. Find the point in which the tangent to the function is parallel to the line $y = 2x + 3$. Show the point, the tangent and the line on the graph.

   g. Find the point in which the tangent to the function is parallel to the line $y = -5x + 3$. Show the point, the tangent and the line on the graph.

   h. Find the equation of the tangent to the function at the point with $x = 1$. Sketch the tangent on graph.

   i. Find the equation of the tangent and normal to the function at the point with $x = 0$. Sketch the tangent and normal on graph.

   j. Find the equation of the tangent and normal to the function at the point with $x = -2$. Sketch the tangent and normal on the graph.

2. Given the function $f(x) = -\dfrac{2}{x} + 1$.

Sketch it.

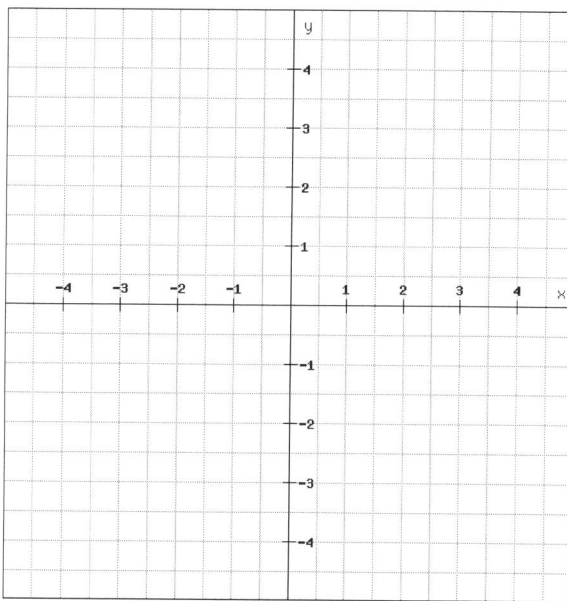

a. Find its derivative.

b. Find the slope of the tangent to the function at the point with x = 1. Show the slope found on the graph.

c. Find the slope of the tangent to the function at the point with x = 0. Show the slope found on the graph.

d. Find the slope of the tangent to the function at the point with $x = \dfrac{1}{2}$. Show the slope found on the graph.

e. Find the point in which the slope of the tangent to the function is –3. Show the point and slope on the graph.

f. Find the point in which the slope of the tangent to the function is $\dfrac{1}{2}$. Show the point and slope on the graph.

g. Find the point in which the tangent to the function is parallel to the line $y = -\dfrac{5}{3}x + 3$. Show the point, the tangent and the line on the graph.

h. Find that point in which the tangent to the function is parallel to the line $y = 6x + 3$. Show the point, the tangent and the line on the graph.

i. Find the equation of the tangent to the function at the point with x = 1. Sketch the tangent on graph.

j. Find the equation of the tangent and normal to the function at the point with x = 0. Sketch the tangent and normal on graph.

k. Find the equation of the tangent and normal to the function at the point with $x = \dfrac{1}{2}$. Sketch the tangent and normal on graph.

211

3. Given the function $f(x) = -x^2 - x$.
   Sketch it.

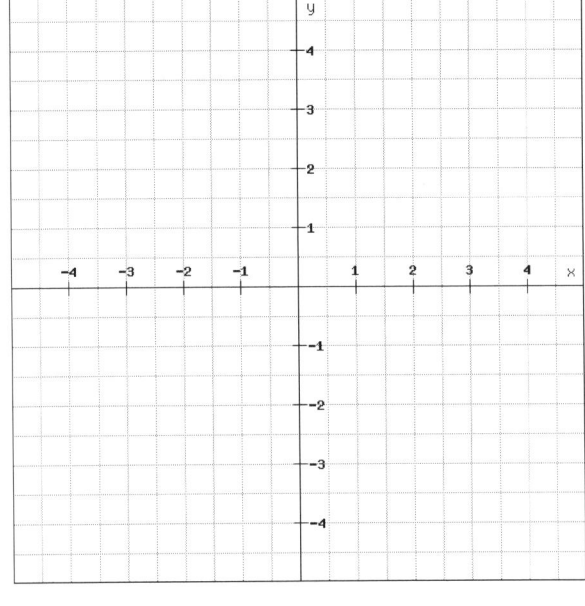

   a. Find its derivative

   b. Find the slope of the tangent to
      the function at the point with x
      = –1. Show the slope found on
      the graph.

   c. Find the slope of the tangent to
      the function at the point with x
      = 2. Show the slope found on
      the graph.

   d. Find the slope of the tangent to
      the function at the point with x = –4. Show the slope found on the
      graph.

   e. Find the point in which the slope of the tangent to the function is 2.
      Show the point and slope on the graph.

   f. Find the point in which the slope of the tangent to the function is –2.3.
      Show the point and slope on the graph.

   g. Find the point in which the tangent to the function is parallel to the line
      $y = 3x + 1$. Show the point, the tangent and the line on the graph.

   h. Find the point in which the tangent to the function is parallel to the line
      $y = -5x + 3$. Show the point, the tangent and the line on the graph.

   i. Find the equation of the tangent to the function at the point with x = –
      1. Sketch the tangent on graph.

   j. Find the equation of the tangent and normal to the function at the point
      with x = 2. Sketch the tangent and normal on graph.

   k. Find the equation of the tangent and normal to the function at the point
      with x = –4. Sketch the tangent and normal on graph.

4. Given the function $f(x) = -3x^2 + 1$. Sketch it.

a. Find its derivative

b. Find $f'(1) = \_\_\_\_$. Show it on the graph.

c. Find $f'(0) = \_\_\_\_$. Show it on the graph.

d. Find $f'(2) = \_\_\_\_$. Show it on the graph.

e. Given that $f'(x) = 3$, find x. Show it on the graph.

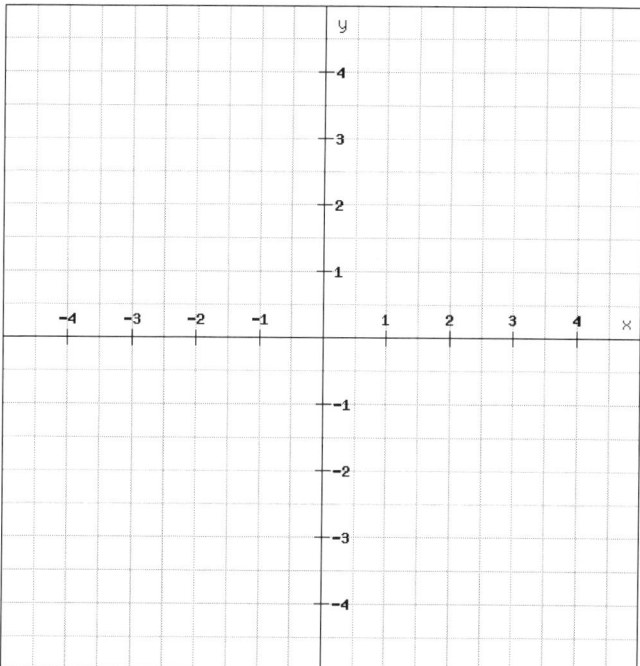

f. Given that $f'(x) = -4$, find x. Show it on the graph.

g. Find the point in which the tangent to the function is parallel to the line $y = -5x + 3$. Show the point and tangent on the graph.

h. Find the equation of the tangent and normal to the function at the point with x = 0. Sketch the tangent and normal on graph.

5. Given the function $f(x) = \dfrac{3}{x-2}$. Sketch it.

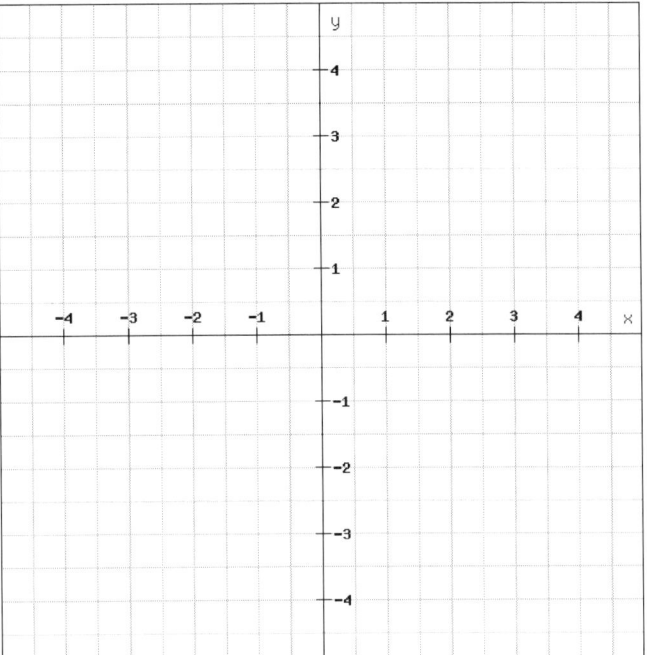

   a. Find its derivative

   b. Find $f'(1) = $ ____. Show it on the graph.

   c. Find $f'(2) = $ ____. Show it on the graph.

   d. Find $f'(\dfrac{1}{2}) = $ ____. Show it on the graph.

   e. Given that $f'(x) = -3$, find x. Show it on the graph.

   f. Given that $f'(x) = \dfrac{1}{2}$, find x. Show it on the graph.

   g. Find the point in which the tangent to the function is parallel to the line $y = -\dfrac{5}{3}x + 3$. Show the point, the line and the tangent on the graph.

   h. Find the equation of the tangent to the function at the point with x = 1. Sketch the tangent on graph.

   i. Find the equation of the tangent and normal to the function at the point with x = 2. Sketch the tangent and normal on graph.

   j. Find the equation of the tangent and normal to the function at the point with $x = \dfrac{1}{2}$. Sketch the tangent and normal on graph.

7.4. – STATIONARY POINTS AND FUNCTION ANALYSIS

Functions may describe production, benefit, position, sugar level, efficiency of an engine, wind resistance or any other magnitude. Usually it is out interest to maximize benefit, efficiency or minimize lost. As a result we are usually most interested in the maximum or minimum points of a function.

1. In a maximum or minimum point of a "smooth" function the slope of the tangent to the function is _____ . Sketch an example:

2. There is one more situation in which the slope of the tangent to the function is

    _____ , such point is called: _____ . Sketch an example:

3. In order to find the stationary points´ x coordinate we equal the _____ to _____

4. To find the stationary points´ y coordinate we _____

5. Once we found the stationary point we have to decide if it's a _____ ,
    _____ or _____ .

6. When f'(a) > 0 it means that f(x) is _____ at the point where x = _____ .

7. When f'(a) < 0 it means that f(x) is _____ at the point where x = _____ .

8. For example given the function $f(x) = x^3 - 3x^2$. Use the derivative to find its local maximum and minimum. Verify your answer using the GDC.

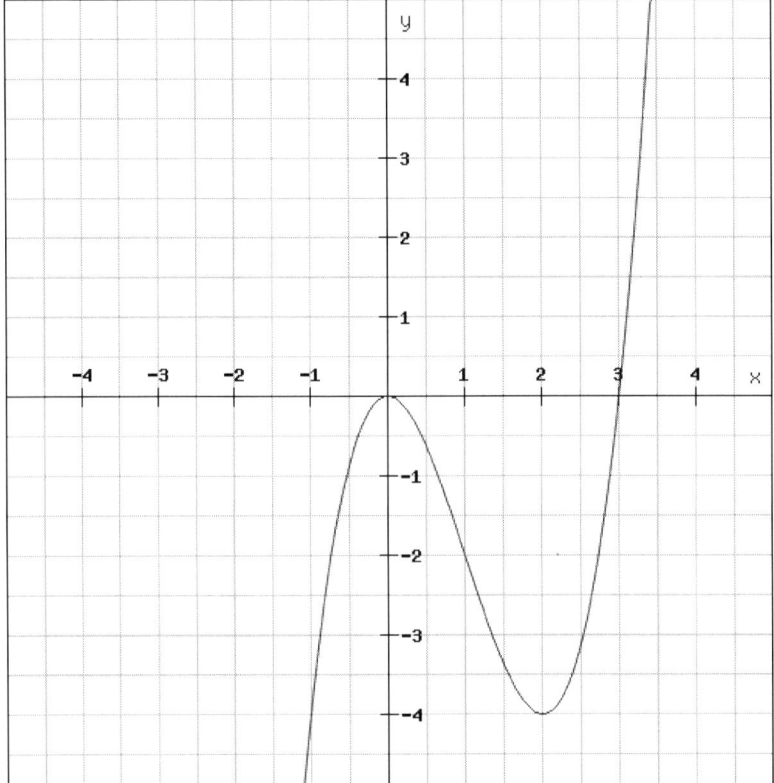

$f'(x) =$

9. Given the function $f(x) = x^4 - 2x^3$.

    a. Sketch the graph for $-2 \le x \le 3$ and $-3 \le y \le 15$

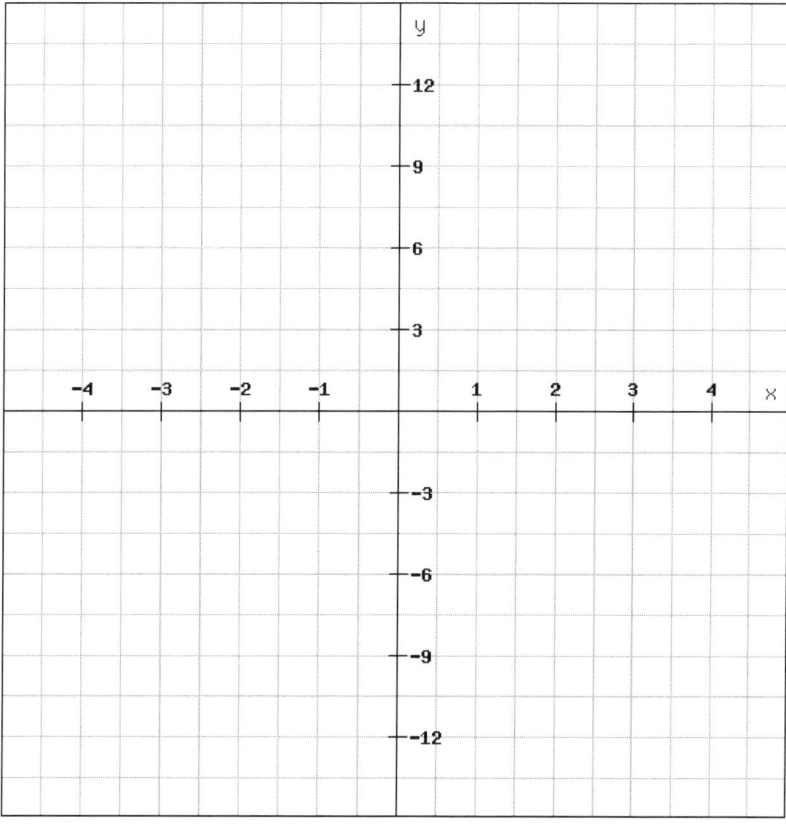

    b. Find: f(2) =   f'(x) =   f'(1.5) =

    c. Write down the coordinates of the local minimum point on the graph of f.

    d. Find the gradient of the tangent to the graph at x = 1.

    e. There is another point on the graph in which the tangent has the same gradient as in x = 1. Find it.

    f. Where is the function increasing?

10. Given the function $f(x) = 10x - x^3$.

    a. Sketch the graph for $-4 \le x \le 4$ and $-15 \le y \le 15$

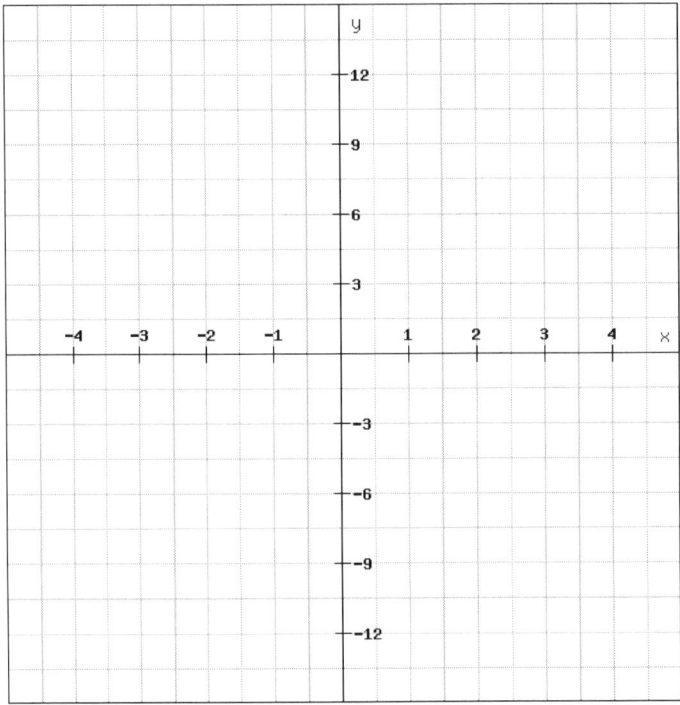

    b. Find $f(-2) =$ $f'(x) =$ $f'(0) =$

    c. Write down the coordinates of the local minimum point on the graph of f.

    d. Find the gradient of the tangent to the graph at its local maximum.

    e. There is another point on the graph in which the tangent has the same gradient as in $x = 3$. Find it.

    f. Find the equation of the tangent and normal to the function at the points where $x = -1$. Sketch the lines on the graph.

    g. Where is the function decreasing?

11. Given the function f(x) = $\dfrac{4}{x^2} + x + 2$

    a. Sketch the graph for $-4 \le x \le 4$ and $-5 \le y \le 15$

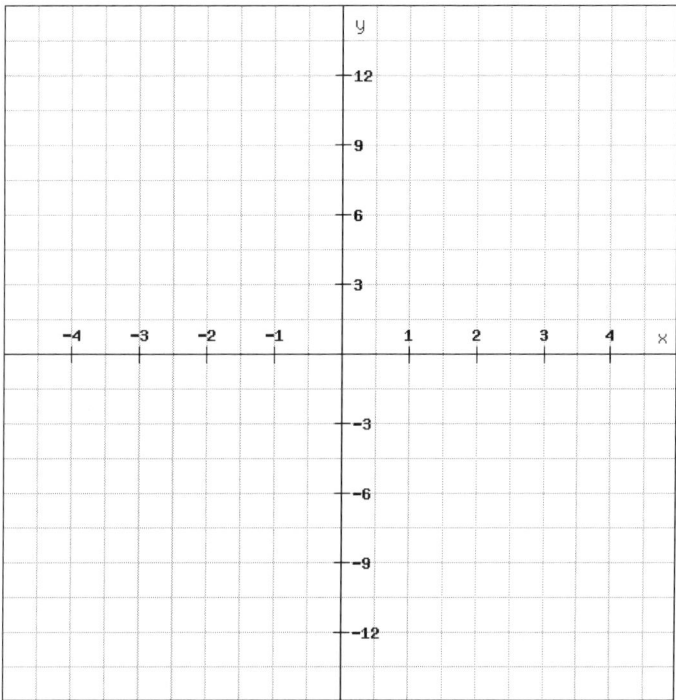

    b. Find f(−2) =   f′(x) =   f′(0) =

    c. f′(1) = _____This value of the derivative means that the

        function is _____ at this point.

    d. The equation of the vertical asymptote is: _____

    e. Write down the coordinates of the local minimums and maximums points
        on the graph of f .

    f. Find the equation of the tangent and normal to the function at the points
        where x = −3. Sketch the lines on the graph.

12. Given the function $f(x) = \dfrac{1}{x+1} + x + 2$

    a. Sketch the graph for $-4 \le x \le 4$ and $-15 \le y \le 15$

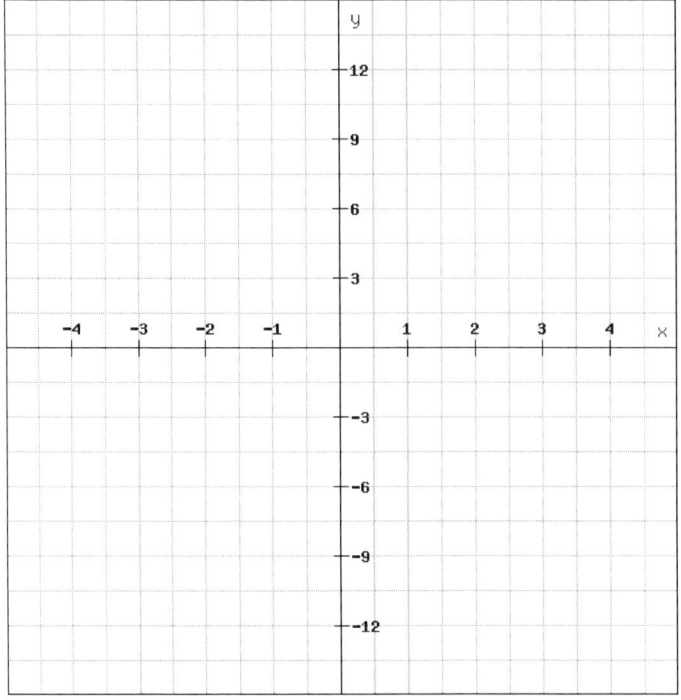

    b. Find: $f(-2) =$ $f'(x) =$ $f'(0) =$

    c. $f'(1) =$ _____ This value of the derivative means that the

        function is _____ at this point.

    d. Write down the coordinates of the local minimum point on the graph of f.

    e. The equation of the vertical asymptote is: _____

    f. Find the gradient of the tangent to the graph at the point where $x = 2$.

    g. Find the equation of the tangent and normal to the function at the points where $x = -2$. Sketch the lines on the graph.

7.5. – OPTIMIZATION PROBLEMS

1. Given a cylinder with a surface area of 54π cm^2

    a. Write an <u>equation</u> for the cylinder's surface area in terms of r and h.

    b. Write a <u>function</u> for the volume of the cylinder in terms of r and h.

    c. Use the <u>equation</u> from part a to express the <u>function</u> only in terms of r.

    d. Use the function to find the radius and height for which the volume of the cylinder is maximum.

2. Given a cuboid with 2 equal sides and a surface area of 100 cm^2

    a. Write an equation for the cuboid surface area in terms of its sides.

    b. Write a function for the volume of the cuboid in terms of its sides.

    c. Use the equation from part a to express the function in terms of one side only.

    d. Use the function to find the length of the sides for which the volume of the cuboid is maximum.

3. The benefit of a certain company can be modeled by the function

$$f(x) = 2^{-x} + 5 - \frac{0.3}{x^2} \quad x \in [0.1, 5]$$

Where x is the amount of money in thousands of Euros invested in marketing. Find the amount of money invested that will maximize the benefit. Find the maximum benefit.

4. The consumption of gasoline of a new engine can be modeled by

$$f(x) = 3^{0.3x} - x + 5 \ x \in [0,15]$$

Where x is the number of revolutions per minute of the engine in thousands.

Find the number of revolutions per minute that will minimize the consumption of gasoline.

5. The elevation power of a wing as a function of angle of attack of the airplane can be modeled by the function

$$f(x) = \left(\frac{x}{4}\right)^2 - 2^{\left(\frac{x}{4}\right)} + \left(\frac{x}{2}\right) + 6 \qquad x \in [0, 22]$$

where x is angle of attack measured in degrees. Find the angle of attack that will maximize the elevation power of the wing.

8.1. – CORRELATION

1. In many occasions variables may be related to each other, for example:

    - Age – Height
    - Level of education – Average income
    - Resistance to wind – gasoline consumption

    Give 3 other examples; discuss the kind of relation that exists between the variables:

2. The relation between variables is called: _____ and if it is _____ it can be classified in the following way:

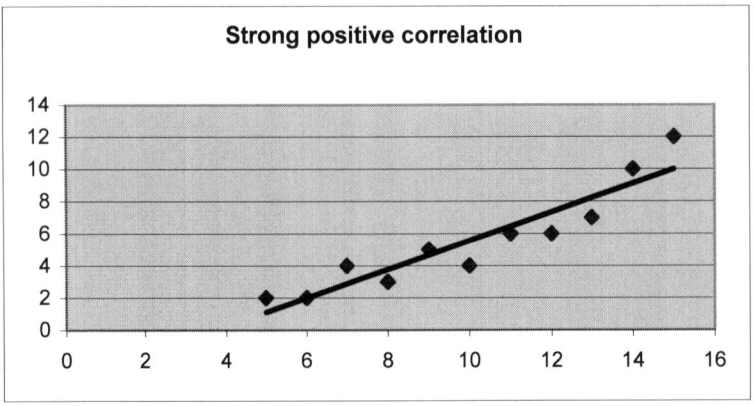

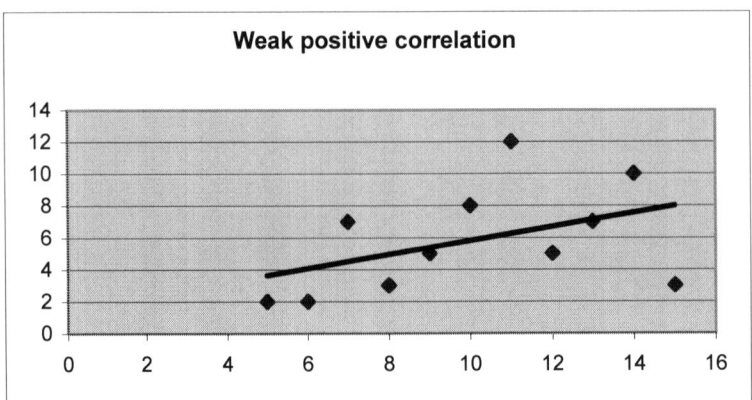

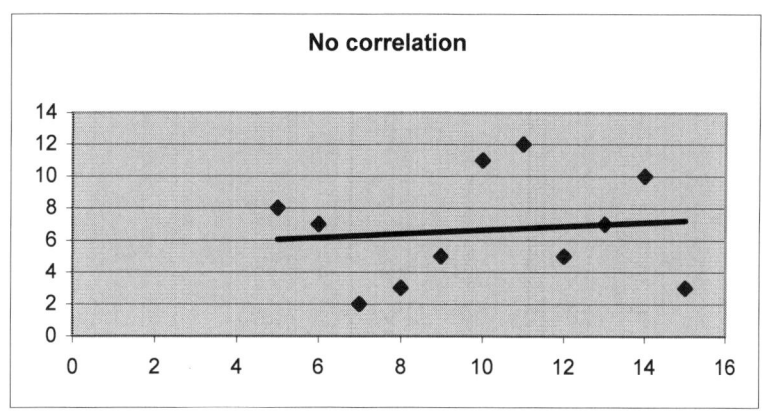

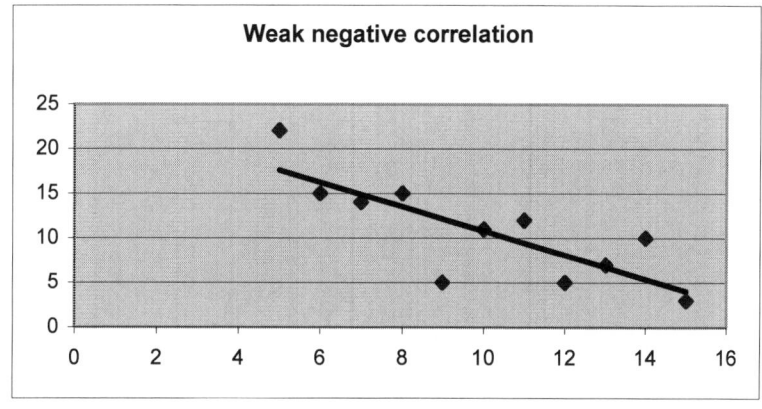

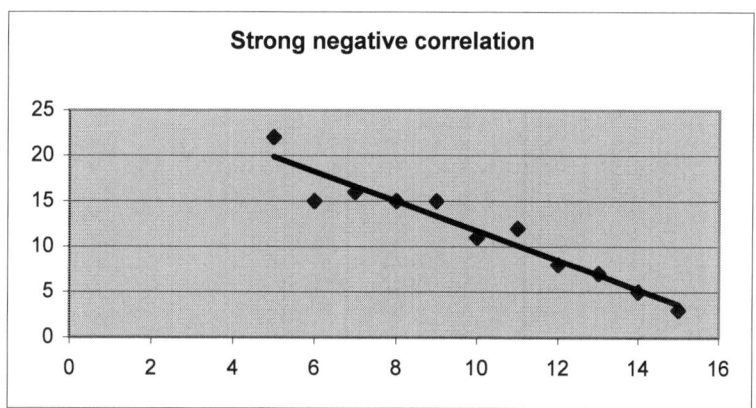

3. This correlation is characterized by a certain number called _____ coefficient (r).

4. In case of a perfect positive correlation the value of r is _____

5. In case of a perfect negative correlation the value of r is _____

6. In case of a no correlation the value of r is _____

7. Finally r is between _____ and _____

8. All of the correlations above mentioned are _____. There can be other

   kinds of correlation for example _____

9. The full name of r is _____

10. If $r \in [0.75,1)$ we say there is a _____ Correlation.

11. If $r \in [0.5,0.75)$ we say there is a _____ Correlation.

12. If $r \in [0.25,0.5)$ we say there is a _____ Correlation.

13. If $r \in (-0.25,0.25)$ we say there is a _____ Correlation.

14. If $r \in (-0.5,-0.25]$ we say there is a _____ Correlation.

15. If $r \in (-0.75,-0.5]$ we say there is a _____ Correlation.

16. If $r \in (-1,-0.75]$ we say there is a _____ Correlation.

17. In a certain math class the following data about students was found:

Name	John	Dean	Elisa	Marc	Heather	Alicia	Raquel	Kevin	Alex	Deena
HW Done (%)	58	90	75	50	40	95	100	85	75	82
Grade (%)	70	80	80	65	55	78	86	89	82	70

    a.   Represent the data on a graph:

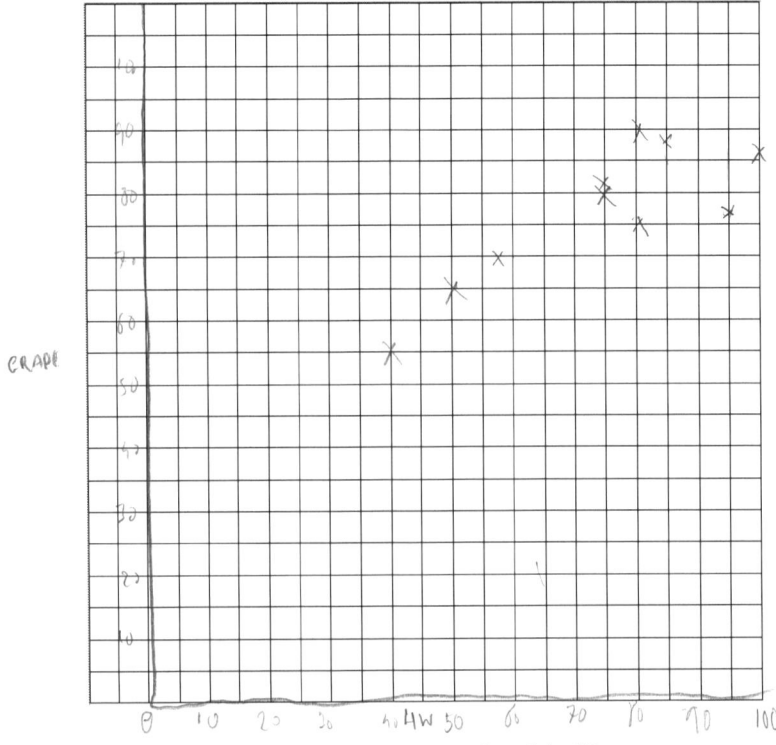

    b.   Is there correlation? _____ what kind? _____

    c.   Try to predict the value of r: _____

d. In order to calculate the value of r first find:

$\bar{x} = $ _____

$\bar{y} = $ _____

Complete the table:

Name	x_i	$(x_i - \bar{x})^2$	y_i	$(y_i - \bar{y})^2$	$x_i y_i$
John	58		70		
Dean	90		80		
Elisa	75		80		
Marc	50		65		
Heather	40		55		
Alicia	95		78		
Raquel	100		86		
Kevin	85		89		
Alex	75		82		
Deena	82		70		
Total					

Use the table to find Sx, Sy and Sxy using the following formulas taken from IB information booklet:

$$S_x = \sqrt{\frac{\sum_{i=1}^{i=n}(x_i - \bar{x})^2}{n}}, \quad S_y = \sqrt{\frac{\sum_{i=1}^{i=n}(y_i - \bar{y})^2}{n}}, \quad S_{xy} = \frac{\left(\sum_{i=1}^{i=n}(x_i y_i) - \frac{\sum_{i=1}^{i=n}x_i \sum_{i=1}^{i=n}y_i}{n} \right)}{n}$$

Sx = _____   Sy = _____ ,   Sxy = _____

Find r using $r = \dfrac{S_{xy}}{S_x S_y}$ r = _____

e. Was your prediction accurate?

f. Find r using your GDC

LINE OF BEST FIT

18. The line of best fit is the straight line that most approximates to the scatter diagram obtained. The equation of the line is given by:

$$y - \overline{y} = \frac{S_{xy}}{\left(S_x\right)^2}(x - \overline{x})$$

19. Write this expression in the forma $y = mx + b$

20. By looking at the expression it can be seen that the slope of the line is m = _____

21. Given the data

Name	John	Dean	Elisa	Marc	Heather	Alicia	Raquel	Kevin	Alex	Deena
HW Done (%)	58	90	75	50	40	95	100	85	75	82
Grade (%)	70	80	80	65	55	78	86	89	82	70

Using your GDC find:

    a.   r = _____

    b.   The line of best fit: _____

22. In a group of students, height and weight correlation was studies. The results are given by the table below.

Height (cm)	Weight (kg)
165	58
170	62
172	80
169	65
188	88
163	52
191	95
177	72

a. Write the equation of the regression line in the form $y = mx + c$

b. Use your equation in part a to predict the weight of a student who is 174cm tall.

c. Write down the correlation coefficient and the kind of correlation that exists.

23. In a group of students the reading speed was studied in relation to age of the student. The results are given by the table below.

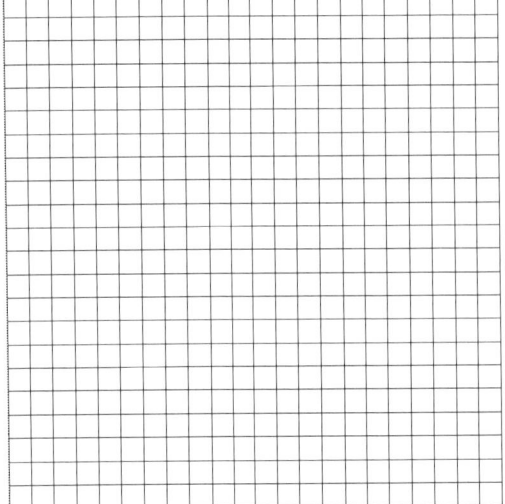

Age (years)	Reading speed (words per minute)
15	98
12	65
17	111
19	120
18	122
16	102
19	143
17	100
13	80
14	85
14	95
15	90

a. Write the equation of the regression line in the form $y = mx + c$

b. Use your equation in part a to predict the reading speed of a student who is 11 years old.

c. Write down the correlation coefficient and the kind of correlation that exists.

d. Draw a scatter diagram to show the data.

e. $\bar{x} =$ ___ = _____ $\bar{y} =$ ___ = _____

f. Plot the point $(\bar{x}, \bar{y})$ on your scatter diagram. Label this point as A.

g. Draw the regression line on the diagram.

8.2. – CHI SQUARED TEST (χ^2)

1. The chi squared test is used to see if a pair of variables is related in a significant way or not. For example, the following data was obtained:

Observed Values:

	Smokers	None-smokers	Total
Male	27	56	
Female	35	78	
Total			

Expected Values:

	Smokers	None-smokers	Total
Male			
Female			
Total			

a. The tables above are called _____

b. The number of _____ is given by _____

c. In this case it is _____

d. The Null Hypothesis (H_o) is _____

e. The Alternative Hypothesis (H_1) is _____

f. Next we will calculate the value of χ^2 using the following expression taken from the information booklet:

$$\chi^2_{calc} = \sum \frac{(f_o - f_e)^2}{f_e}$$

$\chi^2 =$

g. $\chi^2_{critical} = $ _____. Since _____ the _____ hypothesis is _____

2. The chi squared test is used to see if a pair of variables is related in a significant way or not. For example, the following data was obtained:

Observed values:

	High Blood Pressure	Normal Blood Pressure	Low Blood Pressure	Total
Fat	50	56	25	
Thin	35	78	44	
Total				

Expected Values:

	High Blood Pressure	Normal Blood Pressure	Low Blood Pressure	Total
Fat				
Thin				
Total				

a. The tables above are called _____

b. The number of _____ is given by _____

c. In this case it is _____

d. The Null Hypothesis (H_o) is _____

e. The Alternative Hypothesis (H_1) is _____

f. Next we will calculate the value of χ^2 using the following expression taken from the information booklet:

$$\chi^2_{calc} = \sum \frac{(f_o - f_e)^2}{f_e}$$

$\chi^2 =$

g. $\chi^2_{critical} =$ _____. Since _____ the _____ hypothesis is _____

3. A group of students was asked about their favorite color to see if there are differences between male and female. The colors were blue, red, green, white and orange. A χ^2 test was conducted at 5% significance level and the value found was 9.01.

    a. Write down the Null hypothesis.

    b. Write down the Alternative hypothesis.

    c. Write down the number of degrees of freedom.

    d. Write down the critical value for this test.

    e. Reach a conclusion and write it down.

4. The FIFA is doing some research about free kicks to check association between the shoe size (41 – 43, 43 – 45, more than 45) of the player and the outcome (goal/no goal).

    a. Write down the Null hypothesis.

    b. Write down the Alternative hypothesis.

    c. Write down the number of degrees of freedom

5. Some students were asked about their favorite subject. The following information was obtained

	Math	History	English	Total
Male	123	86	102	
Female	81	108	100	
Total				

A χ^2 test was conducted at 5% significance level

a. Write down the Null hypothesis.

b. Write down the Alternative hypothesis.

c. Write down the number of degrees of freedom.

d. Write down the number of students participating.

e. Show (without GDC) the expected value for math female students.

f. Write down the critical value for this test.

g. Use GDC to find χ^2

h. Reach a conclusion and write it down.

6. A certain university wants to determine if a person's choice of studies (science, engineering, social studies or economics) depends on its height (more than 1.70 or less or equal to 1.70)

   a. Write down the Null hypothesis.

   b. Write down the Alternative hypothesis.

   c. Write down the number of degrees of freedom.

   d. 250 students were surveyed, 100 were taller than 1.70 and 90 chose science. Calculate the expected number of scientists shorter than 1.70.

7. A research to determine weather the favorite type of dessert is related to city of residence was conducted in Madrid, Barcelona and Valencia. The types of dessert were ice-cream, chocolate cake and flan. A χ^2 test was conducted at 1% significance level and the value found was 15.6.

   a. Write down the Null hypothesis.

   b. Write down the Alternative hypothesis.

   c. Write down the number of degrees of freedom.

   d. Write down the critical value for this test.

   e. Reach a conclusion and write it down.

8. A new medicine called "Unbroken heart" for heart diseases is being tested and a χ^2 test was conducted. The results

	Used "Unbroken heart"	Did not use "Unbroken heart"	Total
Cured	76	61	
Not Cured	43	45	
Total			

A χ^2 test was conducted at 1% significance level

a. Write down the Null hypothesis.

b. Write down the Alternative hypothesis.

c. Write down the number of degrees of freedom.

d. Write down the number of patients participating.

e. Show (without GDC) the expected value for cured patients that used the new medicine.

f. Write down the critical value for this test.

g. Use GDC to find χ^2

h. Reach a conclusion and write it down.

8.3 – NORMAL DISTRIBUTION

Given the following information about a Group of people:

Weight	[40, 50)	[50, 60)	[60, 70)	[70, 80)	[80, 90)	[90, 100)	[100, 110)
Number of people	4	8	12	11	10	6	2

The histogram that represents this information is:

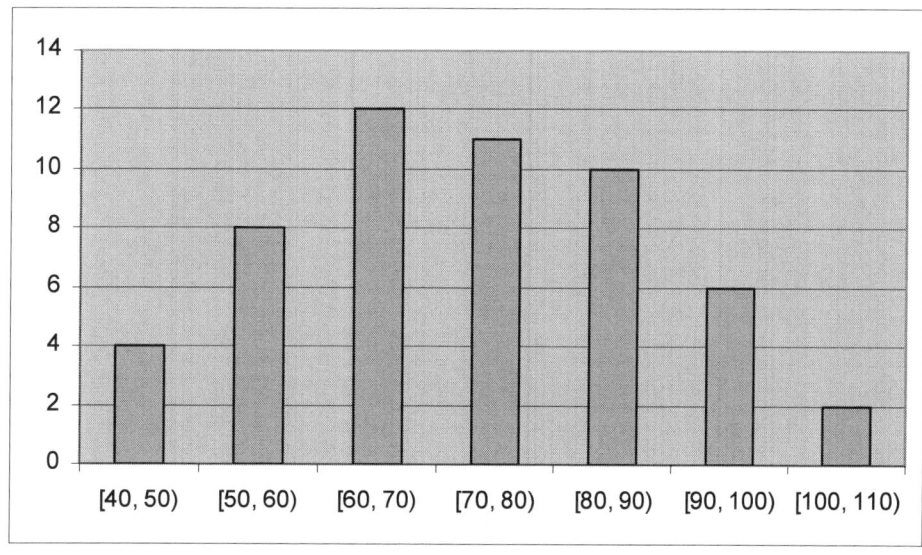

A bigger sample was taken to and the following information was obtained:

Weight	[40, 45)	[45, 50)	[50, 55)	[55, 60)	[60, 65)	[65, 70)	[70, 75)
Number of people	7	12	20	22	30	36	34

Weight	[75, 80)	[80, 85)	[85, 90)	[90, 95)	[95, 100)	[100, 105)	[105, 110)
Number of people	26	16	12	5	3	2	1

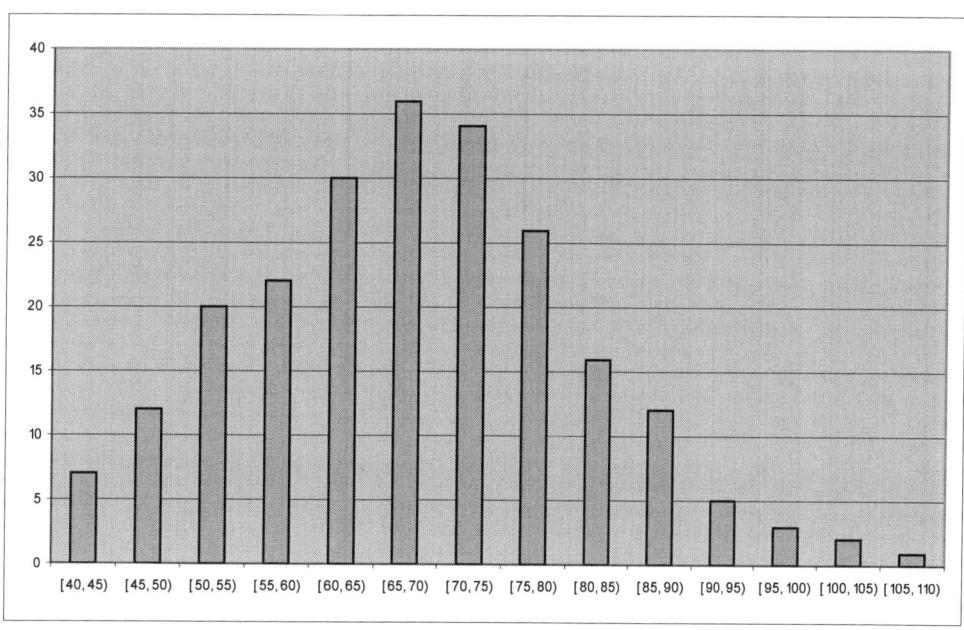

What do you observe? Can you guess how would a bigger sample look like?

1. This distribution of a variable of this type is called the _____

2. The normal distribution is characterized by 2 numbers: The _____

   and the _____ σ .

3. For example, given a few distributions, state the mean and standard deviation in all of them (It is known that $\sigma = 1$ or $\sigma = 2$ in the istributions where it is not indicated.

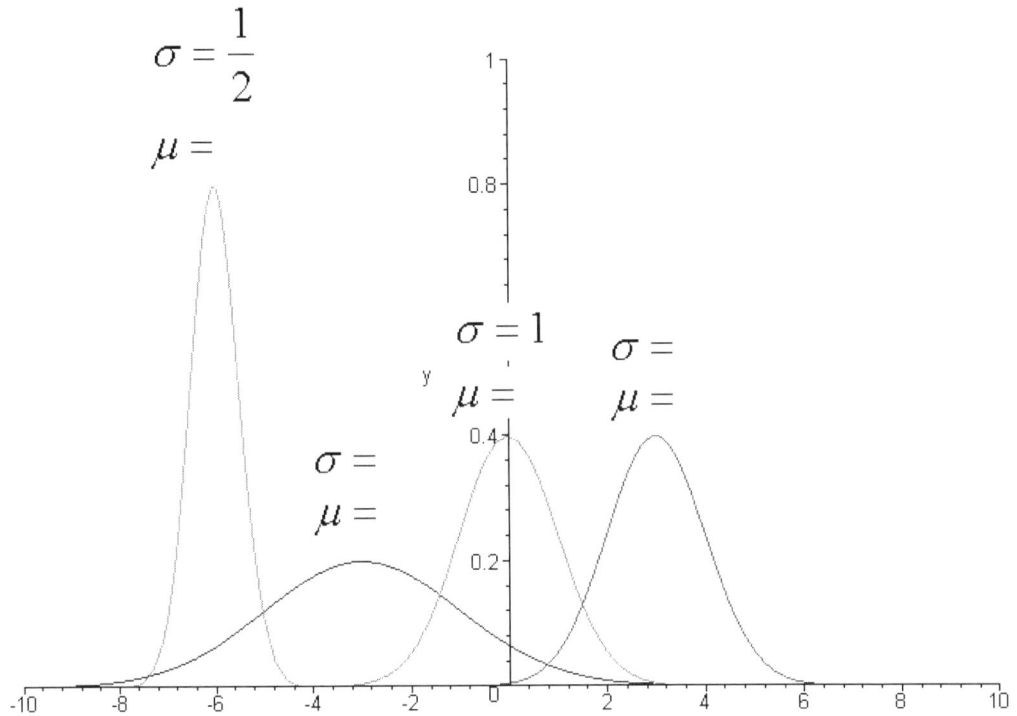

$\sigma = \dfrac{1}{2}$

$\mu =$

$\sigma = 1$ $\sigma =$

$\mu =$ $\mu =$

$\sigma =$

$\mu =$

4. **The standard normal distribution** is the one with $\mu =$ __ $\sigma =$ __

Properties of the normal distribution

5. The area under the graph represents _____ therefore the

   total area under the graph between $-\infty$ and $+\infty$ is _____

6. Normal distribution is symmetric therefore the area on each side of the

   mean is __

7. The distribution will narrower and taller in case _____

8. σ , the _____ , gives an idea about the _____

9. μ , the _____ , indicates the _____

10. In general the area under the curve in the interval $\mu \pm 1\sigma$ is _____

11. In general the area under the curve in the interval $\mu \pm 2\sigma$ is _____

12. In general the area under the curve in the interval $\mu \pm 3\sigma$ is _____

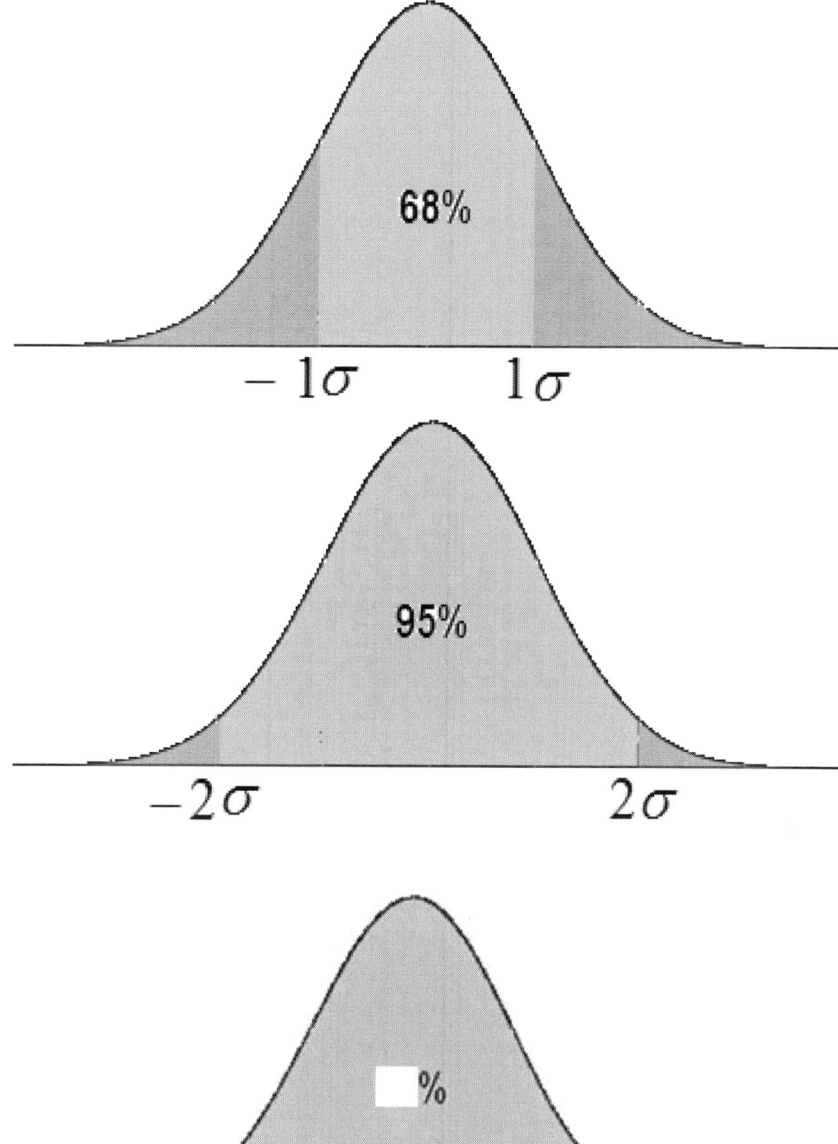

FINDING PROBABILIT FOR $a < X < b$

The amount of time to produce a product follows a normal distribution with mean of 40 minutes and S. D. of 8 minutes.

1. Find the probability that the product is produced between 35 and 50 minutes. Shade the corresponding area on the following diagram. Use GDC to find your answer: normalcdf(35, 50, 40, 8)

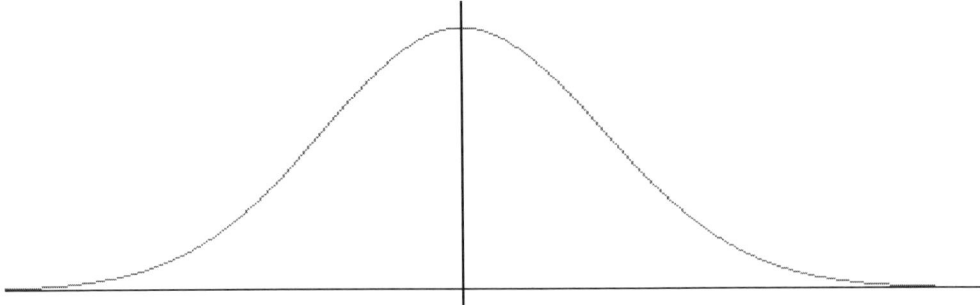

2. Find the probability that the product is produced in more than 38 minutes. Shade the corresponding area on the following diagram. Use GDC to find your answer: normalcdf(38, 1000, 40, 8)

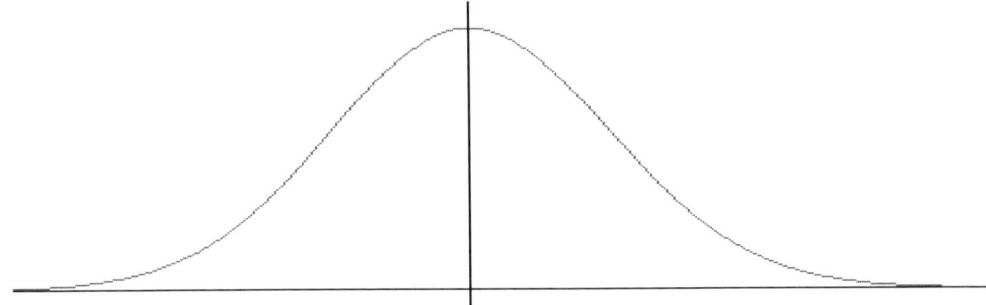

3. Find the probability that the product is produced in less than 34 minutes. Shade the corresponding area on the following diagram. Use GDC to find your answer: normalcdf(–1000,34, 40, 8)

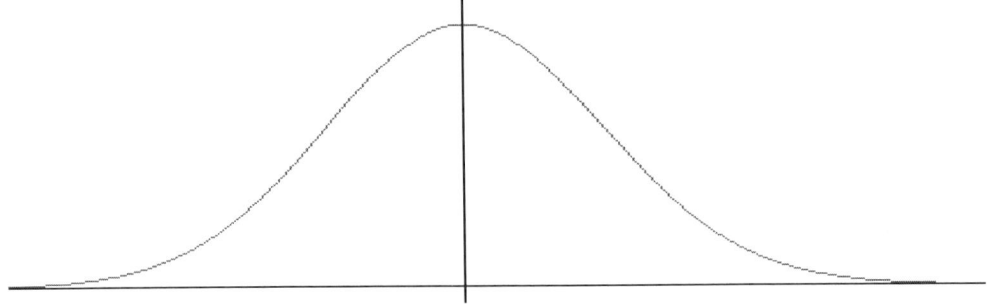

Exercises

1. In a lake there are 3000 fish distributed according to a normal distribution with a mean of 26cm and a standard deviation of 7cm.

    a. Find and shade on the graph the interval in which 68% of the fish lengths are. How many fish in this case?

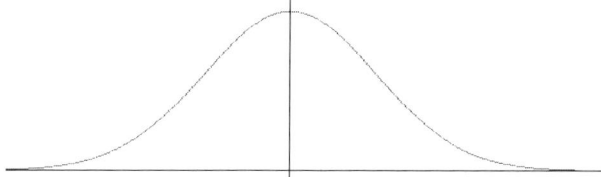

    b. Find and shade on the graph the interval in which 95% of the fish lengths are. How many fish in this case?

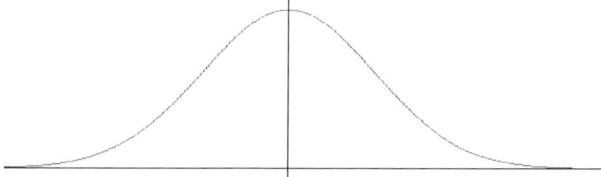

    c. Find and shade on the graph the interval in which 99.7% of the fish lengths are. How many fish in this case?

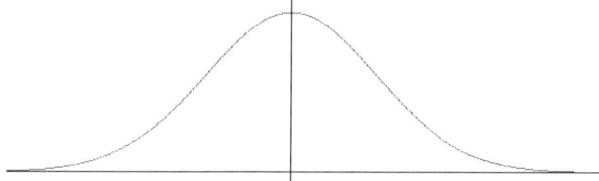

    d. Find and the probability for a fish to measure between 23 and 28 cm. Shade on graph. How many fish in this would you expect in this case to be in this interval?

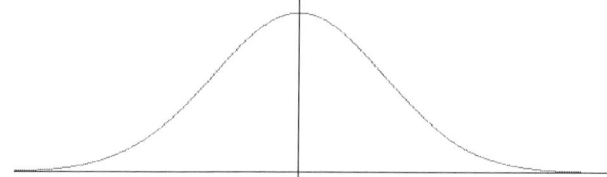

    e. Find and the probability for a fish to measure between 12 and 24 cm. Shade on graph. How many fish in this would you expect in this case to be in this interval?

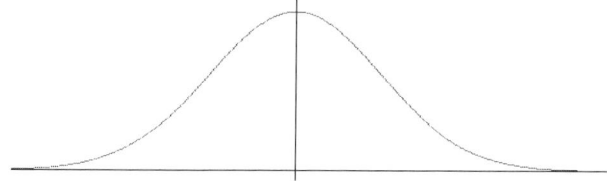

f. Find and the probability for a fish to measure between 27 and 28 cm. Shade on graph. How many fish in this would you expect in this case to be in this interval?

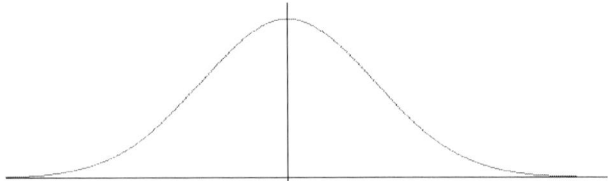

g. Find and shade on graph the probability for a fish to measure more than 26 cm. How many fish in this case?

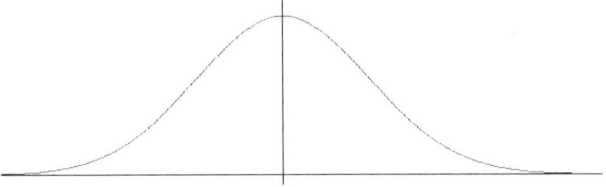

h. Find and shade on graph the probability for a fish to measure exactly 27 cm.

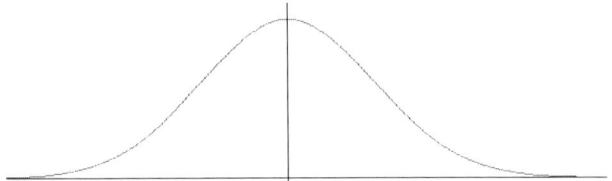

i. Find and shade on graph the probability for a fish to measure exactly 20 cm.

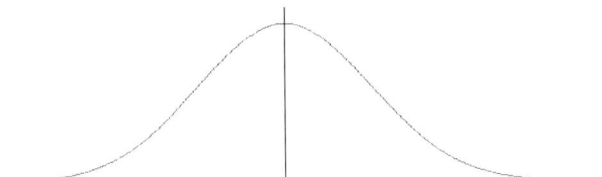

FINDING INVERSE NORMAL PROBABILITIES

1. The amount of time (X) to produce a product follows a normal distribution with mean of 40 minutes and S. D. of 8 minutes.

    a. Find the value of a, if 6% of the value of X are less than a. Shade the corresponding area on the following diagram. Use GDC to find your answer: invNorm(0.06, 40, 8)

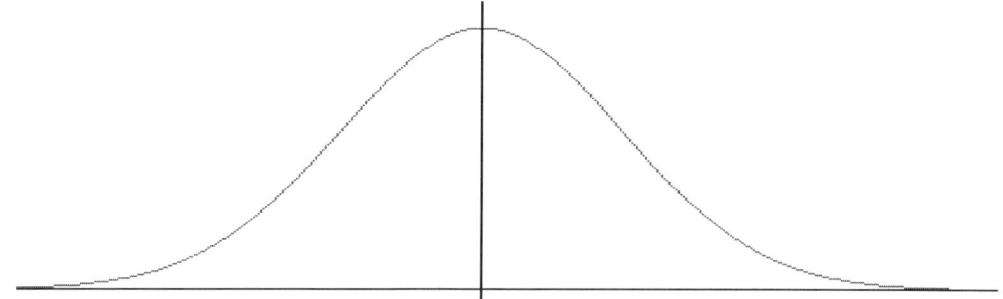

    b. Find the value of a, if 13% of the value of X are more than a. Shade the corresponding area on the following diagram. Use GDC to find your answer: invNorm(0.87, 40, 8)

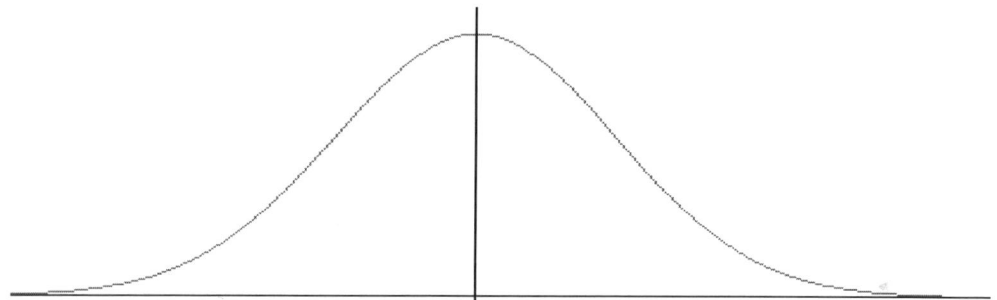

    c. Find the value of a and b if the middle 50% of value of X are between a and b. Shade the corresponding area on the following diagram. Use GDC to find your answer: , invNorm(0.25, 40, 8),   invNorm(0.75, 40, 8)

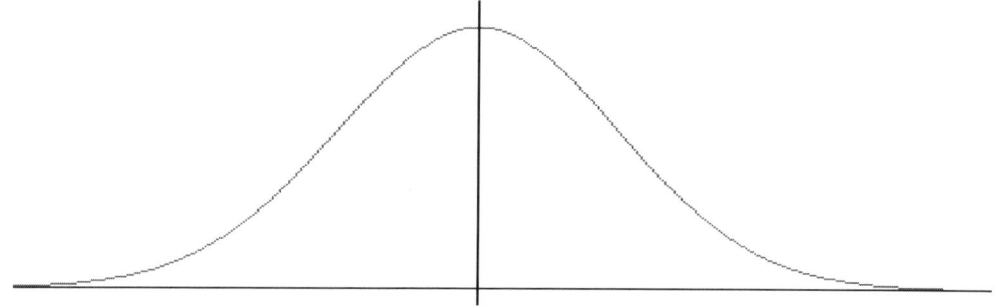

2. In a lake there are 2000 fish distributed according to a normal distribution with a mean of 26cm and a standard deviation of 7cm.

   a. Find and shade the length interval for 80% of the fish. How many fish are expected to be in the interval in this case?

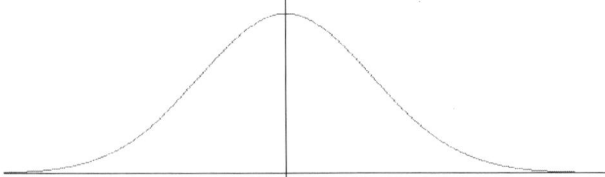

   b. Find and shade the length interval for 90% of the fish. How many fish are expected to be in the interval in this case?

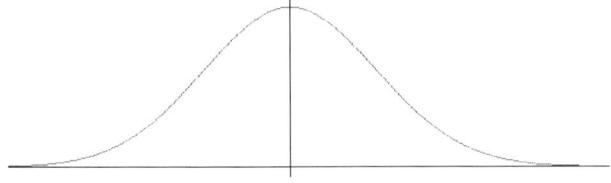

   c. Find and shade the length interval for 75% of the fish. How many fish are expected to be in the interval in this case?

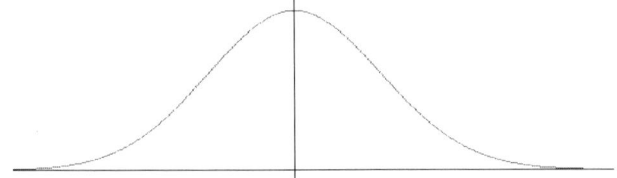

   d. There is a probability of 0.2 that a fish's length is more than q, find q. How many fish are expected to be in the interval in this case?

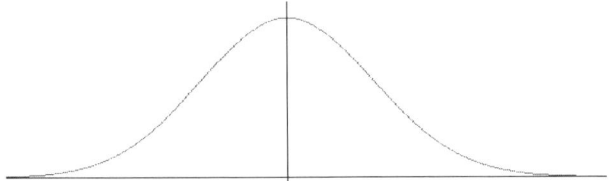

   e. There is a probability of 0.32 that a fish's length is more than w, find w. How many fish are expected to be in the interval in this case?

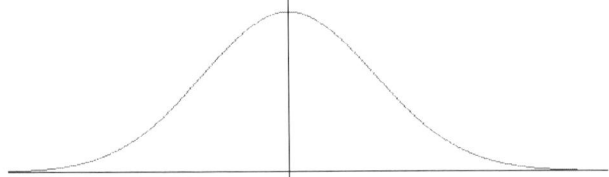

f. There is a probability of 0.4 that a fish's length is between a and b, find a and b. How many fish are expected to be in the interval in this case?

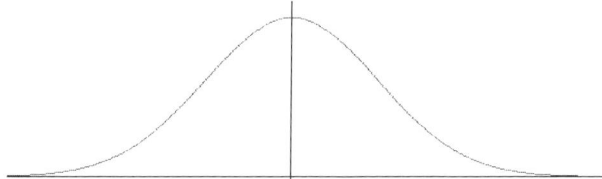

g. There is a probability of 0.2 that a fish's length is between a and b, find a and b. How many fish are expected to be in the interval in this case?

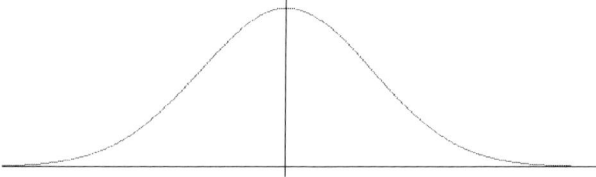

h. There is a probability of 0.1 that a fish's length is less than t, find t. How many fish are expected to be in the interval in this case?

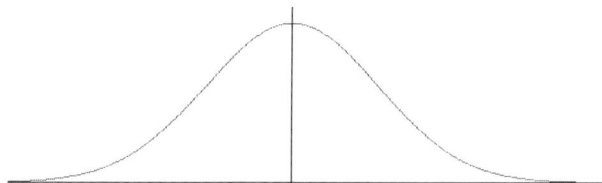

i. Find and shade the interval in which 65% of the fish measure. How many fish are expected to be in the interval in this case?

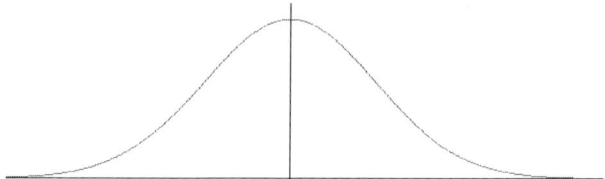

3. In a normal distribution N(0, 1) Find and shade:

   a. $P(Z = 2) =$

   b. $P(Z \geq 2) =$

   c. $P(Z \leq 2) =$

   d. $P(Z \geq -2) =$

   e. $P(Z \leq -2) =$

   f. $P(-2 \leq Z \leq 2) =$

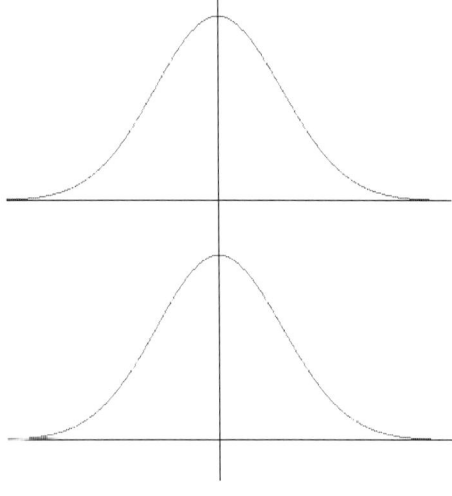

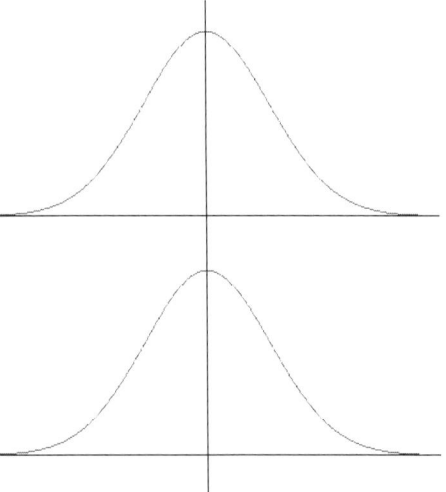

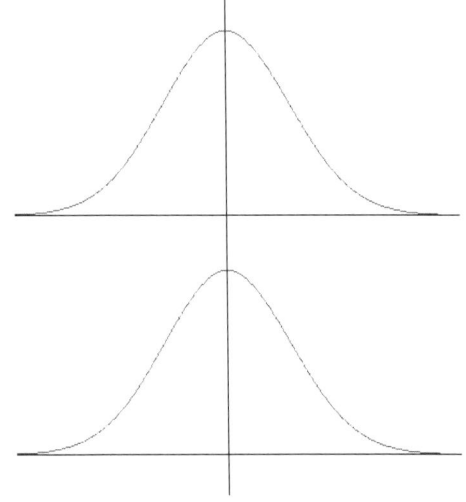

248

4. In a normal distribution N(0, 1) Find and shade:

   a. P(Z = 0.81) =

   b. P(–0.78 ≤ Z ≤ 1.31) =

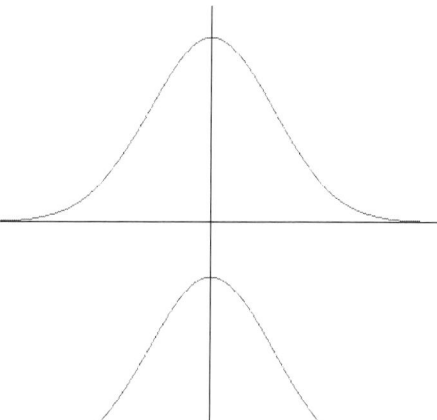

   c. P(–1.31 ≤ Z ≤ 0.78) =

   d. P(0.78 < Z < 1.31) =

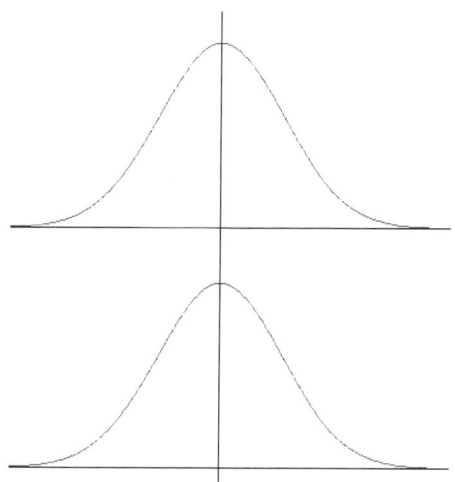

   e. P(–1.31 ≤ Z ≤ -0.78) =

5. In a normal distribution N(24, 6) Find and shade:

   a. P(X = 25) =

   b. P(X ≥ 25) =

   c. P(X ≤ 25) =

   d. P(X ≥ 15) =

   e. P(14 ≤ X ≤ 20) =

   f. P(19 ≤ X ≤ 31) =

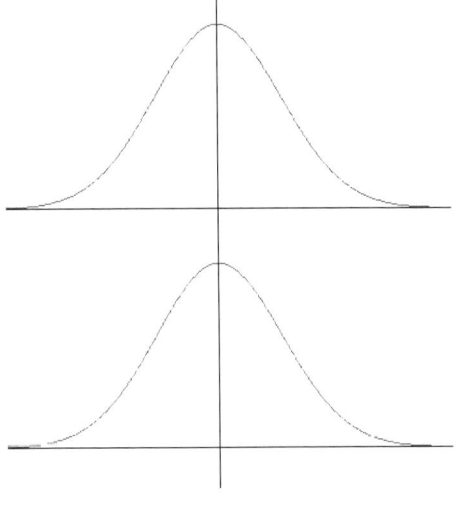

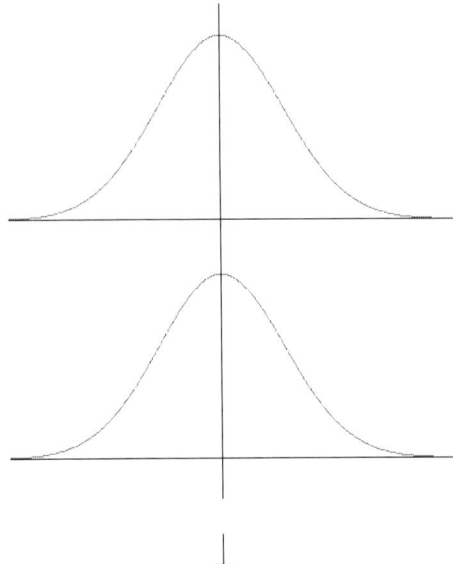

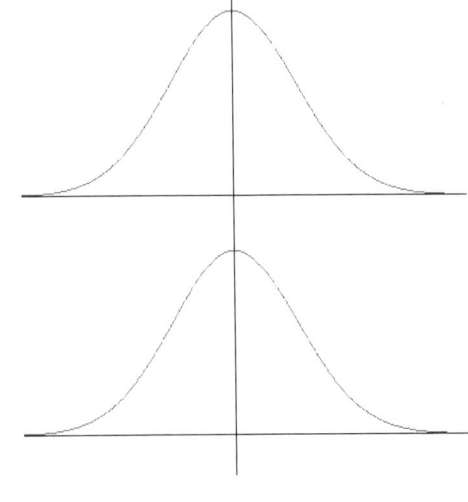

6. The weight of a certain animal is normally distributed with mean of 150 kg and standard deviation of 12 kg.

a. Sketch a diagram for the distribution of weight for the animal.

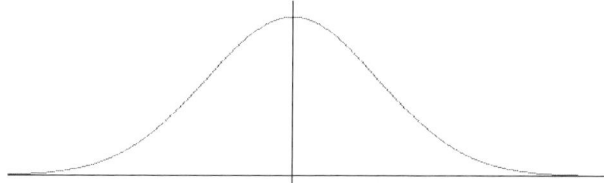

b. We classify the animals in the following way:

Small   weight < 130
Medium   130 ≤ weight < 170
Big   170 ≤ weight

Add these boundaries to your diagram.

c. Find the probability for each one the cases described.

d. There is a probability of 0.2 for an animal to have a weight bigger than q. Find q.

e. In a jungle with 3000 animals how many are expected to have a weight bigger than q?

7. 500 high school students' grades are distributed normally with a mean of 72 and a standard deviation of 6.

    a. Label the mean and 2 standard deviations from the mean.

    b. What percentage of scores are between scores 60 and 70? How many students in this group?

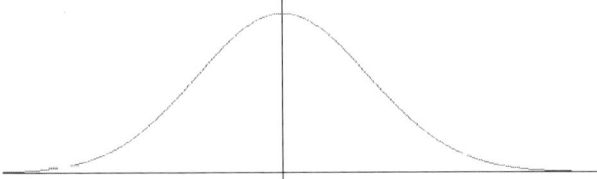

    c. What percentage of scores are between scores 80 and 90? How many students in this group?

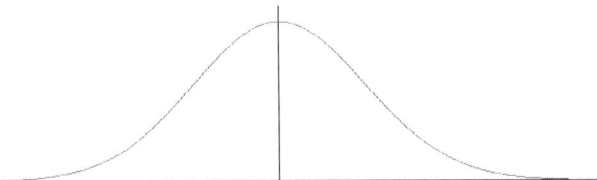

    d. What percentage of scores are between scores 90 and 100? How many students in this group?

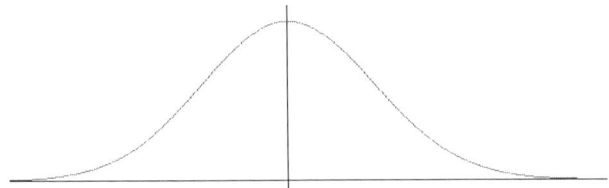

    e. Can students' grades distribute normally? Explain.

8. The time it takes to complete a certain journey is normally distributed with a mean of 50 days and a standard deviation of 4 days.

   a. The probability that the length of the journey lies between 53 and 60 days hours is represented by the shaded area in the following diagram.

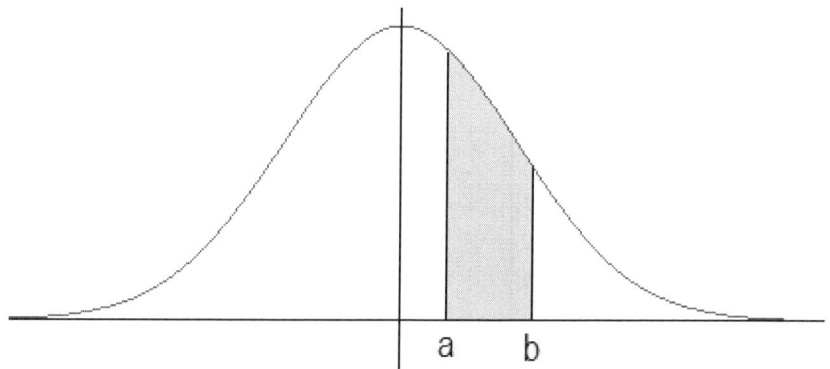

   Write down the values of *a* and *b*.

   b. Find the probability that the length of the journey is more than 57 days.

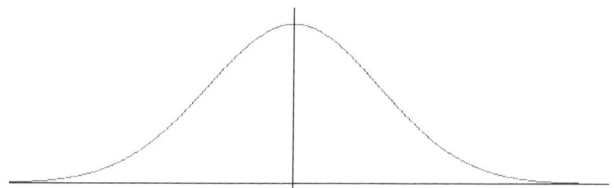

   c. Find the probability that the length of the journey is between 56 and 61 days.

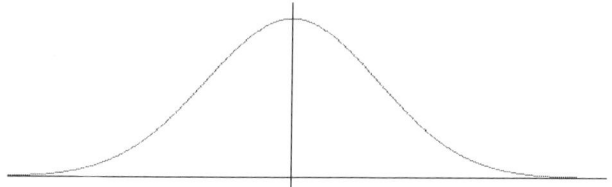

   d. 80% of the travellers complete the journey after x hours. Find x.

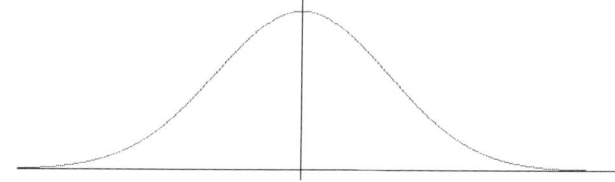

ANSWER KEY
CHAPTER 1 – ALGEBRA

1.1. – TYPES OF NUMBERS

Natural Numbers (N): $N = \{1, 2, 3, 4...\}$

Integers (Z): $Z = \{...-4, -3, -2, -1, 0, 1, 2, 3, 4...\}$

Rational Numbers (Q): $Q = \{\frac{a}{b}, a, b \in Z\}$

Numbers that **can** be written as <u>fractions</u> being both the

numerator and the denominator <u>integers</u>.

Examples: $\frac{1}{1}, \frac{2}{3}, \frac{-7}{3}, \frac{4}{-1}, \frac{0}{2}, 0.55, 0.121212...$

Irrational Numbers (Q'): $Q' \neq \{\frac{a}{b}, a, b \in Z\}$ Numbers that <u>cannot</u> be written as

fractions, being both the <u>numerator</u> and the <u>denominator</u>
integers.

Examples: $\pi, \sqrt{2}, e...$

Real Numbers (R): $R = Q + Q'$ (Rationals and Irrationals)

Exercises:

1. Natural numbers are contained in the <u>Integer</u> numbers.

2. Integer numbers are contained in the <u>Rational</u> numbers

3. Rational numbers are contained in the <u>Real</u> numbers.

4. Irrational numbers are located <u>in the outermost ring</u>.

5. Shade the area in which the irrational numbers are located:

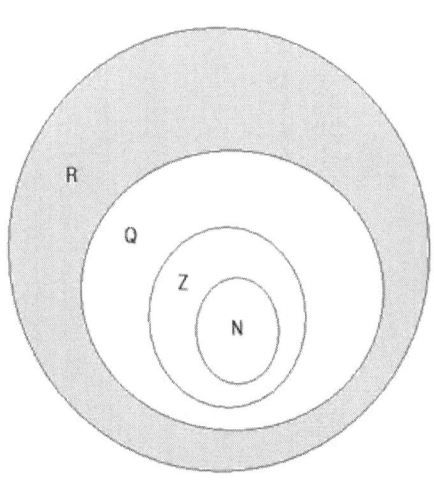

6. True or False:

    a. All Natural numbers are Integers: <u>True</u>

    b. All Real numbers are Natural: <u>False</u>

    c. All Rational numbers are Real: <u>True</u>

    d. All Real numbers are Rational: <u>False</u>

    e. All Integer numbers are Rational: <u>True</u>

    f. All Real numbers are Irrational: <u>False</u>

    g. Some Irrational numbers are Real and some are not: <u>False</u>

    h. Some Irrational numbers are Integers: <u>False</u>

    i. Some integers are negative: <u>True</u>

    j. Some Irrationals are negative: <u>True</u>

    k. Some Natural numbers are negative: <u>False</u>

7. Fill the chart with yes or no (follow the example):

Number	Natural	Integer	Rational	Real
-2	no	yes	yes	yes
Π	no	no	no	yes
$-3.121212....$	no	no	yes	yes
-15.16	no	no	yes	yes
$\sqrt{3}$	no	no	no	yes
$-2\frac{2}{5}$	no	no	yes	yes
$\sqrt[3]{8}$	yes	yes	yes	yes

8. Fill the numbers column with appropriate numbers and yes or no. Follow the example.

Number	Natural	Integer	Rational	Real
−1	no	yes	yes	yes
0.1	no	no	yes	yes
Does not exist	yes	yes	yes	no
$\sqrt{2}$	no	no	no	yes
$\dfrac{1}{2}$	no	no	yes	yes
0	no	yes	yes	yes
0.333...	no	no	yes	yes
Does not exist		yes	no	

4. Convert the following numbers into the form: $\dfrac{n}{m}$

1. $0.333... = \dfrac{1}{3}$

2. $1.111... = \dfrac{10}{9}$

3. $5.3 = \dfrac{53}{10}$

4. $5.2828... = \dfrac{523}{99}$

5. $-2.3535... = \dfrac{233}{99}$

6. $42.67 = \dfrac{4267}{100}$

7. $12.355355... = \dfrac{12343}{999}$

8. $-31.44 = \dfrac{-3144}{100}$

9. $0.125125... = \dfrac{125}{99}$

10. $3.22332233... = \dfrac{32230}{2930}$

11. $1115.36 - \dfrac{111536}{100}$

12. $122.53 = \dfrac{12253}{100}$

13. $1.123123... = \dfrac{1122}{999}$

14. $1.22565656... = \dfrac{12134}{9900}$

15. $1.5696969... = \dfrac{1554}{990}$

16. $5.540404040... = \dfrac{5485}{990}$

5. Given the following diagram:

Write the following numbers in the appropriate location in the diagram:

a. 2.2
b. −5
c. 3
d. $\dfrac{1}{3}$
e. 5
f. −3.3
g. 1.111...
h. $\dfrac{1}{\sqrt{3}}$
i. 2π
j. $1+2\pi$
k. $\sqrt{2}+3$
l. $\dfrac{4}{2}$

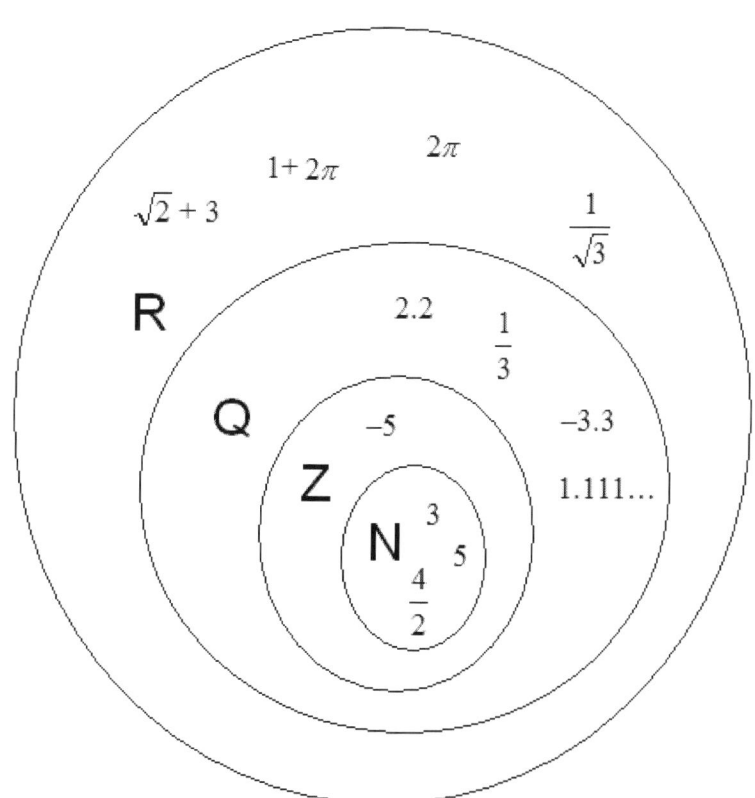

6. Circle the right option. The number −2 is:

    a. Integer and Natural.
    b. Positive
    c. Integer and Rational
    d. Natural and Real
    e. Natural and Rational
    f. None of the above

7. Circle the right option. The number 3.41414141..... is:

    a. Integer and Natural.
    b. Natural
    c. Integer and Real
    d. Rational and Integer
    e. Rational
    f. None of the above

8. Circle the right option. The number 3.41 is:

    a. Integer and Natural.
    b. Integer
    c. **Rational and Real**
    d. Integer and Real
    e. Rational and negative
    f. None of the above

9. Circle the right option. The number $\sqrt{31}$ is:

    a. Integer and Natural.
    b. Integer
    c. Decimal
    d. Integer and Real
    e. Rational
    f. **Irrational**

10. Circle the right option. The number 5 is:

    a. Natural.
    b. Integer
    c. Real
    d. Integer and Natural
    e. Rational and Natural
    f. **All of the above**

1.2. – INTERVAL NOTATION

x ϶ (a, b] or {x| a < x ≤ b} means x is between a and b, not including a and including b.

Exercises:

1. Represent the following Intervals on the real line:

   a. x ϶ (2, 5]

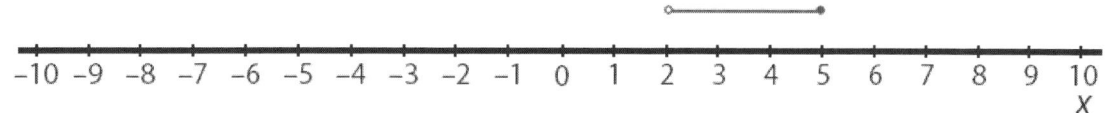

   b. x ϶ (3,6)

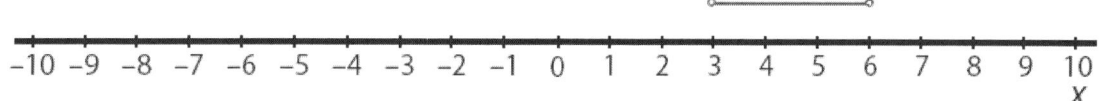

   c. x ϶ [−5,9]

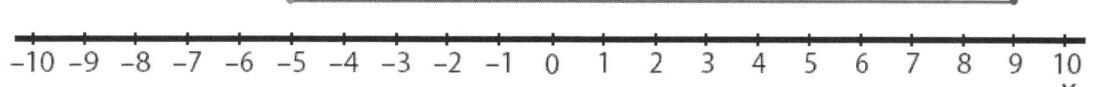

   d. x ϶ [−8,−1)

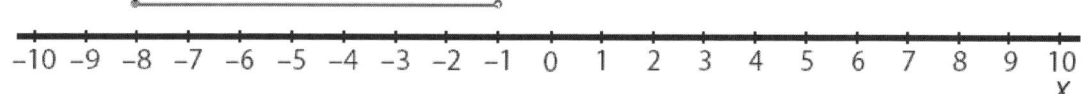

   e. x ϶ [−∞,−1)

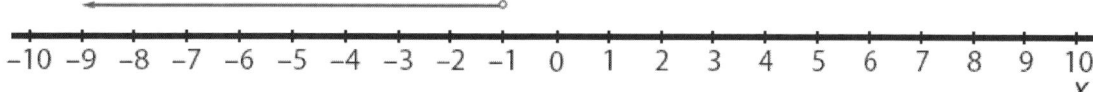

   f. x ϶ [−∞,6]

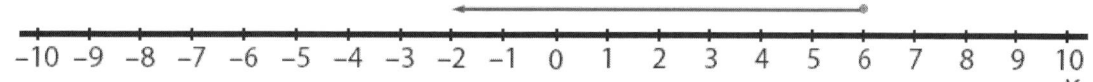

   g. x ϶ (6, ∞]

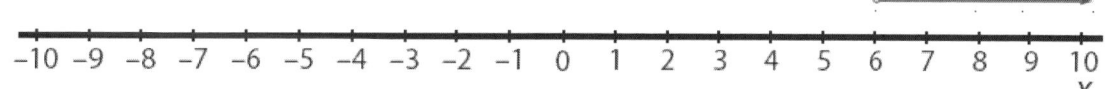

   h. {x| 7 < x < 9}

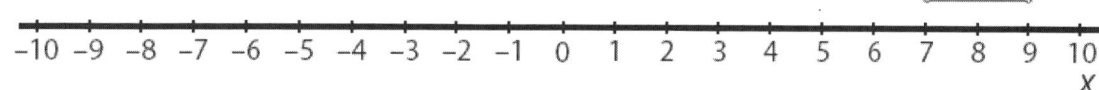

   i. {x| −7 < x < −2}

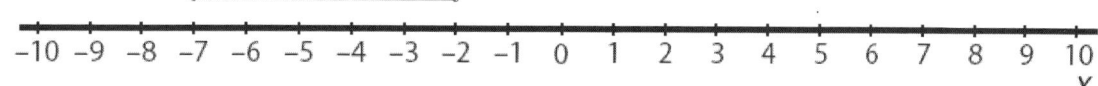

   j. {x| 1 < x < 2}

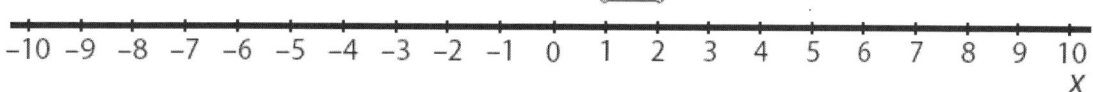

k. $\{x|\ \infty < x < 2\}$ Not Possible

l. $\{x|\ 1 < x < \infty\ \}$

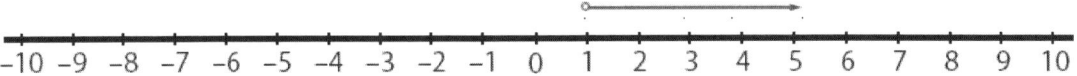

2. Write each one of the Intervals using all types of notations:

a. $x \ni (4, 5) = 4 \le x \le 5$

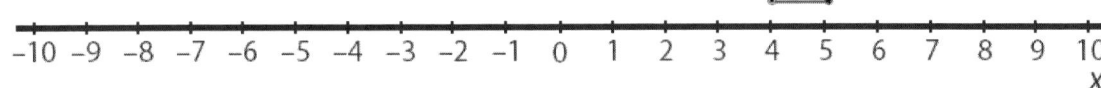

b. $x \ni (-\infty, 5) = x < 5$

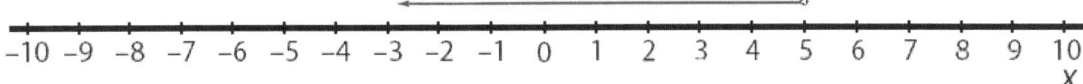

c. $x \ni (4, 5) = 4 < x < 5$

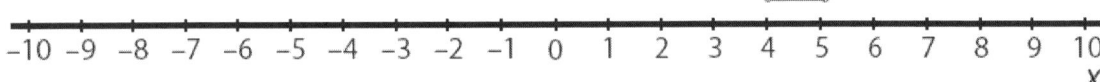

d. $x \ni (3, \infty] = 3 < x$

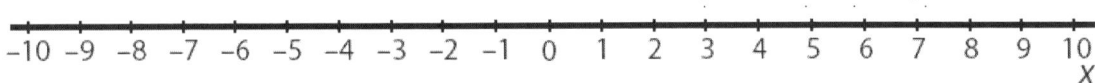

e. $x \ni\ ]-5,9] = -5 < x \le 9$

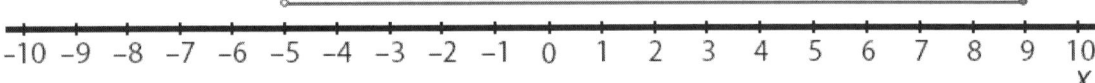

f. $x \ni [-8,-1[\ = -8 \le x < -1$

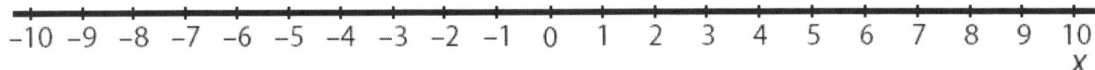

g. $\{x|\ 7 < x < 9\} = x \ni (7, 9)$

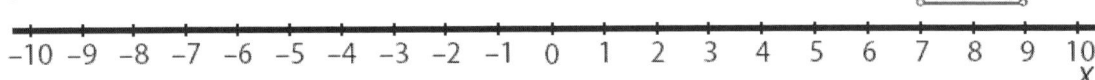

h. $\{x|\ -7 < x < -2\} = x \ni (-7, -2)$

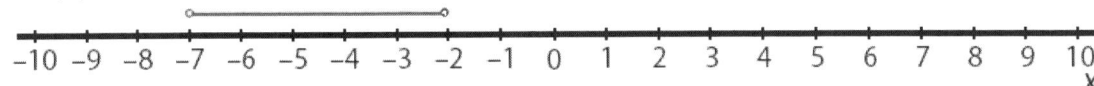

3.

a. Solve the inequality $3x - 7 \le 2$ $x \le 3$

b. Solve the inequality $-x < -2$. $x > 2$

c. Represent both solutions on the real line:

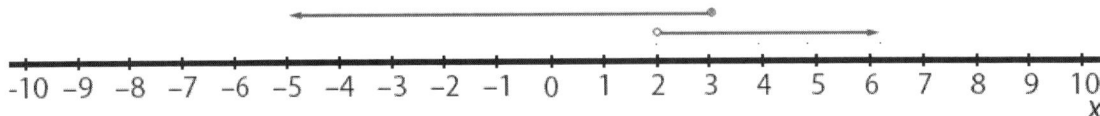

d. State their intersection: $\{x|\ 2 < x \le 3\} = x \ni (2, 3]$

260

4.

   a. Solve the inequality $5x - 2 \leq 2$ $x \leq \dfrac{4}{5}$

   b. Solve the inequality $-2x + 1 > -2$ $x < \dfrac{3}{2}$

   c. Represent both solutions on the real line:

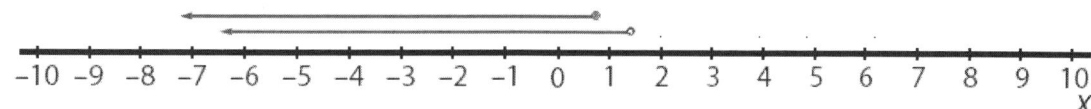

d. State their intersection: $\{x | \infty < x \leq \dfrac{4}{5}\} = x \ni (\infty, \dfrac{4}{5}]$

5.

   d. Solve the inequality $5x - 2 \leq -12$ $x \leq -2$

   a. Solve the inequality $-2x - 3 \leq -2$. $x \geq -\dfrac{1}{2}$

   b. Represent both solutions on the real line:

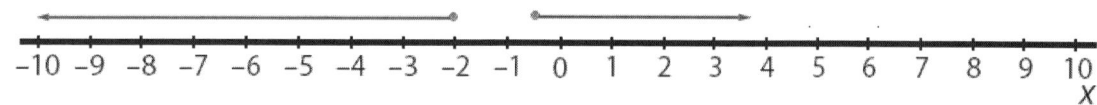

   c. State their intersection: No intersection

1.3. – SIGNIFICANT FIGURES

Determine the number of significant digits in each of the following:

1.	273.20 cm	5	8.	10	1
2.	4513.01 L	6	9.	1.0	2
3.	2.00011 km	6	10.	9.401°C	4
4.	0.0001010450 sec	7	11.	0.2 ml	1
5.	4.75 kg	3	12.	314 kg	3
6.	1.0	2	13.	2000.103 mm	7
7.	10.0	3	14.	704000 h	3

Answer using proper number of significant figures:

11. 3.414 s + 10.02 s + 58.325 s + 0.00098 s = 71.76s

12. 2.326 h – 0.10408 h = 2.222h

13. 10.19 m x 0.013 m = 0.13m^2

14. 140.01 cm x 26.042 cm x 0.0159 cm = 58.0cm^3

15. 80.23 m / 2.4 s = 33m/s

16. 4.301 kg / 1.9 cm^3 = _____2.3kg/cm^3_____

17. A Chemical experiment involves the following substances:
    85.238 g of Iron, 32.1 g of Water, 0.0026 g of Oil, 7.13 g of Glass

    a.   How many significant digits are there in each measurement?
        5.238 g of Iron (4)
        32.1 g of Water (3)
        0.0026 g of Oil (2)
        7.13 g of Glass (3)

    b.   What is the total mass of substances in this experiment?
        124.5 (one decimal place)

    c.   How many significant digits are there in the answer to part b? 4

18. A certain living room was measured to be 12.412m long and 5.212m wide. Determine:

    a. The area of the living room to the correct number of decimal places. <u>64.69 m^2</u>

    b. The area of the living room to 3 significant figures. <u>65.0 m^2</u>

    c. The area of the living room to 4 significant figures. <u>64.69 m^2</u>

    d. The area of the living room to 1 decimal place. <u>65.0 m^2</u>

    e. The perimeter of the living room to the correct number of decimal places. <u>17.624 m</u>

    f. The perimeter of the living room to 3 significant figures. <u>17.6 m</u>

    g. The perimeter of the living room to 4 significant figures. <u>17.62 m</u>

    h. The perimeter of the living room to 1 decimal place. <u>17.6 m</u>

19. You measured 17.40 ml of water in a certain recipient. After a certain experiment 9.0 ml of water was left.

    a. Which measurement is more precise, before or after the experiment? Explain.

       <u>Before, it was accurate to 2 decimal places.</u>

    b. How much water was consumed during the experiment?

       <u>8.4 ml</u>

1.4. – SCIENTIFIC NOTATION

1. How many significant figures does the measurement of 100 mm have? __1__
   However, what if whoever performed the measurement was accurate to within 1
   mm? How can the experimenter report the measurement with the appropriate
   number of significant figures?

2. Reporting the value as 100.0 suddenly turns the term having one significant digit

   into a term having 4

3. The solution to this problem is called "scientific notation". In this case the

   solution to the problem would be: $1.00 \cdot 10^{-1} m$. With this notation, it is clear that

   three significant digits are intended.

4. Typically a <u>number between 1 and 10</u> is placed to the <u>left of the decimal</u>, and

   this number is then <u>multiplied by the appropriate power of 10</u>. Our

   experimenter could report the measured quantity as 10.0×10^1 mm, but the first
   version is more common.

Write the following numbers in scientific notation and indicate the number of
significant figures, later write with 3 significant figures:

1. $1026.90 = \underline{1.02690 \cdot 10^3}$ ___ 3S.F. $\underline{1.03 \cdot 10^3}$

2. $0.03045 = \underline{3.045 \cdot 10^{-2}}$ ___ 3S.F. $\underline{3.05 \cdot 10^{-2}}$

3. $12,000 = \underline{1.2 \cdot 10^4}$ ___ 3S.F. $\underline{1.20 \cdot 10^4}$

4. $0.00690 = \underline{6.90 \cdot 10^{-3}}$ ___ 3S.F. $\underline{6.90 \cdot 10^{-3}}$

Write In scientific notation (use appropriate number of significant figures):

5. $0.11 = \underline{1.1 \cdot 10^{-1}}$

6. $0.015 = \underline{1.5 \cdot 10^{-2}}$

7. $0.0071 = \underline{7.1 \cdot 10^{-3}}$

8. $0.0000001 = \underline{1 \cdot 10^{-7}}$

9. $1.2 = \underline{1.2 \cdot 10^0}$

10. $1.02 = \underline{1.02 \cdot 10^0}$

11. $0.3 = \underline{3 \cdot 10^{-1}}$

12. $0.00004 = \underline{4 \cdot 10^{-5}}$

13. $0.06023 = \underline{6.023 \cdot 10^{-2}}$

14. $0.000345 = \underline{3.45 \cdot 10^{-4}}$

15. $0.00155 = \underline{1.55 \cdot 10^{-3}}$

16. $0.0000204 = \underline{2.04 \cdot 10^{-5}}$

17. $100 = \underline{1 \cdot 10^{2}}$

18. $10100 = \underline{1.01 \cdot 10^{4}}$

19. $11.0 = \underline{1.10 \cdot 10^{1}}$

20. $200 = \underline{2 \cdot 10^{2}}$

21. $201 = \underline{2.01 \cdot 10^{2}}$

22. $10.00 = \underline{1.000 \cdot 10^{1}}$

23. $101.0 = \underline{1.010 \cdot 10^{2}}$

24. $1.200 = \underline{1.200 \cdot 10^{0}}$

25. $1500 = \underline{1.5 \cdot 10^{3}}$

26. $2000 = \underline{2 \cdot 10^{3}}$

27. $51223 = \underline{5.1223 \cdot 10^{4}}$

28. $100.80 = \underline{1.0080 \cdot 10^{2}}$

29. $209.1 = \underline{2.091 \cdot 10^{2}}$

30. $24.18 = \underline{2.418 \cdot 10^{2}}$

31. $5500 = \underline{5.5 \cdot 10^{3}}$

32. $766600 = \underline{7.666 \cdot 10^{5}}$

33. $54000 = \underline{5.4 \cdot 10^{4}}$

34. $44500 = \underline{4.45 \cdot 10^{4}}$

35. $65000 = \underline{6.5 \cdot 10^{4}}$

36. $0.00545 = \underline{5.45 \cdot 10^{-3}}$

37. $0.001545 = \underline{1.545 \cdot 10^{-3}}$

38. $0.00020545 = \underline{2.0545 \cdot 10^{-4}}$

39. $0.050425 = \underline{5.0425 \cdot 10^{-2}}$

40. $0.0050545 = \underline{5.0545 \cdot 10^{-3}}$

41. $70000 = \underline{7 \cdot 10^{4}}$

Calculate giving your answers in scientific notation with the proper number of significant figures.

42. $(6.6 \cdot 10^{-8}) / (3.30 \cdot 10^{-4}) = \underline{2.0 \cdot 10^{-4}}$

43. $(1.56 \cdot 10^{-7}) + (2.43 \cdot 10^{-8}) = \underline{1.80 \cdot 10^{-7}}$

44. $(7.4 \cdot 10^{10}) / (3.7 \cdot 10^{3}) = \underline{2.0 \cdot 10^{7}}$

45. $(2.5 \cdot 10^{-8}) \cdot (3.0 \cdot 10^{-7}) = \underline{7.5 \cdot 10^{-15}}$

46. $(2.67 \cdot 10^{-3}) - (9.5 \cdot 10^{-4}) = \underline{1.72 \cdot 10^{-3}}$

47. $(2.3 \cdot 10^{-4}) \cdot (2.0 \cdot 10^{-3}) = \underline{4.6 \cdot 10^{-7}}$

1.5. – ERROR ANALYSIS

1. As was seen earlier, when performing a measurement an error is always committed. The errors are classified in the following way:

2. Absolute error = $|\text{Measured value} - \text{True Value}|$

3. Relative error = $\left|\dfrac{\text{Measured value} - \text{True Value}}{\text{True Value}}\right|$

4. Percentage error = $\left|100 \cdot \dfrac{\text{Measured value} - \text{True Value}}{\text{True Value}}\right|$

5. An error can be negative (True/**False**).

Exercises

1. 0.33 is used instead of $\dfrac{1}{3}$

    a. Calculate the absolute error committed

    $$\text{Absolute error} = \left|0.33 - \frac{1}{3}\right| = 0.00333$$

    b. Calculate the relative error committed

    $$\text{Relative error} = \left|\frac{0.00333}{\left(\dfrac{1}{3}\right)}\right| = 0.00999$$

    c. Calculate the percentage error committed

    $$\text{Percentage error} = 0.00999 \cdot 100 = 0.999\% \approx 1\%$$

2. 1.41 is used instead of $\sqrt{2}$

    a. Calculate the absolute error committed
    $$\text{Absolute error} = \left|1.41 - \sqrt{2}\right| = 0.00421$$

    b. Calculate the relative error committed
    $$\text{Relative error} = \left|\frac{0.00421}{\left(\sqrt{2}\right)}\right| = 0.00298$$

    c. Calculate the percentage error committed
    $$\text{Percentage error} = 0.00298 \cdot 100 = 0.298\%$$

3. A bathroom scale measures weights to the nearest 0.5 Kg. If we weigh a box that weights 65 Kg.

   a. Calculate the absolute error committed

   Absolute error = $|65.5 - 60| = 0.5 Kg$

   b. Calculate the relative error committed

   Relative error = $\left|\dfrac{0.5}{65}\right| = 0.00769$

   c. Calculate the percentage error committed

   Percentage error = 0.769%

4. A digital bathroom scale measures weights to the nearest 0.1 Kg. If we weigh a cat that weights 1.9 Kg.

   a. Calculate the absolute error committed
   Absolute error = $|1.9 - 2.0| = 0.1 Kg$

   b. Calculate the relative error committed
   Relative error = $\left|\dfrac{0.1}{1.9}\right| = 0.0526$

   c. Calculate the percentage error committed
   Percentage error = 5.26%

5. A certain ruler measures lengths to the nearest millimeter. Find the absolute error, relative error and percentage error committed if we measure lengths of:

   a. 5cm

   A. error = $1mm$ R. error = $\left|\dfrac{1mm}{50mm}\right| = 0.02$ P. error = 2%

   b. 1 cm

   A. error = $1mm$ R. error = $\left|\dfrac{1mm}{10mm}\right| = 0.1$ P. error = 10%

   c. 0.5 cm

   A. error = $1mm$ R. error = $\left|\dfrac{1mm}{5mm}\right| = 0.2$ P. error = 20%

   d. 1 mm

   A. error = $1mm$ R. error = $\left|\dfrac{1mm}{1mm}\right| = 1$ P. error = 100%

   e. In which case(s) would you say the ruler is not very useful? Explain
   Clearly as the size of the object measured is close to the Absolute error the ruler loses efficiency. In the last 2 cases the P. error is very big.

6. Given that x = 0.12, y = 0.0316 and z = 808
   a. State the number of significant figures given for each variable:
      x: 2 SF   y: 3 SF   z: 3 SF
   b. Calculate exactly $\dfrac{z(x^2+\sqrt{y})}{x-y} = 1756.430110$
   c. Write all the values of x, y and z correct to 1 significant figure.
      x = 0.1   y = 0.03   z = 800
   d. Use the values found in c to calculate $\dfrac{z(x^2+\sqrt{y})}{x-y} = 2093.772351$
   e. Find the absolute, relative and percentage error committed (in part d compared with the exact value calculated in b).
      Absolute error = 337   Relative error = 0.192
      Percentage error = 19.2%
   f. Write all the values of x, y and z correct to 2 significant figures.
      x = 0.12   y = 0.032   z = 810
   g. Use the values found in f to calculate $\dfrac{z(x^2+\sqrt{y})}{x-y} = 1779.104601$
   h. Find the absolute, relative and percentage error committed (in part g compared with the exact value calculated in b).
      Absolute error = 22.7   Relative error = 0.0129
      Percentage error = 1.29%
7. Given that x = 560°, y = 1.61 and z = 808

   a. State the number of significant figures given for each variable:
      x: 2 SF   y: 3 SF   z: 3 SF
   b. Calculate exactly $\dfrac{z\sin(x)}{y} \approx -171.6473763$
      (exactly not possible, irrational number!)
   c. Write all the values of x, y and z correct to 1 significant figure.
      x = 600°   y = 2   z = 800
   d. Use the values found in c to calculate $\dfrac{z\sin(x)}{y} = -346.4101616$
   e. Find the absolute, relative and percentage error committed (in part d compared with the exact value calculated in b).
      Absolute error = 175   Relative error = 1.02
      Percentage error = 102%
   f. Write all the values of x, y and z correct to 2 significant figures.
      x = 560°   y = 1.6   z = 810
   g. Use the values found in f to calculate $\dfrac{z\sin(x)}{y} = -173,14769755861979$
   h. Find the absolute, relative and percentage error committed (in part g compared with the exact value calculated in b).
      Absolute error = 1.50   Relative error = 0.00874
      Percentage error = 0.874%
      Pay attention to difference in relative error only by adding 1 more significant figure!

1.6. – INTERNATIONAL SYSTEM OF UNITS

Notation of units units: g – gram, m – metre, s – second

1. Gram is a unit of <u>mass</u>. Other units of <u>mass</u> are: mg, Kg

2. Metre is a unit of <u>length</u>. Other unit s of <u>length</u>. are: mm, cm, Km

3. Second is a unit of <u>time</u>. Other units of <u>time</u> are: minute, hour, day, year

4. Celsius is a unit of <u>temprature</u>. Other units of <u>time</u>.are: Fahrenheit, Kelvin

5. An area has units of <u>mm^2, cm^2, Km^2 in general $length^2$</u>

6. A volume has units of <u>mm^3, cm^3, Km^3 in general $length^3$</u>

7. Velocity has units of <u>m/s, cm/s, Km/hour in general length/time</u>

8. Kilo = <u>1000</u> Mili = <u>1/1000</u>

9. 1 Litre = <u>$1000cm^3$</u> = <u>$1000000000mm^3$</u> = <u>$0.001m^3$</u>

Convert the units in the following exercises, use scientific notation in at least one of each type of exercises:

1. How many metres are 2.5 km?   <u>2500m</u>

2. How many metres are 0.5 km?   <u>500m</u>

3. How many metres are $\frac{1}{3}$ km?   <u>333m</u>

4. How many metres are 56 km?   <u>56000m</u>

5. How many metres are 2500 km?   <u>2500000m</u>

6. How many grams are 1.25 kg?   <u>1250g</u>

7. How many grams are 0.05 kg?   <u>50g</u>

8. How many grams are $\frac{1}{4}$ kg?   <u>250g</u>

9. How many grams are 34.5 kg?   <u>34500g</u>

10. How many grams are 257.31 kg?   <u>257310g</u>

11. How many km are 26 m?   <u>0.026Km</u>

12. How many km are 75 m?   <u>0.075Km</u>

13. How many km are 1000 m?   1Km

14. How many km are $5.2 \bullet 10^7$ m?   52000Km

15. How many km are $5.12 \bullet 10^8$ m?   512000Km

16. How many kg are 5798 g?   5.798Kg

17. How many kg are 115 g?   0.115Kg

18. How many kg are 1000 g?   1Kg

19. How many mg are 2.9 kg?   2900000mg

20. How many mg are 0.4 g?   400mg

21. How many mg are 0.55 kg?   550000mg

22. How many mg are 24 g?   24000mg

23. How many mg are 2660 kg? $2.66 \cdot 10^9 \, mg$

24. How many mg are 2.85 g? $2.85 \cdot 10^3 \, mg$

25. How many mg are 73 g? $7.3 \cdot 10^4 \, mg$

26. How many ms are 3.04 s? $3.04 \cdot 10^3 \, ms$

27. How many ms are 0.5 s? $5 \cdot 10^2 \, ms$

28. How many ms are 1 s? $1 \cdot 10^3 \, ms$

29. How many s are 5 min?   300s

30. How many s are 5 hours?   18000s

31. How many ms are in 2 days?   172800000ms

32. How many ms are 2.5 min?   150000ms

33. How many ms are 1.35 min?   81000ms

34. How many ms are $\dfrac{1}{3}$ min?   20000ms

35. How many ms are 56 min?   3360000ms

36. How many ml are 3.1 litres?   <u>3100ml</u>

37. How many ml are 0.5 litres?   <u>500ml</u>

38. How many litres are there in 120 ml?   <u>0.120L</u>

39. How many litres are there in 5420 ml?   <u>5.420L</u>

40. How many litres are there in 17 ml?   <u>0.017L</u>

41. How many litres are there in 12392 ml?   <u>12.392L</u>

42. How many ms are 5.1 s?   <u>5100ms</u>

43. How many ms are 2.2 min?   <u>132000ms</u>

44. How many ml are 13.12 litres?   <u>13120ml</u>

45. How many ml are 10.05 litres?   <u>10050ml</u>

46. 1 m/s = <u>0.001</u> km/s = <u>3.6</u> km/h

47. 1 km/h = <u>1/3600</u> km/s = <u>1/3.6</u> m/s

48. 2 m/s = <u>0.002</u> km/s = <u>7.2</u> km/h

49. 2 km/h = <u>1/1800</u> km/s = <u>1/1.8</u> m/s

50. How many m/s are 50 km/h? <u>13.9 m/s</u>

51. How many m/s are 0.5 km/h? <u>0.139 m/s</u>

52. How many m/s are $\frac{5}{2}$ km/h? <u>0.694 m/s</u>

53. How many m/s are 516 km/h? <u>143 m/s</u>

54. How many km/h are 10 m/s? <u>36 km/h</u>

55. How many km/h are 0.5 m/s? <u>1.8 km/h</u>

56. How many km/h are $\frac{5}{2}$ m/s? <u>9 km/h</u>

57. How many km/h are 280 m/s? <u>77.8 km/h</u>

Celsius – Fahrenheit:

Convert Cº to F

$$F = \frac{9}{5}C^\circ + 32$$

1. −100º = −148F

2. −50º = −58F

3. 0º = 32F

4. 20º = 68F

5. 30º = 86F

6. 100º = 212F

7. 200º = 392F

8. 1000º = 1832F

Convert F to Cº

9. −100F = −73.3º

10. −50F = −45.6º

11. 0F = −17.8º

12. 20F = −6.67º

13. 30F = −1.11º

14. 100F = 37.8º

15. 2000F = 1093.3º

1.7. – CURRENCY CONVERSION

1. The Exchange rate from US dollars to Euros is 1 USD = 0.81 EUR

<u>Important to understand:</u> that if 1 USD = 0.81 EUR then 1.23 USD = 1 EUR (Just divide both sides by 0.81)

    a. Convert 100 USD to Euros   <u>81 EUR</u>

    b. Convert 255 USD to Euros   <u>206.55 EUR</u>

    c. Convert 67 EUR to USD   <u>82.7 USD</u>

    d. Convert 332 EUR to USD   <u>$4.10 \cdot 10^2 USD$</u>

    e. Diana receives 200 CAD (Canadian dollars) for 150 Euros. Calculate the value of 1 USD in CAD.
       <u>200 CAD = 150 EUR</u> $\Rightarrow$
       <u>1.33 CAD = 1 EUR</u> $\Rightarrow$
       <u>1.33 CAD = 1.23 USD</u> $\Rightarrow$
       <u>1.08 CAD = 1 USD</u>

    f. Diana receives 1300 MAR (Martian dollars) for 150 Euros. Calculate the value of 1 USD in MAR.
       <u>1300 MAR = 150 EUR</u> $\Rightarrow$
       <u>8.67 MAR = 1 EUR</u> $\Rightarrow$
       <u>8.67 MAR = 1.23 USD</u> $\Rightarrow$
       <u>7.05 MAR = 1 USD</u>

2. Given that 1 USD = 13.2 MXN (Mexican peso). Richard travels to Mexico with 1200 USD. He changes all his money to MXN and later spends 60% of the amount.

    a. How much MXN is he left with at the end of his trip?

       <u>1 USD = 13.2 MXN</u>
       <u>1200 USD = 15840 MXN</u>
       <u>40% of 15840 = 6336 MXN</u>

    b. Back in the US he changes the MXN he is left with for USD. If the bank charges a commission 3% after the exchange. Calculate how many USD Richard receives.

       <u>1 USD = 13.2 MXN</u>
       <u>480 USD = 6336 MXN</u>
       <u>97% of 480 = 465.6 USD</u>

3. A certain bank presents the following table to clients. The table makes reference to USD:

	Buy	Sell
JPY (Japanese Yenn)	75	85
ARS (Argentina Pesos)	4.4	5.2
COP (Colombian Pesos)	1750	1850

    a. State the amount of JPY obtained for 100 USD.
       7500 JPY

    b. How many USD will be obtained in case the client switches back to USD? What is the lost in percentage.
       88.2 USD, 17.8% lost

    c. A client exchanges 300 ARS to USD and then exchanges the amount obtained to COP. Find the amount of COP obtained.
       300 ARS to USD gives 57.7 USD
       57.7 USD to COP gives 100975 COP

4. The Exchange rate from US dollars to Euros is 1 USD = 0.73 GBP

    a. Convert 560 GBP to USD.
       560 GBP = 767 USD

    b. Jane goes on a trip with 700 USD. She changes the amount to GBP. Later she wins a 100 GBP in a card game and decides to switch back to USD. The bank charges 1% commission on the last operation. Find the amount of GBP Jane will have.
       700 USD = 511 GBP
       611 GBP = 837 USD
       99% of 837 gives 829 USD

5. The following table presents the exchange rate between EURO and different currencies:

1 EURO	89 JPY (Japanese Yenn)
1 EURO	6 ARS (Argentinean Peso)
1 EURO	2005 COP (Colombian Pesos)

    a. State the amount of JPY obtained for 100 EURO.
       100 EUR = 890 JPY

    b. Find the exchanges rate between ARS and COP.
       6 ARS = 2005 COP $\Rightarrow$
       1 ARS = 334 COP

1.8. – SEQUENCES AND SERIES

Given The following sequences, write the first 3 terms and the term in the 20th position. If possible identify the pattern using text (follow example):

1. $a_n = 3n$ $a_1 = 3$ $a_2 = 6$ $a_3 = 9$ $a_{20} = 60$ Pattern: <u>   add 3   </u>

2. $a_n = 3n + 1$ $a_1 = 4$ $a_2 = 7$ $a_3 = 10$ $a_{20} = 61$ Pattern: <u>   add 3   </u>

3. $a_n = 3n - 5$ $a_1 = -5$ $a_2 = -2$ $a_3 = 1$ $a_{20} = 55$ Pattern: <u>   add 3   </u>

4. $a_n = 2n + 1$ $a_1 = 3$ $a_2 = 5$ $a_3 = 7$ $a_{20} = 41$ Pattern: <u>   add 2   </u>

5. $a_n = 2n$ $a_1 = 2$ $a_2 = 4$ $a_3 = 6$ $a_{20} = 40$ Pattern: <u>   add 2   </u>

6. $a_n = 2n - 4$ $a_1 = -2$ $a_2 = 0$ $a_3 = 2$ $a_{20} = 36$ Pattern: <u>   add 2   </u>

7. $a_n = -4n$ $a_1 = -4$ $a_2 = -8$ $a_3 = -12$ $a_{20} = -80$ Pattern: <u>   add -4   </u>

8. $a_n = -4n + 10$ $a_1 = 6$ $a_2 = 2$ $a_3 = -2$ $a_{20} = -70$ Pattern: <u>   add -4   </u>

9. $a_n = -4n - 6$ $a_1 = -10$ $a_2 = -14$ $a_3 = -18$ $a_{20} = -86$ Pattern: <u>   add -4   </u>

10. $a_n = \dfrac{n}{3}$ $a_1 = \dfrac{1}{3}$ $a_2 = \dfrac{2}{3}$ $a_3 = 1$ $a_{20} = \dfrac{20}{3}$ Pattern: <u>   add $\dfrac{1}{3}$ </u>

11. $a_n = \dfrac{n}{2}$ $a_1 = \dfrac{1}{2}$ $a_2 = 1$ $a_3 = \dfrac{3}{2}$ $a_{20} = 10$ Pattern: <u>   add $\dfrac{1}{2}$ </u>

12. $a_n = \dfrac{2n}{5} + 1$ $a_1 = \dfrac{7}{5}$ $a_2 = \dfrac{9}{5}$ $a_3 = \dfrac{11}{5}$ $a_{20} = 9$ Pattern: <u>   add $\dfrac{2}{5}$ </u>

13. $a_n = \dfrac{-3n}{7} + 5$ $a_1 = \dfrac{32}{7}$ $a_2 = \dfrac{29}{7}$ $a_3 = \dfrac{26}{7}$ $a_{20} = \dfrac{-25}{7}$ Pattern: <u>   add $-\dfrac{3}{7}$ </u>

14. $a_n = \dfrac{n}{9} - 5$ $a_1 = \dfrac{-44}{9}$ $a_2 = \dfrac{-43}{9}$ $a_3 = \dfrac{-42}{9}$ $a_{20} = \dfrac{-25}{9}$ Pattern: <u>   add $\dfrac{1}{9}$ </u>

15. $a_n = \dfrac{n}{10} - 1$ $a_1 = \dfrac{-9}{10}$ $a_2 = \dfrac{-8}{10}$ $a_3 = \dfrac{-7}{10}$ $a_{20} = 1$ Pattern: <u>   add $\dfrac{1}{10}$ </u>

16. $a_n = \dfrac{3n}{4} + 2$ $a_1 = \dfrac{11}{4}$ $a_2 = \dfrac{14}{4}$ $a_3 = \dfrac{17}{4}$ $a_{20} = \dfrac{68}{4}$ Pattern: <u>   add $\dfrac{3}{4}$ </u>

17. $a_n = n^2$ $a_1 = 1$ $a_2 = 4$ $a_3 = 9$ $a_{20} = 400$ Pattern: <u>   different   </u>

18. $a_n = n^3$ $a_1 = 1$ $a_2 = 8$ $a_3 = 27$ $a_{20} = 8000$ Pattern: <u>   different   </u>

19. $a_n = 2^n$ $a_1 = 2$ $a_2 = 4$ $a_3 = 8$ $a_{20} = 2^{20}$ Pattern: <u>   multiply by 2   </u>

20. $a_n = -2^n$ $a_1 = -2$ $a_2 = -4$ $a_3 = -8$ $a_{20} = -2^{20}$ Pattern: <u>   multiply by 2   </u>

21. $a_n = 2^{-n}$ $a_1 = \dfrac{1}{2}$ $a_2 = \dfrac{1}{4}$ $a_3 = \dfrac{1}{8}$ $a_{20} = \dfrac{1}{2^{20}}$ Pattern: <u>   multiply by $\dfrac{1}{2}$ </u>

22. $a_n = -2^{-n}$ $a_1 = -\dfrac{1}{2}$ $a_2 = -\dfrac{1}{4}$ $a_3 = -\dfrac{1}{8}$ $a_{20} = -\dfrac{1}{2^{20}}$ Pattern: ___multiply by $\dfrac{1}{2}$___

23. $a_n = (-2)^n$ $a_1 = -2$ $a_2 = 4$ $a_3 = -8$ $a_{20} = 2^{20}$ Pattern: ___multiply by -2_____

24. $a_n = 2^{n-1}$ $a_1 = 1$ $a_2 = 2$ $a_3 = 4$ $a_{20} = 2^{19}$ Pattern: ___multiply by 2_____

25. $a_n = 2^{n+2}$ $a_1 = 8$ $a_2 = 16$ $a_3 = 32$ $a_{20} = 2^{22}$ Pattern: ___multiply by 2_____

26. $a_n = 3 \times 2^n$ $a_1 = 6$ $a_2 = 12$ $a_3 = 24$ $a_{20} = 3 \cdot 2^{20}$ Pattern: ___multiply by 2_____

27. $a_n = -5 \times 2^{n-1}$ $a_1 = -5$ $a_2 = -10$ $a_3 = -20$ $a_{20} = -5 \cdot 2^{19}$ Pattern: ___multiply by 2____

28. $a_n = 5 \times 2^{1-n}$ $a_1 = 5$ $a_2 = \dfrac{5}{2}$ $a_3 = \dfrac{5}{4}$ $a_{20} = \dfrac{5}{2^{19}}$ Pattern: ___multiply by $\dfrac{1}{2}$_____

29. $a_n = (-3)^{2-n}$ $a_1 = -3$ $a_2 = 1$ $a_3 = -\dfrac{1}{3}$ $a_{20} = \dfrac{1}{3^{18}}$ Pattern: ___multiply by $-\dfrac{1}{3}$_____

30. $a_n = 2 \times (-3)^n$ $a_1 = -6$ $a_2 = 18$ $a_3 = -54$ $a_{20} = 2 \cdot 3^{20}$ Pattern: ___multiply by -3_____

31. $a_n = 2 \times (-5)^{n-1}$ $a_1 = 2$ $a_2 = -10$ $a_3 = 50$ $a_{20} = 2 \cdot (-5)^{19}$ Pattern: ___multiply by -5_

32. $a_n = (-3)^{n+1}$ $a_1 = 9$ $a_2 = -27$ $a_3 = 81$ $a_{20} = (-3)^{21}$ Pattern: ___multiply by -3_____

33. $a_n = 1 + 5^{n-2}$ $a_1 = \dfrac{6}{5}$ $a_2 = 2$ $a_3 = 6$ $a_{20} = 1 + 5^{18}$ Pattern: ___different_____

34. $a_n = 3 \times 2^n$ $a_1 = 6$ $a_2 = 12$ $a_3 = 24$ $a_{20} = 3 \cdot 2^{20}$ Pattern: ___multiply by 2_____

35. $a_n = -5 \times 2^{n-1}$ $a_1 = -5$ $a_2 = -10$ $a_3 = -20$ $a_{20} = -5 \cdot 2^{19}$ Pattern: ___multiply by 2_____

36. $a_n = 2 \times 3^n$ $a_1 = 6$ $a_2 = 18$ $a_3 = 54$ $a_{20} = 2 \cdot 3^{20}$ Pattern: ___multiply by 3_____

37. $a_n = 5^{n-2} + 3$ $a_1 = \dfrac{16}{5}$ $a_2 = 4$ $a_3 = 8$ $a_{20} = 3 + 5^{-18}$ Pattern: ___different_____

38. $a_n = (-3)^n$ $a_1 = -3$ $a_2 = 9$ $a_3 = -27$ $a_{20} = 3^{20}$ Pattern: ___multiply by -3_____

39. $a_n = 2 \times (-3)^n$ $a_1 = -6$ $a_2 = 18$ $a_3 = -54$ $a_{20} = 2 \cdot 3^{20}$ Pattern: ___multiply by -3_____

40. $a_n = 2 \times (-5)^{n-1}$ $a_1 = 2$ $a_2 = -10$ $a_3 = 50$ $a_{20} = 2 \cdot (-5)^{19}$ Pattern: ___multiply by -5_____

41. $a_n = (-3)^{n+1}$ $a_1 = 9$ $a_2 = -27$ $a_3 = 81$ $a_{20} = -3^{21}$ Pattern: ___multiply by -3_____

42. $a_n = 1 + 5^{n-2}$ $a_1 = \dfrac{6}{5}$ $a_2 = 2$ $a_3 = 6$ $a_{20} = 1 + 5^{18}$ Pattern: ___different_____

43. The sequences in which the pattern is add/subtract a number are called

    Arithmetic

44. The sequences in which the pattern is multiply/divide (pay attention that dividing by a is the same as multiplying by the inverse) a number are called Geometric

45. (T/**F**) Arithmetic and Geometric sequences are most of the sequences that exist.

46. Give an example of a convergent geometric sequence: 200, 100, 50, 25…

47. Give an example of a divergent geometric sequence: 7, 21, 63, 189…

Arithmetic sequence (Pattern – Add a constant):

General term: $a_n = a_1 + (n-1)d$

Sum: $\quad S_n = \dfrac{n}{2}(2a_1 + (n-1)d)$

Geometric Sequence (Pattern – multiply by a constant):

General term: $a_n = a_1 r^{n-1}$

Sum: $\quad S_n = \dfrac{a(r^n - 1)}{r - 1}$

Given the following sequences:

a. For each one write: arithmetic, geometric convergent, geometric divergent or neither, the <u>next term</u> and their <u>general term</u> (in case they are geometric or arithmetic only).

b. Try to write the general term of the other sequences as well.

48. 1, 2, 3, 4, _5_

$a_n = 1 + (n-1)1$, Arithmetic

$a_n = n$

49. 1, 2, 4, 8, _16_

$a_n = 2^{n-1}$, Geometric

50. 1, 3, 5, 7, ___

$a_n = 1 + (n-1)2$, Arithmetic

$a_n = -1 + 2n$

51. 1, 3, 9, 27, _81_

$a_n = 3^{n-1}$, Geometric

52. 4, 6, 9, 13,5, _20.25_

$a_n = 4\left(\dfrac{3}{2}\right)^{n-1}$, Geometric

53. 4, 1, –2, –5, _–8_

$a_n = 4 + (n-1)(-3)$, Arithmetic

$a_n = 7 - 3n$

54. 5, 0, –4, –7, ___

Neither

55. 10, 1000, 100000, _10000000_

$a_n = 10 \cdot 100^{n-1}$, Geometric

56. 30, 10, $\dfrac{10}{3}$, $\dfrac{10}{9}$, $\dfrac{10}{27}$

$a_n = 30 \cdot \left(\dfrac{1}{3}\right)^{n-1}$, Geometric

57. 2, 10, 50, 250, _1250_

$a_n = 2 \cdot 5^{n-1}$, Geometric

58. 2, 102, 202, 302, _402_

$a_n = 2 + (n-1)100$, Arithmetic

$a_n = -98 + 100n$

59. 1, –1, 1, –1, <u>1</u>

$a_n = (-1)^{n-1}$, Geometric

60. –2, 2, –2, 2, <u>–2</u>

$a_n = -2(-1)^{n-1}$, Geometric

61. 3, –6, 12, –24, <u>48</u>

$a_n = 3(-2)^{n-1}$, Geometric

62. –8, 4, –2, 1, $\underline{\left(-\dfrac{1}{2}\right)}$

$a_n = -8\left(-\dfrac{1}{2}\right)^{n-1}$, Geometric

63. 5, 1, $\dfrac{1}{5}$, $\dfrac{1}{25}$, $\dfrac{1}{\underline{125}}$

$a_n = 5\left(\dfrac{1}{5}\right)^{n-1}$, Geometric

64. 100, 10, 1, $\dfrac{1}{10}$, $\dfrac{1}{\underline{100}}$

$a_n = 100\left(\dfrac{1}{10}\right)^{n-1}$, Geometric

65. $\dfrac{3}{4}$, $\dfrac{3}{8}$, $\dfrac{3}{16}$, $\dfrac{3}{\underline{32}}$

$a_n = \dfrac{3}{4}\left(\dfrac{1}{2}\right)^{n-1}$, Geometric

66. 12, 11, 10, 9, <u>8</u>

$a_n = 12 + (n-1)(-1)$, Arithmetic

$a_n = 13 - n$

67. $\dfrac{4}{9}$, $\dfrac{5}{9}$, $\dfrac{6}{9}$, $\dfrac{7}{\underline{9}}$

$a_n = \dfrac{4}{9} + (n-1)\left(\dfrac{1}{9}\right)$, Arithmetic

$a_n = -98 + 100n$

68. 9, 8, 6, 5, 3, 2, ___

Neither

69. 5, 9, 13, <u>17</u>

$a_n = 5 + (n-1)4$, Arithmetic

$a_n = 1 + 4n$

70. 1, $\dfrac{3}{2}$, $\dfrac{9}{4}$, $\dfrac{27}{8}$, $\dfrac{81}{\underline{16}}$

$a_n = \left(\dfrac{3}{2}\right)^{n-1}$, Geometric

71. 5, $-\dfrac{5}{3}$, $\dfrac{5}{9}$, $-\dfrac{5}{27}$, $\dfrac{5}{81}$

$a_n = 5\left(-\dfrac{1}{3}\right)^{n-1}$, Geometric

72. –1, –2, –3, <u>–4</u>

$a_n = -1 + (n-1)(-1)$, Arithmetic

$a_n = -n$

73. –2, 4, –8, <u>16</u>

$a_n = -2(-2)^{n-1}$, Geometric

74. 70, 20, $\dfrac{40}{7}$, $\dfrac{80}{14}$

$a_n = 70\left(\dfrac{2}{7}\right)^{n-1}$, Geometric

75. 100, 10, 1, $\dfrac{1}{10}$

$a_n = 100\left(\dfrac{1}{10}\right)^{n-1}$, Geometric

76. 100, –10, 1, $\dfrac{-1}{10}$, $\dfrac{1}{100}$

$a_n = 100\left(-\dfrac{1}{10}\right)^{n-1}$, Geometric

77. 3, 24, 192, <u>1536</u>

$a_n = 3 \cdot 8^{n-1}$, Geometric

78. $90, 9, \dfrac{9}{10}, \dfrac{9}{100}$

$a_n = 90 \cdot \left(\dfrac{1}{10}\right)^{n-1}$, Geometric

79. $\dfrac{3}{2}, \dfrac{4}{3}, \dfrac{5}{4}, \dfrac{6}{5}$

Neither, General term:

$a_n = \dfrac{2+n}{1+n}$ Numerator and

denominator are arithmetic.

80. $\dfrac{40}{3}, \dfrac{20}{6}, \dfrac{10}{12}, \dfrac{5}{24}, \dfrac{5}{96}$

$a_n = \dfrac{40}{3}\left(\dfrac{1}{4}\right)^{n-1}$, Geometric

81. $\dfrac{2}{3}, -\dfrac{4}{9}, \dfrac{8}{27}, -\dfrac{16}{81}, \dfrac{32}{243}$

$a_n = \dfrac{2}{3}\left(-\dfrac{2}{3}\right)^{n-1}$, Geometric

82. $-\dfrac{1}{2}, -\dfrac{1}{4}, -\dfrac{1}{8}, -\dfrac{1}{16}, \dfrac{1}{32}$

$a_n = -\dfrac{1}{2}\left(\dfrac{1}{2}\right)^{n-1}$, Geometric

83. $\dfrac{1}{7}, -\dfrac{1}{14}, \dfrac{1}{21}, -\dfrac{1}{28}, \dfrac{1}{35}$

Neither, General term:

$a_n = \dfrac{1}{7n}(-1)^{n-1}$

84. $8, 5, 3, 0,$ ____ ...

Neither

85. $3, \dfrac{3}{4}, \dfrac{3}{16}, \dfrac{3}{64}$

$a_n = 3\left(\dfrac{1}{4}\right)^{n-1}$, Geometric

86. $81, -9, 1, -\dfrac{1}{9}, \dfrac{1}{81}$

$a_n = 81\left(-\dfrac{1}{9}\right)^{n-1}$, Geometric

87. $2, -10, 50, -250$

$a_n = 2(-5)^{n-1}$, Geometric

In each one of the following sequences find the term indicated:

88. $1, 4, 7 ...$ (a_{31}) $\quad a_{31} = 1 + 3 \cdot 30 = 91$

89. $-8, -5, -2 ...$ (a_{37}) $\quad a_{37} = -8 + 3 \cdot 36 = 100$

90. $4, -8, 16 ... (a_{15})$ $\quad a_{15} = 4(-2)^{14}$

91. $32, -8, 2 ... (a_{11})$ $\quad a_{37} = 32\left(-\dfrac{1}{4}\right)^{10}$

92. $68, -34, 17 ... (a_9)$ $\quad a_9 = 68\left(-\dfrac{1}{2}\right)^{8} = \dfrac{68}{256}$

279

93. The 4th term of a geometric sequence is 3, the 6th term is $\dfrac{27}{4}$.

a. Find the ratio of the sequence.

$$a_6 = a_4 r^2$$

$$\frac{27}{4} = 3r^2$$

$$r = \pm\frac{3}{2}$$

b. Find a_1

$$a_4 = a_1 r^3$$

$$3 = \pm\left(\frac{3}{2}\right)^3 a_1$$

$$a_1 = \pm\left(\frac{8}{9}\right)$$

c. Find a_{12}

$$a_{12} = \left(\pm\left(\frac{8}{9}\right)\right)\left(\pm\left(\frac{3}{2}\right)^{11}\right) = \frac{3^9}{2^8}$$

d. Sum the first 15 terms.

$$S_{15} = \frac{\left(\pm\left(\frac{8}{9}\right)\right)\left(\left(\pm\left(\frac{3}{2}\right)\right)^{15} - 1\right)}{\pm\left(\frac{3}{2}\right) - 1}$$

94. The 2nd term of a arithmetic sequence is –2, the 6th term is –4.

a. Find the difference of the sequence.

$$a_6 = a_2 + 4d$$

$$-4 = -2 + 4d$$

$$d = -\frac{1}{2}$$

b. Find a_1

$$a_2 = a_1 + d$$

$$-2 = a_1 - \frac{1}{2}$$

$$a_1 = -\frac{3}{2}$$

c. Find a_{12}

$$a_{12} = a_1 + 11d$$

$$a_{12} = -\frac{5}{2} - \frac{11}{2}$$

$$a_{12} = -\frac{16}{2} = -8$$

d. Sum the first 50 terms.

$$S_{50} = \frac{50}{2}\left(\frac{-6}{2} + \frac{-49}{2}\right) = -\frac{2750}{4}$$

95. The 10th term of a geometric sequence is 5, the 14th term is $\dfrac{80}{81}$

$$a_{14} = a_{10}r^4$$

a. Find the ratio of the sequence.

$$\frac{80}{81} = 5r^4$$

$$r = \pm\frac{2}{3}$$

$$a_{10} = a_1 r^9$$

b. Find a_1

$$5 = a_1\left(\pm\frac{2}{3}\right)^9$$

$$a_1 = 5\left(\pm\frac{3}{2}\right)^9$$

$$a_{10} = a_7 r^3$$

c. Find a_7

$$5 = a_7\left(\pm\frac{2}{3}\right)^3$$

$$a_1 = 5\left(\pm\frac{3}{2}\right)^3 = \pm\frac{135}{8}$$

d. Sum the first 10 terms.

$$S_{10} = \frac{\left(5\left(\pm\frac{3}{2}\right)^9\right)\left(\left(\pm\left(\frac{2}{3}\right)\right)^{10}-1\right)}{\pm\left(\frac{2}{3}\right)-1}$$

96. The 7th term of a arithmetic sequence is 120, the 16th term is 201.

$$a_{16} = a_7 + 9d$$

a. Find the difference of the sequence.

$$201 = 120 + 9d$$

$$d = 9$$

b. Find a_1

$$a_7 = a_1 + 6d$$

$$a_1 = 66$$

c. Find a_{12} $\quad a_{12} = a_1 + 11d = 66 + 99 = 165$

d. Sum the first 50 terms. $\quad S_{50} = \dfrac{50}{2}(132 + 49\cdot9) = 14325$

97. All the terms in a geometric sequence are positive. The first term is 7 and the 3rd term is 28.

$$a_3 = a_1 r^2$$

a. Find the common ratio. $\quad 28 = 7r^2$ $\quad$ Positive since all terms are positive.

$$r = +2$$

b. Find the sum of the first 14 terms. $\quad S_{14} = \dfrac{7\left(2^{14}-1\right)}{2-1} = 114681$

98. The fifth term of an arithmetic sequence is –20 and the twelfth term is –44.

$$a_{12} = a_5 + 7d$$

    a. Find the common difference.

$$d = -\frac{24}{7}$$

$$a_5 = a_1 + 4d$$

    b. Find the first term of the sequence. $\quad -20 = a_1 - \frac{24}{7} \cdot 4$

$$a_1 = -\frac{44}{7}$$

    c. Calculate eighty–seventh term. $\quad a_{87} = a_1 + 86d = -\frac{44}{7} - 86 \cdot \frac{24}{7} = -\frac{2108}{7}$

    d. Sum of the first 150 terms. $\quad S_{150} = \frac{150}{2}(-\frac{88}{7} + 149 \cdot \frac{24}{7}) = \frac{261600}{7}$

99. Sum the following sequences:

    a. $3 + 6 + 9 + 12 + \ldots + 69 =$

First find the number of terms using general term $69 = 3 + (n-1)3; n = 23$

Now, sum the 23 terms: $S_{23} = \frac{23}{2}(6 + 22 \cdot 3) = 828$

    b. $6 + 14 + 22 + 30 + \ldots + 54 =$

First find the number of terms using general term $54 = 6 + (n-1)8; n = 7$

Now, sum the 7 terms: $S_7 = \frac{7}{2}(12 + 6 \cdot 8) = 210$

    c. $5 + \frac{5}{3} + \frac{5}{9} + \ldots =$ $\qquad S_\infty = \frac{a_1(r^\infty - 1)}{r - 1} = \frac{5\left(\left(\frac{1}{3}\right)^\infty - 1\right)}{\left(\frac{1}{3}\right) - 1} = \frac{-5}{\left(-\frac{2}{3}\right)} = -\frac{15}{2}$

Attention that $\left(\frac{1}{3}\right)^\infty \approx 0$

    d. $1 + 2 + 3 + 4 + \ldots + 158 =$

First find the number of terms using general term $158 = 1 + (n-1)1; n = 158$

Now, sum the 158 terms: $S_{158} = \frac{158}{2}(2 + 157 \cdot 1) = 12561$

    e. $9 + 18 + 27 + 36 + \ldots + 900 =$

First find the number of terms using general term $900 = 9 + (n-1)9; n = 100$

Now, sum the 100 terms: $S_{100} = \frac{100}{2}(18 + 99 \cdot 9) = 45450$

f. $80 + 20 + 5 + \ldots = S_\infty = \dfrac{a_1(r^\infty - 1)}{r - 1} = \dfrac{80\left(\left(\frac{1}{4}\right)^\infty - 1\right)}{\left(\frac{1}{4}\right) - 1} = \dfrac{-80}{\left(-\frac{3}{4}\right)} = \dfrac{320}{3}$

Attention that $\left(\dfrac{1}{4}\right)^\infty \approx 0$

100. In a theatre there are 20 seats in the first row, 23 in the 2nd, 26 in the 3rd etc. There are 40 rows in the theatre. Find the total number of seats available.

20, 23, 26 … Arithmetic

$S_{40} = \dfrac{40}{2}(40 + 39 \cdot 3) = 3140\, seats$

101. A ball bounces on the floor. It is released from a height of 160 cm. After the 1st bounce it reaches a height of 120 cm and 90 cm after the 2nd. If the patterns continue find:

   a. The height the ball will reach after the 6th bounce.

   160, 120, 90, … Geometric, $r = \dfrac{120}{160} = \dfrac{90}{120} = \dfrac{3}{4}$

   $a_n = 160 \cdot \left(\dfrac{3}{4}\right)^{n-1}$; $a_7 = 160 \cdot \left(\dfrac{3}{4}\right)^6 = \dfrac{3645}{128} \approx 28.5\, cm$

   Attention that a_7 corresponds to height <u>after</u> the 6th bounce.

   b. The total distance the ball passed after a <u>long period o time</u>.

   $S_\infty = \dfrac{a_1(r^\infty - 1)}{r - 1} = \dfrac{160\left(\left(\frac{3}{4}\right)^\infty - 1\right)}{\left(\frac{3}{4}\right) - 1} = \dfrac{-160}{\left(-\frac{1}{4}\right)} = 640\, cm$

   Attention that $\left(\dfrac{3}{4}\right)^\infty \approx 0$

102. In a certain forest the current population of rabbits is 200 objects. It is know that the population increases by 20% every year.

   a. Find the population of rabbits after a year. $\dfrac{120}{100} \cdot 200 = 240\, rabbits$

   b. Find the population of rabbits after 2 years. $\dfrac{120}{100} \cdot 240 = 288\, rabbits$

   c. What kind of a sequence is it? State the expression for the population after n years. Geometric. $r = \dfrac{120}{100} = \dfrac{6}{5}$ $a_n = 200 \cdot \left(\dfrac{6}{5}\right)^{n-1}$

   d. Find the total number of rabbits after 10 years (assuming none has died).

   $a_{11} = 200 \cdot \left(\dfrac{6}{5}\right)^{10} \approx 1240\, rabbits$

103. In a research it was observed that the number of defective products produced by a machine per year decreases by 10% every year (due to technological improvements). In a certain year the machine made 300 products.

   a. Find the number of defective products produced a year later.

   $$\frac{90}{100} \cdot 300 = 270 \text{ defective}$$

   b. Find the number of defective products produced 2 years later.

   $$\frac{90}{100} \cdot 270 = 243 \text{ defective}$$

   c. What kind of a sequence is it? State the expression for the number of errors committed after n years.

   Geometric. $r = \frac{90}{100} = \frac{9}{10}$ $a_n = 300 \cdot \left(\frac{9}{10}\right)^{n-1}$

   d. Find the <u>total number</u> of bad products produced in the first 8 years.

   $$S_8 = \frac{300\left(\left(\frac{9}{10}\right)^8 - 1\right)}{\left(\frac{9}{10}\right) - 1} \approx 1710 \text{ defective}$$

104. In a certain company the pay scale follows a pattern of an arithmetic sequence (every year). This means:

   a. The salary increases by a certain % every year (True/**False**), explain.

   <u>Since the amount of the increase is fixed, the percentage is not the same one every year. An increase by a percentage corresponds to a geometric sequence.</u>

   b. The salary increases by a certain amount every year (**True**/False), explain

   <u>Since the amount of the increase is fixed, the pattern is identical to an Arithmetic sequence.</u>

1.9. – FINANCIAL APPLICATIONS OF SEQUENCES AND SERIES

COMPOUND INTEREST

1. 1200$ are put in account that gives 2% per year. Calculate the amount of money in the account after:

   a. 1 year. $\text{Amount} = 1200(1.02) = 1224 \text{ \$}$

   b. 2 years. $\text{Amount} = 1200(1.02)^2 = 1248.48 \text{ \$}$

2. To increase an amount A by 5% it should be multiplied by 1.05
3. To increase an amount A by 56% it should be multiplied by 1.56
4. To decrease an amount A by 5% it should be multiplied by 0.95
5. To increase an amount A by 15% it should be multiplied by 1.15
6. To decrease an amount A by 12% it should be multiplied by 0.88
7. To increase an amount A by 230% it should be multiplied by 3.3

8. 1000$ are put in account that takes 5% commission per year. Calculate the amount of money in the account after:

   a. 1 year. $\text{Amount} = 1000(0.95) = 950 \text{ \$}$

   b. 2 years. $\text{Amount} = 1000(0.95)^2 = 902.5 \text{ \$}$

9. 2000$ are being put in a deposit that pays 5% (per year).

   a. Fill the table:

Number of Years	Interest earned at the end of the year	Amount in deposit ($)
0		2000
1	$\frac{5}{100} 2000 = 100$	2100
2	$\frac{5}{100} 2100 = 105$	2205
3	$\frac{5}{100} 2205 = 110.25$	2315.25
4	$\frac{5}{100} 2315.25 = 115.7625$	2431.0125
5	$\frac{5}{100} 2431.0125 = 121.550625$	2552.563125

   b. Observe the numbers in the compound interest column: 2000, 2100, 2205… What kind of a sequence is that? Write its general term.
   Geometric sequence. $a_n = 2000(1.05)^{n-1}$

c. How much money will be in the account after 20 years?

$a_{21} = 2000(1.05)^{20} \approx 5310 \text{ \$}$

Attention that a_{21} corresponds to "after 20 years" as a_1 corresponds to "after 0 years".

d. Discuss the meaning of writing $a_n = a_1 r^{n-1}$ or writing $a_n = a_0 r^n$. Use the exercise as an example.

$a_n = 2000(1.05)^{n-1}$ means a_1 corresponds to "after 0 years" while writing

$a_n = 2000(1.05)^n$ means a_1 corresponds to "after 1 year"

10. A loan of 1200\$ is made at 12% per year compounded semiannually, over 5 years the debt will grow to:

    a. $\$1200(1 + 0.12)^5$
    b. $\$1200(1 + 0.06)^{10}$
    c. $\$1200(1 + 0.6)^{10}$
    d. $\$1200(1 + 0.06)^5$
    e. $\$1200(1 + 0.12)^{10}$

11. A loan of 23200\$ is made at 8% per year compounded quarterly, over 6 years the debt will grow to:

    a. $\$23200(1 + 0.2)^{24}$
    b. $\$23200(1 + 0.08)^6$
    c. $\$23200(1 + 0.02)^{24}$
    d. $\$23200(1 + 0.08)^{24}$
    e. $\$23200(1 + 0.02)^6$

12. A loan of 20\$ is made at 12% per year compounded monthly, over 8 years the debt will grow to:

    a. $\$20(1 + 0.12)^{80}$
    b $\$20(1 + 0.01)^8$
    c. $\$20(1 + 0.012)^{96}$
    d. $\$20(1 + 0.01)^{96}$
    e. $\$20(1 + 0.06)^{12}$

13. A loan of X\$ is made at 12% per year compounded every 4 months, over 5 years the debt will grow to:

    a. $\$X(1 + 0.12)^4$
    b. $\$X(1 + 0.3)^5$
    c. $\$X(1 + 0.12)^{15}$
    d. $\$X(1 + 0.03)^{15}$
    e. $\$X(1 + 0.3)^{15}$

14. A loan of X\$ is made at i% per year compounded every m months, over n years the debt will grow to:

$$Debt = X(1 + \frac{i}{100})^{\frac{12n}{m}}$$

15. Calculate the total amount owing after two years on a loan of 1500$ if the interest rate is 11% compounded

    a. Annually $Amount = 1500(1+\frac{11}{100})^2 \approx 1848\$$

    b. Semiannually $Amount = 1500(1+\frac{11}{200})^4 \approx 1858\$$

    c. Quarterly $Amount = 1500(1+\frac{11}{400})^8 \approx 1864\$$

    d. Monthly $Amount = 1500(1+\frac{11}{1200})^{24} \approx 1867\$$

16. How much will a client have to repay on a loan of 800$ after 2 years, if the 12% interest is compounded annually.

$$Amount = 800(1+\frac{12}{100})^2 = 1003.52\$$$

17. Find the compound interest **earned** by the deposit. Round to the nearest cent. $3000 at 12% compounded semiannually for 10 years

$$AmountObtained = 3000(1+\frac{12}{200})^{20} \approx 9620\$$$

$$AmountEarned = 9620 - 3000 = 6620\$$$

18. How many years will it take to a 100$ to double assuming interest rate is 6%. Compounded semiannually.

$$200 = 100(1+\frac{6}{200})^{2n}$$ So it will take 12 years.

$n \approx 11.7$

19. How many years will it take to a X$ to triple assuming interest rate is 7%. Compounded quarterly

$$3X = X(1+\frac{7}{400})^{4n}$$ So it will take 16 years.

$n \approx 15.8$

20. Find the interest rate given to a certain person in case he made a deposit of 1000$ and obtained 1200$ after 3 years, compounded monthly.

$$1200 = 1000(1+\frac{i}{1200})^{36}$$

$i \approx 6.09$

21. Find the interest rate given to a certain person in case he made a deposit of 2500$ and obtained 3000$ after 10 years, compounded yearly.

$$3000 = 2500(1+\frac{i}{100})^{10}$$

$i \approx 1.84$

ANNUAL DEPRECIATION

1. Depreciation is <u>A decrease in an assets value</u>

2. The value of a car is depreciated by 20% every year. Given its initial price is 10000$, find:
   a. Its value after 1 year. $Value = 10000 \cdot (0.8) = 8000\$$
   b. Its value after 2 years. $Value = 10000 \cdot (0.8)^2 = 6400\$$
   c. Expression for value after n year. $Value = 10000 \cdot (0.8)^n$

3. The value of a flat is depreciated by 12% every year. Given its initial price is 200000$, find:
   a. Its value after 1 year. $Value = 200000 \cdot (0.88) = 176000\$$
   b. Its value after 2 years. $Value = 200000 \cdot (0.88)^2 = 154880\$$
   c. Expression for value after n year. $Value = 200000 \cdot (0.88)^n$

4. Given that the price of a product is 200$ when it's bought and 100$ 4 years later, find the percentage in which it's depreciated per year.
$$100 = 200 \cdot (x)^4$$
$$x \approx 0.841$$
<u>So it is depreciated by approximately 15.9% per year</u>

5. Given that the price of a product is 1400$ when it's bought and 700$ 10 years later, find the percentage in which it's depreciated per year.
$$700 = 1400 \cdot (x)^{10}$$
$$x \approx 0.933$$
<u>So it is depreciated by approximately 6.7% per year</u>

6. The value of a toy is depreciated by 2% every month. Given its current price is 300$, find:
   a. Its value 1 year ago.
   $$300 = x \cdot (0.98)^{12}$$
   $$x \approx 382\$$$
   b. Its value 2 years ago.
   $$300 = x \cdot (0.98)^{24}$$
   $$x \approx 487\$$$
   c. An expression for its value n years ago. $P = \dfrac{300}{(0.98)^{12n}}$
   d. Its initial price assuming it was bought a year and a half ago.
   $$P = \dfrac{300}{(0.98)^{12 \cdot 1.5}}$$
   $$P \approx 432\$$$

2.1. – INTRODUCTION TO STATISTICS

In Statistics we try to obtain some conclusions by observing and/or analyzing data.

1. The set of objects that we are trying to study is called <u>population</u>. the number of elements in the population can be <u>finite</u> or <u>infinite</u>.

2. Usually the <u>population</u> is too big and therefore we obtain a <u>sample</u>.

   This process is called <u>sampling</u>.

3. We use the <u>sample</u> to obtain conclusions about the <u>population</u>.

Types of DATA

1. <u>Categorical</u> data.
2. <u>Numerical</u> data that can be divided to <u>continuous</u> or <u>discrete</u>.

3. <u>Numerical discrete</u> can be counted while <u>numerical continuous</u> data can be <u>measured</u>.

4. Give 3 examples of <u>Categorical</u> data:

   Eye color (blue, green, brown etc.)
   Favorite food (meat, pasta, ice cream etc.)
   Preferred website (whatever.com, whatsup.com etc.)

5. Give 3 examples of <u>numerical discrete</u> data:

   Number of students in a classroom
   Shoe size
   Number of rabbits in the forest

6. Give 3 examples of <u>numerical continuous</u> data:

   Height of people
   Amount of energy in a laser beam
   CO_2 level in the atmosphere

2.2. – FREQUENCY DIAGRAMS & MEASURES OF CENTRAL TENDENCY

1. In a certain math class the following grades were obtained:

    68, 79, 75, 89, 54, 81, 88, 62, 67, 75, 64, 85, 97, 77, 79, 90, 75, 89, 76, 68

    a. State the number of elements in the set: <u>20</u>

    b. What kind of data is this? <u>Numerical discrete</u>
    c. Fill the table:

Grade	Mid – Grade (Mi)	Frequency (fi)	fi · Mi	Cumulative Frequency (Fi)	Fi (%)
51 – 60	55.5	1	55.5	1	5
61 – 70	65.5	5	327.5	6	30
71 – 80	75.5	7	528.5	13	65
81 – 90	85.5	6	513	19	95
91 – 100	95.5	1	95.5	20	100
Total		20	1520		

    d. Is this the only possible choice for the left column of the table? Why? Discuss the advantages and disadvantages of organizing information in such a way.
    <u>No it is not the only possibility. Narrower or wider intervals can be chosen. Narrower interval implies higher accuracy but information may be harder to understand and/or analyze. It also implies more work. Wider interval implies lower level of accuracy but information may be easier to understand and/or analyze. It also implies less work.</u>

    e. Design a new table with a different <u>interval</u>

Grade	Mid – Grade (Mi)	Frequency (fi)	fi · Mi	Cumulative Frequency (Fi)	Fi (%)
51 – 55	53	1	53	1	5
56 – 60	58	0	0	1	5
61 – 65	63	2	126	3	15
66 – 70	68	3	204	6	30
71 – 75	73	3	219	9	45
76 – 80	78	4	312	13	65
81 – 85	83	2	166	15	75
86 – 90	88	4	352	19	95
91 – 95	93	0	0	19	95
96 – 100	98	1	98	20	100
Total		20	1530		

f. Obtain the mean in both cases:

$$\text{Table 1 } \mu = \frac{1520}{20} = 76 \qquad \text{Table 2 } \mu = \frac{1530}{20} = 76.5$$

g. State a formula for the mean: $\mu = \dfrac{\sum_{n} M_i f_i}{n}$

h. The mean of the <u>population</u> is denoted with the Greek letter mu: $\underline{\mu}$

and typically it is <u>unknown</u>. The mean of the <u>sample</u> is denoted by $\underline{\bar{x}}$

i. State the mode of the set: <u>75</u>

j. Find the modal interval in both cases:

<u>Table 1: 71 – 80</u>   <u>Table 2: 76 – 80, 86 – 90 (Bimodal)</u>

k. Find the Median using the original data: <u>76.5</u>

Since there are 20 elements, the mean of elements 10 and 11 is the median. First elements must be put in order:

54 62 64 67 68 68 75 75 75 **76 77** 79 79 81 85 88 89 89 90 97

<u>So median is 76.5</u>

l. Find the median using the tables, discuss your answer. The median is the center of interval where F% ≥ 50% for the first time.

<u>Table 1: 75.5</u>   <u>Table 2: 78</u>

m. In general this method of organizing information is called <u>grouping</u>.

n. The 1st column is called <u>class</u> with upper interval boundary and

<u>lower</u> interval boundary.

o. The 2nd column is called <u>Mid - Class</u>

p. On the following grid paper sketch the corresponding points.

OGIVE

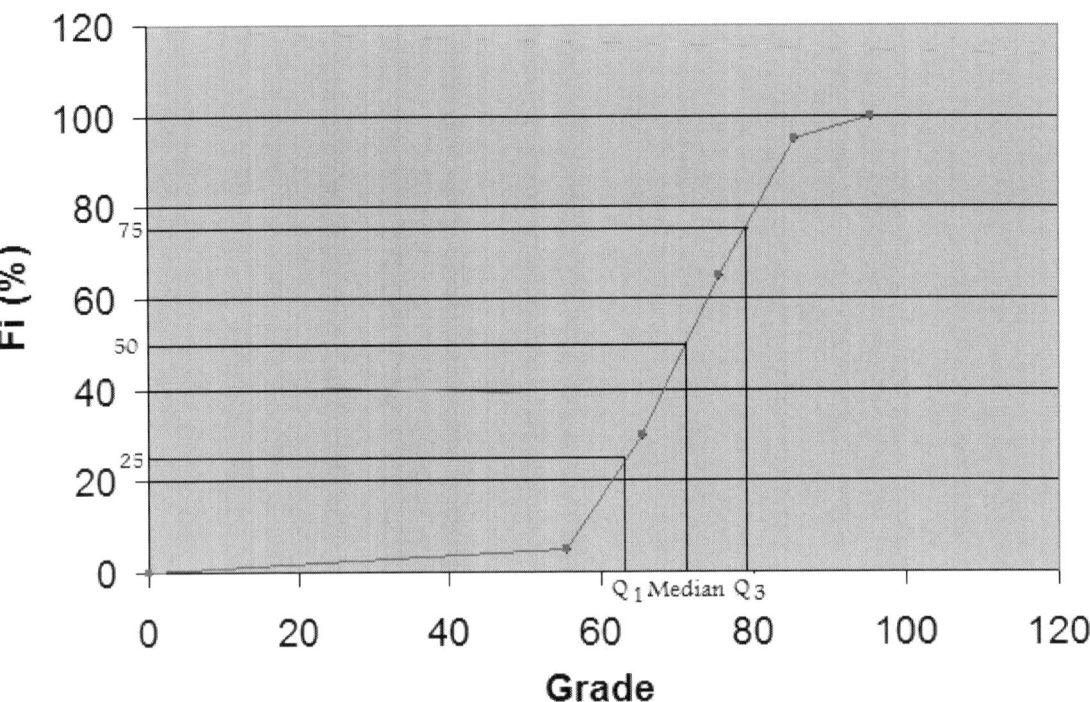

q. This graph is called cumulative frequency curve or <u>Ogive</u>

r. Find the median using the graph: ~ 72

s. Find the first quartile (Q_1) using the graph: Q_1 = ~ 64

t. Find the first quartile (Q_1) using the original data: Q_1 = 68

u. Find the third quartile (Q_3) using the graph: Q_3 = ~ 79

v. Find the first quartile (Q_3) using the original data: Q_3 = 86.5

w. Find P_{30} using the graph: ~ 67 Find P_{65} using the graph: ~ 75

x. The <u>Inter Quartile Range</u> is in general $Q_3 - Q_1$ in this case 86.5–68= 18.5

y. Find the answers to all the different parts using your GDC.

2. In a certain class the following heights (in m) of students were collected:

1.77, 1.60, 1.89, 1.54, 1.77, 1.65, 1.86, 1.51, 1.67, 1.94, 1.73, 1.70, 1.66

   a. State the number of elements in the set: 13

   b. What kind of data is this? Numerical continuous
   c. Fill the table:

Height	Mid – Height (Mi)	Frequency (fi)	fi · Mi	Cumulative Frequency (Fi)	Fi (%)
[1.50 , 1.60)	1.55	2	3.1	2	15.4
[1.60 , 1.70)	1.65	4	6.6	6	46.2
[1.70 , 1.80)	1.75	4	7	10	76.9
[1.80 , 1.90)	1.85	2	3.7	12	92.3
[1.90 , 2.00)	1.95	1	1.95	13	100
Total			22.35		

   d. Obtain the mean: $\mu = \dfrac{22.35}{13} \approx 1.72m$

   e. State the mode of the set: 1.77m

   f. Find the modal interval: bimodal, [1.60 – 1.70), [1.70– 1.80)

   g. Find the Median using the original data: We order the data:

   1.51 1.54 1.60 1.65 1.66 1.67 **1.70** 1.73 1.77 1.77 1.86 1.89 1.94

   There are 13 terms so the median is the 7th, 1.70m

   h. Find the median using the table, discuss your answer.

   The median according to table is the centre of the interval in which Fi% is greater than 50% for the first time. The interval is [1.70– 1.80) so median 1.75.

   i. On the following grid paper sketch the corresponding points.

OGIVE

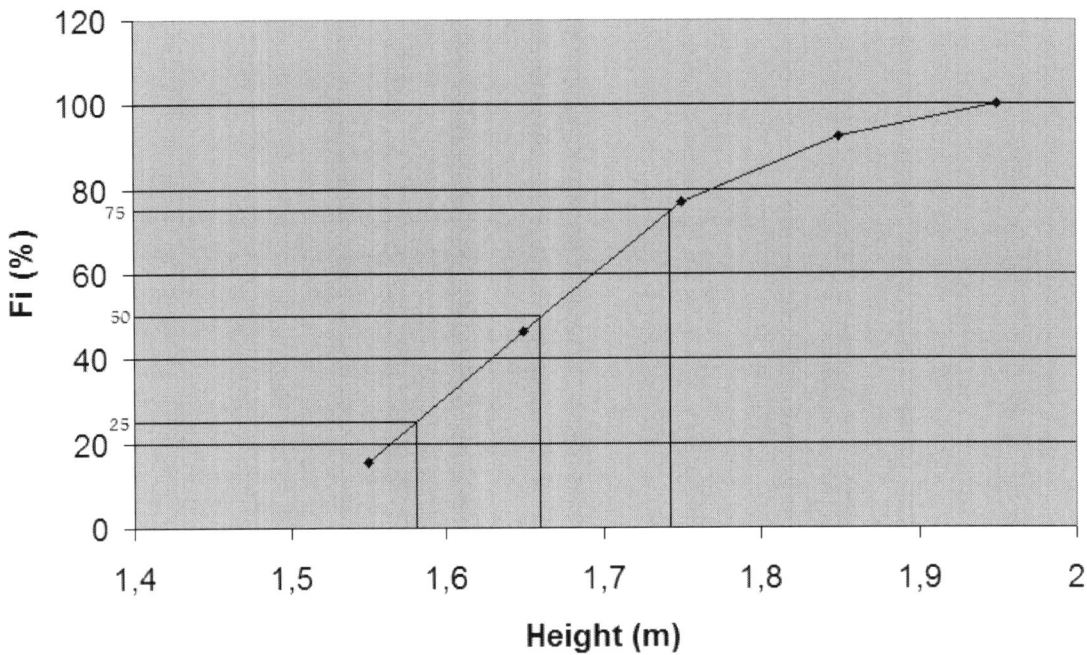

Height (m)

j. This graph is called cumulative frequency curve or <u>ogive</u>

k. Find the median using the graph: $\sim 1.66m$

l. Find the first quartile (Q_1) using the graph: $Q_1 = \sim 1.58m$

m. Find the first quartile (Q_1) using the original data: $Q_1 = \underline{1.625m}$

   We use the ordered data; the middle of the first half of data is 1.625m

   1.51 1.54 **1.60 1.65** 1.66 1.67 <u>1.70</u> 1.73 1.77 1.77 1.86 1.89 1.94

n. Find the third quartile (Q_3) using the graph: $Q_3 = \sim 1.74m$

o. Find the first quartile (Q_3) using the original data: $Q_3 = \underline{1.815m}$

   We use the ordered data; the middle of the second half of data is 1.815m

   1.51 1.54 <u>1.60 1.65</u> 1.66 1.67 <u>1.70</u> 1.73 1.77 **1.77 1.86** 1.89 1.94

p. Find P_{20} using the graph: $\sim 1.67m$ Find P_{80} using the graph: $\sim 1.78m$

q. The <u>Inter Quartile Range</u> is in general $\underline{Q_3 - Q_1}$ in this case $\underline{1.815 - 1.625}$ $= \underline{0.190m}$

r. Find the answers to all the different parts using your GDC.

3. In a certain class students eye color was collected:

Brown, Black, Brown, Blue, Brown, Blue, Green, Brown, Black, Green

a. State the number of elements in the set: <u>10</u>

b. What kind of data is this? <u>Categorical</u>
c. Fill the table:

Eye Color	Mid – Color (Mi)	Frequency (fi)	Fi x Mi	Cumulative Frequency (Fi)	Fi (%)
Brown	N/A	4	N/A	N/A	N/A
Blue	N/A	2	N/A	N/A	N/A
Green	N/A	2	N/A	N/A	N/A
Black	N/A	2	N/A	N/A	N/A
Total	N/A	10	N/A	N/A	N/A

d. Obtain the mean: <u>N/A</u>

e. State the mode of the set: <u>Brown</u>

f. Find the modal interval: <u>N/A</u>

g. Find the Median using the original data: <u>N/A</u>

h. Find the median using the table, discuss your answer. <u>N/A</u>

i. Find the answers to all the different parts using your GDC. <u>N/A</u>

j. Represent the information in a histogram:

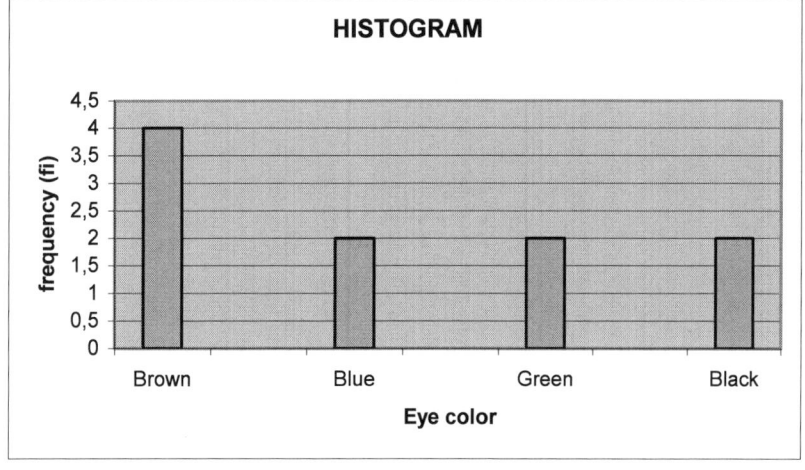

295

BOX PLOT

1.

2. The results for 100 m dash competition are displayed in the following diagram:

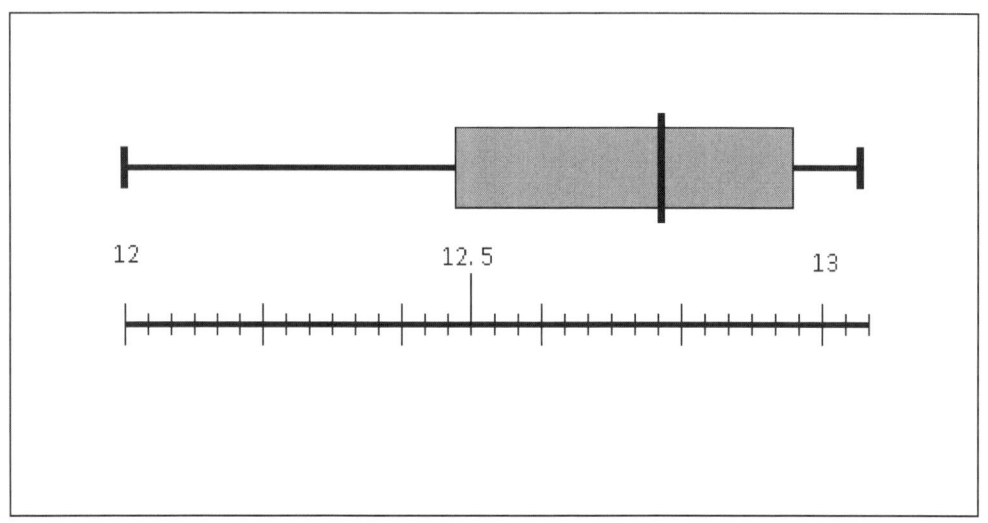

Answer:

   a. Min = <u>12</u>   Max = <u>13.1</u>

   b. Q_1 = <u>12.5</u> Q_2 = Med = <u>12.8</u> Q_3 = <u>13.0</u>

   c. Range = <u>1.1</u>

   d. Inter quartile range = <u>0.5</u>

3. Given that in a certain classroom the heights of the students in cm are: 168, 178, 166, 191, 188, 181, 174, 159, 179, 173, 171, 166, 185, 184, 169. Draw a box-and-whisker plot using the graph below.

Using GDC:

Min = 159cm Q$_1$ = 168cm Q$_2$ = Med = 174cm Q$_3$ = 184cm Max = 191cm

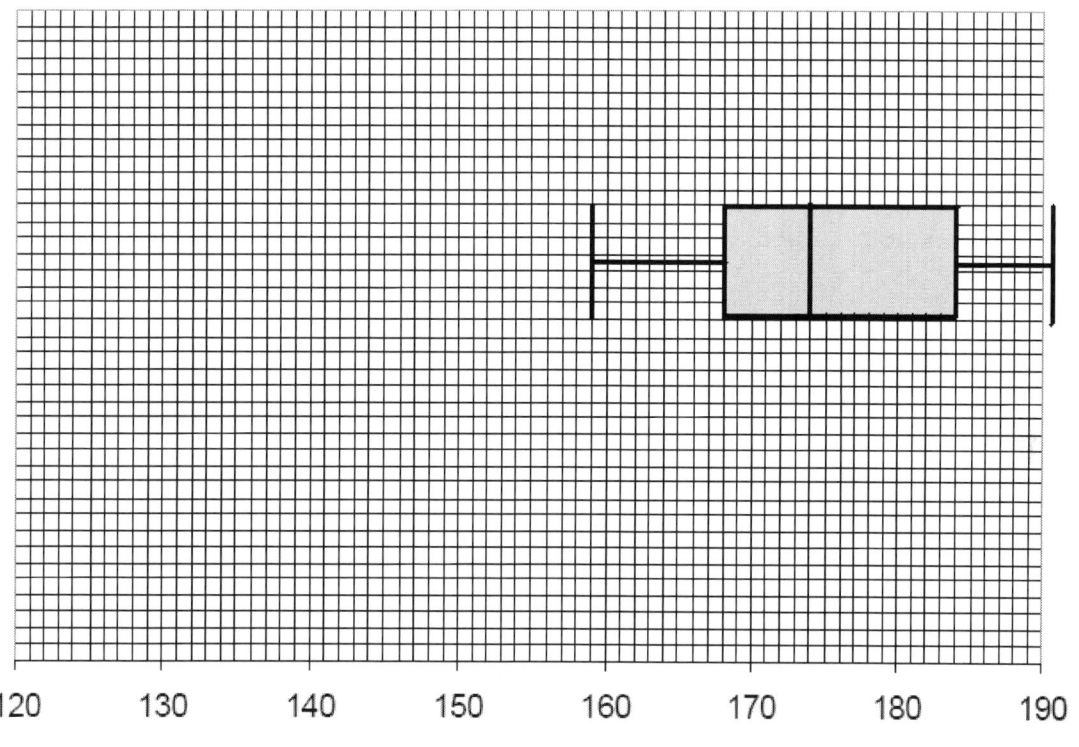

| 120 | 130 | 140 | 150 | 160 | 170 | 180 | 190 |

height in cm

4. In a factory a few machines are being classified according to the number of defective products produced. The following data was collected:

Machine	A	B	C	D	E	F	G	H	I
Number of defective products	0	2	4	1	5	2	1	3	2

Using GDC:

    a. Mean =2.22   Median = 2   Mode = Machine E

    b. Min = 0   Max = 5

    c. Q$_1$ = 1   Q$_2$ = Med = 2   Q$_3$ = 3.5

    d. Range = 5   Inter quartile range = 2.5

STEM AND LEAF DIAGRAMS

1. The following stem and leaf diagram gives the heights of a group of high school students (in cm):

Introducing all the heights into GDC: 157, 157, 159, 164 …

Stem	Leaf
15	7 7 9
16	4 5 6 7 7 8
17	1 3 3 4 8 8
18	2 3 4 8 9 9
19	0 1 3

    a. Find the number of students in the classroom <u>24</u>

    b. Mean =<u>175cm</u> Median = <u>174cm</u> Mode = <u>157, 167,178,189 cm</u>

    c. Min = <u>157cm</u>   Max = <u>193cm</u>

    d. Q_1 = <u>167cm</u> Q_2 = Med = <u>174cm</u> Q_3 = <u>186cm</u>

    e. Range = <u>36cm</u>   Inter quartile range = <u>19cm</u>

    f. What percentage of students is less than 165cm tall? $\dfrac{4}{24} \approx 16.6\%$

2. The following stem and leaf diagram gives the grades of a group of high school students in math:

Introducing all the grades into GDC: 51, 53, 55, 55, 58, 60 …

Stem	Leaf
5	1 3 5 5 8
6	0 1 3 5 6 6 7
7	1 3 4 7 8
8	0 1 1 3 7 8 8
9	2 6 8

    a. Find the number of students in the classroom <u>27</u>

    b. Mean = <u>72.9</u> Median = <u>73</u> Mode = 55, 66, 81, 88

    c. Min = <u>51</u> Max = <u>98</u>

    d. Q_1 = <u>61</u> Q_2 = Med = <u>73</u> Q_3 = <u>83</u>

    e. Range = <u>47</u>   Inter quartile range = <u>22</u>

    f. 60 is the passing grade in the class room. How many students failed? <u>5</u>

    g. What percentage of students obtained 85 or more? $\dfrac{6}{27} \approx 22.2\%$

2.3. – MEASURES OF DISPERSION

1. In a certain Biology test the following results were obtained: 80, 80, 80, 80,

    a. Obtain the mean: $\mu = \underline{80}$

    b. Represent the results using a histogram:

    c. The standard deviation of a set of numbers is defined by:

    $$\sigma = \sqrt{\frac{\sum_i f_i(x_i - \mu)^2}{n}} = \sqrt{\frac{f_1(x_1 - \mu)^2 + f_2(x_2 - \mu)^2 + ...}{n}}$$

    In this case

    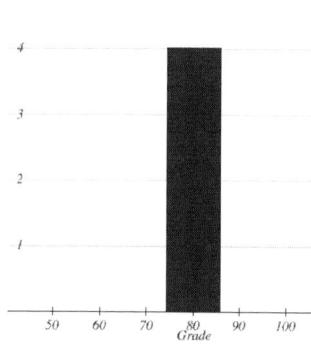

    $$\sigma = \sqrt{\frac{1(80-80)^2 + 1(80-80)^2 + 1(80-80)^2 + 1(80-80)^2}{4}} = 0$$

    d. How spread is this group of grades? <u>It is not spread at all, that means 0 standard deviation.</u>

2. In a certain Physics test the following results were obtained: 70, 80, 80, 90

    a. Obtain the mean: $\mu = \underline{80}$

    b. Represent the results using a histogram:

    c. The standard deviation of a set of numbers is defined by:

    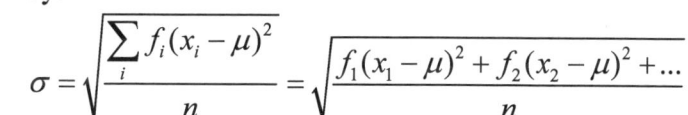

    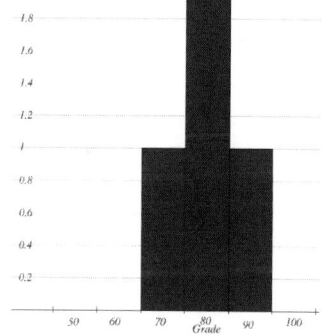

    In this case $\sigma = \sqrt{\dfrac{1(70-80)^2 + 2(80-80)^2 + 1(90-80)^2}{4}} = \dfrac{\sqrt{200}}{2} \approx 7.07$

    d. How spread is this group of grades? Is it more spread than the previous one?

    <u>As can be seen both distributions have the same mean but the 2nd one is more spread, its S.D. is approximately 7.07.</u>

3. In a certain math class the following grades were obtained:

   68, 79, 75, 89, 54, 81, 88, 62, 67, 75, 64, 85, 97, 77, 79, 90, 75, 89, 76, 68

   a. State the number of elements in the set: <u>20</u>
   b. What kind of data is this? <u>Numerical discrete</u>
   c. Fill the table:

Grade	Mid – Grade (Mi)	Frequency (fi)	fi · Mi	$(Mi - \mu)^2$	$fi(Mi - \mu)^2$
51 – 60	55.5	1	55.5	$(55.5 - 76)^2$	$1(55.5 - 76)^2$
61 – 70	65.5	5	327.5	$(65.5 - 76)^2$	$5(65.5 - 76)^2$
71 – 80	75.5	7	528.5	$(75.5 - 76)^2$	$7(75.5 - 76)^2$
81 – 90	85.5	6	513	$(85.5 - 76)^2$	$6(85.5 - 76)^2$
91 – 100	95.5	1	95.5	$(95.5 - 76)^2$	$1(95.5 - 76)^2$
Total		20	1520		1895

   d. Obtain the mean: μ = <u>76</u>

   e. The numbers in the 6th column give us an idea about the <u>contribution</u> of each <u>interval</u> to the spread of the data.

   f. The sum of the numbers in the 6th column gives us an idea about the <u>total spread</u> of the data. In case this number is 0 it means that <u>the data is not spread at all (like in example 1)</u> for example:

   g. Use the table to find the Variance:
   $$Variance = \sigma^2 = \frac{\sum_i f_i(x_i - \mu)^2}{n} = \frac{1895}{20} = 94.75$$

   h. Use the table to find the Standard Deviation S.D.:
   $$S.D. = \sigma = \sqrt{\frac{\sum_i f_i(x_i - \mu)^2}{n}} = \sqrt{\frac{1895}{20}} \approx 9.73$$

   i. Write down the formula for the Variance of a population (σ^2): <u>see part g.</u>

   j. Write down the formula for the SD of a population (σ): <u>see part h.</u>

   k. Write down the difference between μ and $\bar{x}$: <u>μ stands for the mean of the population, $\bar{x}$ stands for the mean of a sample.</u>

   l. Write down the difference between σ and S_x: <u>σ stands for the S.D. of the population, S_x stands for the S.D. of a sample.</u>

4. In a certain class the following heights (in m) of students were collected:

1.77, 1.60, 1.89, 1.54, 1.77, 1.65, 1.86, 1.51, 1.67, 1.94, 1.73, 1.70, 1.66

    a. State the number of elements in the set: <u>13</u>
    b. What kind of data is this? <u>Numerical continuous</u>
    c. Fill the table:

Height	Mid – Height (M_i)	Frequency (f_i)	$F_i \cdot M_i$	$(M_i - \mu)^2$	$f_i(M_i - \mu)^2$
$[1.50 - 1.60)$	1.55	2	3.1	$(1.55 - 1.72)^2$	$2(1.55 - 1.72)^2$
$[1.60 - 1.70)$	1.65	4	6.6	$(1.65 - 1.72)^2$	$4(1.65 - 1.72)^2$
$[1.70 - 1.80)$	1.75	4	7	$(1.75 - 1.72)^2$	$4(1.75 - 1.72)^2$
$[1.80 - 1.90)$	1.85	2	3.7	$(1.85 - 1.72)^2$	$2(1.85 - 1.72)^2$
$[1.90 - 2.00)$	1.95	1	1.95	$(1.95 - 1.72)^2$	$1(1.95 - 1.72)^2$
Total			22.35		0.1677

    d. Obtain the mean: $\mu = \dfrac{22.35}{13} \approx 1.72m$

    e. The numbers in the 6th column give us an idea about the <u>contribution</u> of each <u>interval</u> to the spread of the data.

    f. The sum of the numbers in the 6th column gives us an idea about the <u>total spread</u> of the data. In case this number is 0 it means that <u>the data is not spread at all (like in example 1)</u> for example:

    g. Use the table to find the Variance:
$$Variance = \sigma^2 = \frac{\sum_i f_i(x_i - \mu)^2}{n} = \frac{0.1677}{13} = 0.0129m^2$$

    h. Use the table to find the Standard Deviation (S.D.):

$$S.D. = \sigma = \sqrt{\frac{\sum_i f_i(x_i - \mu)^2}{n}} = \sqrt{\frac{0.1677}{13}} \approx 0.114m$$

    i. Find the answers to all the different parts using your GDC.

5. The weights in kg of 6 different classes (A, B, C, D, E, F) was collected and represented in the following histograms:

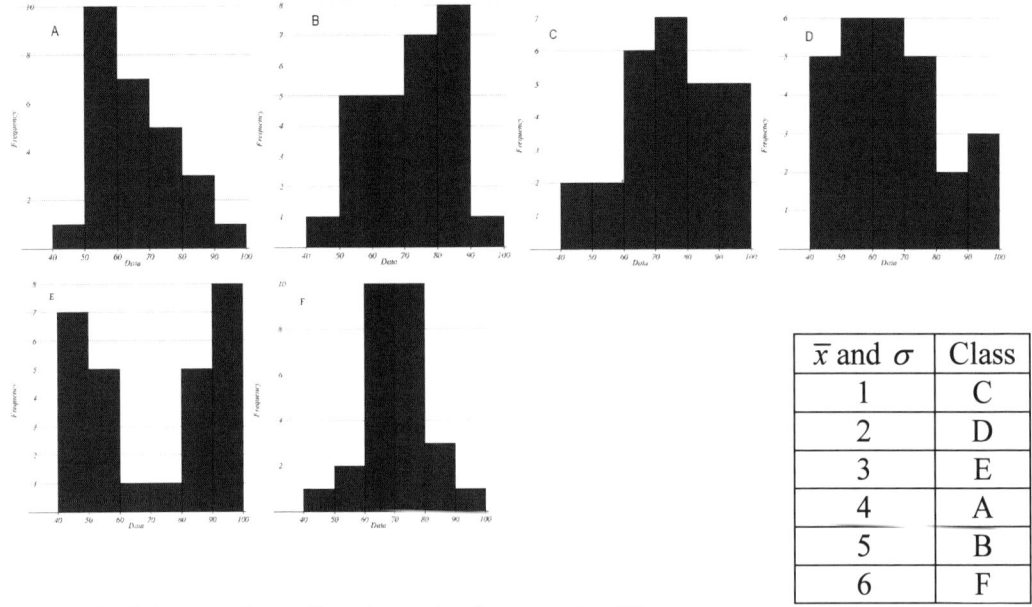

$\bar{x}$ and σ	Class
1	C
2	D
3	E
4	A
5	B
6	F

a. Find the number of students in the sample: <u>27</u>
b. Which distribution will the highest SD: <u>E (corresponds to 3)</u>
c. Which distribution will the lowest SD: <u>F (corresponds to 6)</u>

6. In a certain class students eye color was collected:

Brown, Black, Brown, Blue, Brown, Blue, Green, Brown, Black, Green

a. State the number of elements in the set: <u>10</u>
b. What kind of data is this? <u>Categorical</u>
c. Fill the table:

Eye Color	Mid – Color (Mi)	Frequency (fi)	Fi · Mi
Brown	N/A	4	N/A
Blue	N/A	2	N/A
Green	N/A	2	N/A
Black	N/A	2	N/A
Total	N/A	10	N/A

d. What can you say about the measures of spread in this case?

<u>There is no meaning to spread in case of categorical data.</u>

3.1. – SET THEORY

1. A set is <u>a collection of different objects</u>

2. Give 3 examples of sets:

   a. {chair, table, shelf}
   b. {1, 2, 3…}
   c. {Jeff, Ron, Alex, …}

3. Consider the set {2, 4, 6, …}

   a. This is the set of <u>even numbers</u>. The next element is <u>8</u>

   b. In this set the number of elements is <u>infinite</u>. It is an <u>infinite</u> set

4. Consider the set {1, 8, 27, …}

   a. This is the set of <u>perfect cubes</u>. The next element is <u>64</u>

   b. In this set the number of elements is <u>infinite</u>. It is an <u>infinite</u> set

5. Consider the set {Asia, Africa, …}

   a. This is the set of <u>continents</u>. The next element is <u>America</u>.

   b. In this set the number of elements is <u>6</u>. It is a <u>finite</u> set

6. A **subset** is <u>a set such that each of its elements is contained in a bigger (or equal) set</u>. It is denoted by $A \subseteq B$

7. Given the set L = {A, B, C}

    a. State all the possible subsets of L. include the empty set.

    <u>L1 = {A, B, C}</u>

    <u>L2 = {A, B}</u>

    <u>L3 = {A, C}</u>

    <u>L4 = {B, C}</u>

    <u>L5 = {A}</u>

    <u>L6 = {B}</u>

    <u>L7 = {C}</u>

    <u>L8 = {}</u>

    b. All the subsets except <u>L1</u> are called **proper subsets denoted by** $A \subset B$

    c. Explain the difference between a subset and a proper subset.

    <u>A proper subset is smaller than the original set, a subset may be equal (like L1)</u>

    d. $A \not\subset B$ means <u>not a proper subset</u>

    e. <u>$A \not\subseteq B$</u> means that A is NOT a subset of B

8. M is the set of perfect square smaller than a 100.

    a. List the elements of M <u>{1, 4, 9, 16, 25, 36, 49, 64, 81}</u>

    b. List the subset Q of even numbers in M <u>{4, 16, 36, 64}</u>

9. N is the set of prime numbers between 10 and 30.

    a. List the elements of M <u>{11, 13, 17, 19, 23, 29}</u>

    b. List the subset Q of even numbers in M <u>{}</u>

10. The **universal set** is particular for each problem and

contains all the relevant objects for the problem. Usually it is

denoted by the letter U.

11. The universal set for the students in the classroom is

U = {_____, _____, _____, _____, ...} fill the names of the students in your
classroom.

12. Given the sets U = {John, Raquel, Felix, Shan, Mila, Jessy, Pamela} and the
subset of U: B = {Shan, Mila}.

State the complement of the set B' = {John, Raquel, Felix, Jessy, Pamela}

13. The **complement of a** set A is the set that contains all the elements of U that
are not in A.

14. The **intersection** of 2 sets is the set that contains all the elements that belong
to both of them at the same time. It is denoted by $A \cap B$.

15. The **union** of 2 sets is the set that contains all the elements that belong to
either A or B or both. It is denoted by $A \cup B$

16. For example if S = {1, 2, 3, 4, 5, 6, 7, 8, 9} and M = {2, 6, 10, 12}

   a. $S \cap M = \{2, 6\}$

   b. $S \cup M = \{1, 2, 3, 4, 5, 6, 7, 8, 9, 10, 12\}$

17. Given the sets U = {John, Raquel, Felix, Shan, Mila, Jessy, Pamela} and the
subset of U: B = {Shan, Mila}.

   a. $U \cap B = \{Shan, Mila\}$.

   b. $U \cup B = \{John, Raquel, Felix, Shan, Mila, Jessy, Pamela\}$

Venn diagrams

Event	Set Language	Venn diagram	Probability result
Complementary event (A')	Not A		$P(A') = 1 - P(A)$
The intersection of A and B (A∩B)	Set of elements that belongs to A and B		$P(A \cup B) = P(A) + P(B) - P(A \cup B)$
The union of A and B (A∪B)	Set of elements that belongs to A or B or both		
If (A∩B) = ∅ A and B are said to be: mutually exclusive	The sets A and B are Mutually exclusive		$P(A \cup B) = P(A) + P(B)$ $P(A \cap B) = 0$

18. Given N, the set of natural numbers, Z the set of integers, Q the set of rationals and R the set of Real numbers.

   a. Write down an element of the set N∩Z: <u>1</u>

   b. Write down an element of the set Q∩Z: <u>0</u>

   c. Write down an element of the set Q∩Z': <u>0.5</u>

   d. Write down an element of the set Q'∩Z: <u>not possible</u>

   e. Write down an element of the set R∩Q: <u>2</u>

   f. Write down an element of the set R∩Q': <u>π</u>

   g. Write down an element of the set N∩N': <u>Not possible</u>

19. Consider the sets: $U = \{x \in N\}$

$A = \{x \in N \,|\, 11 < x < 21\}$, B={multiples of 4}, and C ={13, 16, 18, 20}

 a. Write all the elements of the set A∩B: {12, 16, 20}

 b. Write all the elements of the set A∩C: {13, 16, 18, 20}

 c. Write all the elements of the set B∩C: {16, 20}

 d. Write all the elements of the set B∪C: {multiples of 4, 13, 18}

 e. Write all the elements of the set A∩(B'∪C): {13, 14, 15, 16, 17, 18, 19, 20}

 f. Write all the elements of the set A∩(B∪C'): {12, 14, 15, 16, 17, 19, 20}

 g. Write all the elements of the set A∩B∩C'): {12}

 h. True/**False**: $11 \in A$ **True**/False: $11 \in A'$

 i. **True**/False: $13 \in A \cap C$ **True**/False: $30 \notin B$

 j. **True**/False: $12 \in A \cap B$ **True**/False: $30 \notin C$

 k. True/**False**: $B \subset A$ **True**/False: $C \subset A$

20. Given the Venn diagram. Shade A∩B

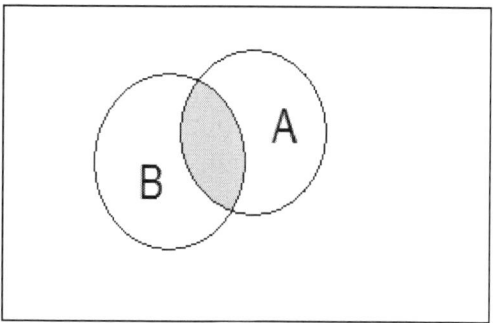

21. Given the Venn diagram. Shade A∩B'

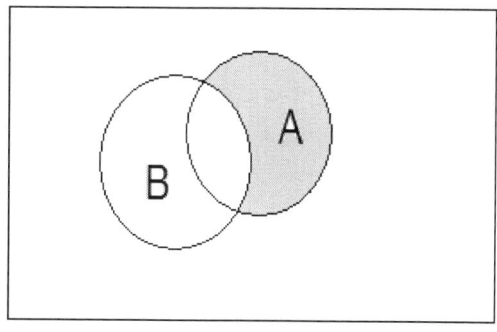

22. Given the Venn diagram. Shade B'

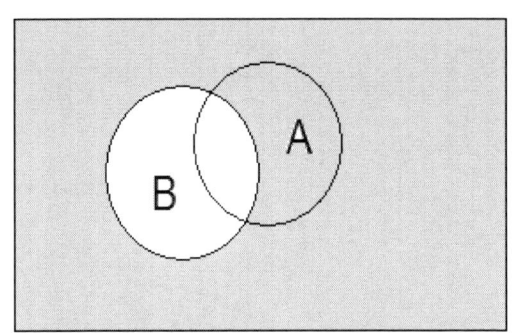

23. Given the Venn diagram. Shade A' ∩ B'

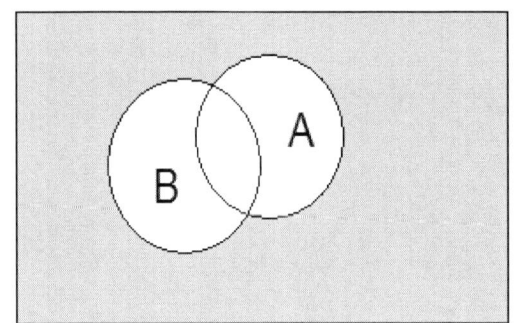

24. Given the Venn diagram. Shade A ∪ B

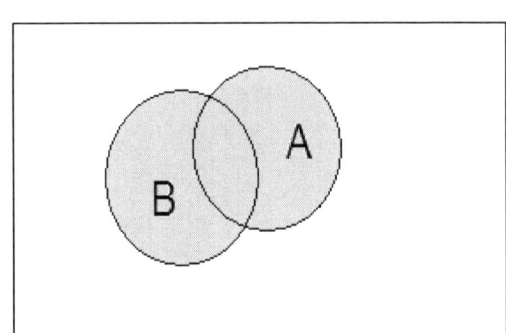

25. Given the Venn diagram. Shade A' ∪ B

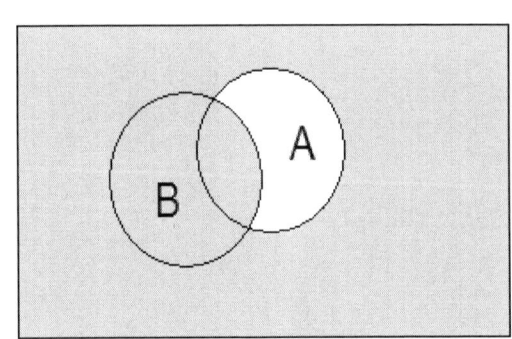

26. Given the Venn diagram. Shade A' ∪ B'

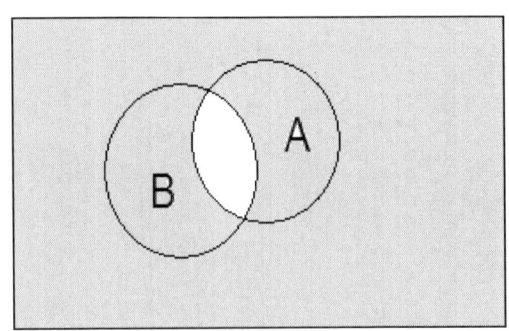

27. Given the Venn diagram. Shade A ∪ B

28. Given the Venn diagram. Shade A ∪ B'

29. Given the Venn diagram. Shade A ∩ B'

30. Given the Venn diagram. Shade A ∩ B   (None - Empty)

31. Given the Venn diagram. Shade A ∩ B ∩ C   (None - Empty)

32. Given the Venn diagram. Shade $(A \cup B) \cap C$

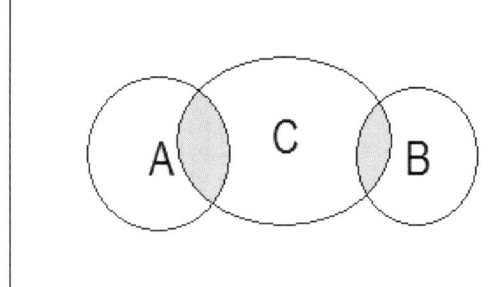

33. Given the Venn diagram. Shade $(A' \cup B) \cap C$

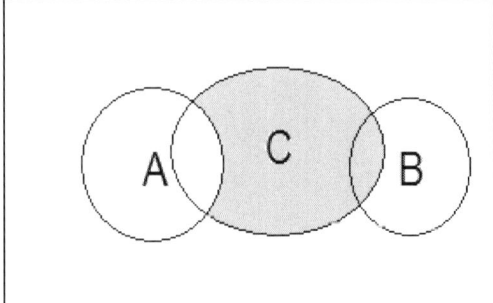

34. Given the Venn diagram. Shade $(A \cup B) \cap C'$

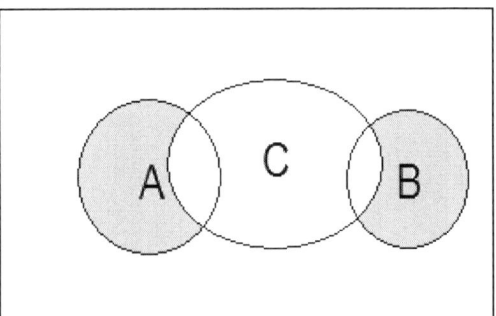

35. Given the Venn diagram. Shade $A \cap B \cap C$

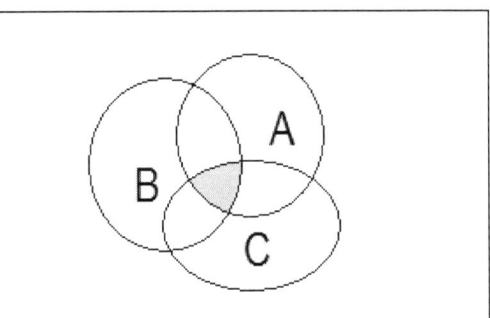

36. Given the Venn diagram. Shade $(A \cap B) \cap C'$

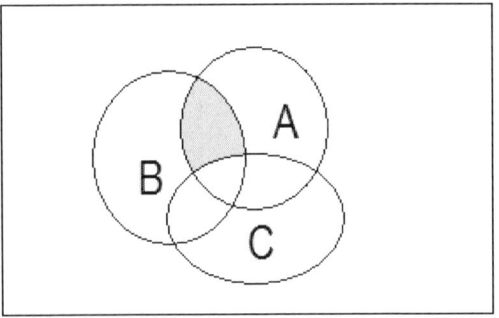

37. Given the Venn diagram. Shade $(A' \cap B) \cap C$

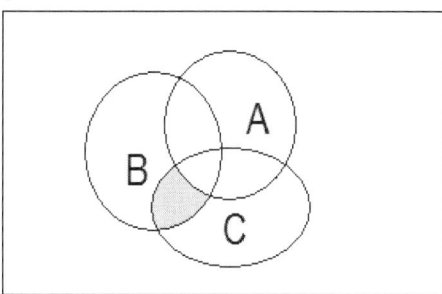

38. Given the Venn diagram. Shade $(A \cap B') \cap C$

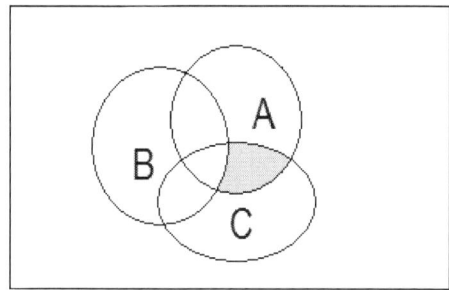

39. 50 drivers were asked about the favourite car colour. 3 choices were given: Red (X), Blue (Y) and White (Z). The results were:

        15 liked all three
        3 liked red and blue only
        9 liked red and white only
        7 liked blue and white only
        2 liked red only
        5 liked white only
        1 liked blue only

   a. Represent this information in a Venn diagram. Fill the Venn diagram with all the corresponding numbers.

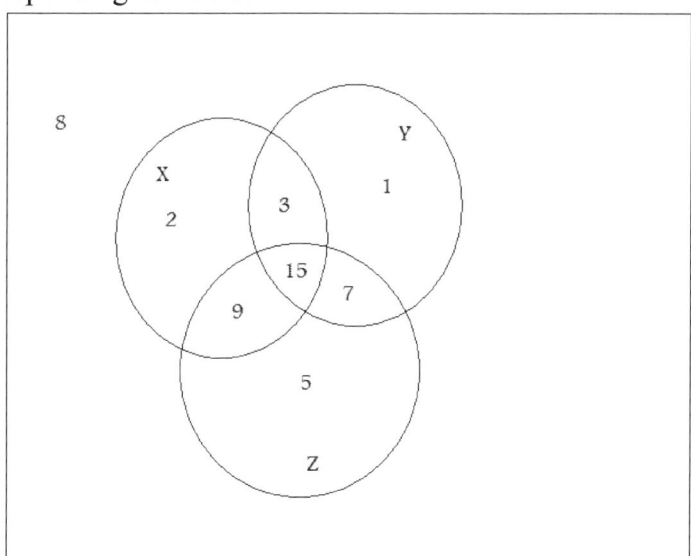

   b. Write down the percentage of drivers that did not like any of the 3 colours.

$$\frac{8}{50} = 16\%$$

40. Given the sets U = {Real numbers}, A={Negative numbers}, Z={Integers}

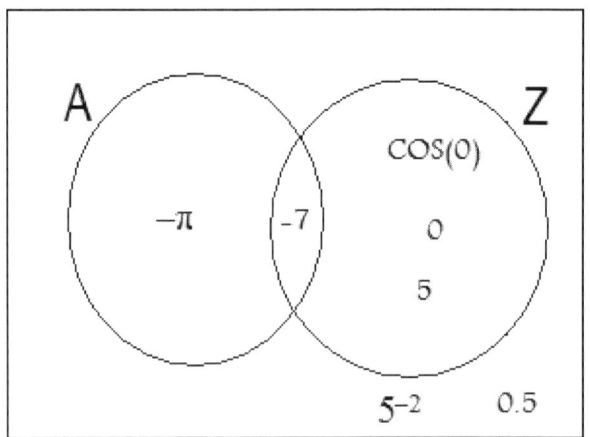

Write the following numbers in the correct region: cos(0), 0.5, –π, 5^{-2}, –7, 0

41. In a certain hospital in which there are 70 nurses, 20 work in cardiac surgery (C) and 15 others in the intensive care unit (I). 8 nurses work in both units.

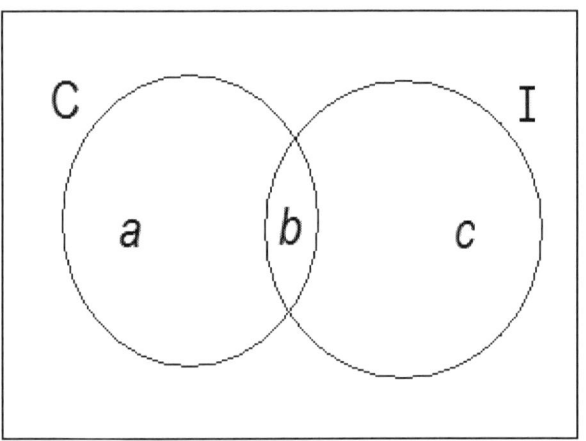

a. a = 12   b = 8   c = 7

b. Calculate the number of nurses that work outside of the cardiac surgery or intensive care units.

Nurses outside = 70 – (20 + 35 – 8) = 23

3.2. – LOGIC

1. Logic is a way to describe situations or knowledge in a way that allows drawing new conclusions. It is useful in computer programming, artificial intelligence and better understanding of language.

2. For example:

   a. All swimmers can swim fast
   b. Daniel is a swimmer

   Therefore by using logic, Daniel can <u>swim fast</u>.

3. p: A proposition that is either true or false

   Example: <u>Today it will rain</u>

   Example: <u>Tomorrow it will be sunny</u>

   Example: <u>5 is a rational number</u>

   Example that is not a proposition: <u>Let's have a party</u>

   Example that is not a proposition: <u>Could you watch my dog please</u>

4. $\neg p$ Negation of p

   Example: if p is <u>Today it will rain</u> $\neg p$ is <u>Today it will not rain</u>

   Example: if p is <u>Jack likes ice cream</u> $\neg p$ is <u>Jack does not like ice cream</u>

   Example: if p is <u>5 is a rational number</u> $\neg p$ is <u>5 is not a rational number</u>

5. Compound statements: A compound statement is: <u>a statement made of two or more propositions</u>.

6. $q \wedge p$ Conjunction: q and p

   Assuming p: <u>Today it will rain</u>   q: <u>Tomorrow it will be sunny</u>

   Example: <u>Today it will rain and Tomorrow it will be sunny</u>

   Assuming p: <u>Today it will rain</u>   q: <u>5 is a rational number</u>

   Example: <u>Today it will rain and 5 is a rational number</u>

313

7. $q \vee p$ Disjunction: q or p

         Assuming p: Today it will rain   q: Jack likes ice cream

    Example: Today it will rain or Jack likes ice cream

         Assuming p: Today it will rain   q: Tomorrow it will be sunny

    Example: Today it will rain or Tomorrow it will be sunny

8. $q \underline{\vee} p$ Exclusive Disjunction: q or p but not both

         Assuming p: Today it will rain   q: Jack likes ice cream

    Example: Today it will rain or Jack likes ice cream but not both

         Assuming p: Today it will rain   q: Tomorrow it will be sunny

    Example: Today it will rain or tomorrow it will be sunny but not both

9. $p \Rightarrow q$ Implication

         Assuming p: Today it is cloudy   q: Tomorrow it will be sunny

    Example: If today it is cloudy then tomorrow it will be sunny

         Assuming p: Jeff likes apples   q: Jeff likes bananas

    Example: If Jeff likes apples then Jeff likes bananas

10. $p \Leftarrow q$ Converse of an Implication

         Assuming p: Today it is cloudy   q: Tomorrow it will be sunny

    Example: If tomorrow it will be sunny then today it is cloudy

         Assuming p: Jeff likes apples   q: Jeff likes bananas

    Example: If Jeff likes bananas then Jeff likes apples

11. $\neg p \Rightarrow \neg q$ Inverse of an Implication

         Assuming p: Today it is cloudy   q: Tomorrow it will be sunny

    Example: If today it is not cloudy then tomorrow it will not be sunny

         Assuming p: Jeff likes apples   q: Jeff likes bananas

    Example: If Jeff doesn't likes apples then Jeff doesn't likes bananas

12. $\neg p \Leftarrow \neg q$ Contrapositive of an Implication

   Assuming p: <u>Today it is cloudy</u>   q: <u>Tomorrow it will be sunny</u>

Example: <u>If tomorrow it will not be sunny then today it is not cloudy</u>

   Assuming p: <u>Jeff likes apples</u>   q: <u>Jeff likes bananas</u>

Example: <u>If Jeff doesn't like bananas then Jeff doesn't likes apples</u>

13. $p \Leftrightarrow q$ Equivalence of p and q

Two statements p, q are equivalent if p <u>implies q and q implies p</u>

If $p \Rightarrow q$ and $p \Leftarrow q$ are both <u>true</u> we can say that <u>they are equivalent</u>

Example:

Assuming p: <u>Today it is cloudy</u>   q: <u>Tomorrow it will rain</u>

$p \Rightarrow q$ <u>If today it is cloudy then tomorrow it will rain</u>

$p \Leftarrow q$ <u>If tomorrow it will rain then today it is cloudy</u>

If both statements are true we can say $p \Leftrightarrow q$

14. Valid arguments: An argument is valid if the conclusion follows the statements, even if the statements are incorrect. For example:

   a. Oranges are white
   b. White fruit are sweet

Therefore by logic, <u>Oranges are sweet</u>

15. There is a deep analogy between set theory and logic. For example:

Disjoint: A red chair is never blue, that can be observed in the following sets exercise:

Sketch the corresponding Venn diagram to the following sets:

A: Set of red chairs
B: Set of blue chairs
C: Set of red chairs with wheels
D: Set of high chairs

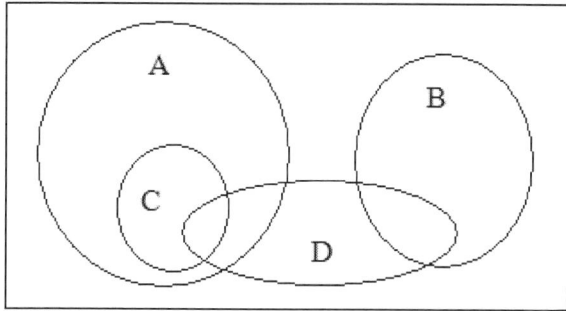

TRUTH TABLES

1. A truth table is a way to show the possibilities of a statement.

2. For example:

   q: Tuesday it will rain
   p: Wednesday it will rain
   r: Thursday it will rain

p	q	$\neg p$	$\neg q$	$q \wedge p$	$q \vee p$	$q \veebar p$
T	T	F	F	T	T	F
F	T	T	F	F	T	T
T	F	F	T	F	T	T
F	F	T	T	F	F	F

p	q	r	$\neg r$	$\neg q \wedge r$	$(\neg r \vee p) \wedge q$	$\neg(q \veebar p)$
T	T	T	F	F	T	T
F	T	T	F	F	F	F
T	F	T	F	F	F	F
F	F	T	F	F	F	T
T	T	F	T	F	T	T
F	T	F	T	F	T	F
T	F	F	T	T	F	F
F	F	F	T	T	F	T

3. Tautology: When a statement is always <u>true</u> it is considered a tautology.

4. Logical contradiction: When a statement is always <u>false</u> it is considered a logical contradiction.

p	$\neg p$	$p \wedge \neg p$	$\neg(p \wedge \neg p)$
T	F	F	T
F	T	F	T

5. Implication:

p	q	$q \Rightarrow p$
T	T	T
F	T	T
T	F	F
F	F	T

6. Converse

p	q	$q \Leftarrow p$
T	T	T
F	T	F
T	F	T
F	F	T

7. Given the logic propositions:
   p: Daniel eats ice cream   q: Daniel plays soccer

   a. $q \wedge p$ <u>Daniel plays soccer and Daniel eats ice cream</u>

   b. $q \wedge \neg p$ <u>Daniel plays soccer and Daniel does not eat ice cream</u>

   c. $q \underline{\vee} p$ <u>Daniel plays soccer or Daniel eats ice cream but not both</u>

   d. $q \Rightarrow p$ <u>If Daniel plays soccer then Daniel eats ice cream</u>

   e. $q \Rightarrow \neg p$ <u>If Daniel plays soccer then Daniel doesn't eat ice cream</u>

8. Consider the propositions p and q. Complete the table

p	r	$\neg r$	$p \Rightarrow \neg r$	$\neg p$	$\neg p \Rightarrow r$	$(p \Rightarrow \neg r) \Leftrightarrow (\neg p \Rightarrow r)$
T	T	F	F	F	T	F
T	F	T	T	F	T	T
F	T	F	T	T	T	T
F	F	T	T	T	F	F

9. Consider the propositions p and q. Complete the table

p	r	$\neg p$	$p \Rightarrow \neg r$
T	T	F	
T	F	F	
F	T	T	
F	F	T	

10. Given the logic propositions:

p: Maria loves to dance.   q: Maria will dance for 2 hours.
r: Maria will go swimming.

a. Maria does not like to dance $\underline{\neg p}$

b. If Maria loves to dance then she will dance for 2 hours $\underline{p \Rightarrow q}$

c. Maria doesn't love to dance therefore she will not dance for 2 hours $\underline{\neg p \Rightarrow \neg q}$

d. Maria will dance for 2 hours or she will go swimming $\underline{q \vee r}$

e. Maria will dance for 2 hours or she will go swimming but not both $\underline{q \underline{\vee} r}$

f. Maria will dance for 2 hours and she will go swimming $\underline{q \wedge r}$

g. $(q \wedge \neg r) \Rightarrow \neg p$

<u>If Maria will dance for 2 hours and she will not go swimming then she doesn't love to dance</u>

11. Given the logic propositions:

p: a number is an integer

q: a number can be divided by 2

r: a number is odd

Write in symbolic form:

a. If a number is an integer and it is not odd then it can be divided by 2

$(p \wedge \neg r) \Rightarrow q$

b. Write the contrapositive of the previous statement. $\neg(p \wedge \neg r) \Leftarrow \neg q$

If a number can't be divided by 2 then it is not an integer and it is odd

c. Write in words:

$(q \vee r) \Rightarrow p$ If a number can be divided by 2 or it is odd then it is an integer

$p \Rightarrow (q \vee r)$ If a number is an integer then it can be divided by 2 or it is odd

12. complete the table:

p	r	$\neg r$	$\neg r \wedge p$	$\neg p$	$(\neg r \wedge p) \vee (\neg p)$	$(\neg r \wedge p) \vee (\neg p) \Rightarrow r$
T	T	F	F	F	F	T
F	T	F	F	T	T	T
T	F	T	T	F	T	F
F	F	T	F	T	T	F

4.1. – PROBABILITY

Exercises
1. In an unbiased coin what is P(head) ? <u>0.5</u>

   This probability is called <u>"theoretical probability"</u>

2. Explain the difference between theoretical probability and "regular" probability.
   <u>Theoretical probability is calculated, predicted. "regular" probability is
   measured in an experiment. The probability for head is theoretically 0.5, we
   would need to repeat an experiment an infinite number of times to make sure it
   is. In reality the coin has some small probability to lend on its thin side (more
   than 0) so it is not really 0.5 for head…</u>

3. Throw a drawing pin at least 15 times and fill the table:
   <u>This experiment should be done in class</u>

4. The definition of probability is:

   $$P(A) = \frac{\text{Number of times A ocurred}}{\text{Total numberof times experiment repeated}}$$

Properties of probability
1. $\underline{\mathbf{0}} \leq P(A) \leq \underline{\mathbf{1}}$
2. $P(U) = \underline{\mathbf{1}}$

Exercises
1. The events A and B are such $P(A) = 0.2$, $P(B) = 0.4$ and $P(A \cup B) = 0.5$. Find:
   a. $P(A \cup B) = P(A) + P(B) - P(A \cap B)$

   $0.5 = 0.2 + 0.4 - P(A \cap B);$ $P(A \cap B) = 0.1$

   b. $P(B') = 1 - P(B) = 0.6$

   c. Sketch the corresponding Venn diagram.

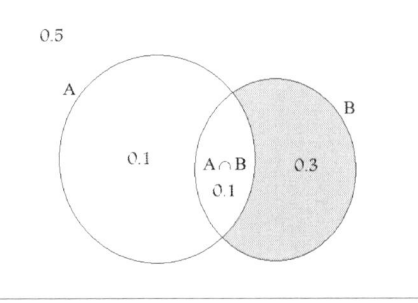

   d. $P(A' \cap B)$ is the size of the shaded area so 0.3

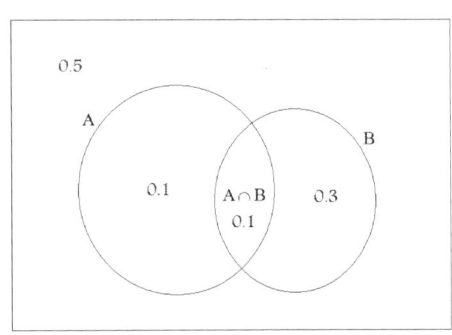

e. $P(A' \cap B')$ is the size of the shaded area so 0.5

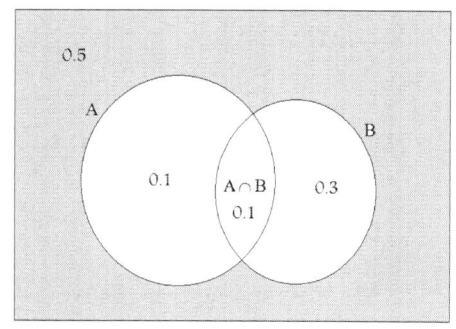

f. Are the events A and B Independent? Explain. <u>In case events are independent $P(A \cap B) = P(A) P(B)$, in this case $0.1 \neq (0.2)(0.4)$ therefore these events are not independent.</u>

2. The events A and B are such $P(A) = 0.15$, $P(B) = 0.3$ and $P(A \cup B) = 0.4$, Find:

   a. $P(A \cap B) =$; $P(A \cup B) = P(A) + P(B) - P(A \cap B)$

   $0.4 = 0.15 + 0.3 - P(A \cap B)$; $P(A \cap B) = 0.05$

   b. $P(B') = 1 - P(B) = 0.7$

   c. Sketch the corresponding Venn diagram.

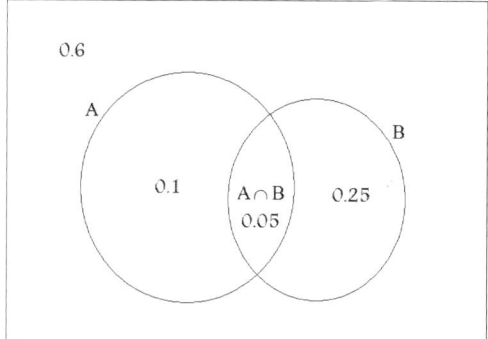

   g. $P(A' \cap B)$ is the size of the shaded area so 0.25

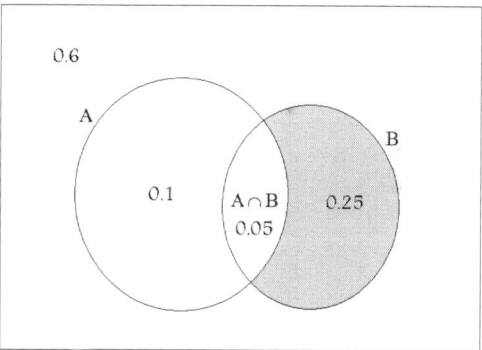

   h. $P(A' \cap B')$ is the size of the shaded area so 0.6

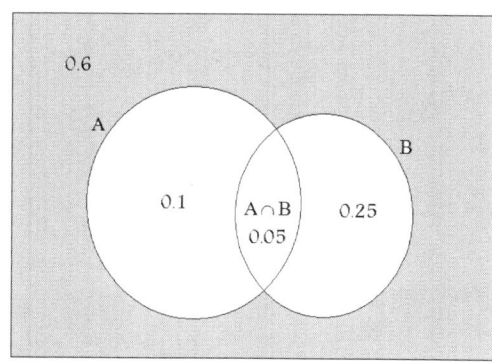

   d. Are the events A and B Independent? Explain. <u>In case events are independent $P(A \cap B) = P(A) P(B)$, in this case $0.05 \neq (0.15)(0.3)$ therefore these events are not independent.</u>

3. The events A and B are such $P(A) = 0.3$, $P(B) = 0.6$ and $P(A \cup B) = 0.9$, Find:

a. $P(A \cap B)$
   $P(A \cup B) = P(A) + P(B) - P(A \cap B)$
   $0.9 = 0.6 + 0.3 - P(A \cap B)$; $P(A \cap B) = 0$ That means no intersection
   So events are mutually exclusive.

b. $P(B') = 1 - P(B) = 0.4$

c. Sketch the corresponding Venn diagram.

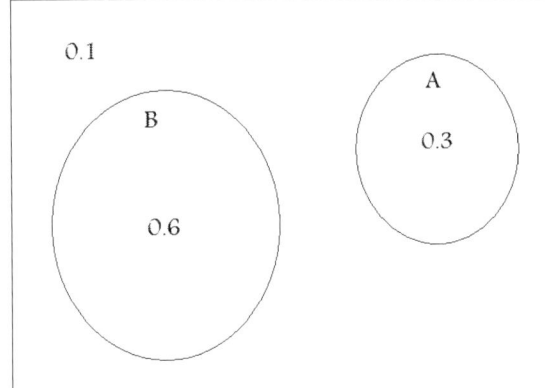

d. $P(A' \cap B) = P(B) = 0.6$ (the size of the shaded area)

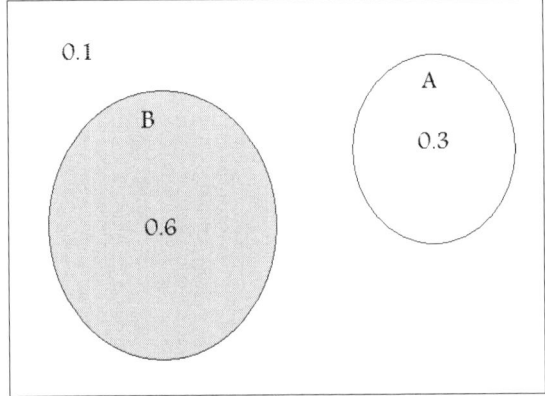

e. $P(A' \cap B') = 0.1$ (the size of the shaded area)

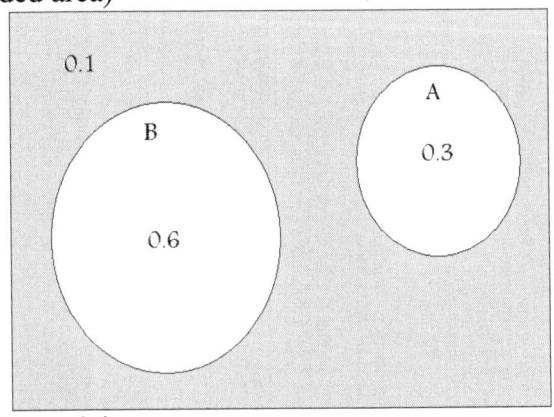

f. Are the events A and B Independent? Explain.
   In case events are independent $P(A \cap B) = P(A)\,P(B)$, in this case
   $0 \neq (0.3)(0.6)$ therefore these events are not independent.

4. The events A and B are such $P(A) = 0.2$, $P(B) = 0.9$ and $P(A \cap B) = 0.1$, Find:

    a. $P(A \cup B)$

       $P(A \cup B) = P(A) + P(B) - P(A \cap B)$

       $P(A \cup B) = 0.2 + 0.9 - 0.1$; $P(A \cup B) = 1$, that means there is no "outside" the events "fill" the entire rectangle.

    b. $P(B') = 1 - P(B) = 0.1$

    c. Sketch the corresponding Venn diagram.

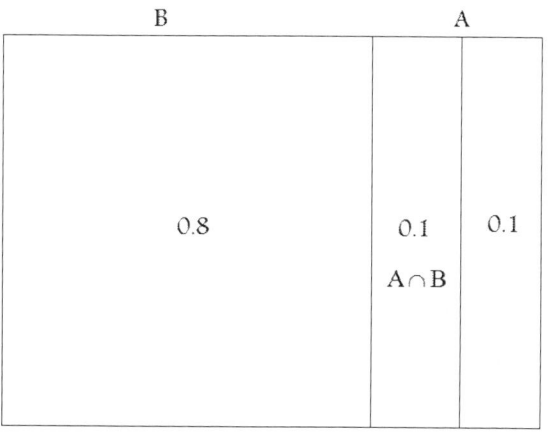

    d. $P(A' \cap B) = 0.8$(the size of the shaded area)

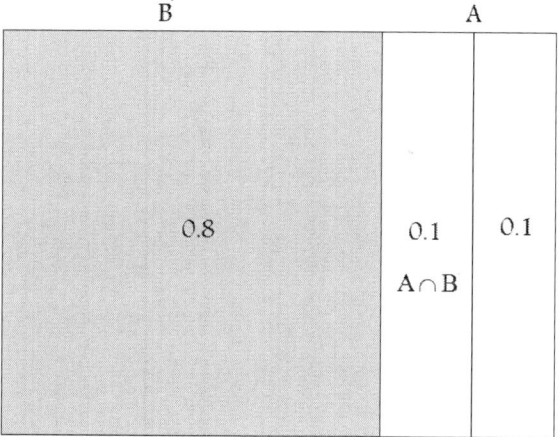

    e. $P(A' \cap B') = 0$

       There is no "outside"

    f. Are the events A and B Independent? Explain.

       In case events are independent $P(A \cap B) = P(A) \, P(B)$, in this case $0.1 \neq (0.2)(0.9)$ therefore these events are not independent.

5. 20% of certain city census consume alcohol regularly, 40% do sport regularly and 10% do both.

 a. Represent the information in a diagram.

 $P(A \cup S) = P(A) + P(S) - P(A \cap S)$

 $P(A \cup S) = 0.2 + 0.4 - 0.1; \quad P(A \cup S) = 0.5$

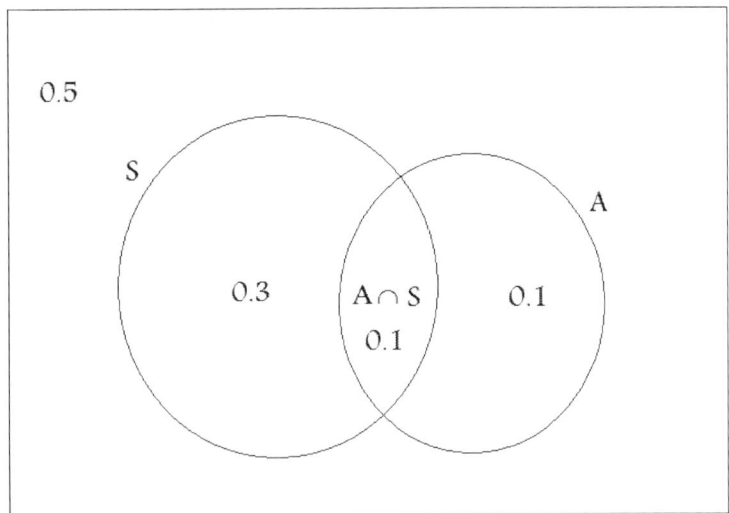

 b. Calculate the probability that someone chosen at random only drinks alcohol regularly.

 P(A only) = 0.1 (see venn diagram)

 c. Calculate the probability that someone chosen at random only drink alcohol regularly or only practices sport regularly (but not both).

 P(A or S but not both) = 0.1 + 0.3 = 0.4 (see venn diagram)

 d. Calculate the probability that someone picked at random does not drink alcohol nor practices sport regularly.

 $P(A' \cap S') = 0.5$ (The "outside")

6. $P(A) = 0.46, P(B) = 0.33, P(A \cap B) = 0.15$.

 a. Represent the information in a diagram.

 $P(A \cup B) = 0.46 + 0.33 - 0.15 = 0.64$

 b. Find the probability that an event is not A nor B.

 $P(A' \cap B') = 1 - 0.64 = 0.36$

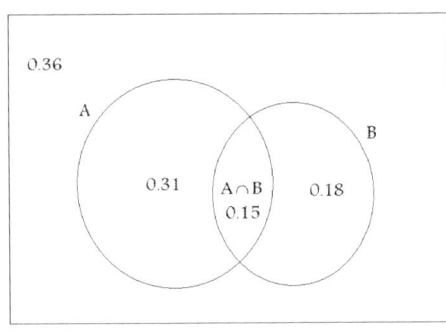

CONDITIONAL PROBABILITY

Exercises

1. What is the difference between independent events and mutually exclusive events?
   Mutually exclusive events cannot exist at the same "time" $P(A \cap B) = 0$
   In independent events $P(A \cap B) = P(A)P(B)$ (The intersection is not 0 in general)

2. Give an example of independent events.
   Each time the ball of casino roulette is launched is an independent event of previous launches.

3. In a certain town the probability of a rainy day is 0.58 and the probability of strong wind is 0.76. If these are independent events, find the probability of:

   a. A rainy windy day.
      $P(R \cap W) = P(R)P(W) = (0.58)(0.76) = 0.4408$

   b. A dry windy day.
      $P(R' \cap W) = P(R')P(W) = (0.42)(0.76) = 0.3192$

   c. A dry and not windy day.
      $P(R' \cap W') = P(R')P(W') = (0.42)(0.24) = 0.1008$

   d. 2 consecutive rainy days.
      $P(R \cap R) = P(R)P(R) = (0.58)(0.58) = 0.3364$

   e. 2 consecutive windy rainy days.
      $P(R \cap W)\ P(R \cap W) = (0.4408)(0.4408) = 0.194$

Lattice diagrams

4. Two dice numbered one to six are rolled onto a table.

   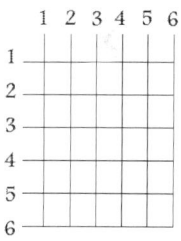

   a. Sketch a corresponding diagram.

   b. Find the probability that the sum is 7.

      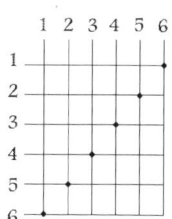

      $$P(\text{Sum} = 7) = \frac{6}{36}$$

   c. Find the probability that the sum is more than 7.

      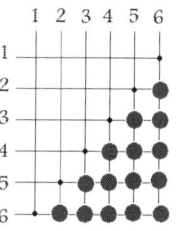

      $$P(\text{Sum} > 7) = \frac{15}{36} b$$

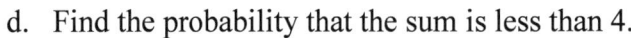

d. Find the probability that the sum is less than 4.

$$P(\text{Sum} < 4) = \frac{3}{36}$$

e. Find the probability that the sum is even.

$$P(\text{Sum} = \text{even}) = \frac{18}{36}$$

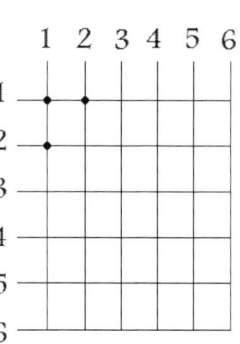

f. Find the probability of obtaining a sum of five <u>given</u> that the sum is seven or less.

Conditional probability: $P(A|B) = \dfrac{P(A \cap B)}{P(B)}$ in this case:

$$P(sum = 5 | sum \leq 7) = \frac{P(sum = 5 \cap sum \leq 7)}{P(sum \leq 7)} = \frac{\left(\dfrac{4}{36}\right)}{\left(\dfrac{21}{36}\right)} = \frac{4}{21}$$

g. Find the probability of obtaining a sum of 4 <u>given</u> that the sum is even.

Conditional probability: $P(A|B) = \dfrac{P(A \cap B)}{P(B)}$ in this case:

$$P(sum = 4 | sum = even) = \frac{P(sum = 4 \cap sum = even)}{P(sum = even)} = \frac{\left(\dfrac{3}{36}\right)}{\left(\dfrac{18}{36}\right)} = \frac{3}{18}$$

5. A die and coin are rolled on a table.

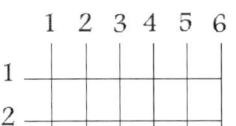

a. Sketch a corresponding diagram.

b. Find the probability of getting Tail and an even number.

$$P(T \cap Even) = \frac{3}{12}$$

c. Find the probability of getting Tail and a 4. $P(T \cap 4) = \dfrac{1}{12}$

d. Find the probability of obtaining a 5 knowing that a tail was obtained.

Conditional probability: $P(A|B) = \dfrac{P(A \cap B)}{P(B)}$ in this case:

$$P(5|T) = \frac{P(5 \cap T)}{P(T)} = \frac{\left(\dfrac{1}{12}\right)}{\left(\dfrac{6}{12}\right)} = \frac{1}{6}$$

6. If the probability of tail is 0.53, find the probability of at least one tail in 2 throws.

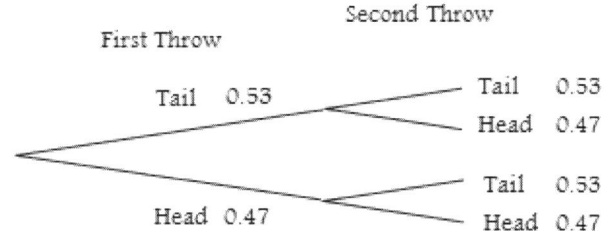

$$P(T \cap T) + P(T \cap H) + P(H \cap T) = (0.53)^2 + (0.53)(0.47) + (0.47)(0.53) = 0.7791$$

Can be done easier:

$$1 - P(H \cap H) = 1 - (0.47)^2 = 0.7791$$

7. An urn contains 8 cubes of which 5 are black and the rest are white.

   a. What is the probability to draw a white cube? $P(W) = \dfrac{3}{8}$

   b. Draw a tree diagram in case a 1st cube is drawn, it is **NOT replaced** and then another cube is drawn. Indicate all the probabilities on the tree diagram.

   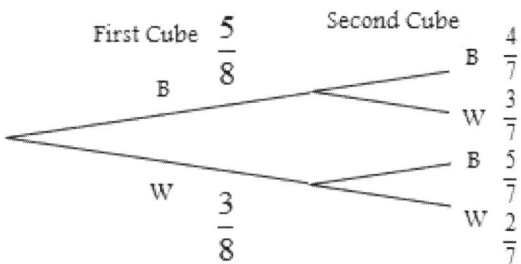

   c. Calculate the probability to draw 2 consecutive black cubes.

   $$P(B \cap B) = \frac{5}{8} \cdot \frac{4}{7} = \frac{20}{56}$$

   d. Calculate the probability to draw **at least** 1 black cube.

   $$P(B \cap B) + P(B \cap W) + P(W \cap B) = \frac{50}{56}$$

   Can be done easier:

   $$1 - P(W \cap W) = 1 - \frac{3}{8} \cdot \frac{2}{7} = 1 - \frac{6}{56} = \frac{50}{56}$$

   e. Given that the first cube drawn was white, calculate the probability that the 2nd is black.

   Conditional probability: $P(A|B) = \dfrac{P(A \cap B)}{P(B)}$ in this case:

   $$P(2ndB|1stW) = \frac{P(2ndB \cap 1stW)}{P(1stW)} = \frac{\left(\dfrac{3}{8} \cdot \dfrac{5}{7}\right)}{\left(\dfrac{3}{8}\right)} = \frac{5}{7}$$

8. A bag contains 3 red balls, 4 blue balls and 5 green balls. A ball is chosen at random from the bag and is not replaced. A second ball is chosen. Find the probability of choosing one green ball and one blue ball in any order.

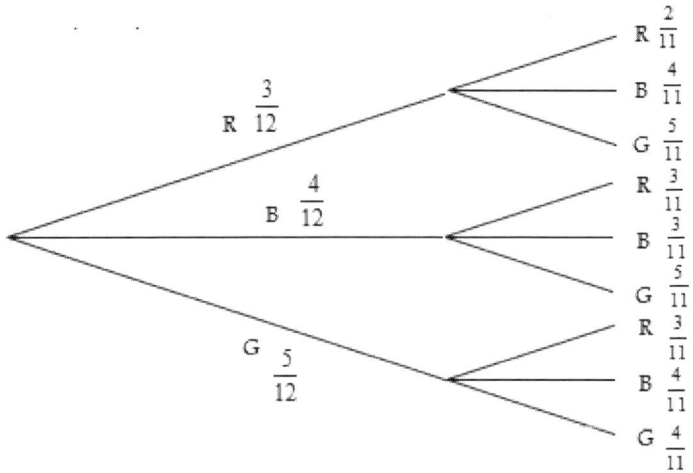

$$P(B \cap G) + P(G \cap B) = \frac{4}{12} \cdot \frac{5}{11} + \frac{5}{12} \cdot \frac{4}{11} = \frac{40}{132}$$

9. Given that events A and B are independent with $P(A \cap B) = 0.4$ and $P(A \cap B') = 0$. Find $P(A \cup B)$.

   $P(A \cap B') = 0$ means that A is inside B (it has no intersection with the "outside" of B), the Venn diagram is:

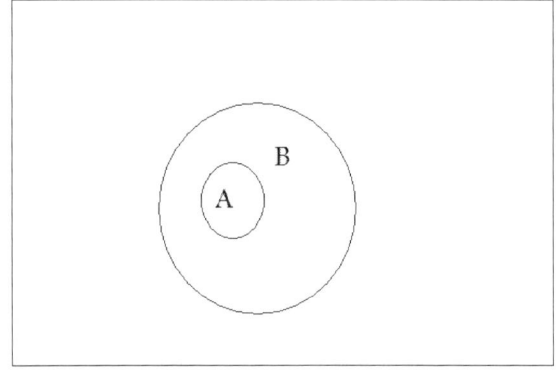

   In consequence:
   $P(A \cup B) = P(B)$
   $P(A \cap B) = P(A) = 0.4$

   Since events are independent
   $P(A \cap B) = P(A) P(B)$
   $0.4 = (0.4)P(B)$
   $P(B) = 1 = P(A \cup B)$.

10. Given that $P(A) = 0.4$, $P(B) = 0.7$ and $P(A \cup B) = 0.8$. Find:

   a. $P(A \cap B)$
       $P(A \cup B) = P(A) + P(B) - P(A \cap B)$
       $0.8 = 1.1 - P(A \cap B);$ $P(A \cap B) = 0.3$

   b. $P(A \mid B)$
       $$P(A|B) = \frac{P(A \cap B)}{P(B)} = \frac{0.3}{0.7} = \frac{3}{7}$$

   c. Determine if A and B are independent events.
       Check if $P(A \cap B) = P(A) P(B)$ is satisfied:
       $0.3 \neq (0.4)(0.7)$ so events are not independent.

11. Given that P(A) = 0.4, P(B) = 0.6 and P(A ∪ B) = 0.76.

    a. Find P($A \cap B$)
       P(A ∪ B) = P(A) + P(B) − P(A ∩ B)
       0.76 = 0.4 + 0.6 − P(A ∩ B) ;   P(A ∩ B) = 0.24

    b. Are events A and B mutually exclusive? Explain.
       The events are not mutually exclusive since their intersection exists
       and it is bigger than 0.

    c. Are events A and B independent?
       Check if *P(A ∩ B)* = P(A) P(B) is satisfied:
       0.24 = (0.4)(0.6) so events are independent.

12. The events A and B are independent, where A is the event "it will rain today"
and B is the event "We will go out for pizza". It is known that

$$P(B) = 0.3, P(A \mid B) = 0.6, P(A \mid B') = 0.5.$$

    a. Complete the following tree diagram.

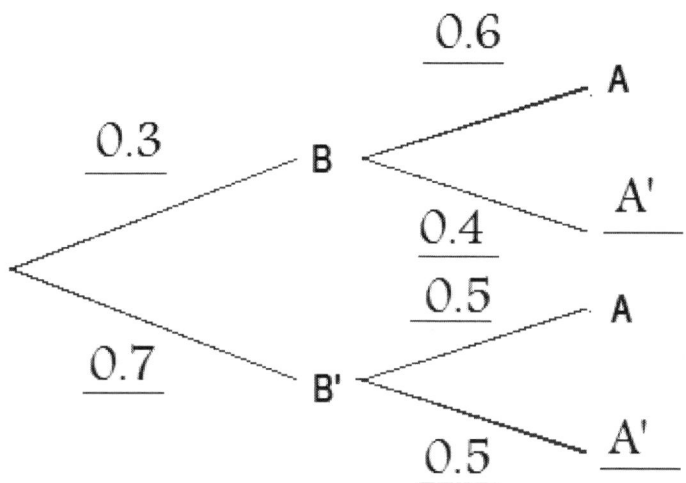

    b. Calculate the probability that it rains knowing we went out for
pizza.

       P(A | B) = 0.6

5.1. – INTRODUCTION TO FUNCTION

1. Write the definition of a function in your own words:

    A one to one or one to many relation between "things" (variables),

2. Write 2 examples of relations that <u>are</u> functions:

    <u>Day of the week</u> → <u>color of my shirt</u>
    <u>Word</u> → <u>First letter of word</u>
    <u>Time</u> → <u>Temperature</u>

3. Draw a sketch of the functions that describe those relations. Can you write the mathematical expression to describe them?

    Only the last example is "mathematical enough" to find an expression:
    f(t) = Asin(kt) + B (this will be discussed later). Approximate sketch can be:

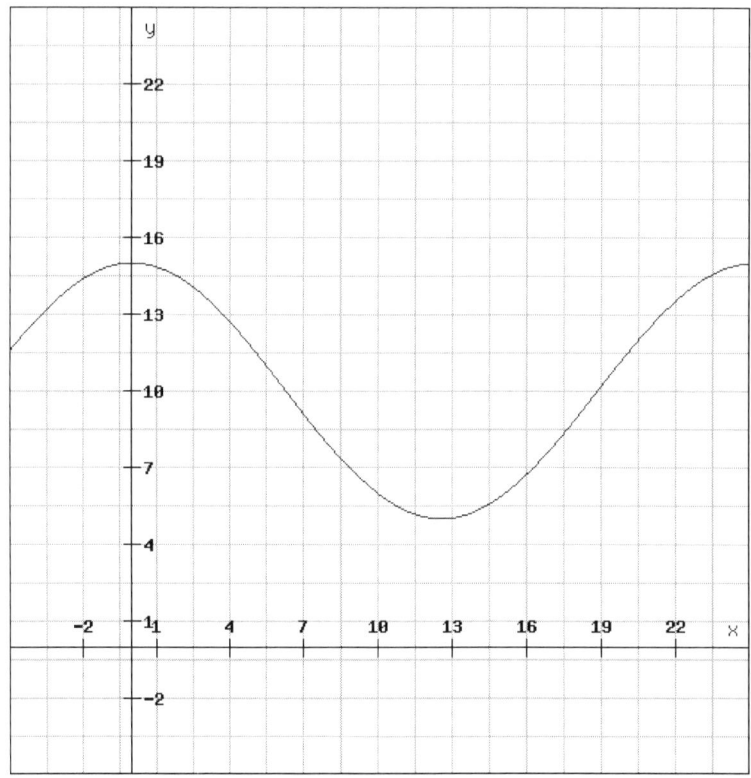

4. Write 2 examples of relations that <u>are not</u> functions:

    <u>Name of person</u> → <u>Personal information</u>   (one to many)
    <u>Name of City</u> → <u>Names of habitants</u>   (one to many)

5. Which one of the following graphs cannot represent function:

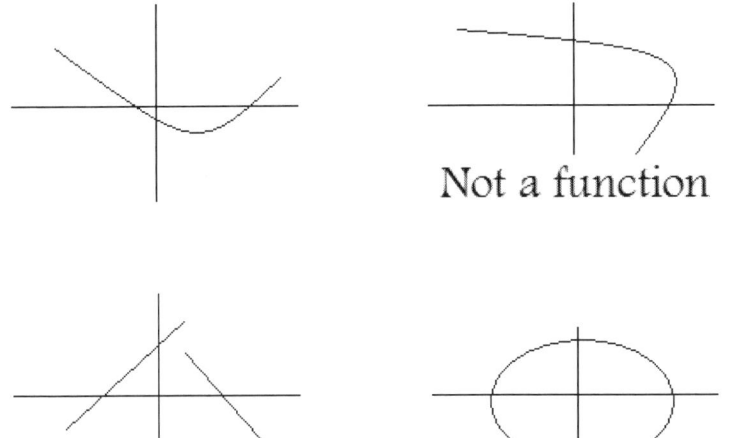

Not a function

Not a function

6. Draw an example of a curve that is not a function:

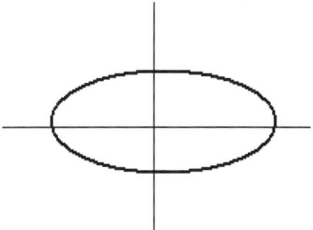

7. Draw an example of a curve that is a function:

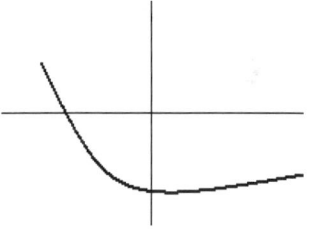

8. The domain of a function is the: <u>The set of allowed values of the independent variable ("what x can be")</u>

9. The Range of a function is the: <u>The set of allowed values of the dependent variable ("what y can be")</u>

10. Given the Height – age curve for a human.

    a.   Sketch an approximate graph:

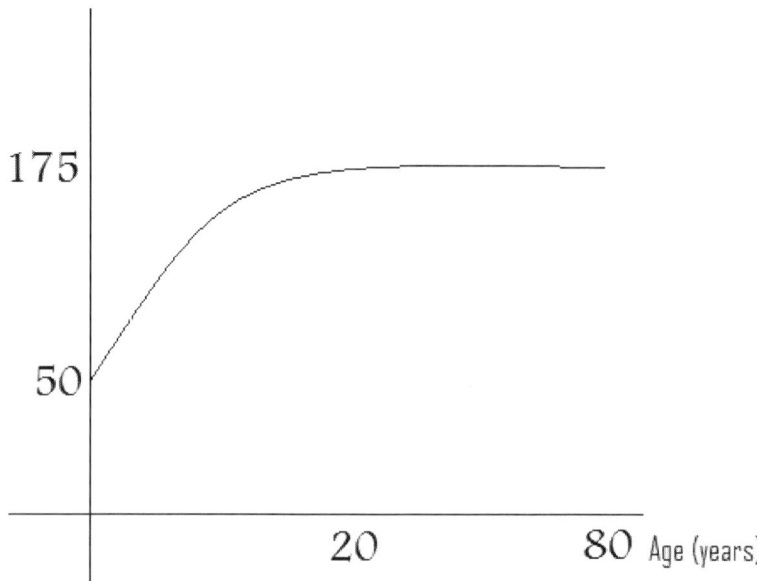

    b.   In your sketch Height(0) = <u>50cm</u>, it is the height of <u>a new born baby</u>

    c.   In your sketch Height(t) = 100cm. Then t is: <u>2 years</u>

    d.   State its domain: <u>*Age* ∍ [0,80]</u>

    e.   State its range: <u>*Height* ∍ [50,175]</u>

11. Out of the following relations circle the ones that are functions:

    a. **<u>Person's name</u> → <u>Person's age</u>**
    b. **<u>City</u> → <u>Number of habitants</u>**
    c. City → Names of habitants
    d. **<u>Family</u> → <u>Home Address</u>**
    e. **<u>Satellite's name</u> → <u>Position of satellite</u>**
    f. **<u>Time</u> → <u>Position of object</u>**
    g. **<u>One</u> → <u>One</u>**
    h. One → Many
    i. **<u>Many</u> → <u>One</u>**

12. Given the function:

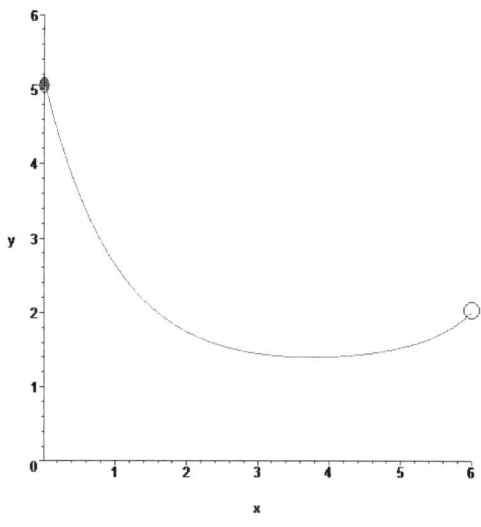

a. f(0) = <u>5</u>

b. f(2) = <u>1.8</u>= f(<u>5.5</u>)   (many to one)

c. f(7) = <u>Does not exist</u>

d. f(x) = 3, x = <u>0.8</u>

e. f(x) = 2, x = <u>1.5</u>

f. State its domain: $x \ni [0,6)$

g. State its range: $f(x) \ni [1.5,5]$

h. Is this function one to one? One to many? Explain.
   <u>This is many to one. There are many values of x with the same y.</u>

13. Given the function:

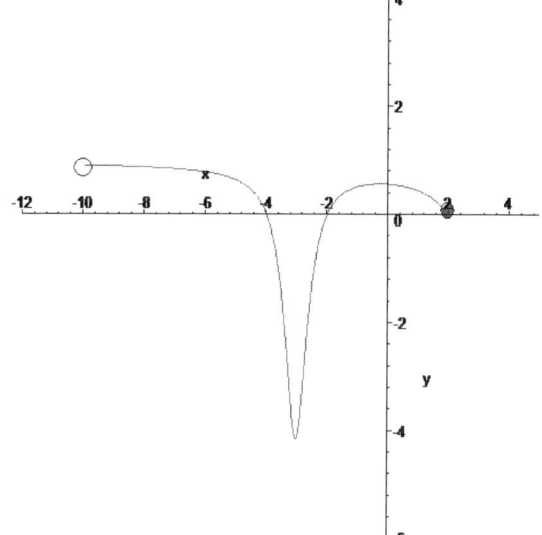

a. f(x) = 0, x = −4,−2,2 (many to one)

b. f(0) = 0.5 = f(<u>−5</u>)

c. f(−8) = <u>0.8</u>

d. f(−3) = <u>−4</u>

e. f(−4) = 0 = f(<u>−2</u>)

f. f(3) = Doesn't exist.

g. State its domain: $x \ni (-10, 2]$

h. State its range: $f(x) \ni [-4,1)$

i. Is this function one to one? One to many? Explain.
   <u>This is many to one. There are many values of x with the same y.</u>

14. Given the following function:

Domain   Range

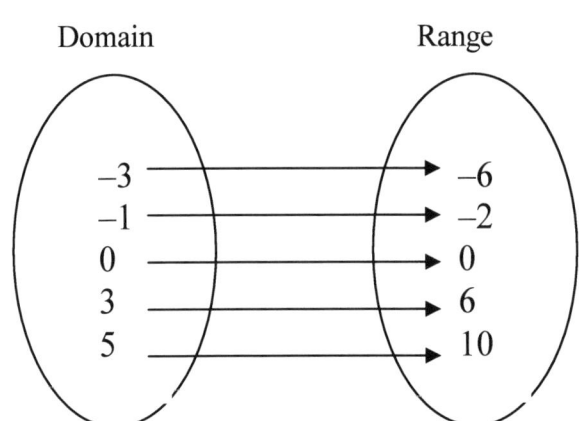

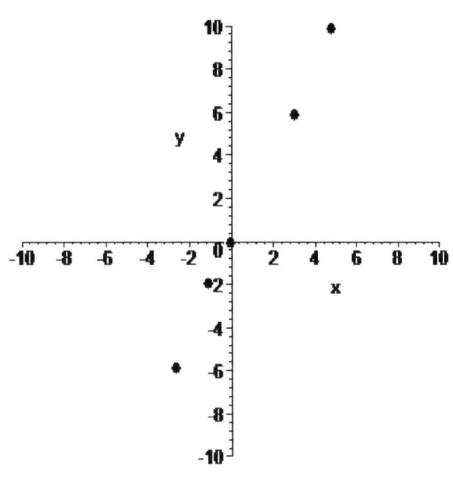

a. What are the allowed values for the independent variable (The domain)?
   $\{-3,-1,0,3,5\}$

b. What are the allowed values for the dependent variable (The range)?
   $\{-6,-2,0,6,10\}$

c. Sketch the function on the graph.

d. Can you write a mathematical expression to express this function?

   $f(x) = 2x$

15. Given the following function:

Domain   Range

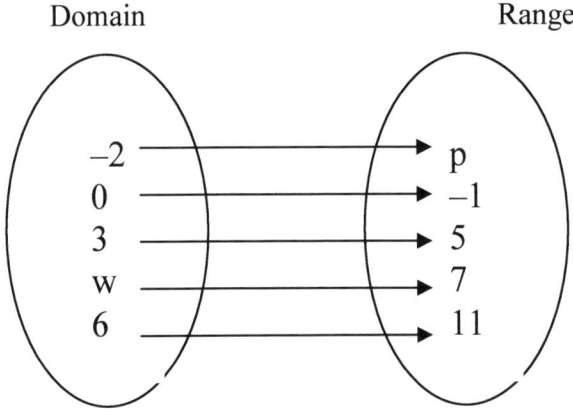

a. Can you write a mathematical expression to express this function?

   $f(x) = 2x - 1$

b. Find p. Find w. $p = -5, w = 4$

334

16. Use the graph below to answer the following:

    a. $f(0) = \underline{1}$

    b. $f(7) = \underline{-1}$

    c. $f(2) = \underline{1.5}$

    d. Is $f(-1/2)$ positive or negative? <u>Positive</u>

    e. For what values of x is $f(x) = 0$ $x = \underline{-3.9, -2, 6}$

    f. Is $f(1) > f(7)$? <u>Yes</u>

    g. For what values of x is $f(x) > 0$? $\underline{x \ni (-\infty, .4) \cup (-2, 6)}$

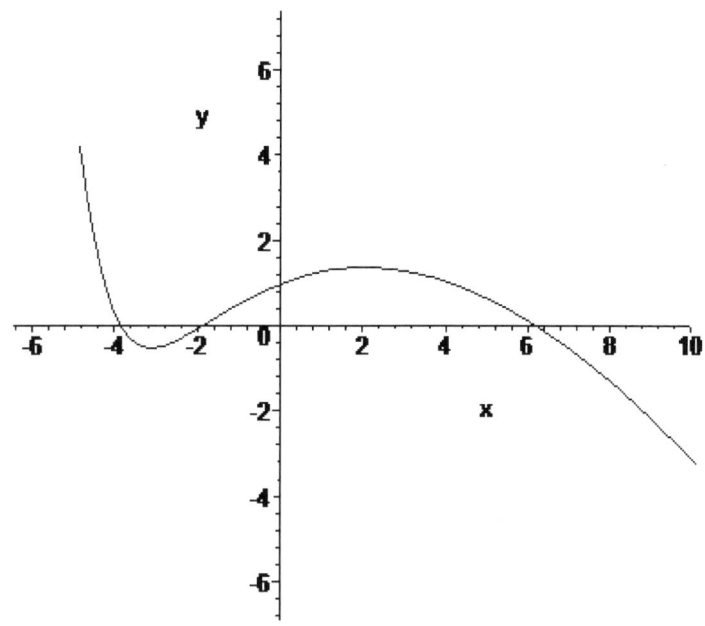

17. Functions can be represented using: <u>Graphs</u> or <u>Expressions</u>

18. The following graph models the concentration of a drug injected into the blood as a function of the time (in minutes) since the injection. $t = 0$ corresponds to the time of injection.

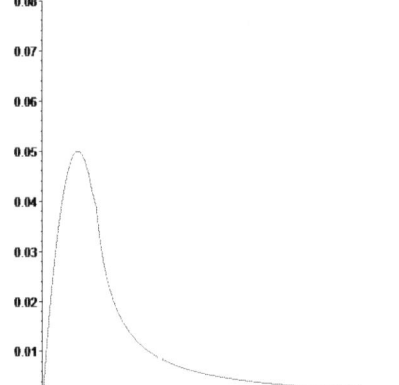

a. What is the concentration of the drug 4 hours after the injection? <u>0.008</u>

b. During what period of time is the concentration increasing? $t \ni (0,1)$

c. After how long is the concentration maximum? <u>1 min</u>

d. When is the concentration greater than 0.02? $t \ni (0.3, 2)$ <u>min</u>

e. State the domain and range of the function.

Domain: $t \ni [0,10]$

Range: $C(t) \ni [0, 0.05]$

19. The graph below models the temperature in C° on a particular day as a function of time since midnight.

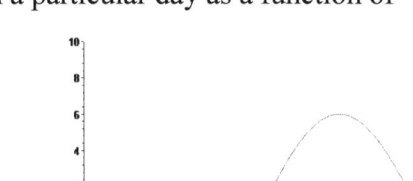

a. What was the temperature at 4:00 a.m.? <u>−5°</u>

b. When was the temperature 4 degrees? <u>15:00, 22:00</u>

c. When was the temperature below freezing? (less than 0 degrees) $t \ni (0,12)$

d. When was the temperature increasing? $t \ni (6,18)$

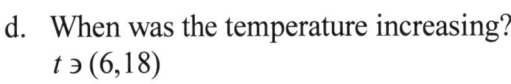

f. State the domain and range of the function.

Domain: $t \ni [-1, 24]$

Range: $T(t) \ni [-6, 6]$

5.2. – LINEAR FUNCTIONS

1. Given the function: f(x) = –5

X	–5	–4	–3	–2	–1	0	1	2	3	4	5
f(x)	–5	–5	–5	–5	–5	–5	–5	–5	–5	–5	–5

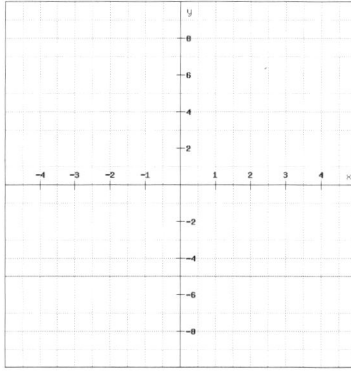

- Sketch the points of the chart on a graph (use a ruler).

- State the domain of the function: $x \in R$

- State the y intercept (sketched on the graph: (0, –5)

- State the x intercept: None

- The function is increasing on the interval: Never

- The function is decreasing on the interval: Never

- Sketch the function of the graph used for the points initially drawn

- State the range of the function: $f(x) \in \{-5\}$

2. Given the function: f(x) = x + 3

x	–5	–4	–3	–2	–1	0	1	2	3	4	5
f(x)	–2	–1	0	1	2	3	4	5	6	7	8

- Sketch the points of the chart on a graph (use a ruler).

- State the domain of the function: $x \in R$

- State the y intercept (sketched on the graph: (0, 3)

- State the x intercept: (–3,0)

- The function is increasing on the interval: $x \in R$

- The function is decreasing on the interval: Never

- Sketch the function of the graph used for the points initially drawn

- State the range of the function: $f(x) \in R$

3. Given the function: f(x) = –2x – 5

x	–5	–4	–3	–2	–1	0	1	2	3	4	5
f(x)	5	3	1	–1	–3	–5	–7	–9	–11	–13	–15

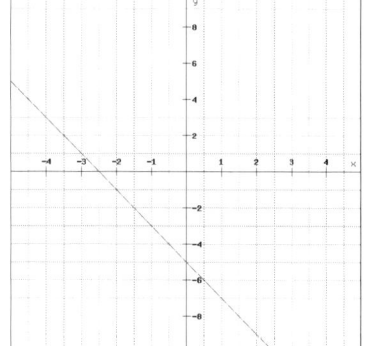

- Sketch the points of the chart on a graph (use a ruler).

- State the domain of the function: $x \in R$

- State the y intercept (sketched on the graph: (0, –5)

- State the x intercept: $\left(\dfrac{5}{2}, 0 \right)$

- The function is increasing on the interval: Never

- The function is decreasing on the interval: $x \in R$

- Sketch the function of the graph used for the points initially drawn

- State the range of the function: $f(x) \in R$

4. Given the function: f(x) = 4x – 3

x	–5	–4	–3	–2	–1	0	1	2	3	4	5
f(x)	–23	–19	–15	–11	–7	–3	1	5	9	13	17

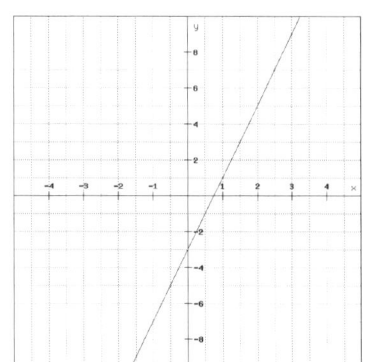

- Sketch the points of the chart on a graph (use a ruler).

- State the domain of the function: $x \in R$

- State the y intercept (sketched on the graph: (0, –3)

- State the x intercept: $\left(\dfrac{3}{4}, 0 \right)$

- The function is increasing on the interval: $x \in R$

- The function is decreasing on the interval: Never

- Sketch the function of the graph used for the points initially drawn

- State the range of the function: $f(x) \in R$

5. Given below are the equations for five different lines. Match the function with its graph.

Function	On the graph
f(x) = 20 + 2x	**B**
g(x) = 4x + 20	**C**
s(x) = –30 + 2x	**A**
a(x) = 60 – x	**D**
b(x) = – 2x + 60	**E**

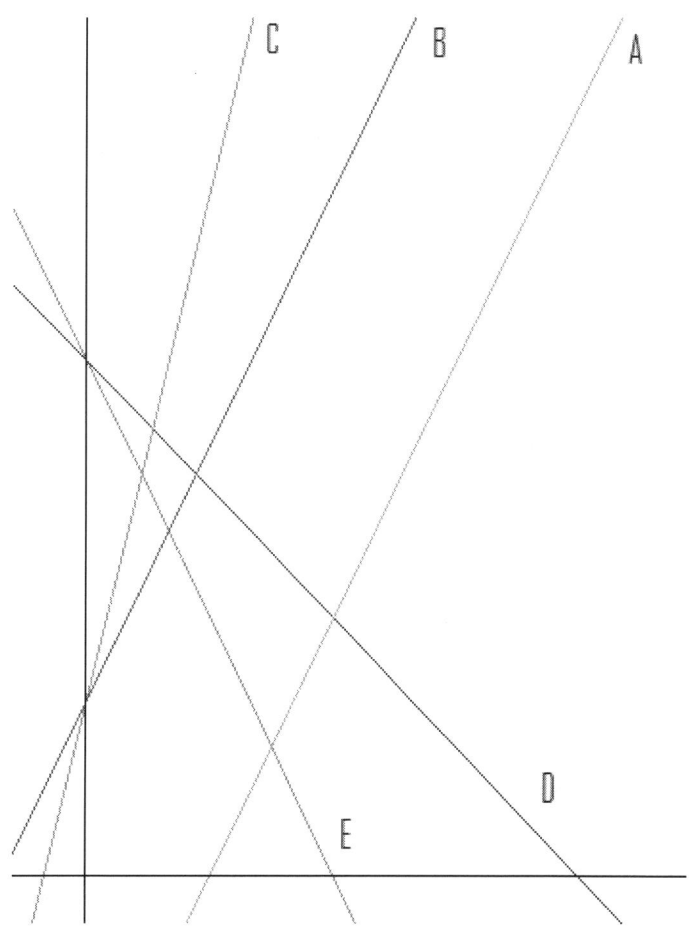

6. The general functions that describes a straight line is <u>f(x) = mx + b</u>

7. We know a function is a straight line because <u>x is to the power of 1 only</u>

8. The y–intercept (also called vertical intercept), tells us where the line crosses the <u>y axis</u>. The corresponding point is of the form <u>(0 , b)</u>.

9. The x–intercept (also called horizontal intercept), tells us where the line crosses the <u>x axis</u>. The corresponding point is of the form (p , 0).

10. If m > 0, the line <u>increases</u> left to right. If <u>m < 0</u> the line decreases left to right.

11. In case the line is horizontal m is <u>zero</u> and the line is of the form <u>f(x) = b</u>

12. The larger the value of m is, the <u>steeper</u> the graph of the line is.

13. Given the graph, write, the slope (m), b and the equation of the line:

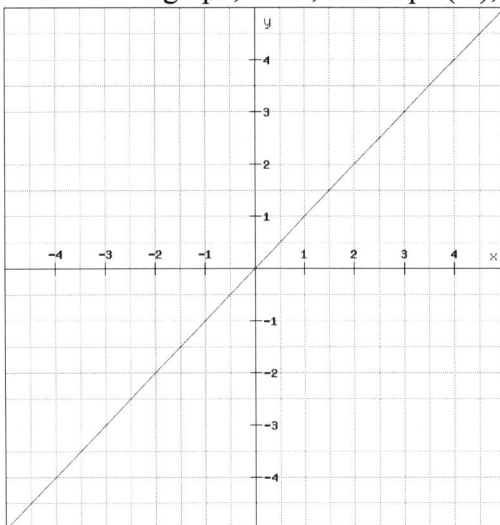

m = 1   b = 0   f(x) = x   m = -2   b = 0   f(x) = -2x

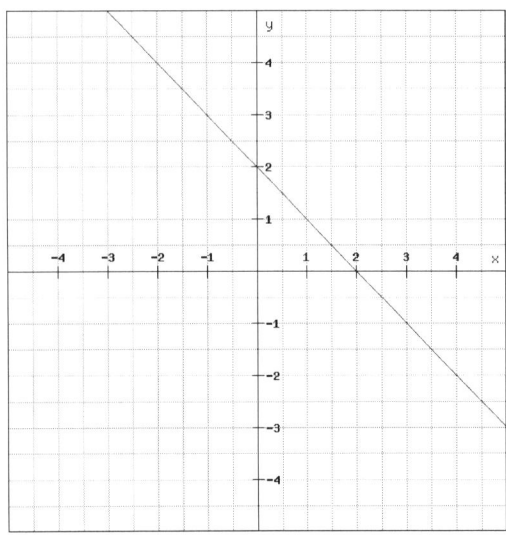

m = −1   b = 2   f(x) = −x + 2   m = 1   b = 2   f(x) = x + 2

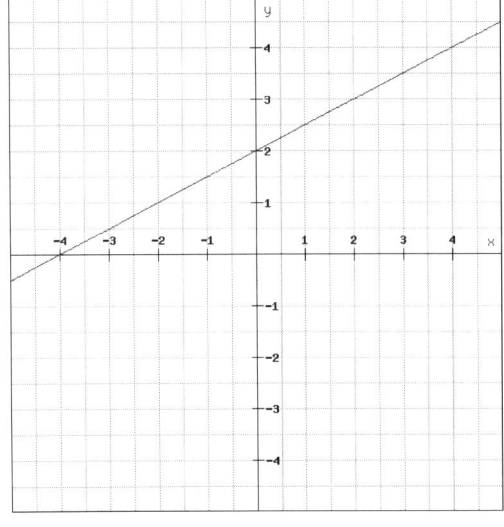

$m = \dfrac{1}{2}$ b = 2 $f(x) = \dfrac{1}{2}x + 2$ $m = -\dfrac{1}{2}$ b = −2 $f(x) = -\dfrac{1}{2}x - 2$

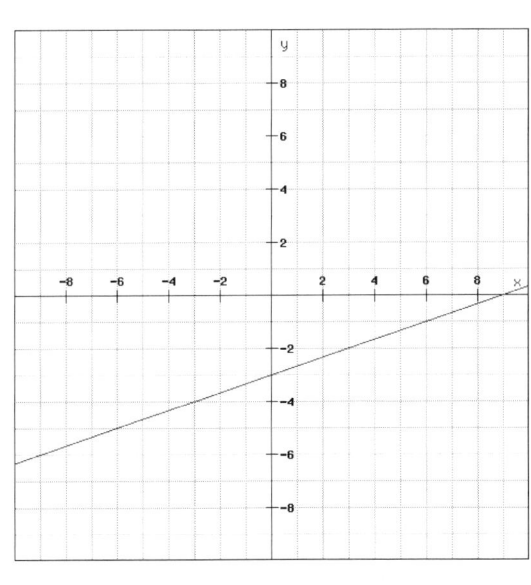

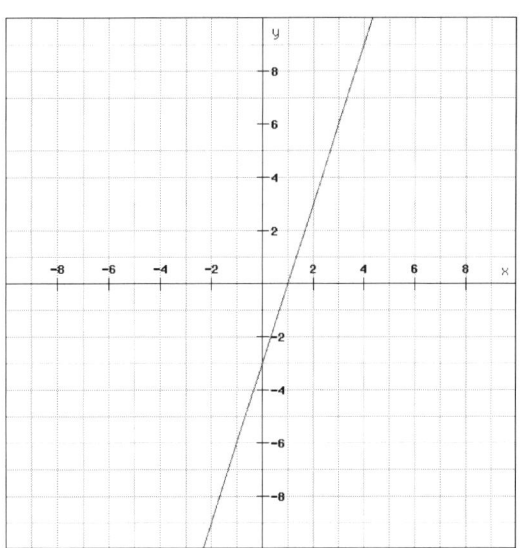

m = $\dfrac{1}{3}$　　　b = –3　　　f(x) = $\dfrac{1}{3}$x – 3　　　m = 3　　　b = –3　　　f(x) = 3x – 3

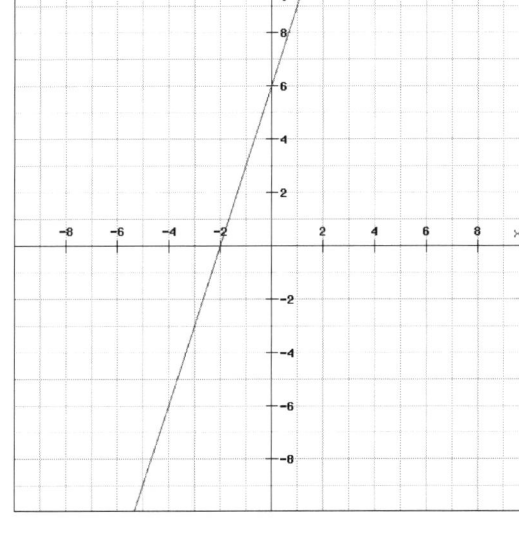

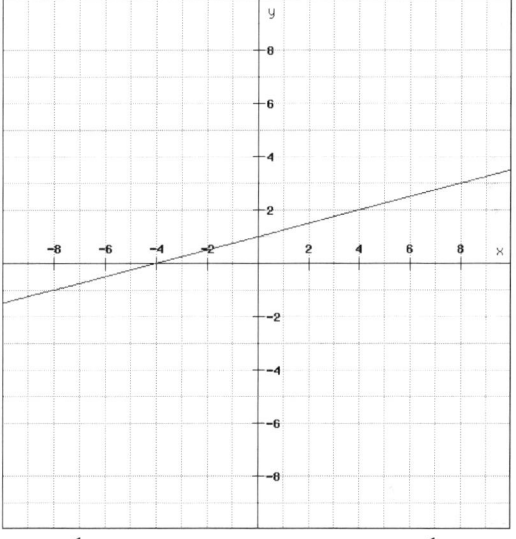

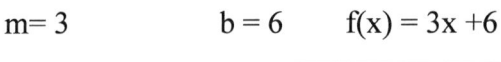

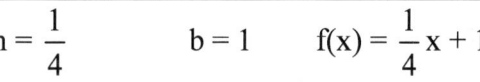

m = 3　　　b = 6　　　f(x) = 3x +6　　　m = $\dfrac{1}{4}$　　　b = 1　　　f(x) = $\dfrac{1}{4}$x + 1

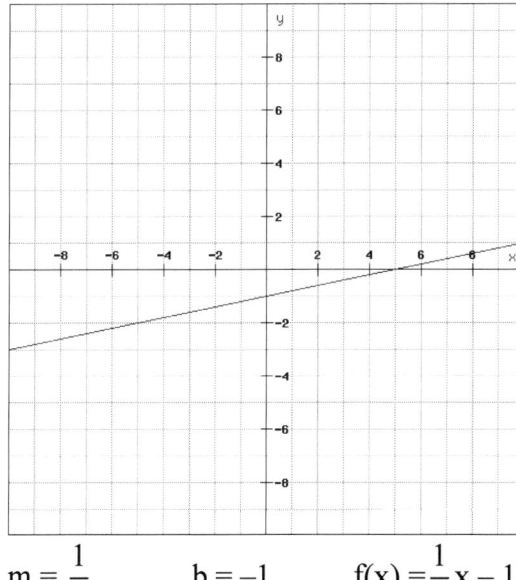

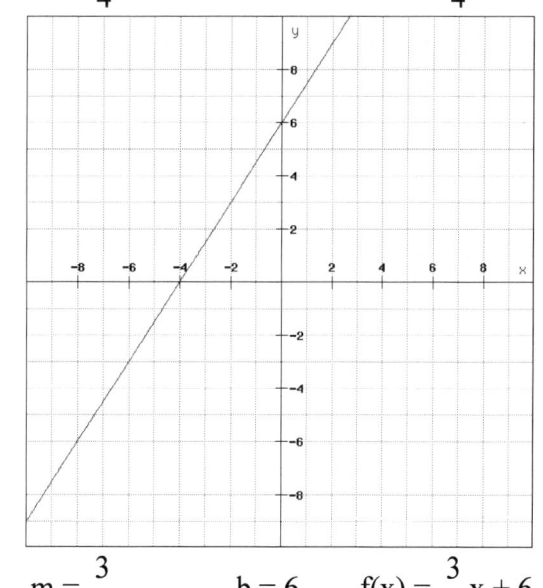

m = $\dfrac{1}{5}$　　　b = –1　　　f(x) = $\dfrac{1}{5}$x – 1　　　m = $\dfrac{3}{2}$　　　b = 6　　　f(x) = $\dfrac{3}{2}$x + 6

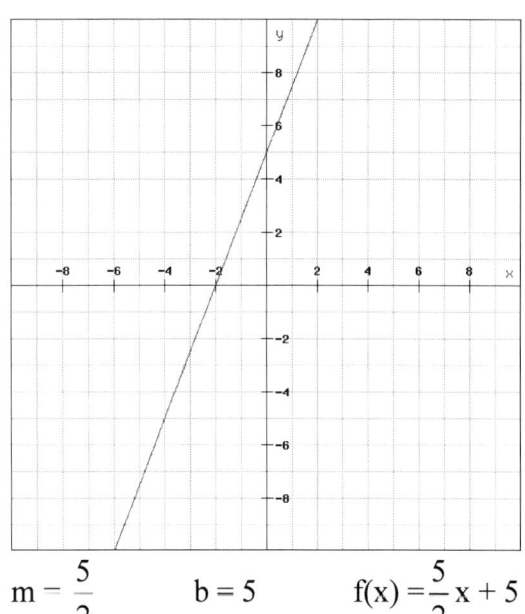

$$m - \frac{5}{2} \qquad b = 5 \qquad f(x) = \frac{5}{2}x + 5$$

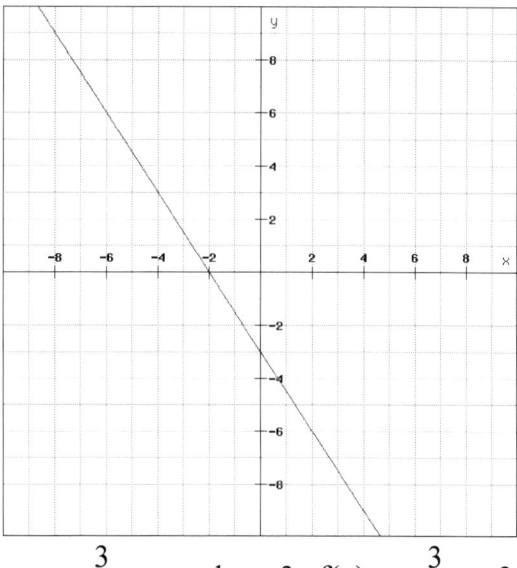

$$m = -\frac{3}{2} \qquad b = -3 \qquad f(x) = -\frac{3}{2}x - 3$$

Analyze the following functions:

1. f(x) = 1

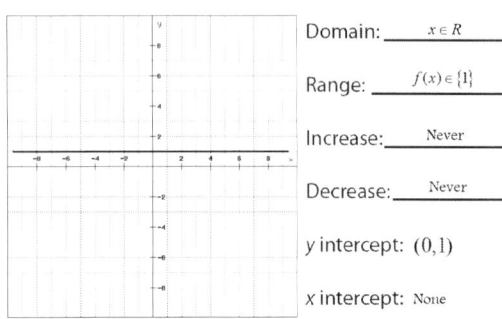

Domain: _____ $x \in R$ _____

Range: _____ $f(x) \in \{1\}$ _____

Increase: _____ Never _____

Decrease: _____ Never _____

y intercept: $(0,1)$

x intercept: None

4. f(x) = 0

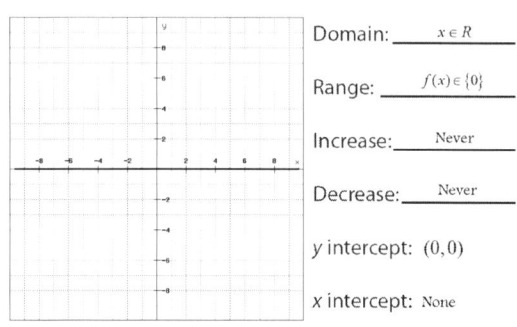

Domain: _____ $x \in R$ _____

Range: _____ $f(x) \in \{0\}$ _____

Increase: _____ Never _____

Decrease: _____ Never _____

y intercept: $(0,0)$

x intercept: None

2. f(x) = 2

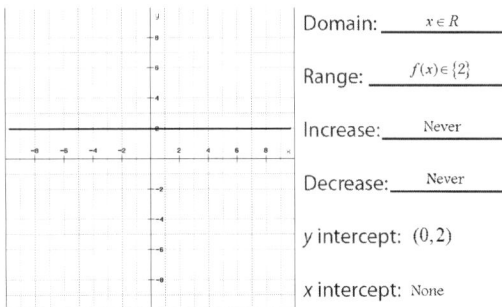

Domain: _____ $x \in R$ _____

Range: _____ $f(x) \in \{2\}$ _____

Increase: _____ Never _____

Decrease: _____ Never _____

y intercept: $(0,2)$

x intercept: None

5. f(x) = x

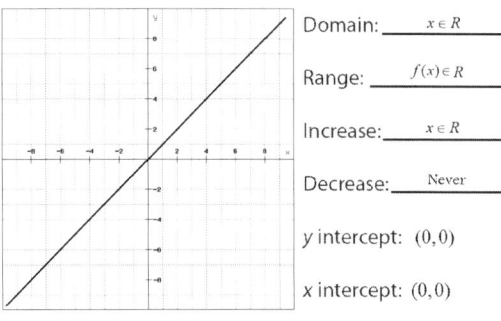

Domain: _____ $x \in R$ _____

Range: _____ $f(x) \in R$ _____

Increase: _____ $x \in R$ _____

Decrease: _____ Never _____

y intercept: $(0,0)$

x intercept: $(0,0)$

3. f(x) = −1

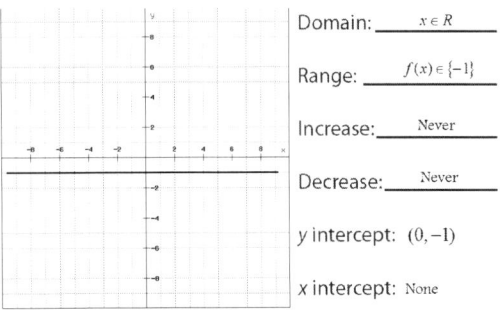

Domain: _____ $x \in R$ _____

Range: _____ $f(x) \in \{-1\}$ _____

Increase: _____ Never _____

Decrease: _____ Never _____

y intercept: $(0,-1)$

x intercept: None

6. f(x) = x+1

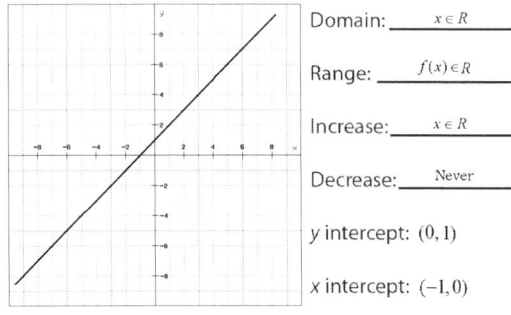

Domain: _____ $x \in R$ _____

Range: _____ $f(x) \in R$ _____

Increase: _____ $x \in R$ _____

Decrease: _____ Never _____

y intercept: $(0,1)$

x intercept: $(-1,0)$

7. f(x) = −x

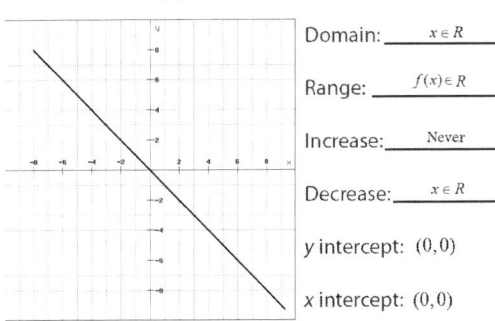

Domain: $x \in R$

Range: $f(x) \in R$

Increase: Never

Decrease: $x \in R$

y intercept: (0,0)

x intercept: (0,0)

8. f(x) = − x − 2

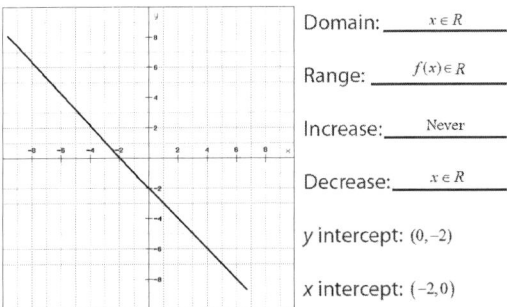

Domain: $x \in R$

Range: $f(x) \in R$

Increase: Never

Decrease: $x \in R$

y intercept: (0,−2)

x intercept: (−2,0)

9. f(x) = 2x

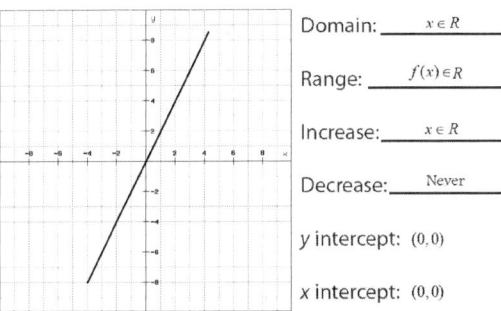

Domain: $x \in R$

Range: $f(x) \in R$

Increase: $x \in R$

Decrease: Never

y intercept: (0,0)

x intercept: (0,0)

10. f(x) = 3x − 5

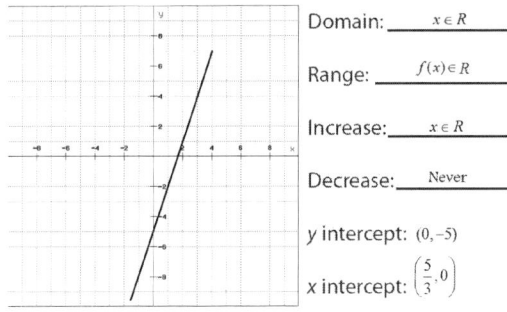

Domain: $x \in R$

Range: $f(x) \in R$

Increase: $x \in R$

Decrease: Never

y intercept: (0,−5)

x intercept: $\left(\frac{5}{3}, 0 \right)$

11. f(x) = 3 − 2x

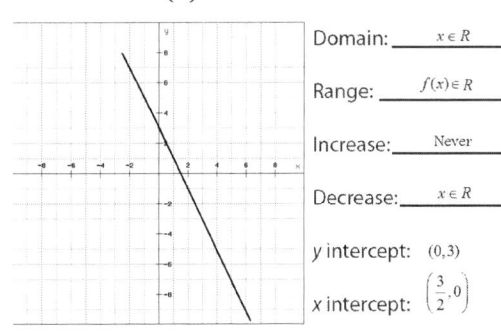

Domain: $x \in R$

Range: $f(x) \in R$

Increase: Never

Decrease: $x \in R$

y intercept: (0,3)

x intercept: $\left(\frac{3}{2}, 0 \right)$

12. f(x) = $\frac{x}{3}$

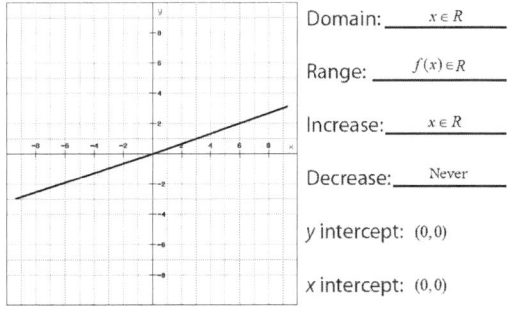

Domain: $x \in R$

Range: $f(x) \in R$

Increase: $x \in R$

Decrease: Never

y intercept: (0,0)

x intercept: (0,0)

13. f(x) = 2x + 1

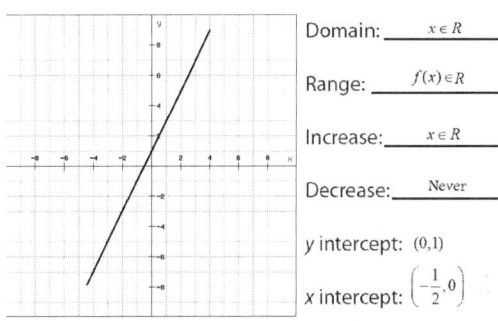

Domain: $x \in R$

Range: $f(x) \in R$

Increase: $x \in R$

Decrease: Never

y intercept: (0,1)

x intercept: $\left(-\frac{1}{2}, 0 \right)$

14. f(x) = 2x − 2

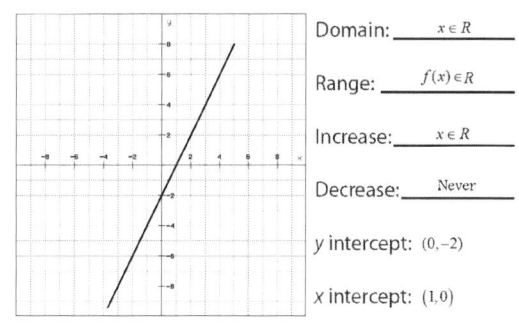

Domain: $x \in R$

Range: $f(x) \in R$

Increase: $x \in R$

Decrease: Never

y intercept: (0,−2)

x intercept: (1,0)

15. f(x) = 3x + 5

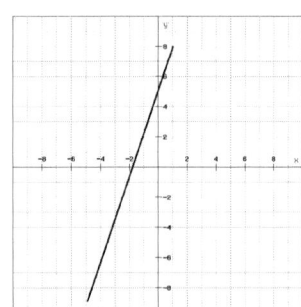

Domain: $x \in R$

Range: $f(x) \in R$

Increase: $x \in R$

Decrease: Never

y intercept: $(0,5)$

x intercept: $\left(-\frac{5}{3}, 0\right)$

16. f(x) = $\dfrac{x}{2}$ − 5

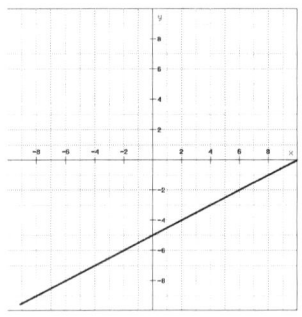

Domain: $x \in R$

Range: $f(x) \in R$

Increase: $x \in R$

Decrease: Never

y intercept: $(0,-5)$

x intercept: $(10,0)$

17. f(x)= $\dfrac{x}{4}$ + 6

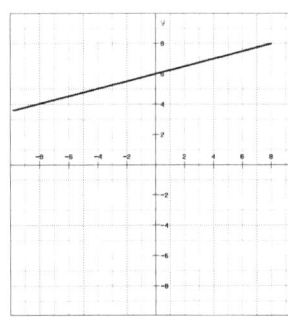

Domain: $x \in R$

Range: $f(x) \in R$

Increase: $x \in R$

Decrease: Never

y intercept: $(0,6)$

x intercept: $(-24,0)$

18. f(x) = $\dfrac{3}{2}$ x − 5

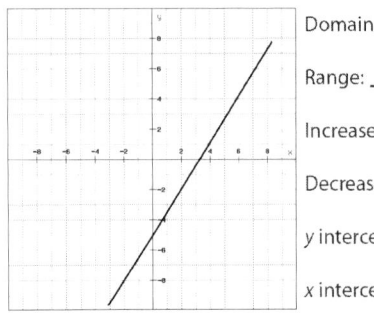

Domain: $x \in R$

Range: $f(x) \in R$

Increase: $x \in R$

Decrease: Never

y intercept: $(0,-5)$

x intercept: $\left(\frac{10}{3}, 0\right)$

19. f(x) = $-\dfrac{3}{2}$ x − $\dfrac{3}{2}$

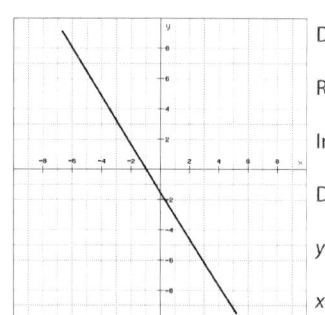

Domain: $x \in R$

Range: $f(x) \in R$

Increase: Never

Decrease: $x \in R$

y intercept: $\left(0, -\frac{3}{2}\right)$

x intercept: $(-1,0)$

20. f(x) = $-\dfrac{1}{2}$ x − $\dfrac{3}{2}$

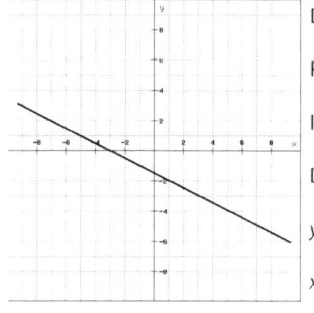

Domain: $x \in R$

Range: $f(x) \in R$

Increase: Never

Decrease: $x \in R$

y intercept: $\left(0, -\frac{3}{2}\right)$

x intercept: $(-3,0)$

21. f(x) = $\dfrac{7}{2}$ x − $\dfrac{1}{4}$

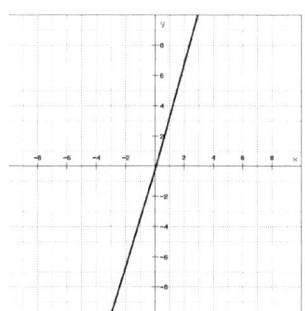

Domain: $x \in R$

Range: $f(x) \in R$

Increase: $x \in R$

Decrease: Never

y intercept: $\left(0, -\frac{1}{4}\right)$

x intercept: $\left(\frac{1}{14}, 0\right)$

22. f(x) = $-\dfrac{9}{5}$ x + $\dfrac{8}{3}$

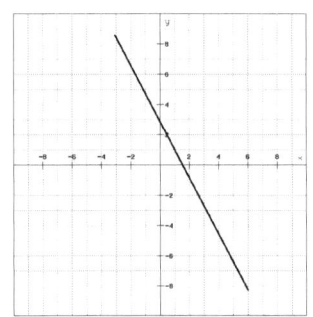

Domain: $x \in R$

Range: $f(x) \in R$

Increase: Never

Decrease: $x \in R$

y intercept: $\left(0, \frac{8}{3}\right)$

x intercept: $\left(\frac{40}{27}, 0\right)$

23. 3x + 2y = 2

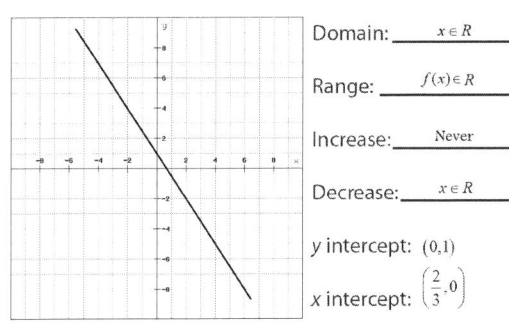

Domain: _____ $x \in R$ _____

Range: _____ $f(x) \in R$ _____

Increase: _____ Never _____

Decrease: _____ $x \in R$ _____

y intercept: $(0,1)$

x intercept: $\left(\frac{2}{3}, 0\right)$

24. 4x– 2y –3 = 1

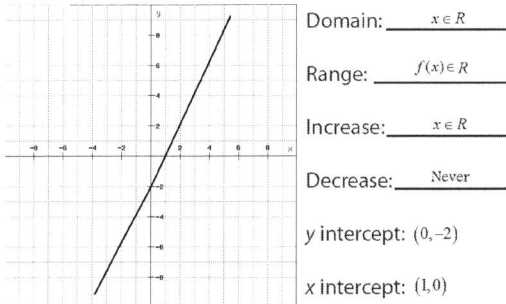

Domain: _____ $x \in R$ _____

Range: _____ $f(x) \in R$ _____

Increase: _____ $x \in R$ _____

Decrease: _____ Never _____

y intercept: $(0,-2)$

x intercept: $(1,0)$

25. –2y + 3x = –5

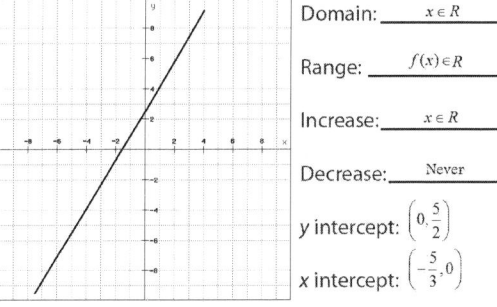

Domain: _____ $x \in R$ _____

Range: _____ $f(x) \in R$ _____

Increase: _____ $x \in R$ _____

Decrease: _____ Never _____

y intercept: $\left(0, \frac{5}{2}\right)$

x intercept: $\left(-\frac{5}{3}, 0\right)$

26. y – x = 2

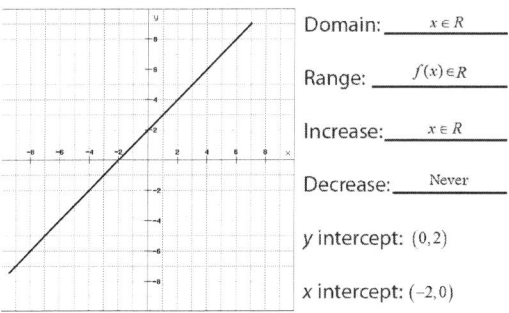

Domain: _____ $x \in R$ _____

Range: _____ $f(x) \in R$ _____

Increase: _____ $x \in R$ _____

Decrease: _____ Never _____

y intercept: $(0,2)$

x intercept: $(-2,0)$

27. y + 2x –3 = 1

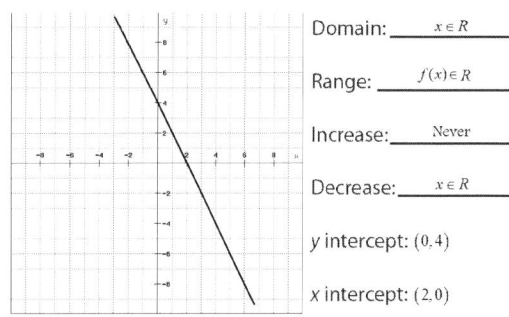

Domain: _____ $x \in R$ _____

Range: _____ $f(x) \in R$ _____

Increase: _____ Never _____

Decrease: _____ $x \in R$ _____

y intercept: $(0,4)$

x intercept: $(2,0)$

28. 5y + 5x = 5

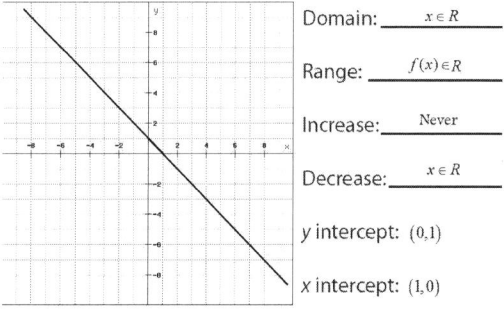

Domain: _____ $x \in R$ _____

Range: _____ $f(x) \in R$ _____

Increase: _____ Never _____

Decrease: _____ $x \in R$ _____

y intercept: $(0,1)$

x intercept: $(1,0)$

29. 2x – 2y –3 = 1

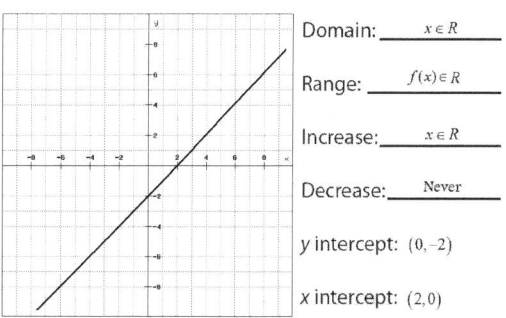

Domain: _____ $x \in R$ _____

Range: _____ $f(x) \in R$ _____

Increase: _____ $x \in R$ _____

Decrease: _____ Never _____

y intercept: $(0,-2)$

x intercept: $(2,0)$

30. x – 2y – 150 = 0

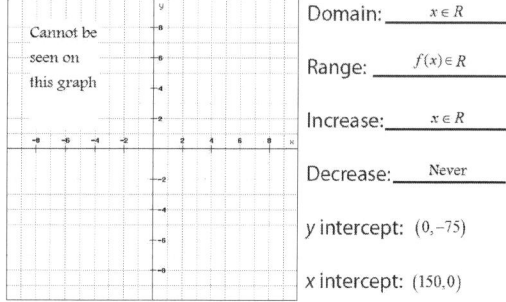

Cannot be seen on this graph

Domain: _____ $x \in R$ _____

Range: _____ $f(x) \in R$ _____

Increase: _____ $x \in R$ _____

Decrease: _____ Never _____

y intercept: $(0,-75)$

x intercept: $(150,0)$

31. Write the equation of the line that has a slope of 2 and passes through the point (2, 4) in the forms: y = mx + b and ax + by + c = 0, (a, b $\in Z$)

$$y = 2x; 2x - y = 0$$

32. Write the equation of the line that has a slope of $-\dfrac{1}{2}$ and passes through the point (–2, –3) in the forms: y = mx + b and ax + by + c = 0, (a, b $\in Z$)

$$y = \frac{1}{2}x - 2; x - 2y - 4 = 0$$

33. Write the equation of the line that has a slope of $-\dfrac{5}{2}$ and passes through the point (–1, 2) in the forms: y = mx + b and ax + by + c = 0, (a, b $\in Z$)

$$y = -\frac{5}{2}x - \frac{1}{2}; 5x + 2y + 1 = 0$$

34. Find the equation of the line that passes through the points (1, 1), (2, 4), indicate its y and x intercepts and sketch it. Write its equation in the forms: y = mx + b and ax + by + c = 0, (a, b $\in Z$)

$$y = 3x - 2; 3x - y - 2 = 0$$

35. Find the equation of the line that passes through the points (–1, –5), (4, 3), indicate its y and x intercepts and sketch it. Write its equation in the forms: y = mx + b and ax + by + c = 0, (a, b $\in Z$)

$$y = \frac{8}{5}x - \frac{17}{5}; 8x - y - 17 = 0$$

36. Find the equation of the line that passes through the points (–5, 1), (–2, 4), indicate its y and x intercepts, sketch it and write it in both forms y = mx + b and ax + by + c = 0, (a, b $\in Z$)

$$y = x + 6; -x + y - 6 = 0$$

37. Write the equation of the line that is parallel to the line y = 5x – 2 and passes through the point (–2, –1). Write its equation in the forms: y = mx + b and ax + by + c = 0, (a, b $\in Z$)

$$y = 5x + 9; -5x + y - 9 = 0$$

38. Write the equation of the line that is parallel to the line y = –0.5x – 1 and passes through the point (–3, 6). Write its equation in the forms: y = mx + b and ax + by + c = 0, (a, b ∈ Z)

$$y = -\frac{1}{2}x + \frac{9}{2}; x + 2y - 9 = 0$$

39. Sketch and write the equation of the line with a slope of $-\frac{1}{5}$ that passes through the point (0,2).

$$y = -\frac{1}{5}x + 2; x + 5y - 10 = 0$$

40. Sketch and write the equation of the lines with a slope: $1, 2, -3, -1, -\frac{1}{2}, -\frac{1}{3},$ that passes through the point (0,0).

$$y = x; y = 2x; y = -3x; y = -x; y = -\frac{1}{2}x; y = -\frac{1}{3}x$$

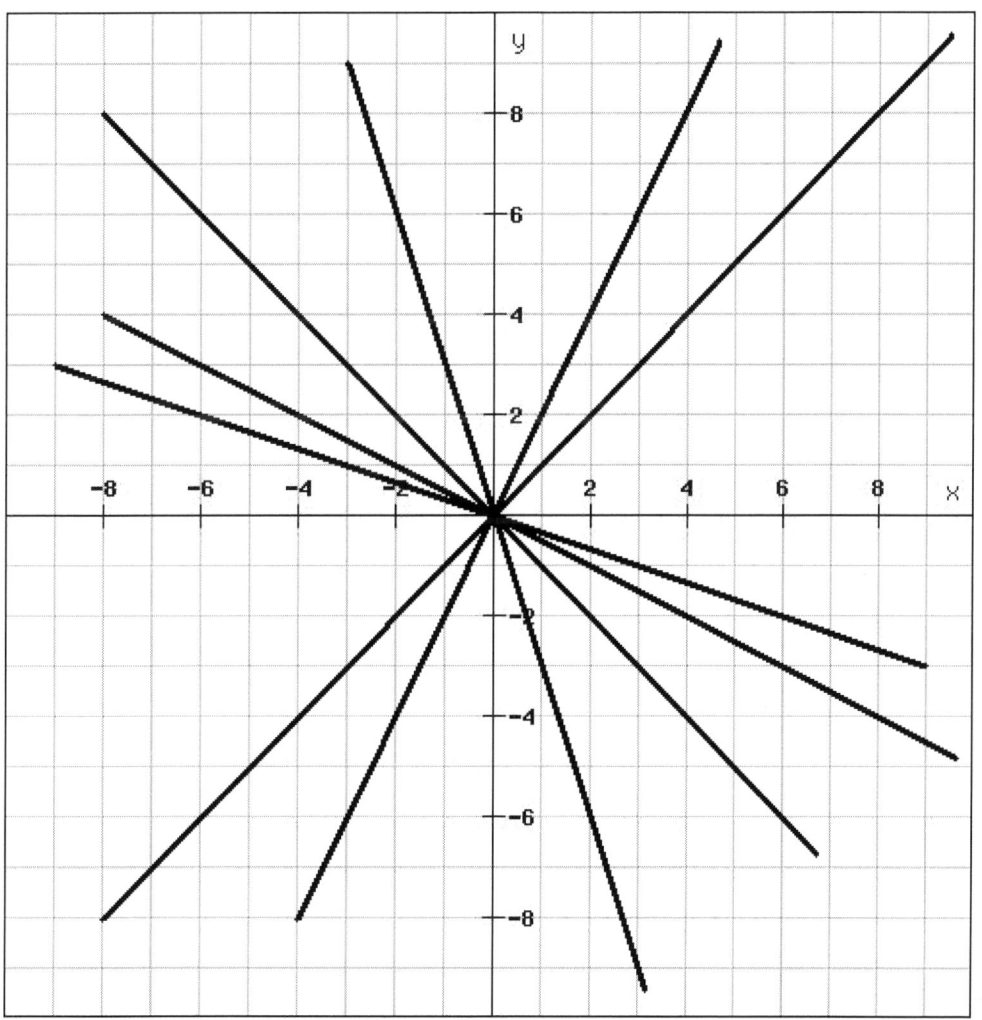

347

41. Sketch and write the equation of the line with a slope of –3 that passes through the point (0,–3).

$$y = -3x - 3$$

42. Sketch and write the equation of the line with a slope of 2 that passes through the point (2,0)

$$y = 2x - 4$$

43. Sketch and write the equation of the line with a slope of $-\dfrac{1}{2}$ that passes through the point (–2,0)

$$y = -\dfrac{1}{2}x - 1$$

44. Sketch and write the equation of the line with a slope of 2 that passes through the point (–4,2)

$$y = 2x + 10$$

45. Find the intersection between the lines f(x) = 2x – 3 and f(x) = –5x –2

$$2x - 3 = -5x - 2$$

$$x = \dfrac{1}{7}$$

$$\left(\dfrac{1}{7}, -\dfrac{19}{7}\right)$$

46. Find the intersection between the lines f(x) = –12x – 13 and f(x) = 15x +20.

$$-12x - 13 = 15x + 20$$

$$x = -\dfrac{33}{27}$$

$$\left(-\dfrac{33}{27}, \dfrac{5}{3}\right)$$

DISTANCE AND MIDPOINT BETWEEN 2 POINTS

47. Given the points (1, 2) and (5, 8). Find the distance between them. Find the midpoint. Sketch to illustrate your answer.

$$\text{Distance} = \sqrt{16 + 36} = \sqrt{52}$$
$$\text{Midpoint} = (3, 5)$$

48. Given the points (–3, 2) and (5, –6). Find the distance between them. Find the midpoint. Sketch to illustrate your answer.

$$\text{Distance} = \sqrt{64 + 64} = \sqrt{128}$$
$$\text{Midpoint} = (1, -4)$$

49. Given the points (–1, –6) and (–5, –1). Find the distance between them. Find the midpoint. Sketch to illustrate your answer.

$$\text{Distance} = \sqrt{16 + 25} = \sqrt{41}$$
$$\text{Midpoint} = \left(-3, -\frac{7}{2}\right)$$

PERPENDICULAR LINES ($m\,m_\perp = -1$)

50. Find the equation of a line perpendicular to the line $y = 3x – 2$ that passes through the point (3, 12). Sketch to illustrate your answer.

$$y = -\frac{1}{3}x + 13$$

51. Find all the lines perpendicular to the line $y = –3x + 4$. Fin the ones that passes through the point (–3, 1). Sketch to illustrate your answer.

$$y = \frac{1}{3}x + 2$$

52. Find a line perpendicular to the line $y = -\frac{2}{5}x + 1$ that passes through the point (–1, –7). Sketch to illustrate your answer.

$$y = \frac{5}{2}x - \frac{9}{2}$$

53. Given that the slope of one of the lines is 3 and that the lines are perpendicular, find the **exact** coordinates of the point of intersection of the two lines.

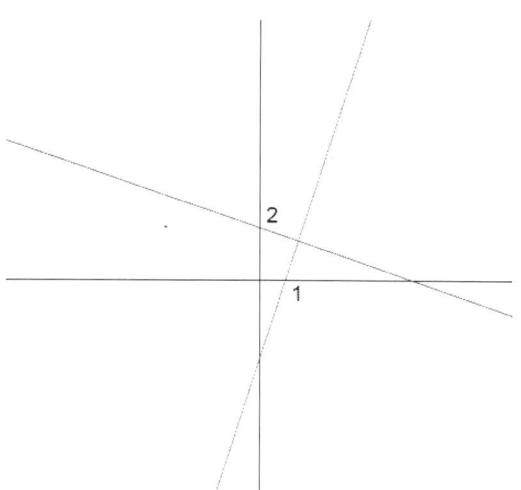

Increasing line (plug (1,0):

$y = 3x - 3$

Decreasing line:

$y = -\dfrac{1}{3}x + 2$

Intersection:

$3x - 3 = -\dfrac{1}{3}x + 2$

$x = \dfrac{3}{2}$

$\left(\dfrac{3}{2}, \dfrac{1}{2} \right)$

Application

1. The price of a new toy (in US$) is C(t) = 20 – 0.5t, t given in days.

    a. Sketch the corresponding graph.

    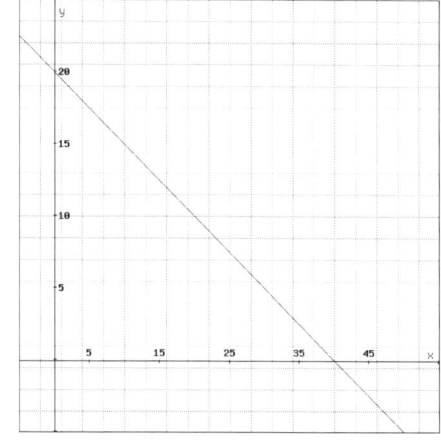

    b. What was the initial price of the toy?

        20$

    c. Find the price of the toy after 10 days

        15$

    d. What is the domain of the function, argument the answer, $t \in [0, 40]$

        Price cannot be negative.

    e. What is the range of the function? $C \in [0, 20]$

    f. What is the meaning of 0.5? Does it have units? What are they?

        0.5 $/ day, it is the daily reduction of the price.

350

2. You need to rent a car for one day and to compare the charges of 3 different companies. Company I charges 20$ per day with additional cost of 0.20$ per mile. Company II charges 30$ per day with additional cost of 0.10$ per mile. Company III charges 70$ per day with no additional mileage charge.

a. Write the cost function for each one of the companies.

$$C_I = 20 + 0.2x$$
$$C_{II} = 30 + 0.1x$$
$$C_{III} = 70$$

b. Sketch all 3 graphs on the same axes system.

c. Comment on the circumstances in which renting a car from each one of the companies is best.

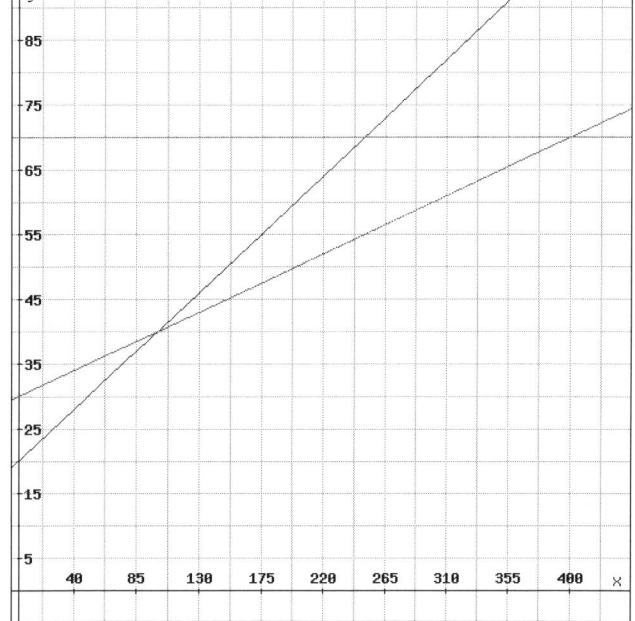

The black line represent the cheapest price:

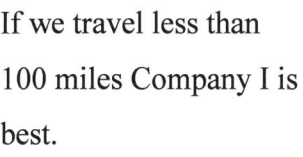

It is important to find the intersection points between: lines I, II and lines II, III.

I, II: (100, 40)

II, III (400, 70)

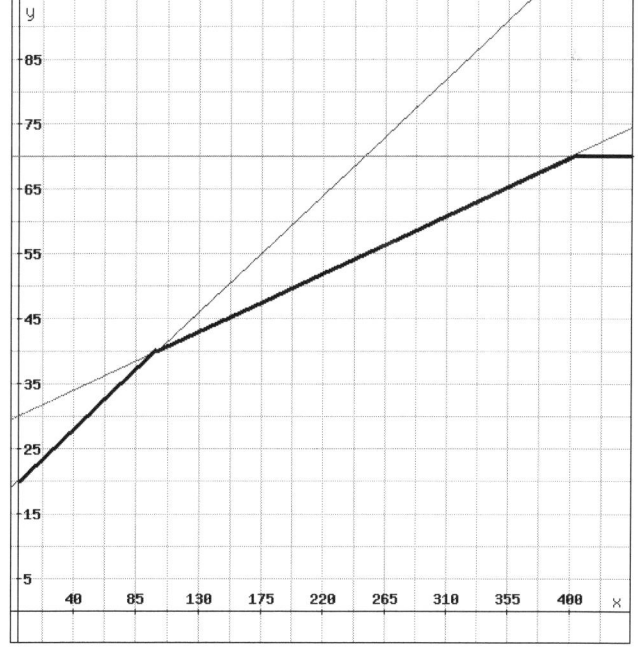

If we travel less than 100 miles Company I is best.

If we travel between 100 and 400 miles Company II is best.

If we travel more than 400 miles Company III is best.

5.3. – QUADRATIC FUNCTIONS

1. Given the functions: $f(x) = x^2$, $g(x) = x^2 - 2$. Complete the following table:

x	−5	−4	−3	−2	−1	0	1	2	3	4	5	6
f(x)	25	16	9	4	1	0	1	4	9	16	25	36
g(x)	23	14	7	2	−1	−2	−1	2	7	14	23	34

- Sketch the points of the table on a graph (use a ruler).

- State the domain of the function: $x \in R$

- State the y intercept (sketched on the graph): $f(x):(0,0); g(x):(0,-2)$

- State the x intercept(s): $f(x):(0,0); g(x):(\sqrt{2},0),(-\sqrt{2},0)$

- Write in all possible forms:

$$f(x) = x^2 \qquad g(x) = x^2 - 2 = (x+\sqrt{2})(x-\sqrt{2})$$

- Find the max/**min** point(s): $f(x):(0,0); g(x):(0,-2)$

- The function is increasing on the interval: $f(x): x \in (0,\infty); g(x): x \in (0,\infty)$

- The function is decreasing on the interval: $f(x): x \in (-\infty,0); g(x): x \in (-\infty,0)$

- State the range of the function: $f(x) \in [0,\infty); g(x) \in [-2,\infty)$

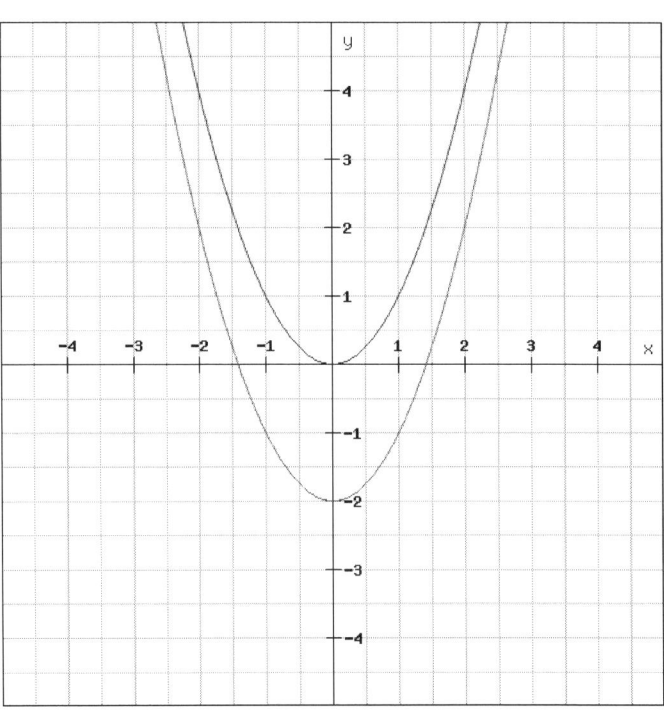

2. Given the functions: f(x) = (x − 2)², g(x) = (x + 3)² − 2. Complete the following table:

x	−5	−4	−3	−2	−1	0	1	2	3	4	5	6
f(x)	49	36	25	16	9	4	1	0	1	4	9	16
g(x)	2	−1	−2	−1	2	7	14	23	34	47	62	79

- State the domain of the function: $x \in R$

- State the y intercept (sketched on the graph): $f(x):(0,4); g(x):(0,7)$

- State the x intercept(s): $f(x):(2,0); g(x):(\sqrt{2}-3,0),(-\sqrt{2}-3,0)$

- Write in all possible forms:

$$f(x) = (x-2)^2 = x^2 - 4x + 4$$
$$g(x) = (x+3)^2 - 2 = (x-(\sqrt{2}-3))(x-(-\sqrt{2}-3)) = x^2 + 6x + 7$$

- Find the max/**min** point(s): $f(x):(2,0); g(x):(-3,-2)$

- The function is increasing on the interval: $f(x): x \in (2,\infty); g(x): x \in (-3,\infty)$

- The function is decreasing on the interval: $f(x): x \in (-\infty,2); g(x): x \in (-\infty,-3)$

- State the range of the function: $f(x) \in [0,\infty); g(x) \in [-2,\infty)$

- State its axes of symmetry: $f(x): x = 2; g(x): x = -3$

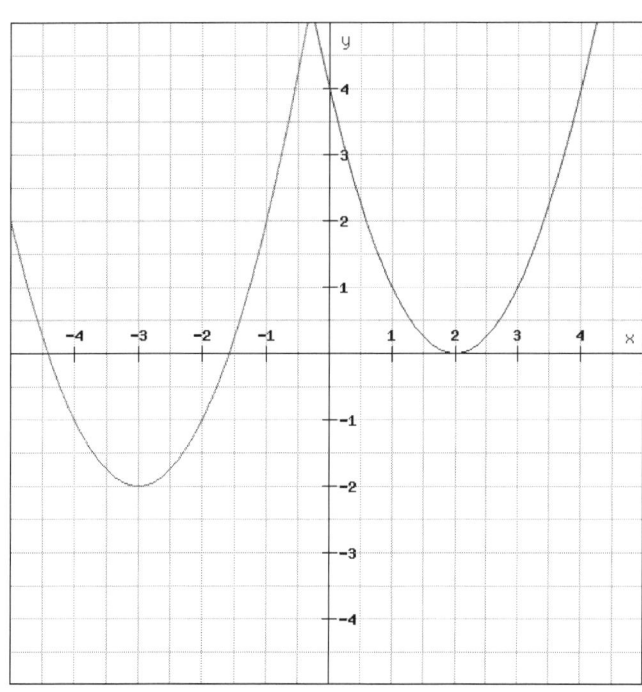

3. Given the function: $f(x) = (x + 2)(x - 4)$, $g(x) = 2(x + 2)(x - 4)$ Complete the following table:

x	−5	−4	−3	−2	−1	0	1	2	3	4	5	6
f(x)	27	16	7	0	−5	−8	−9	−8	−5	0	7	16
g(x)	54	32	14	0	−10	−16	−18	−16	−10	0	14	32

- State the domain of the function: $x \in R$

- State the y intercept (sketched on the graph): $f(x):(0,-8); g(x):(0,-16)$

- State the x intercept(s): $f(x):(-2,0),(4,0); g(x):(-2,0),(4,0)$

- Write in all possible forms:

$$f(x) = (x+2)(x-4) = x^2 - 2x - 8 = (x-1)^2 - 9$$

$$g(x) = 2(x+2)(x-4) = 2x^2 - 4x - 16 = 2(x-1)^2 - 18$$

- Find the max/**min** point(s): $f(x):(1,-9); g(x):(1,-18)$

- The function is increasing on the interval: $f(x): x \in (1,\infty); g(x): x \in (1,\infty)$

- The function is decreasing on the interval: $f(x): x \in (-\infty,1); g(x): x \in (-\infty,1)$

- State the range of the function: $f(x) \in [-9,\infty); g(x) \in [-18,\infty)$

- State its axes of symmetry: $f(x): x = 1; g(x): x = 1$

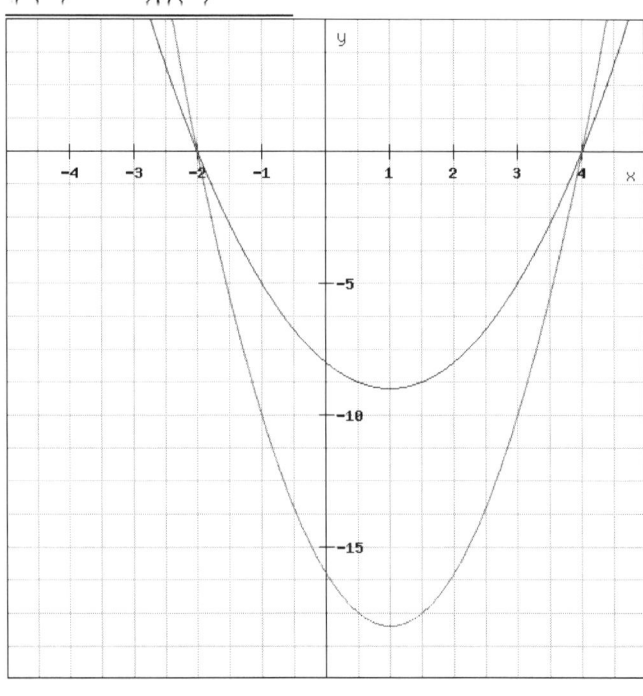

In general, a quadratic function f can be written in several different ways:

a. $f(x) = ax^2 + bx + c$ **standard form**, where a, b and c are constants
b. $f(x) = a(x-r)(x-s)$ **factored form**, where a, r and s are constants
c. $f(x) = a(x-h)^2 + k$ **vertex form**, where a, h and k are constants

Example:

Vertex form: $f(x) = 3(x-2)^2 - 3$
Partial factored form: $f(x) = 3(x-1)(x-3)$
Standard form: $f(x) = 3x^2 + 12x + 9$

Complete the sentences:

1. The graph of a quadratic function is called a <u>Parabola</u>

2. In factored form, the numbers r and s represent <u>the x-coordinates of the x</u> <u>intercepts</u> of f.

3. In vertex form, the point (h, k) is called the <u>vertex</u> of the parabola. The axis of symmetry of the parabola is the line <u>x = h</u>

4. The graph of the parabola opens upwards if <u>a > 0</u> and downwards if <u>a < 0</u>

5. In case $f(x) = x^2 + 1$, the function can be written in <u>1</u> form(s) only. Why? <u>No x intercepts so no factored form. Vertex and standard are identical.</u>

6. In case $f(x) = x^2 - 1$, the function can be written in <u>2</u> form(s) only. Show your answer: <u>Vertex and standard are identical.</u>

7. A parabola has its vertex at the point (2, 3) and goes through the point (6, 11). Find the expression of the function.

    $f(x) = a(x-2)^2 + 3; 11 = a(6-2)^2 + 3; a = \dfrac{1}{2}$

    $f(x) = \dfrac{1}{2}(x-2)^2 + 3$

8. A parabola has its vertex at the point (– 2, 4) and passes through the point (2, – 6). Find the expression of the function.

    $f(x) = a(x+2)^2 + 4; -6 = a(2+2)^2 + 4; a = -\dfrac{10}{16} = -\dfrac{5}{8}$

    $f(x) = -\dfrac{5}{8}(x+2)^2 + 4$

9. Write the analytical expression that corresponds the following functions in all possible forms, assume $a = 1$ or -1 in all cases:

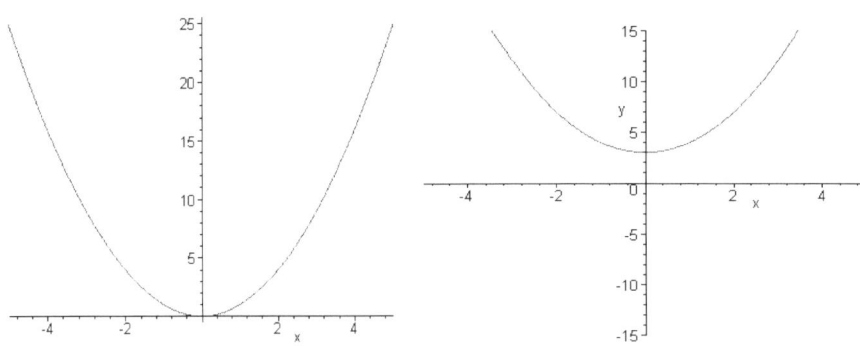

Range: _____ $f(x) \in [0, \infty)$ _____
Vertex form: _____ $f(x) = x^2$ _____
Factorized form: _____ $f(x) = x^2$ _____
Standard form: _____ $f(x) = x^2$ _____

Range: _____ $f(x) \in [3, \infty)$ _____
Vertex form: _____ $f(x) = x^2 + 3$ _____
Factorized form: _____ None _____
Standard form: _____ $f(x) = x^2 + 3$ _____

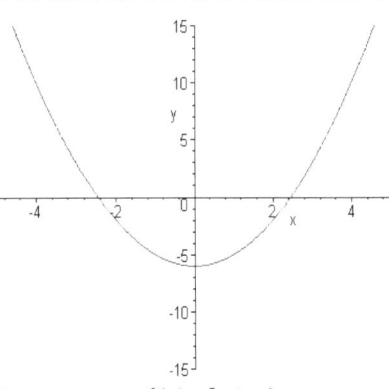

Range: _____ $f(x) \in [-6, \infty)$ _____
Vertex form: _____ $f(x) = x^2 - 6$ _____
Factorized form: _____ $f(x) = (x - \sqrt{6})(x + \sqrt{6})$ _____
Standard form: _____ $f(x) = x^2 - 6$ _____

Range: $f(x) \in [-1, \infty)$; $f(x) \in [-2, \infty)$
Vertex form: $f(x) = x^2 - 1$; $f(x) = x^2 - 2$
Factorized form: $f(x) = (x-1)(x+1); f(x) = (x - \sqrt{2})(x + \sqrt{2})$
Standard form: $f(x) = x^2 - 1$; $f(x) = x^2 - 2$

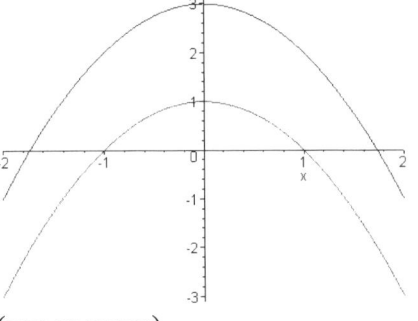

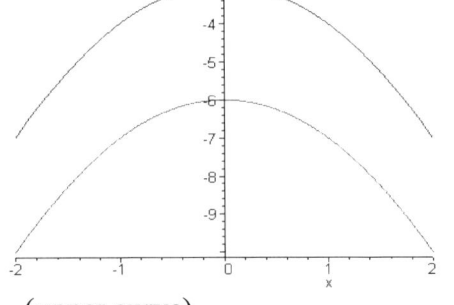

(upper curve)

Range: _____ $f(x) \in [-\infty, 3)$ _____
Vertex form: _____ $f(x) = -x^2 + 3$ _____
Factorized form: _____ $f(x) = -(x - \sqrt{3})(x + \sqrt{3})$ _____
Standard form: _____ $f(x) = -x^2 + 3$ _____

(upper curve)

Range: _____ $f(x) \in [-\infty, -3)$ _____
Vertex form: _____ $f(x) = -x^2 - 3$ _____
Factorized form: _____ None _____
Standard form: _____ $f(x) = -x^2 - 3$ _____

10. Complete the tables:

Function	On the graph
$f(x) = x^2$	B
$f(x) = \dfrac{x^2}{2}$	C
$f(x) = \dfrac{x^2}{3}$	D
$f(x) = 2x^2$	A

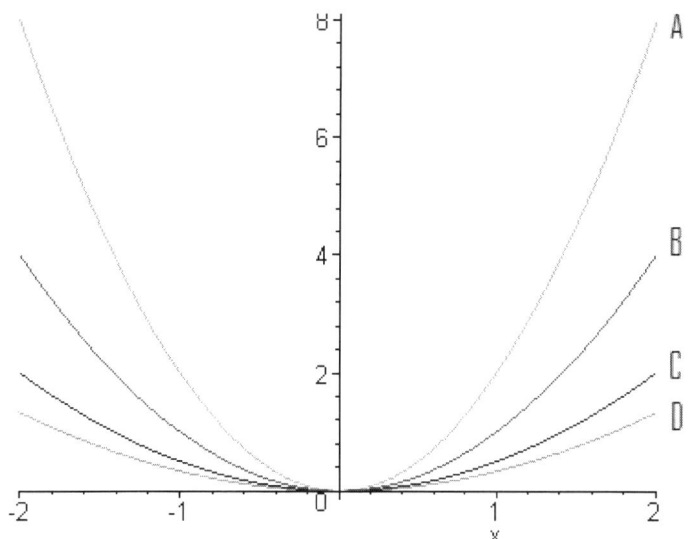

11. Complete the table:

Function	On the graph
$f(x) = x^2 + 2$	B
$f(x) = x^2 - 2$	C
$f(x) = x^2 - 3$	D
$f(x) = 2x^2 + 2$	A

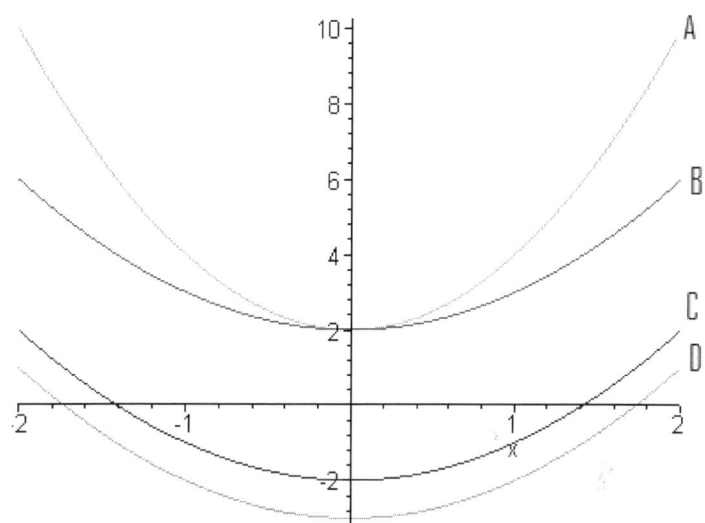

12. Complete the table:

Function	On the graph
$f(x) = -x^2 + 2$	C
$f(x) = x^2 - 4$	D
$f(x) = -x^2 + 3$	B
$f(x) = 2x^2 + 2$	A

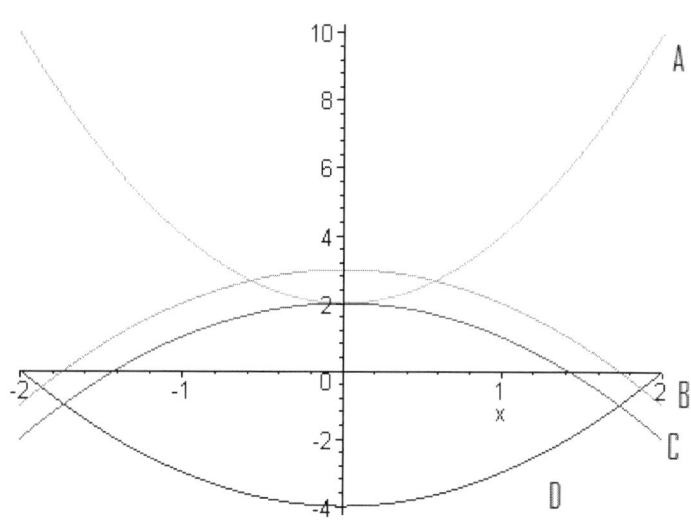

13. Write the expression of the function in all possible forms, indicate the range assume $a = 1$ or -1 in all cases. Use GDC to check your answer.

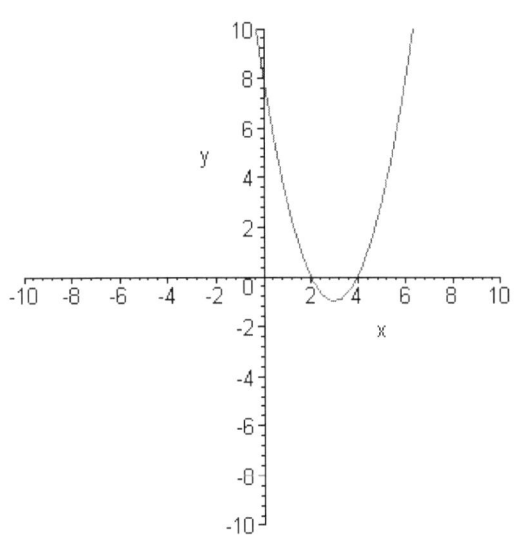

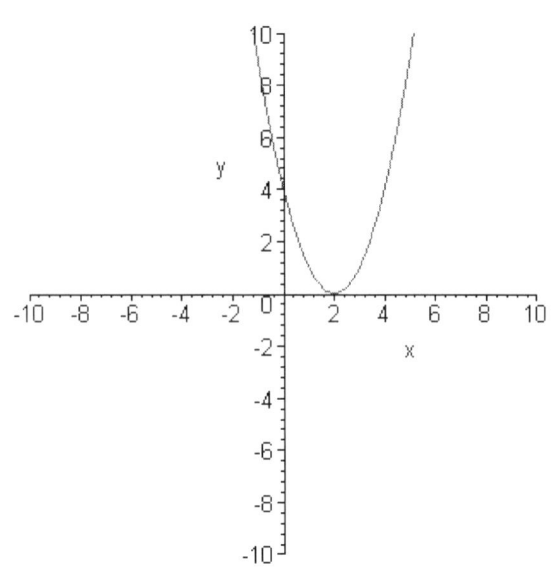

Range: $f(x) \in [-1, \infty)$ Range: $f(x) \in [0, \infty)$

Vertex form: $f(x) = (x-3)^2 - 1$ Vertex form: $f(x) = (x-2)^2$

Factorized form: $f(x) = (x-2)(x-4)$ Factorized form: $f(x) = (x-2)(x-2)$

Standard form: $f(x) = x^2 - 6x + 8$ Standard form: $f(x) = x^2 - 4x + 4$

14.

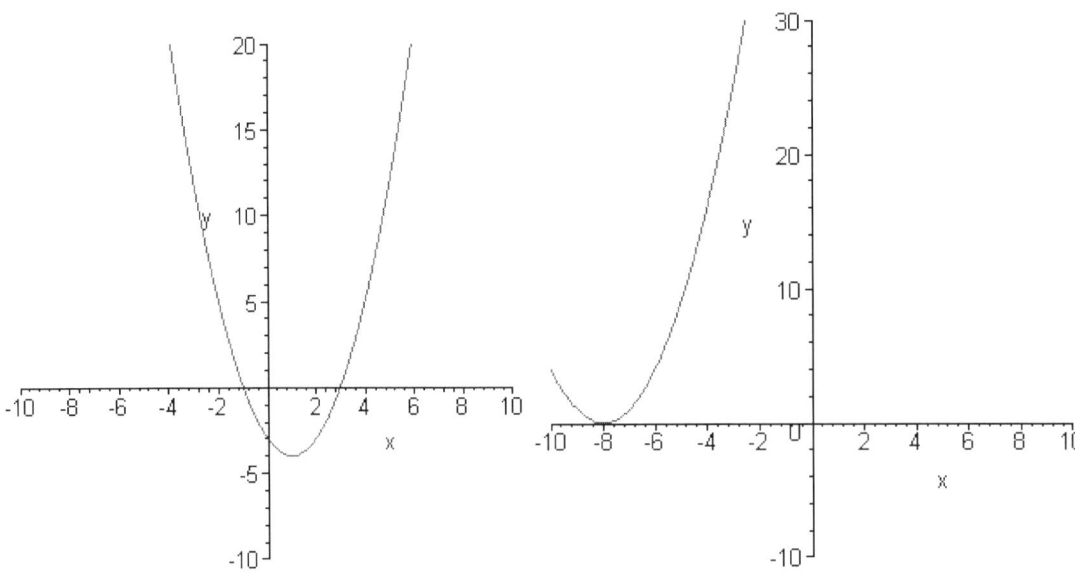

Range: $f(x) \in [-4, \infty)$ Range: $f(x) \in [0, \infty)$

Vertex form: $f(x) = (x-1)^2 - 4$ Vertex form: $f(x) = (x+8)^2$

Factorized form: $f(x) = (x+1)(x-3)$ Factorized form: $f(x) = (x+8)(x+8)$

Standard form: $f(x) = x^2 - 2x - 3$ Standard form: $f(x) = x^2 + 16x + 64$

15.

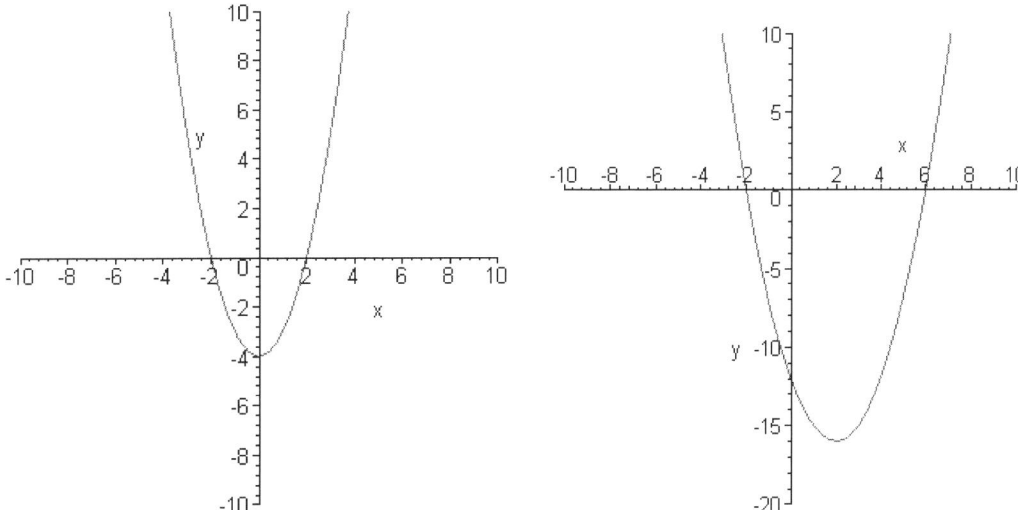

Range: _____ $f(x) \in [-4, \infty)$ _____   Range: _____ $f(x) \in [-16, \infty)$ _____

Vertex form: _____ $f(x) = x^2 - 4$ _____   Vertex form: _____ $f(x) = (x-2)^2 - 16$ _____

Factorized form: _ $f(x) = (x+2)(x-2)$ _   Factorized form: _____ $f(x) = (x+2)(x-6)$ _____

Standard form: _____ $f(x) = x^2 - 4$ _____   Standard form: _____ $f(x) = x^2 - 4x - 12$ _____

16.

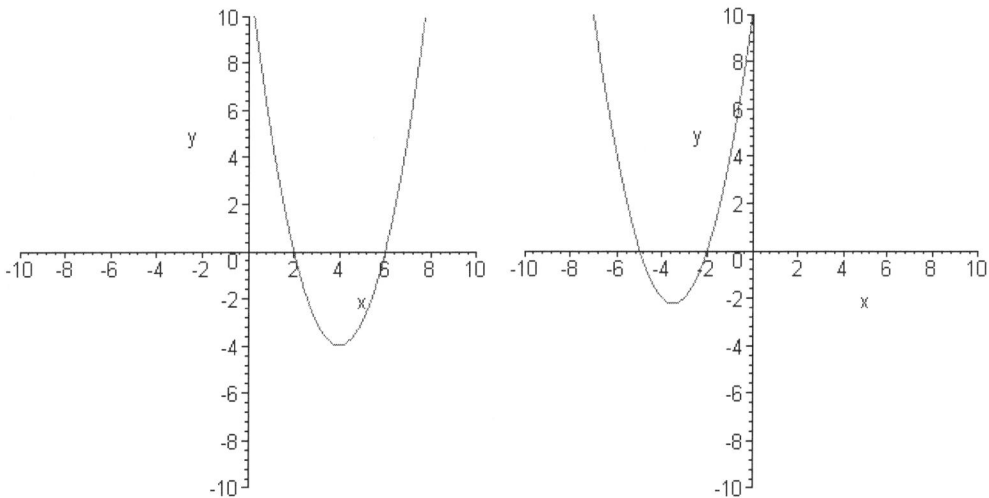

Range: _____ $f(x) \in [-4, \infty)$ _____   Range: _____ $f(x) \in [-\frac{9}{4}, \infty)$ _____

Vertex form: _____ $f(x) = (x-4)^2 - 4$ _____   Vertex form: _____ $f(x) = \left(x + \frac{7}{2}\right)^2 - \frac{9}{4}$ _____

Factorized form: _____ $f(x) = (x-2)(x-6)$ _____   Factorized form: _____ $f(x) = (x+2)(x+5)$ _____

Standard form: _____ $f(x) = x^2 - 8x + 12$ _____   Standard form: _____ $f(x) = x^2 + 7x + 10$ _____

17.

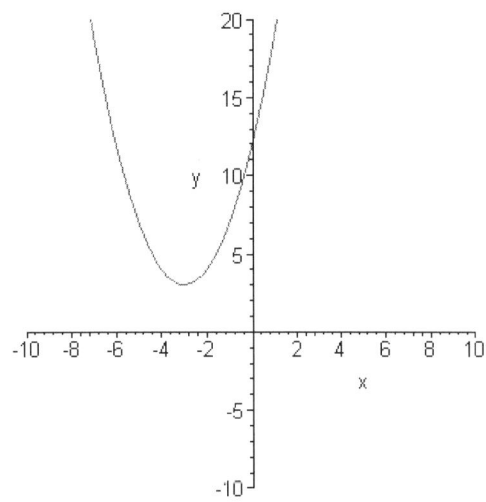

Range: $f(x) \in [3, \infty)$

Vertex form: $f(x) = (x+3)^2 + 3$

Factorized form: *None*

Standard form: $f(x) = x^2 + 6x + 12$

Range: $f(x) \in [-6, \infty)$

Vertex form: $f(x) = (x-4)^2 - 6$

Factorized form: $f(x) = (x - (\sqrt{6}+4))(x - (-\sqrt{6}+4))$

Standard form: $f(x) = x^2 - 8x + 10$

18.

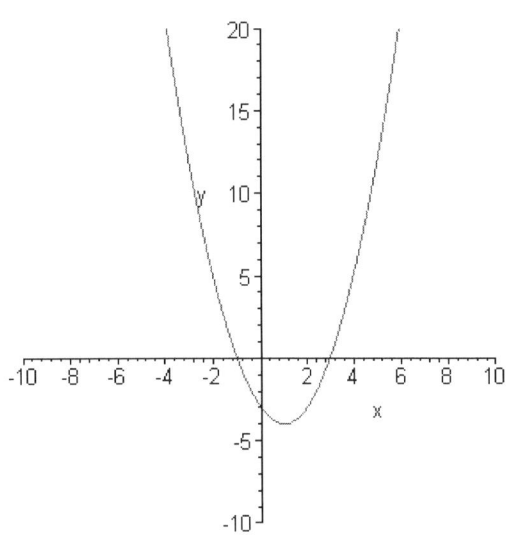
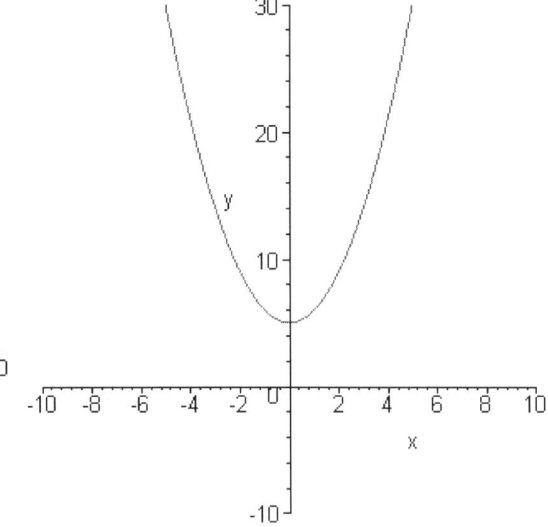

Range: $f(x) \in [-4, \infty)$

Vertex form: $f(x) = (x-1)^2 - 4$

Factorized form: $f(x) = (x-3)(x+1)$

Standard form: $f(x) = x^2 - 2x - 3$

Range: $f(x) \in [5, \infty)$

Vertex form: $f(x) = x^2 + 5$

Factorized form: *None*

Standard form: $f(x) = x^2 + 5$

19.

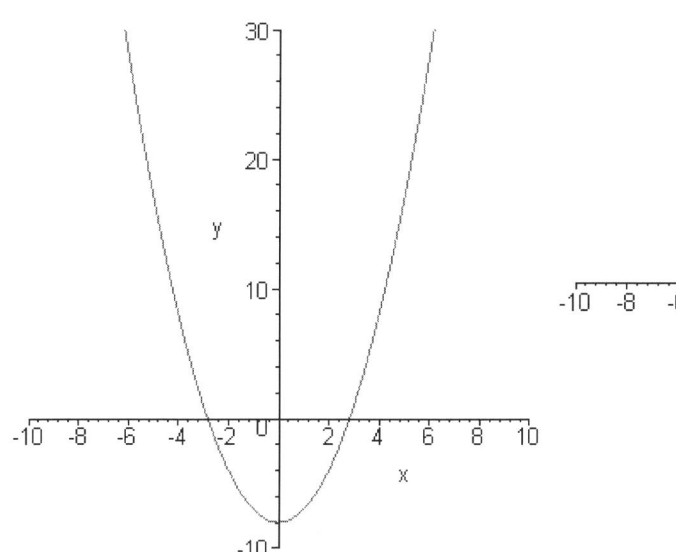

Range: _$f(x) \in [-8, \infty)$_____

Vertex form: _$f(x) = x^2 - 8$_____

Factorized form: _$f(x) = (x - \sqrt{8})(x + \sqrt{8})$__

Standard form: _$f(x) = x^2 - 8$_____

Range: _$f(x) \in [-9, \infty]$_____

Vertex form: _$f(x) = (x+1)^2 - 9$_____

Factorized form: _$f(x) = (x - 2)(x + 4)$_____

Standard form: _$f(x) = x^2 + 2x - 8$_____

20.

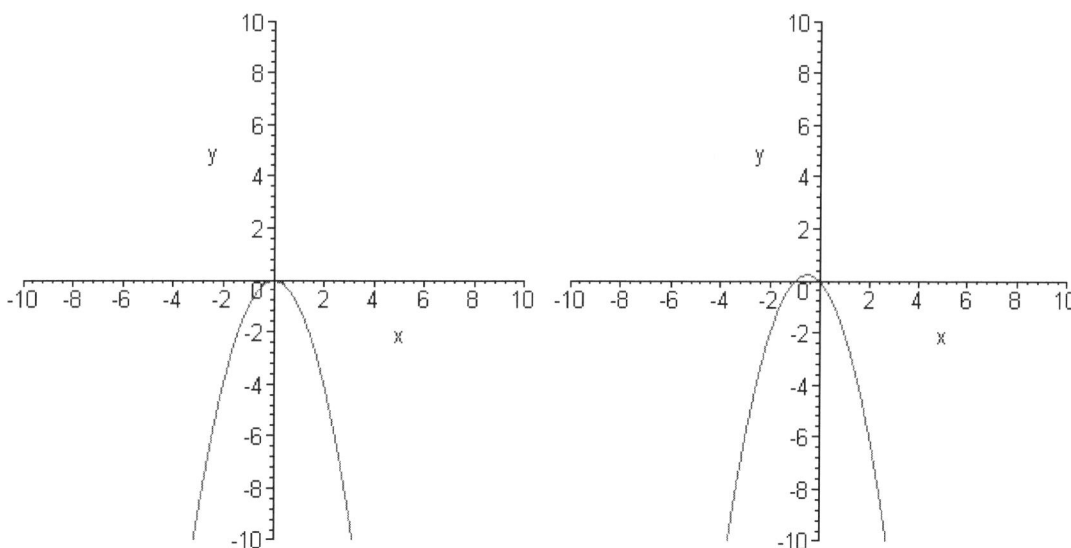

Range: _$f(x) \in (-\infty, 0]$_____

Vertex form: _$f(x) = -x^2$_____

Factorized form: _$f(x) = -x^2$_____

Standard form: _$f(x) = -x^2$_____

Range: _$f(x) \in (-\infty, \frac{1}{4}]$_____

Vertex form: _$f(x) = -\left(x + \frac{1}{2}\right)^2 + \frac{1}{4}$_____

Factorized form: _$f(x) = -x(x + 1)$_____

Standard form: _$f(x) = -x^2 - x$_____

21.

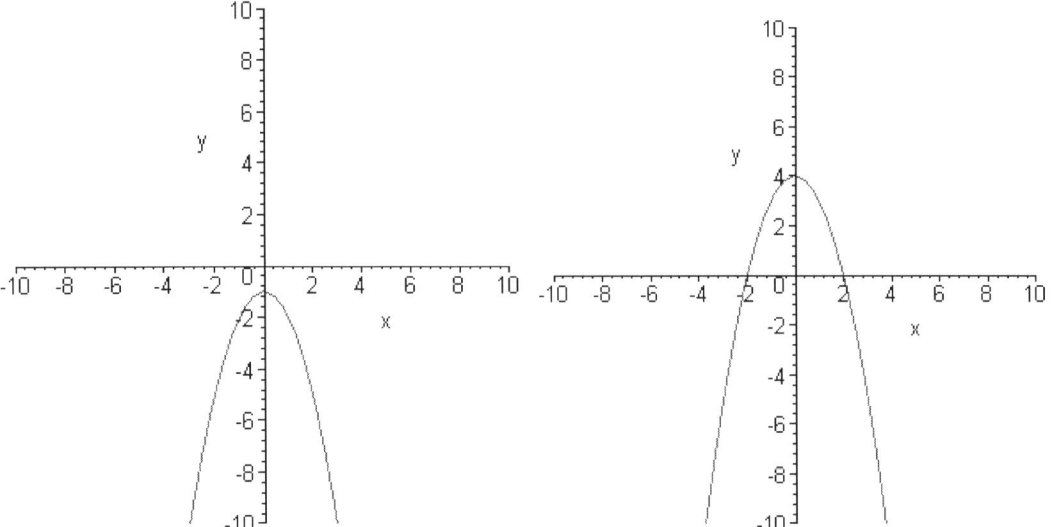

Range: $f(x) \in (-\infty, -1]$

Vertex form: $f(x) = -x^2 - 1$

Factorized form: *None*

Standard form: $f(x) = -x^2 - 1$

Range: $f(x) \in (-\infty, 4]$

Vertex form: $f(x) = -x^2 + 4$

Factorized form: $f(x) = -(x-2)(x+2)$

Standard form: $f(x) = -x^2 + 4$

22.

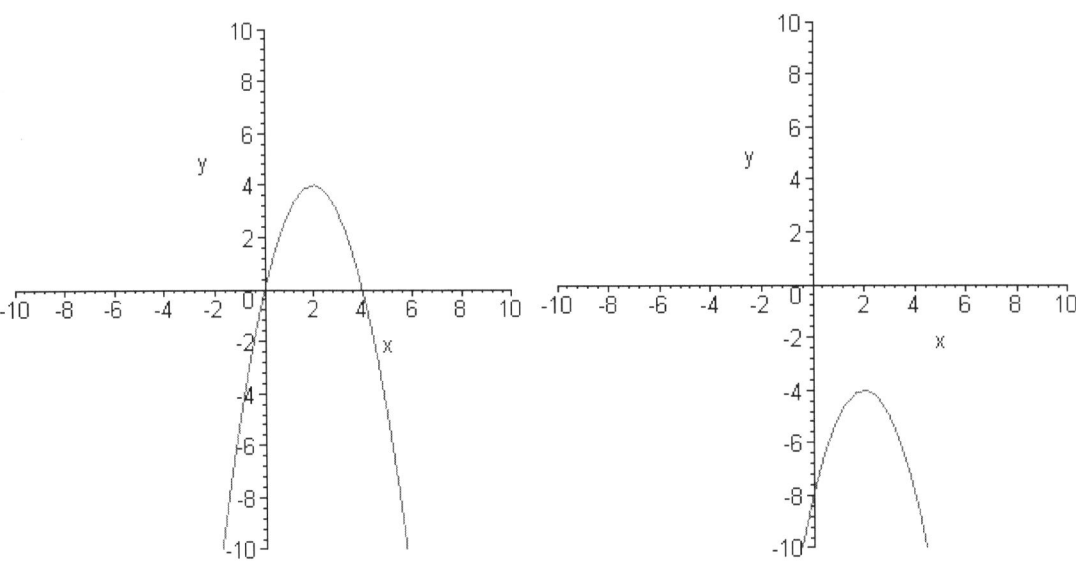

Range: $f(x) \in (-\infty, 4]$

Vertex form: $f(x) = -(x-2)^2 + 4$

Factorized form: $f(x) = -x(x-4)$

Standard form: $f(x) = -x^2 + 4x$

Range: $f(x) \in (-\infty, -4]$

Vertex form: $f(x) = -(x-2)^2 - 4$

Factorized form: *None*

Standard form: $f(x) = -x^2 + 4x - 8$

23.

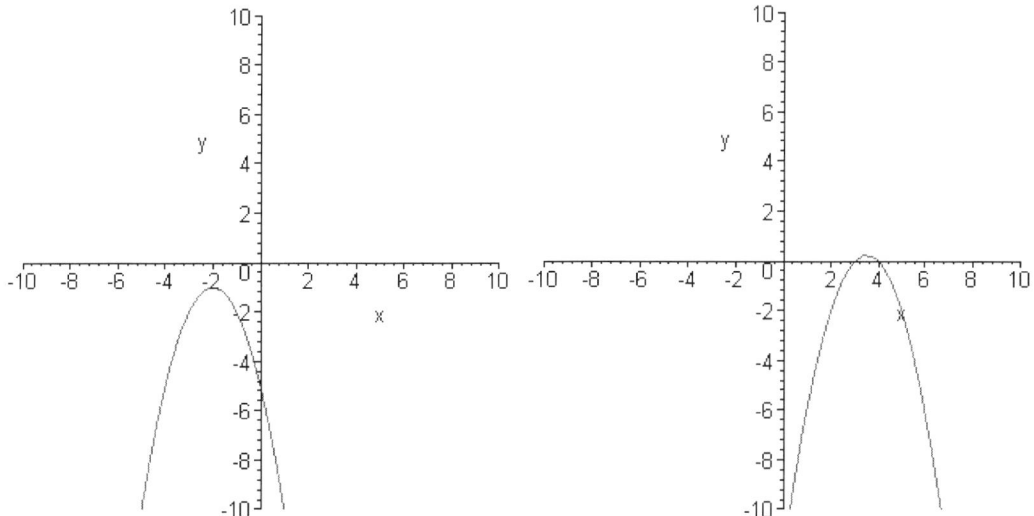

Range: $f(x) \in (-\infty, -1]$

Vertex form: $f(x) = -(x+2)^2 - 1$

Factorized form: None

Standard form: $f(x) = -x^2 - 4x - 5$

Range: $f(x) \in (-\infty, \frac{1}{4}]$

Vertex form: $f(x) = -\left(x - \frac{7}{2}\right)^2 + \frac{1}{4}$

Factorized form: $f(x) = -(x-3)(x-4)$

Standard form: $f(x) = -x^2 - 7x - 12$

24.

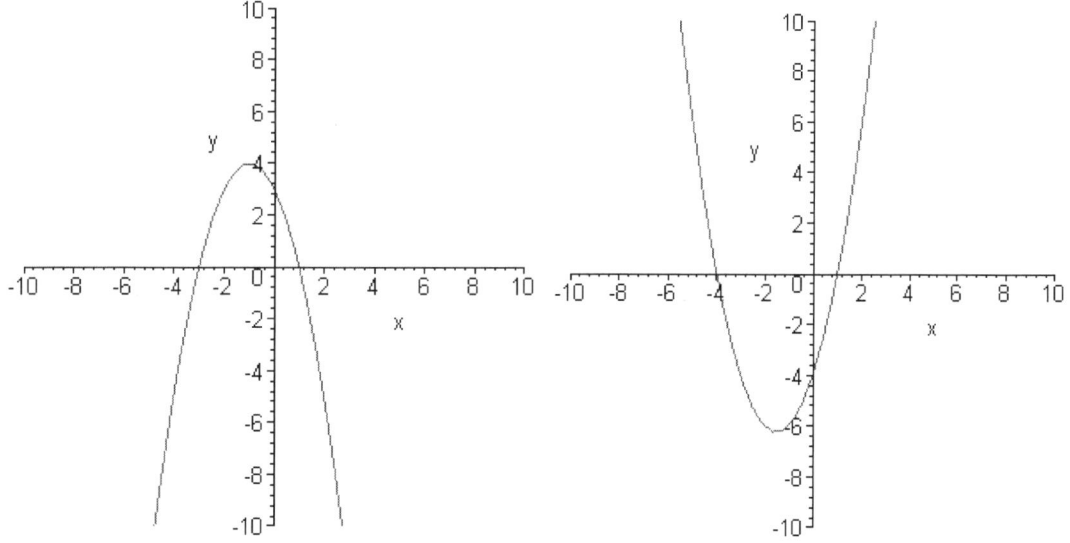

Range: $f(x) \in (-\infty, 4]$

Vertex form: $f(x) = -(x+1)^2 + 4$

Factorized form: $f(x) = -(x-1)(x+3)$

Standard form: $f(x) = -x^2 - 2x + 3$

Range: $f(x) \in (-\frac{25}{4}, \infty]$

Vertex form: $f(x) = \left(x + \frac{3}{2}\right)^2 - \frac{25}{4}$

Factorized form: $f(x) = (x-1)(x+4)$

Standard form: $f(x) = x^2 + 3x - 4$

25.

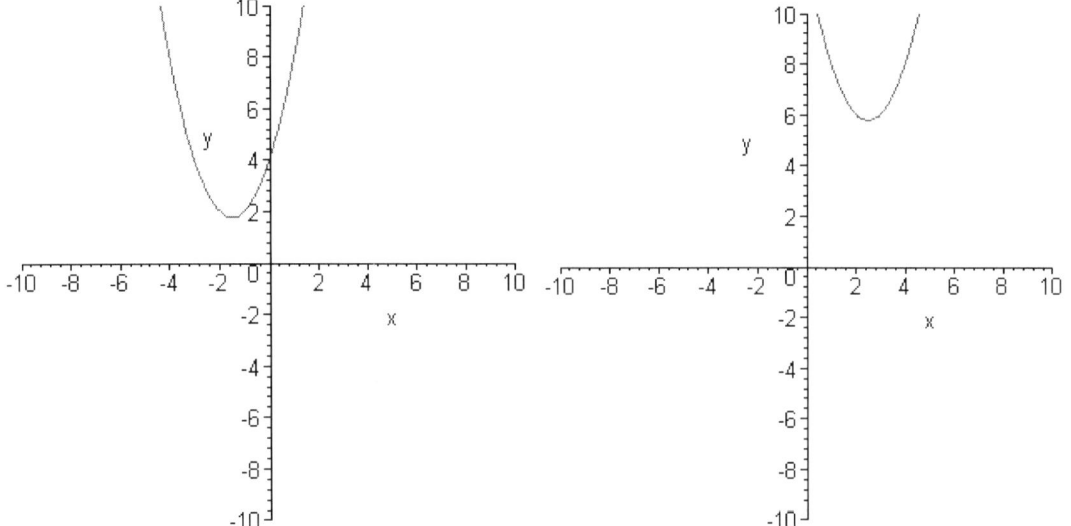

Range: ___$f(x) \in [\frac{7}{4}, \infty)$___

Vertex form: ___$f(x) = \left(x + \frac{3}{2}\right)^2 + \frac{7}{4}$___

Factorized form: ___*None*___

Standard form: ___$f(x) = x^2 + 3x + 4$___

Range: ___$f(x) \in [\frac{23}{4}, \infty)$___

Vertex form: ___$f(x) = \left(x + \frac{5}{2}\right)^2 + \frac{23}{4}$___

Factorized form: ___*None*___

Standard form: ___$f(x) = x^2 + 5x + 12$___

Analyze the following functions; use GDC to verify your answers.

26. f(x) = −3

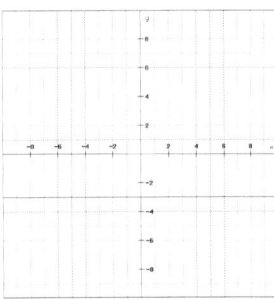

$Vertex \quad Form : None(Linear)$

$Factorized \quad Form : None(Linear)$

$Domain : x \in R \quad Range : f(x) \in \{-3\}$

$y \operatorname{int} : (0, -3) \quad Vertex : None$

$x \operatorname{int} : None$

$Increase : Never \quad Decrease : Never$

27. f(x) = 5x

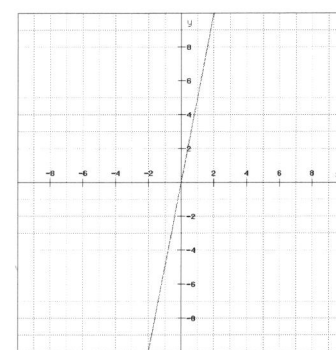

Vertex   Form : *None*(*Linear*)

Factorized   Form : *None*(*Linear*)

Domain : $x \in R$ *Range* : $f(x) \in R$

y int : $(0,0)$ *Vertex* : *None*

x int : $(0,0)$

Increase : $x \in R$ *Decrease* : *Never*

28. f(x) = x² + 8x + 19

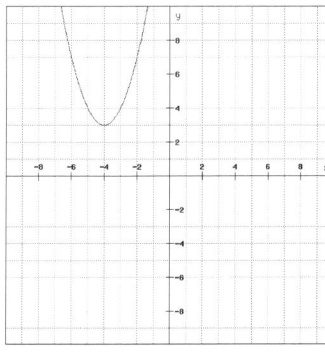

Vertex   Form : $f(x) = (x+4)^2 + 3$

Factorized   Form : *None*

Domain : $x \in R$ *Range* : $f(x) \in [3, \infty)$

y int : $(0,19)$ *Vertex* : $(-4,3)$

x int : *None*

Increase : $x \in (-4, \infty)$ *Decrease* : $x \in (-\infty, 4)$

29. f(x) = 10x² − 8x − 2

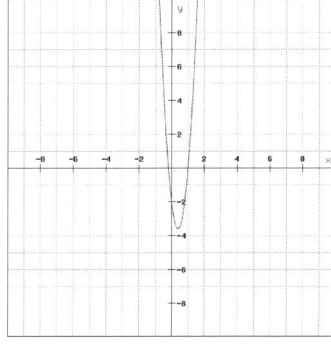

Vertex   Form : $f(x) = 10\left(x - \dfrac{2}{5}\right)^2 - \dfrac{90}{25}$

Factorized   Form : $f(x) = 10\left(x + \dfrac{1}{5}\right)(x-1)$

Domain : $x \in R$ *Range* : $f(x) \in [-\dfrac{90}{25}, \infty)$

y int : $(0,-2)$ *Vertex* : $(\dfrac{2}{5}, -\dfrac{90}{25})$

x int : $(-\dfrac{1}{5}, 0), (1,0)$

Increase : $x \in (\dfrac{2}{5}, \infty)$ *Decrease* : $x \in (-\infty, \dfrac{2}{5})$

30. f(x) = x² + 4x + 1

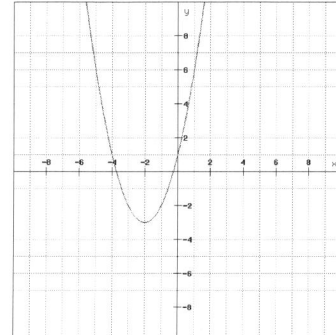

Vertex   Form : $f(x) = (x+2)^2 - 3$

Factorized   Form : $f(x) = \left(x - (\sqrt{3} - 2)\right)\left(x - (-\sqrt{3} - 2)\right)$

Domain : $x \in R$ *Range* : $f(x) \in [-3, \infty)$

y int : $(0,1)$ *Vertex* : $(-2,-3)$

x int : $(\sqrt{3} - 2, 0), (-\sqrt{3} - 2, 0)$

Increase : $x \in (-2, \infty)$ *Decrease* : $x \in (-\infty, -2)$

31. $f(x) = 4x^2 - 14x + 6$

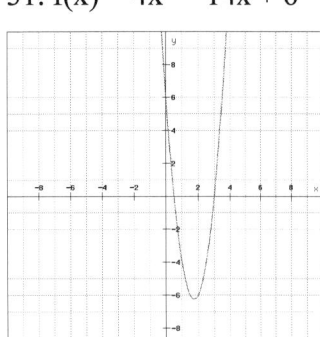

$Vertex\ \ Form: f(x) = 4\left(x - \dfrac{7}{4}\right)^2 - \dfrac{25}{4}$

$Factorized\ \ Form: f(x) = 2\left(x - \dfrac{1}{2}\right)(x - 3)$

$Domain: x \in R\ \ \ Range: f(x) \in [-\dfrac{25}{4}, \infty)$

$y\,\text{int}: (0,6)\ \ Vertex: (\dfrac{7}{4}, -\dfrac{25}{4})$

$x\,\text{int}: (\dfrac{1}{2}, 0), (3, 0)$

$Increase: x \in (\dfrac{7}{4}, \infty)\ \ Decrease: x \in (-\infty, \dfrac{7}{4})$

32. $f(x) = 2x^2 - 3x - 5$

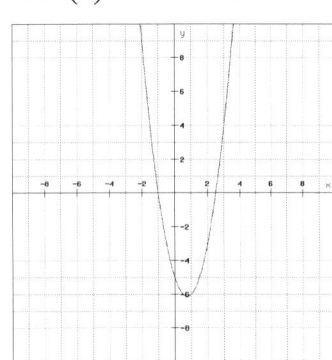

$Vertex\ \ Form: f(x) = 2\left(x - \dfrac{3}{4}\right)^2 - \dfrac{49}{8}$

$Factorized\ \ Form: f(x) = 2\left(x - \dfrac{5}{2}\right)(x + 1)$

$Domain: x \in R\ \ \ Range: f(x) \in [-\dfrac{49}{8}, \infty)$

$y\,\text{int}: (0,-5)\ \ Vertex: (\dfrac{3}{4}, -\dfrac{49}{8})$

$x\,\text{int}: (\dfrac{5}{2}, 0), (-1, 0)$

$Increase: x \in (\dfrac{3}{4}, \infty)\ \ Decrease: x \in (-\infty, \dfrac{3}{4})$

33. $f(x) = x^2 + 3x - 10$

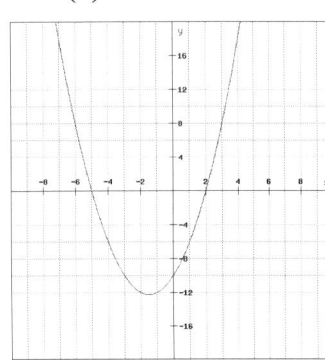

$Vertex\ \ Form: f(x) = \left(x + \dfrac{3}{2}\right)^2 - \dfrac{49}{4}$

$Factorized\ \ Form: f(x) = (x + 5)(x - 2)$

$Domain: x \in R\ \ \ Range: f(x) \in [-\dfrac{49}{4}, \infty)$

$y\,\text{int}: (0,-10)\ \ Vertex: (-\dfrac{3}{2}, -\dfrac{49}{4})$

$x\,\text{int}: (-5, 0), (2, 0)$

$Increase: x \in (-\dfrac{3}{2}, \infty)\ \ Decrease: x \in (-\infty, -\dfrac{3}{2})$

34. $f(x) = x^2 + 7x - 1$

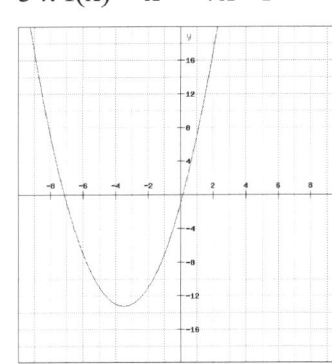

$Vertex \quad Form: f(x) = \left(x + \dfrac{7}{2}\right)^2 - \dfrac{53}{4}$

$Factorized \quad Form: f(x) = \left(x - \left(\sqrt{\dfrac{53}{5}} - \dfrac{7}{2}\right)\right)\left(x - \left(-\sqrt{\dfrac{53}{5}} - \dfrac{7}{2}\right)\right)$

$Domain: x \in R \quad Range: f(x) \in [-\dfrac{53}{4}, \infty)$

$y\,int: (0, -1) \quad Vertex: (-\dfrac{7}{2}, -\dfrac{53}{4})$

$x\,int: (\sqrt{\dfrac{53}{5}} - \dfrac{7}{2}, 0), (-\sqrt{\dfrac{53}{5}} - \dfrac{7}{2}, 0)$

$Increase: x \in (-\dfrac{7}{2}, \infty) \quad Decrease: x \in (-\infty, -\dfrac{7}{2})$

35. $f(x) = x^2 + 2x + 7$

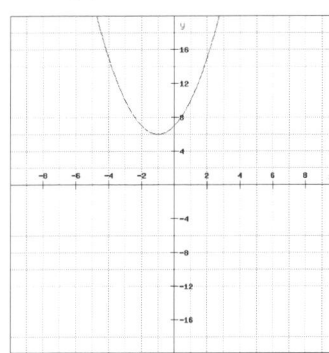

$Vertex \quad Form: f(x) = (x + 1)^2 + 6$

$Factorized \quad Form: None$

$Domain: x \in R \quad Range: f(x) \in [6, \infty)$

$y\,int: (0, 7) \quad Vertex: (-1, 6)$

$x\,int: None$

$Increase: x \in (-1, \infty) \quad Decrease: x \in (-\infty, -1)$

36. $f(x) = x^2 + x - 1$

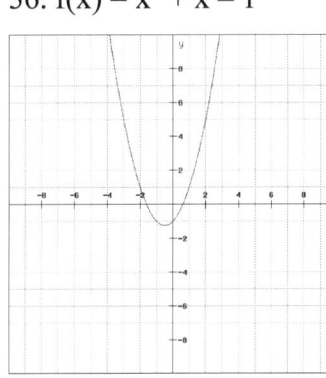

$Vertex \quad Form: f(x) = \left(x + \dfrac{1}{2}\right)^2 - \dfrac{5}{4}$

$Factorized \quad Form: f(x) = \left(x - \left(\sqrt{\dfrac{5}{4}} - \dfrac{1}{2}\right)\right)\left(x - \left(-\sqrt{\dfrac{5}{4}} - \dfrac{1}{2}\right)\right)$

$Domain: x \in R \quad Range: f(x) \in [-\dfrac{5}{4}, \infty)$

$y\,int: (0, -1) \quad Vertex: (-\dfrac{1}{2}, -\dfrac{5}{4})$

$x\,int: (\sqrt{\dfrac{5}{4}} - \dfrac{1}{2}, 0), (-\sqrt{\dfrac{5}{4}} - \dfrac{1}{2}, 0)$

$Increase: x \in (-\dfrac{1}{2}, \infty) \quad Decrease: x \in (-\infty, -\dfrac{1}{2})$

37. $f(x) = x^2 + 2x + 1$

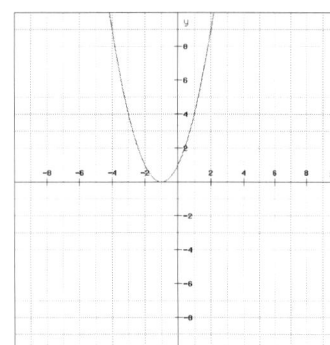

Vertex Form : $f(x) = (x+1)^2$

Factorized Form : $f(x) = (x+1)(x+1)$

Domain : $x \in R$ *Range* : $f(x) \in [0, \infty)$

$y\,\text{int} : (0,1)$ *Vertex* : $(-1, 0)$

$x\,\text{int} : (-1, 0)$

Increase : $x \in (-1, \infty)$ *Decrease* : $x \in (-\infty, -1)$

38. $f(x) = x^2 + 1$

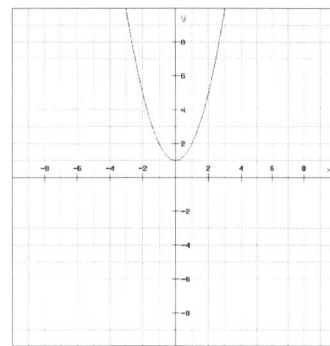

Vertex Form : $f(x) = x^2 + 1$

Factorized Form : *None*

Domain : $x \in R$ *Range* : $f(x) \in [1, \infty)$

$y\,\text{int} : (0,1)$ *Vertex* : $(0, 1)$

$x\,\text{int} : \textit{None}$

Increase : $x \in (0, \infty)$ *Decrease* : $x \in (-\infty, 0)$

39. $f(x) = x^2 - 1$

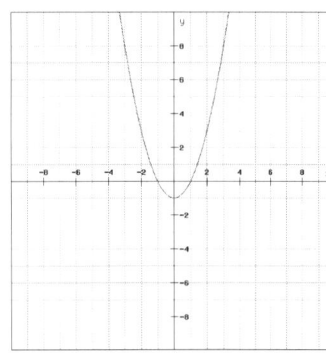

Vertex Form : $f(x) = x^2 - 1$

Factorized Form : $f(x) = (x+1)(x-1)$

Domain : $x \in R$ *Range* : $f(x) \in [-1, \infty)$

$y\,\text{int} : (0,-1)$ *Vertex* : $(0, -1)$

$x\,\text{int} : (-1, 0), (1, 0)$

Increase : $x \in (0, \infty)$ *Decrease* : $x \in (-\infty, 0)$

40. $f(x) = x^2 + 3x$

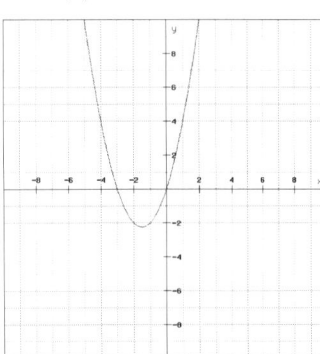

Vertex Form : $f(x) = \left(x + \dfrac{3}{2}\right)^2 - \dfrac{9}{4}$

Factorized Form : $f(x) = x(x+3)$

Domain : $x \in R$ *Range* : $f(x) \in [-\dfrac{9}{4}, \infty)$

$y\,\text{int} : (0,0)$ *Vertex* : $(-\dfrac{3}{2}, -\dfrac{9}{4})$

$x\,\text{int} : (-3, 0), (0, 0)$

Increase : $x \in (-\dfrac{3}{2}, \infty)$ *Decrease* : $x \in (-\infty, -\dfrac{3}{2})$

41. $f(x) = x^2 + 5x$

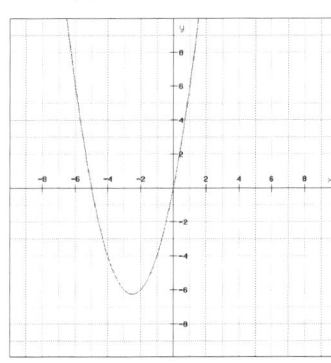

$Vertex\ Form: f(x) = \left(x + \dfrac{5}{2}\right)^2 - \dfrac{25}{4}$

$Factorized\ Form: f(x) = x(x+5)$

$Domain: x \in R \quad Range: f(x) \in [-\dfrac{25}{4}, \infty)$

$y\,int: (0,0) \quad Vertex: (-\dfrac{5}{2}, -\dfrac{25}{4})$

$x\,int: (-5,0), (0,0)$

$Increase: x \in (-\dfrac{5}{2}, \infty) \quad Decrease: x \in (-\infty, -\dfrac{5}{2})$

42. $f(x) = x^2 - 3x$

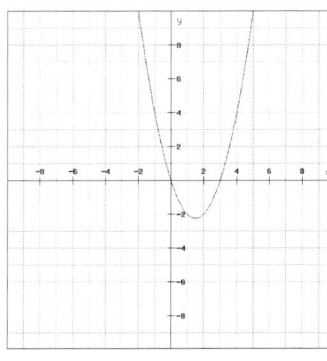

$Vertex\ Form: f(x) = \left(x - \dfrac{3}{2}\right)^2 - \dfrac{9}{4}$

$Factorized\ Form: f(x) = x(x-3)$

$Domain: x \in R \quad Range: f(x) \in [-\dfrac{9}{4}, \infty)$

$y\,int: (0,0) \quad Vertex: (\dfrac{3}{2}, -\dfrac{9}{4})$

$x\,int: (0,0), (3,0)$

$Increase: x \in (\dfrac{3}{2}, \infty) \quad Decrease: x \in (-\infty, \dfrac{3}{2})$

43. $f(x) = x^2 - 7x$

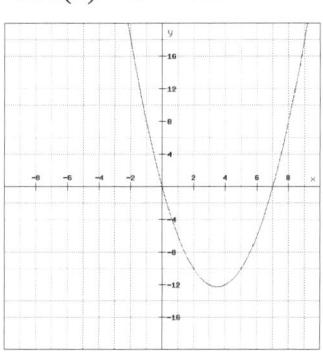

$Vertex\ Form: f(x) = \left(x - \dfrac{7}{2}\right)^2 - \dfrac{49}{4}$

$Factorized\ Form: f(x) = x(x-7)$

$Domain: x \in R \quad Range: f(x) \in [-\dfrac{49}{4}, \infty)$

$y\,int: (0,0) \quad Vertex: (\dfrac{7}{2}, -\dfrac{49}{4})$

$x\,int: (0,0), (7,0)$

$Increase: x \in (\dfrac{7}{2}, \infty) \quad Decrease: x \in (-\infty, \dfrac{7}{2})$

44. $f(x) = x^2 + 4x + 6$

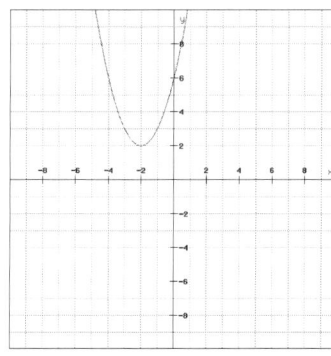

$Vertex\ Form: f(x) = \left(x + 2\right)^2 + 2$

$Factorized\ Form: None$

$Domain: x \in R \quad Range: f(x) \in [2, \infty)$

$y\,int: (0,6) \quad Vertex: (-2,2)$

$x\,int: None$

$Increase: x \in (-2, \infty) \quad Decrease: x \in (-\infty, -2)$

45. $f(x) = -2x^2 - 16x - 29$

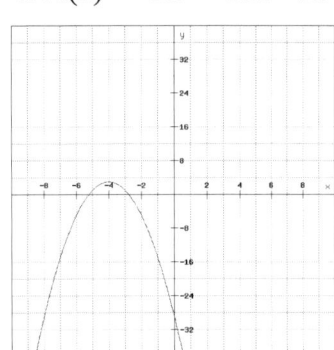

$Vertex \quad Form : f(x) = -2(x+4)^2 + 3$

$Factorized \quad Form : f(x) = -2\left(x - \left(\sqrt{\dfrac{3}{2}} - 2\right)\right)\left(x - \left(-\sqrt{\dfrac{3}{2}} - 2\right)\right)$

$Domain : x \in R \quad Range : f(x) \in (-\infty, 3]$

$y\,int : (0, -29) \quad Vertex : (-4, 3)$

$x\,int : (\sqrt{\dfrac{3}{2}} - 2, 0), (-\sqrt{\dfrac{3}{2}} - 2, 0)$

$Increase : x \in (-\infty, -4) \quad Decrease : x \in (-4, \infty)$

46. $f(x) = x^2 - 6x + 4$

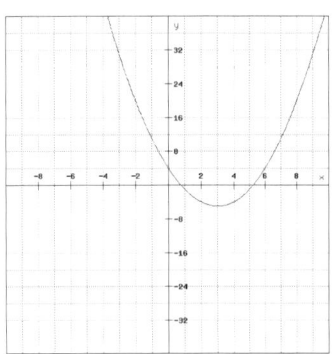

$Vertex \quad Form : f(x) = (x - 3)^2 - 5$

$Factorized \quad Form : f(x) = \left(x - (\sqrt{5} + 3)\right)\left(x - (-\sqrt{5} + 3)\right)$

$Domain : x \in R \quad Range : f(x) \in [-5, \infty)$

$y\,int : (0, 4) \quad Vertex : (3, -5)$

$x\,int : (\sqrt{5} + 3, 0), (-\sqrt{5} + 3, 0)$

$Increase : x \in (3, \infty) \quad Decrease : x \in (-\infty, 3)$

47. $f(x) = x^2 - 7x + 2$

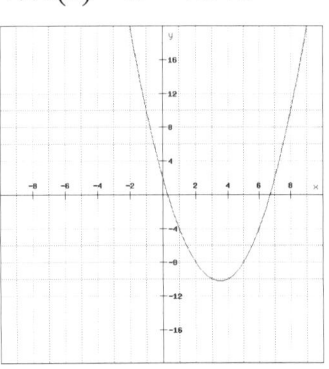

$Vertex \quad Form : f(x) = \left(x - \dfrac{7}{2}\right)^2 - \dfrac{41}{4}$

$Factorized \quad Form : f(x) = \left(x - \left(\sqrt{\dfrac{41}{4}} + \dfrac{7}{2}\right)\right)\left(x - \left(-\sqrt{\dfrac{41}{4}} + \dfrac{7}{2}\right)\right)$

$Domain : x \in R \quad Range : f(x) \in [-\dfrac{41}{4}, \infty)$

$y\,int : (0, 2) \quad Vertex : (\dfrac{7}{2}, -\dfrac{41}{4})$

$x\,int : (\sqrt{\dfrac{41}{4}} + \dfrac{7}{2}, 0), (-\sqrt{\dfrac{41}{4}} + \dfrac{7}{2}, 0)$

$Increase : x \in (\dfrac{7}{2}, \infty) \quad Decrease : x \in (-\infty, \dfrac{7}{2})$

48. $f(x) = x^2 + 3x + 10$

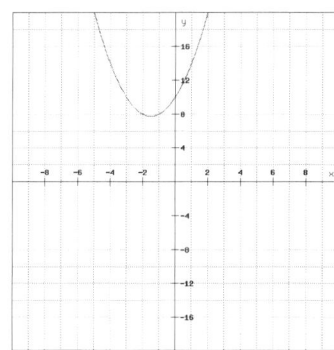

Vertex   Form : $f(x) = \left(x + \dfrac{3}{2}\right)^2 + \dfrac{49}{4}$

Factorized   Form : *None*

Domain : $x \in R$ *Range* : $f(x) \in [\dfrac{49}{4}, \infty)$

y int : $(0,10)$ *Vertex* : $(-\dfrac{3}{2}, \dfrac{49}{4})$

x int : *None*

Increase : $x \in (-\dfrac{3}{2}, \infty)$ *Decrease* : $x \in (-\infty, -\dfrac{3}{2})$

49. $f(x) = x^2 + 5$

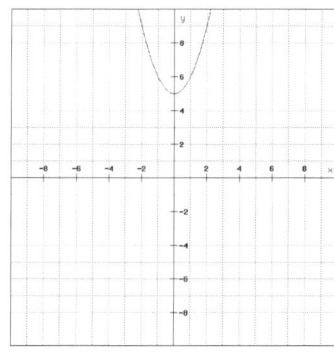

Vertex   Form : $f(x) = x^2 + 5$

Factorized   Form : *None*

Domain : $x \in R$ *Range* : $f(x) \in [5, \infty)$

y int : $(0,5)$ *Vertex* : $(0,5)$

x int : *None*

Increase : $x \in (0, \infty)$ *Decrease* : $x \in (-\infty, 0)$

50. $f(x) = x^2 - 3$

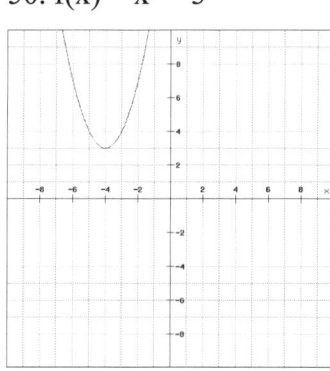

Vertex   Form : $f(x) = x^2 - 3$

Factorized   Form : $f(x) = (x + \sqrt{3})(x - \sqrt{3})$

Domain : $x \in R$ *Range* : $f(x) \in [-3, \infty)$

y int : $(0, -3)$ *Vertex* : $(0, -3)$

x int : $(-\sqrt{3}, 0), (\sqrt{3}, 0)$

Increase : $x \in (0, \infty)$ *Decrease* : $x \in (-\infty, 0)$

51. $f(x) = x^2 - 7x$

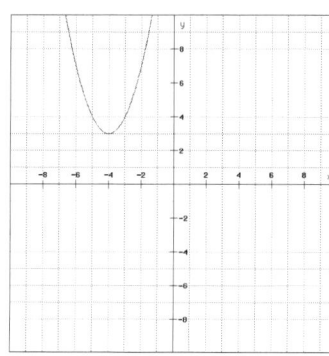

Vertex   Form : $f(x) = \left(x - \dfrac{7}{2}\right)^2 - \dfrac{49}{4}$

Factorized   Form : $f(x) = x(x - 7)$

Domain : $x \in R$ *Range* : $f(x) \in [-\dfrac{49}{4}, \infty)$

y int : $(0,0)$ *Vertex* : $(\dfrac{7}{2}, -\dfrac{49}{4})$

x int : $(0,0), (7,0)$

Increase : $x \in (\dfrac{7}{2}, \infty)$ *Decrease* : $x \in (-\infty, \dfrac{7}{2})$

52. f(x) = x² + 3x −5

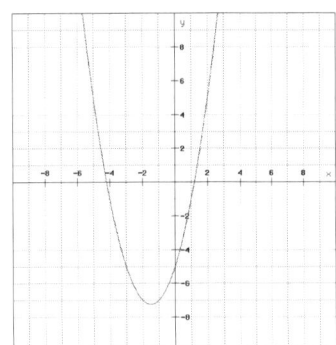

$Vertex\ Form: f(x) = \left(x + \dfrac{3}{2}\right)^2 - \dfrac{29}{4}$

$Factorized\ Form: f(x) = \left(x - \left(\sqrt{\dfrac{29}{4}} - \dfrac{3}{2}\right)\right)\left(x - \left(-\sqrt{\dfrac{29}{4}} - \dfrac{3}{2}\right)\right)$

$Domain: x \in R \quad Range: f(x) \in [-\dfrac{29}{4}, \infty)$

$y\,int: (0, -5) \quad Vertex: (-\dfrac{3}{2}, -\dfrac{29}{4})$

$x\,int: (\sqrt{\dfrac{29}{4}} - \dfrac{3}{2}, 0), (-\sqrt{\dfrac{29}{4}} - \dfrac{3}{2}, 0)$

$Increase: x \in (-\dfrac{3}{2}, \infty) \quad Decrease: x \in (-\infty, -\dfrac{3}{2})$

53. f(x) = 5x² − 3

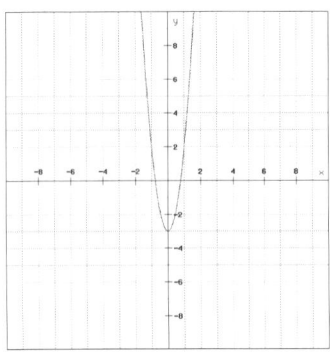

$Vertex\ Form: f(x) = 5x^2 - 3$

$Factorized\ Form: f(x) = 5\left(x - \sqrt{\dfrac{3}{5}}\right)\left(x + \sqrt{\dfrac{3}{5}}\right)$

$Domain: x \in R \quad Range: f(x) \in [-3, \infty)$

$y\,int: (0, -3) \quad Vertex: (0, -3)$

$x\,int: (-\sqrt{\dfrac{3}{5}}, 0), (\sqrt{\dfrac{3}{5}}, 0)$

$Increase: x \in (0, \infty) \quad Decrease: x \in (-\infty, 0)$

54. f(x) = 5x² − 10x

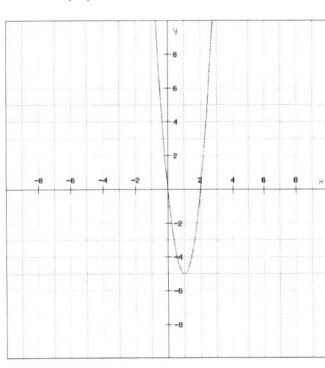

$Vertex\ Form: f(x) = 5(x-1)^2 - 5$

$Factorized\ Form: f(x) = 5x(x-2)$

$Domain: x \in R \quad Range: f(x) \in [-5, \infty)$

$y\,int: (0, 0) \quad Vertex: (1, -5)$

$x\,int: (0, 0), (2, 0)$

$Increase: x \in (1, \infty) \quad Decrease: x \in (-\infty, 1)$

55. f(x) = −5x²

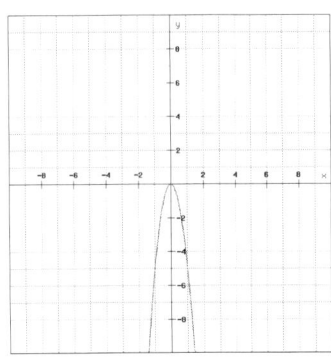

$Vertex\ Form: f(x) = -5x^2$

$Factorized\ Form: f(x) = -5x^2$

$Domain: x \in R \quad Range: f(x) \in (-\infty, 0]$

$y\,int: (0, 0) \quad Vertex: (0, 0)$

$x\,int: (0, 0)$

$Increase: x \in (-\infty. 0) \quad Decrease: x \in (0, \infty)$

56. $f(x) = -x^2 + 6x - 8$

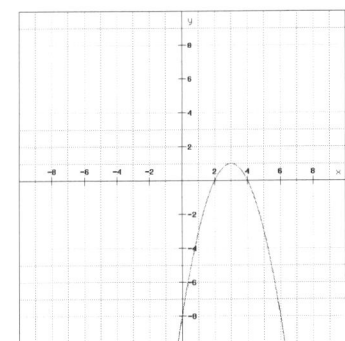

$Vertex\ \ Form: f(x) = -(x-3)^2 + 1$

$Factorized\ \ Form: f(x) = -(x-2)(x-4)$

$Domain: x \in R\ \ \ Range: f(x) \in (-\infty, 1]$

$y\,\text{int}: (0, -8)\ \ Vertex: (3, -1)$

$x\,\text{int}: (2, 0), (4, 0)$

$Increase: x \in (-\infty, 3)\ \ \ Decrease: x \in (3, \infty)$

57. $f(x) = -x^2 - 6x + 2$

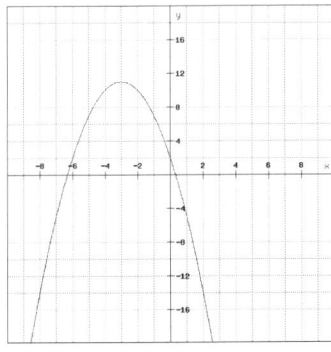

$Vertex\ \ Form: f(x) = -(x+3)^2 + 11$

$Factorized\ \ Form: f(x) = -\left(x - \left(\sqrt{11} - 3\right)\right)\left(x - \left(-\sqrt{11} - 3\right)\right)$

$Domain: x \in R\ \ \ Range: f(x) \in (-\infty, 11]$

$y\,\text{int}: (0, 2)\ \ Vertex: (-3, 11)$

$x\,\text{int}: (\sqrt{11} - 3, 0), (-\sqrt{11} - 3, 0)$

$Increase: x \in (-\infty, -3)\ \ \ Decrease: x \in (-3, \infty)$

58. $f(x) = -x^2 + x - 5$

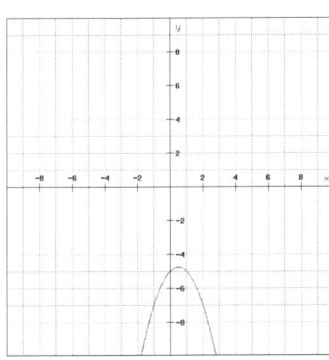

$Vertex\ \ Form: f(x) = -\left(x - \dfrac{1}{2}\right)^2 - \dfrac{19}{4}$

$Factorized\ \ Form: None$

$Domain: x \in R\ \ \ Range: f(x) \in \left(-\infty, -\dfrac{19}{4}\right]$

$y\,\text{int}: (0, -5)\ \ Vertex: \left(\dfrac{1}{2}, -\dfrac{19}{4}\right)$

$x\,\text{int}: None$

$Increase: x \in \left(-\infty, \dfrac{1}{2}\right)\ \ \ Decrease: x \in \left(\dfrac{1}{2}, \infty\right)$

59. $f(x) = -x^2 - 4x - 4$

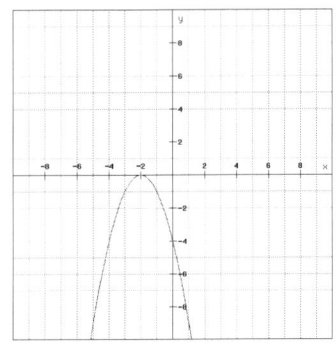

$Vertex\ \ Form: f(x) = -(x+2)^2$

$Factorized\ \ Form: f(x) = -(x+2)(x+2)$

$Domain: x \in R\ \ \ Range: f(x) \in (-\infty, 0]$

$y\,\text{int}: (0, -4)\ \ Vertex: (-2, 0)$

$x\,\text{int}: (-2, 0)$

$Increase: x \in (-\infty, -2)\ \ \ Decrease: x \in (-2, \infty)$

60. $f(x) = -x^2 + 3$

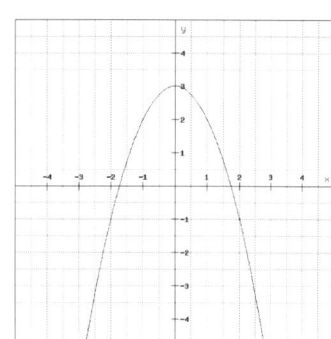

Vertex Form: $f(x) = -x^2 + 3$

Factorized Form: $f(x) = -(x + \sqrt{3})(x - \sqrt{3})$

Domain: $x \in R$ *Range*: $f(x) \in (-\infty, 3]$

y int: $(0, 3)$ *Vertex*: $(0, 3)$

x int: $(\sqrt{3}, 0), (-\sqrt{3}, 0)$

Increase: $x \in (-\infty, 0)$ *Decrease*: $x \in (0, \infty)$

61. $f(x) = 3x^2$

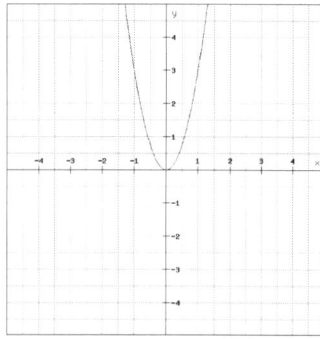

Vertex Form: $f(x) = 3x^2$

Factorized Form: $f(x) = 3x^2$

Domain: $x \in R$ *Range*: $f(x) \in [0, \infty)$

y int: $(0, 0)$ *Vertex*: $(0, 0)$

x int: $(0, 0)$

Increase: $x \in (0, \infty)$ *Decrease*: $x \in (-\infty, 0)$

62. $f(x) = x^2 + 3x + 4$

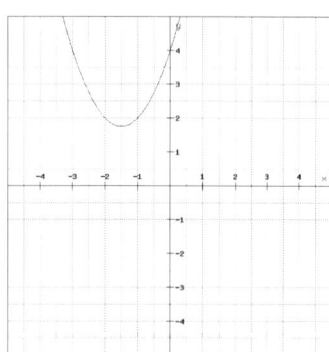

Vertex Form: $f(x) = \left(x + \dfrac{3}{2}\right)^2 + \dfrac{7}{4}$

Factorized Form: $None$

Domain: $x \in R$ *Range*: $f(x) \in [\dfrac{7}{4}, \infty)$

y int: $(0, 4)$ *Vertex*: $(-\dfrac{3}{2}, \dfrac{7}{4})$

x int: $None$

Increase: $x \in (-\infty, -\dfrac{3}{2})$ *Decrease*: $x \in (-\dfrac{3}{2}, \infty)$

63. $f(x) = -4x + 3$

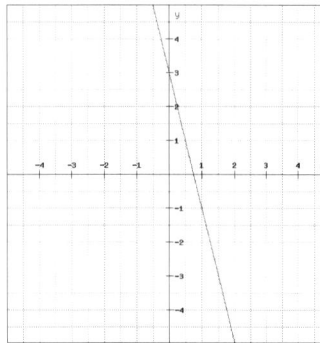

Vertex Form: $None(Linear)$

Factorized Form: $None(Linear)$

Domain: $x \in R$ *Range*: $f(x) \in R$

y int: $(0, 3)$ *Vertex*: $None$

x int: $(\dfrac{3}{4}, 0)$

Increase: $Never$ *Decrease*: $x \in R$

64. $f(x) = x^2 - 2$

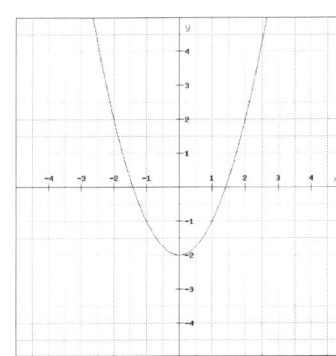

Vertex Form: $f(x) = x^2 - 2$

Factorized Form: $f(x) = (x - \sqrt{2})(x - \sqrt{2})$

Domain: $x \in R$ *Range*: $f(x) \in [-2, \infty)$

$y$int: $(0, -2)$ *Vertex*: $(0, -2)$

$x$int: $(-\sqrt{2}, 0), (\sqrt{2}, 0)$

Increase: $x \in (0, \infty)$ *Decrease*: $x \in (-\infty, 0)$

65. $f(x) = x^2 - 2x$

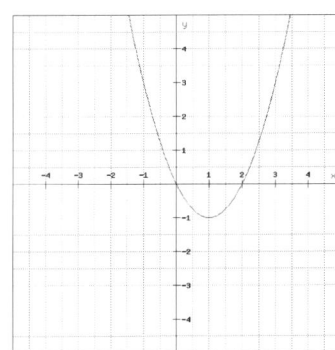

Vertex Form: $f(x) = (x - 1)^2 - 1$

Factorized Form: $f(x) = x(x - 2)$

Domain: $x \in R$ *Range*: $f(x) \in [-1, \infty)$

$y$int: $(0, 0)$ *Vertex*: $(1, -1)$

$x$int: $(0, 0), (2, 0)$

Increase: $x \in (1, \infty)$ *Decrease*: $x \in (-\infty, 1)$

66. What are the coordinates of the vertex of $y = 7(x + 3)^2 + 4$? <u>(-3, 4).</u> State its axes of symmetry: <u>x = -3</u>

67. What are the coordinates of the vertex of $y = -2(x - 4)^2 + 2$? <u>(4, 2).</u> State its axes of symmetry: <u>x = 4</u>

68. What value of b makes the expression $x^2 + 8x + b$ a perfect square? State its axes of symmetry: <u>b = 16</u>

69. When a quadratic function can be written as a perfect square on the graph it

means that <u>its vertex is on the x axis and it has a single x intercept.</u>

70. what are the zeros of the quadratic relation $y = 10x^2 - 20x$. State its axes of symmetry: <u>zeros: x = 0, x = 2, axes of symmetry x = 1</u>

71. Find the roots (zeros) of the equation $20(6 + 5x)(12 - x) = 0$. State its axes of symmetry:Roots: $x = -\dfrac{6}{5}, x = 12,$ axes of symmetry: $x = \dfrac{27}{5}$

72. The quadratic equation is used to find the <u>zeros (x intercepts)</u> of the quadratic function. in case this equation has no solutions it means the quadratic function is completely <u>above</u> or <u>below</u> the x axis and the value of $b^2 - 4ac$ <u>is negative</u>. In case $b^2 - 4ac$ is <u>positive</u> the quadratic function will have <u>2 zeros (2 x intercepts)</u> and lastly if $b^2 - 4ac$ is <u>zero</u> the quadratic function will have <u>1 zero</u>.

If $b^2 - 4ac > 0$ there are <u>2 zeros (2 x intercepts)</u> Example: $f(x) = x^2 - 10x + 2$

If $b^2 - 4ac = 0$ there are <u>1 zero (1 x intercept)</u> Example: $f(x) = x^2 - 6x + 9$

If $b^2 - 4ac < 0$ there are <u>no zeros (no x intercepts)</u> Example: $f(x) = x^2 + 4x + 1$

73. Under what conditions will the parabola with equation $y = a(x - h)^2 + k$ have two x–intercepts? <u>$k < 0$</u>

74. How many zeros does the quadratic relation $y = -1.7(x + 13.2)^2 - 3.1$ have? <u>Opens down, vertex below x axes so no zeros</u>

75. A parabola has its vertex in the third quadrant and opens down. Write a possible function for it. <u>$f(x) = -(x + 2)^2 - 1$</u>

76. Write the equation, in vertex form, of a parabola that has its vertex in the second quadrant, contains two zeros, and is narrower than $y = x^2$

<u>$f(x) = -2(x + 2)^2 + 3$</u>

77. Write the equation, in vertex form, of a parabola that has its vertex in the third quadrant, contains two zeros, and is wider than $y = x^2$

<u>$f(x) = \dfrac{1}{2}(x + 2)^2 - 3$</u>

78. Give   the relation $y = -4(x - 2)^2 + 7$, state its axes of symmetry: <u>x = 2</u>

79. Determine the value of the vertex of the relation $y = -(x - 3)(x + 1)$. Is the vertex a maximum or a minimum? State its axes of symmetry:
<u>Maximum: (1, 4), axes of symmetry x = 1</u>

Applications

80. The height of a ball kicked upwards is given by $h(t) = 40t - 16t^2$ meters, $t \in [0, 2.5]$ where t is measured in seconds.

    a. Sketch the corresponding function, label the axes.

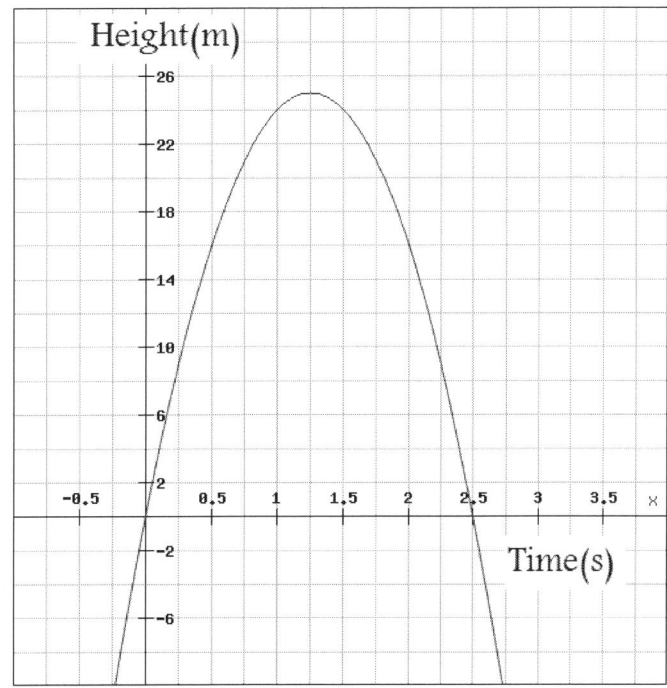

    b. Calculate h(1) and give a practical interpretation to your answer.

       h(1) = 24m, the height of the ball after 1 second.

    c. Calculate the zeros of h(t) and explain the meaning in the context of the problem.

       t = 0s, t = 2.5s, the instants in which the height of the ball is kicked. Right in the beginning and after it fell back.

    d. Solve the equation h(t) = 10 and explain the meaning of the solutions in the context of the problem.

       $h(t) = 40t - 16t^2 = 10$; $t \approx 0.28s$, $t \approx 2.22s$ the instants in which the height of the ball is 10m once on the way up and once on the way down.

    e. Obtain the maximum height of the ball and the instant in which it reaches it.

       The vertex of the parabola is (1.25, 25) so the maximum height is 25m

81. The efficiency of an engine as a function of the concentration of a certain chemical component is given by $f(x) = -0.5x^2 + x, 0 \le x \le 2$.

f. Sketch the function in its domain.

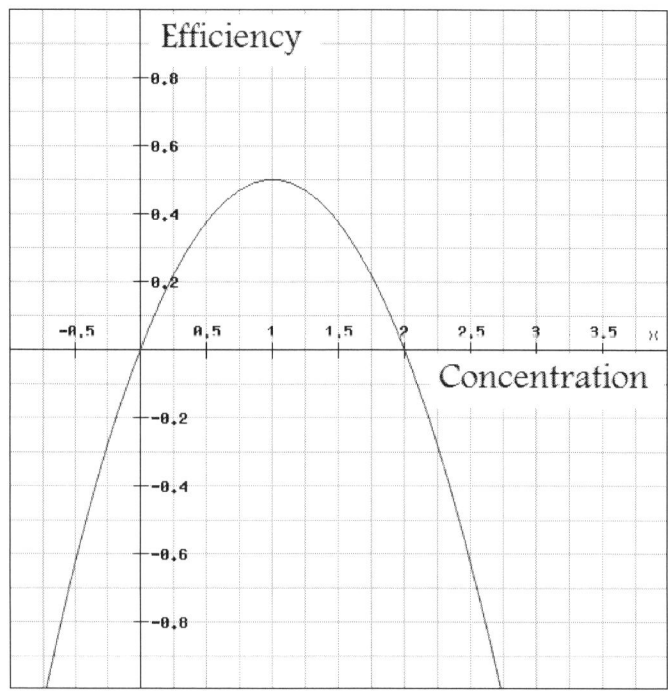

g. Find the concentration of the chemical for which the efficiency is maximized. What is the efficiency in this case?

The vertex of the parabola is (1, 0.5) so the concentration required is 1 and the efficiency is 0.5

82. A hundred meters of fencing is available to enclose a rectangular field along side of a River, What dimensions will produce the maximum area that can be enclosed?

A(x) = x(100 – 2x)

Parabola whose maximum is

(25, 1250) so the dimensions are:

25m width and 50m length

X   X

100–2x

5.4. – EXPONENTIAL FUNCTIONS

1. Given the functions: $f(x) = 2^x$, $g(x) = 3^x$, Complete the following chart:

x	−5	−4	−3	−2	−1	0	1	2	3	4	5	6
f(x)	$\dfrac{1}{32}$	$\dfrac{1}{16}$	$\dfrac{1}{8}$	$\dfrac{1}{4}$	$\dfrac{1}{2}$	1	2	4	8	16	32	64
g(x)	$\dfrac{1}{243}$	$\dfrac{1}{81}$	$\dfrac{1}{27}$	$\dfrac{1}{9}$	$\dfrac{1}{3}$	1	3	9	27	81	243	729

- Sketch the points of the table on a graph.

- State the domain of the function: $x \in R$

- State the y intercept (sketched on the graph: $f(x):(0,1); g(x):(0,1)$

- State the x intercept(s): None

- Write the equation of the horizontal asymptote: y = 0 (in both cases)

- Function is increasing on the interval: $x \in R$, decreasing on the interval: Never

- Find the max/min point(s): None, always increasing

- State the range of the function: $f(x) \in (0,\infty); g(x) \in (0,\infty)$

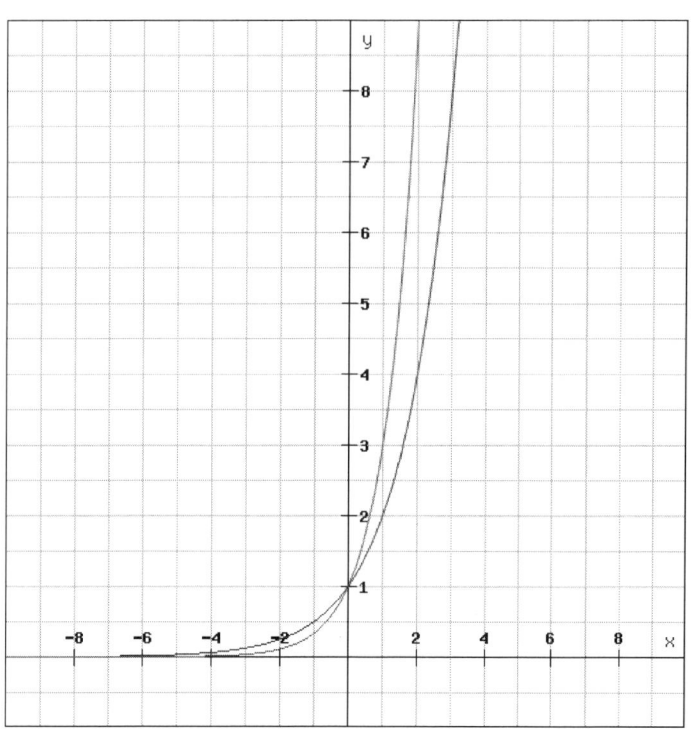

2. Given the functions: f(x) = 2^{-x}, g(x) = 3^{-x}, Complete the following chart:

x	−5	−4	−3	−2	−1	0	1	2	3	4	5	6
f(x)	32	16	8	4	2	1	$\frac{1}{2}$	$\frac{1}{4}$	$\frac{1}{8}$	$\frac{1}{16}$	$\frac{1}{32}$	$\frac{1}{64}$
g(x)	243	81	27	9	3	1	$\frac{1}{3}$	$\frac{1}{9}$	$\frac{1}{27}$	$\frac{1}{81}$	$\frac{1}{243}$	$\frac{1}{729}$

- Sketch the points of the table on a graph.

- State the domain of the function: $x \in R$

- State the y intercept (sketched on the graph: $f(x):(0,1); g(x):(0,1)$

- State the x intercept(s): None

- Write the equation of the horizontal asymptote: y = 0 (in both cases)

- Function is increasing on the interval: Never, decreasing on the interval: $x \in R$

- Find the max/min point(s): None, always decreasing

- State the range of the function: $f(x) \in (0,\infty); g(x) \in (0,\infty)$

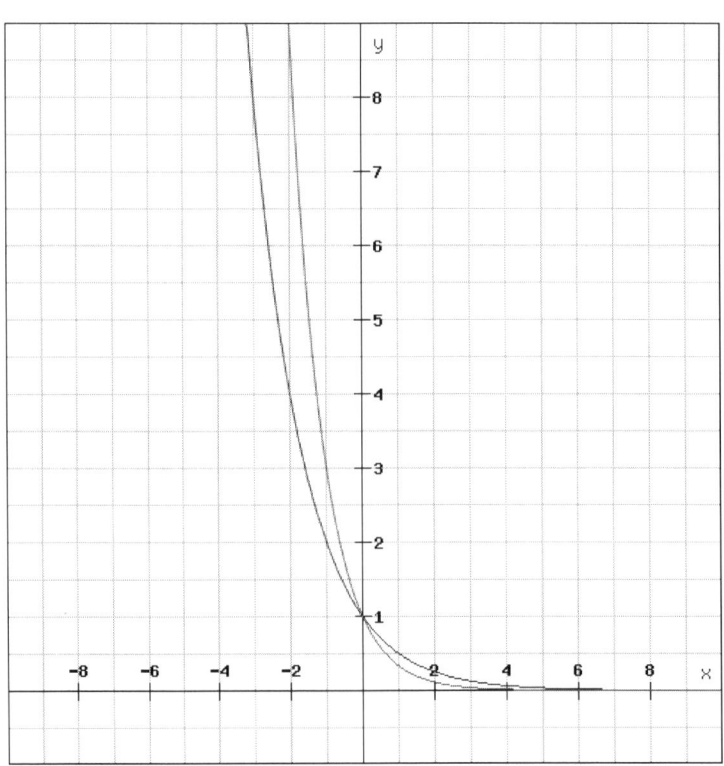

3. Given the functions: $f(x) = -2^x$, $g(x) = -3^x$, Complete the following chart:

x	−5	−4	−3	−2	−1	0	1	2	3	4	5	6
f(x)	−32	−16	−8	−4	−2	−1	$-\dfrac{1}{2}$	$-\dfrac{1}{4}$	$-\dfrac{1}{8}$	$-\dfrac{1}{16}$	$-\dfrac{1}{32}$	$-\dfrac{1}{64}$
g(x)	−243	−81	−27	−9	−3	−1	$-\dfrac{1}{3}$	$-\dfrac{1}{9}$	$-\dfrac{1}{27}$	$-\dfrac{1}{81}$	$-\dfrac{1}{243}$	$-\dfrac{1}{729}$

- Sketch the points of the table on a graph.

- State the domain of the function: $\underline{x \in R}$

- State the y intercept (sketched on the graph: $\underline{f(x):(0,-1); g(x):(0,-1)}$

- State the x intercept(s): <u>None</u>

- Write the equation of the horizontal asymptote: <u>y = 0 (in both cases</u>

- Function is increasing on the interval: <u>Never</u>, decreasing on the interval: $\underline{x \in R}$

- Find the max/min point(s): <u>None, always decreasing</u>

- State the range of the function: $\underline{f(x) \in (-\infty, 0); g(x) \in (-\infty, 0)}$

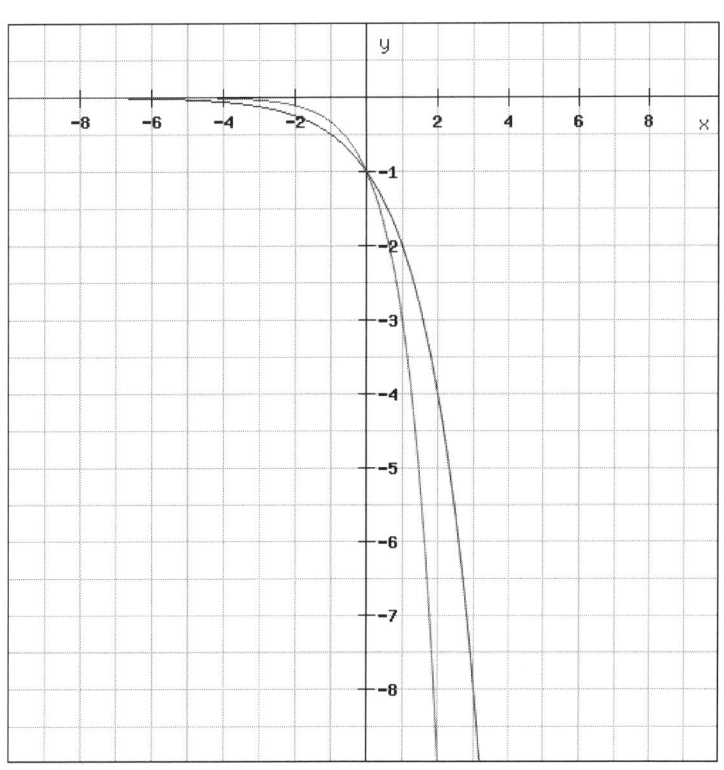

381

4. Given the functions: $f(x) = -2^{-x}$, $g(x) = -3^{-x}$, Complete the following chart:

x	−5	−4	−3	−2	−1	0	1	2	3	4	5	6
f(x)	−32	−16	−8	−4	−2	−1	$-\dfrac{1}{2}$	$-\dfrac{1}{4}$	$-\dfrac{1}{8}$	$-\dfrac{1}{16}$	$-\dfrac{1}{32}$	$-\dfrac{1}{64}$
g(x)	−243	−81	−27	−9	−3	−1	$-\dfrac{1}{3}$	$-\dfrac{1}{9}$	$-\dfrac{1}{27}$	$-\dfrac{1}{81}$	$-\dfrac{1}{243}$	$-\dfrac{1}{729}$

- Sketch the points of the table on a graph.

- State the domain of the function: $x \in R$

- State the y intercept (sketched on the graph: $f(x):(0,-1); g(x):(0,-1)$

- State the x intercept(s): None

- Write the equation of the horizontal asymptote: y = 0 (in both cases

- Function is increasing on the interval: $x \in R$, decreasing on the interval: Never

- Find the max/min point(s): None, always increasing

- State the range of the function: $f(x) \in (-\infty, 0); g(x) \in (-\infty, 0)$

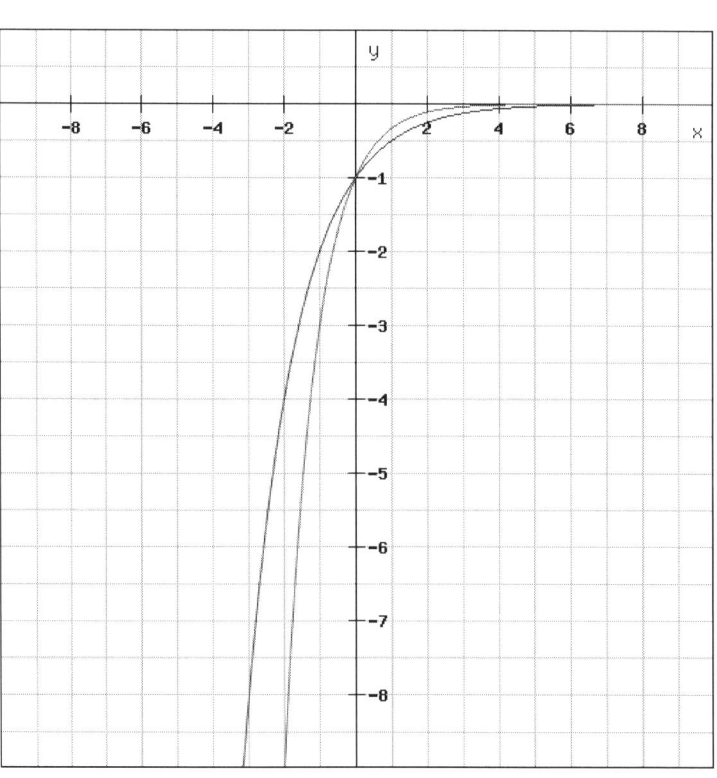

5. Given the functions: $f(x) = -5 \times 4^{-2x} + 1$, Complete the following chart:

x	−5	−4	−3	−2	−1	0	1	2	3	4	5
f(x)	$-5\cdot4^{10}+1$	$-5\cdot4^{8}+1$	$-5\cdot4^{6}+1$	$-5\cdot4^{4}+1$	-79	-4	$\dfrac{11}{16}$	$\dfrac{-5}{4^{4}}+1$	$\dfrac{-5}{4^{6}}+1$	$\dfrac{-5}{4^{8}}+1$	$\dfrac{-5}{4^{4}}+1$

- Sketch the points of the table on a graph.

- State the domain of the function: $x \in R$

- State the y intercept (sketched on the graph: $(0, -4)$

- State the x intercept(s): $(\dfrac{\ln(5)}{4\ln(2)}, 0)$

- Write the equation of the horizontal asymptote: $y = 1$

- Function is increasing on the interval: $x \in R$, decreasing on the interval: Never

- Find the max/min point(s): None, always increasing

- State the range of the function: $f(x) \in (-\infty, 1)$

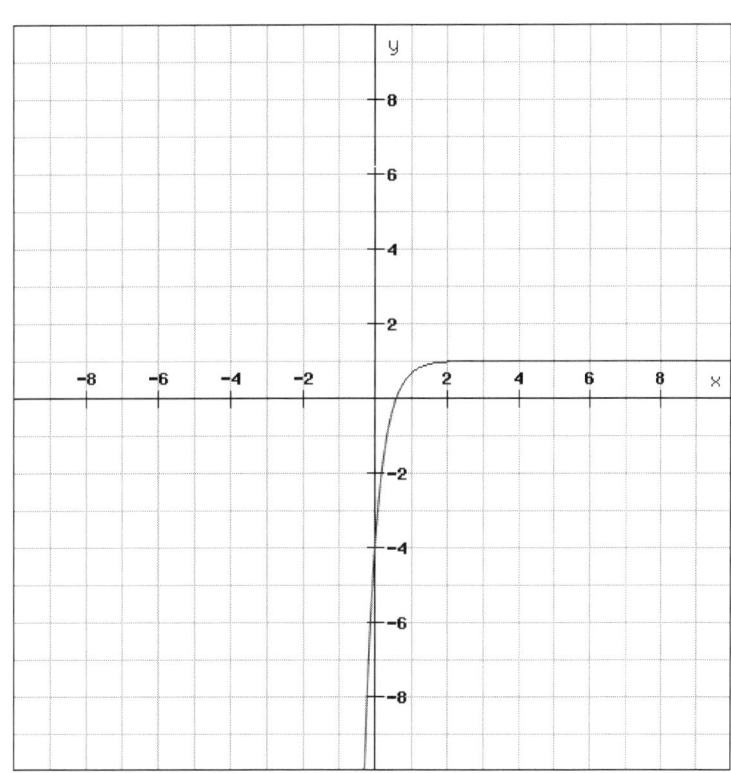

383

6. Given the graph of the function $f(x) = \left(\dfrac{1}{2}\right)^x = (2^{-1})^x = 2^{-x}$ sketch, on the same set of axes, the graphs of the functions:

$$g(x) = \left(\dfrac{1}{2}\right)^{x-2} = (2^{-1})^{x-2} = 2^{2-x} = 4 \cdot 2^{-x}$$

$$d(x) = \left(\dfrac{1}{2}\right)^x - 2 = 2^{-x} - 2$$

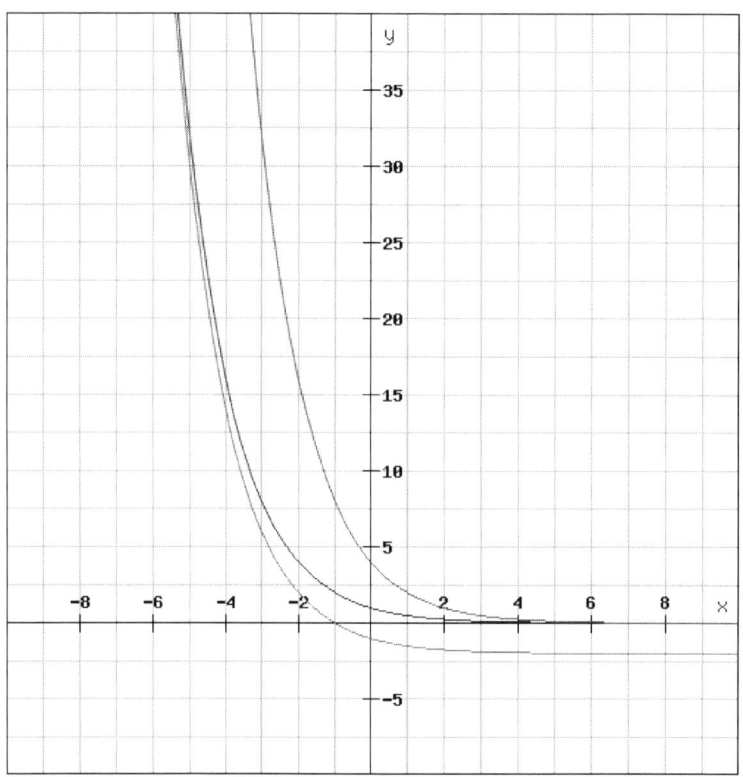

7. Given the graph, complete the table below:

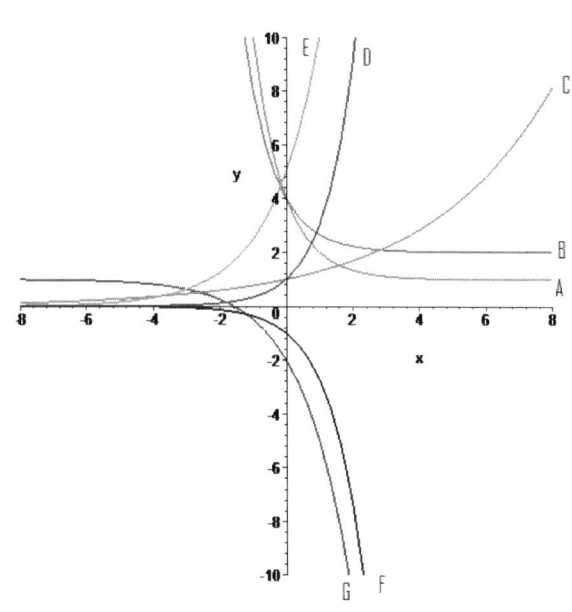

Function	On the graph
$f(x) = 5 \times 2^x$	E
$f(x) = 2 + 2 \times 3^{-x}$	B
$f(x) = 3 \times 3^{-x} + 1$	A
$f(x) = (1.3)^x$	C
$f(x) = -e^x$	F
$f(x) = 3^x$	D
$f(x) = -3 \times 2^x + 1$	G

Analyze the functions, using your GDC:

1. $f(x) = 4^x$

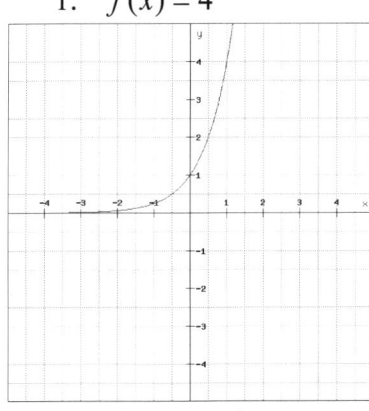

Domain : $x \in R$ *Range* : $f(x) \in (0, \infty)$

y int : $(0,1)$ *Increase* : $x \in R$

x int : *None* *Decrease* : *Never*

Horizontal *Asymptote* : $y = 0$

2. $f(x) = -3^x$

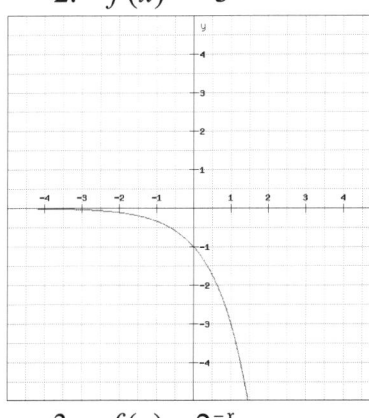

Domain : $x \in R$ *Range* : $f(x) \in (-\infty, 0)$

y int : $(0,-1)$ *Increase* : *Never*

x int : *None* *Decrease* : $x \in R$

Horizontal *Asymptote* : $y = 0$

3. $f(x) = 2^{-x}$

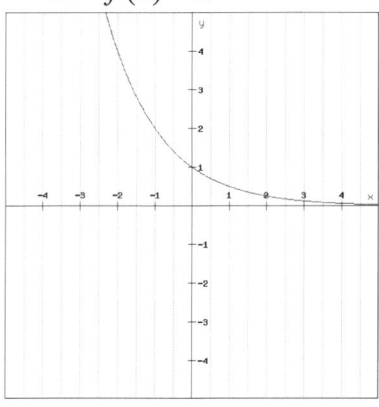

Domain : $x \in R$ *Range* : $f(x) \in (0, \infty)$

y int : $(0,1)$ *Increase* : *Never*

x int : *None* *Decrease* : $x \in R$

Horizontal *Asymptote* : $y = 0$

4. $f(x) = -2^{-x}$

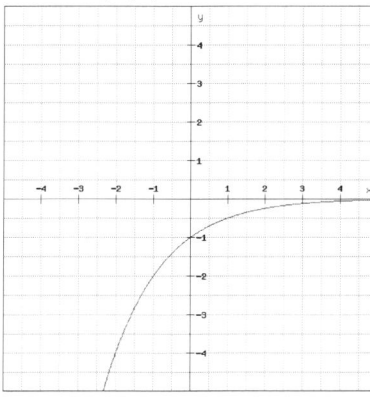

Domain : $x \in R$ *Range* : $f(x) \in (-\infty, 0)$

y int : $(0,-1)$ *Increase* : $x \in R$

x int : *None* *Decrease* : *Never*

Horizontal *Asymptote* : $y = 0$

5. $f(x) = \left(\dfrac{1}{4}\right)^x$

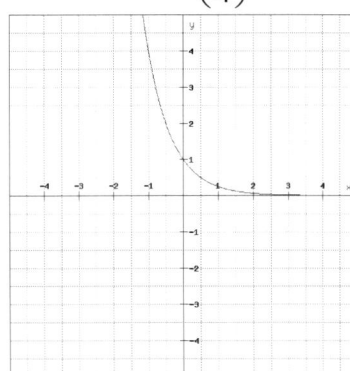

Domain : $x \in R$ *Range* : $f(x) \in (0, \infty)$

$y$int : $(0,1)$ *Increase* : *Never*

$x$int : *None*   *Decrease* : $x \in R$

Horizontal   Asymptote : $y = 0$

6. $f(x) = 3\left(\dfrac{2}{7}\right)^x$

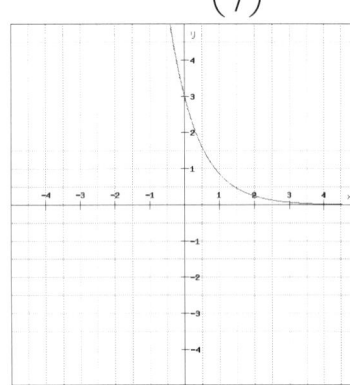

Domain : $x \in R$ *Range* : $f(x) \in (0, \infty)$

$y$int : $(0,3)$ *Increase* : *Never*

$x$int : *None*   *Decrease* : $x \in R$

Horizontal   Asymptote : $y = 0$

7. $f(x) = -2^{x+5}$

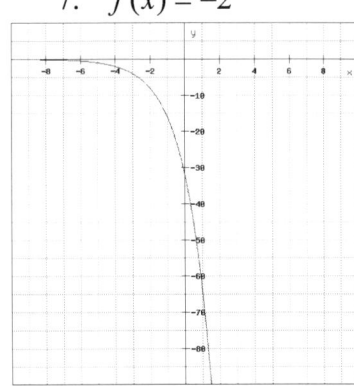

Domain : $x \in R$ *Range* : $f(x) \in (-\infty, 0)$

$y$int : $(0,-32)$ *Increase* : *Never*

$x$int : *None*   *Decrease* : $x \in R$

Horizontal   Asymptote : $y = 0$

8. $f(x) = \left(\dfrac{2}{3}\right)^x$

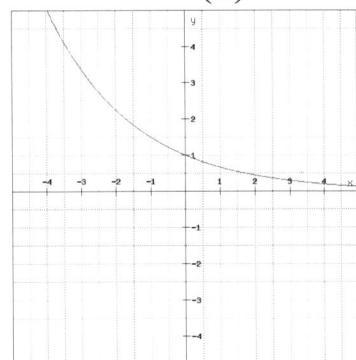

Domain : $x \in R$ *Range* : $f(x) \in (0, \infty)$

$y$int : $(0,1)$ *Increase* : *Never*

$x$int : *None*   *Decrease* : $x \in R$

Horizontal   Asymptote : $y = 0$

9. $f(x) = 3 \cdot 7^{x-4}$

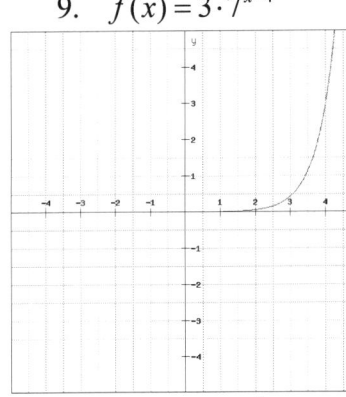

$Domain: x \in R$ $Range: f(x) \in (0, \infty)$

$y \, int: (0, \dfrac{3}{7^4})$ $Increase: x \in R$

$x \, int: None$ $Decrease: Never$

$Horizontal \quad Asymptote: y = 0$

10. $f(x) = -7^{x-2} + 2$

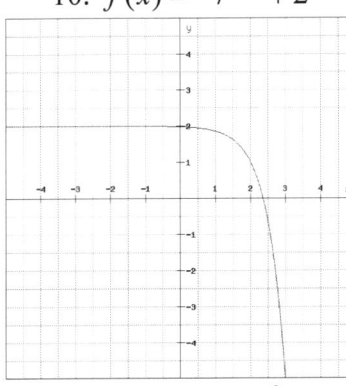

$Domain: x \in R$ $Range: f(x) \in (-\infty, 2)$

$y \, int: (0, \dfrac{97}{49})$ $Increase: Never$

$x \, int: (\approx 2.36, 0)$ $Decrease: x \in R$

$Horizontal \quad Asymptote: y = 2$

11. $f(x) = 2 \cdot 5^{-x-2} - 5$

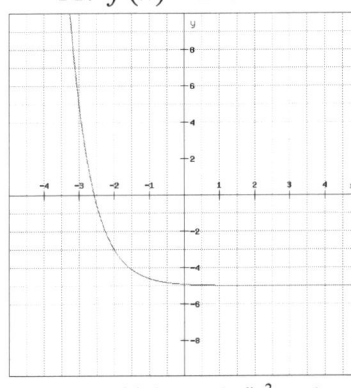

$Domain: x \in R$ $Range: f(x) \in (-5, \infty)$

$y \, int: (0, -\dfrac{123}{25})$ $Increase: Never$

$x \, int: (\approx -2.57, 0)$ $Decrease: x \in R$

$Horizontal \quad Asymptote: y = -5$

12. $f(x) = -3^{-x-3} + 4$

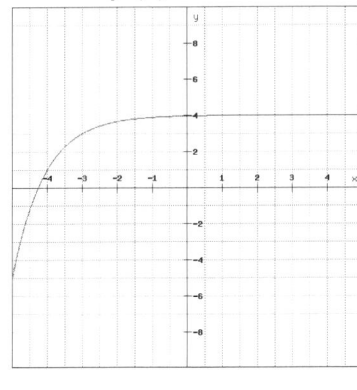

$Domain: x \in R$ $Range: f(x) \in (-\infty, 4)$

$y \, int: (0, \dfrac{107}{27})$ $Increase: x \in R$

$x \, int: (\approx 4.26, 0)$ $Decrease: Never$

$Horizontal \quad Asymptote: y = 4$

13. $f(x) = -e^x$

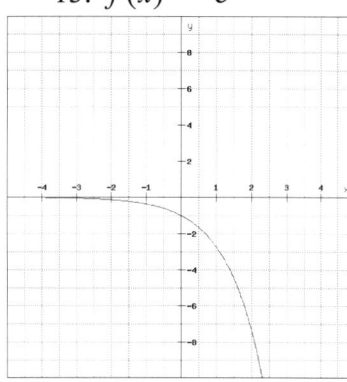

$Domain: x \in R \quad Range: f(x) \in (-\infty, 0)$

$y\,int: (0, -1) \quad Increase: Never$

$x\,int: None \quad Decrease: x \in R$

$Horizontal \quad Asymptote: y = 0$

14. $f(x) = e^{x+2}$

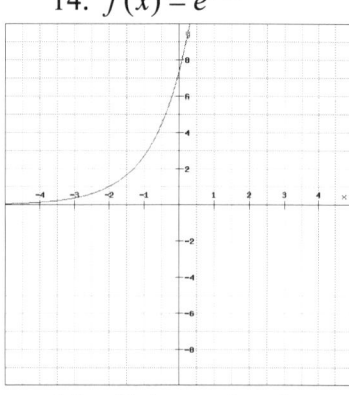

$Domain: x \in R \quad Range: f(x) \in (0, \infty)$

$y\,int: (0, e^2) \quad Increase: x \in R$

$x\,int: None \quad Decrease: Never$

$Horizontal \quad Asymptote: y = 0$

15. $f(x) = -e^x + 4$

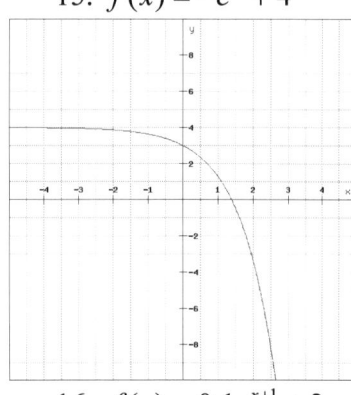

$Domain: x \in R \quad Range: f(x) \in (-\infty, 4)$

$y\,int: (0, 3) \quad Increase: Never$

$x\,int: None \quad Decrease: x \in R$

$Horizontal \quad Asymptote: y = 4$

16. $f(x) = 0.1e^{x+1} + 2$

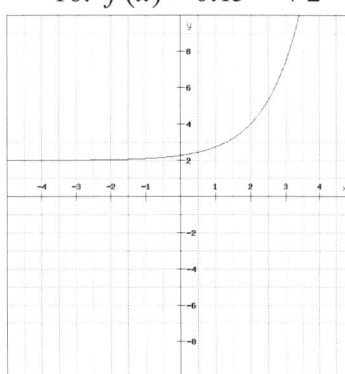

$Domain: x \in R \quad Range: f(x) \in (2, \infty)$

$y\,int: (0, e^2) \quad Increase: x \in R$

$x\,int: None \quad Decrease: Never$

$Horizontal \quad Asymptote: y = 2$

17. $f(x) = 2e^{2x+1} - 4$

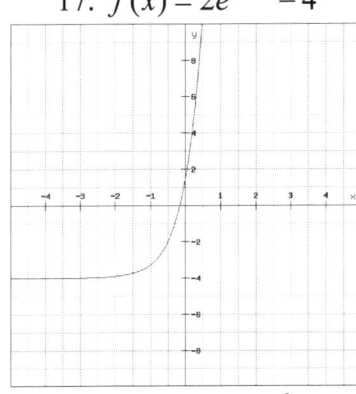

$Domain: x \in R \quad Range: f(x) \in (-4, \infty)$

$y\,int: (0, 2e - 4) \quad Increase: x \in R$

$x\,int: (\approx -0.153, 0) \quad Decrease: Never$

$Horizontal \quad Asymptote: y = -4$

18. $f(x) = -2 \cdot 6^{x-2} - 1$

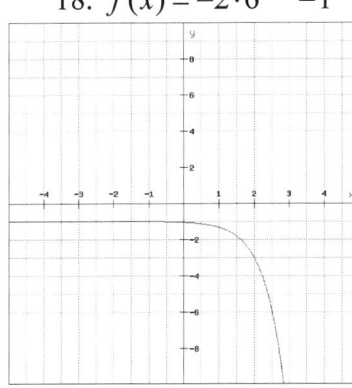

$Domain: x \in R \quad Range: f(x) \in (-\infty, -1)$

$y\,int: (0, -\dfrac{19}{18}) \quad Increase: Never$

$x\,int: None \quad Decrease: x \in R$

$Horizontal \quad Asymptote: y = -1$

19. $f(x) = 2 \cdot 3^{x-2} - 5$

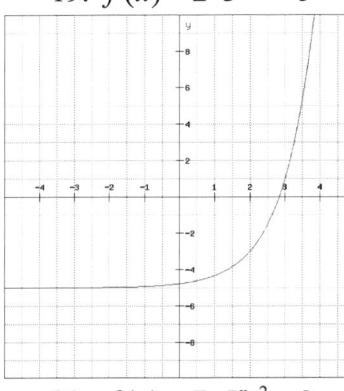

$Domain: x \in R \quad Range: f(x) \in (-5, \infty)$

$y\,int: (0, -\dfrac{43}{9}) \quad Increase: x \in R$

$x\,int: (\approx -0.153, 0) \quad Decrease: Never$

$Horizontal \quad Asymptote: y = -5$

20. $f(x) = 7 \cdot 5^{x-2} + 2$

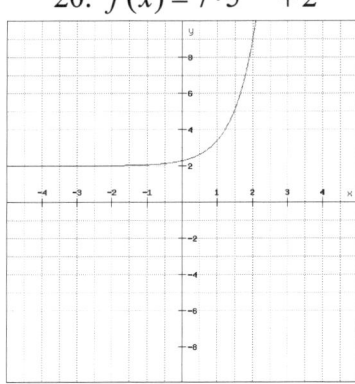

$Domain: x \in R \quad Range: f(x) \in (2, \infty)$

$y\,int: (0, \dfrac{57}{25}) \quad Increase: x \in R$

$x\,int: None \quad Decrease: Never$

$Horizontal \quad Asymptote: y = 2$

21. $f(x) = -2 \cdot 3^{-2x+1} + 4$

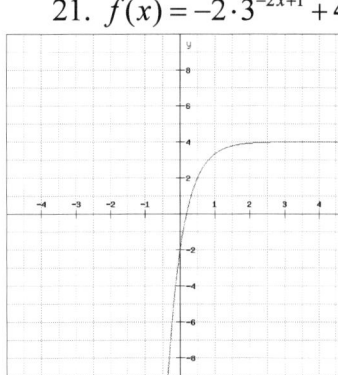

$Domain: x \in R \quad Range: f(x) \in (-\infty, 4)$

$y\,int: (0, -2) \quad Increase: x \in R$

$x\,int: (\approx 0.185, 0) \quad Decrease: Never$

$Horizontal \quad Asymptote: y = 4$

Applications

1. The number of products sold during the year 2012 in a certain store can be modeled by the following function where t is given in months (t = 1 corresponds the month of January).

$$T(t) = 800 \times (1.02)^{(2.3)t} - 50$$

a. Find the number of products sold in March.

$$T(3) = 800 \times (1.02)^{(2.3)3} - 50 \approx 867 \underline{Products}$$

b. Sketch the function.

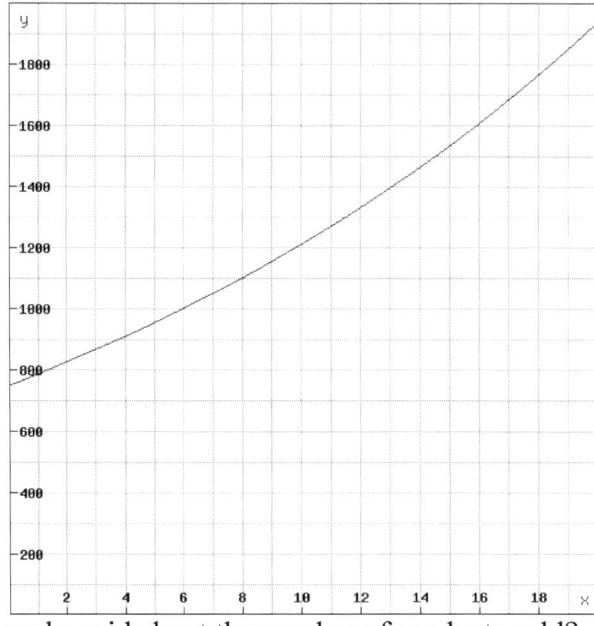

c. What can be said about the number of products sold?

It increases exponentially.

d. When will the number of products sold exceed 1000 for the first time?

$$1000 = 800 \times (1.02)^{(2.3)t} - 50; t \approx 5.97 \underline{\text{ so after 6 months.}}$$

2. The temperature of boiling liquid can be modeled by the following function where t is given in minutes.

$$T(t) = 80 \times \left(\frac{9}{8}\right)^{-2t} + 10$$

a. Find the initial temperature of the liquid. $T(0) = 80 \times \left(\frac{9}{8}\right)^{0} + 10 = 90°$

b. Find the temperature of the liquid after 2 minutes.

$$T(t) = 80 \times \left(\frac{9}{8}\right)^{-4} + 10 \approx 59.9°$$

c. What will the temperature of the liquid after a long time? Give a practical interpretation to this temperature.

$$T(99999) = 80 \times \left(\frac{9}{8}\right)^{-2t} + 10 \approx 0 + 10 = 10°$$

The liquids gets colder approaching the temperature of its surroundings.

d. Sketch the function.

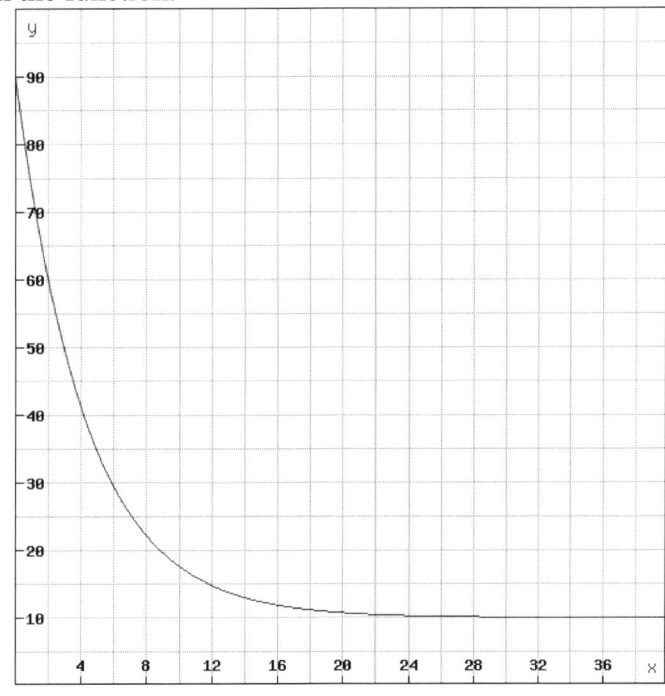

e. How long will it take the temperature of the liquid reach 42°?

$$42 = 80 \times \left(\frac{9}{8}\right)^{-2t} + 10; t \approx 3.89 \, min$$

3. The population of a rapidly–growing country starts at 4 million and increases by 10% each year.

   a. Complete the table below:

t(years)	P, population (in millions)	ΔP, increase in population (in millions)
0	4	0.4
1	4.4	0.44
2	4.84	0.484
3	5.324	0.5324
4	5.8564	0.58564

   b. Do you identify a pattern? Can you write a general expression of the population (P) as a function of the time (t)?

$$P(t) = 4 \cdot (1.10)^t$$

   c. Sketch its graph:

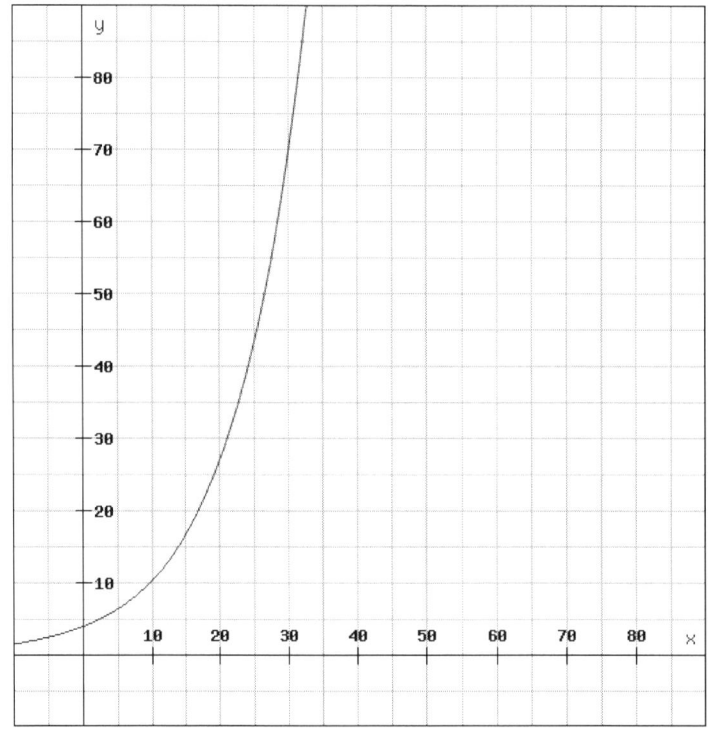

4. A chemical reaction starts with 200 grams of radioactive substance that decays by 20% per year.
   a. First, complete the table below.

t (years)	0	1	2	3	4
Q (grams)	200	160	128	102.4	81.92

   b. Find the expression of the function A(t), A the amount of substance and t the time in years.

   $$A(t) = 200 \cdot (0.8)^t$$

   c. Sketch its graph.

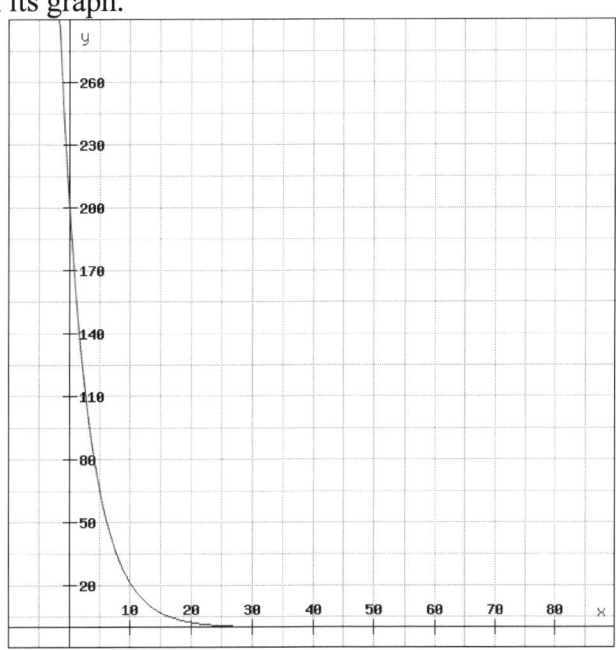

5. Suppose you invest 10000$ in the year 2000 and the investment earns 5.5% annually.

   a. a. Find the expression of the function A(t), A the amount of money and t the time in years.

   $$A(t) = 10000 \cdot (1.055)^t$$

   b. What will be the investment worth in 2010, 2020, 2030?

   $$A(t) = 10000 \cdot (1.055)^{10} \approx 1.71 \cdot 10^3 \$$$

   $$A(t) = 10000 \cdot (1.055)^{20} \approx 2.92 \cdot 10^3 \$$$

   $$A(t) = 10000 \cdot (1.055)^{30} \approx 4.99 \cdot 10^3 \$$$

6.1. – DEFINITION OF TRIGONOMETRIC FUNCTIONS

Definition of Sin(x):

As can be deduced from the unit circle in the <u>first</u> and <u>second</u> quadrants the Sin(x) function is <u>positive</u>, while in the <u>third</u> and <u>forth</u> quadrants it is <u>negative</u>.

Definition of Cos(x):

As can be deduced from the unit circle in the <u>first</u> and <u>forth</u> quadrants the Cos(x) function is <u>positive</u>, while in the <u>second</u> and <u>third</u> quadrants it is <u>negative</u>

Exercises:

In each one of the cases sketch the unit circle and the corresponding angle and then find the corresponding value:

1. $\text{Sin}(0^\circ) = \underline{0}$

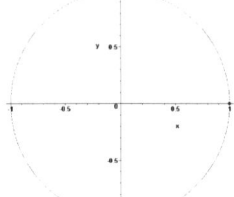

2. $\text{Cos}(0^\circ) = \underline{1}$

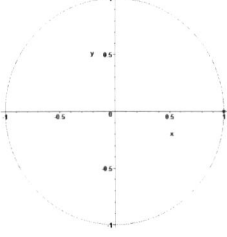

3. $\text{Sin}(90^\circ) = \underline{1}$

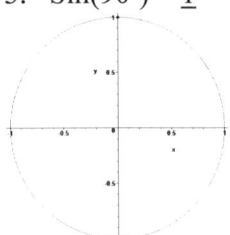

4. $\text{Cos}(225^\circ) = -\dfrac{1}{\sqrt{2}}$

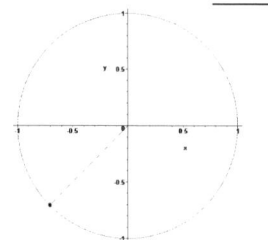

5. $\text{Sin}(225^\circ) = -\dfrac{1}{\sqrt{2}}$

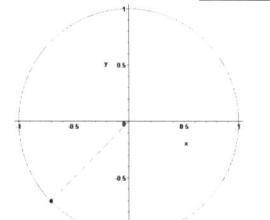

6. $\text{Cos}(210^\circ) = -\dfrac{\sqrt{3}}{2}$

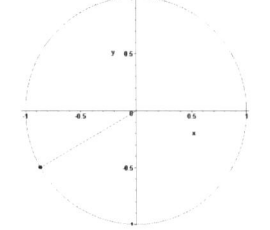

7. $\text{Sin}(210^\circ) = -\dfrac{1}{2}$

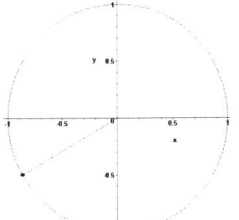

8. $\text{Cos}(225^\circ) = -\dfrac{1}{\sqrt{2}}$

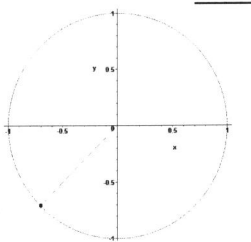

9. $\text{Sin}(-225^\circ) = \dfrac{1}{\sqrt{2}}$

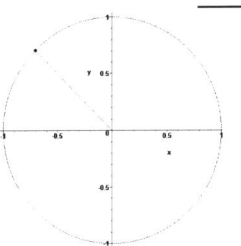

10. $\text{Cos}(210^\circ) = -\dfrac{\sqrt{3}}{2}$

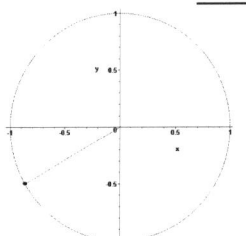

11. $\text{Sin}(-210^\circ) = -\dfrac{1}{2}$

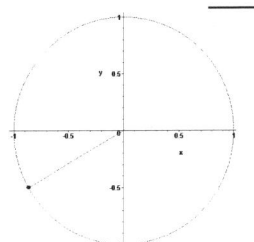

12. $\text{Cos}(90^\circ) = \underline{0}$

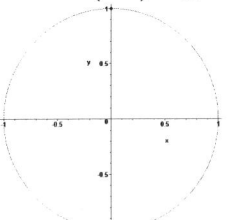

13. $\text{Sin}(270^\circ) = \underline{-1}$

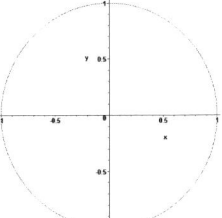

14. $\text{Cos}(270^\circ) = \underline{0}$

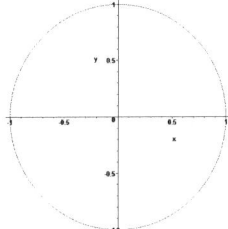

15. $\text{Sin}(360^\circ) = \underline{0}$

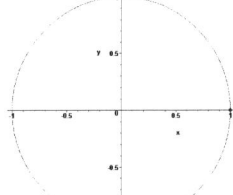

16. $\text{Cos}(180^\circ) = \underline{-1}$

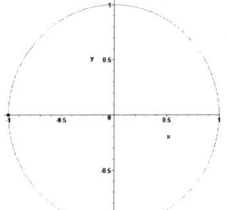

17. $\text{Sin}(180^\circ) = \underline{0}$

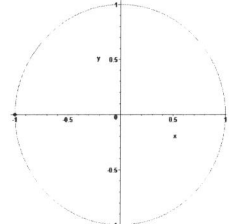

18. $\text{Cos}(-45°) = \dfrac{1}{\sqrt{2}}$

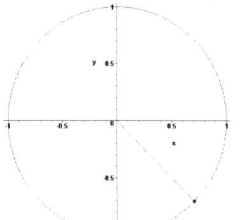

19. $\text{Cos}(300°) = \dfrac{1}{2}$

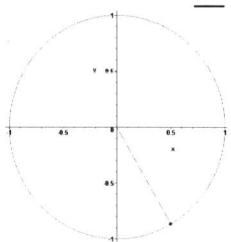

20. $\text{Sin}(300°) = -\dfrac{\sqrt{3}}{2}$

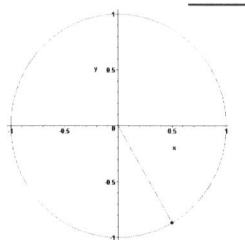

21. $\text{Sin}(330°) = -\dfrac{1}{2}$

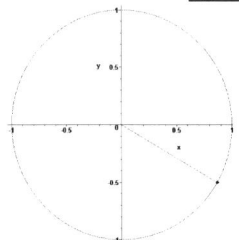

22. $\text{Cos}(390°) = \dfrac{\sqrt{3}}{2}$

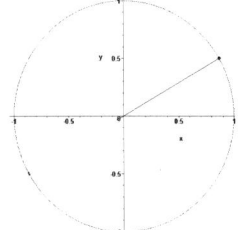

23. $\text{Cos}(135°) = -\dfrac{1}{\sqrt{2}}$

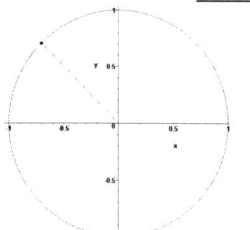

24. $\text{Sin}(135°) = \dfrac{1}{\sqrt{2}}$

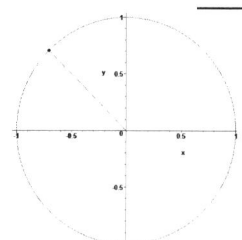

25. $\text{Sin}(45°) = \dfrac{1}{\sqrt{2}}$

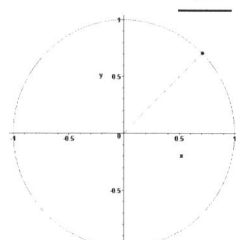

26. $\text{Cos}(70°) \approx 0.342$

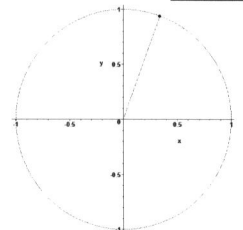

27. $\text{Cos}(130°) = \approx -0.643$

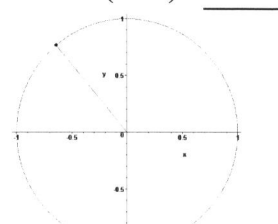

28. $\text{Cos}(1°) = \approx 0.999$

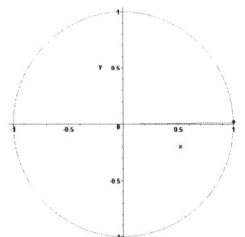

6.2. – SINE AND COSINE RULE

<u>The sine rule:</u> For any triangle, given the sides a, b and c and their corresponding opposite angles, A, B and C:

$$\frac{Sin(A)}{a} = \frac{Sin(B)}{b} = \frac{Sin(C)}{c}$$

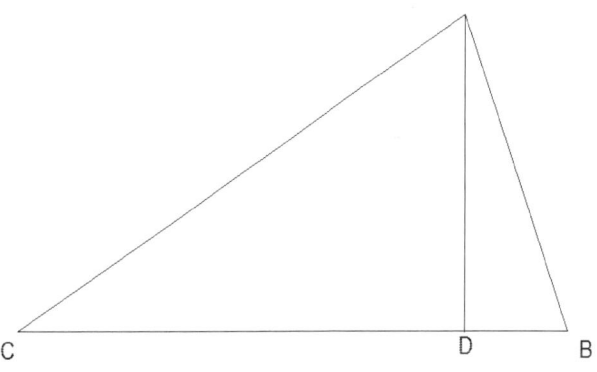

How many equations are written above? <u>3</u>

I. 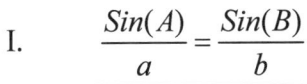 $\dfrac{Sin(A)}{a} = \dfrac{Sin(B)}{b}$

II. $\dfrac{Sin(A)}{a} = \dfrac{Sin(C)}{c}$

III. $\dfrac{Sin(B)}{b} = \dfrac{Sin(C)}{c}$

Given the following triangle:

a. Find AD in terms of AC and the angle C.

$$\underline{AD = AC\sin(C)}$$

b. Find the Area of the triangle in terms of BC, AC and the angle C.

$$\underline{S_{ABC} = \frac{BC \cdot AC\sin(C)}{2}}$$

c. Conclusion:

<u>**Area of any triangle is given by half of the product of 2 of its sides multiplied by the sine of the angle between those sides**</u>

$$\underline{S_{ABC} = \frac{a \cdot b\sin(\alpha)}{2}}$$

Exercises

1. Sketch a right angled triangle with angles: M, N, G and sides x, y, z. Write the Sine and Cosine rule for this triangle.

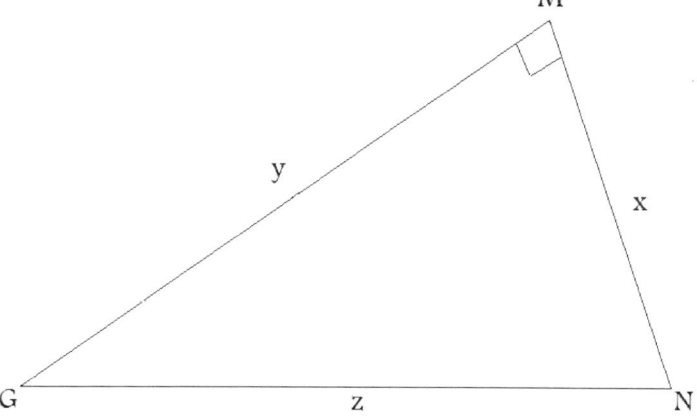

$$\frac{Sin(G)}{x} = \frac{Sin(N)}{y} = \frac{Sin(M)}{z}$$

$$x^2 = y^2 + z^2 - 2yz\cos(G)$$

$$y^2 = x^2 + z^2 - 2xz\cos(N)$$

$$z^2 = y^2 + x^2 - 2yx\cos(M)$$

2. Find all the missing sides, angles and area of the triangles below. If there is more than one set of solutions, try to find them all.

$$12^2 = 8^2 + 10^2 - 2 \cdot 8 \cdot 10\cos(G)$$

$$G \approx 82.8°$$

$$10^2 = 8^2 + 12^2 - 2 \cdot 8 \cdot 12\cos(S)$$

$$S \approx 55.8°$$

$$M = 180° - 82.8° - 55.8° = 41.4°$$

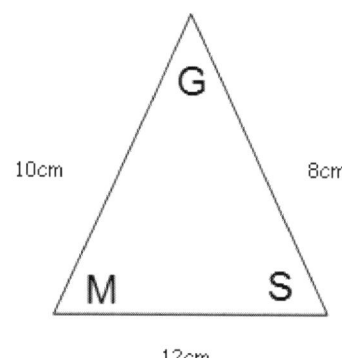

$$x^2 = 11^2 + 10^2 - 2 \cdot 11 \cdot 10\cos(30)$$

$$x \approx 5.52cm$$

$$5.52^2 = 11^2 + 10^2 - 2 \cdot 11 \cdot 10\cos(G)$$

$$G \approx 85.1°$$

$$M = 180° - 30° - 85.1° = 64.9°$$

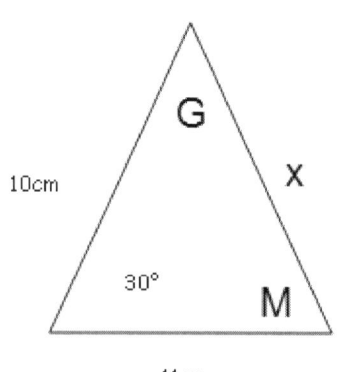

3. Find all the sides, angles and the area of the following triangles:

Ambiguous Case (2 possible solutions)

$6^2 = 8^2 + x^2 - 2 \cdot x \cdot 8 \cos(40°)$

$x_1 \approx 3.04 cm$

$x_2 \approx 9.22 cm$

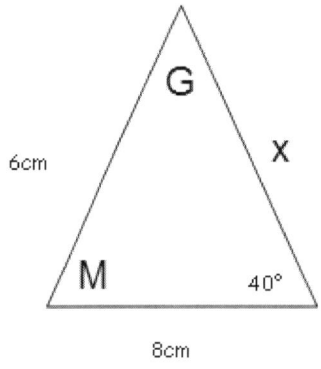

$8^2 = 6^2 + 3.04^2 - 2 \cdot 3.04 \cdot 8 \cos(G)$

$G_1 \approx 121°$

$M_1 = 180° - 121° - 40° = 19°$

$8^2 = 6^2 + 9.22^2 - 2 \cdot 9.22 \cdot 8 \cos(G)$

$G_2 \approx 59.0°$

$M_2 = 180° - 59° - 40° = 81°$

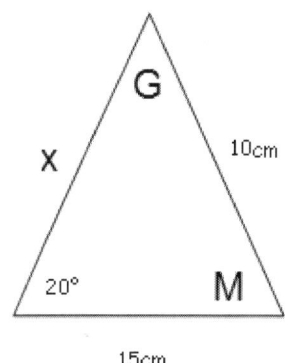

$\dfrac{\sin(20°)}{10} = \dfrac{\sin(G)}{15}$

$G \approx 30.9°$

$M = 180° - 30.9° - 20° = 129.1°$

$x^2 = 10^2 + 15^2 - 2 \cdot 10 \cdot 15 \cos(129.1°)$

$x \approx 22.7 cm$

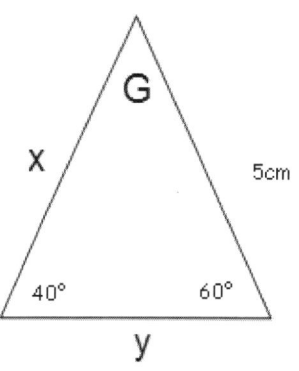

$G = 180° - 40° - 60° = 80°$

$\dfrac{\sin(40°)}{5} = \dfrac{\sin(60)}{x}$

$x \approx 6.74 cm$

$\dfrac{\sin(40°)}{5} = \dfrac{\sin(80)}{y}$

$y \approx 7.66 cm$

4. Find all the sides, angles and the area of the following triangles:

This triangle can have any size as only angles are given

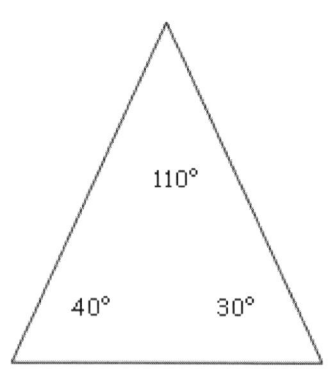

Ambiguous Case (2 possible solutions

$$5^2 = 9^2 + x^2 - 2 \cdot x \cdot 9 \cos(20^\circ)$$

$$x_1 \approx 4.52 cm$$

$$x_2 \approx 12.4 cm$$

$$\frac{\sin(20^\circ)}{5} = \frac{\sin(G)}{9}$$

$$G_1 \approx 28.6^\circ$$

$$G_2 \approx 180 - 28.6^\circ = 151.4^\circ$$

$$M_1 = 180^\circ - 20^\circ - 28.6^\circ = 131.4^\circ$$

$$\underline{M_2 = 180^\circ - 20^\circ - 151.4^\circ = 8.6^\circ}$$

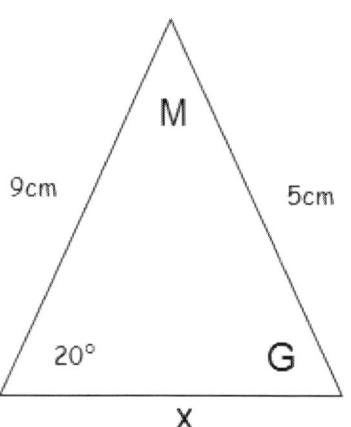

This triangle cannot exist as
the sum 5 + 6 is smaller than 13

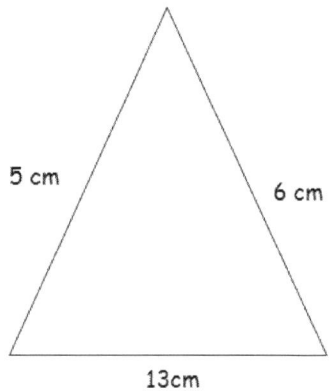

$$\frac{\sin(50^\circ)}{15} = \frac{\sin(G)}{12}$$

$G \approx 37.8^\circ$

$M = 180^\circ - 37.8^\circ - 50^\circ = 92.2^\circ$

$x^2 = 12^2 + 15^2 - 2 \cdot 12 \cdot 15 \cos(92.2^\circ)$

$x \approx 19.6 cm$

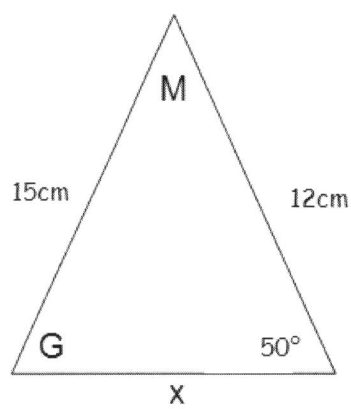

$x^2 = 12^2 + 8^2 - 2 \cdot 12 \cdot 8 \cos(40^\circ)$

$x \approx 7.81 cm$

$$\frac{7.81}{Sin(40^\circ)} = \frac{8}{Sin(G)}$$

$G \approx 41.2^\circ$

$M = 180^\circ - 41.2^\circ - 40^\circ = 98.8^\circ$

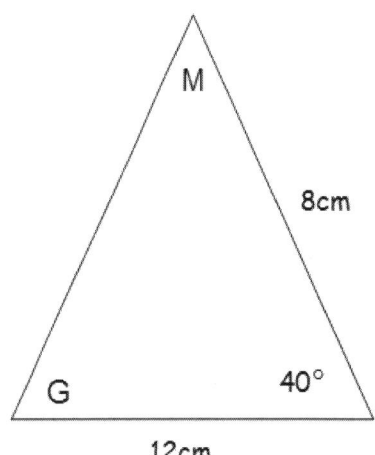

$x^2 = 13^2 + 6^2 - 2 \cdot 13 \cdot 6 \cos(20^\circ)$

$x \approx 7.64 cm$

$$\frac{7.64}{Sin(20^\circ)} = \frac{6}{Sin(G)}$$

$G \approx 15.6^\circ$

$M = 180^\circ - 15.6^\circ - 40^\circ = 134.4^\circ$

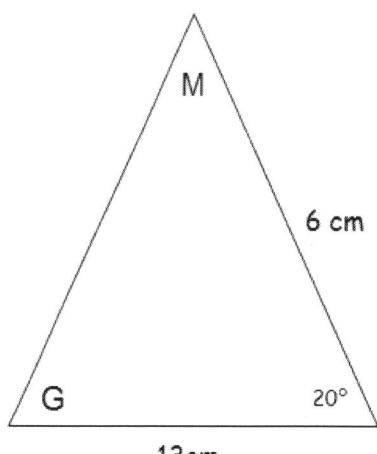

6.3. – TRIGONOMETRIC RATIOS

1. Find x and y in the following cases:
   a.

   $$\sin(25°) = \frac{5}{y}$$

   $$y \approx 11.8$$

   $$\tan(25°) = \frac{5}{x}$$

   $$\underline{x \approx 10.7}$$

   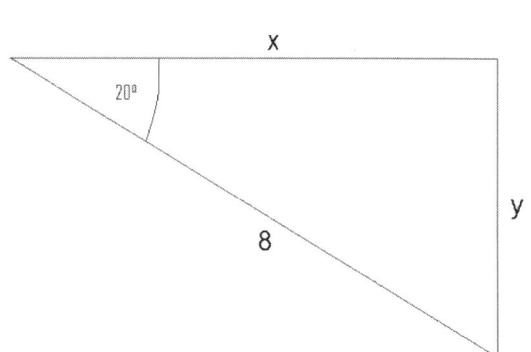

   b.

   $$\sin(20°) = \frac{y}{8}$$

   $$y \approx 2.74$$

   $$\cos(20°) = \frac{x}{8}$$

   $$\underline{x \approx 7.52}$$

2. The Triangle in the diagram (not to scale) is <u>not</u> right angled, find x and y.

   Not right angled, must use cos rule:

   $$Y^2 = 40^2 + 10^2 - 2 \cdot 40 \cdot 10 \cos(35)$$

   $$Y \approx 32.3$$

   $$\frac{10}{Sin(x)} = \frac{32.3}{Sin(35)}$$

   $$\underline{x \approx 10.2°}$$

   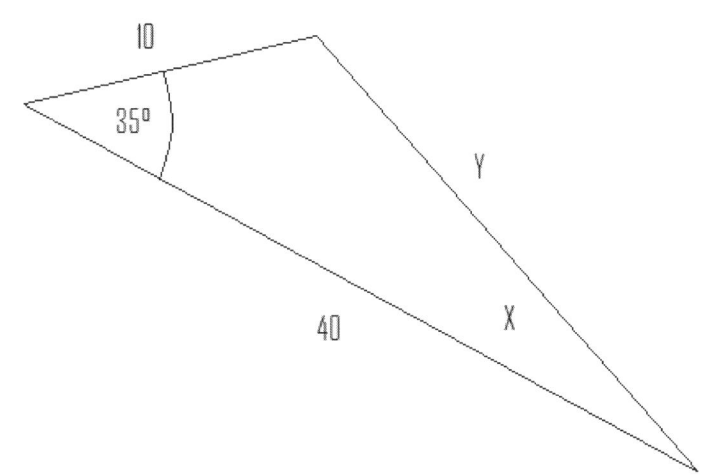

3. The shade formed by building is 100m long. The depression angle of the light as it approaches the ground is 40°.

   a. Sketch a diagram that describes the situation.
   b. Find the height of the building.

$$\tan(40°) = \frac{h}{100}$$

$$h \approx 83.9m$$

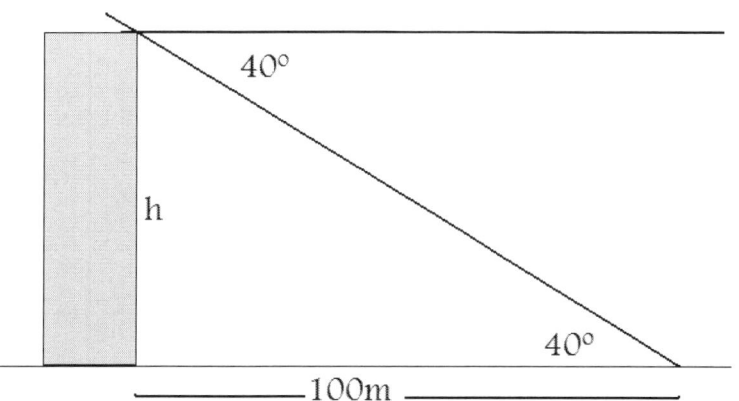

4. John who lives next the river wanted to measure its width without crossing the river. He did some measurements and obtained the following data:

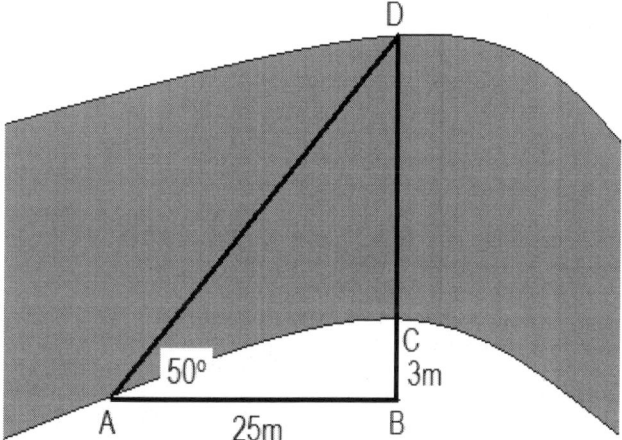

AB = 25m, BC = 3m, B = 90°

Find the width of the river.

$$\tan(50°) = \frac{DB}{25}$$

$$h \approx 29.8m$$

$$Width = DC = DB - 3 = 29.8 - 3 = 26.8m$$

5. The height of building is 120m. The depression angle of the light as it approaches the ground is 30°.

    a. Sketch a diagram that describes the situation.
    b. Find the length of the shade on the ground.

$$\tan(30°) = \frac{120}{x}$$

$$h \approx 208m$$

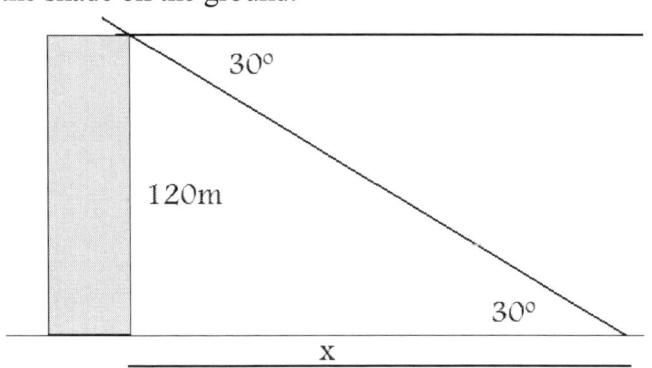

6. In its search for food the lion is observing a certain prey located 2 m above the ground. The lion's head forms an angle of 12° with the ground as he looks at his prey.

    a. Sketch a diagram that describes the situation.
    b. Find the distance from the lion's mouth to its prey.

$$\sin(12°) = \frac{2}{x}$$

$$x \approx 9.62m$$

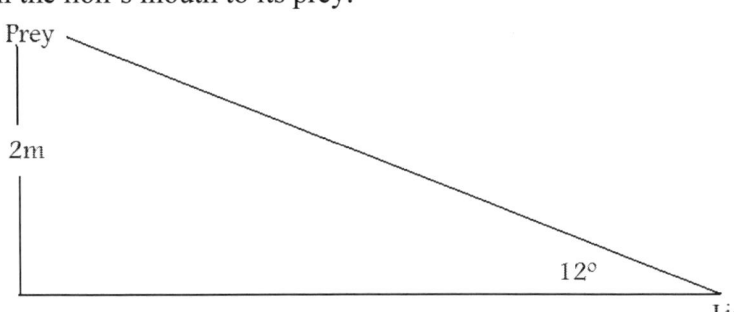

7. Measuring the height and distance of objects:

$$\tan(20°) = \frac{h}{AD}$$

$$\tan(18°) = \frac{h}{AD+4}$$

Solving system using the numerical values of tan(18°) and tan(20ª) or graphically gives:

$$h \approx 12.1$$

$$AD \approx 33.3$$

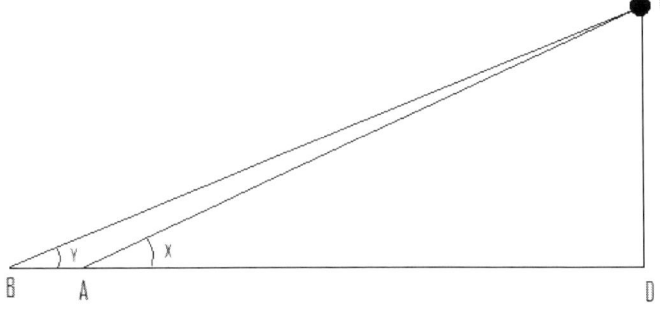

6.4. – 3D GEOMETRY

1. Sketch each one of the solids and fill the blanks.

    a. Cuboid   Volume $= abc$ Surface Area $= 2(ab+ac+bc)$

    a, b and c the sides of the cuboid.

    b. Right pyramid   Volume $= \dfrac{A_{base}h}{3}$ Surface Area $= A_{base} + L(LateralArea)$

    a and h the side of the base and the height of the pyramid.

    c. Right prism   Volume $= A_{base}h$ Surface Area $= 2A_{base} + L(LateralArea)$

    d. Right cone   Volume $= \dfrac{\pi r^2 h}{3}$ Surface Area $= \pi(r^2 + rh)$

    e. Cylinder   Volume $= \pi r^2 h$ Surface Area $= 2\pi r^2 + 2\pi rh$

    f. Sphere   Volume $= \dfrac{4}{3}\pi r^3$ Surface Area $= 4\pi r^2$

    g. Hemisphere   Volume $= \dfrac{2}{3}\pi r^3$ Surface Area $= 2\pi r^2$

2. In the design process of a certain lamp the following diagram is obtained.

    Assuming the sun is directly above the lamp and length of the shadow on the ground is 2.5 meters.

    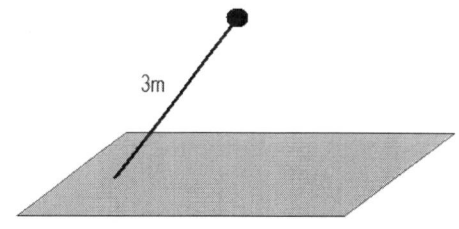

    a. Find the angle between the lamp and the ground.

    $\cos(x) = \left(\dfrac{2.5}{3}\right)$

    $x \approx 33.6°$

    b. Find the height of the lamp above the ground.

    $\sin(33.6) = \left(\dfrac{h}{3}\right)$

    $h \approx 1.66m$

3. Given the following diagram (not to scale): ABCD is a rectangle AB = 20 cm, BC = 12 cm, EA = BF = 14 cm. EM = 5 cm.

   a. Find the angle between NB and the base ABCD.

   First find DB = $\sqrt{544}$ cm, ND = 9 cm, then working in triangle NBD:
   $$\tan(\alpha) = \left(\frac{ND}{DB}\right) = \left(\frac{9}{\sqrt{544}}\right)$$
   $$\alpha \approx 21.1°$$

   b. Find the length of the segment MC. $\sqrt{544}$
   c. Find the area of MNBC

   $$A = BC \cdot BM = 12 \cdot \sqrt{481} cm^2$$

   d. Find the volume of the cuboid.

   $$V = 20 \cdot 12 \cdot 14 = 3360 cm^3$$

   e. Find the surface area of the cuboid.

   $$S = 2(20 \cdot 12 + 20 \cdot 14 + 12 \cdot 14) = 1376 cm^2$$

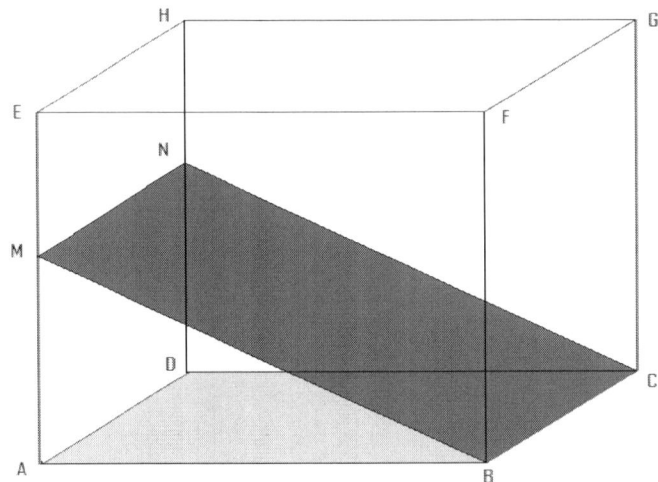

2. Given the following diagram (not to scale): ABCD is a square AB = 10 cm. CG = BF = 12 cm. M is the midpoint of DB.

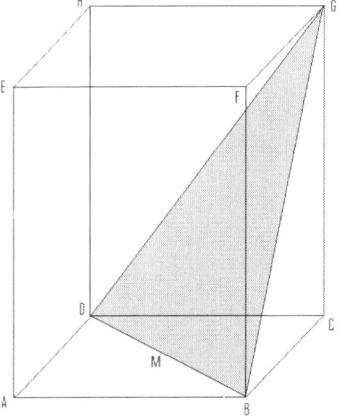

   a. Find the length DB.

$$DB = \sqrt{200}\,cm$$

   b. Find the angle between DG and the base ABCD.

Working in triangle DGC:

$$\tan(\alpha) = \left(\frac{GC}{DC}\right) = \left(\frac{12}{10}\right)$$

$$\alpha \approx 50.2°$$

   c. Find the angle between GM and the base ABCD.

Working in triangle GMC:

$$\tan(\beta) = \left(\frac{GC}{CM}\right) = \left(\frac{12}{\left(\frac{\sqrt{200}}{2}\right)}\right)$$

$$\beta \approx 59.5°$$

   d. Find the area of BDG.
First we find MG working in triangle MGC:

$$MG = \sqrt{12^2 + \left(\frac{\sqrt{200}}{2}\right)^2} = \sqrt{194}$$

Then:

$$A_{BDG} = \frac{DG \cdot MG}{2} = \left(\frac{\left(\frac{\sqrt{200}}{2}\right)\sqrt{194}}{2}\right) = 5\sqrt{97}\,cm^2$$

3. In the design process of a modern building a sphere of 5m radius is put on top a cylinder with a radius twice as big. The height of the building is 30m.

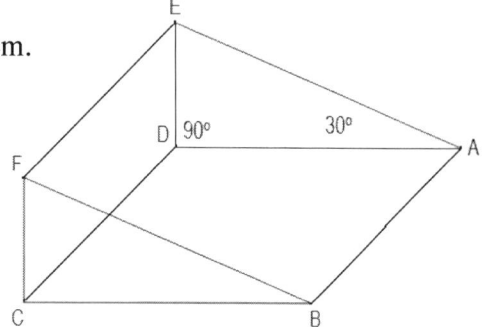

a. Find the volume of the sphere. $V = \frac{4}{3}\pi 5^3 = \frac{500\pi}{3}\ cm^3$

b. Find the height of the cylinder. $h = 30 - 10 = 20m$

c. Find the volume of the building. $V = \frac{500\pi}{3} + 2000\pi\ cm^3$

d. Find the surface area of the building that that is exposed to fresh air.

$A = A_{sphere} + A_{cylinderTop} + A_{cylinderSide} = 100\pi + 100\pi + 400\pi = 600\pi\ cm^2$

4. Given the following right prism. AB = 12cm, AE = 15cm.

a. The length of AD.

In triangle ADE: $\cos(30°) = \left(\frac{AD}{AE}\right) = \left(\frac{AD}{15}\right)$

$AD = \frac{15\sqrt{3}}{2} \approx 13.0$

b. The length of ED.

In triangle ADE: $\sin(30°) = \left(\frac{DE}{AE}\right) = \left(\frac{DE}{15}\right); DE = 7.5cm$

c. The length of AF.
In triangle ACD:

$AC^2 = AD^2 + CD^2; AC^2 = \left(\frac{15\sqrt{3}}{2}\right)^2 + (12)^2; AC = \sqrt{\frac{1251}{4}} \approx 17.7cm$

In triangle ACF:

$AF^2 = CF^2 + AC^2; AF^2 = (7.5)^2 + \left(\sqrt{\frac{1251}{4}}\right)^2; AF = 3\sqrt{41} \approx 19.2cm$

d. The angle FAB. $\tan(\delta) = \left(\frac{FB}{BA}\right) = \left(\frac{15}{12}\right); \delta \approx 51.3°$

e. The surface area of the prism.

$A = 2A_{triangle} + A_{base} + A_{top} + A_{back} = \frac{450\sqrt{3}}{8} + 90\sqrt{3} + 180 + 90 = 270 + \frac{585\sqrt{3}}{4} \approx 523cm^2$

5. An old tower is made of a cone put on top of a cylinder. The radius of both is 5m. The height of the cylinder is 10m. The height of the cone is 60% of the cylinder's height.

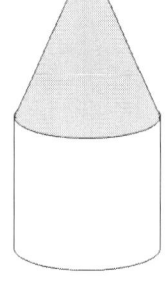

   a. Find the height of the tower.

   $h = 10 + 6 = 16m$

   b. Find the volume of the tower.

   $V = V_{cone} + V_{cylinder} = \dfrac{150\pi}{3} + 250\pi = 300\pi \ cm^3$

6. Given the following diagram (not to scale): ABCD is a rectangle AB = 9 cm. BC = 7 cm. EF = 10 cm is the height of the right pyramid.

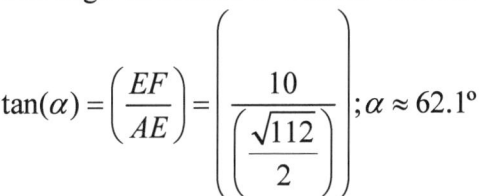

   a. The length AE. $AE = \dfrac{\sqrt{112}}{2} cm$

   b. The length AF. $AF = \sqrt{\left(\dfrac{\sqrt{112}}{2}\right)^2 + (10)^2} = \sqrt{128} cm$

   c. The angle between AF and the base ABCD.

   $\tan(\alpha) = \left(\dfrac{EF}{AE}\right) = \left(\dfrac{10}{\left(\dfrac{\sqrt{112}}{2}\right)}\right); \alpha \approx 62.1°$

   d. The length MF.

   $MF = \sqrt{EM^2 + EF^2} = \sqrt{(4.5)^2 + (10)^2} = \dfrac{\sqrt{481}}{2} \approx 11.0cm$

   e. The angle between MF and the base ABCD.

   $\tan(\beta) = \left(\dfrac{EF}{EM}\right) = \left(\dfrac{10}{4.5}\right); \beta \approx 65.8°$

   f. The area of FBC. $A_{FBC} = \dfrac{\left(7 \cdot \dfrac{\sqrt{481}}{2}\right)}{2} = \dfrac{7\sqrt{481}}{4} \approx 38.4cm^2$

   g. Find the volume of the pyramid. $V = \dfrac{7 \cdot 9 \cdot 10}{3} = 210cm^3$

   h. Find the surface area of the pyramid.

   $S_{pyramid} = 2A_{FBC} + 2A_{ABF} + A_{ABCD} \approx 76.8 + 91.4 + 63 \approx 231cm^2$

7.1. – RATE OF CHANGE

Example 1: Oil prices, represented as a function of time P(t):

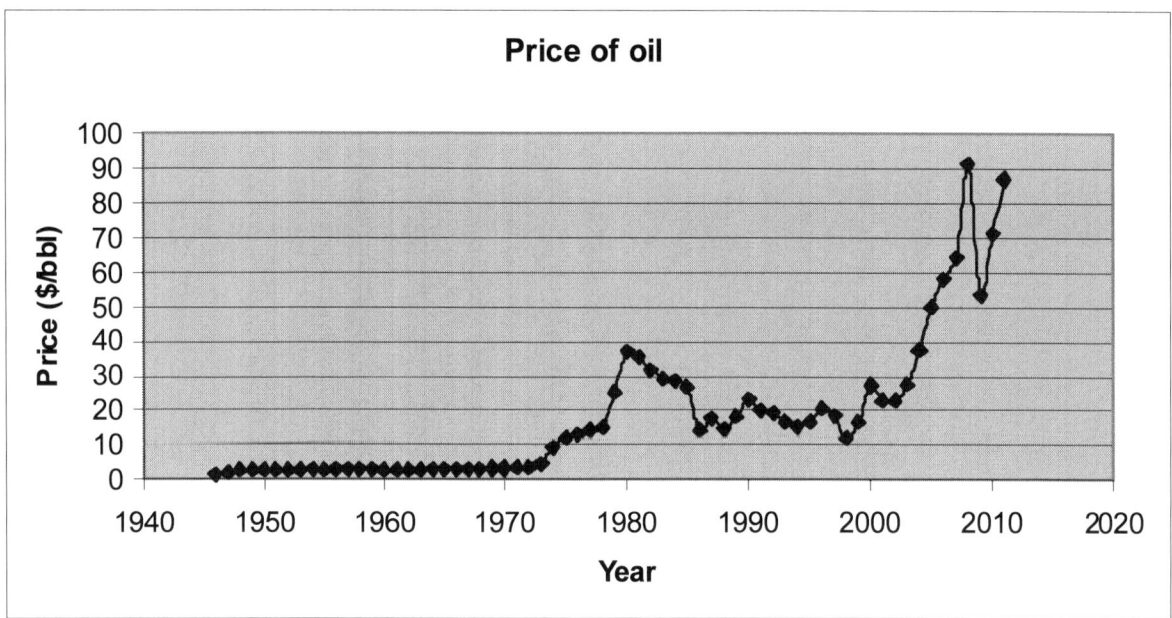

1. As you can see there have been periods of time in history in which the prices have changed slowly, Identify one of them: $t \in (1950, 1970)$

2. In other periods the prices have been changing very quickly, identify one positive change: $t \in (2003, 2005)$ and one negative change: $t \in (2008, 2009)$

3. In this graph what are the <u>units</u> of the <u>change</u> of price: $\left[\dfrac{\$}{bbl \cdot year} \right]$

4. Find the <u>average rate of change</u> in oil prices between 1970 and 1985. Is this average similar to the real change in prices? Explain your answer.

    $Av_{1970-1985} = \dfrac{24}{15} = 1.6 \; \frac{\$}{bbl \cdot year}$ <u>It is not similar to real change as the prices went up and down during that period of time.</u>

5. Find the average rate of change between 1945 and 2005, how can this change be represented graphically?

    $Av_{1945-2005} = \dfrac{48}{60} = 0.8 \; \frac{\$}{bbl \cdot year}$ <u>The average rate of change is the slope of the line the connects the two points.</u>

Example 2: Population of 20 – 29 year olds in southern Europe for example, represented as a function of time P(t):

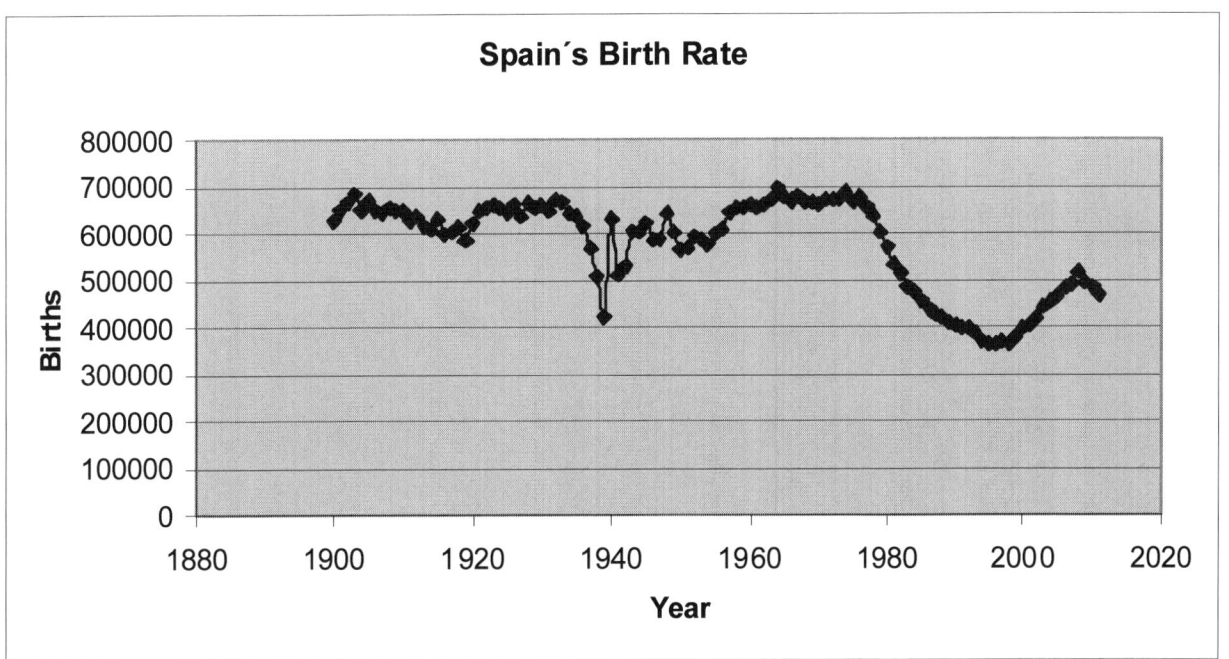

6. During what period of time the fastest change occurs? $t \in (1939, 1940)$

7. In this graph what are the <u>units</u> of the <u>change</u> of birth: $\left[\dfrac{Births}{year} \right]$

8. Find the <u>average rate of change</u> between 1960 and 2000. Is this average similar to the real change in births? Explain your answer.

$$Av_{1960-2000} = -\frac{260000}{40} = -6500 \frac{Births}{year}$$ <u>It shows some similarity to the real tendency.</u>

9. Find the average rate of change between 2000 and 2010, how can this change be represented graphically?

$$Av_{2000-2010} = \frac{100000}{10} = 10000 \frac{Births}{year}$$ <u>The average rate of change is the slope of the</u>

<u>line the connects the two points.</u>

7.2. – DEFINITION OF DERIVATIVE

Given the function Temp(x) = –x(x – 4) with the points P = (2, 4) and Q = (a, f(a)). Temp is the temperature on the top of a certain mountain, t is given in hours.

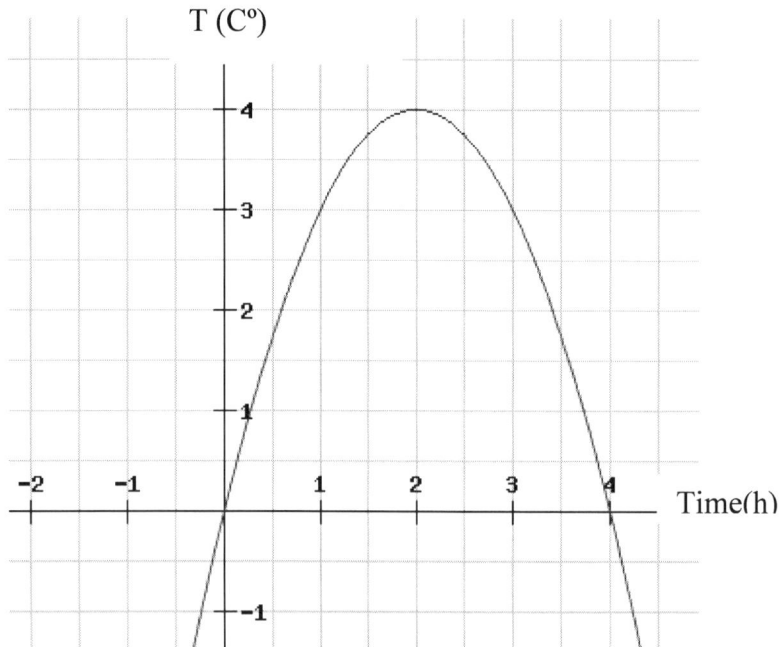

1. Complete the y coordinate of point Q in case a = 3. $Q = (3,3)$

2. If a = 2.5 find the slope of the line that connects the points Q and P (and sketch the line).

   $Q = (2.5, 3.75); P = (2, 4)$

   $m = -0,5$

3. If a = 2.1 find the slope of the line that connects the points Q and P (and sketch the line on the same graph).

   $Q = (2.1, 3.99); P = (2, 4)$

   $m = -0.1$

4. If a = 2.01 find the slope of the line that connects the points Q and P (and sketch the line on the same graph).

   $Q = (2.01, 3.9999); P = (2, 4)$

   $m = -0.01$

5. If a = 2.001 find the slope of the line that connects the points Q and P (and sketch the line on the same graph).

   $Q = (2.001, 3.999999); P = (2, 4)$

   $m = -0.001$

6. Fill the following table:

a	2.5	2.1	2.01	2.001
Slope of QP	$-0,5$	$-0,1$	$-0,01$	$-0,001$

What is your conclusion?

As Q approaches P the slope of the line QP tends to 0 (the slop at P).

7. What does the slope **between 2 points** represent? Make reference to temperature and give units.

   <u>The average rate of change. Average change of temperature with height.</u>

8. What does the slope of the tangent to the function **at a certain point** represent? Make reference to temperature and give units.

   <u>The instantaneous rate of change. Instantaneous change of temperature with height.</u>

The derivative is the <u>slope of the tangent to a function at a certain point.</u>

Find the derivative of the following functions

1. $f(x) = 3$ $\qquad$ $\dfrac{df}{dx} = f'(x) = 0$

2. $g(x) = 2x - 2$ $\qquad$ $\dfrac{dg}{dx} = g'(x) = 2$

3. $f(x) = -\dfrac{x}{2} + 1$ $\qquad$ $\dfrac{df}{dx} = f'(x) = -\dfrac{1}{2}$

4. $f(x) = -x^2 + 4x$ $\qquad$ $\dfrac{df}{dx} = f'(x) = -2x + 4$

In this case the value of the derivative depends on the <u>point,</u> for example:

$\underline{f'(0) = 4 \quad f'(1) = 2 \quad f'(2) = 0}$

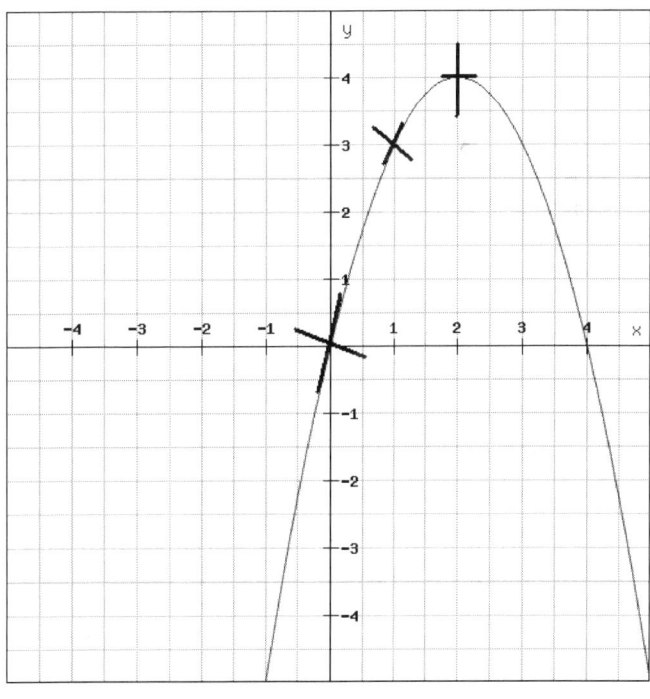

Sketch the tangent and normal in each one of the cases. State the slope of the normal in each case:

$\underline{m_{normal(x=0)} = -\dfrac{1}{4} \quad m_{normal(x=1)} = -\dfrac{1}{2} \quad m_{normal(x=0)} = undefined}$

413

5. Given the function, sketch the tangent in each one of the points:

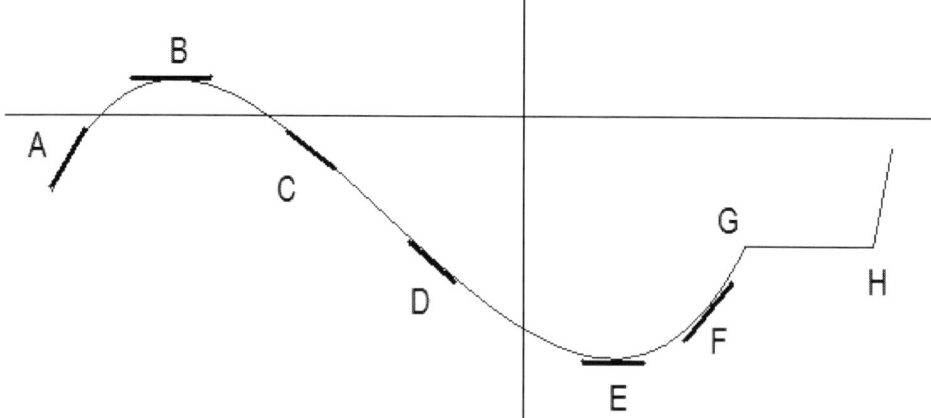

At points G and H the tangent is not well defined and cannot be sketched.

Fill the blanks with the words positive, negative, zero or doesn't exist. The value of the derivative at point

A is positive   B is zero   C is negative   D is negative

E is zero   F is positive   G is D.E.   H is D.E.

6. $f(x) = x - 3x^2 + \dfrac{2}{x} + 3$

$\dfrac{df}{dx} = f'(x) = 1 - 6x - 2x^{-2}$

$f'(0) = undefined$

$f'(-2) = 1 + 12 - \dfrac{1}{2} = 12.5$
_____

7. $V(r) = 5 - 4r^{-2} - 3r + \dfrac{4}{3r^3}$

$\dfrac{dV}{dr} = V'(r) = 8r^{-3} - 3 - 4r^{-4}$

$V'(-1) = -8 + 3 - 4 = -9$

$V'(3) = \dfrac{8}{27} - 9 - \dfrac{4}{81} \approx -8.75$
_____

8. $S(c) = \dfrac{-2}{c^2} - c^{-3} + 10$

$\dfrac{dS}{dc} = S'(c) = 2c^{-3} + 3c^{-4}$

$S'(-3) = -\dfrac{2}{27} + \dfrac{3}{81} = -\dfrac{3}{81}$

$S'(1) = 5$
_____

9. $f(x) = 7x^3 - 3 + \dfrac{5}{x^2}$

$f'(x) = 21x^2 - 10x^{-3}$

$f'(2) = 84 - \dfrac{10}{8} = 82.75$

$f'(-2) = 84 + \dfrac{10}{8} = 85.25$
_____

414

Find the derivatives of the following functions

1. $f(x) = -2$ $\qquad$ $\underline{f'(x) = 0}$

2. $f(x) = x$ $\qquad$ $\underline{f'(x) = 1}$

3. $f(x) = 5x$ $\qquad$ $\underline{f'(x) = 5}$

4. $f(x) = 5kx + 1$ $\qquad$ $\underline{f'(x) = 5k}$

5. $f(x) = -2x$ $\qquad$ $\underline{f'(x) = -2}$

6. $f(x) = -2x - 3$ $\qquad$ $\underline{f'(x) = -2}$

7. $f(x) = -2x + 3$ $\qquad$ $\underline{f'(x) = -2}$

8. $f(x) = x^2 + 3x - 10$ $\qquad$ $\underline{f'(x) = 2x + 3}$

9. $f(x) = x^2 + 7x - 1$ $\qquad$ $\underline{f'(x) = 2x + 7}$

10. $f(x) = bx^6 + 2x + 7$ $\qquad$ $\underline{f'(x) = 6bx^5 + 2}$

11. $f(x) = x^{22} + x - 1$ $\qquad$ $\underline{f'(x) = 22x^{21} + 1}$

12. $f(x) = x^4 + 2x + 1$ $\qquad$ $\underline{f'(x) = 4x^3 + 2}$

13. $f(x) = x^5 + x$ $\qquad$ $\underline{f'(x) = 5x^4 + 1}$

14. $f(x) = x^{22} - \dfrac{1}{x}$ $\qquad$ $\underline{f'(x) = 22x^{21} + x^{-2}}$

15. $f(x) = x^2 - 2x + \dfrac{1}{x^2}$ $\qquad$ $\underline{f'(x) = 2x - 2 - 2x^{-3}}$

16. $f(x) = a\,x^5 - 2x^4 - \dfrac{5}{x^2} + \dfrac{1}{x^3}$ $\qquad$ $\underline{f'(x) = 5ax^4 + 8x^3 + 10x^{-3} - 3x^{-4}}$

17. $f(x) = 5x^2 - 10x + \dfrac{1}{x^2}$ $\qquad$ $\underline{f'(x) = 10x - 10 - 2x^{-3}}$

18. $f(x) = -5x^{20} - \dfrac{1}{x^2} + \dfrac{3}{x^3}$ $\qquad$ $\underline{f'(x) = 100x^{19} + 2x^{-3} - 9x^{-4}}$

19. $f(x) = -bx^4 - 4x^2 - 4 + \dfrac{5}{x^2}$ $f'(x) = -4bx^3 - 8x - 10x^{-3}$

20. $f(x) = -x^{-2} + 3x$ $f'(x) = 2x^{-3} + 3$

21. $f(x) = 5 - 15x^{-2} - 3x^{-5} + \dfrac{1}{x^5}$ $f'(x) = 30x^{-3} + 15x^{-6} - 5x^{-6}$

22. $f(x) = \dfrac{5}{2}x^{-3} - b6x + \dfrac{1}{2x^2} + 7$ $f'(x) = -\dfrac{15}{2}x^{-4} - 6b + \dfrac{1}{2}x^{-3}$

23. $f(x) = \dfrac{1}{6}x^3 - 3 + \dfrac{3}{x^2} - 5$ $f'(x) = \dfrac{1}{2}x^2 - 3x^{-3}$

24. $f(x) = -12x - 13 + 3bx + 4 + 3x^{-3} + \dfrac{44}{6x^2} - 51$

$f'(x) = -12 + 3b - 9x^{-3} - \dfrac{44}{3}x^{-3}$

25. $f(x) = x^2 + 9x - 4 + 3x^2 + \dfrac{2}{7x^{12}} - 12$

$f'(x) = -2x + 9 + 6x - \dfrac{24}{7}x^{-13}$

26. $f(x) = 8x + 8 + \dfrac{11}{3x^4} + 345$

$f'(x) = 8 - \dfrac{44}{3}x^{-5}$

27. $f(x) = -x^3 + 6x^{22} - 8 - x + \dfrac{8}{3x^7} - 135$

$f'(x) = -3x^2 + 132x^{21} - 1 - \dfrac{56}{3}x^{-8}$

7.3. – TANGENTS AND NORMALS TO FUNCTIONS

1. Given the function $f(x) = 2x^2$. Sketch it.

   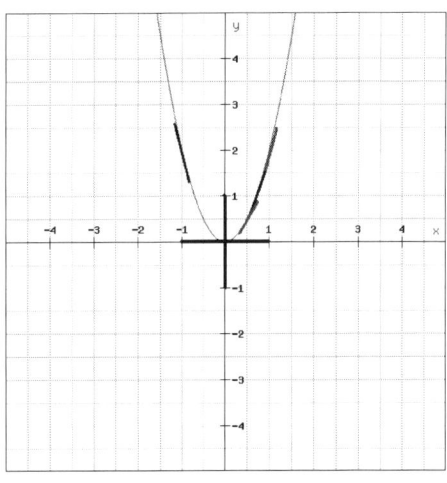

   a. $f'(x) = 4x$

   b. $f'(1) = 4$

   c. $f'(-1) = -4$

   d. $f'(x) = 4x = 3; x = \dfrac{3}{4}; \left(\dfrac{3}{4}, \dfrac{9}{8}\right)$

   e. $f'(x) = 4x = -4; x = -1; (-1, 2)$

   f. $f'(x) = 4x = 2; x = \dfrac{1}{2}; \left(\dfrac{1}{2}, \dfrac{1}{2}\right)$

   g. $f'(x) = 4x = -5; x = -\dfrac{5}{4}; \left(-\dfrac{5}{4}, \dfrac{25}{8}\right)$

   h. $m = f'(1) = 4; po\operatorname{int} = (1, 2); y = 4x + b; y = 4x - 3$

   i. $Tangent : m = f'(0) = 0; po\operatorname{int} = (0, 0); y = 4x + b; y = 0$

   $Normal : x = 0$

   j. $Tangent : m = f'(-2) = -8; po\operatorname{int} = (-2, 8); y = -8x + b; y = -8x - 8$

   $Normal : m = \dfrac{1}{8}; po\operatorname{int} = (-2, 8); y = \dfrac{1}{8}x + b; y = \dfrac{1}{8}x + \dfrac{33}{4}$

2. Given the function $f(x) = -\dfrac{2}{x} + 1$.

   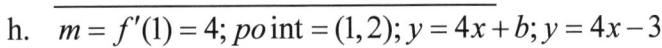

   a. $f'(x) = \dfrac{2}{x^2}$

   b. $f'(1) = 2$

   c. Out of domain, not possible.

   d. $f'\left(\dfrac{1}{2}\right) = 8$.

   e. $f'(x) = \dfrac{2}{x^2} = -3$ no solution, no such point exists.

   f. $f'(x) = \dfrac{2}{x^2} = \dfrac{1}{2} : x = \pm 2; (2, 0), (-2, 2)..$

   g. $f'(x) = \dfrac{2}{x^2} = -\dfrac{5}{3}$ This equation has no solution, no such point exists.

   h. $f'(x) = \dfrac{2}{x^2} = 6 : x = \pm \dfrac{1}{\sqrt{3}}; \left(\dfrac{1}{\sqrt{3}}, 1 - \dfrac{2\sqrt{3}}{3}\right), \left(\dfrac{1}{\sqrt{3}}, 1 + \dfrac{2\sqrt{3}}{3}\right)$.

   i. $m = f'(1) = 2; po\operatorname{int} = (1, -1); y = 2x + b; y = 2x - 3$

   j. Out of domain, not possible.

   k. 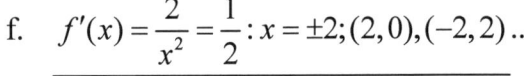 $Tangent : m = f'\left(\dfrac{1}{2}\right) = 8; po\operatorname{int} = \left(\dfrac{1}{2}, -3\right); y = 8x + b; y = 8x - 7$

   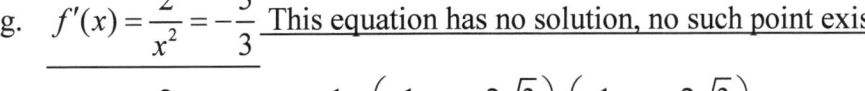 $Normal : m = -\dfrac{1}{8}; po\operatorname{int} = \left(\dfrac{1}{2}, -3\right); y = -\dfrac{1}{8}x + b; y = -\dfrac{1}{8}x + 1$

168

3. Given the function $f(x) = -x^2 - x$.

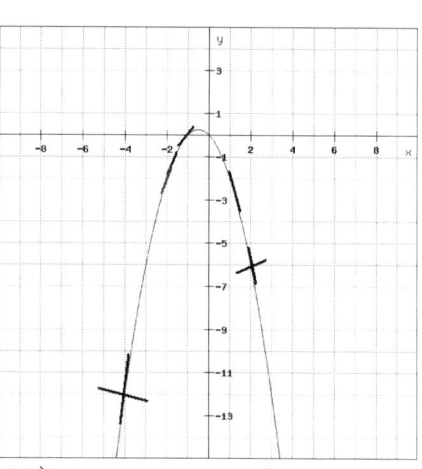

   a. $f'(x) = -2x - 1$
   b. $f'(-1) = 1$
   c. $f'(2) = -5$
   d. $f'(-4) = 7$

   e. $f'(x) = -2x - 1 = 2; x = -\dfrac{3}{2}; \left(-\dfrac{3}{2}, -\dfrac{3}{4}\right)$

   f. $f'(x) = -2x - 1 = -2.3; x = 0.65; (0.65, -1.0725)$

   g. $f'(x) = -2x - 1 = 3; x = -2; (-2, -2)$

   h. $f'(x) = -2x - 1 = -5; x = 2; (2, -6)$

   i. $m = f'(-1) = 1; po\operatorname{int} = (-1, 0); y = x + b; y = x + 1$

   j. $Tangent: m = f'(2) = -5; po\operatorname{int} = (2, -6); y = -5x + b; y = -5x + 4$

   $Normal: m = \dfrac{1}{5}; po\operatorname{int} = (2, -6); y = \dfrac{1}{5}x + b; y = \dfrac{1}{5}x - \dfrac{32}{5}$

   k. $Tangent: m = f'(-4) = 7; po\operatorname{int} = (-4, -12); y = 7x + b; y = 7x + 16$

   $Normal: m = -\dfrac{1}{7}; po\operatorname{int} = (-4, -12); y = -\dfrac{1}{7}x + b; y = -\dfrac{1}{7}x - \dfrac{88}{7}$

4. Given the function $f(x) = -3x^2 + 1$. Sketch it.

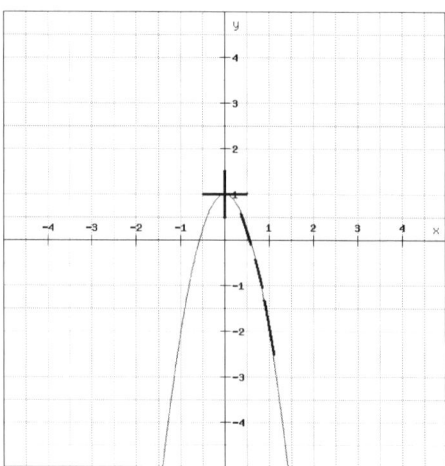

   a. $f'(x) = -6x$
   b. $f'(1) = \underline{6}$
   c. $f'(0) = \underline{0}$
   d. $f'(2) = \underline{-12}$

   e. $f'(x) = -6x = 3; x = \dfrac{1}{2}; \left(\dfrac{1}{2}, \dfrac{1}{4}\right)$

   f. $f'(x) = -6x = -4; x = \dfrac{2}{3}; \left(\dfrac{2}{3}, -\dfrac{1}{3}\right)$

   g. $f'(x) = -6x = -5; x = \dfrac{5}{6}; \left(\dfrac{5}{6}, -\dfrac{13}{12}\right)$

   h. $Tangent: m = f'(0) = 0; po\operatorname{int} = (0, 1); y = 1$

   $Normal: x = 0$

5. Given the function $f(x) = \dfrac{3}{x-2}$. Sketch it.

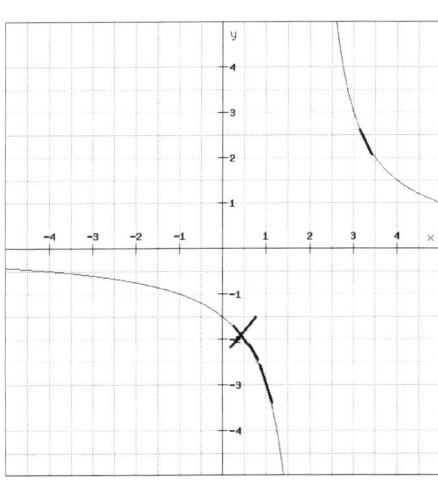

   a. $f'(x) = \dfrac{-3}{(x-2)^2}$

   b. $\underline{f'(1) = -3}$

   c. $f'(2) = \underline{\text{Does not exist.}}$

   d. $f'(\dfrac{1}{2}) = -\dfrac{4}{3}$

   e. $f'(x) = \dfrac{-3}{(x-2)^2} = -3; x_1 = 1, x_2 = 3; (1,3), (3,1)$,

   f. $f'(x) = \dfrac{-3}{(x-2)^2} = \dfrac{1}{2}$ $\underline{\text{No solution, no such point.}}$

   g. $f'(x) = \dfrac{-3}{(x-2)^2} = -\dfrac{5}{3}; (x-2)^2 = \dfrac{9}{5}; x = 2 \pm \dfrac{3}{\sqrt{5}}; \left(2 + \dfrac{3}{\sqrt{5}}, \sqrt{5}\right), \left(2 - \dfrac{3}{\sqrt{5}}, -\sqrt{5}\right)$

   h. $f'(1) = -3; po\mathrm{int} = (1, -3); y = -3x + b; y = -3x$

   i. $\underline{\text{Does not exist, out of domain}}$

   j. $Tangent: m = f'(\dfrac{1}{2}) = -\dfrac{4}{3}; po\mathrm{int} = \left(\dfrac{1}{2}, -2\right); y = -\dfrac{4}{3}x + b; y = -\dfrac{4}{3}x - \dfrac{4}{3}$

      $Normal: m = \dfrac{3}{4}; po\mathrm{int} = \left(\dfrac{1}{2}, -2\right); y = \dfrac{3}{4}x + b; y = \dfrac{3}{4}x - \dfrac{19}{8}$

7.4. – STATIONARY POINTS AND FUNCTION ANALYSIS

1. In a maximum or minimum point of a "smooth" function the slope of the tangent to the function is <u>zero</u>. Sketch an example:

2. There is one more situation in which the slope of the tangent to the function is <u>zero</u>, such point is called: <u>horizontal inflection point</u>. Sketch an cxample:

3. In order to find the stationary points´ x coordinate we equal the <u>derivative</u> to <u>zero</u>

4. To find the stationary points´ y coordinate <u>we plug the x value found into function</u>

5. Once we found the stationary point we have to decide if it's a <u>maximum, minimum</u> or <u>horizontal inflection point</u> .

6. When f'(a) > 0 it means that f(x) is <u>increasing</u> at the point where <u>x = a.</u>

7. When f'(a) < 0 it means that f(x) <u>decreasing</u> at the point where <u>x = a.</u>

8. For example given the function f(x) = $x^3 - 3x^2$. Use the derivative to find its local maximum and minimum. Verify your answer using the GDC.

$$f'(x) = 3x^2 - 6x = 0$$
$$x(3x - 6) = 0; x = 0, x = 2$$
$$f(0) = 0; (0,0)$$
$$f(2) = -4; (2,-4)$$

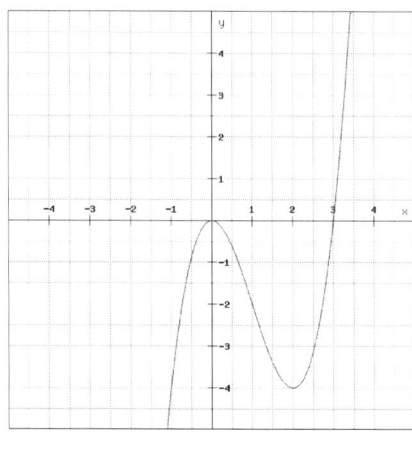

On graph the points (0,0) and (2, –4) can be observed as a max and min correspondingly

9. Given the function $f(x) = x^4 - 2x^3$.

   a. Sketch the graph for $-2 \le x \le 3$ and $-3 \le y \le 15$

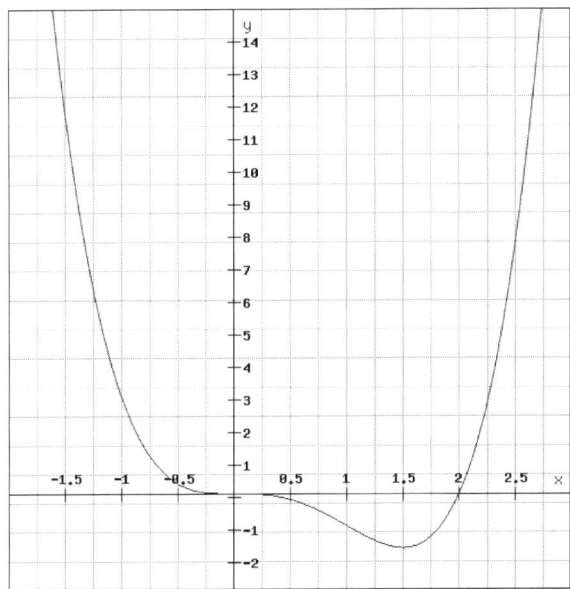

   b. Find: <u>$f(2) = 0$</u>   <u>$f'(x) = 4x^3 - 6x^2$</u>   <u>$f'(1.5) = 0$</u>

   c. The coordinates of the local minimum on the graph of f <u>$(1.5, -1.6875)$</u>

   d. Find the gradient of the tangent to the graph at $x = 1$. <u>$f'(1) = -2$</u>

   e. There is another point on the graph in which the tangent has the same
       gradient as in $x = 1$. Find it.
       $$f'(x) = 4x^3 - 6x^2 = -2$$
       $$x = 1, x = -\frac{1}{2}$$
       <u>$f(-\frac{1}{2}) = \frac{5}{16}; (-\frac{1}{2}, \frac{5}{16})$</u>

   f. Where is the function increasing?

       <u>$x \in (1.5, \infty)$</u>

10. Given the function f(x) = 10x – x³.

  a.   Sketch the graph for −4 ≤ x ≤ 4 and −15 ≤ y ≤ 15

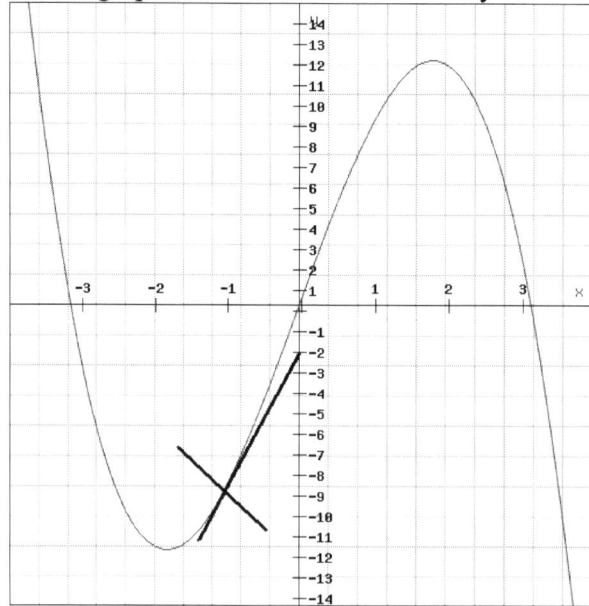

  b.   Find   <u>f(−2) = -12</u>   <u>f'(x) = 10 – 3x²</u>   <u>f'(0) = 10</u>

  c.   Write down the coordinates of the local minimum point on the graph of f .

$$f'(x) = 10 - 3x^2 = 0; x = \pm\sqrt{\frac{10}{3}}; \left(-\sqrt{\frac{10}{3}}, 20\sqrt{\frac{30}{81}}\right)$$

  d.   Find the gradient of the tangent to the graph at its local maximum. <u>0</u>

  e.   There is another point on the graph in which the tangent has the same
       gradient as in x = 3. Find it.
       $f'(3) = -17 = 10 - 3x^2; x = -3; (-3, -3)$

  f.   Find the equation of the tangent and normal to the function at the points
       where x = −1. Sketch the lines on the graph.
       $Tangent : m = f'(-1) = 7; (-1, -9); y = 7x + b; y = 7x - 2$

       $Normal : m = -\frac{1}{7}; (-1, -9); y = -\frac{1}{7}x + b; y = -\frac{1}{7}x - \frac{64}{7}$

  g.   Where is the function decreasing?

$$x \in (-\infty, -\sqrt{\frac{10}{3}}) \cup (\sqrt{\frac{10}{3}}, \infty)$$

11. Given the function f(x) = $\dfrac{4}{x^2} + x + 2$

a. Sketch the graph for $-4 \le x \le 4$ and $-5 \le y \le 15$

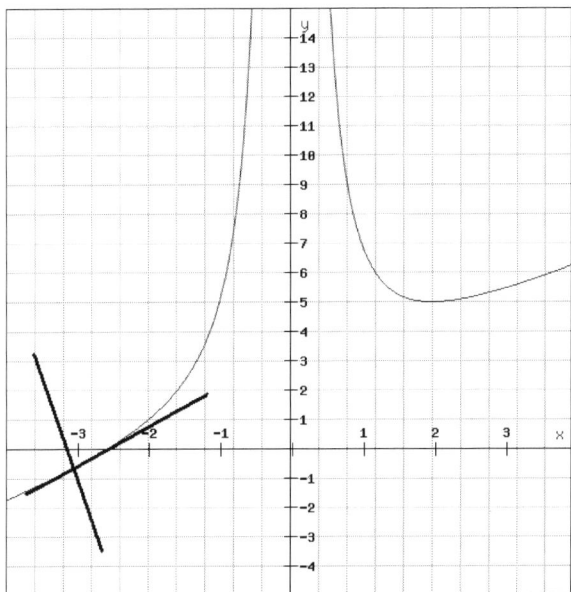

b. Find <u>f(−2) = 4</u>   f′(x) = $\dfrac{-8}{x^3} + 1$

   f′(0) = out of domain, does not exist.

c. f′(1) = -7 This value of the derivative means that the function is <u>decreasing</u> at this point.

d. The equation of the vertical asymptote is: <u>x = 0</u>

e. Write down the coordinates of the local minimums and maximums points on the graph of f.

$$f'(x) = \frac{-8}{x^3} + 1 = 0; x = 2, f(2) = 5; (2,5); \min imum$$

f. Find the equation of the tangent and normal to the function at the points where x = −3. Sketch the lines on the graph.

$$Tangent: m = f'(-3) = \frac{35}{27}; (-3, -\frac{5}{9}); y = \frac{35}{27}x + b; y = \frac{35}{27}x + \frac{30}{9}$$

$$Normal: m = -\frac{27}{35}; (-3, -\frac{5}{9}); y = -\frac{27}{35}x + b; y = -\frac{27}{35}x - \frac{904}{315}$$

12. Given the function $f(x) = \dfrac{1}{x+1} + x + 2$

   a. Sketch the graph for $-4 \le x \le 4$ and $-15 \le y \le 15$

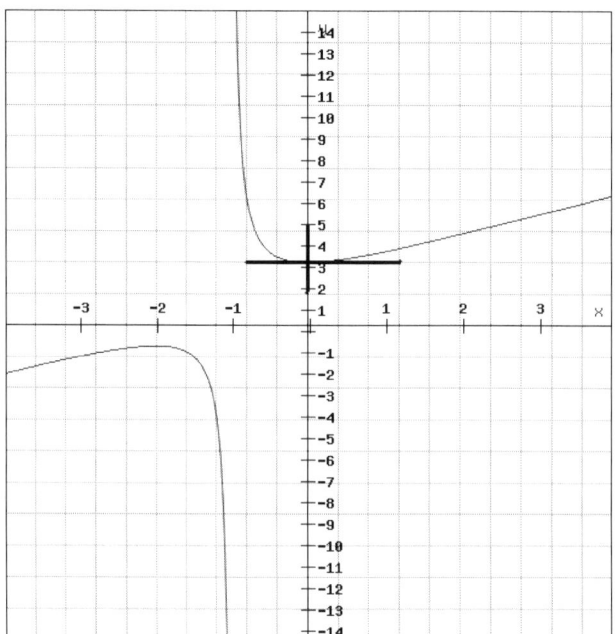

   b. Find: $\underline{f(-2) = -1}$ $\qquad$ $f'(x) = \dfrac{-1}{(x+1)^2} + 1$ $\qquad$ $\underline{f'(0) = 0}$

   c. $f'(1) = \dfrac{3}{4}$ This value of the derivative means that the function is <u>increasing</u> at this point.

   d. Write down the coordinates of the local minimum point on the graph of f.
   $$f'(x) = \dfrac{-1}{(x+1)^2} + 1 = 0; x = 0, x = -2; f(0) = 3(0,3)\min; f(-2) = -1, (-2,-1)\max$$

   The equation of the vertical asymptote is: <u>x = -1</u>

   e. Find the gradient of the tangent to the graph at the point where $x = 2$.
   $$f'(2) = \dfrac{8}{9}$$

   f. Find the equation of the tangent and normal to the function at the points where $x = -2$. Sketch the lines on the graph.
   $Tangent : m = f'(-2) = 0; (-2,-1); y = -1$

   $Normal : x = 0$

7.5. – OPTIMIZATION PROBLEMS

1. Given a cylinder with a surface area of 54π cm^2

   a. Write an <u>equation</u> for the cylinder's surface area in terms of r and h.
   $$S = 2\pi r^2 + 2\pi rh = 54\pi$$

   b. Write a <u>function</u> for the volume of the cylinder in terms of r and h.
   $$V = 2\pi r^2 h$$

   c. Use the <u>equation</u> from part a to express the <u>function</u> only in terms of r.
   From equation in part a isolating h gives: $h = \dfrac{27}{r} - r$
   $$V(r) = 2\pi r^2 \left(\frac{27}{r} - r \right) = 54\pi r - 2\pi r^3$$
   Into volume: _____

   d. Use the function to find the radius and height for which the volume of the cylinder is maximum.
   $$V'(r) = 54\pi - 6\pi r^2 = 0; r = 3; h = 6$$

2. Given a cuboid with 2 equal sides and a surface area of 100 cm^2

   a. Write an equation for the cuboid surface area in terms of its sides.
   $$S = 4x^2 + 2xy = 100$$

   b. Write a function for the volume of the cuboid in terms of its sides.
   $$V = x^2 y$$

   c. Use the equation from part a to express the function in terms of one side only.
   $$4x^2 + 2xy = 100; y = \frac{50}{x} - 2x;$$
   $$V(x) = x^2 \left(\frac{50}{x} - 2x \right) = 50x - 2x^3$$
   _____

   d. Use the function to find the length of the sides for which the volume of the cuboid is maximum.
   $$V'(x) = 50 - 6x^2 = 0; x = \sqrt{\frac{25}{3}}, y = \frac{20\sqrt{3}}{3}$$

3. The benefit of a certain company can be modeled by the function

$$f(x) = 2^{-x} + 5 - \frac{0.3}{x^2} \quad x \in [0.1, 5]$$

Where x is the amount of money in thousands of Euros invested in marketing. Find the amount of money invested that will maximize the benefit. Find the maximum benefit.

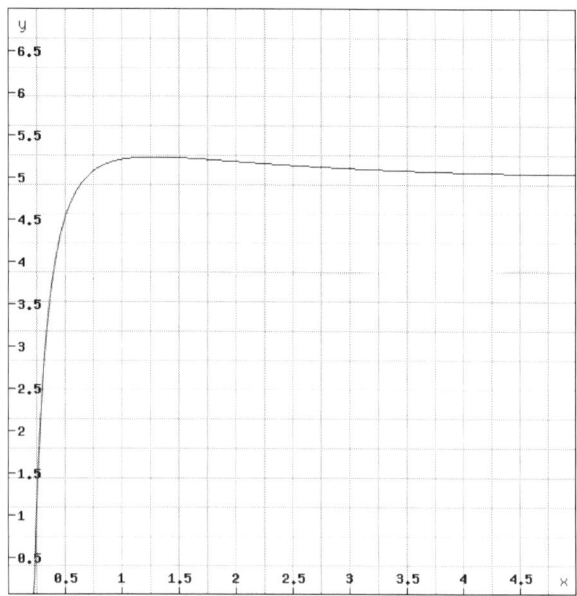

Using GDC, graph the function, as can b e seen and found with GDC, the maximum is at x ≈ 1.28 so investment should be 1280 euros. The benefit would be 5.23 so 5230 euros.

4. The consumption of gasoline of a new engine can be modeled by

$$f(x) = 3^{0.3x} - x + 5 \quad x \in [0, 15]$$

Where x is the number of revolutions per minute of the engine in thousands. Find the number of revolutions per minute that will minimize the consumption of gasoline.

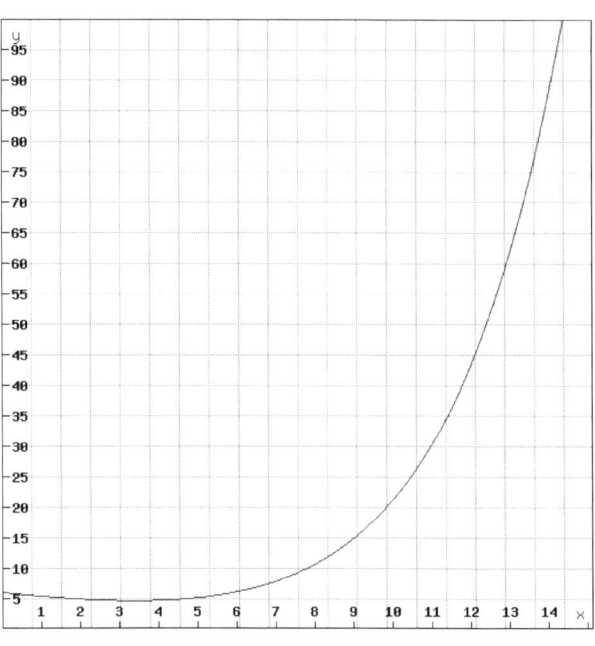

Using GDC, graph the function, as can be seen and found with GDC, the number of revolutions per minute the minimizes consumption is x ≈ 5.24 so should be 5240 RPM. The consumption would be 5.38.

5. The elevation power of a wing as a function of angle of attack of the airplane can be modeled by the function

$$f(x) = \left(\frac{x}{4}\right)^2 - 2^{\left(\frac{x}{4}\right)} + \left(\frac{x}{2}\right) + 6 \qquad x \in [0, 22]$$

where x is angle of attack measured in degrees. Find the angle of attack that will maximize the elevation power of the wing.

Using GDC, graph the function, as can be seen and found with GDC, the angle of attack that maximizes elevation is x ≈ 15.2°.

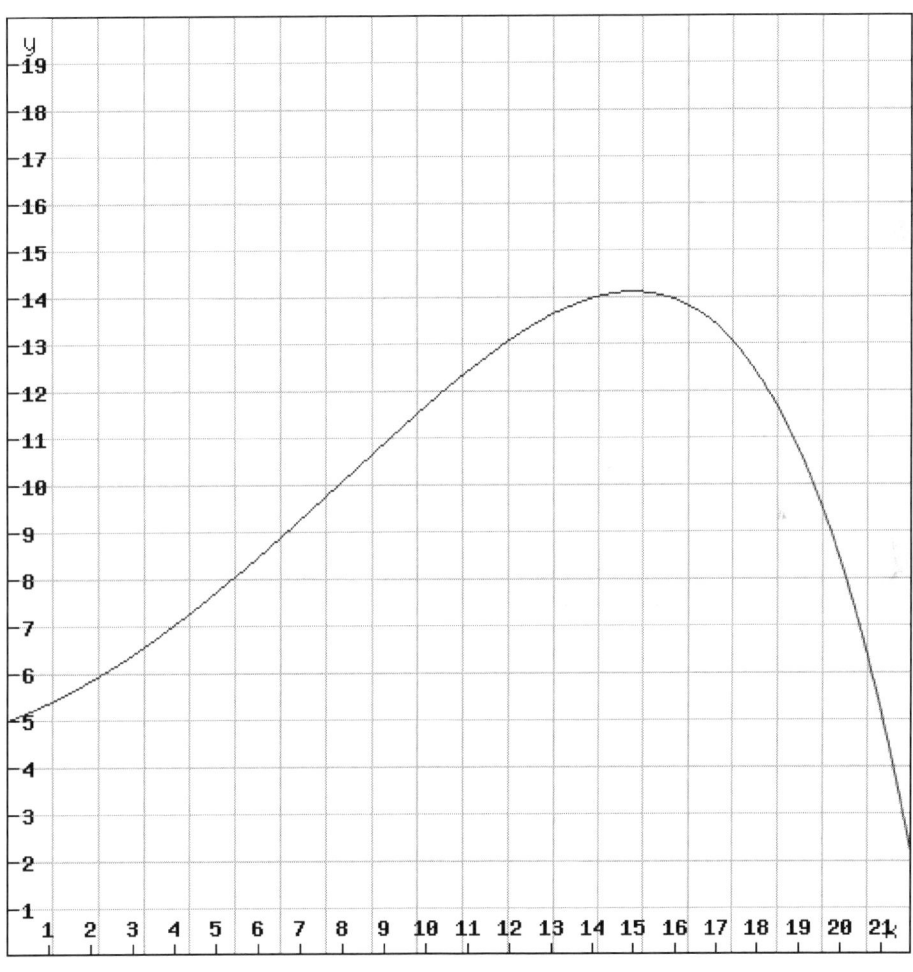

8.1. – CORRELATION

1. In many occasions variables may be related to each other, for example: Give 3 other examples; discuss the kind of relation that exists between the variables:

   Year – mean temperature
   Humidity level – wind speed
   Name of a student – shoe size

2. The relation between variables is called: <u>correlation</u> and if it is <u>linear</u> it can be classified in the following way:

3. This correlation is characterized by a certain number called <u>correlation</u> coefficient (r).

4. In case of a perfect positive correlation the value of r is <u>1</u>

5. In case of a perfect negative correlation the value of r is <u>–1</u>

6. In case of a no correlation the value of r is <u>0</u>

7. Finally r is between <u>–1 and 1</u>

8. All of the correlations above mentioned are <u>linear</u> There can be other kinds of correlation for example <u>logarithmic, exponential, quadratic etc.</u>

9. The full name of r is <u>Pearson product–moment correlation coefficient</u>

10. If $r \in [0.75, 1)$ we say there is a <u>strong positive</u> Correlation.

11. If $r \in [0.5, 0.75)$ we say there is a <u>moderate positive</u> Correlation.

12. If $r \in [0.25, 0.5)$ we say there is a <u>weak positive</u> Correlation.

13. If $r \in (-0.25, 0.25)$ we say there is a <u>no</u> Correlation.

14. If $r \in (-0.5, -0.25]$ we say there is a <u>weak negative</u> Correlation.

15. If $r \in (-0.75, -0.5]$ we say there is a <u>moderate negative</u> Correlation.

16. If $r \in (-1, -0.75]$ we say there is a <u>strong negative</u> Correlation.

17. In a certain math class the following data about students was found:

Name	John	Dean	Elisa	Marc	Heather	Alicia	Raquel	Kevin	Alex	Deena
HW Done (%)	58	90	75	50	40	95	100	85	75	82
Grade (%)	70	80	80	65	55	78	86	89	82	70

a. Represent the data on a graph:

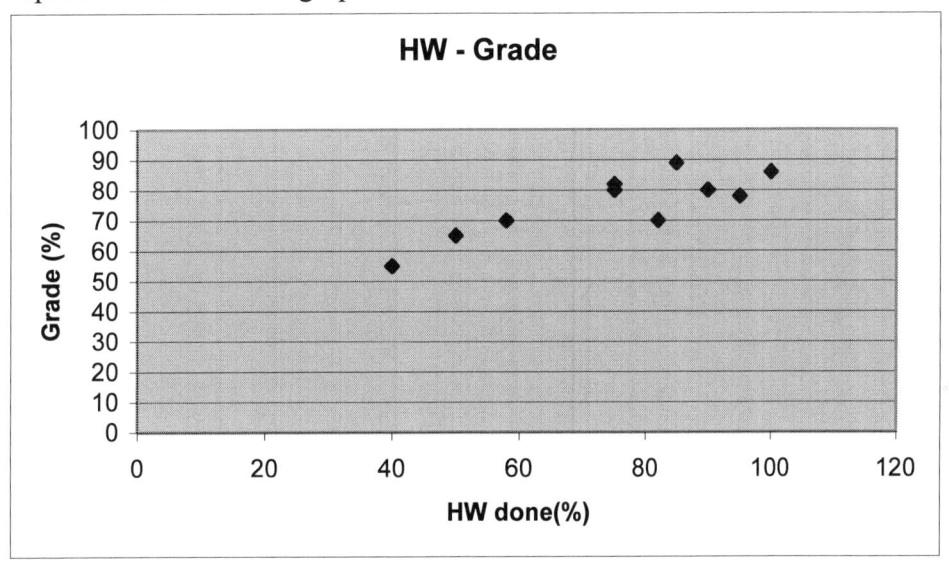

b. Is there correlation? <u>It seems strong positive correlation</u>

c. Try to predict the value of r: <u>0.85? guessing..</u>

d. In order to calculate the value of r first find:

$\bar{x} = \underline{75}$ $\bar{y} = \underline{75.5}$

Complete the table:

Name	x_i	$(x_i - \bar{x})^2$	y_i	$(y_i - \bar{y})^2$	$x_i y_i$
John	58	289	70	30.25	4060
Dean	90	225	80	20.25	7200
Elisa	75	0	80	20.25	6000
Marc	50	625	65	110.25	3250
Heather	40	1225	55	420.25	2200
Alicia	95	400	78	6.25	7410
Raquel	100	625	86	110.25	8600
Kevin	85	100	89	182.25	7565
Alex	75	0	82	42.25	6150
Deena	82	49	70	30.25	5740
Total		3538		972.5	58175

Use the table to find Sx, Sy and Sxy using the following formulas taken from IB information booklet:

$$S_x = \sqrt{\frac{3538}{10}} \approx 18.8, \; S_y = \sqrt{\frac{972.5}{10}} \approx 9.86, \; S_{xy} = \frac{\left(58175 - \frac{750 \cdot 755}{10}\right)}{10} \approx 155$$

Find r using $r = \dfrac{S_{xy}}{S_x S_y} = \dfrac{155}{(18.8)(9.86)} \approx 0.836$

e. Was your prediction accurate? <u>Not bad...</u>

LINE OF BEST FIT

18. The line of best fit is the straight line that most approximates to the scatter diagram obtained. The equation of the line is given by:

$$y - \overline{y} = \frac{S_{xy}}{\left(S_x\right)^2}(x - \overline{x})$$

19. Write this expression in the forma y = mx + b

$$y = \frac{S_{xy}}{\left(S_x\right)^2}x + \overline{y} - \frac{S_{xy}}{\left(S_x\right)^2}\overline{x}$$

20. The slope of the line is m = $\dfrac{S_{xy}}{\left(S_x\right)^2}$

Name	John	Dean	Elisa	Marc	Heather	Alicia	Raquel	Kevin	Alex	Deena
HW Done (%)	58	90	75	50	40	95	100	85	75	82
Grade (%)	70	80	80	65	55	78	86	89	82	70

21. Given the data

a. <u>R ≈ 0.836</u>

b. The line of best fit: <u>y = 0.438x + 42.6</u>

22. In a group of students, height and weight correlation was studies. The results are given by the table below.

Height (cm)	Weight (kg)
165	58
170	62
172	80
169	65
188	88
163	52
191	95
177	72

a. Write the equation of the regression line in the form $y = mx + c$
   $y = 1.38x - 169$

b. Use your equation in part a to predict the weight of a student who is 174cm tall.
   $y = 1.38(174) - 169 = 71.12kg$

c. Write down the correlation coefficient and the kind of correlation that exists.
   $R = 0.941$

23. In a group of students the reading speed was studied in relation to age of the student. The results are given by the table below.

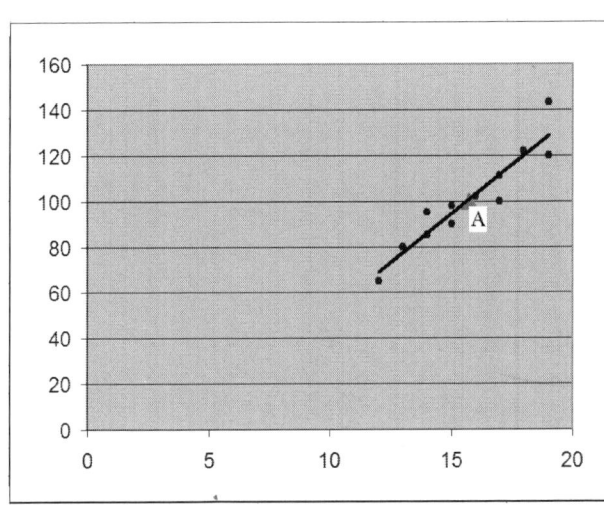

Age (years)	Reading speed (words per minute)
15	98
12	65
17	111
19	120
18	122
16	102
19	143
17	100
13	80
14	85
14	95
15	90

a. Write the equation of the regression line in the form $y = mx + c$
   $y = 8.56x - 33.9$

b. Use your equation in part a to predict the reading speed of a student who is 11 years old.
   $y = (8.56)11 - 33.9 = 60.26$

c. Write down the correlation coefficient and the kind of correlation that exists.
   $R = 0.941$

d. Draw a scatter diagram to show the data.

e. $\bar{x} = \dfrac{89}{12} \approx 15.8$ _____ $\bar{y} = \dfrac{1211}{12} \approx 101$

f. Plot the point ($\bar{x}$, $\bar{y}$) on your scatter diagram. Label this point as A.

g. Draw the regression line on the diagram.

8.2. – CHI SQUARED TEST (χ^2)

1. The chi squared test is used to see if a pair of variables is related in a significant way or not. For example, the following data was obtained:

Observed Values:

	Smokers	None-smokers	Total
Male	27	56	83
Female	35	78	113
Total	62	134	196

Expected Values:

	Smokers	None-smokers	Total
Male	$\frac{62}{196}\cdot 83 \approx 26.3$	$\frac{134}{196}\cdot 83 \approx 56.7$	83
Female	$\frac{62}{196}\cdot 113 \approx 35.7$	$\frac{134}{196}\cdot 113 \approx 77.3$	113
Total	62	134	196

a. The tables above are called <u>contingency tables</u>

b. The number of <u>degrees of freedom</u> is given by $\upsilon = (R-1)(C-1)$

c. In this case it is $\upsilon = (2-1)(2-1) = 1$

d. The Null Hypothesis (H_o) is <u>Gender and smoking are independent</u>

e. The Alternative Hypothesis (H_1) is <u>Gender and smoking are dependent</u>

f. Next we will calculate the value of χ^2 using the following expression taken from the information booklet:

$$\chi^2{}_{calc} = \sum \frac{(f_o - f_e)^2}{f_e} = \frac{(26.3-27)^2}{27} + \frac{(35.7-35)^2}{35} + \frac{(56.7-56)^2}{56} + \frac{(77.3-77)^2}{77} \approx 0.0421$$

g. $\chi^2{}_{critical} = 3.841$. Since $\chi^2{}_{critical} > \chi^2{}_{calc}$ the null hypothesis is accepted (the alternative is rejected) so <u>Gender and smoking are independent</u>
- <u>Assuming 95% level of certainty (5% significance level).</u>

2. The chi squared test is used to see if a pair of variables is related in a significant way or not. For example, the following data was obtained:

Observed values:

	High Blood Pressure	Normal Blood Pressure	Low Blood Pressure	Total
Fat	50	56	25	131
Thin	35	78	44	157
Total	85	134	69	288

Expected Values:

	High Blood Pressure	Normal Blood Pressure	Low Blood Pressure	Total
Fat	$\frac{85}{288} \cdot 131 \approx 38.7$	$\frac{134}{288} \cdot 131 \approx 61.0$	$\frac{69}{288} \cdot 131 \approx 31.4$	131
Thin	$\frac{85}{288} \cdot 157 \approx 46.3$	$\frac{134}{288} \cdot 157 \approx 73.0$	$\frac{69}{288} \cdot 157 \approx 37.6$	157
Total	85	134	69	288

a. The tables above are called <u>contingency tables</u>

b. The number of <u>degrees of freedom</u> is given by $\upsilon = (R-1)(C-1)$

c. In this case it is $\upsilon = (2-1)(3-1) = 2$

d. The Null Hypothesis (H_o) is <u>weight and blood pressure are independent</u>

e. The Alternative Hypothesis (H_1) is <u>weight and blood pressure are dependent</u>

f. Next we will calculate the value of χ^2 using the following expression taken from the information booklet:

$$\chi^2_{calc} = \sum \frac{(f_o - f_e)^2}{f_e} = \frac{(38.7-50)^2}{50} + \frac{(61.0-56)^2}{56} + \frac{(31.4-25)^2}{25} + \frac{(46.3-35)^2}{77} +$$

$$\frac{(73.0-78)^2}{78} + \frac{(37.6-44)^2}{44} \approx 8.53$$

g. $\chi^2_{critical} = 5.991$. Since $\chi^2_{critical} < \chi^2_{calc}$ the alternative hypothesis is accepted (the null is rejected) weight and blood pressure are dependent

- Assuming 95% level of certainty (5% significance level).

3. A group of students was asked about their favorite color to see if there are differences between male and female. The colors were blue, red, green, white and orange. A χ^2 test was conducted at 5% significance level and the value found was 9.01.

a. Write down the Null hypothesis:
   Gender and preferred color are independent

b. Write down the Alternative hypothesis.
   Gender and preferred color are dependent

c. Write down the number of degrees of freedom.
   $v = (2-1)(5-1) = 4$

d. Write down the critical value for this test. $\chi^2_{critical} = 9.488$

e. Reach a conclusion and write it down.
   Since $\chi^2_{critical} > \chi^2_{calc}$ the null hypothesis is accepted (the alternative is rejected) Gender and preferred color are independent

4. The FIFA is doing some research about free kicks to check association between the shoe size (41 – 43, 43 – 45, more than 45) of the player and the outcome (goal/no goal).

a. Write down the Null hypothesis.
   Shoe size and free kick result are independent

b. Write down the Alternative hypothesis.
   Shoe size and free kick result are dependent

c. Write down the number of degrees of freedom
   $v = (2-1)(3-1) = 2$

5. Some students were asked about their favorite subject. The following information was obtained

	Math	History	English	Total
Male	123	86	102	311
Female	81	108	100	289
Total	204	194	202	600

A χ^2 test was conducted at 5% significance level

a. Write down the Null hypothesis.
   <u>Gender and favorite subject are independent</u>

b. Write down the Alternative hypothesis.
   <u>Gender and favorite subject are dependent</u>

c. Write down the number of degrees of freedom.
   $\upsilon = (2-1)(3-1) = 2$

d. Write down the number of students participating. <u>600</u>

e. Show (without GDC) the expected value for math female students.
   $\dfrac{204}{600} \cdot 289 \approx 98.3$

f. Write down the critical value for this test. $\chi^2_{critical} = 5.991$

g. Use GDC to find χ^2 $\chi^2_{calc} \approx 10.4$

h. Reach a conclusion and write it down.
   <u>Since $\chi^2_{critical} < \chi^2_{calc}$ the alternative hypothesis is accepted (the null is rejected) Gender and favorite subject are dependent</u>

6. A certain university wants to determine if a person's choice of studies (science, engineering, social studies or economics) depends on its height (more than 1.70 or less or equal to 1.70)

  a. Write down the Null hypothesis.
     <u>Height and choice of studies are independent</u>

  b. Write down the Alternative hypothesis.
     <u>Height and choice of studies are dependent</u>

  c. Write down the number of degrees of freedom.
     $\upsilon = (2-1)(4-1) = 3$

  d. 250 students were surveyed, 100 were taller than 1.70 and 90 chose science. Calculate the expected number of scientists shorter than 1.70.

	Science	engineering	social studies	economics	
Height>1.70					100
Height≤1.70	$\frac{90}{250} \cdot 150 = 54$				150
Total	90				250

7. A research to determine weather the favorite type of dessert is related to city of residence was conducted in Madrid, Barcelona and Valencia. The types of dessert were ice-cream, chocolate cake and flan. A χ^2 test was conducted at 1% significance level and the value found was 15.6.

  a. Write down the Null hypothesis.
     <u>Favorite dessert and city of residency are independent</u>

  b. Write down the Alternative hypothesis.
     <u>Favorite dessert and city of residency are dependent</u>

  c. Write down the number of degrees of freedom.
     $\upsilon = (3-1)(3-1) = 4$

  d. Write down the critical value for this test.
     $\chi^2_{critical} = 13.277$ (1% significance level)

  e. Reach a conclusion and write it down.
     <u>Since $\chi^2_{critical} < \chi^2_{calc}$ the alternative hypothesis is accepted (the null is rejected) Favorite dessert and city of residency are dependent</u>

8. A new medicine called "Unbroken heart" for heart diseases is being tested and a χ^2 test was conducted. The results

	Used "Unbroken heart"	Did not use "Unbroken heart"	Total
Cured	76	61	137
Not Cured	43	45	88
Total	119	106	225

A χ^2 test was conducted at 1% significance level

a. Write down the Null hypothesis.
   Using "Unbroken heart" and curing heart diseases are independent

b. Write down the Alternative hypothesis.
   Using "Unbroken heart" and curing heart diseases are dependent

c. Write down the number of degrees of freedom.
   $v = (2-1)(2-1) = 1$

d. Write down the number of patients participating.
   225

e. Show (without GDC) the expected value for cured patients that used the new medicine.
   $\dfrac{119}{225} \cdot 137 \approx 68.8$

f. Write down the critical value for this test.
   $\chi^2_{critical} = 6.635$ (1% significance level)

g. Use GDC to find χ^2

   $\chi^2_{calc} \approx 0.69$

h. Reach a conclusion and write it down.
   Since $\chi^2_{critical} > \chi^2_{calc}$ the NULL hypothesis is accepted (the alternative is rejected) Using "Unbroken heart" and curing heart diseases are independent

8.3 – NORMAL DISTRIBUTION

1. This distribution of a variable of this type is called the <u>Normal</u>

2. The normal distribution is characterized by 2 numbers: The <u>mean μ</u>

    and the <u>standard deviation (SD)</u> σ.

3. For example, given a few distributions, state the mean and standard
    deviation in all of them (It is known that $\sigma = 1$ or $\sigma = 2$ in the
    distributions where it is not indicated.

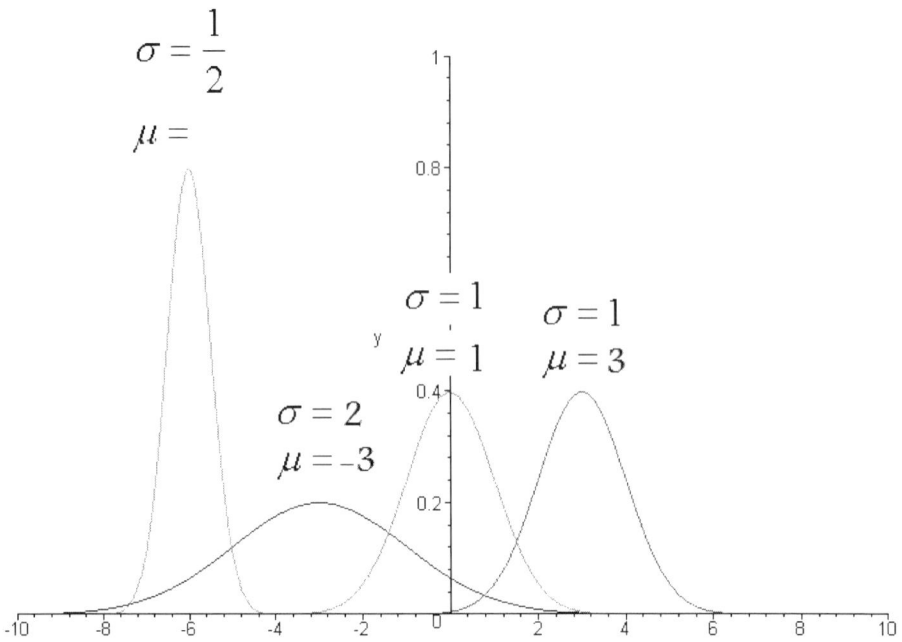

4. **<u>The standard normal distribution</u>** is the one with $\mu = 1$ $\sigma = 1$

Properties of the normal distribution

5. The area under the graph represents <u>probability</u> therefore the

   total area under the graph between $-\infty$ and $+\infty$ is <u>1</u>

6. Normal distribution is symmetric therefore the area on each side of the

   mean is <u>0.5</u>

7. The distribution will narrower and taller in case <u>SD is smaller</u>

8. σ, the <u>standard deviation</u>, gives an idea about the <u>spread</u>

9. μ, the <u>mean</u>, indicates the <u>center of the distribution</u>

10. In general the area under the curve in the interval $\mu \pm 1\sigma$ is <u>68%</u>

11. In general the area under the curve in the interval $\mu \pm 2\sigma$ is 95<u>%</u>

12. In general the area under the curve in the interval $\mu \pm 3\sigma$ is <u>99%</u>

FINDING PROBABILIT FOR $a < X < b$

The amount of time to produce a product follows a normal distribution with mean of 40 minutes and S. D. of 8 minutes.

1. $P(35 < x < 50) = 0.628$

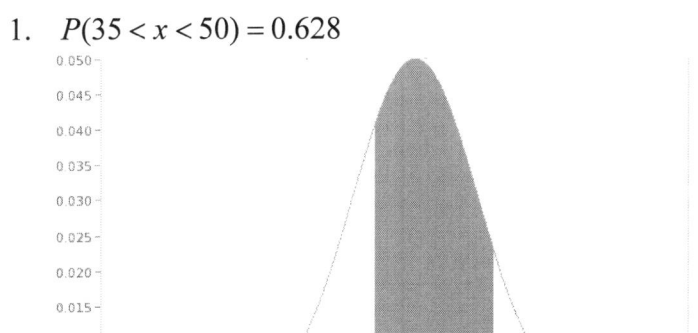

2. $P(38 < x < \infty) = 0.599$

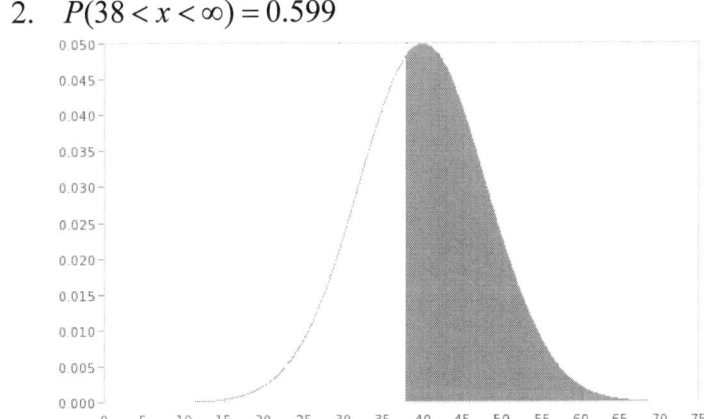

3. $P(\infty < x < 34) = 0.227$

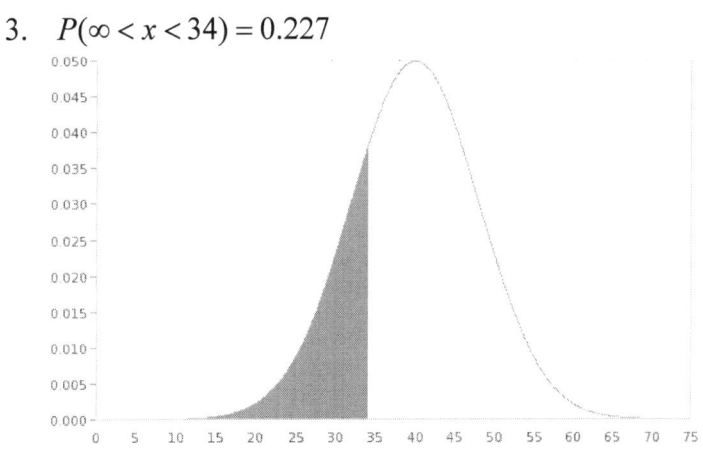

439

Exercises

1. In a lake there are 3000 fish distributed according to a normal distribution with a mean of 26cm and a standard deviation of 7cm.

a. 68% corresponds 1 SD so $P(19 < x < 33) = 0.68$; 68% of 3000 is 2040 fish

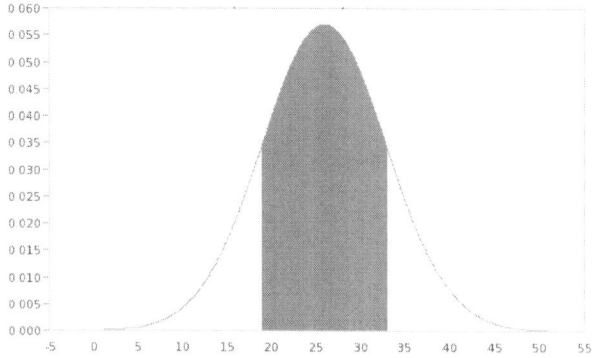

b. 95% corresponds 2 SD so $P(12 < x < 40) = 0.95$; 95% of 3000 is 2850 fish

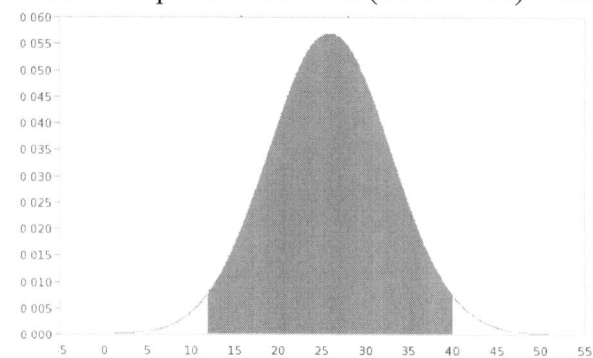

c. 99.7% corresponds 2 SD so $P(5 < x < 47) = 0.997$; 99.7% of 3000 is 2991 fish

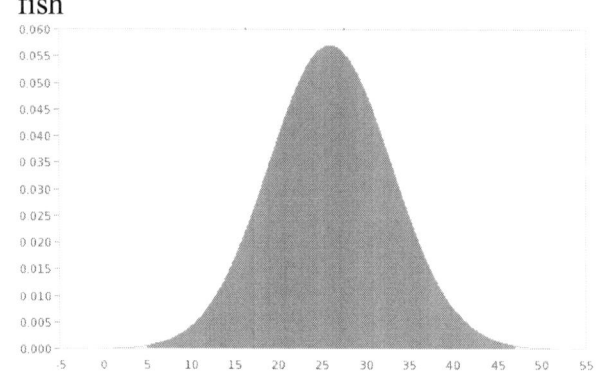

d. $P(23 < x < 28) = 0.278$; 27.8% of 3000 is 834 fish

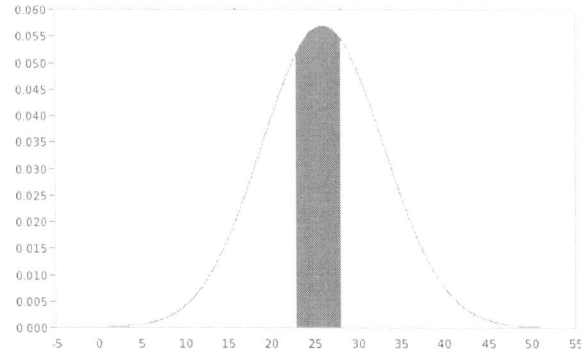

e. $P(12 < x < 24) = 0.365$; 36.5% of 3000 is 1095 fish

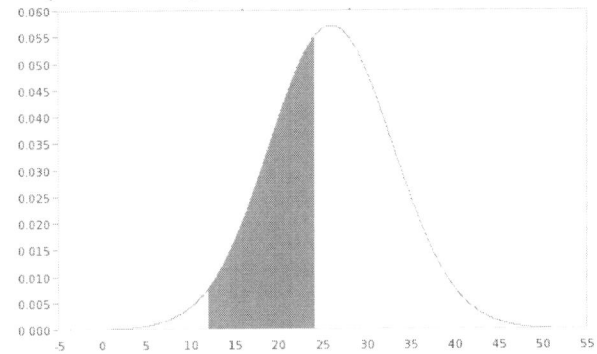

f. $P(27 < x < 28) = 0.0557$; 5.57% of 3000 is 167 fish

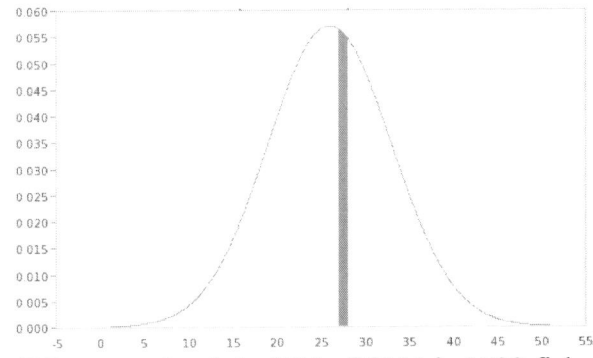

g. $P(2 < x < \infty) = 0.5$; 50% of 3000 is 1500 fish

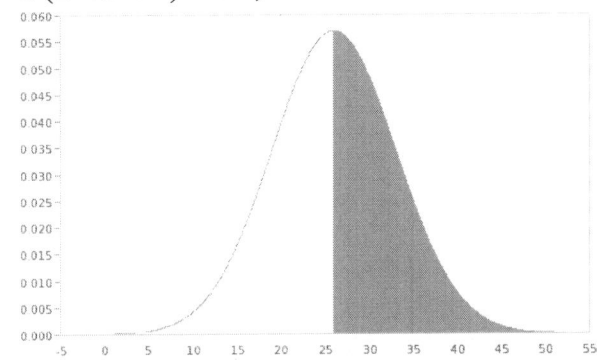

h. Find and shade on graph the probability for a fish to measure exactly 27 cm. <u>The probability to find a certain value is 0! Only an interval will have a value greater than 0.</u>

i. Find and shade on graph the probability for a fish to measure exactly 20 cm. <u>The probability to find a certain value is 0! Only an interval will have a value greater than 0.</u>

FINDING INVERSE NORMAL PROBABILITIES

1. The amount of time (X) to produce a product follows a normal distribution with mean of 40 minutes and S. D. of 8 minutes.

    a. invNorm(0.06, 40, 8) ≈ 27.6

    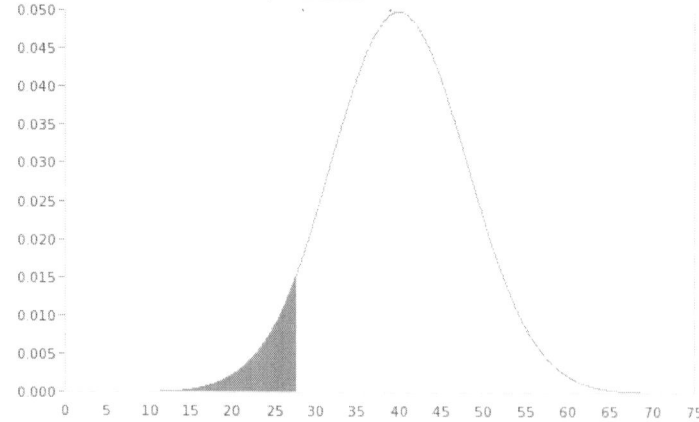

    b. invNorm(0.87, 40, 8) ≈ 49.0

    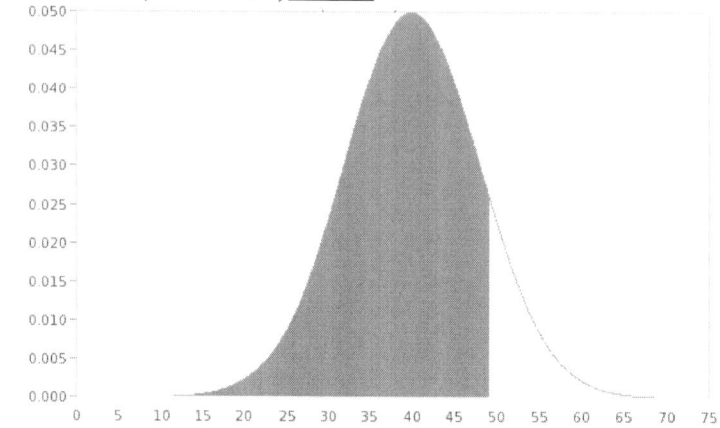

    c. invNorm(0.25, 40, 8) ≈ 34.6, invNorm(0.75, 40, 8) ≈ 45.4
       The central 50% are located in the interval [34.6, 45.4]

    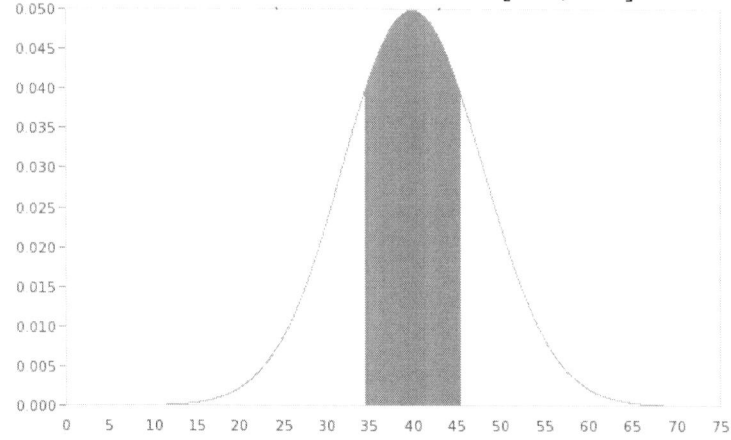

2. In a lake there are 2000 fish distributed according to a normal distribution with a mean of 26cm and a standard deviation of 7cm.

a. invNorm(0.10, 26, 7) ≈ 17.0,   invNorm(0.90, 26, 7) ≈ 35.0
The central 80% are located in the interval [17.0, 35.0]; 80% of 2000 are 1600 fish

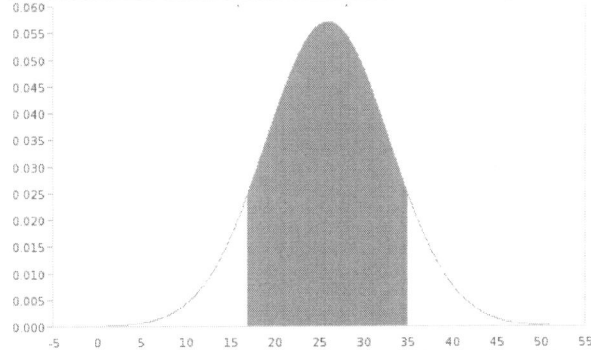

b. invNorm(0.05, 26, 7) ≈ 14.5,   invNorm(0.95, 26, 7) ≈ 37.5
The central 90% are located in the interval [14.5, 37.5]; 90% of 2000 are 1800 fish

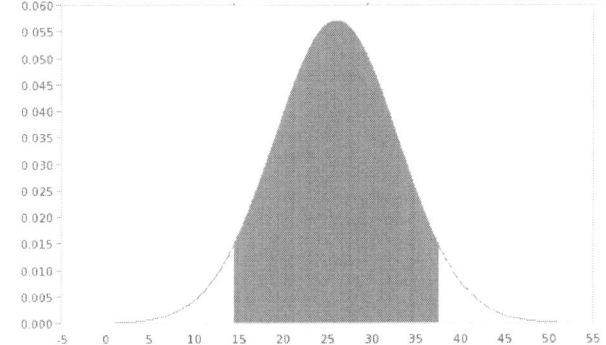

c. invNorm(0.125, 26, 7) ≈ 17.9,   invNorm(0.875, 26, 7)≈ 34.1
The central 75% are located in the interval [17.9, 34.1]; 75% of 2000 are 1500 fish

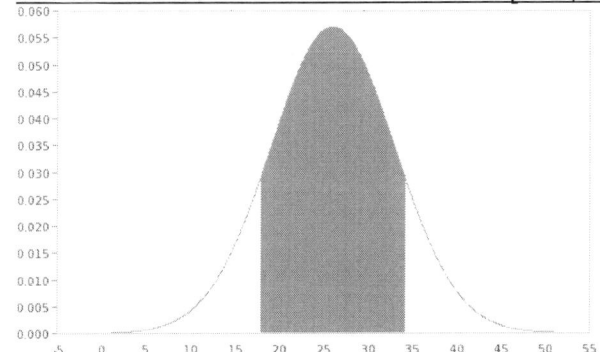

d. invNorm(0.8, 26, 7) ≈ 31.9 = q; 0.2 of 2000 are 400 fish

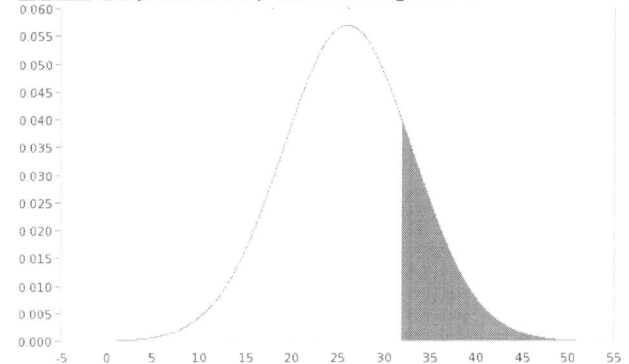

e. $\underline{\text{invNorm}(0.68, 26, 7) \approx 29.3 = w; \; 0.32 \text{ of } 2000 \text{ are } 640 \text{ fish}}$

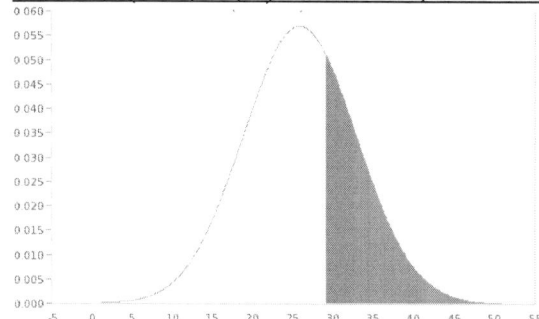

f. $\underline{\text{invNorm}(0.3, 26, 7) \approx 22.3 = a, \quad \text{invNorm}(0.7, 26, 7) \quad \approx 29.7 = b}$
$\underline{\text{The central } 40\% \text{ are located in the interval } [22.3, 29.7]; \; 40\% \text{ of } 2000 \text{ are } 800 \text{ fish}}$

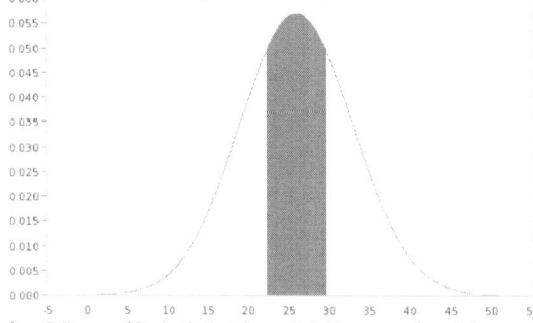

g. $\underline{\text{invNorm}(0.4, 26, 7) \approx 24.2 = a, \quad \text{invNorm}(0.6, 26, 7) \quad \approx 27.8 = b}$
$\underline{\text{The central } 20\% \text{ are located in the interval } [24.2, 27.8]; \; 20\% \text{ of } 2000 \text{ are } 400 \text{ fish}}$

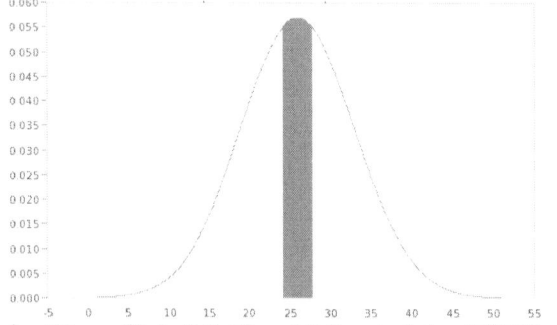

h. $\underline{\text{invNorm}(0.1, 26, 7) \approx 17.0 = t; \; 0.1 \text{ of } 2000 \text{ are } 200 \text{ fish}}$

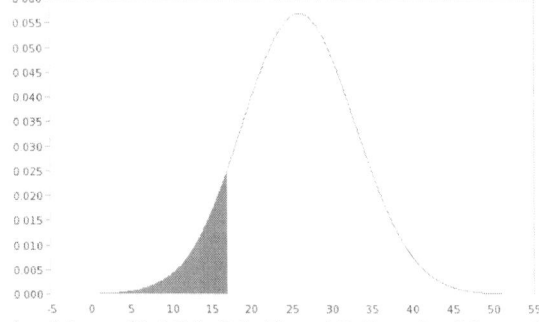

i. $\underline{\text{invNorm}(0.175, 26, 7) \approx 19.5, \quad \text{invNorm}(0.825, 26, 7) \approx 34.1}$
$\underline{\text{The central } 65\% \text{ are located in the interval } [19.5, 34.1]; \; 65\% \text{ of } 2000 \text{ are } 1300 \text{ fish}}$

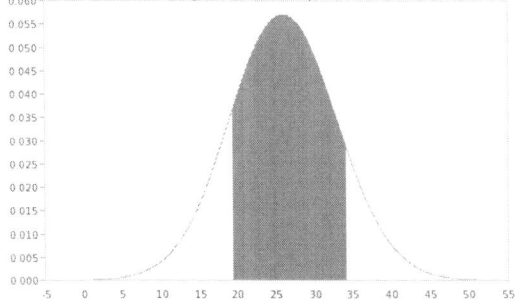

3. In a normal distribution N(0, 1) Find and shade:

    a. $P(Z = 2) = 0$

    b. $P(Z \geq 2) = 0.0228$

    c. $P(Z \leq 2) = 1 - 0.0228 = 0.9772$

    d. $P(Z \geq -2) = P(Z \leq 2) = 0.9772$

    e. $P(Z \leq -2) = P(Z \geq 2) = 0.0228$

    f. $P(-2 \leq Z \leq 2) = 1 - 0.0228 - 0.0228 = 0.9544$

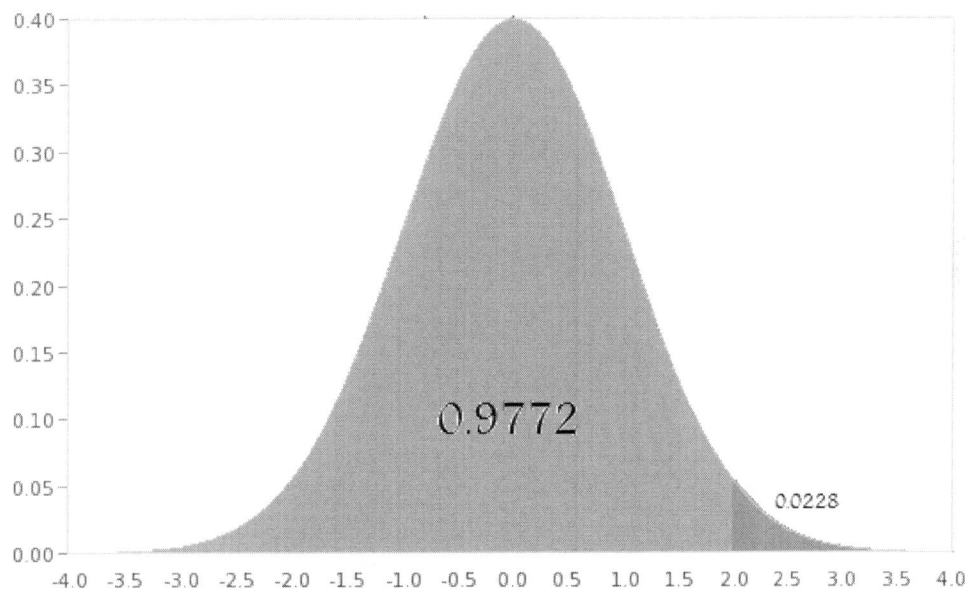

4. In a normal distribution N(0, 1) Find and shade:

    a. $P(Z = 0.81) = 0$

    b. $P(-0.78 \leq Z \leq 1.31) = \text{ShadeNorm}(-0.78,1.31,1,0) = 0.6872$

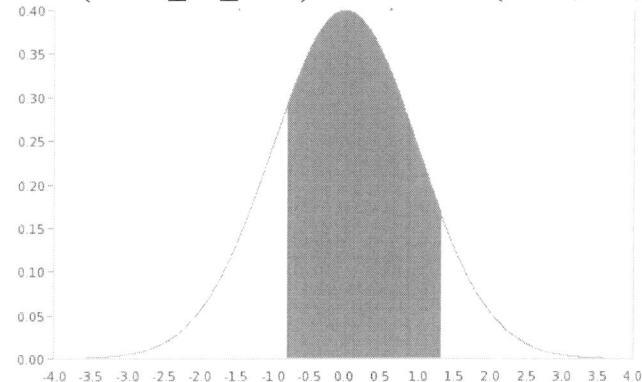

    c. $P(-1.31 \leq Z \leq 0.78) = P(-0.78 \leq Z \leq 1.31) = \text{ShadeNorm}(-1.31,0.78, 1,0) = 0.6872$

d. P(0.78 < Z < 1.31) = ShadeNorm(0.78, 1.31, 1,0) = 0.123

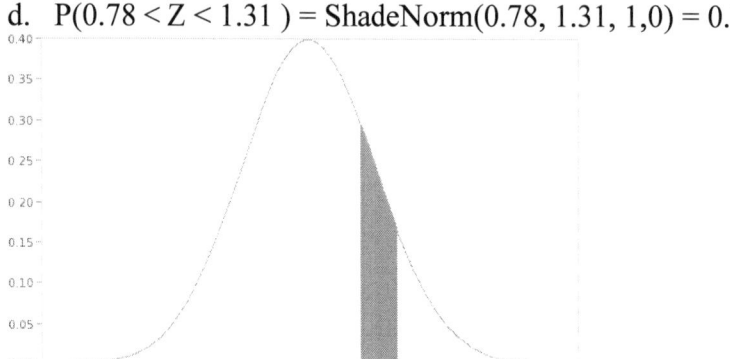

e. P(−1.31 ≤ Z ≤ −0.78) = P(0.78 < Z < 1.31) = 0.123

5. In a normal distribution N(24, 6) Find and shade:

a. P(X = 25) = 0
b. P(X ≥ 25) = ShadeNorm(25, 1000, 24,6) = 0.434

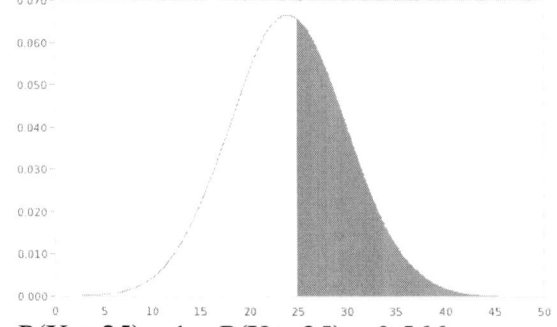

c. P(X ≤ 25) = 1 − P(X ≥ 25) = 0.566

d. P(X ≥ 15) = ShadeNorm(15, 1000, 24,6) = 0.933

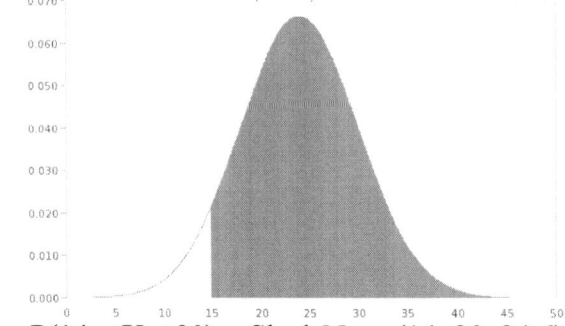

e. P(14 ≤ X ≤ 20) = ShadeNorm(14, 20, 24,6) = 0.205

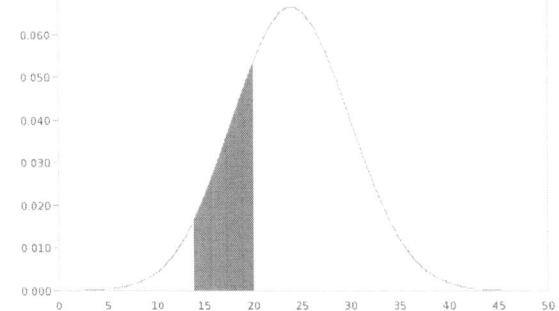

f. P(19 ≤ X ≤ 31) = ShadeNorm(19, 31, 24,6) = 0.676

6. The weight of a certain animal is normally distributed with mean of 150 kg and standard deviation of 12 kg.

   a. Sketch a diagram for the distribution of weight for the animal.

   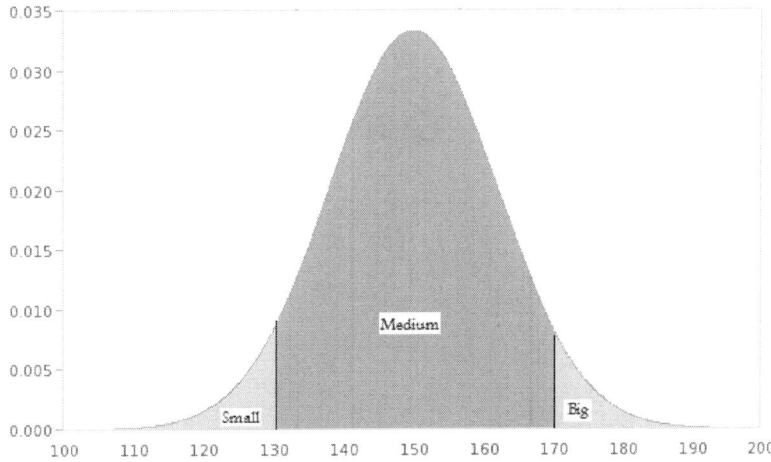

   b. We classify the animals in the following way:

   c. Find the probability for each one the cases described.
      Small: ShadeNorm(0, 130, 150,12) = 0.0478
      Medium   ShadeNorm(130, 170, 150,12) = 0.904
      Big   ShadeNorm(170, 1000, 150,12) = 0.0478

   d. invNorm(0.8, 150, 12) ≈ 160 = q

   e. 0.2 of 3000 = 600 animals

7. 500 high school students' grades are distributed normally with a mean of 72 and a standard deviation of 6.

   a. 2 SD from mean is the interval [60, 84]

   b. ShadeNorm(60, 70, 72, 6) ≈ 0.347
      0.347 of 500 ≈ 174 students

   c. ShadeNorm(80, 90, 72, 6) ≈ 0.0899
      0.0899 of 500 ≈ 45 students

   d. ShadeNorm(90, 100, 72, 6) ≈ 0.00135
      0.00135 of 500 ≈ 1 student

   e. Normal distribution extends from minus infinity to infinity, grades only extend between 0 and 100 so in reality using the normal distribution is an approximation, cannot be exact.

8. The time it takes to complete a certain journey is normally distributed with a mean of 50 days and a standard deviation of 4 days.

    a. a = 53, b = 60

    b. ShadeNorm(57, 1000, 50, 4) ≈ 0.401

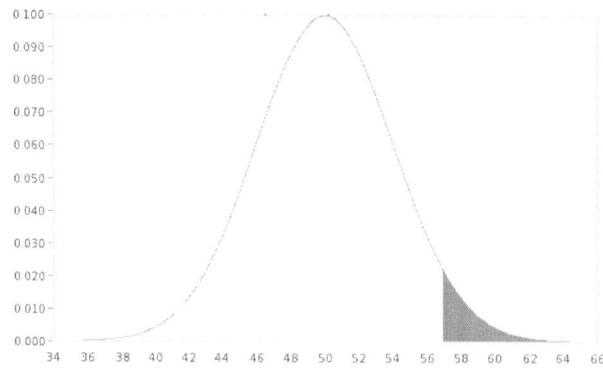

    c. ShadeNorm(56, 61, 50, 4) ≈ 0.0638

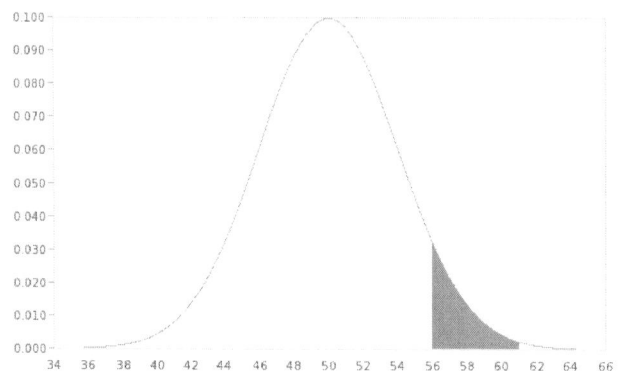

    d. invNorm(0.8, 50, 4) ≈ 53.4

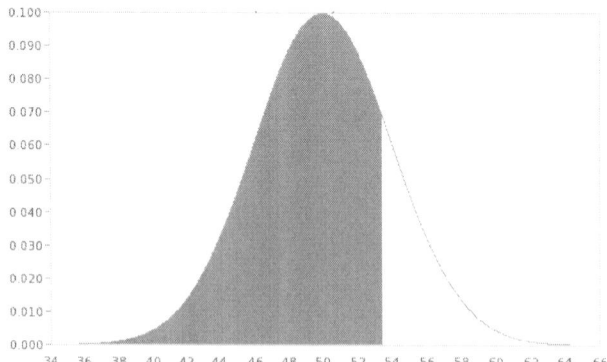

10399635R00247

Printed in Great Britain
by Amazon.co.uk, Ltd.,
Marston Gate.